# Business Strategies for Economies in Transition

# Business Strategies for Economies in Transition: Book of Readings on CEE Countries

Edited by

Petr G. Chadraba and Reiner Springer

Cambridge Scholars Publishing

Business Strategies for Economies in Transition: Book of Readings on CEE Countries,
Edited by Petr G. Chadraba and Reiner Springer

This book first published 2008

Cambridge Scholars Publishing

12 Back Chapman Street, Newcastle upon Tyne, NE6 2XX, UK

British Library Cataloguing in Publication Data
A catalogue record for this book is available from the British Library



ISBN (10): 1-4438-0049-X, ISBN (13): 978-1-4438-0049-5

# TABLE OF CONTENTS

## Section II: Advertising



## Section III: Finance and Banking

## Section V: Case

# FOREWORD

This book contains a collection of papers from the Conference on Business and Marketing Strategies for CEE Countries organized jointly by the Institute of International Business of Wirtschaftsuniversität Wien and the College of Commerce of DePaul University, Chicago and held annually in Vienna, Austria. Because of rapidly changing economic environments in Central and Eastern European countries, we chose papers from the last 3 conferences. Our goal is to offer educational material to academics whose interest is focused on issues related to economies in transition.

The book is divided into four sections – Finance and Banking, Human Resource Management, Marketing and Advertising. It also includes a case study. We chose these four areas since they seem to be most impacted by the transformation. Unlike accounting, these disciplines reflect more the subjectivity of human behavior. The economic transition, which took place in Central and Eastern Europe starting in 1990, was as much about changing human behavior as it was about changing the economic systems. Many of the articles in this book illustrate the slow change in people's attitudes toward the new economic system and the new business practices. While the markets in CEE countries may carry the same products as the western markets do, the consumers' views toward market driven economies and western style business concepts still differ, even after 17+ years of change. The case study illustrates some of the problems companies may expect when entering markets that are in transition. Additionally, the case shows the danger of making assumptions about similarities among markets and/or countries, based on limited and superficial variables.

The articles in this book cover a variety of business topics. Due to the past economic structure in these countries, western style business concepts had to be adjusted and tailored to the local conditions. Even today, the environment is in transition. Distribution channels differ; consumer's brand preferences change and in many cases the demand is shifting back to domestic, cheaper, brands. We also see differences in the perception of what is unethical, or illegal. In general the attitudes toward these issues seem more liberal. Consumers also appear more cynical about businesses' role in the economy and the society.

We can safely say that the economic transformation has taken hold on the macro level. Ten formerly communist countries in CEE are now members of the European Union. The macro economic indicators of these countries are mostly within the EU guidelines and some of them have already adopted the Euro. However, as the research indicates, the micro economic indicators are still in the transitional stage. It is taking somewhat longer than expected for the changes to be fully adopted on the micro level.

The four sections of the book are arranged according to business disciplines typically dividing the various departments within business universities. This arrangement allows professors from the different departments to select specific articles relevant to their topic. These articles show the process that business institutions, as well as consumers, go through in transitional economies. The articles give us a real picture of the transitional process, which we never before have had. We are now able to use real business examples; we can point to these articles when teaching new business concepts in countries, which may still be in transition. There are still a number of formerly communist countries that are only beginning to transfer their economies. This book can serve as a valuable guide to teachers in those countries by giving them factual evidence relevant to theoretical concepts.

All of the articles and the case study within this book describe business issues, which arose while countries were transforming their economic systems from a centralized to a market driven economy. However, we feel that this book can be used as a teaching tool in countries moving from undeveloped to a developed economic state. Any progress, which brings significant change to the status quo, will impact the citizens of these countries. The response of these people will directly impact their chance of a successful economic development. A number of the articles in this book can be used to determine what type of a consumer response we can expect. Issues such as foreign direct investment, foreign made products taking market share from local manufacturers and competition from foreign enterprises, are all global concepts. These issues are common to transforming economies and are also relevant to economies which are in the developmental stage.

Petr G. Chadraba, PhD
College of Commerce
Chicago, Il. USA
DePaul University

Prof. Dr. Reiner Springer
Institute of International Business
Vienna, Austria
Wirtschaftsuniversität Wien

# SECTION I:

# MARKETING MANAGEMENT

# CURRENT TRENDS IN THE MARKETING STRATEGIES OF AUSTRIAN FIRMS IN CENTRAL AND EASTERN EUROPE

ARNOLD SCHUH

## Abstract

In this paper the findings of an online survey on trends in the marketing strategies of Austrian companies in Central and Eastern Europe for the 2006-09 period are presented. Austrian companies are very optimistic about the future market developments in CEE. Their interest is shifting from Central Europe to South-Eastern Europe and more to the East. By increasing the marketing budget and moving to more direct forms of local presence the competitive position shall be improved. Regional integration is growing as it is documented by the broad adoption of extended home market concepts. International marketing program standardization is already high and further on the rise. Flexibility in local marketing seems to be secured by granting the local management a high degree of autonomy in decision-making.

## Introduction

Most of business and management research on Central and Eastern Europe (CEE) had been focused on the entry and expansion activities of Western firms in the 1990s. The fundamental changes in the institutional framework and the economic transition process offered ample opportunity for interesting research on how firms behave in transition economies (Springer & Schuh, 1999; Schuh & Pacolt, 2000). Now that most of the countries have gone through the major phases of the transition process or even completed them the interest among researchers seems to be waning – the CEE countries have become "normal" market economies that have lost their exceptional status. But from an evolutionary perspective of corporate development, it is still interesting to learn how the Western MNCs have been responding to the fundamental changes of the markets and how they deal with the new constellations in the markets today.

In the first decade, after the fall of the Iron Curtain, the early entrants were confronted with a lot of uncertainty concerning the institutional framework, the progress in the transition process and the future development of the markets in this region (Schuh, Klausegger & Schreiber, 1994). At the beginning, the management was preoccupied with finding the right country markets, entry method and marketing strategy for each individual market. However, the constellation has changed over the past years: The business infrastructure has improved constantly, the institutional environment has stabilized, especially in those eight CEE countries which became member of the EU in 2004, and the risk that the reforms will stall and the countries will return to their former planned economy and socialist system has diminished (EBRD, 2002 and 2005). At the same time, some of the early entrants have become regional players by building a remarkable presence in many countries of the region. It is fair to assume that the priorities in the business and marketing strategies of these regional players changed in the meantime and that they are probably more interested now in optimizing their presence in the region rather than in further expansion into new countries. Given the broad presence in the region companies have started to think about better coordinating and integrating their operations (Kozminski & Yip, 2000; Ferencikova & Schuh, 2003).

## Objective of Study and Research Design

The purpose of this paper is to identify current trends in the marketing strategies of Austrian firms in CEE for the 2006-2009 period. Research questions center around three areas: (a) perceived attractiveness of country markets in CEE, (b) thrust, objectives and priorities in marketing strategies, and (c) degree of regional integration and organizational issues. The definition of CEE for this study includes all countries of the region except the Baltic states and the CIS states – however, Russia and Ukraine are included given their importance for the Austrian economy. The following sub-regions were used throughout the questionnaire:

- Central Europe: Czech Republic, Hungary, Poland, Slovak Republic, and Slovenia.
- South-Eastern Europe: Bulgaria, Croatia, and Romania.
- West Balkan: Albania, Bosnia-Herzegovina, Macedonia, and Serbia-Montenegro.

The research questions were addressed in an online survey. The design and implementation of the survey was subject of a project seminar at the Institute for Marketing Management in the Summer Term 2006. Target persons were managers in charge of marketing activities in CEE at Austrian companies. The names of Austrian firms operating in CEE were partly provided by the foreign trade organization of the Austrian Chamber of Commerce (WKÖ) and partly the outcome of our own research. Target companies were contacted by phone or email in order to identify the manager responsible for the CEE operations. A personal invitation to participate was then sent out in two waves in May and July 2006. Reminder emails followed 7-10 days in the case of non-response. A total of 317 Austrian firms were contacted. 78 persons participated in the survey and 50 of them completed all questions. This represents a participation rate of 15.8%.

## Findings

### Market Attractiveness and Country Risk

All business planning starts with an assessment of the current market situation and an outlook on future market developments. In this study this step is captured by measuring the attractiveness of country markets today and in 2009. Interviewees were asked to rate CEE markets in terms of their market attractiveness, i.e. to rate to what degree a CEE market offers promising sales opportunities for companies of their industry. The results for the year 2006 show (Figure 1) that Central Europe is leading the rating (4.82 on a six-point scale) followed by Russia (4.54) and South-Eastern Europe (4.52). Ranked next to this leading group are the Ukraine (3.98) and the West Balkan (3.32). The future of the region is seen even brighter: all countries/sub-regions can improve their ratings for 2009 except of Central Europe, which slides from 4.82 to a still attractive 4.50. From the perspective of the Austrian firms South-Eastern Europe (4.92) is moving to the top of the rating with Russia (4.76) close behind. Strong improvements are anticipated for Ukraine and the West Balkan (Figure 1).

**Figure 1: Market attractiveness ratings by country/sub-region**

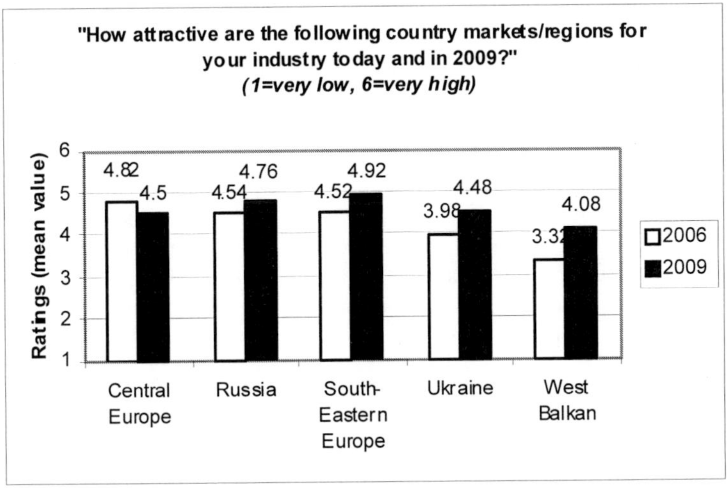


When analyzing the results by economic sector, marked differences show up: Service companies rate the market attractiveness of Central Europe (service firms 5.08 vs. manufacturing industry 4.41), South-Eastern Europe (4.96 vs. 3.88) and the West Balkans (3.83 vs. 2.76) significantly higher than the respondents of the manufacturing industry (Table 4). This could be due to a time lag in the general market development, which is normally led by an up-swing of the manufacturing industry before the (business) services sector begins to expand. Another explanation is that the results mirror the "follow your customer" principle describing the phenomenon in the internationalization process that (business) service providers often follow their (manufacturing industry) clients into foreign market. Thus, markets for services take off later what is reflected in a postponed attractiveness rating.

Large companies (>500 employees) judge Russia and Ukraine significantly higher than smaller companies (<500 employees). Larger companies appear to be stronger attracted by larger markets and are better prepared to cope with the higher resource requirements and risks involved. Moreover, we found that companies which are present with their products in the geographically and culturally more distant markets of Russia and Ukraine show a significant better assessment of the market attractiveness than those which are not present there (Table 1). This result is in accordance with internationalization theory as described by the "Uppsala School" (Johanson & Wiedersheim-Paul, 1975). A firm that is active in a foreign market knows the market better, so it is easier for this firm to spot market opportunities and to cope with risks typical for this market.

**Table 1: Market attractiveness ratings split by presence in Russia and Ukraine**

| Differences in the assessment of market attractive-ness (six-item scale)* | 2006 | | 2009 | |
|---|---|---|---|---|
| | Company present | Company not present | Company present | Company not present |
| Russia | 5.18 | 3.73 | 5.25 | 4.14 |
| Ukraine | 4.60 | 3.36 | 5.00 | 3.96 |

* *All differences are significant on a p<0.05 level (Table 5)*

The Figures 2 and 3 give a more detailed overview of the most attractive and risky CEE markets in the next three years. Interviewees were asked to name the three most attractive and risky markets. Country risk relates to the likelihood that unstable political, economic, and social conditions in a foreign market will have a negative impact on the business operations of an international company active in this market. The results are fairly consistent with regard to the leading group irrespective if you just take the first ranked countries or the accumulated responses for a country in all top-3 ranks: Russia, Czech Republic, Poland, and Romania are regarded as the most attractive country markets of the region (Figure 2). Ukraine and Hungary are forming the runner ups followed by Bulgaria, Serbia-Montenegro, and Croatia (when counting the combined top 3 responses). The most risky markets of the region are Albania, Russia, Ukraine, Serbia-Montenegro, and Bosnia-Herzegovina based on the responses for the three most risky markets (Figure 3).

**Figure 2: Ranking of the most attractive country markets in the next 3 years**

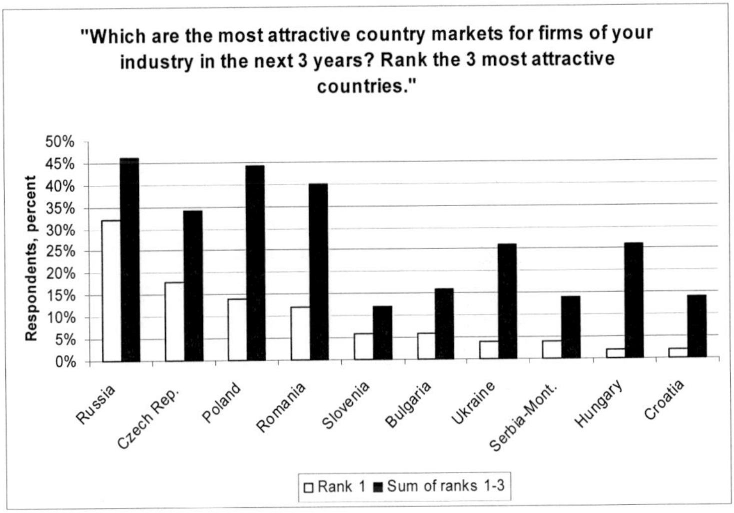


**Figure 3: Ranking of the most risky country markets in CEE**

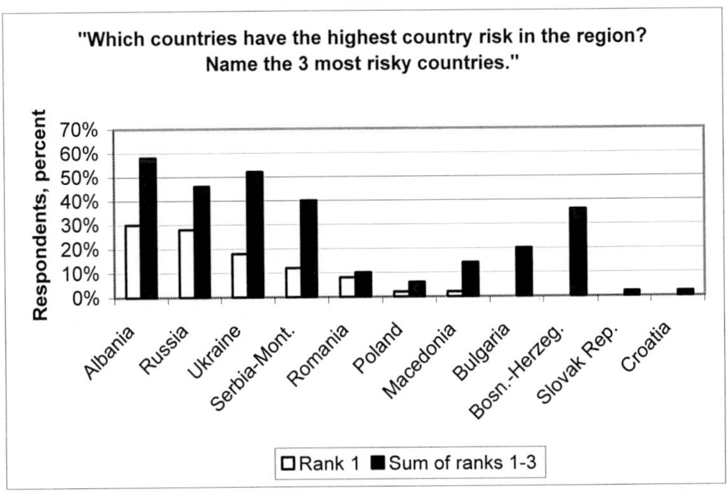

Market attractiveness seems to correlate strongly with the size of the market in terms of population. With Russia, Poland, Romania, and fifth ranked Ukraine the most populous countries are on top of the list. This shift of interest is insofar noteworthy as Austrian companies were strongly focused on Central European countries in the 1990s. We still find the highest degree of presence there. While Poland and Romania are barely mentioned among the most risky countries, companies have to be very careful when planning to enter Russia or Ukraine. These countries, especially Russia, rank high on the market attractiveness scale but at the same time are among the most risky countries. 28% of respondents view Russia as the most risky country in CEE, 18% say the same about Ukraine. Companies that already are or want to become active there have to pay special attention to the management of business risks in those two countries.

Austrian companies also expect an increasing level of intensity of competition in the next three years (Figure 4). The mean value will rise from 4.02 in 2006 to 5.18 on a six-item scale by 2009. Today only 28% of respondents regard the intensity of competition as 'high' or 'very high'. Until 2009 this proportion will nearly triple to 86% of respondents. Thus, it is not surprising that 44% of respondents expect to see more consolidation in their industry in CEE.

**Figure 4: Intensity of competition in the most important CEE markets in 2006 and 2009**

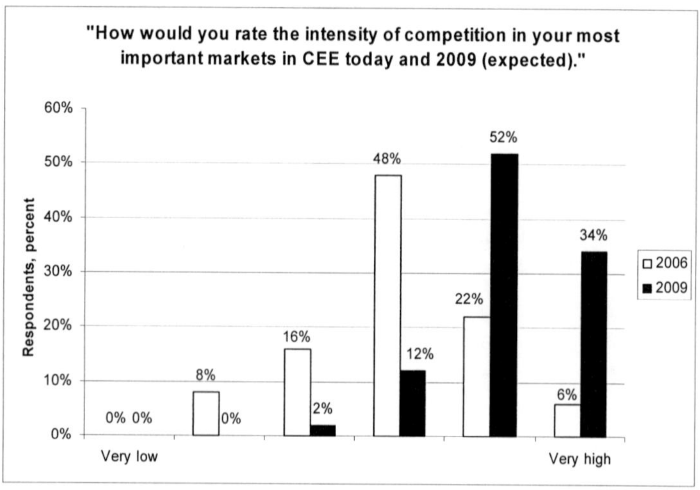

## Thrust, Objectives and Priorities in Marketing Strategy

The central section of the questionnaire deals with the thrust, objectives, and priorities in marketing planning for the 2006-2009 business period. The questions covered issues such as the direction of the growth strategy, the trade-off between market share growth and profitability, trends in the form of presence, and in the level of standardization of the international marketing-mix. Before presenting the findings, a few key facts are given which characterize the presence of the respondents in the region:

- The respondents are present with their products and services in 9 countries in CEE on average.
- The strongest presence can be found in the four neighboring countries of Austria where more than 82% of the respondents are active. About three quarters are already present in Poland and South-Eastern Europe, more than half are present in Russia and Ukraine today.
- The most important markets in terms of sales are the Czech Republic, Hungary, Poland, Russia and Romania (Figure 5)

**Figure 5: Most important country markets of the respondents in 2006**

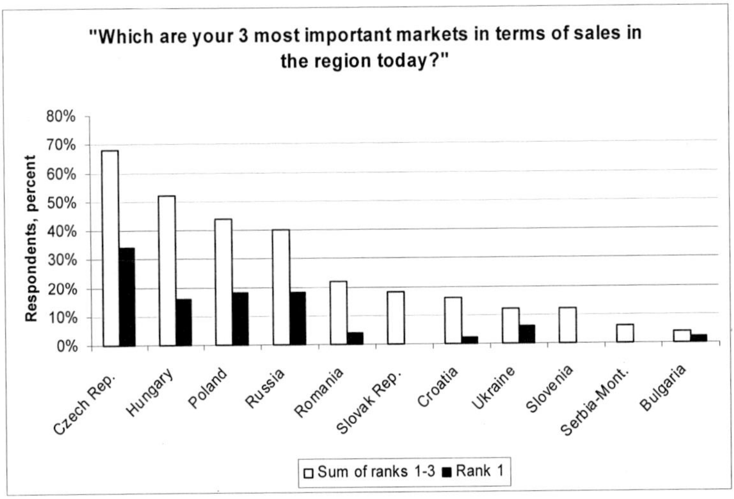


Despite the broad presence in the region the Austrian companies plan to continue with their expansion. This includes the expansion into new country markets, the broadening of the range of goods offered as well as the targeting of new customer segments (Table 2). 76% of the respondents intend to enter new country markets in CEE, 80% plan to broaden the range of products offered and 72% plan to address new customer groups. Only about a quarter of the respondents is satisfied with the current market coverage and does not plan any expansion in new markets until 2009. Virtually none of the companies wants to withdraw from any of the countries.

**Table 2: Direction of development in the marketing planning for CEE until 2009**

| *Direction of development until 2009* / *Decision area* | Increase | Hold | Reduce |
|---|---|---|---|
| Number of countries in CEE | 76% | 24% | 0% |
| Range of products offered | 80% | 18% | 2% |
| Number of customer segments targeted | 72% | 28% | 0% |

The overview of the competitive positions provides a mixed picture. The companies are nearly evenly distributed across the available categories ranging from weak to very strong competitive positions. However, a clear trend is visible to improve the competitive position by 2009. While only 42% of respondents are among the top-3 players in their industry in more than 50% of the countries today, this number shall increase to 52% until 2009.

The results on thrust and priorities in the marketing planning are quite revealing (Figure 7). After more than a decade of expansion into CEE the question arises if the companies want to grow now by building the existing business or by expanding into new countries. The findings show that the emphasis is now placed on the local market expansion (54%) rather than on the expansion into new countries of the region (22%). Despite all the predominant growth orientation the companies do not forget profitability. Only 16% approve of the statement that increasing the market share is more important than improving profitability (all 'strongly agree' and 'agree' responses together), whereas 50% disagree. Furthermore, the majority of respondents are still in an investment mood: 60% reject the notion that the time for investing is over and that it is now time to harvest. The continued expansion is supported by an increase in the marketing budget (sales force, advertising, promotion). In particular, the manufacturing industry shows a significantly higher willingness to expand marketing expenditures (4.12 on a five-item scale) than the services sector (3.42) and the trade sector (3.11).

**Figure 6: Overview of the current and intended competitive position**

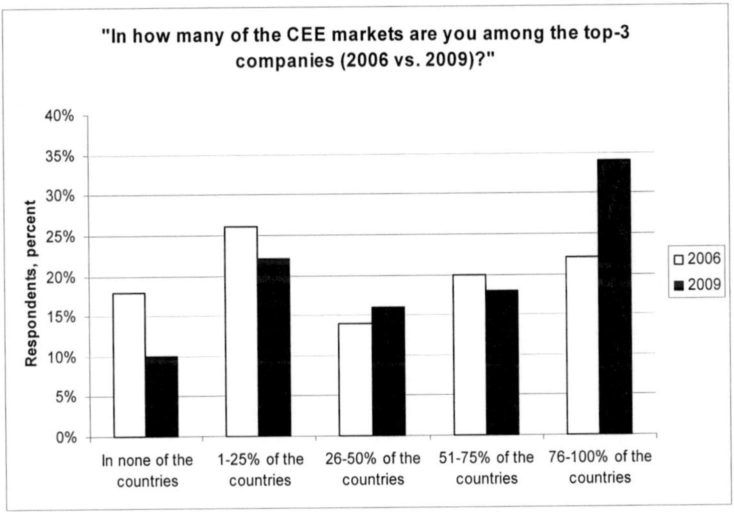


As far as the possible shift of value added activities from Austria to CEE is concerned, no marked interest can be found; only 16% of respondents plan to do it. This reserved attitude is quite a surprise given the ongoing public discussion about shifting production from Western to Eastern European locations ("nearsourcing"). It is possible that the broad range of quoted value added activities (production, product development, support and back-office activities) led to this response. By offering a broader definition of value added activities we wanted to address the situation of the service sector where the outsourcing of back-office activities (e.g. financial services) has become quite common. But the analysis by industry sector did not reveal any differences.

**Figure 7: Objectives and priorities in the marketing planning for CEE**

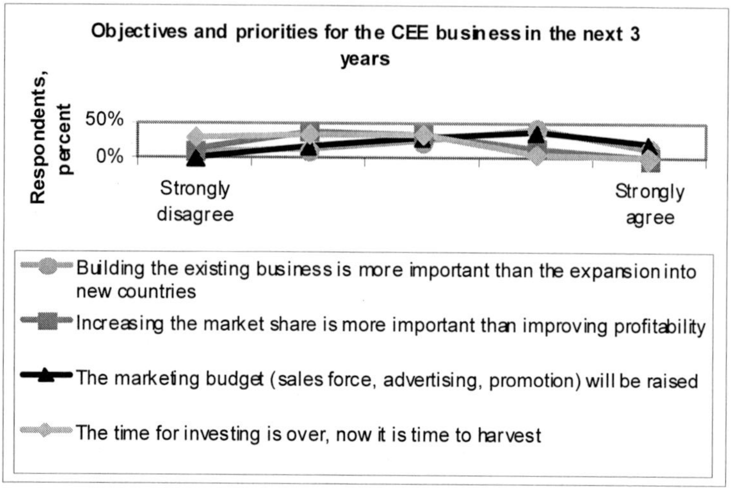


**Figure 8: No major shift of value added activities from Austria to CEE within the next three years**

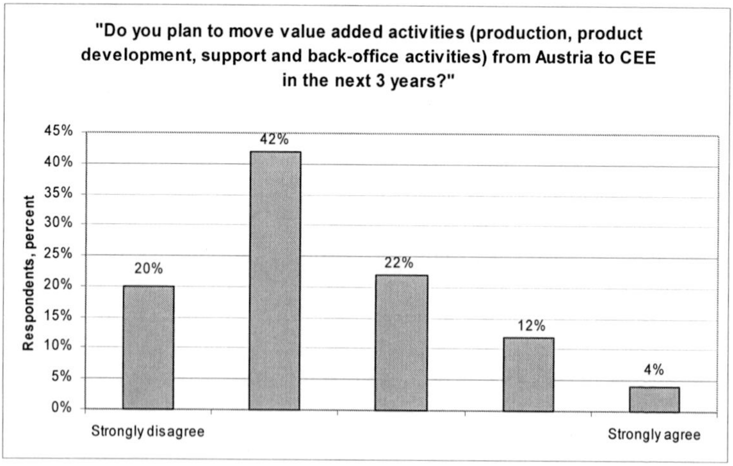

With regard to the mode of entry/operation a trend towards a more direct presence in the CEE market and, mainly limited to the service sector, towards cooperation/joint venture with local partners can be spotted (Figure 9 and 10). The results only include those modes of operation that are relevant for a company. The highest ratings can be found for fully owned subsidiaries with production (3.43 on a five-item scale), sales subsidiaries (3.42), and the acquisition of local competitors (3.37). There is also a tendency towards cooperating with local partners (3.23), while the cooperation with international partners is rather declining. The use of sole agents/importers is declining as well as the use of licensing, franchising, and contract manufacturing. In general, the patterns are not very pronounced. This may be attributed to an already high degree of direct presence in the markets through fully owned subsidiaries and the gradual character of internationalization in general, i.e. radical changes in the mode of operation are rather seldom.
A detailed analysis reveals that the trends vary by industry sector (Table 4). The cooperation/joint venture with local partners is significantly higher rated by service providers (3.86) than by manufacturers (2.79) and by the trade (2.38). Contract manufacturing is more important for smaller companies (3.18) than for bigger ones (2.33).

**Figure 9: Trends in the mode of operations (1)**

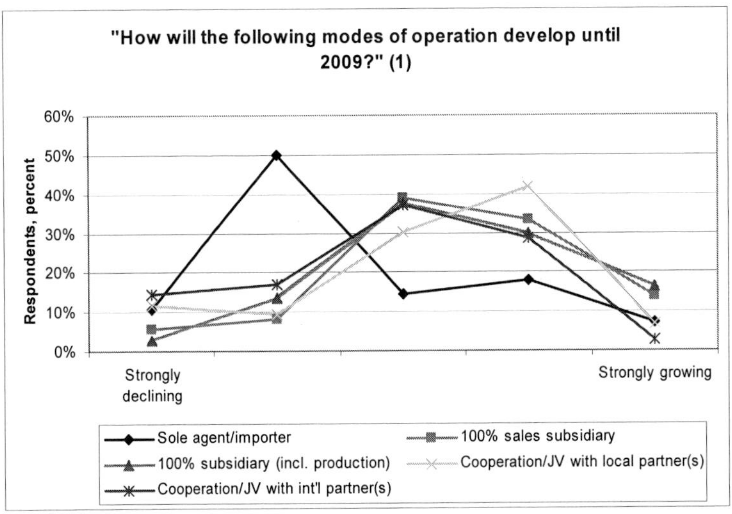

**Figure 9: Trends in the mode of operations (2)**

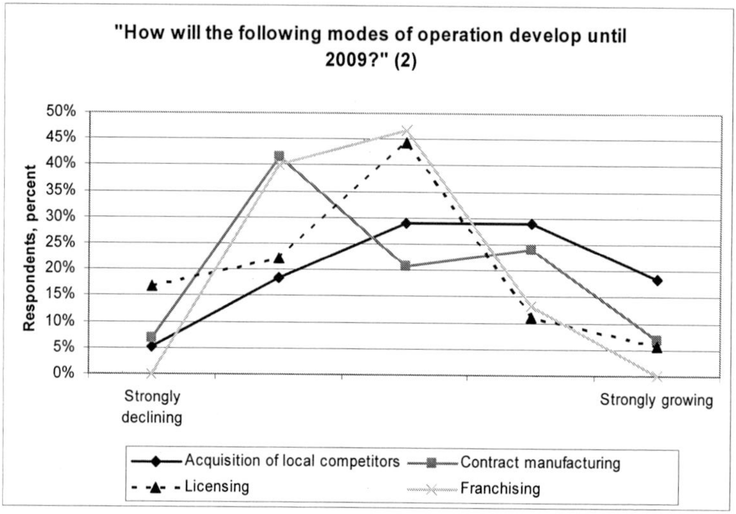


The question of standardization vs. localization of the international marketing program is a central aspect of all international marketing planning. The results show already a high level of standardization of most of the elements studied in 2006 (Figure 10). Corporate design (5.18 on a six-item scale) and brands (4.96) are ranked highest, followed by type of products offered (4.52) and type of distribution channel used (4.48). The lowest values can be found for advertising (4.26) and price positioning (3.88) – but they are still leaning towards the standardization end. These results correspond with existing empirical evidence of a high level of marketing standardization in CEE (Schuh, 2000). A comparison of the means of 2006 with 2009 indicates an even further increasing level of standardization over the next years. This high level of marketing standardization matches well the picture of a growing regional integration as manifested in the high adoption rates of the "extended home market" concept and the high proportion of companies that describe themselves as a "regional player".

**Figure 10: Level of marketing program standardization in 2006 and 2009**

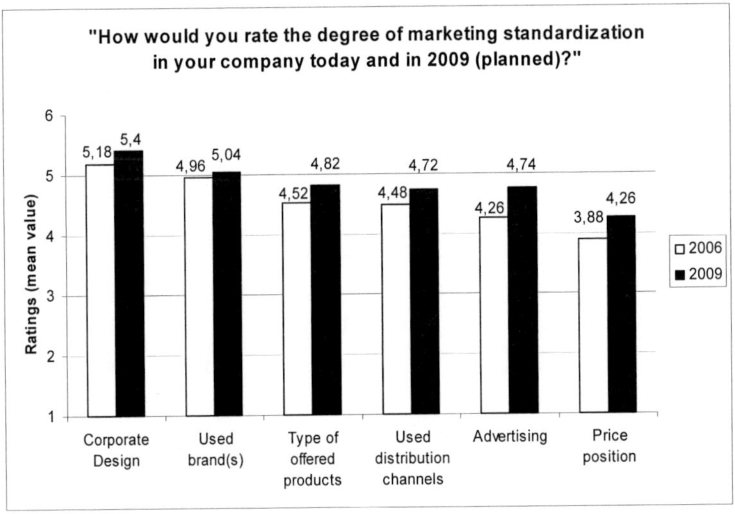


## Regional Integration and Control of Cee Activities

There exists the notion in the international business literature that after a phase of expansion companies start to think about a stronger regional coordination and integration of their operations (Heenan & Perlmutter, 1979; Morrison & Roth, 1992). In particular, the CEE region seems to be an ideal candidate for regionalization (Ferencikova & Schuh, 2003; Kozminski & Yip, 2000; Schuh, 2007). Starting point for the forming of a regional cluster normally is a group of neighboring countries with a lot of similarities in terms of market development, marketing infrastructure and consumer behavior and strong inter-regional trade. Asked if they regard the activities in the Central European countries together with the Austrian home market activities as core market and the Central European region as "extended home market", 86% of respondents agreed (percentages for 'strongly agree' and 'agree'; Figure 11). Especially, retailers & wholesalers show a strong tendency towards regional integration (4.67 on a five-item scale) compared to services (4.33) and manufacturing industry (4.06).

**Figure 11: The activities in Central Europe are already part of the "extended home market"**

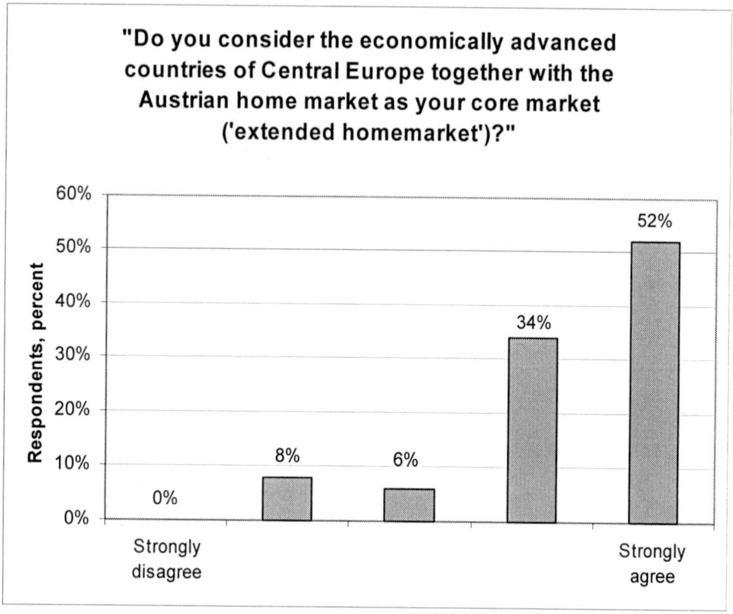


In addition, 72% of the respondents regard themselves as a "regional player" (Figure 12). Regional player was defined as a company with a broad market presence and a leading market position in CEE. The self-description as "regional player" is significantly higher for the group with a strong competitive position and for larger companies (Tables 3 and 4).

**Figure 12: A majority of respondents describes itself as a "regional player"**

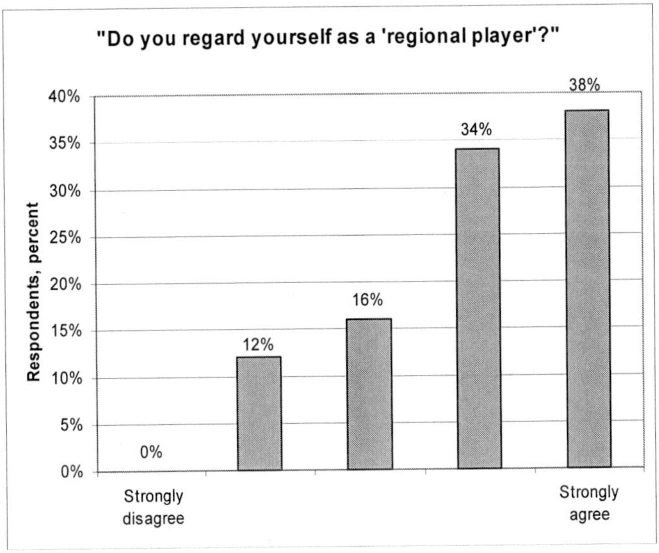


Given the high level of international marketing program standardization and the strong tendency towards regional integration the question arises how Austrian companies adapt to local market conditions. One option that is often used by (consumer good) companies operating in CEE is the multi-tier product/brand strategy (Dahm, 1995; Schuh & Holzmüller, 2003). In order to reach the price-sensitive segments of the markets, often an additional product line is offered under a separate brand (Batra, 1997). However, this type of marketing strategy is not very common among Austrian companies. Only 32% of respondents are using it already today, until 2009 this proportion will rise to 44%. The parallel offering of an additional regional product line can be found more often in retailing & wholesaling (3.11 on a five-item scale) and in the services sector (3.00) than among manufacturers (2.06; Table 3).

The last section of the questionnaire covered aspects of control of CEE marketing activities. In particular, the influence of the parent company or centre on local marketing decisions was of interest. The results show a slight decrease in central control of the CEE business for the coming three years. 40% disagree with the statement that the centre will get more strongly involved in the steering of the CEE business, while 26% agree. Asked to rate the autonomy of local management in marketing decision-making today and in 2009, 84% of respondents view it as 'high' and 'very high' today and expect an even higher degree of autonomy (88%) in 2009.

**Figure 13: The already high autonomy of local management in marketing decision-making will still slightly grow until 2009**

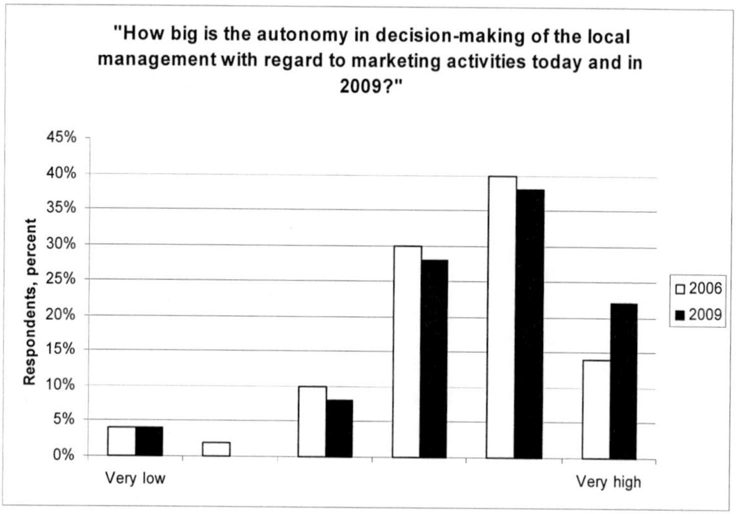


## Conclusions

The findings show a very optimistic outlook of Austrian companies for the CEE business in the next three years. The companies express a pronounced growth orientation along all planning dimensions: they intend to enter new countries, introduce new products and tap new customer groups. The biggest markets in CEE, namely Russia, Poland and Romania, draw the greatest interest. While in the 1990s most attention was given to Central Europe, now the new growth markets can be found in South-Eastern Europe and more in the East (Russia and to a certain degree Ukraine). In terms of presence and sales the Central European markets Czech Republic, Hungary, and Poland are still the most important for the Austrian companies and are viewed by a majority as part of the extended home market. When asked about priorities in the direction of growth, building the business in existing markets is seen as more important than the expansion into new country markets. As a strong increase of the intensity of competition is looming in their major markets in CEE, the respondents are determined to improve their competitiveness. Thus, they are prepared to continue with investing in CEE markets and to raise marketing budgets.

According to internationalization theory a trend towards a direct presence in the foreign markets can be observed in the course of the internationalization process of the firm. The Austrian companies of our sample follow this pattern. It seems that the Austrian companies want to improve their position in the markets and to have a better control over the implementation of their business and marketing strategy. Fully owned subsidiaries, sales subsidiaries, and acquisitions of local competitors are those modes of operation that are on the rise. Cooperation with local competitors is increasing in importance among service providers. Sole agents and importers, licensing, franchising, and contract manufacturing will decline over the next years. However, we have to be careful in the generalization of the conclusions as the sample contains many pioneers (64% of respondents entered CEE before 1996) and regional players. So the data mirrors to a high degree the specific business conditions of these pioneers among the Austrian companies rather than the challenges and responses of new or later entrants into CEE.

The results also provide additional evidence for the high level of international marketing program standardization. Although the level is already very high now, a further increase is expected. This finding complements the surprisingly broad usage of the extended home market concept. The Central European markets are regarded as core markets and are treated in a similar way as the Austrian home market. Together with the fact that nearly three quarters of respondents describe themselves as regional players this indicates a trend towards stronger regional integration. These findings raise the question how flexibility or adaptation to local market conditions is taken into account in local marketing, which seems to be increasingly determined by standardization and regional integration. One possibility, namely the offering of a separate regional product line ("multi-tier product/brand strategy"), is not very common among the companies of the sample (with the exception of retailers & wholesalers). Yet, it has to be said that an increasing number of companies is considering its introduction or extension in the next years. It seems that the solution can be found in the organizational design of the parent-subsidiary relationship. In the majority of companies local management is granted a high degree of autonomy in local marketing decision-making. So the results point at a combination of centrally developed and provided product and marketing concepts with a high autonomy in decision-making as far as local marketing issues are concerned. Local management is relatively free in finding the best implementation for a centrally developed strategy in the local market.

The study offers plenty of ideas for future research. First of all, it would be interesting to find out how the business conditions and strategies of late and new entrants differ from the ones of the pioneer companies in CEE. The prime mover advantage was often mentioned as critical determinant for success in CEE (Arnold & Quelch, 1998; Schuh, 2000). New entrants face a very different market situation today: marketing infrastructure, market structures, and consumer behavior in general have steadily converged to Western standards. The intensity of competition has risen and new entrants meet entrenched competitors that have gained valuable experience in the last years. On the other hand, risks associated with instability and rapid changes in the economic and political environment have lowered. On which success factors should strategies of new entrants be based today? When the regional players are selected as subject of research, then regional integration offers plenty of interesting questions. Although a majority views itself as a regional player, the role and form of regional integration is still subject of discussion (Schuh, 2007). This includes questions regarding regionalization strategy as well as the regional organization (e.g., regional headquarters).

## Appendices

Internationalization theory holds that certain characteristics of companies determine their internationalization behavior. Industry or economic sector, size of the firm, the existing international experience and presence as well as the competitive strength affect the perceived market attractiveness and country risk, the choice of market entry method (or mode of operation) and marketing strategy (Kutschker & Schmid, 2006). Therefore, additional analyses were conducted by relevant groupings in order to detect significant differences. Table 3 provides some background information on the sample. In the Tables 4 and 5 significant differences for important group splits are listed.

For the analyzes by sub-groups the following splits were used:

- Economic sector: Manufacturing Industry (manufacturing industry, power generation); Trade (wholesaling and retailing); Services (services and real estate industry, construction, transport & logistics)
- Size of firm: Small & medium sized = less than 500 employees/Large = more than 500 employees
- Degree of presence in CEE: Low = products are present in 1-9 countries/High = present in 10-14 countries
- Competitive strength: Low = in 0-50% of countries among top-3 companies/High = 51-100% of countries

**Table 3: Characteristics of company sample**

| **Industry** | | | | | | |
|---|---|---|---|---|---|---|
| | Manu-facturing | Services & real estate | Wholesaling & retailing | Transport & logistics | Constructio n | Power generatio n |
| Frequency | 16 | 16 | 9 | 5 | 3 | 1 |
| Percentage | 32% | 32% | 18% | 10% | 6% | 2% |
| **Total number of employees** | | | | | | |
| | 1-100 | 101-500 | 501-1000 | 1001-2500 | >2500 | |
| Frequency | 8 | 17 | 4 | 7 | 14 | |
| Percentage | 16% | 34% | 8% | 14% | 28% | |
| **Total sales (in Euro)** | | | | | | |
| | <2 Mio. | 2-10 Mio. | 11-100 Mio. | 101-500 Mio. | >500 Mio. | |
| Frequency | 3 | 4 | 19 | 11 | 13 | |
| Percentage | 6% | 8% | 38% | 22% | 26% | |

*MA = market attractiveness, int. = international, 1-s. = one-sided test of significance (2-sided test is standard)*

**Table 4: Significant differences by economic sector**

| | Mean values | | | t-test (p-values) Significance level α = 0,05 | | |
|---|---|---|---|---|---|---|
| | Manufact. (n=17) | Trade (n=9) | Services (n=24) | Manufact. vs. Trade | Manufact. vs. Services | Trade vs. Services |
| MA Central Europe 2006 | 4.41 | | 5.08 | | 0.043 | |
| MA South-East Eu. 2006 | 3.88 | | 4.96 | | 0.015 | |
| MA West Balkan 2006 | 2.76 | | 3.83 | | 0.015 | |
| Increase of mkt. budget | 4.12 | 3.11 | 3.42 | 0.005 | 0.026 | |
| Multi-tier product line 2006 | 2.06 | 3.11 | 3.00 | 0.030 (1-s.) | 0.011 (1-s.) | |
| Multi-tier product line 2009 | 2.53 | 3.67 | | 0.039 | | |
| Cooperation w. local partners | 2.79 | 2.38 | 3.86 | | <0.001 | <0.001 |
| Cooperation w. int. partners | | 2.00 | 3.26 | | | 0.021 |
| Franchising | | 2.00 | 3.00 | | | 0.020 |

*MA = market attractiveness, int. = international, 1-s. = one-sided test of significance (2-sided test is standard)*

**Table 5: Overview of significant differences by selected sub-groups**

| | Mean values | | t-test (p-values) Significance level α = 0.05 |
|---|---|---|---|
| **Significant differences by company size** | | | |
| | Small & medium sized (n=25) | Large companies (n=25) | |
| MA Russia 2006 | 4.12 | 4.96 | 0.035 |
| MA Ukraine 2006 | 3.52 | 4.44 | 0.013 |
| Regional Player | 3.76 | 4.20 | 0.033 (1-s.) |
| Multi-tier product line 2006 | 3.04 | 2.36 | 0.037 (1-s.) |
| Contract manufacturing | 3.18 | 2.33 | 0.040 |
| **Significant differences by degree of presence in CEE** | | | |
| | Low presence in CEE (n=24) | Strong presence in CEE (n=26) | |
| MA Russia 2006 | 3.96 | 5.08 | 0.004 |
| MA Ukraine 2006 | 3.50 | 4.42 | 0.013 |
| Sales subsidiary | 3.06 | 3.70 | 0.063 |
| **Significant differences by presence in Russia/Ukraine** | | | |
| | Presence given (n=28) | No presence in country (n=22) | |
| MA Russia 2006 | 5.18 | 3.73 | <0.001 |
| MA Ukraine 2006 | 4.60 | 3.36 | 0.001 |
| MA Russia 2009 | 5.25 | 4.14 | 0.010 |
| MA Ukraine 2009 | 5.00 | 3.96 | 0.015 |
| **Significant differences by competitive position** | | | |
| | Weak comp. position (n=29) | Strong comp. position (n=21) | |
| Regional Player | 3.66 | 4.43 | 0.007 |
| Multi-tier product line 2009 | 3.45 | 2.57 | 0.022 |

*MA = market attractiveness, 1-s. = one-sided test of significance (2-sided test is standard)*

## Acknowledgements

I would like to thank the students of my seminar on "Doing Business in Central and Eastern Europe" of the Summer Term 2006 who were involved in address search, invitation of target persons, and the online implementation of the survey: Christian Faber, Bernhard Frank, Florian Huber, Carina Langer, Stefan Seebacher, Susanne Schwarz, Tobias Sickinger, Lukas Steiner und Mario Taboga.

## References

Arnold, D. and Quelch, J.A. (1998) New Strategies in Emerging Markets. Sloan Management Review, Fall 1998, 7-20.

Batra, R. (1997) Marketing Issues and Challenges in Transitional Economies. Journal of International Marketing, 5/4, 95-114.

Dahm, M. (1995) Strategische Marktbearbeitungsentscheidungen internationaler Markenartikelunternehmen am Beispiel Ungarns. Der Markt, 34/3, 122-132.

EBRD (1999) Transition report 1999: Ten years of transition. London: EBRD.

—. (2005) Transition report 2005: Business in transition. London: EBRD.

Ferencikova, S. and Schuh, A. (2003) Regionalization in Central and Eastern Europe: A Discussion of Strategic and Organizational Aspects of Its Implementation. Ekonomicky Casopis - Journal of Economics, 51/5, 592-611.

Heenan, D. and Perlmutter, H. (1979) Multinational organization development. Reading: Addison-Wesley.

Johanson, J. and Wiedersheim-Paul, F. (1975) The internationalization of the firm – Four Swedish cases. The Journal of Management Studies, 12/3, 305-322.

Kozminski. A. and Yip. G. (2000) Strategies for Central and Eastern Europe. New York: St. Martin's Press.

Kutschker, M. and Schmid, S. (2006) Internationales Management. 5th ed., München: Oldenbourg.

Morrison, A. and Roth, K. (1992) The regional solution: an alternative to globalization. Transnational Corporation, 1/2, 37-55.

Schuh, A., Klausegger, C. and Schreiber, M. (1994) Aktuelle Problemfelder und Strategien österreichischer Unternehmen bei der Marktbearbeitung in Mittel-Osteuropa. Der Markt, 33/131, 178-190.

Schuh, A. (2000) Global standardization as a success formula for marketing in Central and Eastern Europe? Journal of World Business, 5/2, 133-148.

Schuh, A. and Holzmüller, H. (2003) Marketing Strategies of Western Consumer Goods Firms in Central and Eastern Europe. In Stüting, H.-J., Dorow, W., Claasen, F. and Blazejewski (eds.): Change Management in Transition Economies – Integrating Corporate Strategy, Structure and Culture, New York: Palgrave Macmillan, 176-188.

Schuh, A. (2007) Regionalization in Central and Eastern Europe: Searching for Regiocentric Orientations in MNC Strategies. Journal of East-West Business, 13/1 & 2 (forthcoming).

Schuh, A. and Pacolt, O. (2000) Management Research on Central and Eastern Europe: Key Research Areas During the 1989-1999 Period. In Chadraba. P. and Springer. R. (eds.), Proceedings of the 8th Annual Conference on Marketing Strategies for Central and Eastern Europe. Vienna: WU Wien, 360-370.

Springer, R. and Schuh, A. (1999) Osteuropamarketing: Spezifika. Themenschwerpunkte und Entwicklungstendenzen. In Schneider. W. (ed.), Betriebswirtschaftliche Forschung an der Wirtschaftsuniversität – Konzepte, Befunde und Ausblick. Wien: Ueberreuter, 219-234.

# The Empirical Research of the Theoretical Framework of Marketing Mix Standardization and Adaptation for International Markets

BEATA ŠEINAUSKIENĖ
AND REGINA VIRVILAITĖ

## Abstract

Though marketing mix standardization and adaptation is one of the most researched and questioned subjects in the field of international marketing, the continuing debates and contradictory results of empirical studies just confirm the relevance of this subject and the need for further studies.

The goal of this paper is to propose and examine the theoretical framework that could serve as a practical technique facilitating the decision making process in relation with marketing mix standardization and adaptation for international markets. The proposed framework is tested empirically by investigating Poland and Baltic States' IT markets. The results show that particular framework could be applied as a guide for the international companies facing the marketing mix formulation challenge.

## Introduction

Standardization and adaptation issues of international marketing mix have been debated extensively for more then four decades. However it has not resulted in clear theoretical backgrounds, moreover contradictory findings are reporting that the empirical research is still at the early stage of the development.

From the practitioner's point of view, standardization and adaptation theoretical models often are general and too complex to be put into practice.

The existing literature presents the findings of international marketing standardization studies carried mainly in Western European countries. Marketing mix standardization and adaptation issues in Central and Eastern Europe region are little investigated and the existing studies concern mainly Western companies experience and their strategies pursued in the particular CEE region.

The globalization and integration process also cause the growth of new local business leaders striving to expand internationally inside and outside the CEE region and this situation increases the interest in the research of marketing mix standardization and adaptation issues in the particular context.

This paper attempts to contribute to the debates on marketing mix standardization and adaptation issues and seeks to promote the application of theoretical framework.

At the beginning, a brief overview is given of theoretical models of marketing mix standardization and adaptation for international markets. Then the new research framework is proposed and tested empirically by investigating Poland's IT market in relation to marketing mix standardization and adaptation issues. The method of this research is the case study.

## Theoretical Background

### Marketing Mix standardization versus adaptation: three schools of thought

Within the field of international marketing, there has been a longstanding debate over the extent of marketing mix standardization or adaptation. Based on the literature review, three schools of thought can be distinguished in the context of marketing mix standardization and adaptation. One of the main proponents of marketing standardization, Theodore Levitt (1983, p. 93) asserted that "the world's needs and desires have been irrevocably homogenized" whereas proponents of marketing mix adaptation argue that complete standardization is hardly conceivable or even not feasible at all due to still undeniable existence of cultural, political, economical differences among various countries (Douglas and Wind, 1987; Kotler 1986, Hill and Still, 1984). These two initially extreme and opposite approaches namely adaptation and standardization eventually evolved into more moderate contingency perspective stating that marketing mix adaptation and standardization are not two disembodied absolutes and have to be perceived as two contraries of the same continuum where both approaches coexist. Contingency perspective treats adaptation or standardization as a matter of degree where standardization or adaptation degree can vary and appear anywhere on this continuum. The contingency school of thought was that way round enabling to relate these two extremities noting that degree of standardization or adaptation is contingent upon various external environmental and internal organizational factors.

## Marketing Mix standardization and adaptation models

Both standardization and adaptation models met in the literature are a comment on contingency approach and point up differences only in a sense of an initial strategic goal of the company where standardization models represent the preconceived positive attitude toward standardization and adaptation models support the adaptation as the most efficient approach.

**Figure 1. Marketing mix standardization and adaptation models for international markets**

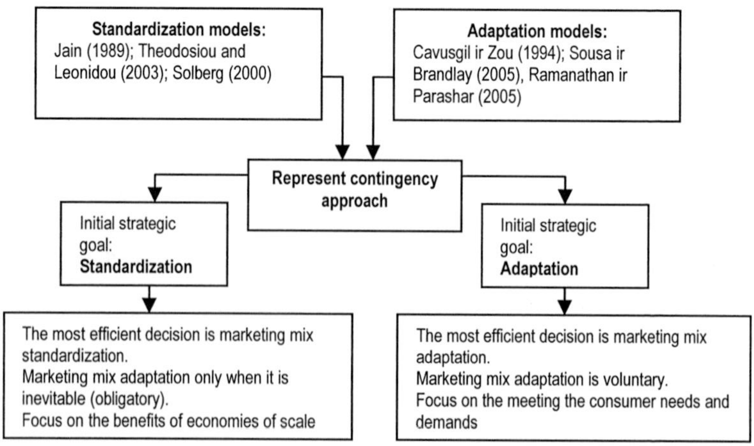

The theoretical models met in the literature can be divided into ***static models*** (reflecting marketing mix standardization or adaptation relationship with antecedent factors and effectiveness) and ***dynamic models***, emphasizing "soft", intangible variables - perceptional and behaviors aspects (company knowledge, experience, organizational culture, psychic distance) so enabling to conceive marketing mix standardization or adaptation as a changing, dynamic and cyclic process.

## Influencing Factors

In reviewing a literature we find a large number of influencing factors. Categorization and generalization is very difficult because of the subtle differences among the studies in term of definitions, measurement or context of research (Waheeduzzaman, 2004). Nevertheless it is evident that these factors are of several levels respectively covering products, company, industry, and market and macro environmental aspects.

The classification of detailed influencing factors identified by various authors (Jain, 1989; Cavusgil and Zou, 1994; Waheeduzzaman, 2004), showing under which condition what decision suits better, was summarized and presented in table no.1 using recent generalization of Theodosiou and Leonidou (2003).

**Table 1. Influencing factors and their impact on standardization and adaptation decisions**

| Influencing factors | Standardize | Adapt |
|---|---|---|
| **Macro environmental factors:**<br>Political, legal, economical, socio-cultural environment | Similar | Different |
| **Market factors:**<br>Market share occupied in different foreign markets<br>Consumers' purchasing power | small<br>similar | large<br>different |
| **Consumer factors:**<br>Consumer behaviour, life style<br>Willingness to pay premium for differentiated goods<br>Usage conditions<br>Identification of similar segments | homogenous<br>low<br>similar<br>possible | heterogeneous<br>high<br>different<br>impossible |
| **Competition factors:**<br>Competition intensity<br>Competitive position in separate foreign markets<br>Marketing infrastructure | low<br>similar<br>similar | high<br>different<br>different |
| **Product factors:**<br>Importance of the scale of economy<br>Product type<br>Consumer goods<br>Positioning strategy<br>Product life cycle | high<br>industrial<br>durable<br>similar<br>similar | low<br>consumer<br>non durable<br>different<br>different |
| **Organizational factors:**<br>International involvement level<br>Company resources<br>International business experience (home-host scenario)<br>International business experience (intermarket scenario) | Many or big markets<br>small<br>low<br>extensive | Few or small markets<br>large<br>extensive<br>small |
| **Managerial factors:**<br>Organisational structure<br>Managerial orientation (attitudes) | centralization<br>ethno-centric, region-centric, geo-centric | autonomy<br>polycentric |

## Theoretical Framework of Marketing Mix Standardization and Adaptation for International Markets

The researchers of dynamic models assume that contradictory findings of different research in the field of marketing mix standardization and adaptation may reflect the fact that some aspects have been overlooked

(Solberg, 2000). More mechanical measures of the degree of standardization (or the static models) may conceal more fundamental organization dimensions, such as market knowledge, decision-making process (Solberg, 2000).

In order to take advantage of the best features of both types of models it is consider appropriate to interlink these models by integrating dimensions (***psychic distance, organizational culture, knowledge and international experience***) of dynamic models into the structure of the static models.

**Figure 2. Merging of static and dynamic models.**

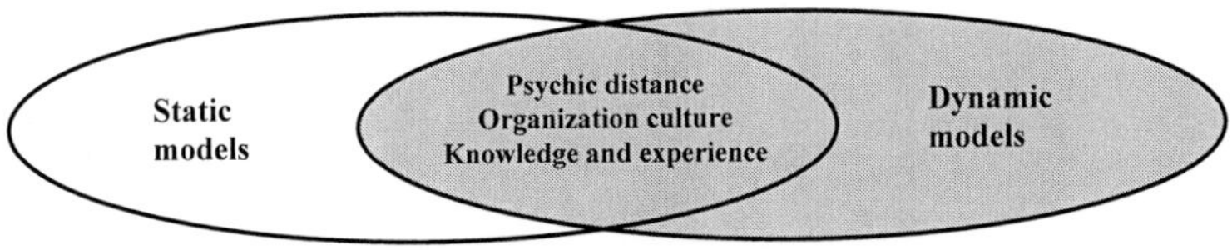


Hence, the research model is derived from conjunction of static and dynamic models. Psychic distance is the individual's perception of the differences between the home country and the foreign country (Sousa and Bradley, 2005). Psychic distance may vary over time depending on acquired knowledge and experience about the international market. Having little experience and poor knowledge about the international market may cause an inappropriate perception about the impact of influencing factors and the company will make a decision that will not be adequate to the external situation and the company will be forced to change it. It could be assumed that the company will change the initial decision only in case it has a sufficient level of knowledge that is acquired along with the international experience.

**Figure 3. The theoretical framework of marketing mix standardization and adaptation for international markets**

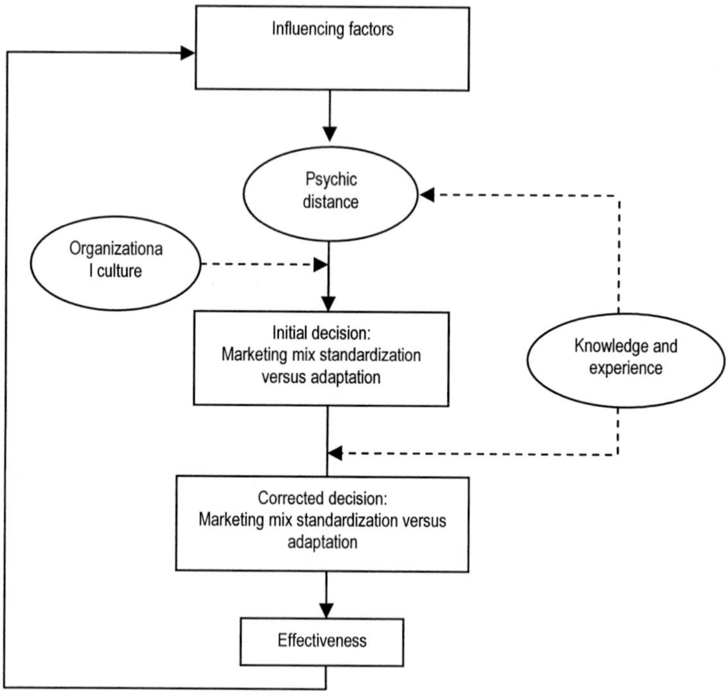


In the next section this new-fangled theoretical framework is tested empirically by investigating Poland's IT market in relation to marketing mix standardization and adaptation issues.

## The Empirical Research of the Theoretical Framework of Marketing Mix Standardization and Adaptation for International Markets

### ELKO Group profile

IT distributor Joint Stock Company ELKO Group operates in 9 countries - Croatia, Estonia, Latvia, Lithuania, Romania, Russia, Slovakia, Slovenia, and Ukraine. The headquarters of ELKO Group are located in Riga

(Latvia), and function as the heart of the company's administration, logistics, finance, marketing, and IT support. ELKO Group offers a full range of IT products – components, peripheral equipment, PCs and notebooks, servers and network solutions - from more than 80 world-leading producers. ELKO Group is among the three biggest distributors of Intel products in Eastern Europe, the biggest distributor of Sony storage products and among the top five distributors of Seagate and Western Digital hard drives in the whole Europe.

## General Situation of IT market in CEE region

The review of peculiarities and trends of the IT market of the Central and East European region show quite a number of similarities. It can be asserted that IT market growth in this region is promoted by the economic growth of these countries (on average, three times as big as that of West European countries). In general terms, the IT market in this region is in the stage of continuous growth. Development of the IT market and the IT saturation level is in direct relationship with economic and social advance of these countries. The highest saturation degree has been fixed in Slovenia, the lowest in Russia and Ukraine. All countries of the region mentioned are characteristic of the fact that it is the computer hardware components that comprise the largest segment. In all countries, except Ukraine, where the situation is aggravated by high duties, the sales of this segment have been affected by low IT level penetration. Even though the companies' acquisition of computer hardware in many countries has already reached the European Union average, household segment is still lagging behind this average. This segment proceeds to be one of the biggest, though the growth rate is going to slow down. New opportunities and the growth of new related segments have been evident – these are rapidly growing sales of software, IT services as well as IT solutions, which naturally result from computer installation. Even though the decisive factor in purchase decision is the price, the demand for more sophisticated IT products is likely to grow, the consumers will accept them willingly and will be able to buy them as the style of life is changing and living standards are improving. With the disappearance of boundaries between IT and household electronic goods, the traditional IT products portfolio is supplemented by household electronic goods, while growing IT literacy creates conditions and preconditions to sell personal computers and its components by using new channels of retail trade chains, i.e. in large supermarkets and consumer goods centers.

## Research design and findings

We are going to analyze which marketing mix solution of the selected company can be applied in the Polish market on the basis of the theoretical framework of marketing mix standardization and adaptation in the international market. Since the subject matter of this work is the application of marketing mix standardization and adaptation solutions in the international market, the purposefulness of the company's activity and the process of selecting international markets will not be analyzed, this aspect being considered only with respect to how much it is related to the subject of marketing mix standardization and adaptation.

ELKO Group started its business in Latvia where the head office of the international company is set up. The first expansion of the company led to the neighboring Baltic countries. Consequently, ELKO accumulated the greatest experience in the Baltic countries' markets. The company is familiar with the markets of this region, because of its presence here for more than ten years. Around 80 percent of the product range offered by the company is similar in all international markets the company operates. Considering market development, competition intensity and countries risk degree; the widest range of products is applied in the Baltic region. On the basis of specific features of the markets of Central and East European region, it can be said that Baltic countries can be treated as the sample representing the IT market of the Central and East European region. The countries of this region are characteristic of similar economic development, social and political background, as they are EU members (except Romania and Croatia), also, the IT products life cycle is quite comparable. Even though the sales volumes in Russia and Ukraine in absolute value significantly exceed those in the Baltic and other countries' markets, the Group Expansion Method is not likely to be suitable in selecting new markets of foreign countries, in our case the Polish market. The Group Method of market selection is based on the assumption that one of the markets is a reference market. The reference market is selected with regard to the sales volumes of this foreign market as well as to the company perspective in this market. The same goods in Russian and Ukrainian markets are in the earlier stages of their life cycle; therefore, the expansion method of the neighboring countries would be more appropriate. Specific features of this method is the fact that one market is selected as reference (this may be home market or the already existing foreign market), while the market selection of foreign countries is based on the similarities of economic, social, and cultural environment. Selection of this type is pursued on the basis of accumulated experience (Kuvykaite, 1998: 60). As it was mentioned, the greatest experience and most profound knowledge are accumulated in the home markets of the company's country and the markets of the neighboring foreign countries. Since the company occupies a solid position in the home market of the country (the biggest company in Latvia) and the neighboring countries are perceived as closely related psychologically, thus, sharing similar political, legal and economic environment, the company, in an effort to avoid risk, is in the first place likely to test and realize all new strategic solutions related to the marketing mix in the markets of this region. It is also essential that this region of Baltic countries represents the latest development stage of IT market in the region covered by ELKO Group. In considering the Polish market, therefore, the assumption that it is most relevant to select the markets of Baltic countries as evaluation reference for the Polish IT market can be made.

***External and Internal Factors***

With regard to consistency of the framework worked out, we will first carry out the analysis of internal and external factors of the countries under consideration, i.e. Poland and the Baltic countries.

***Macro environment factors - economic, political and institutional environment***. Although Lithuania, Latvia, Estonia and Poland are considerably different in terms of population, density, social as well as demographic conditions, all of these countries share the same status of the EU membership and CBSS (Council of the Baltic Sea States). The EU membership provides single market, harmonizes economic policy and abolishes entry barriers and duties as well as stipulates similar economic, political and institutional environment.

In estimating the basic economic indexes, it is evident that the GDP growth rate of both Poland (4.2 %) and Baltic states (6.3-10%) is higher compared to that of EU countries (25 in number), which is 2%. Although the GDP growth rate index in Poland is lower (4.2%), the expenditure growth rate for IT technologies in Poland and Baltic are very similar (Lithuania 10 %, Latvia 9.3 %, Poland 10%).

**Table 2. GDP growth rate and IT spending forecast, 2005**

| Country | GDP growth rate, % | IT spending forecast |
|---|---|---|
| Russia | 6.0 % | 19 % |
| Ukraine | 4.3% | 15% |
| Latvia | 9.0% | 9,3% |
| Estonia | 7.9% | 6,3% |
| Lithuania | 6,5% | 10% |
| Slovakia | 6.3% | 9% |
| Slovenia | 4.0% | 8% |
| Croatia | 4.1% | 9% |
| Romania | 5.2% | 11% |
| Poland | 4.2% | 10% |
| EU (25 countries) | 2% | 4% |

Growth rate source: International Monetary Fund (http://www.imf.org/
IT spending forecast source: www.IDC.lt

***Macro environment factors- cultural environment.*** For the analysis of cultural environment we will make use of World Values Review Map. On the basis of data of the World Values Survey (1990-1993) 43 communities participating in the survey were located in the semantic area according to two dimensions, i.e. traditional values versus secular-rational values, and survival values versus self-expression values. "Cultural Map of the world" confirms that the countries are not accidentally located within the space enclosed by these two dimensions; rather they demonstrate particular cultural stereotypes. The segmentation of these cultural regions is based on the synthesis of geographical, historical and religion categories.

**Figure 4. Cultural Map of the World. Source:**
http://www.worldvaluessurvey.org/

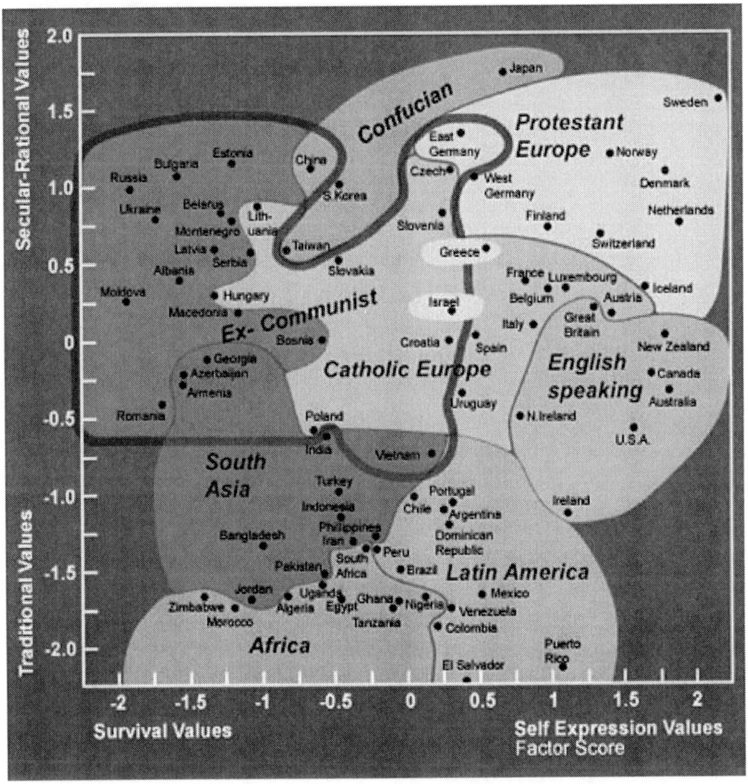


It is evident that Poland at the moment is rather far away from Baltic countries in the value map. Although both Lithuania and Poland occur in the same cluster of values, they are considerably distant from each other with respect to traditional/secular-rational values. What concerns survival/self expression values, Poland is located nearer the self expression values, which shows that the need for self-expression and life quality are valued higher than economic and physical security.

***Market factors***. In fixing the target markets, ELCO Group does not merely refer to the grouping of countries based on their economic development. The company is looking for similar segments. There can be identified the same segments respectively computer hardware components (for PC manufacturing/assembling) and retail computers and computer components (for reselling in retail trade) in Central Eastern Europe market.

**Table 3. Market share occupied by ELKO Group**

| Region | Market share occupied, 2005, % (derived data) |
|---|---|
| Baltic Countries | 12,1 |
| CIS | 2,3 |
| East Europe region | 3,2 |

Derived data source: www.idc.lt; www.infobalt.lt, http://www.ceeitandtelecom.com; www.elkogroup.com

We can see that the market share occupied by ELKO Group in all regions is relatively small. Also it can be maintained that the competitive position of the company with respect to the covered market share differs from region to region (in the Baltic States 12.1%, while in the region of CIS only 2.3 %). Scientific literature says that the companies covering relatively small market shares in different countries tend to standardize their own marketing mix.

The Polish IT market in the year 2005 grew by around 10 %. Poland is the second largest IT market in the Central and East European region and one of the most aggressive in launching IT development initiatives. The largest IT market share in this country is covered by the industrial sector (23.5 %). The communications, banking and public sectors are considerably behind.

The market of hardware components in the year 2003 constituted USD1.5 billion or 47% of overall IT products market. The Polish companies occupy 55 % of the market share of desktop PC, where most of these computers are assembled by small local companies. The international brands predominate in the market of notebooks and in other high-end IT products. The demand for locally produced (assembled) hardware provides favorable conditions for suppliers of hardware components (IT distributors).

Also, highly promising in the Polish market is network equipment and computer periphery. In recent years the growth of software sales has been relatively slow .The sales of this segment are expected to grow in the nearest future since large modernization projects of public sector are under way. The IT services sector has been growing each year.

***Market factors – consumer market potential.*** The rate of PC acquisition in households and enterprises reflect the penetration level of IT in the market or the IT market potential of households and enterprises.

**Figure 5. Household PC acquisition, %; source: Eurostat data, 2005; Russia, Romania data, 2003**

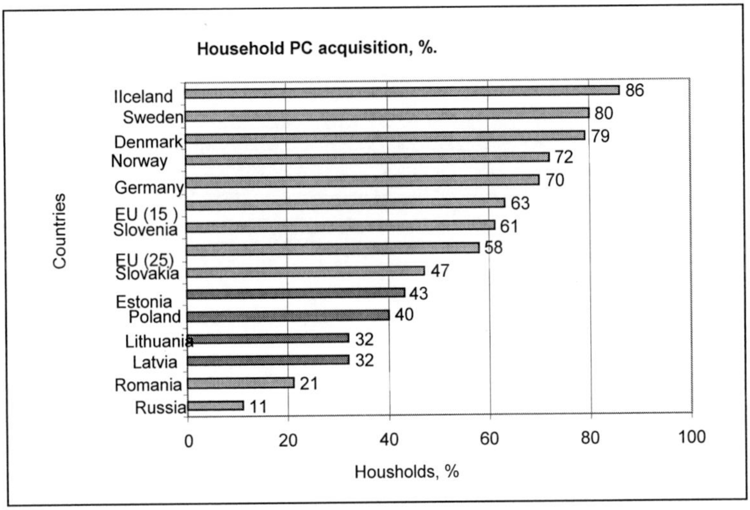


In Poland the number of households owning a PC between year 2002 and 2005 doubled (Indicators for the Information society in the Baltic region, 2005). In countries with relatively low level of PC acquisition in 2002, the growth rate of this index was the highest. The household PC acquisition percentage in Poland between 2002 and 2004 doubled to reach 36 %. Accordingly, in Lithuania this index grew by 11% and in the year 2004 as many as 27 % of households had a personal computer at home. According to data of 2005 we can see that the home market saturation degree in Baltic countries and Poland is quite alike. In Latvia and Lithuania this index is slightly lower (32 %), while in Estonia slightly higher (43%) than in Poland (40%). The home market segment in both Baltic States and Polish markets are significantly behind compared to the average of older EU states (63%). Taking into consideration the growth rate until know, this segment is likely to become one of the most rapidly growing in these markets. The household Internet usage index not only reveals the potential of certain goods in the markets (network cameras, internet telephony), but also characterizes consumers of the markets in many respects. Internet usage in the households is closely related to computer literacy as well as income of the inhabitants. Internet penetration in the home market reflects in a sense the consumer's life style. Therefore, it is relevant to measure the Internet penetration level in these countries.

**Figure 6: Households having access to Internet, %; source: Eurostat, 2005; Russia data, 2003**

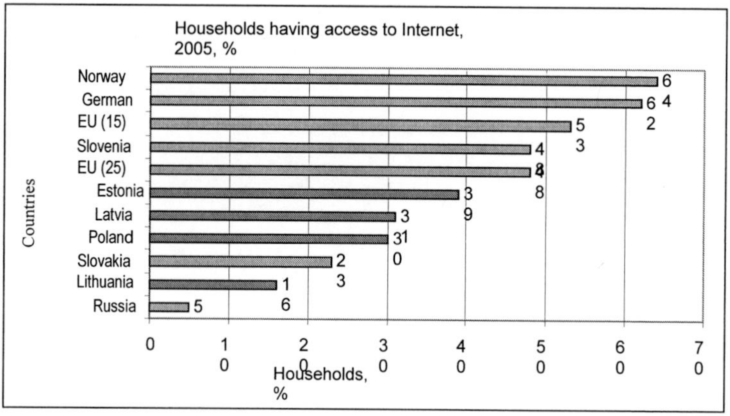


With reference to statistical data, it may be suggested that the common household Internet penetration average in the Baltic States (29%) is very close to the Polish index (30%). Another similar situation is in Latvia (31%) and Poland (30%). In the Polish and Latvian cases, consumers specify that the main reasons restricting the Internet usage at home is high cost of Internet installation and usage (Report of the Nordic Council of Ministers, Information Society Indicators, 2005). Polish users (over 50%) point out the cost as the main reason. Another barrier specified by Polish respondents identified by as many as 40% of them, is the lack of skills or a low computer literacy level. In Latvia 37% of the respondents indicated high cost of hardware, and 24% say that the main reason of low level usage is the cost of Internet services (Report of the Council of Ministers of Nordic countries, Information Society Indicators, 2005).

***Market factors - enterprises' market potential.*** The enterprises' PC and software acquisition reflects IT penetration level in business and public sectors and indicates saturation level of this market. However, this market is characteristic of its periodic nature, i.e. the sales liven up every three years (according to the market experts out-of-date hardware is replaced by a new one).

**Figure 7: Enterprise PC acquisition, %; source: Eurostat, 2005**

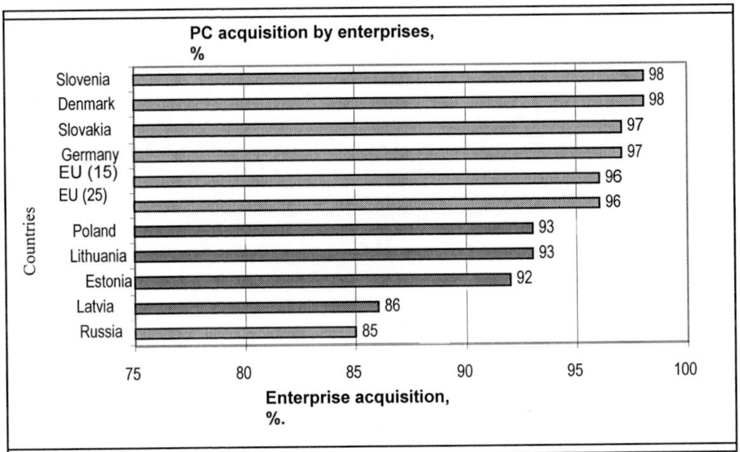


The same level of PC acquisition is recorded in Poland and Lithuania (93%), the lowest in Latvia (86%). What is more, it can be seen that in terms of PC acquisition by the enterprises, Latvia and Lithuania are but very little behind the general European average. However, due to rapid economic growth of the compared countries, expansion of companies, information societies and e-governments as well as due to the need of renovation of computer hardware owned by public and private sectors, it is very likely that this sector will also grow, but at a slightly decelerated rate.

**Figure 8: Enterprise access to Internet, %; source: Eurostat, 2005; Russia data, 2003**

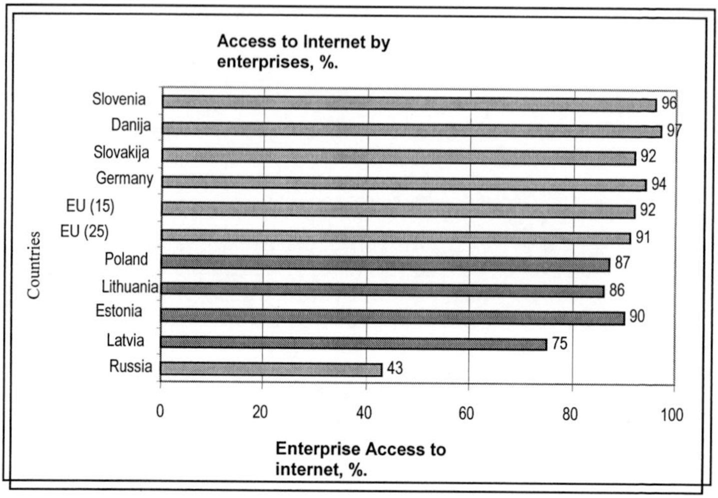


The rate of enterprises' access to the Internet in Baltic countries is rather diverse. The most advanced in this respect is Estonia (90%). Internet access rate by enterprises in Poland and Lithuania is very close (87% and 86%, respectively).

***Consumers' factors***. Consumers strongly influence every element of marketing mix (Theodosiou and Leonidou, 2003; Jain, 1989). With reference to the data of secondary sources (Doing Business in Poland, Country Commercial Guide, 2006, IDC 2005, 2006) it can be said that consumers of Baltic countries and Poland are very cost-sensitive, this being related to the consumers' income, which in the countries analyzed is rather low. Cost is the most essential factor in the decision-making process of purchasing. The image and reputation of international brands play a significant role only in major projects of corporate clients. The customers' cost-sensitivity is also confirmed by the Report of Nordic Councils of Minister (Information Society Indicators, 2005), which states that the main barrier for Polish and Baltic consumers in using the Internet is the high price of hardware and internet services. It should be mentioned here that global vendors, in an effort to avoid "grey import", apply standardized prices in Europe, and significant income differences among consumers of different countries result in limited demand due to unequal purchasing power. The consumers' purchasing power in different countries is represented in Figure 9.

**Figure 9: Cost of a PC as % of household income, source: Eurostat, 2003; Pal Gaspar, 2004**

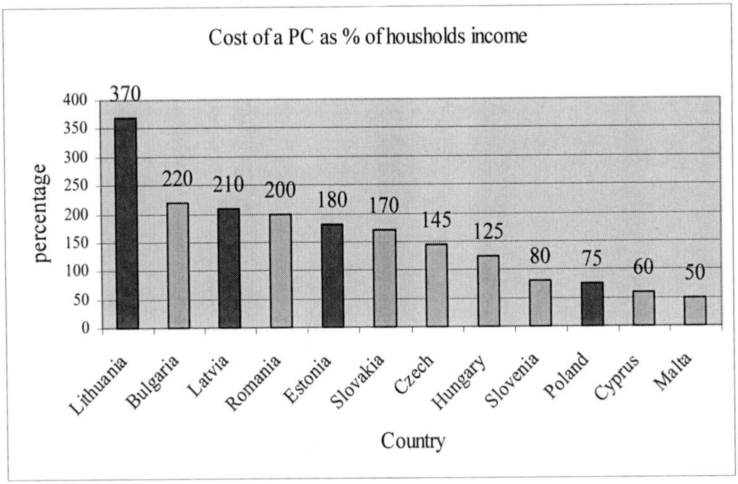


With reference to the above statistics it can be maintained that the purchasing power in the Polish and Baltic States markets is very uneven. In Lithuania the cost of PC acquisition is almost three times and in Latvia five times as big as in Poland. The demand for IT products in Polish and Baltic State markets demonstrates high elasticity with regard to prices, thus, Polish and Baltic States consumers, in respect to the cost-sensitivity aspect, are quite comparable.

The economy of the countries under consideration, consumers income and computer literacy are growing as well as the sales of personal computers, especially notebooks of widely known international brands, consequently, there is a tendency that quality considerations gradually gaining of special value in the purchasing decision making. The households having already acquired basic computer equipment continue to buy associated products and services. Therefore, the demand for computer peripheral and home electronics is also growing.

The same segments are found among the consumers of Polish and Baltic countries, i.e. hardware components (designed for computer manufacture/assembling), PC and computer components for reselling (packaged for retail trade), home electronics (new segment). Hardware products are sophisticated, therefore, their usage conditions are alike everywhere.

**Figure 10: Share of the population with basic computer skills related to computer use. Percent of population aged 16-74.**

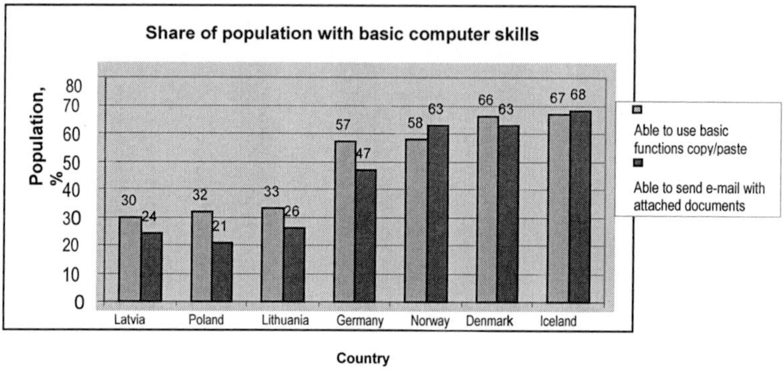


Source: Report of the Nordic Council of Ministers, Information Society Indicators, 2005

The study of computer literacy statistics shows that Polish and Baltic consumers share the same level of computer literacy, which is rather low (Latvia 30%. Poland 32%, Lithuania 33%) compared to West European countries.

***Competition factors - competition intensity***. In our case computer hardware is described as the product of low differentiation. The situation in both the Baltic States and Poland is analogous, i.e. big number of wholesalers, offering the products of the same brand (information provided by Gigabyte representative for Baltic countries). Naturally, the market under study is characterized by a high intensity of competition. The growth of IT market is slowing down. While in 2001-2002 it was around 20%, in the year 2005 it was about 10% (Poland and Lithuania). The slowing-down of the IT market growth results in more intensified competition.

The studied markets show the same structure of consumers and the phenomena of companies' restructurization. Though Poland has about 5000 IT companies, only 25 of them employ more than 250 people. Most companies are small. The Lithuanian market contains about 500 active companies, out of which only 20 are dominating. The markets of both regions are dominated by several major and influential retailers and computer assemblers. The distributors' replacement costs are low for retailers and manufacturers – they have several alternative suppliers for the procurement of the same goods. All IT distributors offer the same or very similar prices and services, identical trade terms and conditions for fulfillment and delivery. Almost all minor players of the market merge into major companies to withstand competition, or they choose to leave the scene.

Baltic countries and Poland are characteristic of a well-developed distribution network, i.e. IT distributors, computer assemblers, system integrators and retail companies. Even the same wholesalers such as GNT, Tech Data are operating in the wholesale market. As to large retail trade networks, major international retailers occupy solid positions in the Polish markets (Tesco), while the Baltic countries market is dominated by local retail traders (VP Market, RIMI).

***Product's factors - the importance of scale economy***. It is really great for the ELKO Group case. Big consolidated orders ensure discounts and lower incoming logistics costs. ELKO Group undertakes to present the negotiated sales plans to the represented vendors. The more uniform the product range is in different markets, the greater is the possibility to achieve the better sales results of particular vendor products'. Marketing support is provided with regard to sales plans (marketing budget for promotion, training, work-shops, bonuses, etc.)

***Product's factors - product type***. The company operates in the market "business to business". The main area of activity is distribution of IT products; therefore, the company does not influence the product modification process. Since the company has a portfolio of diverse products designed for the main segments of IT market, it is in a position to vary the product portfolio and adapt it to specific market features of an individual country by maintaining greater variety of computer components (Ukraine) in one country and highlighting the variety of notebooks, computer periphery and home electronics designed for retail trade (Baltic countries, East European countries). However, the company normally includes into its portfolio only those products that are in demand in all countries.

***Product's factors - product life cycle.*** Although in principle, the same tendencies (slowdown in computer components sales, sales boom of notebooks, digital technologies, home electronics goods, software, IT services) prevail in East and Central European countries, some differences can be detected in comparing the countries separately.

**Table 4. Share of different segments as the IT expenditure, %**

| Country | Computer hardware | Software | IT services |
|---|---|---|---|
| Russia | 70 % | 10,6 % | 19,4% |
| Ukraine | 86% | | |
| Slovenia | 58% | | |
| Poland | 48% | | |
| Baltic countries | 50% | 30% | 20% |

Source: derived data from IDC press releases: www.idc.lt, 2005; Poland Country Commercial Guide, 2006; Baltic countries – experts' estimations

By comparing the data presented in Table 4, it can be claimed that computer hardware goods in Poland and Baltic countries are in the later stage of their life cycle than the same goods in Russia or Ukraine (70% and 86% respectively). The share of computer hardware in the common IT expenses portfolio is similar both in the Baltic countries (50%) and Poland (48%). In the study of hardware varieties, similar sales tendencies can be seen among the same products groups. The sales of notebooks in Estonia grew by 60-80 % (Country Commercial Guide, 2006), in Lithuania by 70% (NK magazine, 2004) and in Poland 60% (Poland Country Commercial Guide, 2005). The summarized situation of IT portfolio in the Polish and Baltic markets is represented in Figure 11.

**Figure 11. IT product classification based on Boston Consultancy Group Matrix**

| Market growth rate | | | |
|---|---|---|---|
| | High | **Stars**<br>Retail IT goods, notebooks of international brands computer peripheral (LCD monitors, LCD TV, printers, multimedia, digital photo and video cameras, MP3 players) | **Question marks**<br>Networking |
| | Low | **Cash Cow**<br>Computer components for PC assemblers and system integrators (computer components – CPU, HDD, MB, graphical cards, memories, cases) | **Dogs**<br>CRT monitors, inkjet printers, low performance CPU, low capacity HDD. |
| | | High sales volumes | Low sales volumes |

***Product's factors - positioning.*** International brands represented by ELKO Group are positioned in the way they are positioned by the manufacturers. If the Sony or Seagate brands are presented to foreign markets, they are positioned in the same way in all the markets (top quality, highest price).

International brands play the greatest role in the IT products market. Analyzing the sales of international brands of major vendors in different countries, we can judge about the popularity and awareness of these brands, consumer preferences and standardization opportunities of marketing mix.

It is evident that both Polish and Baltic markets are dominated by two major international brands of LCD monitors (Samsung and LG). The leading brands respectively Samsung and LG position in the Polish market are weaker (in Poland they both occupy 34.6%, in Lithuania 51.5%, in Estonia 65.9%, and in Latvia 37.8% of all LCD monitor market). The offered range of LCD monitor brands for the Polish and Lithuanian markets is equally wide. Consequently, the threat of substitutes is also equally great.

**Table 5. Market share of LCD monitors by brands, 1st quarter, 2005**

| Estonia | % | Latvia | % | Lithuania | % | Poland | % |
|---|---|---|---|---|---|---|---|
| Samsung | 43,6% | Samsung | 24,6% | Samsung | 34,8% | Samsung | 21,8% |
| LG | 22,3% | BenQ | 13,3% | LG | 16,7% | LG | 12,7% |
| ViewSonic | 16,2% | LG | 13,2% | BenQ | 13,1% | Philips | 8,6% |
| HP | 3,2% | AG Neovo | 12,6% | ProView+MAG | 9,7% | Belinea | 8,1% |
| Acer | 3,1% | HP | 7,8% | AG Neovo | 7,6% | AG Neovo | 7,3% |
| Hyundai | 1,5% | Relisys | 7,8% | HP | 5,6% | Fujitsu Siemens | 6,3% |
| CTX | 1,5% | GNR+DiFusion | 5,5% | Philips | 5,3% | BenQ | 4,5% |
| Yakumo | 1,3% | Acer | 3,5% | Xerox | 1,3% | NEC | 4,5% |
| Ordi | 1,3% | ProView+MAG | 2,6% | Acer | 0,7% | HP | 4,1% |
| ProView+MAG | 1,2% | Hyundai | 1,7% | iiyama | 0,6% | Actina | 3,8% |
| Prestigio | 0,9% | Sony | 1,7% | Dell | 0,6% | Dell | 3,7% |
| Fujitsu Siemens | 0,9% | Dell | 1,4% | CTX | 0,6% | iiyama | 2,9% |
| Hitachi | 0,9% | CTX | 1,2% | Sony | 0,5% | Hyundai | 1,9% |
| BenQ | 0,7% | Hansol | 0,9% | Hyundai | 0,5% | Acer | 1,4% |
| miro | 0,7% | Fujitsu Siemens | 0,9% | Fujitsu Siemens | 0,5% | ProView+MAG | 1,4% |
| Philips | 0,1% | Belinea | 0,3% | Prestigio | 0,3% | Sony | 1,1% |
| LaCie | 0,03% | Philips | 0,2% | Hitachi | 0,3% | IBM | 0,7% |
| | | DTK | 0,2% | Belinea | 0,2% | CTX | 0,6% |
| | | | | NESO | 0,1% | miro | 0,5% |
| | | | | NEC | 0,1% | Vobis | 0,5% |

Source: Bryan Norris Associates, 2005m

***Organizational factors - international involvement level.*** ELKO Group is operating in nine countries of Central and East European region. The company is one of the leading in East European region. The size and weight of the company is described by the fact that it is one of the biggest distributors of Intel products in Eastern Europe, the biggest distributor of Sony storage products and one of the five biggest distributors of Seagate and Western Digital (the world hard disks leading manufacturers) in the region. So, the company's international involvement level is sufficiently high.

***Organizational factors - company's resources.*** Low profitability of IT market (especially for hardware components) is stipulated by low differentiation of product portfolio, low distributors' substitution costs, intensive competition and continuous decreasing product prices. Low product margins stipulate relatively small resources owned by the company. Therefore, the company pursues promotion only if the manufacturers render financial support to this initiative. Relatively small resources (determined by IT market profitability) tend to limit the company's potential to adapt the elements of marketing mix in different foreign markets.

***Organizational factors - experience of international business (intermarket scenario).*** The company has been operating internationally for more than ten years. Due to the growing markets of Central and East Europe, the company's attempts to internationalize brought a success, which is proved by the annual growth of sales volume.

**Figure 12: ELKO Group sales revenue, source: www.elkogroup.com**

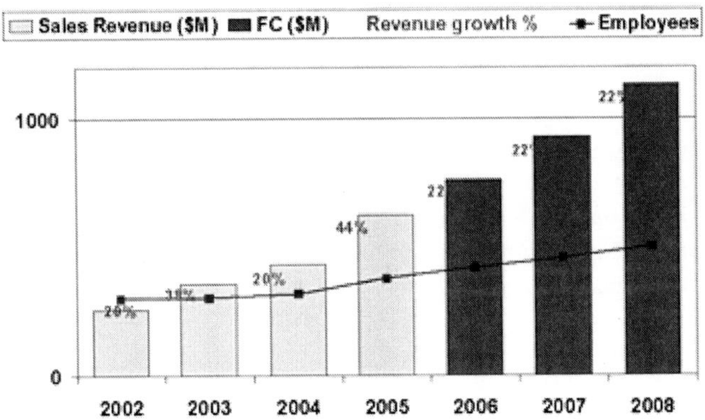


ELKO Group was among the first IT distributor in the Baltic countries. International experience of more than ten years proves considerable experience in East and Central European markets. Continuously growing international experience resulted in more profound knowledge of these markets. Due to the experience acquired, the company expanded to neighboring psychologically close markets (Russia, Ukraine).

***Managerial factors.*** Organizational management structure of ELKO Group is functional. The company applies unified process management system in all its subsidiaries. A high degree of management centralization is inherent to the company; however, with a view not to abandon the available markets and promote local markets integration, the company has deregulated some value chain functions to delegate more power to local subsidiaries. Every project, or idea, however, initiated by the subsidiary, is implemented only upon the approval of the head office. Any initiatives for marketing mix adaptation originated by local companies are first considered in the head office and get a go-ahead only if they are in accordance with international strategic goals of the company.

**Figure 13: ELKO Group value chain**

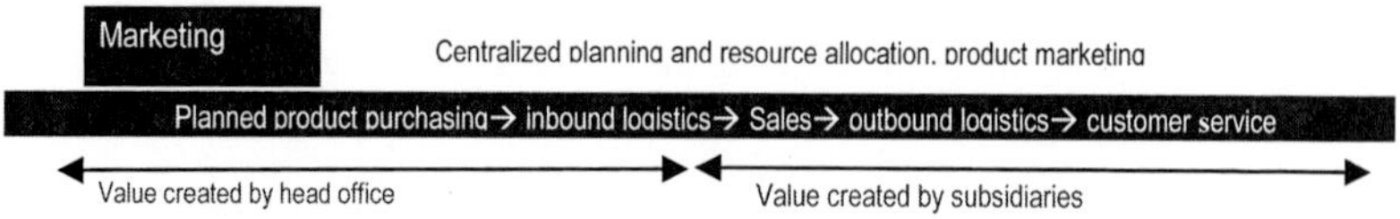


Thus, the marketing mix formation process is highly centralized and standardized (centralized and standardized are marketing planning procedures), whereas marketing mix elements (especially promotion and distribution - outgoing logistics) may be both standardized and adapted with a view to the needs, barriers, resources and international strategic goals of the company.

***Managerial factors - company's managerial orientation.*** Regional-centered orientation is inherent to the company where regional similarities are recognized, and regional strategies are being developed. Managerial orientation determines the company's mission, organizational management structures, organizational culture and provides the opportunity to forecast strategic solutions of the company.

***Psychic distance***

This is individual awareness of differences between home and foreign markets. Decisions related to marketing mix standardization and adaptation may vary depending on whether the company enters the psychologically close or psychologically distant foreign markets. Marketing mix standardization and adaptation are greatly influenced and stipulated by the psychological distance of managers with respect to foreign markets (Sousa and Bradley, 2005).

Psychic distance is the aspect of perception. It strongly depends on the disposal of information on the international market. With reference to primary statistical data of the previous section, the information supplied by secondary sources and experts' assessment, it can be said that there exist numerous similarities between Polish and Baltic markets: similar IT products saturation degree in consumers' markets, similar level of computer acquisition by the enterprises. According to the Internet penetration level and the factors affecting low penetration level in the households, Polish and Baltic markets as well as consumers are akin (price is one of the most key factors in making a purchasing decision). The enterprises' segment level in its relative expression is in close proximity both in Baltic countries and Poland. Equally low computer literacy level is inherent for both Polish and Baltic consumers.

Computer hardware products are in the same stage of product life cycle in the countries under consideration, therefore, it may be said that the Polish IT market has favorable conditions for standardization of IT product portfolio. Summarizing the competition factors, we maintain that great competition intensity is characteristic for the IT market in Poland and the Baltic countries as well. It is a different cultural environment and different purchasing power that slightly increase psychic distance to the Polish market.

After comparing Polish and Baltic markets, generalization of external (macro environment, market, consumers, competition, product) and internal (organizational and managerial) factors influencing marketing mix standardization and adaptation and reflecting psychic distance, is represented in Table 6.

**Table 6: Generalization of factors influencing marketing mix standardization and adaptation decisions**

| Influencing factors | Standardize | Adapt |
|---|---|---|
| **Macro environmental factors:** | | |
| Political - legal, economical environment | alike (S) | |
| Cultural environment | | different (A) |
| **Market factors:** | | |
| Market share occupied in separate foreign country | small (S) | |
| Consumer purchasing power | | different (A) |
| **Consumer factors:** | | |
| Consumer IT literacy | alike (S) | |
| Consumers' willingness to pay premium for differentiated goods | low (S) | |
| Usage conditions | similar (S) | |
| Identification of the same segments | possible (S) | |
| **Competition factors:** | | |
| Competition intensity | | high (A) |
| Competitive position in separate countries | | different (A) |
| Marketing infrastructure (methods) | similar (S) | |

| **Product factors:**<br>Importance of economies of scale<br>Product type (computer components)<br>Product type in respect to consumption durability<br>Positioning strategy<br>Brand awareness<br>The stage of product life cycle | high (S<br>industrial (S)<br>durable goods (S)<br>similar (S)<br>alike (S)<br>similar (S) | |
|---|---|---|
| **Organizational factors:**<br>International involvement level<br>Resources operated<br>Experience in international business (intermarket scenario) | many markets (S)<br>small (S)<br>extensive (S) | |
| **Managerial factors:**<br>Organization structure<br>Managerial orientation (attitudes) | centralization (S)<br>region-centric (S) | |
| **Total** | S = 18 | A = 4 |

Comparing Polish and Baltic countries markets as well as evaluating the effect of internal and external factors on marketing mix standardization and adaptation decisions, it can be said that 18 detailed factors establish favorable conditions for marketing mix standardization and 4 factors encourage the company to adapt marketing mix. Therefore, standardization barriers include different cultural environment, different purchasing power, highly intensified competition and different competitive position of the company in foreign markets.

Since high-tech goods (in our case IT goods) are not much affected by cultural differences, it may be assumed that cultural differences in the case under consideration are eliminated, and psychic distance with regard to Poland is increased mainly by different purchasing power and the company's different competitive position in the foreign market. In conclusion, it may be said that psychic distance regarding Poland (compared to the Baltic countries) is negligible. Theoretical studies revealed that small psychic distance in the primary stage of entering the market usually stipulates marketing mix standardization. However, the primary decision is stipulated not only by psychic distance, but, rather, by organizational culture, which will be discussed below.

***Organizational culture***

ELKO Group is a typical systemic organization with an inherent hierarchical structure, low level of autonomy, centralized and formalized structure. The company's systemic orientation minimizes its possibilities to accept risk. Development processes of such companies are first pursued where the psychic distance is not big. Due to this assumption, the companies of this type when entering the new market do not apply marketing mix modifications. Therefore, it is possible to predict that the first decision of the ELKO Group on entering the Polish market will be to standardize the marketing mix as much as possible according to the one applied in the already covered market. So, taking into consideration the regional-centered orientation of the company we can predict that the company when entering the Polish market will tend to adapt only those elements of marketing mix (promotion, outgoing logistics, pricing), which actually require fewer resources and are easier to be adapted without changing the established structure of the company and its processes.

Being systemic and not likely to accept risk, the company takes more time to adapt to changes. From horizontal (standardized marketing mix) to migration strategies (marketing mix adaptation) the company passes though perceptional strategies. The subsidiaries in Lithuania and Estonia have been raising problems and speaking about the need to expand the product range for many years in reaction to newly emerging associated and profitable segments, nevertheless, the head office ignored these suggestions for a some time and considered the claims unreasonable arguing that the Lithuanian, Latvian and Estonian markets are similar, and if such needs are not relevant in Latvia, they should not be relevant in Lithuania. As the company's sales in Lithuanian and Estonian markets declined and its competitive position in the mentioned markets slackened, the ELKO Group recognized the existing problem and managed to find the solution by shifting strategic priorities from computer components to IT goods of "Retail" group (new related, growing and more profitable segments, i.e. digital audio, video equipment, notebooks).

***Initial decision of marketing mix standardization and adaptation***

On fixing the psychic distance with respect to Poland and identifying restrictions stipulated by organizational culture, we will evaluate the possibilities of marketing mix elements application for the Polish market.

The possibilities of the Baltic countries marketing mix elements application in the Polish market are represented in Table 7. They are evaluated from 0 to 5 points. The highest point (5) is given to marketing mix element in the reference market (in our case – markets of Baltic countries). The permissible deviation limit is 4 points. If the application possibilities of marketing mix elements of the reference market are evaluated from 4 to 5 points, the marketing mix element may be standardized.

**Table 7: The evaluation of the possibilities of marketing mix (Baltic countries) application in the Polish market**

| Forein market | Marketing mix | | | | | | | | | | | | | | | | | | | | | | | |
|---|---|---|---|---|---|---|---|---|---|---|---|---|---|---|---|---|---|---|---|---|---|---|---|---|
| | Product | | | | | | Price | | | | | | Distribution | | | | | | Promotion | | | | | |
| | 0 | 1 | 2 | 3 | 4 | 5 | 0 | 1 | 2 | 3 | 4 | 5 | 0 | 1 | 2 | 3 | 4 | 5 | 0 | 1 | 2 | 3 | 4 | 5 |
| Baltic countr ies | | | | | | | | | | | | | | | | | | | | | | | | |
| Poland | | | | | | | | | | | | | | | | | | | | | | | | |

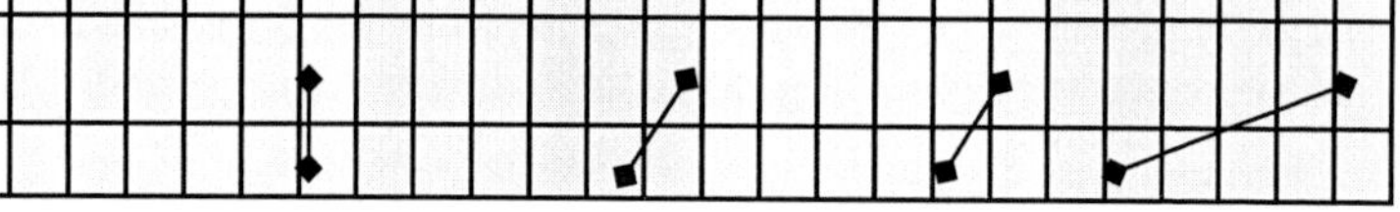

***Product.*** Since the company's activity is limited to wholesale trade (distribution) and it does not produce goods itself, naturally, it is not in a position to modify them. What concerns modification, the problem is the selection of products portfolio (assortment) in compliance with the needs of the foreign market. In our case, due to the similarities of Baltic and Polish markets described above (the same segments, the same stage of product life cycle, the similar brand awareness), the same portfolio of products can be applied in the Polish market. Different purchasing power, however, is a signal that marketing mix adaptation would be more acceptable. Considering greater purchasing power of Polish consumers, expansion of the product range with products meant for a more expensive segment might be realized. However, due to the organizational structure (systemic organization), the company is not likely to resort to such measures, at least in the primary stage, because of limited resources, perceived risk and relatively poor knowledge of the new market.

***Price.*** With a view to avoid "grey import", the manufacturers sell their products to all markets at the same price. Therefore, purchasing price will be the same. However, the selling price and the product's margin will have to be adapted to the conditions of the local market because of intensified competition (prices applied by competitors, prices of substitutes).

***Distribution***. ELKO Group is characterized by high centralization level of management and operational processes. Ingoing logistics (unified transportation schemes, fixed timetables for orders and arrivals of cargo, common regional warehouses) is standardized across all international markets. Outgoing logistics (local distribution) is adapted due to specific features of individual markets. Since Poland and the Baltic countries are found to have similar distribution systems, it is likely that in the first stage the same distribution system model can be equally applied in the Polish market.

***Promotion.*** Since the uniqueness with respect to the product, price and distribution is difficult to obtain due to the characteristic features of IT distribution business, it is promotion that remains to be the only element readily modified, the adaptation of which might be turned into competitive advantage of the company. Owing to the cultural differences mentioned above, different purchasing power and strategic attitude to promotion, marketing mix promotion element will be adapted for Polish market. Both Poland and Lithuania show the same competitive intensity in IT market. Consequently, in forming the marketing mix for the Polish market, it is appropriate to note that intensified competition directly and positively affect adaptation solutions related to promotion (Theodosiou and Leonidou, 2003).

In conclusion, we maintain that in entering the Polish market, the following marketing mix elements may be standardized: product portfolio, price and distribution. The highest degree of standardization can be achieved for the product. Promotion element regarding cultural differences and the company's marketing strategy in other markets should be adapted.

## Knowledge and Experience

Theoretical analysis showed that marketing mix standardization and adaptation is a continuous, dynamic process, cyclic movement between initial and corrected solution of the marketing mix. This process as well as the possible gap between initial and corrected solution is largely influenced by the knowledge on the market as well as by the company's international experience. These two dimensions vary with time. This is confirmed by the ELKO Group experience and dynamics of solutions. The company gradually switches from full standardization (applied initially) to more individual/local approach. It finds new opportunities and more readily adapts to the international market by adopting and studying the experience of local companies.

The primary solution was formed with reference to the available knowledge on the market (secondary data analysis, experts' evaluation) and the company's experience in foreign markets. The decision whether or not the primary solution of marketing mix is adequate for the external situation, is possible only upon its realization. Again, only after some time it will be possible to decide how the marketing mix standardization and adaptation decisions for Poland will be changed. Therefore, empirical substantiation of the theoretical framework of marketing mix standardization and adaptation is finished in this work with the solution of the primary stage. The analysis of the corrected decision influenced by new knowledge and the acquired experience as well as the evaluation of decision effectiveness is possible only after some period of time. Therefore, the stages of the corrected decision, effectiveness and its impact on the new decision could be the goal of further continuous empiric study. In this work empiric substantiation of the theoretical model of marketing mix standardization and adaptation covers only some stages of proposed theoretical framework, i.e. the analysis of internal and external factors, psychic distance, organizational culture and the initial decision on marketing mix influenced by the primary knowledge about the market. These stages are represented in Fig. 16 in the area marked in different color.

**Figure 14: The empirical substantiation of theoretical framework of marketing mix standardization and adaptation in international markets**

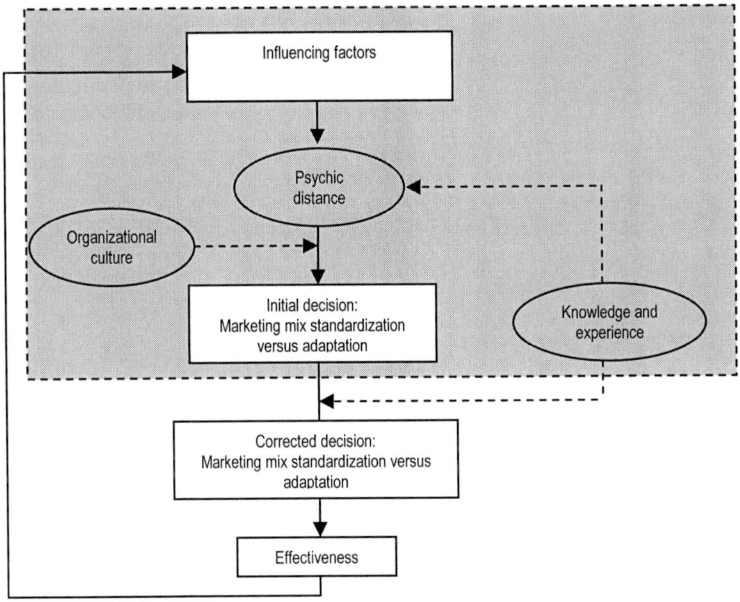


# Conclusions

The empiric research has led to the following conclusions:

1. Marketing mix standardization and adaptation process is a continuous process, dynamic cyclic movement between initial and corrected decision, therefore, the theoretical framework worked out in this study, joins together static and dynamic theoretical models by integrating the variables of dynamic models into the structure of static models.

2. The worked out theoretical framework of marketing mix adaptation and standardization encompasses not only the perceptible external and internal factors influencing the decision and the consequences of this solution, but, also, more subtle

aspects of perception (psychic distance), organizational behavior, the company's knowledge and experience, thus, promoting the awareness of marketing mix standardization and adaptation as a dynamic and time-varying process.

3. On comparing the Polish and Baltic IT markets as well as evaluating the impact of internal (organizational and managerial) and external (macro environment, market, product, consumers, competition) factors on marketing mix standardization and adaptation decisions, we maintain that the majority of detailed factors create favorable conditions for marketing mix standardization, while such factors as different cultural environment and purchasing power, highly intensified competition and different competitive position of the company in the international markets are barriers for standardization.

4. Small psychic distance between Polish and Baltic markets is determined by the similarities in economic, political and legal environment stipulated by EU membership, similar degree of consumers and enterprises' market saturation with IT products, analogues cost-sensitivity, equally low level of computer literacy, the same Internet penetration level, identical stage of the product life cycle and equally high competitive intensity in the IT market.

5. Systemic type of the company and its hierarchical structure stipulate the company's preconceived attitudes, i.e. on entering the new Polish market, ELKO Group is going to strive for the highest possible marketing mix standardization in accordance with the one applied in the already covered markets, and to adapt only those elements (promotion, outgoing logistics, pricing) which require smaller resources and more readily respond to adaptation without changing the company's established structure and processes.

6. On entering the Polish market, the standardization of product portfolio, price and distribution are possible. The highest standardization degree is achieved for price. The promotion element with regard to cultural differences, competition intensity and marketing strategy applied in other markets should be adapted.

7. Since the analysis of the corrected decision influenced by new knowledge and the acquired experience, as well as the evaluation of the decision effectiveness are possible only after some period of time, the empiric substantiation of the theoretical model of marketing mix standardization and adaptation in this work is finished with the stage of initial decision. The stages of corrected decision, its efficiency and effect on new solutions could be the aim of further continuous empiric research.

## References

Cavusgil, S.T., Zou, S. (1994), "Marketing strategy-performance relationship: an investigation of the empirical link in export market venture", Journal of Marketing, Vol. 58 No.1, pp.1-21.

Douglas, S.P., Wind, Y. (1987), "The myth of globalization", *Colombia Journal of World Business*, Winter, pp.19-29.

Hill, John S. and Still, Richard R. (1984). Adapting Products to LDC Taste. Harvard Business Review 62(March–April):92–101

Jain, S.C. (1989), "Standardization of international marketing strategy: some hypotheses", *Journal of Marketing*, Vol. 53 No.1, pp.70-9.

Kotler, P. (1986), "Global standardization-courting danger", *Journal of Consumer Marketing*, Vol. 3 No.2, pp.13-15.

Kuvykaite R., (1998), Tarptautinis Marketingas. "Technologija".

Levitt, T. (1983), "The globalization of markets", *Harvard Business Review*, Vol. 61 No.3, pp.92-102.

Ramanathan A., Parashar M. (2005), A Typology of Format Adaptation Strategies in Comparative Retailing,

Solberg, C.A. (2000), "Educator insights: standardization or adaptation of the international marketing mix: the role of the local subsidiary/representative", *Journal of International Marketing*, Vol. 8 pp.78-98.

Sousa, Carlos M. P. and Frank Bradley, "Global Markets: Does Psychic Distance Matter?", Journal of Strategic Marketing, Forthcoming

Theodosiou, M. and Leonidou, L.C. (2003) 'Standardization versus Adaptation of International Marketing Strategy: An Integrative Assessment of the Empirical Research', International Business Review, 12:2, 141-171

Waheeduzzaman, A. N., Dube, Leon, Trends and Development in Standardization Adaptation Research. Journal of Global Marketing; 2004, Vol. 17 Issue 4, p23, 30p

http://fita.org/countries/poland.html
http://marketing.byu.edu/htmlpages/ccrs/proceedings05/ramanathan-parashar.doc.
http://paiz.gov.pl/index/?id=a0a080f42e6f13b3a2df133f073095dd#reports
http://strategis.ic.gc.ca/epic/internet/inimr-ri.nsf/en/gr109813e.html
http://www.american.edu/initeb/rw9257a/market.htm#ictmarket
http://www.ceemarket.com/index.php?c=POLAND&item=cee_basic_data
http://www.cs.cas.cz/itstar/files/FactorsAndImpacts.pdf
http://www.eito.com/download/EITO%202006%20%20ICT%20market%20March%202006.pdf
http://www.idc.com/getdoc.jsp?containerId=pr2006_03_09_145047
http://www.imf.org
http://www.macworld.com/news/2006/03/09/pcmarket/index.php
http://www.poltradeindia.org/it_sector.htm
http://www.std.lt/uploads/docs/Indicators.pdf
http://www.trademeeting.com/Default.asp?ID=1493
www.elkogroup.com
www.IDC.lt
www.infobalt.lt
www.std.lt
www.worldvaluessurvey.org

# Industrial Clusters, Foreign Direct Investment and Regional Disparities in CEE

Harald Zschiedrich and Agata Gajda

## Abstract

The rapid changing of the international competition is now changing the drivers of the Foreign Direct Investment (FDI). Although the traditional main determinants of FDI as market size, wage differences, highly developed infrastructure and natural resources remain relevant, FDI tends to be fairly concentrated geographically. In this context, regional industrial and knowledge-based Clusters are playing an increasing role as a main driver for FDI into CEE´s. This paper deals with some Clusters in the automotive industry and will demonstrate the development of different Regions within Poland: Wielkopolska and Podkarpackie. Our investigations have shown that where agglomeration economies are significant, the rest of the CEE's are of a little relevance for foreign investors.

Although there is widening of regional disparities within CEE economies as a result of FDI, we can observe first signs of reducing the gaps between regions in these countries.

## Introduction

Although the traditional factors driving FDI to the CEEC's as large markets, possession of natural and high qualified human resources and low labour cost – remain relevant, these drivers, which were dominating at the beginning of the transformation, are diminishing now in importance.

The competition for FDI and location of production is no longer between national economies as a whole, but between strongly networked regions – so called "Industrial Clusters".

Industrial Clusters are high concentrations of firms, banks and research institutions benefiting from synergy effects created by a dense network of competitions, buyers and suppliers. Such agglomerations are able to attract more FDI and relocation of production capacities.

International experience has shown that clusters of high innovative activity (as Silicon Valley in California, Automotive Cluster in Graz, Electronic Cluster in Dresden, Biotechnology in Cambridge, Strasbourg, Munich and Software Exporting Cluster in Dublin) have a great advantage in attracting FDI. Not only in the western countries, but also in the CEEC's foreign investors seek to take advantage of new dynamic clusters to relocate production (for example Automotive Clusters in Bratislava, Mlada Boleslav and Györ, Electronic Cluster Szekesfehervàr or Mechanical engineering Cluster in Brno).

In joining and supporting Industrial Clusters in CEE multinational firms add to its competitiveness, strength and economic dynamism. But on the other hand, we have to take in consideration that where agglomeration economies are significant, the rest of the countries is of little relevance to the FDI decision. Thus it is necessary to compensate this negative employment effects and to take measures for reducing the growing regional disparities both on the national level (for example Szechenyi Programm in Hungary) and on the EU-level (Cohesion-Funds).

Clusters are playing an important role, in the economic development of CEEC's, particularly in the technology intensive branches. We can observe a substantial widening of regional disparities in the result of increasing FDI inflows. "Some 92% of the people in the new Member States live in regions with GDP per head below 75% of the EU 25 average and over two-thirds in regions where it is under half the average"[1].

As our own investigations and case studies have shown, Foreign Direct Investment (FDI) can potentially play a key role in reducing regional disparities as a means of transferring technology and know-how to lagging regions[2]. But FDI tends to go disproportionately to the stronger rather than the weaker parts of the EU-member states. This fact is not a new phenomenon. Agglomeration processes has already been the subject of a number of models of the "New Economic Geography" (P. Krugman).

## Why Regional Clusters in CEE?

"Clustering" is today a main feature of economic and regional policy not only in many EU-countries but also worldwide. Only during the last years, for example in Germany, the provincial government in Bavaria has supported 19 successful clusters in technology-intensive sectors with the aim to increase innovative potentials in the region Bavaria. In the result of "clustering" it became possible to strengthen the value-added chains between final producers, suppliers and customers, particularly in such fields as the following: biotechnology, environment, food, wood and forest, chemical cluster, medicine technique, information and communication techniques, aerospace. Another example is Steiermark in Austria. Here the provincial government overhauled its development strategy and created a cluster networking linking various parts of the automotive industry, which proved effective. Furthermore, in Sweden, the government has shifted in recent years to supporting the development of "growth poles" and clusters in different regions whereas previously it was centred on maintaining a high level of public sector activity in the northern, sparsely populated regions in order to combat outward migration[3].

What the new EU-member states from CEE can learn from the experience of "Clustering" in western countries?

1) Clusters as locational advantages play an increasing role in determining the location of international production systems, and hence FDI patterns. Understanding the patterns of FDI and the driving forces of production location in different industries and within international production systems and international value-added chains is important for formulating effective strategies and policies with respect to FDI-inflows into CEE.

2) Economics activities always had a tendency to cluster. Firms have been attracted to sites where other firms are already located to take advantage of existing external economies-markets, factors of production, specialized skills, intangible assets, suppliers, bank institutions, research institutes and, especially high developed innovative capabilities. (For example; Silicon Valley in California, "Saxony" Valley for semiconductors in Dresden, Wireless Valley in Stockholm, Biotechnology Cluster in the region Heidelberg, Automotive Clusters in Graz, Bratislava, Mlada Boleslav, Wolfsburg, Stuttgart).

3) Using Clusters to attract FDI into CEE-countries requires a new approach, going beyond the first and second generations of investment promotion policies (World Investment Report 2001: Promoting Linkages). The current (third) generation of FDI-promotion policies takes the enabling framework for FDI and a productive approach towards attracting FDI as a starting point. This new promoting approach includes that a CEE-country can nurture specific clusters that build on the country's competitive advantages. The key to success of the new FDI promotion strategy is that they actually address one of the basic economic FDI determinants while understanding the changing location strategies of Transnational Corporations (TNCs)[4].
4) Clusters are not only important for the location of the TNC - headquarters. Experience in Western countries has shown that they are also play a crucial role for the dynamic and successful development of SMEs: "It has been spurred by evidence on the dynamism of SME's located in industrial districts as well as in many developing countries, the growth of high technology clusters in developed countries and the case of clustering as a tool of industrial strategy and new industrial policy. It is therefore to be expected that the location of TNC's in home and host economies reflects agglomeration forces"[5].
5) There is a close interdependence between the existence of strong cluster regions and the intention to relocate production capacities abroad. We should take in consideration that a well organized "clustering" – for example in Japanese economy – is one of the reasons for manufacturing resilience in Japan and a much less number of relocation of production to the neighbour countries (China, Vietnam) in comparison with German firms relocating production to CEE countries.

High value production depends not only on a good qualified workforce but also on a strong network of specialist subcontractors to provide parts and services: "If our client has a problem, it is helpful that they have such a short distance to come to talk about it" (Keni Furuhushi; CEO of Kosiden, an Osaka-based electronics parts manufacturer). Cluster theory suggests: The more manufactures that decide to stay, the better for technological competitiveness. In this way new products can be rapidly improved (High level of innovation). Commercially sensitive technology remains in Japan and lower-end manufacturing takes place abroad (For example: Canon produces basic photocopier in China, but toner cartridges in Japan)[6]. Close

Cooperations within the regional networks (Clusters) is one of the reasons that Japanese companies maintain a relatively high number of employees in Japan. This does mean that firms in Japan employ a steady number of workers at home, even as they have expanded its overseas workforce, most of them in Asia. The reason is, that many customers insist that the crucial part of the value added chain is being made in Japan to ensure a high quality.

## What are the main characteristics of clusters?

The features of a cluster are extreme innovativeness, a high standard of education, a large service industry, an excellent infrastructure, high concentrations of resources and capabilities. In sum: Clusters are concentrations of companies (national and international) in one or few sectors (branches), benefiting from synergies created by a dense network of competitions, buyers and suppliers. Clusters comprise demanding buyers, specialized suppliers (above all in the automotive industry), sophisticated human resources, finance, banking, and well-developed support institutions. (See: Experience of Investment Development Agency in Ireland). Such concentrations of resources and capabilities can attract more and "efficiency-seeking" FDI to the more advanced host countries in CEE[7]. Thus an international location choice-made by multinational firms or TNC's – is today not so much a choice, for example – between Poland and Slovakia as total as for example, between the Poznan or Bratislava Region. The following scheme gives an overview about the main characteristics of a regional cluster:

**Scheme 1:** Characterics of regional clusters as catalysts for industrial development in CEE

| **Characteristics of regional Clusters** | |
|---|---|
| Core idea: | Dynamic transactions betw een synergic firms and w ithin value-chains that create competitive advantages |
| Policy aims: | Creating and leveraging synergies betw een firms and other factors to attract more FDI for such regions |
| Policy instruments: | Netw ork and cluster programs, formation of industrial parts and special economic zones |
| Challenges / Problems: | - Failure to bring national SME's and other TMC's together<br>- Failure to recognize potential synergies |

## Regional Disparities and FDI

The issue of uneven development of the regions has been actively discussed for the last ten years[8]. A new push of discussion emerged in connection with the EU-membership of the states in CEE. In some countries (for example Hungary "Szechenyi Programm" 2002 and Lithuania "The Regulation of Regional Development" 2000) were declared special programmes to accelerate a well-balanced development of separate regions and decrease of social and economic disparities between the regions within the countries. Experience has shown that a lot of regions are suffering from structural weakness, which does limit their competitiveness and their ability to attract Foreign Direct Investment.

Focusing on European economies in the most papers there are no signs that FDI has contributed to a strong reducing of income and development gap in EU-countries. On the contrary: "Clustering" as a result of Foreign Direct Investment inflows has strengthened the trend deepening the regional disparities. Not only in the CEEC's but also in the "old" western EU-member states we can observe uneven distribution of FDI inflows: In Germany – for example – FDI was concentrated in a limited number of

"Länder" (regions); with Nordrhein-Westphalia, Hesse und Baden-Würtemberg accounting 71% of all inward FDI inflows and Bayern and Hamburg for another 20%. By contrast; the five objective 1 Regions in Eastern Germany accounted for only just over 2% of the total FDI inflows into Germany[9].

The same tendency is evident in the Central European Countries. Within all of these countries the dates indicate a relatively high degree of concentration of FDI in and around capital and other large cities (Budapest, Bratislava, Prague, Poznan, Warsaw, Brno...). In Hungary, over two-third of inward FDI went to the Budapest region, in Czech Republic 60% went to Prague region and the surrounding region (Strědni Cechy) and in Slovakia some 65% went to Bratislava.

**Table 1: Distribution of inwared FDI by region in selected new EU Member States (in % of country totals); Source: Third Report on economic and social cohesion, Luxembourg 2005, p.111**

| Czech Republic | | Hungary | | Poland | | Slovakia | |
|---|---|---|---|---|---|---|---|
| Praha | 49.3 | Közep-Magyarország | 67.7 | Mazowieckie | 24.3 | Bratislavský | 63.2 |
| Střední Čechy | 10.7 | Közep-Dunántúl | 9.4 | Śląskie | 13.5 | Východné Slovensko | 18.8 |
| Jihozápad | 7.6 | Nyugat-Dunántúl | 7.5 | Wielkopolskie | 11.6 | Západné Slovensko | 10.3 |
| Severozápad | 8.2 | Észak-Magyarország | 6.2 | Dolnośląskie | 8.4 | Stredné Slovensko | 7.7 |
| Severovýchod | 6.6 | Del-Alföld | 4.0 | Pomorskie | 7.3 | | |
| Jihovýchod | 8.4 | Eszak-alföld | 3.5 | Łódzkie | 5.9 | | |
| Střední Morava | 5.2 | Dél-dunántúl | 1.8 | Małopolskie | 5.6 | | |
| Moravskoslezko | 4.0 | | | Kujawkso-Pomorskie | 4.1 | | |
| | | | | Zachodniopomorskie | 3.9 | | |
| | | | | Lubelskie | 2.8 | | |
| | | | | Podkarpackie | 2.5 | | |
| | | | | Świętokrzyskie | 2.3 | | |
| | | | | Warmińsko-mazurskie | 2.3 | | |
| | | | | Lubuskie | 2.2 | | |
| | | | | Opolskie | 1.8 | | |
| | | | | Podlaskie | 1.6 | | |

Particularly strong disparities we can find in Hungary, where the large FDI inflows ten years ago were concentrated exclusively on the western and central regions of Hungary. This trend has still increased the attractiveness of Western Hungarian regions for FDI. On the other hand, the regional disparities have increased (only 12% of all FDI-inflows to Hungary went to the Eastern regions!) The experience of Hungary has shown that the western investors are above all interested in investment into clusters regions (agglomeration effects!)[10].

In Poland FDI-inflows are less concentrated, because there are a number of large cities. Nevertheless, the capital city region Mazowieckie (696 investors) accounted a quarter of total FDI-inflows and other two regions (Lodzkie and Wielkopolskie – 244 investors), both of which contain large cities (Lódz and Poznan).

**Table 2: Foreign Direct Investment inflows by regions in Poland; Source: PAIiIZ, 2004**

| Region (Wojevodschaft) | Numer of investment projects |
|---|---|
| Pomorskie | 144 |
| Zachodniopomorskie | 95 |
| Warmińsko-mazurskie | 57 |
| Kujaw kso-Pomorskie | 111 |
| Podlaskie | 36 |
| Lubuskie | 63 |
| Wielkopolskie | 242 |
| Mazow ieckie | 801 |
| Łódzkie | 160 |
| Dolnośląskie | 207 |
| Lubelskie | 59 |
| Św iętokrzyskie | 54 |
| Opolskie | 47 |
| Śląskie | 390 |
| Małopolskie | 141 |
| Podkarpackie | 2,5 |

## Case Study 1: Automotive Cluster CEE

CEE is now growing an automotive Cluster which has a higher speed of development in comparison with the traditional centres of the car industry in Western Europe. The main locations of this Regional Cluster are in Czech Republic, Slovakia, Poland, Hungaria and partly also in Romania (supplier industry).

These locations have attracted FDI not only for the Original Equipment Manufactures (OME) but also more and more for the car supplier firms. The automotive Cluster in CEE is more important as a production location than as a sales market. There are signs that car industry output and exports in CEE have been increasingly generated by foreign subsidiaries. Only few of these enterprises with foreign capitals are the result of international relocation with capacities from the EU-15 to the New Member States. Slovakia for example has been widely publicized recently as a very attractive FDI location for the car industry with two large investment projects in the process of competition (2005-2007). Thus the main players in the competition for a "Clustering" in the automotive industry among the CEE locations are Poland, Hungary, Slovakia, Czech Republic and Romania among the Southeast European countries.[11]

Considering Clusters as a dense network of firms, research institutions and supplier companies with high technology and investment intensity, the automotive industry is very suitable for "Modern Clustering" (see Table 3).

Enterprise cooperations, especially the building of "development" and "System-Clustering" are playing an increasing role. There is a new trend that supplier firms in CEE are obliged to offer not only several parts but also more and more modules ("System suppliers").

## Preconditions for "Clustering" in the CEE – Automotive Industry

The main reason for the successful development of CEE-automotive industry was the increasing FDI-activity of foreign companies. 80% of all investment, which was following in this branch, was generated by western firms. In Hungary this share of foreign firms amounts even 100%. Western firms are benefiting from the high qualification of employers and relative low labour costs. In the automotive industry the share of labour costs amounts to 15 – 25% in dependence from type / model of cars (see table 4 + 5).

**Table 3: Technology Intensity [a] and FDI Intensity [b] by Industry 2004 (percent);**

| Industry | Technology intensity | FDI Intensity |
|---|---|---|
| *Technology-intensive industries average* | 6.8 | 22.5 |
| Motor Cars | 8.5 | 29.7 |
| Instruments | 8.3 | 17.2 |
| Electrical machinery | 7.2 | 22.0 |
| Chemicals, refineries | 5.1 | 28.0 |
| Non-electrical machinery | 4.8 | 15.5 |
| *Less technology-intensive industries average* | 2.4 | 7.7 |
| Rubber and plastics | 3.2 | 11.9 |
| Metal and metal products | 2.7 | 3.7 |
| Wood, paper, printing and publishing | 2.6 | 2.3 |
| Textilies, apparel, leather | 2.3 | 17.1 |
| Stone, clay, glass | 2.2 | 14.4 |
| Food beverages, tobacco | 1.6 | 3.2 |
| Other manufacturing (incl. Furniture) | 1.9 | 1.1 |

[a] Innovation expenditures / sales - [b] Stock of outward FDI / gross domestic capital stock

Source: Aschhoff et al. (2006); Deutsche Bundesbank (2006); Statistisches Bundesamt (2006)

**Table 4: Labour cost in the Czech Automotive industry (in Euro); Source: L. Kaufmann / D. Panhans; Managementhandbuch: Mittel- und Osteuropa; Gabler Vertrag Wiesbaden 2006; p. 237**

| Position | Low Level | Higher Level |
|---|---|---|
| Plant Manager | 3.000 | 10.000 |
| Assembler Manager | 1.900 | 4.700 |
| Supervisor | 1.100 | 1.800 |
| Design engeneer | 710 | 1.800 |
| Logistic Manager | 1.500 | 3.100 |
| Human Ressource Manager | 1.400 | 3.800 |
| Financial Controller | 1.800 | 4.700 |
| Assembler Worker | 280 | 530 |

Considering the distribution of worldwide employment in the automotive industry a considerable share of employment is falling to the CEEC's (see table 5).

**Table 5: Employment of the world Automotive industry by countries (2004); Source: U. Jürgens; Strukturveränderungen von Arbeit und Beschäftigung in der internationalen Automobilindustrie; VDA 2005; S 350 ff**

| > 500 thsd. | | 50 - 99 thsd. | |
|---|---|---|---|
| U.S.A | 1.126,2 | Czech Rep. | 94,9 |
| Germany | 869,9 | South Africa | 78,2 |
| Japan | 721,1 | Sweden | 75,3 |
| Russian Fed. | 537,0 | Poland | 74,2 |
| China * | 1.850,0 | Romania | 61,1 |
| **100 - 499 thsd.** | | **< 49 thsd.** | |
| France | 279,6 | Indonesia | 49,5 |
| India | 251,1 | Belgium | 43,5 |
| Brazil | 249,7 | Hungary | 39,5 |
| UK | 215,9 | Austria | 30,2 |
| South Korea | 197,9 | Netherlands | 26,9 |
| Italy | 171,9 | Slovak Rep. | 22,7 |
| Spain | 168,8 | Portugal | 22,7 |
| Turkey | 168,0 | Other** (<10 thsd.) | 32,7 |
| Canada | 153,0 | | |
| Mexico | 138,1 | | |

* Data of year 2000

** Bulgaria, Denmark, Finland, Ireland, Slovenia

Industrial Clustering needs well-developed production capacities. Already today Slovakia and Czech Republic belong to these countries that are leaders in the car production ahead of the national population (table 6)

**Table 6: Automotive production (Cars and utility vehicles); Source: G. Wolf; Fahrzeugindustrie in CEE, Produktionsstandorte sind langfristig wichtiger als die Absatzmärkte; Bank – Austria Creditanstalt, Report 2/2005; p. 13**

| Automotive production | 2004 in 1.000 | 2004 Anteile | 1997 - 2004 Veränderung |
|---|---|---|---|
| EU - 25 | 18,332 | 29% | 6% |
| *EU - 15* | 16,854 | 26% | 4% |
| Deutschland | 5,570 | 9% | 11% |
| Frankreich | 3,666 | 6% | 42% |
| Österreich | 249 | 0% | 131% |
| *Neue EU-Mitglieder* | 1,478 | 2% | 52% |
| Polen | 599 | 1% | 56% |
| Tschechien | 448 | 1% | 22% |
| Slowakei | 224 | 0% | 434% |
| Ungarn | 124 | 0% | 54% |
| Slowenien | 132 | 0% | 37% |
| USA | 11,989 | 19% | -1% |
| Japan | 10,512 | 16% | -4% |
| China | 5,071 | 8% | 221% |
| **Insgesamt** | **63,959** | **100%** | **17%** |

Apart from the Cluster in the Czech Republic, the boom in automobile industry production is also present in Slovakia, Poland and Hungary, producing altogether over 1 million cars:

**Table 7: Production capacities of some Regional automobile locations in CEE (10); Source: R. Landmann; Automotive Cluster in CEE; Volkswagen Conference; Presentation 2005**

| Ranking | Country | Cluster Region | Year of foundation | Lead | Volume | MA (OEM) |
|---|---|---|---|---|---|---|
| 1 | CZ | Mladá Boleslav | 1991 | Skoda | 437.000 | 19.300 |
| 2 | CZ | Kolin | 2002 | Peugeot, Citroen, Toyota | 300.000 (geplant) | 3.000 |
| 3 | SK | Trnava | 2003 | Peugeot, Citroen, Toyota | 300.000 (geplant) | 3.500 |
| 4 | SK | Bratislava | 1991 | VW | 281.000 | 8.400 |
| 5 | SK | Zilina | 2004 | Hyundai - Kia | 250.000 (geplant) | 3.000 |
| 6 | PL | Tychy | 1992 | Fiat | 204.000 | 3.200 |
| 7 | PL | Poznan | 1993 | VW | 120.000 (2004) | 4.400 |
| 8 | HU | Esztergom | 1992 | Suzuki | 89.000 | 2.400 |
| 9 | PL | Gliwice | 1998 | Opel | 77.000 | 2.000 |
| 10 | HU | Györ | 1993 | Audi | 34.000 | 5.000 |

As already mentioned, TNC's have invested heavily in the automobile industry in the CEECs. About one tenth of inward FDI stocks in Hungary, Poland and the Czech Republic are in the automotive industry.

As the large component suppliers have followed car producers, a dynamic manufacturing Cluster with high output and export potential has already developed. For example, in the Czech Republic the export of Skoda cars amounts to 10 % of the total Czech economy exports (!).

Further investments in the new EU-member states are expected from large carmakers (Volkswagen, Toyota) and component suppliers (R. Bosch, Delphi, Continental, ZF-Group, Magna, Du Pont, PPG-Industries, Brose etc.). Why it is realistic to expect more FDI in the next years to the automotive Cluster CEE?

There are several encouraging factors including increasing sales of cars in CEE, expected strong economic growth, relative low labour costs in comparison with western producers in Germany, France, a high skilled workforce, a low tax environment, as well as several investment incentives.

In 2005 the average effective top statuary tax rate on corporate income in the Czech Republic, Hungary and Poland was 20,1 %, compared to the average tax rate of 36,6 % in France, Germany and Italy (see table 8).

**Table 8: Tax Rate on corporate income (2005 in per cent); Source: World Investment Report 2006, p.92**

| Country | Level of Tax Rate |
|---|---|
| France | 33,8 |
| Germany | 38,6 |
| Italy | 37,3 |
| Czech Republic | 26 |
| Hungary | 17,5 |
| Poland | 19 |

Wages in the new EU-member states of CEE were in 2005 / 2006 about 70% lower than those in the EU-15 member states. They can be expected to remain at this level, although from country to country there are different developments in wages (For example in 2007 there was demand in the Skoda / VW Company in CR to increase wages by 25%). Thus, all in all, automobile production in CEE expected to double within the next years, from 1,6 million (2005) to 3,2 million vehicles (2010), increasing the share of the new EU-10 member states in total EU-production to 17%! To sum it up, it can be said, that the automotive Cluster in CEE offers a lot of advantages:

**Table 9: Advantages by CEE automotive Cluster; Source: R. Landmann; Automotive Cluster Osteuropa; Deloitte Consulting GmbH; 2004**

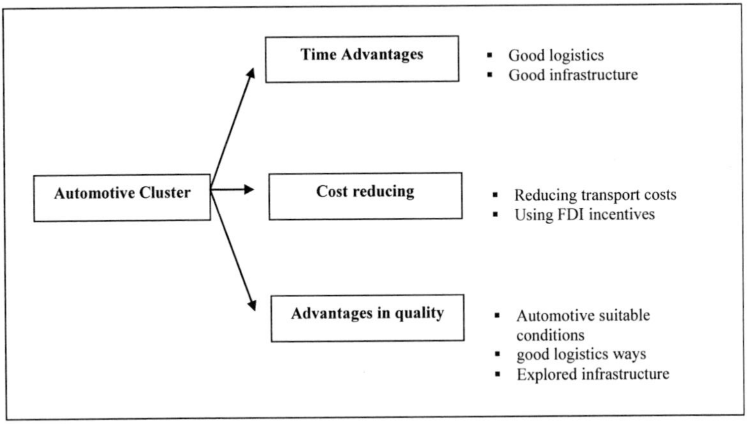


## Results and Lessons from The Automotive Cluster in CEE

The mushrooming of Greenfield investments, Greenfield firms, domestic services and East-West Joint Ventures can be very well illustrated by the development of the automobile industry in some CEEC's. This process was laid by the creation of the Skoda – Volkswagen Joint Venture in 1991. The emerging automobile Cluster around the Mlada Boleslav Region led to a booming market for the Czech production of car components. The high dynamic growth of Skoda-Auto in CR spilled over the whole automobile industry, which grew at an average rate of 12 per cent (in real value added). The share of Skoda-Auto exports in the total volume of CR exports amounts to 10%! Thanks to the close cooperation between the "core" enterprise VW Wolfsburg and the Skoda firm in Mlada Boleslav and to the accompanying learning process ("Tandem leadership Management"), local suppliers of components and car related services became so competitive that the Czech economy has been attracting a lot of FDI.

Until recently, cross border cooperation between automobile firms in CEE was not so intensive and the dependence on the suppliers in the western

EU-member states dominated both production and trade. Dramatic change begins when three additional plants start operating: Consortium Toyota – Peugeot – Citroen and Hyundai in Slovakia, and the total production of cars in the CEE Region has reached almost 2,5 million cars per year in 2007.

The new supply strategies are now based on a greater use of locally produced components, on local business services and deeper intraregional integration of firms (see table 10). The increasing complexity of international cooperation and competition in the automotive industry in the Budapest – Praha – Bratislava – Poznan – Warsaw Regions should create all advantages of industrial Clusters (agglomeration effects): Specialized suppliers, the pooling of specialized labour markets, Knowledge spillovers and strong leaders at the end of the supply chain.

**Table 10: Overview about Supplier locations in CEE; Source: VDA; 2004**

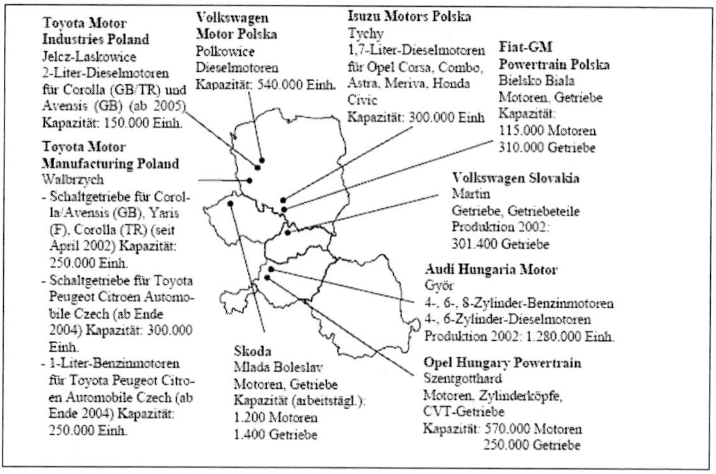


The experience from the emerging automobile Cluster in Central and Eastern Europe has shown that comparative advantage in cheap labour does not appear to be any longer, the main motivation to invest in CEE.

Instead of economizing on variable costs such as wages, the strategic objective in modern industries is to seek out fixed cost reductions and external economies associated with Regional industrial Clusters. Thus, a firm that tried to enter automobile industry in a location outside the above mentioned Cluster Regions in CEE – would have an immediate disadvantage because it would be burdened with additional fixed and transaction costs that would most likely be much higher than any gains from lower wage costs.

## Summary

1. Small CEE economies (Hungary, CR, and Slovakia) with a lot of firms with only local or regional importance, should seek first to establish a strategic link to a "core" company (Volkswagen, Opel, Audi, Suzuki, Toyota) in order to be able to gradually develop an integrated local hub.
2. Drivers for the FDI were not only the lower level of labour cost, but also a wide spectrum of factors such increasing potential of consumer market (75 Mio. consumer in CEE countries), customer union, tax conditions industrial traditions and experience, nearness to the EU-15 markets an FDI Promotion programmes, longer working times etc.
3. FDI contributed to the development of competitive supplier-industries. These industries provide not only the car manufacturer within the automotive Clusters, but also other automotive locations worldwide. More than 50% of worldwide leading suppliers firms have their own manufacturing in CEE.
4. Considering the increasing processes of international "Outsourcing" and "Offshoring" in the automotive industry, the supplier firms are more and more responsible for greater shares in the value added chains of car manufacturers (relocation of processes to specialized development firms; above all software). CEE supplier firms benefited from the increasing cost pressure, made by the final car manufacturers. Thus the supplier industry in CEE – especially in Hungary and Romania – is the winner. For example, the production volume of supplier sector was already 84% of the total volume of automotive industry in Hungary (100.000 employees).
5. Clustering in CEE automotive industry was until now different. Despite the high concentration of car production in Central and

Western Hungary, larger automotive Clusters were not developed because the most Western firms buy the necessary parts and components abroad (with the exception of Suzuki). Thus the local content of Hungarian suppliers is relatively low. Only the Györ Region became a really Cluster Region thanks to the large FDI activities of AUDI AG. Compared with other CEE-locations in Hungary is missing a big car producer with a large assemble factory (with exception of AUDI in Györ).

6. In the Czech Republic, Volkswagen / Skoda company promoted Clustering with the help of special programs for settlement of supplier firms (East-West Joint Ventures). This Cluster Region was helpful in creating of efficient relations between the manufacturer and the local supplier firms ("Value-added partnerships"). Meanwhile 200 German suppliers went to the Czech Republic and have close cooperation's with local firms. The geographic space of this Regional Cluster is furthermore also useful for the car producers in the southern parts of Germany. In some cases the deliveries from Mlada-Boleslav Cluster Region need less time in comparison with the time of delivery from the German Headquarter location. Thus the Cluster Region North Bohemia became a very import hub for the supplier industry.

## Case Study 2: Knowledge-based Cluster and FDI in the Region of Wielkopolska

There is no clear definition for the term "knowledge-based Cluster", although the most important features and determinants have been presented in numerous OECD Reports (1992-2002) and World Investment Reports (2005: Transnational Corporations and Internationalization of R&D; p. XXIV).

The main characteristics of a knowledge-based Cluster are:

- Presence of a knowledge-based infrastructure
- High level of an intensive exchange of knowledge in a certain local/regional dimension
- Factor "knowledge" has a great importance in the value-added-chains
- Attracting Foreign Direct Investment (FDI) as a component for building of knowledge-based Cluster[1].

International experience has demonstrated that while major actors of knowledge-based economies, such as governments, investment and research agencies, and international enterprises, play an important role, regional dimension also heavily influences knowledge-based Clusters. "After all, it is at the regional or local levels that such knowledge-based Cluster elements as social capital and corporate culture assume their fullest form, while valuable resources include not only codified knowledge but also tacit knowledge"[1].

The building of a knowledge-based Cluster in the Region of Wielkopolska is resulting from the initiative of Prof. A. Kuklinski, who organized a panel discussion on: "Wielkopolska in the fuel of challenges of a knowledge-based economy" (November 2001). The idea was that Wielkopolska would need a knowledge-based economy in order to be a dynamic European region in a global economy.
The main preconditions for a knowledge-based Cluster in the Region of Wielkopolska are:

- Enterprises with high international competitiveness which make use of knowledge to gain new competitive advantages (Volkswagen, Beiersdorf Polska, Bertelsmann etc.)
- Educational system (Adam Mickiewicz University, Academy of Economics: Centre of Regional Economic Research; Poznan Polytechnic Institute etc.)
- Research and Development Sector (Poznan Scientic-Technological Park, the newly founded Wielkopolska Institute, Institute of Socio-Economic Geography, Agricultural Academy)
- Regional and Local government bodies
- Special Voivodship Marshal's Office using the experience of European Regional Innovation strategy and the experience made by IDA in Ireland, Wielkopolska Chamber of Industry and Commerce, Wielkopolska Capital Club, Poznan Club of German investors, Department of Voivodship's Development Strategy and Promotion of the Marshal's Office, Regional Development Agency.

The building of a knowledge-based Cluster is generating a lot of challenges facing Wielkopolska enterprises, including international investors (Outlays for R&D, Training courses in Marketing, Inv. Management, purchases of licenses, building of close links between SME, TNC, R&D units, universities, Research institutes, including "import" of modern knowledge, increasing activities of polish enterprises with strong participation of FDI in the field of knowledge transfer).

All in all, the knowledge-based Cluster offers the Region of Wielkopolska good opportunities for integration with the European Union as a whole.

Enterprises with participation of the FDI play an important role for the building of "regional growth poles of a knowledge-based Cluster", as stated above. In the region exist (2006) 3.000 firms with the participation of foreign capital (Volkswagen, Reemtsma, Beiersdorf, MAN, Glaxo, Smithline, Wrigley, Exide, Bridgestone, Philips, etc.)[1]. Foreign firms invested in this region 4 Mld. USD, approximately 5% of all FDI in Poland. The main sectors attracting FDI are the: Food, Chemical Industry, Electronics, and Transport, Machine building, Polygraph industries etc. The greatest influx of FDI was observed during 1995-2000 (Volkswagen, Bertelsmann, Beiersdorf, and Wrigley). Starting in 2006 to the present, a decline in the FDI has been noted in this region. This decline may prove a barrier for further development of the knowledge-based Cluster in Region of Wielkopolska. The diminishing FDI can be attributed to a variety of reasons including but not limited to: the absence of highly developed regional planning, the lack of attractive space for western investors, the poor image of administration in this region, (for example: deficits and barriers in enlarging the production capacities by Volkswagen and statements about relocations of production from Poznan to other regions in CEE[1]). However, the Region of Wielkopolska is positioned well in comparison with other Polish regions attracting FDI, ranking number 5 in a recent study.

**Table 11: Ranking in attracting FDI by different Voivodships in Poland; Source: Kalinowski: "Atrakcyjność inwestycyjna województw i podregionów Polski 2006, IBnGR, Gdańsk 2006, p.20**

| | |
|---|---|
| 1. Śląskie | 9. Opolskie |
| 2. Mazowieckie | 10. Lubuskie |
| 3. Dolnośląskie | 11. Kujawsko-Pomorskie |
| 4. Małopolskie | 12. Warmińsko-Mazurskie |
| 5. Wielkopolskie | 13. Podkarpackie |
| 6. Pomorskie | 14. Świętokrzyskie |
| 7. Lódzkie | 15. Lubelskie |
| 8. Zachodniopomorskie | 16. Podlaskie |

Upon analyzing the strong and weak characteristics of the Region of Wielkopolska as a developing knowledge-based Cluster in the European Union, the local, regional and European authorities should continue to concentrate on reducing the weaknesses in this region (see: table 12).

**Table 12:** Strengths and Weakness of the Region of Wielkopolska; Source: Mikołajczyk, J., "Mocne I słabe strony Wielkopolski jako miejsca lokalizacji inwestycji zagranicznych" in Firma I Rynek-Zeszyt Naukowy ZSB, Szczecin, 2007, p.23

| Strengths | Weakness |
|---|---|
| Geographical position | |
| • communication channel between East and West<br>• multifunctional agglomeration of Poznan<br>• attractive investment area<br>• cultural heritage | • peripheral connection with the main developed centers in Europe<br>• connections possibilities predominantly with the central part of the region (Poznan)<br>• weak connections between the north an south part of the region and the centre<br>• absence of offers with prepared investment areas<br>• absence of regional policy |
| Infrastructure (communication) | |
| • connection East-West, motorway A2, railway line E30<br>• modern airport "Ławica"<br>• dynamic development of the logistic infrastructure<br>• good natural conditions for the riverine traffic | • bad road conditions<br>• lack of highly developed expressway network<br>• low number of the route diversion<br>• poor use of the favorable waterway-system |

| Population | |
|---|---|
| • qualified labor<br>• work-related activity of the residents<br>• high number of students<br>• low unemployment rate | • peripheral areas- high level of unemployment<br>• low educational level outside the metropolis<br>• learning opportunity do not correspond to the market requirement<br>• low level of the cooperation between the education unit and the business<br>• limited access to the infrastructure (information society) |
| Economy | |
| • inflow of FDI<br>• qualified labor<br>• social climate<br>• quality of the technical infrastructure<br>• potential and activity of the SME<br>• meaningful potential R&D<br>• expense of the administration unit | • different allocation FDI (intraregional)<br>• undeveloped connections between companies/enterprises<br>• low number of enterprises with high technology<br>• high labor costs<br>• inadequately capitalization of the active enterprises |

## Case Study 3:

## Can FDI contribute to reduce the development gaps in CEE? The Case of Podkarpackie Region in Poland

Focusing on the international discussion about the effects of FDI, there are not any direct signs that FDI has contributed to reduce of the development gaps in the EU-countries. Thus remote regions in CEE that qualify for EU-regional support, including support for FDI inflows, have until now not performed better in terms of employment, international competitiveness, labour productivity and export power.

The results of numerous analyses and investment researches in Poland have shown that the main benefits of the FDI inflows triggered by regional integration are likely to be (geographically) centrally located ( Mazowieckie with Warszawa as well as Śląskie and Łódzkie).

The main reasons for the reception of a business activity in Poland are: transport infrastructure, the absence of competition, qualified and motivated manpower and size of the polish market as well as geographical position and labor costs. Among other things, the market proximity and the agglomeration effects belong to the wide important reasons.

The first impacts of FDI in Poland are visible. The period 1993-2002 shows positive development of the activity. The number of the employees in companies with foreign participation clearly increases.

Thus, on the one hand from the point of view of regional development, FDI is likely to cement development gaps already existing between central and lagging regions in Poland (east part of the country). On the other hand, as the economic development of Podkarpackie Region has shown, the rising competition (FDI) between different regions in Poland like also CEEC's may well motivate the local administration units and authorities to introduce various instruments/incentives of regional policy (special economic zones/ technology parks) to influence the pattern and direction of FDI inflows.

## Podkarpackie – main economic characteristics

Podkarpackie is located on the east part of Poland and, as numerous comparative analysis of Poland have shown, belongs to the structurally lagging regions of the country. The following table summarize the main information correspond to the year 2006 about this region.

**Table 13: Characteristics of Podkarpackie Region; Source: GUS, www.wup-rzeszow.pl, www.region.rze.pl**

| Inhabitants | 2,1 Mio. |
|---|---|
| Unemployment rate | 16,7% |
| Average salary | ca. 496 euro |
| Country of origin of the investors | USA, Germany, Austria, France, Nederland |
| Sectors | Consumer products, processing industry, synthetic materials, timber industry, vulcanized rubber products |
| Main investors | Kronospan, Goodyear, United Technologies Corporation, Tesco, Media Markt, Heineken |

As disadvantage to this region, the lack of big economic centers (agglomeration zones) can be named which could clearly increase the investment attractiveness of the region and play the role of development centers. As a result it could show positive effects on the economic situation of the region as a whole. For example, the capital city Warszawa (Mazowieckie Region) that appears an important economic centre with technological and financial facilities and it's meaning and function as metropolis. Podkarpackie Region is embossed in opposite to Mazowieckie Region through a multiplicity of medium-sized as well as small cities where the inhabitant number amounts to less as 10.000. As it was mentioned, transport infrastructure belongs to the main factors involve the investment decisions regarding any business activity in Poland. Nowadays makes the improvement of the route of transport in Podkarpackie one of the top priorities. Thanks to the access to the EU financial resources, the first projects could be already realized. The following table represents the strong ones and the weak sides of the Podkarpackie Region:

**Table 14: Strengths and Weakness of the Podkarpackie Region; Source: Regionalna Strategia Innowacji województwa Podkarpackiego na lata 2005-2013, 2004**

| Strengths | Weakness |
|---|---|
| • Implementation and realization the EU-Norms (quality, safety, environmental protection) | • Lack of regional and national coordination of tasks of several units |
| • Numerous private and public colleges, facilities for research and development | • Lacking cooperation with the foreign associates and partners |
| • Different economic structure, traditional and ecological rural economy | • Relative weakly developed technical infrastructure |
| • Implementation of new management methods in the already established companies | • Lack of strategic thinking and development planning |
| • Tradition and success in sectors: electro machine sector, flight sector, household appliances, chemical industry | • Lack of cooperation and trust |
| • Relative low costs of activity, good image of the companies acting in the region | • Small and middle enterprises (SME)- low degree of innovation |
| • Access to new technologies, cooperation with the foreign research centers | • low labour cost (can be seen as a main strength of the region) |
| • High commitment of different institutions to support of the innovations | |

Regarding the geographic situation of the Podkarpackie Region (eastern part of Poland), it shows numerous and important possibilities and chances for the future cooperation and investment with the companies from the Ukraine and Slovakia (cross border cooperation networks). Contact with Eastern Europe can even be, but also not only for Poland of big importance. Countries that intend to widen their business activities.

Two special economic zones play a big role for the attractiveness of the region: EURO-PARK MIELEC (Mielecka) and EURO-PARK WISŁOSAN (Tarnobrzeska).

**Scheme 2: Special Economic Zones in Poland; Source: PAIiIZ, Rocznik 2004**

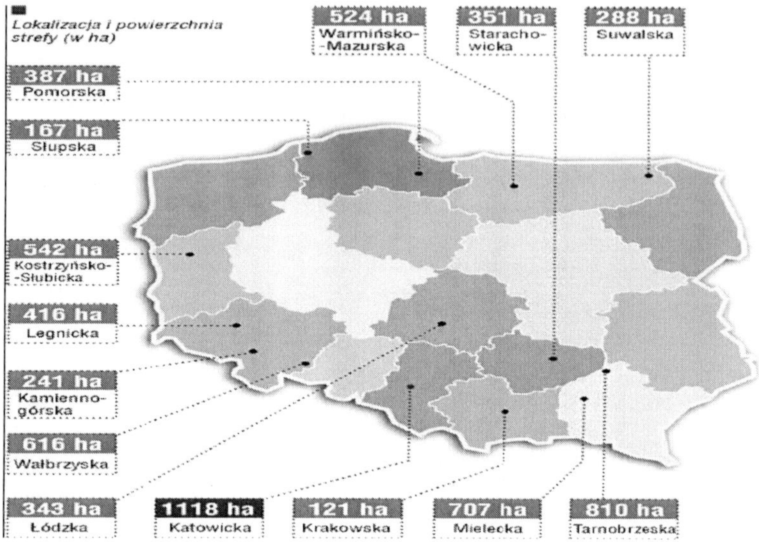


According to the law conditions in Poland (Sejm 1994) in the Special Economic Zones the firms can use the advantages of the following economic incentives:

- full relief from corporate income tax which is equal to half of the period for which the zone has been established
- 50% tax relief during the second half of the life time of the zone
- simplified procedures for selling property
- a 10 year exemption from real estate tax and from VAT liability for goods manufactured in the zone and then sold in the domestic market

The Special Zone EURO-PARK WISŁOSAN is placed in Tarnobrzeg city and has been set up back in 1997. It was scheduled to be an important tool for restructuring of large industrial areas as: sulphur mining and processing, metallurgy and hardware production. According to the statement of annual report for the year 2005, there are more than 10.000 people employed, more that 6.000 jobs of them are new jobs.

The Special Zones EURO-PARK MIELEC deserved a special attention. It was considered a showcase in the country. The following textbox demonstrate the spectrum of used incentives in this Special Economic Zone.

Euro Park Mielec

In September 1995, the Polish government designated Mielec as the country's first Special Economic Zones. The three hectare zone was developed as a response to the unemployment caused by mass layoff in the aerospace industry which had been the main source of economic activity in this remote area of eastern Poland.

The zone was set up to operate for a period of 20 years. Complete exemption from income tax is available to investors locating there for a period of 10 years, with a 50% reduction for the remaining period. For smaller investment projects benefits include the immediate and full write-off all investments made in the SEZ or alternatively revenues from export sales against current taxable earnings. Exemption is also provided from real estate tax. A network of double taxation treaties between Poland and other countries around the world makes this an attractive package for FDI projects.

The physical and human capital available in the area adds to the investment incentives. The Mielec name is associated historically with the manufacture of aviation equipment and the experience of labour force is attractive to incoming production operations- The presence of an airfield, railway siding and access to the national road network also add to the marketability of the site.

Responsibility for management of Euro Park has been assigned for the Industrial Development Agency (ARP SA) which works closely with PAIZ to attract foreign companies to do business there.

Source: Euro-Park Mielec Promotional Material

The increasing FDI inflow to Podkarpackie Region and the growing number of firms with participation of foreign capital contributes to degrease of the differences regarding the incomes and economic development between the structurally lagging Podkarpackie Region and the central regions in Poland.

The period 2000-2006 shows the first impacts of the foreign investments in the region as well the effects on the labor market. The activities of the self-administration units should concentrate more at the promotion of the region outside and on the cooperation with the neighbor regions and countries. The project "Dolina Lotnicza" has a big meaning for the innovative economic system in the region. It was summoned in 2003, by the companies that are active with the aviation industry. Organization and development of an effective delivery network also like promotion of

Polish aviation industry belong to the important intents. This idea has to do very narrowly with the building of innovative cluster. This problem was already represented in this paper.

Nowadays there is still an opinion that the east regions of Poland belong to the backwards regions. But this classification cannot be treated as a final categorization. Regions that for 20 years were presumed to be underdeveloped are now showing business skills and dynamic. The key benefits concerning the geographical position and connection opportunities between East and West Europe should be used. The process already started. First effects can be seen in the next years.

## Concluding Remarks

Results on regional location of FDI have shown that FDI-inflows went disproportionately to the economic stronger regions. The neoclassical views focused on trade creation and diversion, but rarely examined the effects of regional integration on FDI. Modern regional integration is expected to influence the international competitiveness of the region firms, whereas neoclassical views focused on more static efficiency of the regions resource allocation. All in all it can be argued that there are no evidences that FDI contributed to reducing the income, productivity, development and competitiveness gap within the CEEC's. On the contrary: FDI into CEE tend to cement the development gap already existing between stronger (central) and weaker (remote) regions. The increasing competition for FDI between countries and regions of Central and Eastern Europe requires from national governments and local/regional authorities to introduce various policies to influence the patterns of FDI. Greenfield Investment or Merger and Acquisitions, have different impact on regional development. Much depends on the FDI-motivations: "If the reason has to do with supplying a relatively large market in geographical terms, then multinational firms might be open to persuasion where in a particular country or broad geographical region it decides to locate. A national government might then have little difficulty in persuading a multinational to locate in less favoured area. If the reason, however, has to do with the specific attraction of a particular place, then it can often be difficult for a national government to persuade the multinational concerned to locate elsewhere if the place in question is not in line with overall regional development policy. In this case, the risk might be to discourage the multinational from investing in the country concerned at all. This tends to be a particular dilemma for governments in the CEE countries, where there is a potential trade-off between wanting investment to go toward the less developed regions to provide a stimulus and help them catch up, and the fact that investment tends naturally to be attracted to the regions which are most dynamic."[1] Experience has shown that in some CEE-countries national governments tend to prefer a higher economic growth for the country as a whole compared with a decrease of regional disparities.

The EU-commission has proposed a new cohesion policy for the period 2007- 2013. It will be not so easy to solve the "target conflict" between two economic aims of EU structural policies:

- Promoting "Clustering" as a catalysator for economic growth in the CEECs.
- Reducing disparities and promoting a more balanced regional development.

All in all it can be summarized that there are until now no signs that FDI contributed to reducing the regional disparities in the new EU-member states. Thus it is necessary to concentrate the enormous volume of European structural funds (308 Bln. Euros in the period 2007-2013) on the following aims:

– Convergence of the economically weakest regions.
– Increase of the regional competitiveness.
– Regional cooperation and integration in the enlarged EU (27).

## Endnotes

[1] A new partnership for cohesion: Third report of economic and social cohesion. European Commission 2004.
[2] Zschiedrich, H. „Ausländische Direktinvestitionen und regionale Cluster", München, 2006
[3] Third EU-Report on economic and social Cohesion 2004, Luxembourg 2005, p. 97
[4] World Investment Report 2001: Promoting Linkages, United Nation, New York and Geneva 2001, p. XX.
[5] World Investment Report 2001, p. 59.
[6] Masters of the craft : How japanese industry beat off law cost competition, Financial Times, 5 may 2005
[7] World Investment Report 2001, p. XIX.
[8] Koko A. / Gustavson P. "Regional Integration, FDI and Regional Developement", in European Investments Bank, Papers, Volume 9, N° 1,

Luxembourg 2004; Third Report on Economic and Social Cohesion, European Commission, Luxembourg 2004; Cibulskiene and Butkus M. "Estimation of uneven development of lithuanian regions" in Osteuropa-Wirtschaft, N° 2/2006; Thomas M. / Woderick R.: "Regionale Disparitäten und endogene Bildung neuen Sozialkapitals", in Berliner Debatte N° 5/2006.

[9] Third EU Report on Economic and Social Cohesion, 2004, p. 98

[10] Günther, J. / Quast-Jajesnak, D.: Ausländische Direktinvestitionen im 20. Jahrhundert, Berliner Wissenschaftsverlag, 2006, p. 268.

[11] G. Hyna: FDI-WiWi Database in CEE, 2006, "Increasing Significance of Repatriated and Reinvesting Earnings", p. 9 (WIIW)

## References

Alecke, B./ Untiedt, G.: EU-Osterweiterung und regionale Weltbewerbfähigkeit, IFO-Schnelldienst München, Nr. 22/2003.

Butkus, M. / Cibulskiene, Estimation of uneven Development of Lithuanian Regions in the Aspect of Economic Growth; Osteuropa-Wirtschaft, Heft 2/2006, Berlin.

EUROPEAN Investment Bank, Report 2006, Luxembourg 2006.

European Commission: A new Partnership for Cohesion: Convergence – Competitiveness – Cooperation, Third Report on Economic and Social Cohesion, Luxembourg (Printed in Belgium) 2005.

Gajda, A., Die Rolle von Foreign Direct Investment bei der Überwindung regionaler Disparitäten – am Beispiel der polnischen Wirtschaft, University of Applied Science (FHTW) Berlin 2006.

Günther, G. / Jajesnak-Quast, D.: Willkommene Investiven oder nationaler Ausverkauf?, Berliner Wissenschaftsverlag, Berlin 2006.

Kokko, A. / Gustavson P.: Regional Integration, FDI and Regional Development, European Investment Bank Papers, Volume 9, N° 1, 2004, Luxembourg.

Scherer, R. / Bieger, Th.: Clustering – das Zauberwort der Wirtschaftsförderung, Verlag P. Haupt Bern. Stuttgart-Wien, Herausgeber Universität St Gallen (Schweiz) 2004.

Stirböck, C.: Agglomeration Tendencies in EU-Regions: Where does Capital go? Zentrum für europäische Wirtschaftsforschung, Mannheim 2002, Diskussion Paper N° 02-28.

Szechenyi Plan: Ungarns Entwicklungsplan, Ungarisches Wirtschaftsministerium, Budapest 2002.

World Investment Report 2001: Promoting Linkages, United Nations, New York and Geneva, 2001.

Zschiedrich, H.: Internationales Management in der Märkten Mittel- und Osteuropas, R. Hampp Verlag, München 2004.

—. Ausländische Direktinvestitionen und Regionale Industriecluster, R. Hampp Verlag, München 2006.

Zschiedrich, H. / Kunzmann H.: Regionale Industriecluster – Hoffnungsträger wirtschaftlichen Wachstums; Wirtschaft und Gesellschaft, Wien Nr. 2/2005.

Zschiedrich, H.: Regionale Industriecluster – Anziehungspunkt ausländischer Direktinvestitionen, Osteuropa-Wirtschaft, Berlin, Nr. 4/2003.

Zukowska-Gagelmann, K.: Productivity Spillovers from Foreign Direct Investment – The Case of Poland, Europäischer Verlag der Wissenschaften 2003

# INWARD-OUTWARD INTERNATIONALIZATION: CASE OF RUSSIA

DARIA PODMETINA AND JUHA VÄÄTÄNEN

## Abstract

Russia is close and far. Russia is new and old. Plenty of controversial publications in the last ten years impress us with different stories; reveal different sides of country and people, economy and politics, past and future. The research angles widely vary depending on who is writing and who is reading. Russian business–terrifying and intriguing; success and defaults; reality and myths.

Russians have arrived in the international arena to play big games. Who are the "Russian international players"? What are they looking for in the international markets? What are their main goals and target markets? Why and how they internationalize? What strategies they use? Or do they use any strategy? These questions are of the top interest of authors targeting to increase knowledge about Russian internationalization.

Authors present that Russian internationalization is a two-way street that has many faces. Russian large exporters of natural resources, export-import trade companies, companies creating production-processing supply chains with establishing part of their operations abroad, service companies providing knowledge transfer, information technologies firms outsourcing its services, franchisees and licensees of large foreign companies, small and medium sized firms – born globals in different branches of business.

## Introduction

The Russian economy has seen a strong trend of internationalization in the last decade. The process of the internationalization in Russia has not only encompassed an inward internationalization such as the development of foreign direct investment (FDI) and the imports of goods and services, but also an outward internationalization – the exports development and establishment of the production units abroad. As a result, the integration of Russia to the world economy has become more profound.

In the recent years Russian foreign direct investment (FDI) statistics have shown a miracle, FDI outflows have exceeded the inflows. In 2000, 2001 and 2002 investment outflows exceeded inflows and were cumulatively 1.5 billion USD (EIU, 2003). The reason behind this is the very aggressive internationalization of the largest Russian oil companies, which have enjoyed the high oil prices in recent years. The excess profits have in many cases been invested to foreign markets.

The long time of the isolation from the international business, centralization of planning and the "state orders" system limited the internationalization of the Soviet companies. Foreign trade was the state prerogative in the Soviet era. Soviet companies used to be in the international cooperation mostly with the CMEA socialist countries. CMEA was established in the year 1949 for the purpose of the current and perspective plans coordination. In fact, CMEA could be qualified as an attempt for the common market creation, development of the economic collaboration and mutual benefit partnership.

The multilateral clearing system was implemented for the payments in the trade with foreign partners. All – Union Industrial Associations (VPO), managed by the GOSPLAN (main state planning body in USSR), were settled down in the Soviet republics and in the CMEA countries. VPO associations were international organizations by the nature. There were also Soviet companies with organizational and managerial structure common for multinational corporations (MNCs); of course, they were not called MNCs because of the political reasons. For example, INGOSSTRAKH (Insurance agency), had subsidiaries, affiliates and associate firms in the USA, Netherlands, Great Britain, France, Germany and Austria. Also the state transnational company "NaftaMoskva" ("Sojuznefteexport" in the Soviet period) had subsidiaries in Finland, Belgium, Great Britain, Denmark, Italy, Switzerland and Germany.

The situation has changed significantly after the dissolution of the Soviet Union, and last 10 years can be characterized by the increasing participation of Russian companies in the world business. Liberalization of foreign trade, caused by political and economic reforms, provided for the many Russian companies new opportunities to participate in the international business, export products to the international markets, attract foreign investments and establish joint ventures.

The intensified globalization and integration processes worldwide and the development of technology are the basis for the increased interest in the research on the internationalization of companies providing services in the large and developing information technology (IT) market. The new Russia has started to play a more significant role in the international cooperation and technology exchange. The Russian IT market has been growing for the last five years (11% in 2002). However, the demand for high tech products is still relatively low in Russia, which instigates IT companies to outsource their operations internationally.

Authors aim to present that Russian internationalization is a two-way street that has many faces. Russian large exporters of natural resources, export – import trade companies, companies creating production-processing supply chains with establishing part of their operations abroad, service companies providing knowledge transfer, information technologies firms outsourcing its services, franchisees and licensees of large foreign companies, small and medium sized firms – born globals in different branches of business.

This paper discusses various case studies and previous research conducted by authors on the Russian internationalizing process in different periods of time and aims to draw a picture of Russian business internationalization.

1. *Exports* remain as the most significant Russian international operations. For January – August 2005 exports from Russia achieved 152 billion USD, which is 36% more than for the same period of 2004. The volume of the largest companies exports are amazing as well in their growth. The ten largest Russian exporters make about 50% of exports of whole Russia.

2. To authors' opinion Russian inward internationalization - *imports*, deserves more attention. Russian imports in the period of January – August 2005 were 60 billion USD, which was 29% more than in the same period of 2004. It's still more than twice less than exports, but it is worthwhile to put attention to the largest importers.

3. Authors' study on Internationalization of *Russian IT companies* includes the 50 biggest Russian IT companies and study of four smaller

software development companies. Outsourcing is studied as the mode of internationalization. In addition to services internationalization theory approach, to the Russian software development companies can be applied Networks Theory and Born Globals concept.

4. In this paper the internationalization modes of largest *Russian oil companies are* analysed. The traditional internationalization method has been exports, but recent years have seen large investments on up-stream such as oil deposits and down-stream such as refineries and retail operations in European markets.

5. And the last case is about Russian companies actively expanding with FDIs on the CIS market. Authors conducted a study about Russian investors in Ukraine. Many of the core industries of Ukraine are practically under control of Russian companies. Experts estimate that 30 – 55% of FDIs comprise legalized Russian and Ukrainian capital from the "offshore" companies.

## Literature Review

Internationalization is a two-way process during which companies become increasingly involved in international activities. This involvement may happen either through international inward operations such as importing and in-licensing, international outward operations such as exporting and out-licensing, or through international cooperation. Thus, the holistic concept of internationalization includes foreign inward, outward and cooperative activities and the possible connections between them, while inward-outward internationalization is a narrower concept excluding internationalization through cooperation (Korhonen, 1999).

Companies internationalize for a number of various reasons. Some companies internationalize due to external reasons, for example their rivals or customers have become globalized (Ohmae, 1990). Other companies internationalize for internally-pushed factors such as to improve the firm's profitability (Gerliner et al., 1989). Johanson and Vahlne (1990) summarize three research areas that have emerged in the literature on internationalization: (1) *FDI theory*, (2) *stage models*, and (3) *network perspective*.

The *FDI theory* has emerged from various theoretical contributions. According to the transaction cost view, firms select the organizational form and location for which overall transaction costs are minimized (Williamson, 1979; Hogaguchi & Toyne, 1990). Dunning (1980; 1988) suggests that cost minimizing is not the only factor influencing internationalization, but also ownership-specific advantages must be obtained.

*The stage models* indicate that internationalization is linked with managerial learning. Internationalization is defined as a step-by-step process from the simplest form (export) to manufacturing abroad (Luostarinen, 1994). This process combines getting experience and knowledge and increasing resource commitment to foreign market.

*The network perspective* draws on the theories of social exchange and focuses on firm behavior in the context of inter-organizational and interpersonal relationships. It emphasizes the role and influence of social relationships in business transactions (Johanson & Vahlne, 1990; 1992). Companies are connected by *networks* developing the interaction between them. In the network context, internationalization means that the firm develops business relationships in networks in other countries through international extension, penetration or international integration (Johanson and Mattson, 1988). The network approach is especially important in turbulent, high technology industries (Johanson and Vahlne, 1990).

## Exporting

Many researchers understand export as an internationalization stage (phase) and the popular point of view that export is the initial stage in the internationalization process. Luostarinen and Welch in the "Internationalization Pattern of the Firm" in 1990 proved that this statement is incorrect (*Luostarinen, Welch, 1990*). They define four internationalization stages: the export stage, the sales subsidiary stage, the licensing stage and the production subsidiary stage. *Export* is the important stage of the internationalization determined as transfer of goods and services across the national borders using direct or indirect methods (*Leonidou, Katsikeas, 1996*).

The dominant market entry mode for Central and Eastern European firms is exporting. From one viewpoint, it is an indicator showing that a particular firm is still at a very early stage of internationalization and lacks the venture capital and experience for a deeper commitment in foreign markets. On the other hand, many target markets, such as Russia and Ukraine, continue to have relatively unstable economies deterring an FDI, whereas domestic production costs and across-border transportation costs are affordable for CEE firms. Exports may predominate because of the need to reduce exposure to risks. Recent experience shows that, even in the case of exporting, the firms' financial health depends on whether the target markets are stable or not. Therefore, the former explanation seems to be the more reliable. Moving to higher stages should bring about more differentiated operations and, having several target markets, will help firms to survive fluctuations in only one target market. At first, however, experiential market and business knowledge has to be acquired (Roolaht, 2002).

Russian exporters sell products to the most attractive market segments providing greater profits; especially it refers to the oil and gas exporting companies, whose exports depend more on the market oil prices fluctuations, and not on the company's exporting strategy. Many Russian exporters have remarkable low cost advantages on the international markets.

## Internationalization of Service / IT companies

There are two major issues companies have to solve when providing services in the international markets: what kind of services to provide and how to create and sustain relationships (networks) with the customers. Selling a service often means personal interaction between the seller and the buyer. A framework for analyzing the tradability of services has been proposed by Richardson (1987). Some perfectly tradable services can be produced in one country and sold in another; some essentially tradable services have to establish a temporary or permanent commercial presence in order to facilitate their sales; others, exchangeable with more difficulty, require the movement of staff for the delivery; the remaining ones have poor tradability because they can only be developed with the creation of local establishments. Today, the development of telecommunication technologies has made it possible to sell services distantly, which decreases the cost significantly. A lot of services, considered earlier as exportable with difficulty in the absence of an appropriate network, are today currently exported without any local support (Leo and Philippe, 2001). Four types of international exchange have been identified, and four types of internationalization of services can be conceived (Leo and Philippe, 2001):

- *Cross-border transaction* without movement of either the provider or the customer (informational distant services or "tele"-services which use the vectors of telecommunications in order to deliver service; the information and consultation of data bank services; software activities, insurance, banks, computer maintenance);
- International transaction by *movement of the provider* to the client's country in order to deliver the service (consultancy, legal or engineering services, transportation);
- International transaction by *customer's movement* into the provider's country in order to obtain the delivery (tourism, health and training);
- International *delivery through foreign affiliates*. All services are a priori concerned with this type of international exchange because the direct investment in the market country becomes a necessity for companies deeply involved in international business. In this category we can find consumer services (restaurants, hairdressing, and beauty salons), mixed services (hotels, cars and equipment renting) and some business-to-business services (legal consultancy, auditing, advertising, and engineering).

The above four types of exchange concern not only service firms but also manufacturing companies when they sustain the commercialization of their goods through services (services associated to goods). In the companies' current life, relations with customers may appear on many occasions (prospecting, presence on the market, service delivery) and they take these various forms (Leo and Philippe, 2001). Today, the development of telecommunication technologies has made it possible to sell services distantly, which decreases the cost significantly. A lot of services, considered earlier as exportable with difficulty in the absence of an appropriate network, are today currently exported without any local support (Leo and Philippe, 2001).

Software development is truly an international business: customers and development companies are scattered around the world. Hawk and McHenry, 2004 defined the elements influencing competitiveness of software industries. The main elements are *demand* (demand from abroad for offshore work, domestic demand for software), *international linkages and trust* (trust – development of relationships, common culture, language; marketing and in-country representation; piracy and copyright- effective laws, protection of intellectual property); *software industry characteristics* (competition – spurring quality, efficiency, etc.; clustering – co-location of several firms; collaboration – through industry associations, etc.); and *domestic Input Factors/ Infrastructure* (human capital – technical skills, education, experience, English; technological infrastructure; capital; R&D).

## FDIs

Many experts regard FDIs beneficial from the point of view of the host country. However, the well being of the host country is not a decisive motive for FDIs: investors are always seeking profit for the risks they take in the FDI framework. Companies invest in foreign production for three basic reasons: to obtain raw materials, to source products at lower cost and to penetrate local markets (*Root, 1994)*.

*Extractive investors* establish foreign subsidiaries to exploit natural resources in order to acquire raw materials for their own industrial operations (backward vertical integration) or for sale on the world market. Ordinarily, these investors sell only a small fraction of their raw materials output in the foreign country of extraction (*Root, 1994).* In Ukraine, the classic examples of this type of FDIs are investing in the mining and metallurgy, oil industry and other extracting industries.

*Sourcing investors* establish foreign operations to manufacture products that are entirely or mainly exported to the home country or to the third countries. The purpose of sourcing investments is to obtain lower-cost supplies of components, parts, or finished goods by taking advantage of abundant endowments of labour, energy, or other inputs in a foreign country *(Root 1994).* Many investors to the Ukrainian processing and production industries are belonging to this group.

*Market investors* account for most investment abroad. Their objective is to penetrate a target market from a production base inside the target country *(Root, 1994).* Companies producing consumer goods and private services in Ukraine like McDonald's, Philip Morris, Kraft Food, Nestlé, mobile operators and many other companies in food processing, tobacco, beverages, breweries, telecommunications, fast food, etc. have entered the Ukrainian market in order to *find new markets*. The main reason for the expansion to the Ukraine is that home markets are already saturated. Profit per every new unit sold is approximately the same in every country, and, if even small part of the Ukrainians would be able to buy their products, the total sales will increase.

For many foreign investors entering Ukraine and other transitional economies markets, it is difficult to specify the type of investment they make. Many foreign companies entering these markets represent mixed type of sourcing and market investors. However, foreign investors in Ukraine normally tend to take a long-term view. Their purpose is to occupy a new niche on the new Ukrainian market. Companies having a long-term experience of doing business in Ukraine are knowledgeable in the Ukrainian specifics, having relatives or other personal networks.

## International Operations of Russian Companies

### Russian exports and exporters

*Russian exports dynamics*[1]. The Russian exports can be characterized by a high growth rate. On the other hand, during the last years of the Soviet Union exports decreased significantly between the years 1989 and 1991, reasoned mostly by the internal economic and political crisis. After the decrease in the Russian foreign trade volumes in 1992, the growth of the exports and the imports has been even higher than the growth of the GDP. The total volume of the Russian exports has doubled in the 10 years period (1992 – 2002). The growth was achieved mostly because of the increase in the exports to the Western European countries, in the same period the Russian exports to the countries of Commonwealth of Independent States (CIS) increased not so noticeably. As a whole the dynamics of the Russian exports have been mainly influenced by world market prices for the exported goods, natural resources' prices on the world markets, inflation in Russia and ruble/dollar exchange rate.

For January – August 2005 exports from Russia achieved 152 billion USD, what is 36% more than for the same period of 2004. Exports to CIS countries were estimated at 20.3 billion USD (14% growth) and exports to other countries – 131.7 billion USD (40% growth).

*Russian exports structure.* Russia is still playing the unenviable role of a "raw-material adjunct" of the world's industrially developed countries. The raw materials producing sector remains the backbone of the Russian economy. Although it employs only 1.5% of the country's workforce, it provides 6% of the Russian GDP and more than 50% of its exports.

Moreover, the sector has absorbed more than 20% of the total of investments in the national economy and more than 60% of investments into the industrial sector. Reliance towards the raw materials producing sector has caused Russian development to be strongly dependent on world market prices for raw materials. The world market prices for oil and petrochemicals have remained high, which has reasoned the boom in the Russian exports. The increase in the Russian exports of oil and fuels in 2000 was 71% accounted by the increase in the prices and only 5% by increase in the actual volumes of the exported material. The average price of petrochemicals exported from Russia increased from 95.8 USD to 174 USD per metric ton. These factors have determined the structure of the Russian exports in general and that of the country's 100 biggest exporters in particular. So, we can state the ineffective commodity structure as the main problem of the Russian exports. The fuels and resources specialization of Russia on the international market, acceptable on the short period of time, does not have an evolution to the more developed forms, which seriously limits expansion possibilities of Russia on the international markets.

The Russian exports structure (excluding CIS countries) for January – August 2005 was as follows: oil and energy goods - 65.6% of total exports (60.2% in 2004), metals – 16.2% (17.6% in 2004), chemical products – 5.7% (6% in 2004), wood, paper and cellulose products – 3.7% (4.2% in 2004). Export structure to CIS countries was as follow: oil and energy goods - 42.4% of total exports (44.4% in 2004), metals – 11.8% (9.6% in 2004), machine and equipment – 19.8% (22.1% in 2004).

*Geography of the Russian exports.* The geography of the Russian exports is rather stable, majoring orientation to the European markets. The share of the exports to EU countries remained quite stable in the analyzed period. There was a decline of 33% in the year 1998 after the default in Russia, then exports share recovered and achieved 38% growth in the year 2002. Considering Russian exports to the EU, there was a decrease in the exports share of Germany (from 29% in 1992 to 22% in 2002), but still Germany is the main Russian trade partner. The exports share of France decreased as well from 10% in 1992 to 6% in 2002. There was a growth of the Italian exports share (from 14% to 20%) and Netherlands (from 11% to 20%). Taking into consideration the share of new EU member countries (Hungary, Poland, Czech Republic, Slovakia, Slovenia, Estonia, Latvia, Lithuania) in the Russian exports, we can conclude that EU's share in Russian export will be increased significantly in 2004 and will achieve approximately the level of 55%. The share of the Russian exports to CIS countries is oriented mostly to three countries which accumulated about 90% of the Russian exports to CIS: Ukraine (37%), Byelorussia (up to 40%) and Kazakhstan (about 16%). Exports to CIS generally decreased from 21% in 1992 to only 14% in 2002. There is a trend for decreasing share of Ukraine in the Russian exports in the recent years (from 40.4% in 1998 to 37% in 2002). The share of Byelorussia increased in the year 2000 up to 40%, but has trend to decrease in 2002 to 36%. Kazakhstan share in the Russian exports to CIS increased from 14% in 1998 to 16% in 2002.

*Russian 20 biggest exporters*[2] accounted 52.4% of the total Russian exports in the year 2001 (Table 1), and represent five main industries: oil and gas industry (82%) – 10 companies, metal industry (16%) – 8 companies, chemical and petrochemical industry (1.28%) – 1 company, and machine building industry (0.99%) – 1 company. And in the comparison with the year 2000 this structure did not changed significantly. Russia's biggest exporting companies have a strong trend to the international expansion. Many of them have significant growth of exports share in total sales, the growth of the exports volumes, and number of export countries.

**Table 1: Russian Exporters in Volumes (million, USD) and in% of Total Russian Exports**

| | 2001 | | 2000 | | 1999 | | 1998 | |
|---|---|---|---|---|---|---|---|---|
| | Exports | % | Exports | % | Exports | % | Exports | % |
| **Top 100** | 62544.5 | 60.7 | 60464.6 | 57.3 | 40069.6 | 52.9 | 43125.6 | 57.6 |
| **Top 50** | 60208.5 | 58.3 | 57538.5 | 54.5 | 33384.1 | 44.1 | 35947 | 48.0 |
| **Top 20** | 54088.3 | 52.4 | 50213.3 | 47.6 | 25148.3 | 33.2 | 27719.1 | 37.0 |
| **Top 10** | 46195.1 | 44.8 | 42104.8 | 39.9 | 19189.5 | 25.4 | 19949.5 | 26.6 |
| **Total exports** | 103200 | 100 | 105600 | 100 | 75700 | 100 | 74900 | 100 |

Many Russian exporting companies have a significant share of exports in the total sales (even up to 90%). The reason for this phenomenon is that the total sales are accounted in USD, and because of the internal / external prices gap, and strong influence of the world prices for the Russian exports, we get such an illusion. If we consider exports and sales (or production) in volumes (cubic meters, tones, etc) we might get other results. As an example, in the year 2000, exports share in the total oil extraction for the main oil companies in Russia was 32% for Lukoil, 38% for Yukos, 34% for TNK, 34% for Slavneft, 47% for Rosneft, 34% for Surgutneftegaz and 32% for Bashneft. Rosneft as a *state owned company* has the highest exports / extraction rate (Table 2).

**Table 2: Top 10 Russian Exporters**[3]

| | Company | Share,% 2005 | 2004 (place) | 2003 (place) |
|---|---|---|---|---|
| 1 | GazExport | 8.39 | 11.47 (1) | 6.02 (2) |
| 2 | LUKOIL | 4.43 | 6.59 (3) | 3.25 (6) |
| 3 | TNK | 4.37 | 5.22 (4) | 2.90 (7) |
| 4 | ROSNEFT | 3.08 | - | - |
| 5 | Surgutneftegaz | 2.54 | 3.64 (5) | 4.46 (3) |
| 6 | NORMETIMPEX | 1.92 | 3.23 (6) | 2.09 (9) |
| 7 | TATNEFT | 1.60 | 1.96 (8) | 2.22 (8) |
| 8 | Novolipetsk Metallurgical kombinat | 1.37 | 2.33 (7) | - |
| 9 | Magnitogorsk Metallurgical kombinat | 1.21 | 1.73 (10) | - |
| 10 | Sibneft | 1.10 | - | - |

## Russian imports and Importers[4]

Russian imports in the period of January – August 2005 were 60 billion USD what is 29.1% more than in the same period of 2004. From CIS countries Russia imported goods for 12.1 billion USD (9.2% growth) and from other countries – 47.9 billion USD (35.4% growth). In the structure of imports for January – August 2005 share of machines and equipment was 46.7% (for the same period of 2004 – 45.1%), chemical products – 18.4% (17.8% in 2004), food products – 17.7% (17.9% in 2004).

Top 10 Russian Importers (Table 3) show us interesting picture of large international companies, mainly machine and equipment producers. These large companies do not see a benefit to produce their spare parts locally –

they import all necessary parts and equipment and realize just assembling locally. This allows them to avoid custom fees when importing ready products to Russia.

**Table 3: Top 10 Russian Importers**

| | Company | Share,% 2005 | 2004 (place) | 2003 (place) |
|---|---|---|---|---|
| 1 | Toyota Motors | 0.66 | 1.39 (1) | - |
| 2 | Magnitogorsk Metallurgical kombinat | 0.53 | 1.08 (2) | 0.71 (4) |
| 3 | Bratsk Alluminium Plant | 0.40 | 0.57 (7) | 0.44 (7) |
| 4 | Rolf Holding | 0.33 | 0.57 (8) | - |
| 5 | Ford Motors Company | 0.32 | 0.60 (6) | - |
| 6 | CIA Internaitonal | 0.29 | - | 0.52 (6) |
| 7 | Centr Vredrenia PROTEK | 0.28 | 0.60 (5) | 0.69 (5) |
| 8 | Megafon | 0.28 | 0.62 (4) | - |
| 9 | Mobile Systems | 0.25 | - | - |
| 10 | Volkswagen Group Rus | 0.25 | 0.52 (10) | - |

## Russian Services companies internationalization

*International operations of biggest Russian IT companies*

In the study concerning operations of Russian 50 biggest IT companies the sample was formed from the 50 biggest Russian IT companies according to the rating made by Expert magazine. Companies were preliminary checked to be correspondent with requirements of the study and only 41 companies were left in the list. The requirements were as follow: available data for the 2001 – 2003 time period; and available information about company's current activity (no bankruptcy procedure started). Russian IT business is traditionally very concentrated in Moscow (capital city) and other large cities like Saint-Petersburg, Yekaterinburg, Novosibirsk and some others. The same situation is reflected in sample companies: the biggest IT companies of Russia are located in Moscow – 75.6% (Table 4) and in Saint-Petersburg (12.2%).

**Table 4: Biggest Russian IT Companies by Location, 2003**

| | Number of companies | % | Sales, mln EUR | Employees | Sales per Employee, 1000 EUR | Sales Growth, % |
|---|---|---|---|---|---|---|
| **Moscow** | 31 | 75.6 | 915.8 | 11,837 | 77.4 | 74.64 |
| **Saint-Petersburg** | 5 | 12.2 | 35.9 | 702 | 51.2 | 56.60 |
| **Novosibirsk** | 2 | 4.9 | 38.9 | 707 | 55.1 | 35.50 |
| **Yekaterinburg** | 1 | 2.4 | 6.6 | 80 | 82.8 | 17.00 |
| **Kazan'** | 1 | 2.4 | 9.5 | 396 | 24.0 | -9.00 |
| **Perm** | 1 | 2.4 | 8.2 | 120 | 68.5 | 111.00 |
| **Total** | 41 | 100 | 1015.0 | 13,842 | 73.3 | 74.64 |

The structure of sales of the biggest IT companies represents quite correspondingly the situation in the Russian IT market. The demand is higher for IT services: 43% of companies have IT services as major business operation; 22% of companies are specialized in software development, and 21% in equipment and software supply. As told before, specialization in services is conditioned by the market demand.

One company from the sample is the affiliate of international company in Russia with sales in more than 120 countries. This company was excluded from the statistical analysis. One company is owned by the government and works only on governmental orders. 69% of the companies sell their products only in Russia (Table 5), 22% sell in Russia and in CIS markets, and only 12% of the companies provide their products on international markets.

**Table 5: Expansion of IT companies**

| | Number of companies | % | Average number of offices |
|---|---|---|---|
| Regional offices | 27 | 69 | 8.5 |
| Foreign affiliates | 12 | 29 | 1.7 |
| Affiliates in CIS | 9 | 22 | 0.9 |
| Only Sales in Russia | 27 | 69 | |
| Sales in Russia and in CIS | 9 | 22 | |
| Sales Internationally | 5 | 12 | |

Regional offices in Russia have more than 69% of companies, and 29% have offices abroad. Sample companies sell in the next CIS countries: Ukraine, Kazakhstan, Belarus, and Azerbaijan. Companies, operating internationally have offices in USA, UK, Poland, Japan, Germany, Latvia, China, Netherlands and France. It is obvious that biggest IT companies prefer expand into Russian regions with *region/local strategy*. Russia is a big country with 89 regions. This area provides extremely good opportunities for growth inside the country.

About 30% of companies sell in the CIS market. The CIS market is traditionally very well known for Russian companies, the infrastructure and business traditions are familiar and close to Russian. 12% of internationalizing companies operate abroad on the base of personal networks, occasionally happened contracts and offers. 5% of them build their strategy depending on foreign customers; these companies are working in the offshore software development (Podmetina, Vaatanen, 2005).

*International operations of Russian software development companies*

During the last decade new and dynamic private Russian service companies have expanded their business operations to foreign markets by applying high skill levels and low cost structures as their main competitive advantage .In the pilot study of four Russia IT companies conducted in January – March 2004 (Podmetina, 2004), the internationalization theories and service internationalization concepts were discussed to explain the Russian software development companies' internationalization by studying outsourcing as one of the internationalization modes. The case companies were selected according to following criteria: they are private

IT companies, established in 1991 or later, headquartered in Saint-Petersburg, and provide software development services for international customers. Below is presented the summary of case companies (Table 6).

**Table 6: Russian software development companies**

| | Company 1 | Company 2 | Company 3 | Company 4 |
|---|---|---|---|---|
| **Founded** | 1993 | 1992 | 1991 | 1991 |
| **Internationalization Started** | 1993 | N / A | 1992 | 1991 |
| **Ownership** | Private | Private | Private | Private |
| **Headquarters** | Saint-Petersburg | Saint-Petersburg | Saint-Petersburg | Saint-Petersburg |
| **Foreign Subsidiaries** | Yes | Yes | Yes | Yes |
| **Subsidiaries' Location** | 2 USA, Scandinavia | 2 USA, Europe | 5 USA, Europe, Scandinavia | 3 Europe, Scandinavia |
| **Outsourcing** | Yes | Yes | Yes | Yes |
| **Geography of Customers** | USA, Canada, Finland, Sweden, Denmark, Norway, Germany, UK, France, Australia | Sweden, Russia, Germany, New Zeland, Denmark, Finland, UK, etc | Denmark, USA, Switzerland, Germany, Sweden, etc | Europe, North – America, Russia |
| **Staff** | 100+ | 140 + | 190 + | 170 + |
| | **Advantages on the international market** | | | |
| Quality | + | + | + | + |
| Technology | + | + | + | + |
| Human Resources | + | + | + | + |
| Location advantage | + | + | | |
| Internationalization | + | | | |
| Company's reliability | + | | + | |
| Cost saving | + | | + | + |
| Time to market | + | | + | + |
| Other | | | | flexibility towards customers, free resources to focus on core business |

For all the analyzed companies, international operations accumulated more than 50% of their business operation. The companies have organized subsidiaries in the USA (3 companies), Europe (4 companies) and in Scandinavia (3 companies). As mentioned above, the demand for software development in the USA and in Europe is higher than the capacity of local firms. This is the basis of the expansion strategy chosen by the case companies. The companies consider reputation and firm's image as important components of international marketing strategy. The companies' strengths in technologies, education, quality certification and teamworking and cost advantages increase their competitiveness in the international markets.

All case companies had started international operations in the year of their establishment or a year later. This has lead to the idea of applying the Born Globals concept. All pilot study case companies also had started their international operations based on strong personal networks with foreign partners, emphasizing trust and teamworking principles in the internal networks. This justifies the application of the Network concept and Born Globals for the research of the Russian IT sector to analyse the internationalization of new fast growing Russian IT firms.

## Russian Oil Companies Internationalization

In one of the previous studies the internationalization modes of largest Russian oil companies (Tables 7 and 8) were analysed (Väätänen, Podmetina, 2004). The aim was to analyse the transition from oil exporters into foreign direct investors on the international markets. For Russian oil companies the traditional internationalization method has been exports, but recent years have seen large investments on up-stream (oil deposits) and down-stream (refineries and retail operations) in European markets. The analysis covered ten largest Russian oil producers, whose production in 2002 was 90% of all Russian oil production.

**Table 7: Russian Biggest Oil Companies, 2002**

| Company | Turnover, mln USD | NPAT[5], mln USD | Employees, 1000 | Production 1 000 brl per day |
|---|---|---|---|---|
| Lukoil | 15449.0 | 1843.0 | 150.0 | 1511 |
| YUKOS | 11373.0 | 3064.0 | 100.0 | 1397 |
| TNK | 6075.4 | 1251.3 | 81.4 | 1076 |
| Surgutneftegaz | 6407.7 | 1587.2 | 98.1 | 985 |
| Tatneft | 3465.9 | 201.2 | 56.9 | 493 |
| Slavneft | 2718.7 | 428.3 | 28.6 | 322 |
| Sibneft | 4776.7 | 1161.5 | 30.0 | 528 |
| Rosneft | 2669.0 | 479.0 | 58.6 | 323 |
| Bashneft | 1426.3 | 186.1 | 46.4 | 241 |
| Sidanko | 2631.3 | n.a. | 29.0 | n.a. |
| Top 10 | | | | 6876 |
| Total Russia | | | | 7601 |

As can be observed in Table 8 below, the Russian oil companies have managed to increase their exports significantly. At the same time their profitability has remained on a high level (Table 7). This combined with high oil world market prices has created significant financial resources for oil companies' internationalization efforts.

**Table 8: Russian Biggest Oil Exporters**

| Company name | Exports (USD mln) | | Exports growth (%) | Export countries 2001 | Share in total exports (%) | |
|---|---|---|---|---|---|---|
| | 2001 | 2000 | | | 2001 | 2000 |
| Lukoil | 6 625 | 6 218 | 6.5 | 32 | 6.4 | 5.9 |
| YUKOS | 5 682 | 5 248 | 8.3 | 40 | 5.5 | 5.0 |
| TNK | 5 597 | 3 478 | 61.0 | 40 | 5.4 | 3.3 |
| Surgutneftegaz | 2 356 | 1 701 | 38.6 | 13 | 2.3 | 1.6 |
| Tatneft | 2 136 | 2 630 | -18.8 | 43 | 2.1 | 2.5 |
| Slavneft | 1 763 | 1 262 | 39.7 | 25 | 1.7 | 1.2 |
| Sibneft | 1 651 | 1 700 | -2.9 | 29 | 1.6 | 1.6 |
| Rosneft | 1 347 | 1 299 | 3.7 | n. a. | 1.3 | 1.2 |
| Bashneft | 872 | 859 | 1.5 | 21 | 0.8 | 0.8 |
| Sidanko | 6 625 | 6 218 | 6.5 | 32 | 6.4 | 5.9 |

In Table 9 below presents a summary of Russian oil companies' international operations. When analyzing upstream operations, five out of ten companies have oil production in foreign countries. Similarly, six out of ten oil companies have acquired refining capacity on foreign markets. Finally when looking sales network/retailing, half of the largest oil companies have foreign distribution operations.

**Table 9: International Operations of Russian Biggest Oil Exporters**

| Company name | Crude Oil Exports | Refining | Production | Sales / Petrol Station network |
|---|---|---|---|---|
| Lukoil | + | + | + | + |
| YUKOS | + | + | + | + |
| TNK | + | + | - | + |
| Surgutneftegaz | + | - | - | - |
| Tatneft | + | + | + | - |
| Slavneft | + | + | + | + |
| Sibneft | + | - | - | - |
| Rosneft | + | + | + | + |
| Bashneft | + | - | - | - |
| Sidanko | + | - | - | - |

*LUKOIL – International operations*

LUKOIL exports its products to 32 countries and its share of exports was 66% of sales in 2003. This company also has exploration and oil production (4% of production abroad) in Azerbaijan, Kazakhstan, Egypt, Columbia, Iran and Saudi-Arabia. 19% of LUKOIL's oil refining is located abroad – in Ukraine, Bulgaria, and Romania. The company has wide retail sales network/petrol stations in 16 countries: in CIS (Azerbaijan, Belarus, Georgia, Moldova, Ukraine), in Europe (Bulgaria, Hungary, Cyprus, Latvia, Lithuania, Poland, Serbia, Romania, Czech Republic, Estonia), and in the USA. LUKOIL has about 50% of its sales abroad (CIS 26%, USA 16% and Europe 8%).

*Yukos – International operations*

Yukos exports its products to 40 countries and its share of exports was over 50% of sales in 2003. Except exporting, the company has exploration in Kazakhstan and oil refining in Lithuania (19% of refining abroad). Company has sales network/petrol stations in Ukraine.

*Rosneft – International Operations*

Rosneft exports its products to 22 countries and its share of exports was 58% of sales in 2003. Except exporting, the company has exploration in Afghanistan, Algeria, Colombia and Kazakhstan and sales network / petrol stations in Bulgaria and Romania.

**Table 9: International Operations of Russian Biggest Oil Exporters**

| Company name | Crude Oil Exports | Refining | Production | Sales / Petrol Station network |
|---|---|---|---|---|
| Lukoil | + | + | + | + |
| YUKOS | + | + | + | + |
| TNK | + | + | - | + |
| Surgutneftegaz | + | - | - | - |
| Tatneft | + | + | + | - |
| Slavneft | + | + | + | + |
| Sibneft | + | - | - | - |
| Rosneft | + | + | + | + |
| Bashneft | + | - | - | - |
| Sidanko | + | - | - | - |

Authors concluded that exports naturally remain the main internationalization mode for Russian biggest oil companies. Higher exports prices attract Russian oil companies, but currently export pipeline capacity is limiting possibility for significant growth of exports.

Internationalization of Russian oil companies has mainly targeted refineries in CIS and oil reserves. CIS is a very traditional home market. In addition internationalization degrees seem to vary greatly between oil companies – Lukoil vs. Surgutneftegas. Companies seem to understand internationalization as a strategic decision – international operations are often managed in separate entities.

## Russian Investors on CIS market

*Russian FDIs in Ukraine*

Many of the core industries of Ukraine are practically under control of Russian companies (Table 10). Russian influence is enormous in the context of FDIs. The moderate 5$^{th}$ place in the official FDI statistics can be explained by the fact that Russian and Ukrainian companies actively use offshore companies in Cyprus, the British Virgin Islands, Switzerland and some other countries to repatriate their flight capital to the home country. Experts estimate that 30–55% of FDIs comprise legalized Russian and Ukrainian capital from the "offshore" companies.

Russian capital is involved in various sectors of Ukrainian industries. Russian – Singapore Group "Amtel" owns 51% shares of Joint Venture Rosava, – the biggest automobile tire producer in Ukraine. Group "Amtel" started the business in Russia as a natural caoutchouc (rubber) supplier from South – East Asia to Russia and other CIS countries. Today it controls six large tire producers and few chemical companies, including one in Ukraine – Khimvolokno in Chernihiv. Rosava exports 70% of its products to Russia. Ukrainian experts estimate, that "Amtel" Group covers nowadays 15% of tire market in Russia and 80% in Ukraine.

Russian investors play a very active role also in some other sectors. "Energetichesky standard" Group has shares of more than ten *regional energy companies* in Ukraine, Sibirski Aluminium has invested to the Nikolaevsky *Aluminium plant,* Avto VAZ Invest has shares of Zaporoghsky aluminium plant. Russian *food companies* have expanded in the Ukrainian market: Wimm-Bill-Dann company owns large milk factories in Kiev, Kharkov, Sumy region; Company Planeta – Management has bought milk factories in Kiev and Kremenchug. Cosmetic company Kalina has purchased "Alye Parusa" in Ukraine.

Russian investment in the Ukrainian market is not surprising. Unlike Western investors, Russian companies are not afraid of possible problems and difficulties linked with investment climate in Ukraine. Russia and Ukraine were parts of the same federation (Soviet Union) until 1991. Thus, Russian investors have special knowledge of Ukraine. Russian expansion into the oil refining of Ukraine is very natural, as Russia is a major oil producer. Vertical integration of Russian oil companies in Ukraine is the same as in Russia – comprising production and retailing of oil products. Ukraine produces only 20% of its oil consumption, while 50% is imported from Russia. Russia satisfies 30% of Ukraine's need of gas. In nuclear fuel the equivalent figure is 100%.

It can be assumed that Russian investment in Ukraine will grow in the future comprising metallurgy, telecommunication, pharmaceutical and other industries. Ukraine is a natural playing field for Russian companies in their internationalization drive in the post-soviet world.

**Table 10. Russian Companies in Ukraine**

| Russian participation | Expansion perspective | Possible risks |
|---|---|---|
| **1. OIL INDUSTRY** | | |
| Russians own four from six Ukrainian oil processing plants, providing 80% of total oil processing in Ukraine:<br>• **Kremenchug Refinery** - ***Tatneft*** (majority owner – m.o.)<br>• **Lisichi Refinery** – ***TNK***, m.o.<br>• **Kherson Refinery**, **Sevastopol Oil Terminal** - ***Alliance group***<br>• **Odessa Refinery** – ***Lukoil***, m.o. | 1. Privatization of oil extracting company **Ukrneft**<br>2. Privatization of refineries<br>3. Privatization of Ukrainian oil transportation system, oil terminals and sea ports terminals<br>4. Participation of Lukoil and TNK in the privatization of **Azmol** company | 1. Competition between Russian companies and large Ukrainian FPG(Financial Industrial Groups)<br>2. Political resistance from USA and EU on oil transportation |
| **2. TELECOMMUNICATIONS** | | |
| Russian companies participate in many mobile operators.<br>• **UMC** – ***MTC***, m.o.<br>• **Kievstar GSM** - ***Alfa Telecom***, 40%<br>• **Golden Telecom** - ***Alfa Telecom***, m.o. | Privatization of Ukrtelecom – national communications operator | 1. No decision on the Ukrtelecom<br>2. Competition between Russian and Ukrainian companies |
| **3. NON - FERROUS METALLURGY** | | |
| With few exceptions, all non – ferrous plants in Ukraine either are owned by Russian companies, or are in the state ownership.<br>• **Nikolaev Aluminous Plant** - **Rusal,** m.o.<br>• **Zaporozhie Aluminium Plant** - ***AvtoVAZ-Invest***, m.o.<br>• **Pobugsky Ferronickel Plant** – ***Nikomed***, m.o. | Privatization of titanium – magnesium plant in Zaporozhie – GAK "TITAN" (the biggest in CIS producer of titanium dioxide), GOK in Dnepropetrovsk (titanium and zirconium ore extraction), developing new fields of rare-earth metals | No political decision on the privatization of mentioned objects |

| | | |
|---|---|---|
| **4. FOOD INDUSTRY** | | |
| Russian companies control over 30% of milk products market:<br>• **Kiev Milk Plant number 3, Kharkov Milk Plant, Burynsky Dried Milk plant – *Wimm-Bill-Dann***, m.o.<br>• **Galakton** and **Kremez** – ***Planet Management,*** m.o. | Purchasing of the Ukrainian companies with popular bands | Low image on the internal consumer market |
| **5. CHEMICAL INDUSTRY** | | |
| • **Lukor** (oil chemicals production) – ***Lukoil,*** *m.o.*<br>• **JV Rosava** (tires) – ***Amtel*** (51%) | Privatization of state fertilizers firms. Purchasing companies on the secondary market. | Competition between Russian and large Ukrainian FPG |
| **6. MACHINE BUILDING** | | |
| Russian participation is not significant still, but share of non – privatized companies is very high.<br>• **Stakhanovsky machine building plant – *Alliance Group*** (m.o.)<br>• **Kharton – *ASKOND*** (24%) | Privatization of Luganskteplovoz, Energy Machine Building, Chernomorsky Shipbuilding company, Agriculture machine building companies | 1. Political obstacle for Russian capital inflow<br>2. Competition between Russian and Ukrainian FPG |
| **7. MILITARY INDUSTRY** | | |
| Privatization in the military industry has not started yet | 1. Privatization of Ukrainian military enterprises.<br>2. Integration of Ukrainian air defence system with Russian defence holdings, mergers of companies in aircraft industry.<br>3. Privatization of Ukrainian aerospace companies | No political decision on the privatization of military companies<br>International competition (in aerospace industry) |

| | | |
|---|---|---|
| **8. ADVERTISING AND MASS MEDIA** | | |
| Russian companies are participating in national TV channels in Ukraine and control about 50% of TV AD market.<br>• TV channel **Inter** – ***Pervyi kanal*** – blocking package<br>• TV channel **STB**, **Weekly** "Delovaja **Stolitsa**", and Radio **"Apelsin"** – ***Lukoil*** (m.o.)<br>• **Video International Ukraine** – ***Video International***<br>• Advertising agencies **IMS and AITI** – ***Carat Group*** (m.o.)<br>• TV channel "**Novyi Kanal**" and radio "**NasheVremya**" – ***Alfa Group*** | 1. Russian publishing companies and periodicals (mainly, journals and magazines) are actively entering Ukrainian market<br>2. Mergers of large Ukrainian advertising agencies by Russian companies | High political risks entering mass media market due to approaching elections (president elections in 2004 and parliament elections in 2006) |
| **9. ENERGY SECTOR** | | |
| Companies with Russian participation control over 25% of Ukrainian energy supplying companies "Oblenergo". Sevastopoloblenergo, Zhitomiroblenergo, Poltavaoblenergo, Khersonoblenergo, Lvovoblenergo, Sumyoblenergo, Kirovogradoblenergo – According to information of Ukrainian mass media, all these companies are owned by shareholders of Russian football club CSKA (so called "Luzhnikovskaya Group") | 1. Privatization of other energy companies – Oblenergo, energy generating companies<br>2. Participation in nuclear fuel creation company in Ukraine<br>3. Purchasing energy companies on the secondary market. Possibly, RAO "EES Russia" will buy majority shares of Kievoblenergo and Rovnooblenergo from AES company (USA) | 1. No political decision on the privatization in energy sector<br>2. Competition between Russian and Ukrainian FPG<br>3. Resistance from the USA and EU |
| **10. GAS INDUSTRY** | | |
| Offshore companies have privatized about half of 50 regional Ukrainian gas distributing companies ("gorgaz" and "oblgaz"). It is | Currently, Russian – Ukrainian consortium is negotiating about getting possibility to manage gas transportation system of | Tough political resistance of USA towards the establishing of |

| | | |
|---|---|---|
| possible, that among those offshore companies shareholders there are Russian companies. | Ukraine (including gas pipelines and gas storages) | such a consortium |
| **11. FINANCIAL MARKET** | | |
| Russians own about 1.4% of Ukrainian banking system assets (by 01.01.2003)<br>• **Alfa-bank Ukraine,** Investment company **"Alfa Capital", KievInvestbank** – ***Alfa-Group***<br>• **Petrokommerts Ukraine** – ***Petrokommerts Bank***<br>• **NRB-Ukraine** - ***NRB*** | Russian investing companies are planning to expand into Ukrainian market, particularly, is it expected that subsidiary of NIKoil will enter Ukrainian stock exchange market. | Ukrainian financial market is underdevelope d |
| **12. FERROUS METALLURGY** | | |
| Russian participation is not significant, excepting metal mining industry and iron-and-steel scrap processing (10% of scrap market) and participation in iron ore GOKs privatization (Lukoil North-West).<br>• **Inguletsky GOK and Yugny GOK**– ***Lukoil North-West*** (more than blocking package of shares)<br>• **Zhitomirvtormet, Khersonvtormet, Nikolaevvtormet, Cherkassyvtormet, Vinnitzavtormet** – **MAIR Group** | Purchasing private metallurgy companies | 1. High politic risks<br>2. Privatization of metallurgy usually is realized considering concrete Ukrainian FPGs<br>3. High prices for energy<br>4. Low capacity of internal metal market |

Source: Adapted from Expert, Special Issue on Ukraine, 2003

*LUKOIL (Russia)*

LUKOIL Company is the leader of the Russian fuel and energy sector. LUKOIL started its operations in the year 1991. It operates in 40 regions of Russia and in 32 foreign countries. Lukoil produces 24% of the total Russian oil and 12% of the oil products. The company owns more than 1100 gasoline stations in Russia and abroad. LUKOIL was in 2001 Russia's number 1 oil producer with total sales of 14.9 billion USD. LUKOIL has continued its growth in 2002 and 2003. Expansion through exploration and acquisitions made LUKOIL the $2^{nd}$ largest public oil company in the world in terms of oil reserves, and the $6^{th}$ largest in terms of oil and gas production volumes. LUKOIL's refineries abroad have combined capacity of 17.8 million tons per year.

Lukoil's foreign refineries are LUKOIL Odessa Refinery (Odessa, Ukraine), LUKOIL Neftokhim Burgas (Burgas, Bulgaria) and Petrotel LUKOIL (Ploesti, Romania). Holding LUKOIL-Ukraine is LUKOIL's subsidiary, combining oil refining and selling oil products: LUKOIL Odessa Refinery (oil processing plant), LITASKO Ukraine (product operator) and a company with foreign investments "LUKOIL Ukraine" (regional sales company). LUKOIL-Ukraine has annual turnover of 600 million USD and sales of approximately 550 thousands tons of oil products in 2003 in Ukraine (440 thousands tons in 2002). Holding employs more than 3000 people.

LUKOIL started business in Ukraine in 1997 when the first gasoline stations "LUKOIL" were opened in Simpferopol and in Sevastopol. Ukrainian subsidiary "LUKOIL-Crimea" was established. Purchase of Odessa Refinery in 1999 has expanded LUKOIL's business in Ukraine. Odessa refinery was built already in 1937. When LUKOIL bought Odessa refinery, it worked only on 30% capacity. In 2001, the oil processing volume doubled and Odessa refinery's share in the Ukrainian oil processing increased to 14.7%. The plant refined 2.5 million tons of crude oil in 2002. The oil refining annual capacity of Odessa plant is 3.6 million tons. In 2002, LUKOIL Odessa Refinery has got international quality certificate ISO-9001: 2000 – the fist one given in oil processing industry in Ukraine. In 2003, LUKOIL Ukraine has got Environmental Management System Certificate ISO 14001 and industrial safety and labor protection certificate OHSAS 18001.

LUKOIL-Ukraine was founded in 1999 in order to develop sales network of LUKOIL's oil products in Ukraine. With this sales unit, LUKOIL finalized the formation of the closed production cycle in Ukraine: raw material supplies, oil processing, transportation and retail sales. In 1999, LUKOIL's Ukrainian network already included 4 gasoline stations owned by the company and 7 stations managed by franchisees. The retail network was extended to 88 gasoline stations in 2001 and further to 164 in 2002. In 2003, LUKOIL-Ukraine invested about 50 million USD in its operations in Ukraine. Nowadays, LUKOIL-Ukraine owns 179 gasoline stations in 17 regions of Ukraine.

*TNK (Russia)*

*TNK International* is a private company that is indirectly owned by two shareholders, *Access Industries/Renova and Alfa Group*. These two companies own 100% of TNK International through their wholly owned TNK Industrial Holdings. *Access Industries* is a New York-based investment firm established in 1986. In conjunction with its Russian affiliate, *Renova*, it serves both as principal investor and operator in a variety of industries both in the United States and abroad. In addition to its headquarters in New York, the Group has offices in the U.K., Russia, Kazakhstan and Ukraine. The company's strategy in the CIS region is to acquire from 25% to 100% of equity in local firms and to increase shareholder value by providing capital, management and technical expertise to the acquired companies. *Alfa Group Consortium* is one of Russia's major financial-industrial groups. The consortium of businesses includes commodities trading, commercial and retail banking, securities trading, investment banking, retail trading and real estate development. *Alfa Bank*, the largest Russian privately owned bank, is the core of the Consortium. *Alfa Eco*, Alfa's wholesale trading subsidiary, is among the largest commodity trading companies in Russia and other CIS-countries specializing in petroleum products, sugar, tea and non-ferrous metals. The consortium of Alfa Group had consolidated revenues of approximately 5.7 billion USD in 2000.

*TNK-BP* was established in February 2003 when one of the world's largest oil companies, British Petroleum, and the Russian Alfa Group in cooperation with Access/Renova Holdings (AAR) announced the formation of a strategic partnership and intention to unite their oil assets in Russia and Ukraine. BP and AAR each own 50% of the TNK-BP shares. The new holding company is the third largest Russian oil company in terms of its reserves and production volume. Annual oil production is about 60 million tons, and five refineries of the company have a total capacity for 50 million tons a year. The holding company has a network of petrol stations throughout Russia and Ukraine in 2100 locations. In July of 2000 TNK acquired Ukrainian oil refinery LINOS. TNK purchased a 67% of LINOS shares for 50 million UAH. This deal included investment commitments by TNK-Ukraine in excess of 100 million USD. The Lisichansk refinery (Lisichansknefteorgsintez, LINOS) is located in the Lugansk Region in eastern Ukraine. The refinery was commissioned in December 1976. The capacity of the Lisichansk refinery is 16 million tons annually. TNK-Ukraine owns also 925 gasoline stations.

**Table 11. TNK in Regions, 2002**

| | Oil Product Sales, thousand tons | Number of Gasoline Stations |
|---|---|---|
| **Moscow and the Moscow Region** | 1 017.6 | 151 |
| **Ryazan Region** | 622.1 | 140 |
| **Orenburg Region** | 562.2 | 100 |
| **Tula Region** | 394.5 | 130 |
| **Kursk Region** | 389.7 | 122 |
| **Kaluga Region** | 321.2 | 130 |
| **Karelia Region** | 180.6 | 32 |
| **Rostov Region** | 480.5 | 69 |
| **Saratov Region** | 598.0 | 97 |
| **Ukraine** | 3 257.4 | 925 |
| **Other regions** | 628.2 | 46 |

*Alliance Group (Russia)*

Alliance Group is a holding company established in 1998. The company has specialized in restructuring and renovation of enterprises in Russia and other CIS-countries. Alliance Group owns 15 production units in 10 regions of Russia, Ukraine, Kazakhstan and Kyrgyzstan. Alliance Group is operating in the Ukrainian machinery production (Stakhanovsky Vagon Building plant), oil processing (Kherson Refinery, Sevastopol Oil Terminal) and oil products supplies. Oil Company Alliance Ukraine (2002) is a daughter company of Oil Company Alliance, part of the holding Alliance Group (Russia).

Alliance Group, Russian company Rosneft and Kazakh company Kazakhoil have signed an agreement on the development of Kherson Refinery, which is the third largest oil processing plant in terms of oil processing volumes in Ukraine. Kherson Refinery Constructed in the 1930s, the plant needs renovation. The plant has annual refining capacity of 7.1 million tons of oil. According to the agreement, Rosneft will supply oil to the Kherson refinery. Kazakhoil Ukraine (via Trading House Ukrnefteproduct) owns 60% of the Kherson Refinery. Alliance Group owns about 26% of the refinery, and manages the plant on the behalf of Kazakhoil. Alliance Ukraine has significantly modernized the refinery and has developed a reconstruction and technical development program for the Kherson Refinery for 2001 – 2010. The program aims to attract about 1 billion UAH (187.6 million USD) investment. About 100 million UAH (18.8 million USD) are already invested in the refinery's modernization.

Kherson refinery supplies its products to the customers in Kherson, Odessa, Nikolaev, Zaporozhie, Dnepropetrovsk, Donetsk, Lugansk, Kiev, Khmelnitsky regions and in Crimea via the network of 150 gasoline stations. The number of gasoline stations is planned to increase to 200. In order to provide Crimea with gasoline, Alliance has bought the Krymnefteproduct company's infrastructure, including 45 gasoline stations and 10 oil and petroleum storages located in Crimea.

*Alfa-Bank (Russia)*

Founded in 1990, Alfa Bank has developed into Russia's largest privately owned bank. Alfa Bank provides a full range of banking services — commercial banking, investment banking, asset management, trade finance and insurance. Alfa Bank has more than 100 branches in Russia and foreign subsidiary offices in Kazakhstan, Ukraine, the Netherlands, the United Kingdom, and the United States. Alfa Bank is one of the five largest financial corporations in Russia.

Alfa Bank Ukraine has interests in the oil industry, telecommunications, trade, banking, insurance business and food industry. Alfa Bank was registered in Ukraine in January 2001. Alfa-Bank aims to develop in Ukraine as a universal bank possessing all types of banking licenses and having developed network of branches. Alfa-Bank was chosen as the leading bank in Ukraine by Investgazeta in 2003. Alfa Bank has expanded into Ukrainian regions. It has opened branches and subsidiaries in Donetsk, Kharkov, Dnepropetrovsk (2002), Nikolaev (2002), Kiev, and representative offices in Zaporozhie, Lvov and in Simpheropol.

Besides traditional commercial banking services, Alfa-Bank keeps one of the leading positions among Russian investment banks by actively investing in real estate business, food industry, telecommunication, television, radio, consumer goods production, trade, tobacco industry, banking, insurance business and pharmaceutical industry. Alfa-Bank purchases companies for the time period from 3 to 6 years in order to increase the company's market value, and after that sells them to strategic investors. Alfa-Bank Ukraine has assets in mass media and pharmaceutical business: Novyi Kanal (New Channel), Nashe Radio (Our Radio), Diorama and Galichpharm.

*Novyi Kanal* was established in 1998, and in five years developed a wide broadcasting network covering 235 towns and villages reaching about 30 million people, of which 85% are urban). Novyi Kanal is in the top three TV channels in Ukraine. *Nashe Radio* was opened in 1997 and is in the top three Ukrainian radio stations. Nashe radio covers 26 towns and about 30 million people. *Diorama* is a publishing house founded in 1998. It prints "Diorama Plus Moskovsky Komsomolets" – one of the most popular weekly socio-political periodicals. The edition of 93 thousand copies is very significant for Ukrainian market. The "Moskovsky Komsomolets" share on the market has achieved 10.7% in April 2003. Galichpharm is one the leading pharmaceutical companies in Ukraine. The company, certified according quality standards ISO 9001:2001, is actively developing. Alfa-Bank is creating a Direct Investment Centre aiming at investing in medium-sized companies with high value added and average annual turnover of 30 – 50 million USD located in Russia and Ukraine. Alfa-Bank plans to invest 10–50 million USD in each project.

*Wimm-Bill-Dann (Russia)*

Wimm-Bill-Dann Foods is the market leader in the dairy and juice products in Russia. Wimm-Bill-Dann has expanded from a leased production line at the Lianozovsky Dairy Plant in 1992 to a publicly listed food conglomerate and employs more than 18,000 people. Wimm-Bill-Dann owns 24 manufacturing facilities in 20 locations in Russia and the Commonwealth of Independent States (CIS), as well as distribution centres in 26 cities in Russia and abroad. The company also distributes its products in Canada, Germany, Israel, the Netherlands, the UK and the United States through both its own distribution network and independent distributors. On February 8, 2002, Wimm-Bill-Dann became the first Russian consumer company to list Level 3 American Depositary Receipts (ADRs) on the New York Stock Exchange and the third Russian company ever to be listed on the NYSE.

In 2000, Wimm-Bill-Dann bought 60% shares of *Kiev City Milk Plant number 3 (KGMZ)*. In November 2002, Wimm-Bill-Dann paid approximately 1.7 million USD for 76% shares of *Burynsky Dried Milk Plant* (Sumy region, Ukraine). Burynsky Dried Milk Plant has been built in 1974 and renovated in 1985. The plant employs 150 people and is able to process 300 tons of milk daily and produce 18 tons of butter.

In July 2002, Wimm-Bill-Dann acquired 75% share of *Kharkov Dairy* – one of the leading in Ukraine milk processing plants for 4.5 million USD. The plant is built in 1973 with capacity of 500 tons daily milk processing. Kharkov Dairy possesses famous brands and has a significant market share (8.7%) on Ukrainian milk markets. Kharkov Dairy produces more than 60 milk product brands. The company produces about 2500 tons of milk products monthly (Amer Nielsen Investigation on 4 main Ukrainian cities).

In 2003, Wimm-Bill-Dann invested 8.1 million USD in the new production line of yogurts on the Kharkov Dairy. On January 26, 2004, Wimm-Bill-Dann announced about the installation of new manufacturing lines at the Company's two dairy plants located in Ukraine. Total investment in equipment was over 13.3 million USD.

*UMC (Russia)*

Ukrainian Mobile Communications (UMC) was officially registered in 1992. Originally, Ukrtelecom owned 51% of shares in UMC, while the rest 49% of the shares were equally divided between Deutsche Telecom (Germany) (16.33%), TeleDanmark (Denmark) (16.33%) and PTT Telecom (Netherlands) (16.33%). In November 2002 Russian company Mobile Telesystems (MTC) announced its purchase of 57.67% shares of UMC. MTC has bought 16.33% UMC's shares from Holland KPN and 16.33% from Deutsche Telecom (55 million USD paid to each company). 25% more were purchased from Ukrtelecom for 84.2 million USD.

*KIEVSTAR (Norway, Russia)*

Kiev Star is a joint stock company established by the Ministry of Energy, the State Committee for Oil, Gas, and Oil Processing, the Ukrainian Railroads (51%), Tiller International (UK) and the Impex Group (Luxembourg). In summer 2003, Russian Alfa – Telecom (the division of Alfa Group) purchased 50.1% shares of Ukrainian company Storm, controlling 32.39% of Kievstar GSM – the largest Ukrainian mobile operator. Kievstar has more than 2 800 000 subscribers and network covers 72% of the country's population. Kievstar's market share is more than 50%.[6]

## Conclusions

As seen from previous examples Russians have arrived in the international arena. The authors hope to have presented that Russian internationalization is a two-way street that has many faces. Russian large exporters of natural resources, export–import trade companies, service companies providing knowledge transfer, information technologies firms outsourcing its services, small and medium sized firms – born globals in different branches of business.

It could be briefly summarized, the main findings of paper as follows:

1. Russian 20 biggest exporters accounted 52.4% of the total Russian exports in the year 2001 (Table 1), and represent five main industries: oil and gas industry (82%) – 10 companies, metal industry (16%) – 8 companies, chemical and petrochemical industry (1.28%) – 1 company, and machine building industry (0.99%) – 1 company. And in the comparison with the year 2000 this structure did not changed significantly. The biggest Russian exporting companies have a strong trend to the international expansion. Many of them have significant growth of exports share in total sales, the growth of the exports volumes, and number of export countries.

2. Top 10 Russian Importers (Table 3) show us interesting picture of large international companies, mainly machine and equipment producers. These large companies do not see benefit to produce their spare parts locally – they import all necessary parts and equipment and realize just assembling locally. This allows them to avoid custom fees when importing ready products to Russia.

3. IT: More than 69% of studied IT companies had regional offices in Russia, and 29% had offices abroad. Studied companies were targeting target the following CIS countries: Ukraine, Kazakhstan, Belarus, and Azerbaijan. Companies, operating on western markets had offices in USA, UK, Poland, Japan, Germany, Latvia, China, Netherlands and France. It is obvious that biggest IT companies also prefer expand into Russian regions

with *region/local strategy*. Russia is a large country with 89 regions and thus provides extremely good opportunities for growth inside the country.

About 30% of the studied companies operated on the CIS market, which is traditionally very well known for Russian companies, since the infrastructure and business traditions are familiar and close to Russian. 12% internationalizing companies operated abroad on the base of personal networks, occasionally happened contracts and offers. 5% of them had build their strategy depending on foreign customers.

Software: All four studied case companies had started international operations in the year of their establishment or a year later. This has lead to the idea of applying the Born Globals concept. All pilot study case companies also had started their international operations based on strong personal networks with foreign partners, emphasizing trust and teamworking principles in the internal networks. This justifies the application of the Network concept and Born Globals for the research of the Russian IT sector to analyse the internationalization of new fast growing Russian IT firms.

4. On the oil sector, exports naturally remain the main internationalization mode for largest Russian oil companies. Higher exports prices attract Russian oil companies, however export pipeline capacity and international quotas limit possibility for exports. Internationalization of Russian oil companies has happened less than expected by the publicity. Foreign acquisitions have mainly targeted refineries in CIS and oil reserves. CIS is still very traditional home market. Internationalization degrees vary greatly between oil companies. However, companies seem to understand internationalization as a strategic decision – international operations are often managed in separate entities.

To conclude, Russian companies have arrived to stay in international markets. The Ukraine example shows well the influence of Russian businesses in CIS-countries. On the western markets we could expect to see more and more Russian companies, when Russia's integration to world economy progresses.

# Notes

[1] Based on the data of Goskomstat of Russia and Federal Customs Service (FCS)
[2] based on the Expert magazine rating
[3] Based on FCS data
[4] Based on FCS data
[5] NPAT – Net Profit After Tax
[6] Official company's data, adapted from www.kyivstar.net

# References

Andersen, O. (1993) On the internationalisation process of firms: a critical analysis. Journal of International Business Studies, Second Quarter, pp. 209-231.

Bell, J. (1995) The internationalisation of small computer firms – a further challenge to "stage" theories. European Journal of Marketing, vol. 29, no. 8, pp. 60-75.

Bell, J., McNaughton, R.,Young, S. (2001) "Born-again global" firms – an extension to the "born global" phenomenon. Journal of International Management, 7, pp. 173-189.

Dunning, John H. (1980) Toward an Eclectic Theory of International Production: Some Empirical Tests, Journal of International Business Studies, 11 (Spring/Summer), pp. 9-31.

—. (1988) The Eclectic Paradigm of International Production: A Restatement and Some Possible Extensions, Journal of International Business Studies, 19 (Spring), pp. 1-31.

Gerlinger, J. M., Beamish, P. W. & da Costa, R. (1989), Diversification Strategy and Internationalization: Implications for MNE Performance, Strategic Management Journal, 10, pp. 109-119.

Hawk, S., McHenry, W. (2004): The Maturation of the Russian Software Industry, to appear in Journal of Information Technology for Development in 2005.

Hogaguchi, H. & Tonye, B. (1990): Setting the Record Straight – Hymer, Internationalization Theory and Transaction Cost Economics, Journal of International Business Studies, 21/3, pp. 487-494.

Johanson, J & Mattson, L. G. (1988): Internationalisation in industrial systems – a network approach, in: strategies in global competition, Ed. By N. Hood & J. E. Vahlne, Routledge: London, pp. 287 – 314.

Johanson, J., Vahlne, J.-E. (1977): The internationalization process of the firm, Journal of International Business Studies, vol. 8, Spring/Summer.

Johanson, J., Vahlne, J.-E. (1990): The mechanism of internationalization, International Marketing Review, 7, no. 4

Knight, G.A., Cavusgil, T.S. (1996) The born global firm: a challenge to traditional internationalization theory. Advances in International Marketing, 8, pp. 11-26

Leo, P. Y. and Philippe, J. (2001): Internationalisation of service activities in Haute-Garonne, The Service Industries Journal, Jan, 2001, 21, 1, pp 63 – 80.

Lovelock C. H. (1983): Classifying services to gain strategic marketing insights, Journal of Marketing, Summer, pp. 9-20.

Lovelock C. H. and Yip G.S. (1996): Developing global strategies for service businesses, California Management Review, Vol. 38, No.2 Winter.

Luostarinen R. (1994), Internationalization of Finnish firms and their response to global challenges, UNU/WIDER Publications, December 1994, ISBN 952-9520-20-4

O'Farrel ,N. P. and Wood, A. P. (1994): International market selection by business service firms: key conceptual and methodological issues, International Business Review, Vol. 3, No 3, pp. 243 – 264.

Pchounetlev V. (2000) Internationalisation strategies of Russian companies, Paper presented at the Second International Conference "Transition and Enterprise Restructuring in Eastern Europe" 17-19 August 2000, Hellerod, Denmark.

Podmetina, D. (2004): Internationalisation of New Service Companies: Case of Russian Information Technology Firms, AIB Conference, UK Chapter, University of Ulster, Ireland.

Podmetina D., Vaatanen J. (2005): Looking for Expansion: Domestic vs. International. Case of Russian Information Technology Business, 6th International Conference on "Enterprise in Transition", Split University, Croatia.

Root , F. (1994), Entry Strategies for International Markets, Lexington Books, New York, 1994

# ECONOMIC GROWTH, FOREIGN INVESTMENTS AND ECONOMIC FREEDOM: A CASE OF TRANSITION ECONOMY

KAJA LUTSOJA AND MARGUS LUTSOJA

## Abstract

The connection between economic freedom and economic growth is relatively controversial. Even if the economic growth can be managed in stable economies, nobody has universal receipt for transition economies. This paper analyses determinant factors of differences in economic growth of transition economies. The data are analyzed by regression model to examine the effect of the components of economic freedom on growth, output and investment.

The main objective of this paper is to test a hypothesis about the impact of economic freedom as one of the main factors of economic growth paying special attention to CEE transition countries.

## Foreword

The theme of economic growth is perhaps the most researched theme in economic literature. There are numerous textbooks and researches on that, but until now no proven correlation between the theory and empirical data for different economic situations can be found. Even if the economic growth can be managed in stable economies, nobody has universal receipt for transition economies or for poorer countries in developing world. This paper analyses determinant factors of differences in economic growth of transition economies. The main focus of the research is a relationship between economic growth, government intervention in the economy and capital flows of foreign investment based on the case of Estonia compared to neighbouring Latvia and Lithuania. Other Central and Eastern Europe Countries that joined EU in 2004 are also analysed to have larger sample, but the important conclusions are drawn mainly based on Baltic countries.

The data are analysed by regression model to examine the effect of the components of economic freedom on growth, output and investment.

Estonia is one of three Baltic States. After regaining independence from the Soviet Union in 1991 there was rapid change from the soviet system to free market economy. Since 1995 economic growth in Baltic countries has been at least 5% a year. The Baltic region holds its position as one of the world's most rapidly developing areas. Despite the speculations on possible overheating of economies with more than 10% growth in 2005 and 2006 the business confidence still remains strong. The negative effects of the recent global downturn have had some impact on Latvia, Lithuania and Estonia, but the growth is still expected to remain at least 4,5 % per year. Estonia has steadily acquired high rankings in the various economic freedom indexes with the other Central and Eastern Europe countries following with some distance.

The accession of 10 new member countries including Estonia to the European Union in May 2004 resulted in policy changes that affected their scores in the 2006 indexes of economic freedom. While implementation of the EU policies on trade, agriculture, regulation, monetary and fiscal policy has been uneven, with few caveats, their trade policy scores now conform to the EU-wide trade policy. As a result, with the exception of Estonia, the scores for the other 9 accession countries have improved.

## Economic Freedom

Whereas the definitions of the economic freedom may differ in nuances, the ingredients of economic freedom are agreed to be personal choice, voluntary exchange, and protection of person and property. When economic freedom is present, the choices of individuals will decide what and how goods and services are produced. Personal ownership is an underlying postulate of economic freedom as such.

Economic freedom is reduced when taxes, government expenditures, and regulations are substituted for personal choice, voluntary exchange, and market coordination. Economic freedom reflects the presence of protective rights, that is, rights that provide individuals with a shield against others who would invade and/or take what does not belong to them. Since they are nonaggression rights, all citizens can simultaneously possess them (Gwartney, Lawson, 2001).

There are three respected major surveys that measure economic liberty on a systematic basis: the Fraser Institute's economic freedom index, Freedom House's economic freedom indicators, and the Heritage Foundation's indices of economic freedom.

*The Fraser Institute's Economic Freedom Index*

Participants at various symposia on economic freedom felt the Gastil-Wright approach might over-emphasize democratic political procedures and civil liberties in measuring economic freedom, and worked tirelessly over several years to develop alternative measures. The culmination of this effort was the publication in 1996 of Economic Freedom of the World: 1975-1995 (Gwartney, Lawson, and Block 1996).

*Freedom House's Economic Freedom Indicators*

Freedom House's efforts to supplement its annual reports on worldwide political and civil liberty eventually culminated in a free-standing publication, World Survey of Economic Freedom: 1995- 1996. Like Gastil and Wright's earlier efforts, the Freedom House index of economic freedom places significant emphasis on certain civil liberties (e.g., whether women or minorities are foreclosed from certain businesses or from owning or transferring property).

*The Heritage Foundation's Indices of Economic Freedom.*

Starting in 1994, the Heritage Foundation began to publish an annual Index of Economic Freedom. Heritage's aim differed slightly from that of other surveys: it sought to provide evidence on the utility (or lack thereof) of externally funded "development assistance" in facilitating growth. Heritage's Index added to the weight of evidence on the relationship of freedom to growth.

## Economic Growth

Numerous scientific collectives study the relationship between the economic freedom and economic growth. Roll and Talbott found a strong relationship between economic freedom and the level of per capita income in a country, concluding that economic freedom is clearly important to a country's development: "Economic participants cannot save in a world of inflationary government-sponsored counterfeiting. They cannot compete with state-sponsored monopolies. They cannot trade efficiently with the existence of high tariffs and phoney official exchange rates. They cannot easily overcome burdensome regulation and corruption. They cannot capitalize future profits in a world devoid of property rights. And they cannot prosper without economic and personal freedoms" (Kingham, Schaefer, 2003).

In the 1950s and 1960s, economist Robert Solow developed a model that would help revolutionize the understanding of growth theory. Solow added technology to the production function equation; however, he added it as a variable that existed exogenously from the neoclassical model's production function equation (Cortright, 2001). This exogenous technology variable was meant to account for any discrepancies between what certain levels of capital and labour would indicate as the output and actual output, especially in cross-country comparisons. More importantly, it provided a vehicle for explaining the rate of growth over time. There is however a major weakness to Solow's model. By keeping technology outside of the equation, Solow's model could not explain "why" or "how", or from where/what technological progress came from (ibid.).

Barro's classical study from 1996 concludes that: "The data now available for a broad panel of countries over 30 years provides the information necessary to isolate determinants of economic growth. With respect to government policies, the evidence indicates that the growth rate of real per capita GDP is enhanced by better maintenance of the rule of law, smaller government consumption, and lower inflation. Increases in political rights initially increase growth but tend to retard growth once a moderate level of democracy has been attained. Greater starting levels of life expectancy and of male secondary and higher schooling also stimulate growth, by lower fertility rates, and by improvements in the terms of trade. For given values of these variables, growth is higher if a country begins with a lower starting level of real per capita GDP; that is, the data reveal a pattern of condition convergence (Barro, 1996).

**Figure 1. Economic growth of 10 accession countries from 1990 to 2008 (official prognosis of growth used for 2008)**

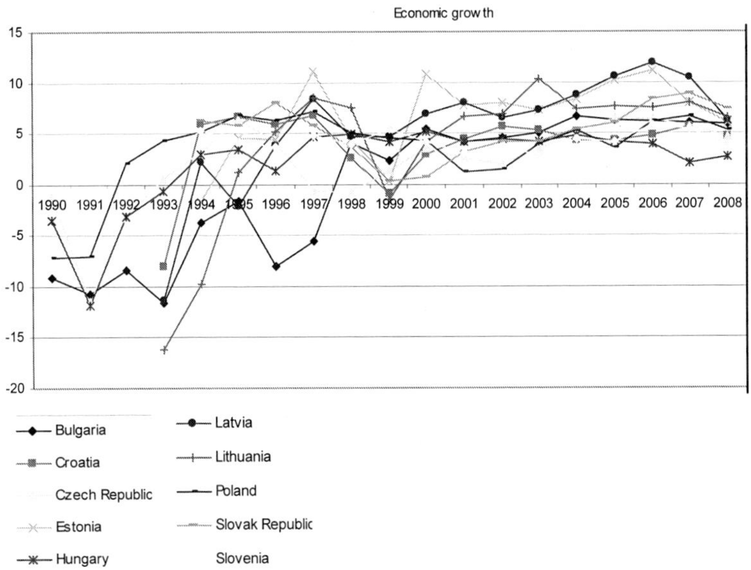


## Investment

The relationship between trade and the investment is not immediately obvious. Yet, the two are linked processes, accounting for big segments of global economic activity. Trade rules mainly relate to the production of goods and services; investment rules regulate the operations of international corporations and financial institutions that see trade and investment as alternative, but complementary routes to global expansion.

Investments between different countries have two basic forms: foreign direct investment (FDI) and international portfolio investment (IPI). FDI can be generally understood as investment by a company domiciled in one country in an asset located in another country with the intent to control the asset and manage it. IPI on the other hand is generally understood as international investment in stocks and shares, bonds or other parts of the financial markets that does not result in a 'controlling stake'. In other words, FDI is by nature active whereas IPI is passive.

Although foreign investment is an important part of the world trade system and probably is important in the development process, it is not a universal medicine for the world economy. Also, some evidence suggests that there is little or no correlation between free investment markets and economic or cultural development

FDI does more likely benefit a developing country than IPI, but it is by no means beneficial in every situation and every time. Governments therefore have every right to decide on circumstances and guide the flows of foreign investment either by means of regulation or by direct intervention.

The paper of Stephen Knowles and Arlene Garces (2000) provides two thoughts on this issue. The first is that the negative correlation between government consumption and economic performance often found by Robert Barro and his colleagues depends crucially on measuring government consumption in international prices. It has been argued that to do this is misleading. Once government consumption is measured in local prices, there is no evidence of any statistically significant relationship between government consumption and output per worker (ibid.).

There are different definitions for the Foreign Direct Investment. FDI is defined as a cross-border investment in which a resident in one economy (the direct investor) acquires a lasting interest in an enterprise in another economy (the direct investment enterprise). By convention, a direct investment is established when the direct investor has acquired 10 percent or more of the ordinary shares or voting power of an enterprise abroad.

We present, hereafter, potential determinants of FDI inflows that have been amply used in the literature. Most analyses of the determinants of FDI inflows have included the size of the host market measured by GDP. The market size has been widely found to be an important, if not the most important, incentive for FDI. A larger market allows a more efficient utilization of resources and the exploitation of economies of scale, and therefore a higher return of investment (Wang, Swain, 1995). Chakrabarti (2001) offers a relatively comprehensive enumeration of works that have proved that the size of the economy is a considerable determinant of FDI inflows for developed as well as developing economies (Chakrabarti, 2001).

However, the market size might be less influential, or even insignificant, if foreign companies are using the host country only as a production base,

taking advantage of the low costs of the host economy in order to export their production more competitively to a third or home markets.
A second potential determinant is the movements in the price level. A large and unsustainable increase in the price level, or high inflation, might reflect instability of the macroeconomic policy of the host country. Such instability creates an uncertain environment for investments
A third frequently noted factor is the strength of the host country's currency measured by the level of exchange rates. A depreciation of the host country currency might attract FDI for the reason that a depreciation of the host country currency favours mergers and acquisitions from foreign firms. Also, the depreciation of currency is favourable if foreign companies aim at re-exporting to home or third countries as producing in the host country enhances competitiveness and investors' wealth rises. However, if the companies intend to sell in the host market, a depreciation of the currency might hinder inflows (Bajo-Rubia, Sosvilla-Rivero, 1994).

In the early 1990s, led largely by Mainland China, countries in Asia received almost half of the FDI directed to the EMCs. Owing largely to the pursuit of economic reforms, the size of the domestic market, and its cost competitiveness, China was successful in receiving large amounts of FDI. In fact, using methods of econometric analysis on FDI is strongly influenced by the dominating amount of FDI into China.

Net FDI flows to EMCs grew at a remarkable average annual rate of 40 percent during 1990–94, and a slower rate of 15 percent during 1995–99. The share of EMCs in global FDI flows increased steadily and on average accounted for a quarter of the global FDI flows through 1994. That proportion has since declined steadily.

To avoid any confusion, we need to emphasise the following two points. First, the sample size is rather small and consequently the accuracy of the results for the purpose of policy implications is restricted. What consists our attempt to enlarge the span and frequency of the sample, data on FDI are not available. Second, we recognize that data on FDI do not reflect exactly the size of inflows and existing foreign investments.

**Figure 2. Foreign direct investments (millions of US$) of 9 accession countries from 1993 to 2006**

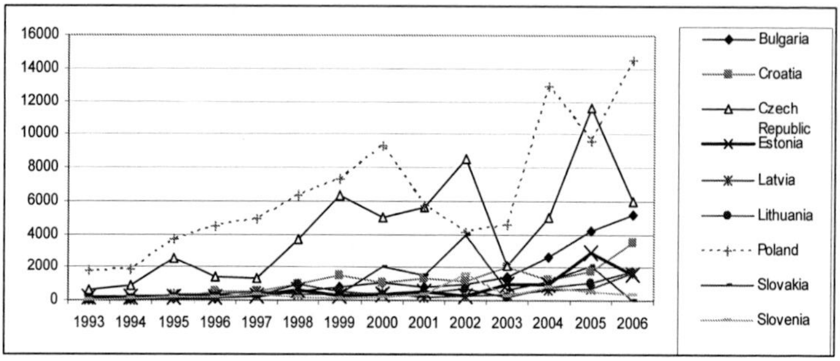


## Estonian Case Compared To Other Baltic Countries

Estonia is open to foreign investment, and foreign investors receive national treatment. The government allows foreigners to invest in all sectors, with requirements restricted to non-discriminatory regulation and documentation. According to the Economist Intelligence Unit, "Estonia's rapid trade and regulatory liberalization and macroeconomic stabilization have produced a positive environment for foreign investment, reinforced by the country's entry into the EU". The government requires licenses for investment in banking, mining, gas and water supply or related structures, railroads and transport, energy, and communications networks, but this requirement has not restricted investment and is applied in a routine, non-discriminatory manner. Foreign direct investment rules regarding real estate, aviation, maritime transport, and security service enterprises were harmonized with European Union.

Regulations in Estonia are transparent and evenly applied. However, due to the small size of Estonia's commercial community, instances of favouritisms are not uncommon despite the regulations and procedures that are designed to limit it. Foreign investment has played a key role in Estonia's economic success. The result has been a huge inflow of foreign direct investment - the per capita figure (more than 5 160 EUR per capita), is one of the highest among the new EU member states.

Estonia has no exchange controls or restrictions on foreign investment. The amount of foreign capital invested in Estonian business enterprise is unlimited and companies can be in full foreign ownership. Foreign companies enjoy equal rights with local ones, including unrestricted repatriation of profits and the right to own property. To encourage companies to expand their business all corporate investments are exempted of corporate income tax from Jan 1, 2000. However, any distributed profits, for example dividends, are taxed at 22%. In respect of the legal system and property rights Estonia is comparable and practically on the same level with Hong Kong, USA and UAE, locating to first 12 countries according to the Fraser Institute's estimation. Being a small and open economy, Estonia does not have a strategy for granting cash incentives to companies. Instead it aims at creating an attractive business and investment climate together with some support on innovation and enhancing the export capabilities of the companies.

Historically there have been large differences in the economic freedom between Estonia, Latvia, Lithuania and other transition countries. The Heritage Foundation's index of economic freedom in the group of transition countries has been with quite similar tendency. The most problematic year for transition countries has been 1996; there we can see the drastic decline in economic freedom index numbers. Within this period the largest change has been in Slovenia: 1,767 index points. Relatively large change has been also in Poland. Changes for other countries have been similar and diminutive. Smallest changes have been in Czech Republic, Russia and Romania (figure 3).

**Figure 3. Index of Economic Freedom 1995-2005**

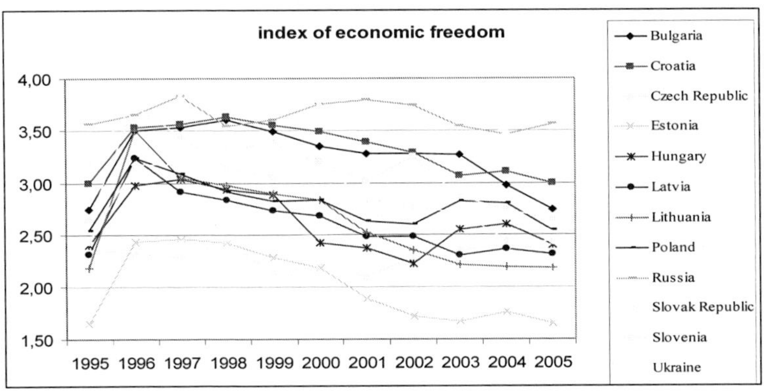

**Figure 4. Index of Economic Freedom 1995 – 2006 recalculated based on 2006 methodology**

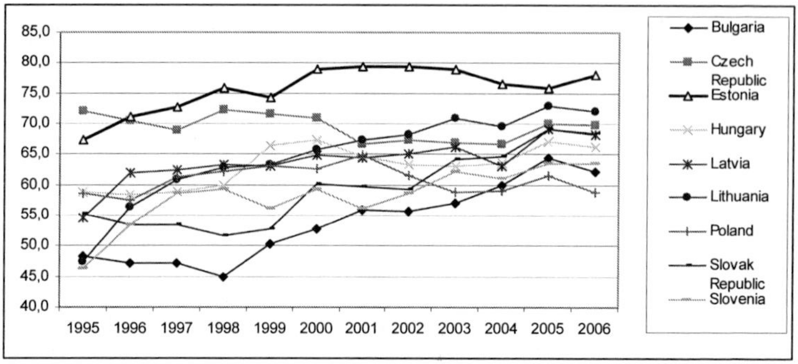


Since accession of the EU these differences have decreased, but Estonia still leads in the index with significant distance between Latvia and Lithuania. However, when looking at the FDI inflows and economic growth, Estonia and Latvia are performing nearly equally or Latvia is even slightly better. It is evident that Estonia and Latvia have large differences in results of the economic freedom index. Despite of that, the actual GDP growth is extremely similar as can be seen on Figure 1. We conclude that this difference demonstrates clearly that the economic freedom in its current estimation methodology does not have strong influence on economic growth, but there should be other factors, which are not measured yet. This conclusion is supported by the analysis of panel data as discussed below.

We need to emphasise that statistical methods do not give any hint on the reasons of such result. We can only guess those reasons:

- The first and most probable reason is that Estonia, Latvia and Lithuania are considered to be one region and the foreign investors are treating them as similar. Similarity is not actually true – differences in culture are notable, starting from the fact that Lithuania is Catholic, Latvia and Estonia Lutheran countries and ending with three different languages from two different language group.
- The second reason is microscopic size of each country in world terms, whereas adding three countries together creates a small

market with 8 million people. Large international corporations may have tendency for such adding together.

- Third likely reason is that although the cultures are different, people of these three countries have extremely similar history and background, size of the economy and geopolitical location.

When we compare annual level of the index for all countries represented in the Heritage Foundation's calculations and estimate the influence of economic freedom to the GDP growth rate, the result is approximately zero relation between the levels and GDP growth during 1995 – 2005. Other authors have predicted that already. When we change the approach and compare the change in index with the GDP growth per capita, then we can see that there exists statistically significant correlation for single countries. For example the correlation between GDP growth rate and change in index number was statistically significant in Slovenia (0.787) and Hungary (0.558). Medium correlation was in data of Czech Republic (0.349) and Slovakia (0.36). There was practically no correlation between the change in index and growth in GDP for Croatia, Bulgaria, Estonia, Latvia, Lithuania, Poland and Romania (all had correlation rounded to 0.08). From this part we can draw a conclusion that it is not justified to formulate the deduction about the effect of economic freedom in transition economy.

Transition countries were re-grouped and separated from total population to find what the different observable patterns are compared to the whole population. Analysis has been made in respect of all component factors included in the Heritage Foundations' index to detect differences in correlations between single factors compared to all other components.

Informal Market score has significantly weaker correlation with all other factors in the group of transition countries than in the whole population. The same appears for Monetary Policy. The correlation is the same numerical for both transition countries and the whole population in Trade. Property Rights has difference and the correlation for transition countries is lower than for the population. The category of Fiscal Burden has conspicuous difference whereas the correlation of that factor with other factors is higher for transition countries than in the population, except for regulations where we can see the opposite – correlation for total population is higher than for transition countries.

It is not sensible to calculate change in different factors and compare that with the growth in GDP because characteristically to the transition countries many factors have remained constant and have zero variability (see appendix). Due to that it is not possible to find which factor has most influence to the growth of GDP. The largest average growth in GDP during the period from 1995 to 2005 has had Latvia and the second is Estonia. These countries are followed by Lithuania and Romania, whereas the smallest average has had Czech Republic and Bulgaria. Both these countries have had periods of negative growth in late 90ties and subsequent average growth does not influence the average sufficiently.

Analysing the variation of the economic freedom index (table 1) shows that the most uneven has it been Estonia – average variability 17.19%. Estonia is followed by Slovakia (12.61) and Slovenia (11.12). The steadiest have been Czech Republic (4.58) and Russia (3.31).

Looking at the components we can see, that the variability of different component indexes is highly different (see appendix 5). Trade has relatively large variability. Largest variations in Trade category have had Lithuania (53.99%), Estonia (49.44%) and Czech Republic (48.06). Steadiest countries have been Croatia (14.27) Slovakia (23.7) and Russia (17.3). Fiscal Burden has less variability and the largest variability has Slovakia (30.62%); the second is Estonia (28.8). The steadiest has been Slovenia (9.77). Other components of the index have few variations. For example, in the Foreign Investment category 4 countries have had the same score during all 11 years under observation, Salaries and Prices category has 5 countries with invariable score, Property Rights has 6 and Regulations has 8 countries with no change at all during 11 years. Regulations category has been the steadiest factor in the index.

The generally accepted point of view in several researches is that transition countries have to have dynamic economic policy to achieve economic growth and the factors of economic freedom should change frequently and in relatively large portions. The change in factor is a consequence of a changing economic environment. If a factor has larger variability, the economy is changed in larger part as expected for the transition countries.

Analysis demonstrates however, that the variability of factors has no statistically significant influence on the growth in GDP. For the model the significance F=0.0807; RSQUARE = 0.798, but the adjusted R2 is -0.816.

We can conclude that there is no factor having statistical reliability. For testing hypothesis about relationship between economic freedom and economic growth we need factors with larger variability for measuring the economic freedom. Different index numbers could be efficient in case of longer time series but unfortunately time series for transition countries are insufficient.

## Conclusions

1. FDI does not depend only on government action and regulations but also on development of the economy. Too fast development of the economy and increase of cost of labour can stop investment. FDI may have a positive impact on the domestic companies, but due to the short time series of statistical data in transition countries the analysis cannot demonstrate a statistically significant relationship. To demonstrate a statistically significant relationship we need to build up lag models, whereas the determination of the lag is complicated due to the relatively different base development.
2. Transition countries in Europe cannot influence FDI by changing their economic environment. FDI is mostly determined by the change in Asian countries. More than ½ of total available FDI is received by Latin America and Asia. European countries have had weak increase trend only.
3. It is impossible to find regularities in the comparison of the economical data and FDI, because each single larger-than-average FDI has a nature of random shock. To find regularities small countries need to be aggregated, but that eliminates also effects of regulations.
4. The economic freedom as estimated by the Heritage Foundation does not have significant correlation with the economic growth. Also, if analysed by different components, none of them has significant correlation with the economic growth. Consequently, there are likely to be other factors than the economic freedom or FDI may play more significant role in actual GDP growth.
5. Comparison of three Baltic countries gives a strong suggestion that despite differences in the economic freedom the foreign investors treat similar countries in terms of the size of the economy in similar geopolitical location similarly.

## References

Bajo-Rubia, O., and S. Sosvilla-Rivero (1994), "An Economic Analysis of Foreign Direct Investment in Spain," Southern Economic Journal, 61(1), pp. 104-117.

Barro, Robert J. Determinants of Economic Growth: A Cross-Country Empirical Study. NBER Working Paper 5698. 1996

Cortright, J. 2001. New Growth Theory, Technology and Learning: A Practitioner's Guide. U.S. Economic Development Administration, Washington, DC. http://www.eda.gov/ImageCache/EDAPublic/documents/pdfdocs/1g3lr_5f7_5fcortright_2epdf/v1/1g3lr_5f7_5fcortright.pdf

Chakrabarti, A., (2001), "The Determinants of Foreign Direct Investment PP. Sensitivity Analyses of Cross-country Regressions," Kyklos, 54(1), pp. 89-114.

Eliezer B. Ayal and Georgios Karras (1998), Components of Economic Freedom And Growth: An Empirical Study., University of Illinois at Chicago. Published in the Journal of Developing Areas, Vol.32, No.3, p 327-338.

Fredrik Carlsson and Susanna Lundström (2001), Economic Freedom and Growth: Decomposing the Effects.. Working Paper in Economics no. 33, Department of Economics Göteborg University.

Clark J.R. , Lee Dwight R. and Sobel Russell S. (2005), *Freedom Barriers to Entry, Entrepreneurship, and Economic Progress* www2.sjsu.edu/depts/economics/faculty/powell/docs/econ206/Growth-Entrepreneurship.pdf/22.01.2006/

Gasiorowski, Marc (2000): „Democracy and Macroeconomic Performance in Underdeveloped Countries. An Empirical Analysis", *Comparative Political Studies* 33, 319-49.

Gastil, Raymond D. (1982): *Freedom in the World.* Westport, Conn.:Greenwood

Gemmel, Norman (1998): „Reviewing the New Growth Literature." *New PoliticalEconomy* 3 (1): 129-33.

Grier, Kevin B., and Gordon Tullock (1989): „An Empirical Analysis of Cross-National Economic Growth, 1951-80", *Journal of Monetary Economics* 24, 259-76.

James Gwartney, Robert Lawson and Erik Gartzke (2005), Economic Freedom of the World 2005 Annual Report, The Fraser Institute.

James Gwartney and Robert Lawson (2001), The Concept and Measurement of Economic Freedom.. Presented to "The Analysis and

Measurement of Freedom: Theoretical, Empirical, and Institutional Perspectives," a Conference held in Palermo, Italy.

James Gwartney, Robert Lawson, Randall Holcombe (1999), Economic Freedom and The Environment for Economic Growth.. Journal of Institutional and Theoretical Economics, vol127(4) pages 643 – .

Steve H. Hanke and Stephen J. K. Walters (1997), Economic Freedom, Prosperity, and Equality: A Survey, Cato Journal, 17-2 pages 117-46. http://www.heritage.org/research/features/index/chapters/htm/Index2006_Chap5.cfm /22.03.2006/

Kormendi, Roger C., and Philip G. Meguire (1985): „Macroeconomic Determinants of Growth. Cross Country Evidence", *Journal of Monetary Economics* 16, 141-163.

Leblang, David A. (1997): „Political Democracy and Economic Growth: Pooled Cross-Sectional and Time Series Evidence", *British Journal of Political Science* 27, 453-72.

Romer, David, (2001), Advanced macroeconomics. Second edition., McGrow-Hill, New York

Schaefer, Brett, D. Jay Kingham. Promoting Growth And Prosperity In The Developing World Through Economic Freedom, Fellow in International Regulatory Affairs, The Heritage Foundation. March 2003. (http://usinfo.state.gov/journals/ites/0303/ijee/schaefer.htm)

Jacob Zipfel (2004), Determinants of Economic Growth, Florida State University. A Thesis submitted to the Department of Political Science in partial fulfilment of the requirements for Honors in the Major.

Volker Bornschier and Hanno Scholtz (2002),Democracy, Economic Growth and Technoeconomic Change – Empirical Evidence for Neglected Indirect Effects. World Congress on Sociology, Brisbane (AUS).

Wang, Z. Q., and N. J. Swain (1995), "The Determinants of Foreign Direct Investment in Transforming Economies PP.

Weede, Erich (1983): „The Impact of Democracy on Economic Growth: Some Evidence from Cross-National Analysis", *Kyklos* 36, 21-39.

http://www.fraserinstitute.ca/economicfreedom/index.asp?snav=ef

http://www.freedomhouse.org/template.cfm?page=70&release=67

http://www.cato.org/pubs/efw/index.html

http://www.heritage.org/index/

# APPENDICES

**Appendix 1. Components of the Index of Economic Freedom (Gwartney, Lawson, Holcombe)**

I. MONEY AND INFLATION (Protection of money as a store of value and medium of exchange)
A. Average Annual Growth Rate of the Money Supply During the Last Five Years Minus the Potential Growth Rate of Real GDP
B. Standard Deviation of the Annual Inflation Rate During the Last Five Years
C. Freedom of Citizens to Own a Foreign Currency Bank Account Domestically
D. Freedom of Citizens to Maintain a Bank Account Abroad

II. ECONOMIC STRUCTURE (Use of markets relative to government)
A. General Government Consumption Expenditures as a Percent of Total Consumption (Private & Government)
B. The Role and Presence of Government-Operated Enterprises
C. Price Controls— the Extent that Businesses are Free to Set Their Own Prices (This variable is included in only the 1990 and 1995 Indexes.)
D. Freedom of Private Businesses and Cooperatives to Compete in Markets (This variable is included only in the 1995 Index.)
E. Equality of Citizens Under The Law and Access of Citizens to a Non-discriminatory Judiciary (This variable is included only in the 1995 Index.)
F. Freedom from Government Regulations and Policies that Cause Negative Real Interest Rates

III. TAKINGS AND DISCRIMINATORY TAXATION (Freedom to keep what you earn)
A. Transfers and Subsidies as a Percent of GDP
B. Top Marginal Tax Rate (and income threshold at which it applies)
C. The Use of Conscripts to Obtain Military Personnel

IV. RESTRAINTS ON INTERNATIONAL EXCHANGE (Freedom of exchange with foreigners)
A. Taxes on International Trade as a Percent of Exports Plus Imports

B. Difference Between the Official Exchange Rate and the Black Market Rate
C. Actual Size of Trade Sector Compared to the Expected Size
D. Restrictions on the Freedom of Citizens to Engage in Capital Transactions with Foreigners

**Appendix 2. A list a subsample of available studies, i.e. the more recent ones, and classified according to some characteristics to find out possible causes for the controversial findings. (Bornschier and Scholtz, 2002)**

| | Author | Operationalisation of democracy | Result | GDP (-1) | Population | Investment | Human capital | Inequality | Political stability | Institutions | Government expenditure | Inflation | Openness | Colonial Heritage |
|---|---|---|---|---|---|---|---|---|---|---|---|---|---|---|
| 1 | Scully | Gastil>D | + | | x | x | | | | | | | | |
| 2 | Knack/Keefer | Gastil | + | x | x | | | | x | x | | | | |
| 3 | Leblang | PolityII | + | x | | | x | | x | | | | | |
| 4 | Pourgerami 1988 | Amnesty | + | | | x | | | | | x | | | x |
| 5 | Kormendi/Meguire | Gastil | (+) | x | | x | | | | | x | x | x | |
| 6 | Grier/Tullock | Gastil>D | (+) 1 | x | x | | | | | | x | x | | |
| 7 | Marsh | Gastil | 0 | x | | x | | x | | | x | | | |
| 8 | Pourgerami 1992 | Gastil | 0 | x | | | | | x | | | | | |
| 9 | Helliwell | Gast/Boll | 0 | x | | x | x | | | | | | | |
| 10 | Alesina/Rodrick | Fields | 0 | x | | | x | x | | | | | | |
| 11 | Barro/Sala-I-Martin | PolII/ Gast | 0 | x | | | x | x | | | | | | |
| 12 | Durham Eff. | Parties | 0 | x | x | x | x | | | x | | | x | |
| 13 | Barro | Gast/Boll | (O) | x | x | x | x | | | x | x | | x | |
| 14 | Obinger | Jagg/ Gurr | O | x | | | x | | | x | x | x | x | x |
| 15 | Martin/Plümper | Jagg/ Gurr | O | x | x | x | x | | | x | x | | x | |
| 16 | Feng | Poll/Boll | 2 | x | x | x | | | x | | | x | x | |
| 17 | Weede | Bollen | (–) | x | | x | x | | | | | | | |
| 18 | Landau | Demo -cracy age>D | – | x | x | | | | x | | x | | | x |

| 19 | Gasiorowski | PolityIII | – | x | x | x | x | x |
|---|---|---|---|---|---|---|---|---|

1. depending on region
2. depending on operationalization of political stability

**Appendix 3.** The various indicators of economic liberty used in these surveys

| **Fraser Institute** | **Freedom House** | **Heritage Foundation** |
|---|---|---|
| Protection of money as a store of value and medium of exchange<br>Low money supply growth<br>Low inflation rate<br>Foreign currency accounts OK<br>Bank accounts abroad OK | Freedom to hold property<br>Private property rights Intellectual property secure<br>Free exchange of property | Freedom of international exchange<br>Low tariffs, trade barriers |
| Freedom to decide what is produced and consumed<br>Low government consumption<br>Few state-owned enterprises<br>Absence of price controls<br>No market entry restrictions<br>Secure property rights, enforceable contracts, non-discriminatory courts<br>No interest rate controls | Freedom to earn a living<br>Free Bargaining associations<br>Absence of wage controls | Freedom to earn a living<br>Low income, corporate taxes<br>Low value-added, other taxes |
| Freedom to earn a living<br>Low transfers/subsidies<br>Low top marginal tax rate<br>No military conscription | Freedom to operate a business<br>Business formation easy<br>No market entry restrictions<br>Absence of price controls | Freedom to decide what is produced and consumed<br>Low government consumption<br>Few state-owned enterprises |

| | | |
|---|---|---|
| Freedom of international exchange<br>Low tariffs<br>No gap between official and black market exchange rates<br>Size of trade sector matches expectations<br>No capital controls | Freedom to invest earnings<br>Market credit allocation<br>Central bank independence<br>No profit/interest controls | Protection of money as a store of value and medium of exchange<br>Low inflation rate |
| | Freedom of international exchange<br>Low tariffs, trade barriers<br>Low travel barriers<br>No exchange controls | Free flows of capital<br>No foreign ownership limits or entry barriers<br>No discrimination between foreign and domestic firms |
| | Freedom to participate in the market economy<br>Antidiscrimination rules<br>Absence of corruption | Open banking system<br>No entry barriers for foreign banks<br>Limited regulation of banking |
| | | Freedom to earn a living, operate a business<br>Absence of wage controls<br>Absence of price controls |
| | | Freedom to hold property<br>Private property rights<br>Low probability of expropriation |
| | | Limited business regulation<br>No market entry restrictions<br>Absence of corruption |
| | | Limited black market |

# The Process Of Firm Internationalization From A Transformational Country Context

Emma Incze

## Abstract

This paper discusses how we can draw upon process thinking from existing internationalization process models and directly explores how the process of internationalization unfolds along time. Central to the study is the general model of entrepreneurial internationalization process, an International Business model that is compared with the processual view of organizations, an Organizational Science model. Primary qualitative data is presented about two multinational companies with non-traditional home base and a process research model is suggested based on existing theory and empirical observation.

## Introduction

Internationalization has been defined as a time-related process since the development of the Uppsala model by Johanson and Vahlne (e.g. Jonahson and Vahlne 1977, 1990, Welch and Luostarinen 1988, Johanson and Mattson 1988). According to this traditional view, internationalization is a gradual process giving a picture of sequential stages. In the last decade as a result of the globalization of markets and the emergence of the 'Born Globals' or 'International New Ventures' (e.g. Oviatt and McDougall 1994) the time-dependency of internationalization was stressed out. Studies about the role of time in addressing the dynamics of the internationalization process have been advanced (Coviello and Munro 1997, Kutschker et. al. 1997, Reuber and Fischer 1997, Jones 1999, 2001, Jones and Coviello 2002, 2005, Hurmerinta-Peltomäki 2003, Hashai and Almor 2004). More recently attention had been paid to the time-based processual view of internationalization (Malnight 1995) and its management (Kutschker et. al. 1997), and the entrepreneurial internationalization process along time (Jones and Coviello, 2002, 2005). All of these studies put forward the development and dynamics of internationalization over time. In addition to the classical international business concepts and constructs these studies have built on theoretical and empirical concepts rooted in the process theories of organizations, such as innovation and change (Van de Ven and Huber 1990, Van de Ven and Poole 1995, Van de Ven and Engleman 2004).

According to Langley (1999), scholars dealing with process research in general can be divided in two groups. One group has chosen to address the dynamics of the processes by formulating a priori process models and testing them. This has been called "weak" process understanding (Chia and Langley 2005, Van de Ven and Poole 2005). Another group has chosen to collect fine-grained qualitative data generally in real time, attempting to extract theory from the ground up (Langley 1999), which has been named the "strong" process understanding. The first approach is rooted in the positivist research philosophy with the final goal of explanation. The second one is the interpretative philosophy that aims at describing and understanding. Most of the international business research publications can be located in the positivist stream characterized by a "weak" process understanding[1]. Interpretative research philosophy has left out the attention and interest of the majority of international business and business management scholars in general[2]. This can be most likely attributed to the simple fact that "explanation is essential to theory and practice" (Pentland 1999, pp. 711). However the so-called "narrow vision" (Sullivan 1998) of international business research has been widened through the use of multidisciplinary approaches and more process oriented research designs. One recent example is the general model of entrepreneurial internationalization process (EIPM) (Jones and Coviello 2005). EIPM describes at a high level of accuracy how time organizes firm internationalization. Analysing the detailed interaction of different activities, events and processes that describe internationalization, one can explore the reasons behind the dynamic profile of internationalization.

This present paper aims at contributing to the processual view of internationalization using a longitudinal research design and a case-study approach (Yin 1984) that was developed to understand the dynamics present within single settings (Eisenhardt 1989). An iteration process between theory and data has been followed leaving room for interpretation of preliminary data before the construction of the final logical structure. Building on EIPM and the "strong" understanding of organizational process (Chia and Langley 2005, Van de Ven and Poole 2005) the paper argues that *in order to understand firm internationalization along time one should observe organizations and their contextual environments as complex interacting processes.* These processes are particularly important for the case of the privatized companies from transformational countries (subject of the present study) that have followed very different paths of transformation (Peng and Heath 1996, Peng 2003) and have operated in business environments with different transformational paths (Szelényi 2004). Moreover the business environment context is important because transformational countries are non-traditional home countries for an MNC.

This paper presents results of two longitudinal case studies of privatized (formerly SOE's) and domestically controlled firms from Hungary, covering a time period of fifteen years. Data on the outflows of foreign direct investment (OFDI) from Hungary (Fig. 1. and Fig. 2) and quantitative empirical research on OFDI from Central and Eastern Europe (e.g. Svetlicic and Jaklic 2003) inform about the importance of internationalization phenomenon of companies from Central and Eastern Europe.

**Fig. 1. Annual Hungarian FDI outflow (source: Ministry of Economy and Transport - MET)**

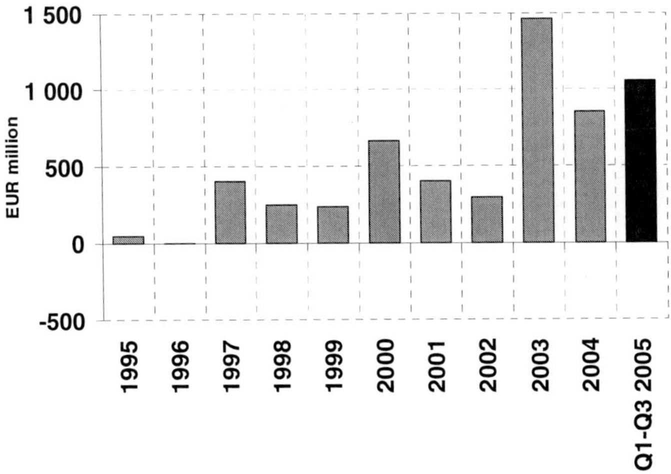

**Fig. 2. Stock of Hungarian FDI abroad (source: MET)**

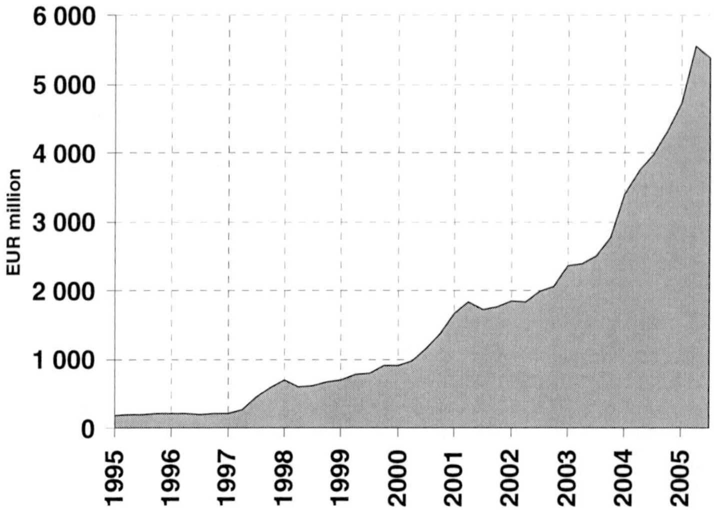


It should be noted that macro data on OFDI cannot distinguish between locally controlled and foreign controlled and managed companies. As a consequence OFDI can be attributed not only to indigenous companies that build their own international strategy but also to local subsidiaries of foreign companies that are integrated in and follow the global or regional strategy of the foreign headquarter (e.g. exports back to the home-market).

Following an iteration process between preliminary data and the theoretical model of entrepreneurial internationalization process and building on concepts of "strong" understanding of organizational processes, a research model to analyze the internationalization process of privatized companies from formerly state-socialist countries is developed. In the end of this paper some discussion is made based on the preliminary findings.

## Literature review

Given the aim of this research to understand and explain the firm internationalization process along time, models that consider firm internationalization along time of internationalization are reviewed.

The traditional model of internationalization process is the Uppsala model (Johanson and Vahlne 1977, 1990). According to this model, internationalization is "a process in which the enterprise gradually increases its international involvement" (Johanson and Vahlne 1990, pp. 11.) The basic assumption of the model is that commitment of resources to international operations and markets is a function of market knowledge. Decisions to commit resources are made in response to perceived problems and/or opportunities on the market that is dependent on the market-specific knowledge. This type of knowledge can be acquired through experience, in other words learning. Consequently the motor of internationalization is the process of learning and that is why firms increase their foreign market commitment step by step and move progressively from closer markets to more distant markets. However the author does not consider explicitly the time dimension, the pattern of internationalization depicted by the model implicitly denote a *predetermined time sequence* (Luostarinen et. al 1994).

The model has been subject of many debates (Björkman and Forsgren 2000). It was criticised mainly because of its deterministic nature (e.g. Reid 1983, Turnbull 1987). It has the tendency to ignore or de-emphasizes strategy and rational decision making as it views decisions as the evolutionary development of an existing state, rather then the result of an explicit economic analysis and decision making. Furthermore it stresses on the risk-avoiding attitude of decision-makers. Another line of the critics pointed out that the model focuses largely on the firm neglecting the business environment, the changes that have occurred during time (e.g. Johanson and Mattsson 1986, 1988, Oviatt and McDougall 1994).

Two different models of internationalization process have been developed as a consequence of the above mentioned criticism: the network model of internationalization (Johanson and Mattsson 1988, Johanson and Mattsson 1992, Forsgren and Johanson 1992) and more recently the international new venture model of internationalization (Oviatt and McDougall 1994, Jones and Coviello 2005).

The network model of internationalization put forward the process of creating and maintaining *relationships* with counterparts in other countries (Johanson and Mattson 1988). According to the model during internationalization the number and strength of the relationships between different parts of the business network increases and relationships are formed in the following sequence: (1) first companies form relationships with counterparts in countries that are new to the firm (international extension), (2) then firms increase their commitment in already established foreign networks (penetration), (3) and third companies integrate their positions in networks in various countries (integration). This succession describes a *predetermined time sequence* again.

The weakness of this model is that it pays less attention to economic motives (Dunning 1995), efficiency and effectiveness (Jones and Coviello 2002). Further on, it has been argued that the model ignores the role of decision-makers and firm characteristics (Chetty and Blankenburg-Holm 2000). It is very difficult to draw general conclusions regarding firm internationalization because according to the model the firm internationalization is dependent on actions and resources of other network members (Björkman and Forsgren 2000). It has been argued that the network model has been developed to understand the market behaviour in general, rather then to explain specific questions like firm internationalization (Björkman and Forsgren 2000). As Perrow stated, the network model deals with networks and not with organizations (Perrow 1997). One can argue that the network model is useful for the analysis of the external factors influencing internationalization, rather than the process of internationalization.

The predetermined sequential pattern of the above "traditional" models of internationalization were challenged especially when the so-called "born global" or "international new venture" (INV) firms appeared. In contrast with the predictions of the previous models that firms initially become successful on their domestic markets and then expand on foreign markets, these firms have looked on the world as their own markets and started to internationalize from inception (McDougall et. al. 2003). They have made use of the resources available on the global market and have sold their products and services on international markets. For researchers of international entrepreneurship, internationalization is in fact the manifestation of the entrepreneurial orientation of firm (i.e. international entrepreneurship) that is "the discovery, enactment, evaluation, and exploitation of opportunities – across national borders to create future goods and services" (McDougall and Oviatt 2003, pg. 7). In the effort to conceptualize the process of internationalization as an entrepreneurial process of behaviour, Jones and Coviello have developed a general model of the *time-based process of entrepreneurial behaviour* (Jones and Coviello 2005). They view internationalization as a development and change process, a "long-term entrepreneurial behavioural phenomenon unique to the experiences of individual firms, and thus avoids prescribing steps or stages" (Jones and Coviello, pg. 297). Time is considered one of the primary dimensions of the general model. Several dimension of time are defined: the chronological time-line; the reference time indicating the specific points in time when internationalization events occur, time sequence, time periods, duration, time intensity, time cyclicality, rate/speed. The authors perceive the internationalization events as the most valid representation of what occurs in internationalization. They distinguish between three types of events associated with the firm internationalization: establishment of a new type of cross-border relationship (i.e. cross-border business modes), establishment of a relationship in a new country (i.e. the place of transference) and cessation of the previously established relationship. Fingerprint patterns refer to the number and range of business modes and the number and distance of countries at a specific point in time. Changes in the composition of modes and countries over a period of time are described as dynamic profiles. The contextual factors considered by the model are performance, the firm, the environment and specifically, the entrepreneur. These factors are decoded in several subsequent variables like financial and non-financial measures of performance, the firm structure, resources, product offer and entrepreneurial orientation, environmental variables of market, industry, dynamism/hostility/intensity and lastly the philosophic view, social capital and human capital of the entrepreneur.

The main strength of the general model is that it builds bridges among existing (economic) theories and (process) models combining the different internal firm factors with the external environmental and firm performance factors thus giving a multi-theoretical, holistic view about *how internationalization takes place*. Another strong point of the model lies in the general nature of it as it is based on contextual constructs (entrepreneur's characteristics, firm characteristics, environmental characteristics, performance characteristics) that are valid for any firm.

In Organizational Science there have been two basic understandings of the concept of process – a "weak" and a "strong" one partially overlapping but also different (Chia and Langley 2005, Van de Ven and Poole 2005). The 'weak' view treat processes as actions of "things" that can be described as variables or states and can be compared, while the "strong" view considers actions and things to be "instantiations of process complexes" (Chia and Langley 2005). Organizational research has been dominated by the first perspective that tends to be more pragmatic, empirically grounded and analytical in orientation. The second perspective has been primarily conceptual and dynamic concepts such as movement, change, perspective, becoming are considered the essence of organizational life. While the first perspective helps us observe and empirically research processes, the latter enables us to appreciate the *sui generis*[3] (of its own kind/genus).

From the above, one can draw the conclusion that EIPM communicates well with the process view of organizations. The latter operates with constructs like events, outcomes, orderings, change, relationships, patterns, profiles and different contextual categories that are some of the key anchor points of process theorizing (e.g. Langley 1999). It is much more difficult to decide on whether the model belongs to the "weak" or the "strong" process understanding. However it is stated that processes are critical to understanding internationalization, and the patterns of internationalization are studied along time, the influencing processes are more or less reduced to "things" more precisely to variables (see Jones and Coviello, Table 1. pp. 296). Most of these conceptual variables are static in their nature (e.g. structure, market characteristics) hence less suitable for process understanding.

Summarizing the above theoretical argumentation one can state that in order to understand the mechanisms behind processes (i.e. internationalization) dynamic concepts and constructs are needed to be observed in a process design fashion.

## Research design and methodology

Process research employs designs that identify or reconstruct the process (Van de Ven and Poole 2005). Iterative case-study approach using an in-depth case method can face this challenge.

Two cases have been selected that are best suited for investigating the process of internationalization over a period of fifteen years for the purpose of theoretical sampling (Eisenhardt 1989). The cases are privatized (formerly SOE's) companies with foreign operations abroad, Hungary being their home base. Why are these cases relevant? With respect to the international empirical literature they are relevant because these firms differ from MNCs originated in developed markets as well as from the MNCs originated in developing countries in several respects. They have started to internationalize with scarce resources and management capabilities in comparison with Western competitors, with "Eastern type" company image on the international (even the regional market of CEE) markets. They are not "born global" or "international new ventures" because they are traditional, formerly state-owned companies and not international from inception. The state ownership but even most the process of ownership change (i.e. privatization) is another characteristic that makes these companies specific. Research has shown that firms from former state-socialist countries followed different paths of development (Peng and Heath 1996, Whitley and Czabán 1998, Peng 2000, 2003). Many local companies from the region have been acquired by foreign direct investors mostly originated in developed economies. In his recent publication Szelényi, the well-known analyst of social transformation of post-socialist countries, postulated that Central and Eastern European countries are deeply embedded in and conditioned by the global economic processes. This is because the "national owner bourgeoisie" of these countries is weaker than that of the western countries, which have the same size and are in the same stage of their development (Szelényi 2004). However, there are indigenous companies that attempt to become lively actors of the global economy. These firms have been able to consolidate their position in the domestic market and to invest abroad. Moreover, some firms succeeded to carry out ambitious strategies to become regional players like the case companies from this paper. They are independent, locally managed and controlled firms that became multinational not through contractual partners of foreign firms as the so-called "dragon multinationals" (Mathews 2002). The collection of data started in 2003 based on in-dept interviews and was continued in 2004 with another series of interviews. In the end of year 2005 another interview series were performed. Indirect data has been collected continuously, analyzing company statements, written materials provided by the individual MNC's as well as materials published in newspapers and webpage's. This repeated measure of events and actions allowed us to directly explore the process of internationalization.

## Internationalization process of OIL

Oil refining, transportation, wholesale and retail of oil and petrochemical products are the core business of OIL founded in 1957. As an international company OIL is one of the few CEE players in the branch active also in exploration and production of oil abroad. However, as a direct investor it concentrates on refining and retail of oil products. The dynamic profile of its internationalization is depicted in Figure 3.

In order to understand the internationalization of OIL, first the market characteristics should be considered. In the period of state socialism oil industry was considered as a strategic sector by each national state, therefore independent refining capacities and logistic systems existed. Consequently, the sector was characterized by parallel capacities and none of the national oil companies possessed the necessary critical mass. It became clear right from the beginning of their privatization process that they could not be competitive unless they are able to reach the necessary critical mass (ten billion dollar capitalization level). Unlike the companies from developed western markets and Russia active in the region that were motivated by market demand and returns, these national oil companies were interested in stabilization of their markets. Consequently, the main influencing factor of foreign market-entry of OIL was to reach the necessary critical mass needed for market stabilization and competitiveness. This was important also from the capital market point of view. In order to remain competitive even in the EU capital market, OIL was interested in reaching a proper level of capitalization before the EU accession. Therefore, fast entry was decisive. One can argue that the hidden (or organizational political) motive behind reaching the critical mass was to become more powerful for the case of an acquisition by a competitor.

**Fig. 3. Internationalization process of "OIL"**

| Date | Location | Mode | Business area | Location | Mode | Business area | Location | Mode | Business area | Location | Mode | Business area | Location | Mode | Business area |
|---|---|---|---|---|---|---|---|---|---|---|---|---|---|---|---|
| 1994-2003 | Romania | Continuous Greenfield | Retail | | | | | | | | | | | | |
| 1995-2000 | Slovakia | Continuous Greenfield | Retail | | | | | | | | | | | | |
| 1995-1999 | Tunis, Egypt, Pakistan, Albania, Greece, Katar, Syria, Yemen | Consortium | R&E | | | | | | | | | | | | |
| 2000 | Tunis, Albania, Egypt, Katar | Divested/ closed | R&E | Slovakia | Sequential acquisition (closed 2004) | Refinery, Wholesale , Retail | Austria, Czech Rep., Poland | Indirect (Slovakia as home) acquistion | Wholesale &Retail | France, Poland, Germany , UK, Italy, Ucraine, Russia | Indirect acquistion (Hungary as home) | Petrochim | | | |
| 2001 | Pakistan, Yemen, Syria, Greece | Divested/ closed (Pakistan& Yemen partial div.) | R&E | Poland | Tender winer, cancelled by the gov. | Refinery, Wholesale , Retail | | | | | | | | | |
| 2002 | Slovakia | Raise contro | Ref, W, R | Russia | Joint venture | Exploration | | | | | | | | | |
| 2003 | Romania | Sequential acquisition (closed 2005) | Retail | Croatia | Partial privatisation acquisition | R&P, Refinery, Wholesale, Retail | Slovenia, Bosnia-Hercegovina, Syria, Egypt, Angola | Indirect acquisition (Croatia as home) | Retail (Slovenia &BH), R&E&P | Austria | Acquisition | Storage facility for wholesale | Serbia | Greenfield | Wholesale &Retail |
| 2004 | Kazakhstan | Consortium | Exploration | Slovakia | Raise contro | Ref, W, R | Austria | Acquisition | W, Retail | | | | | | |
| 2005 | Kazakhstan | Raise contro | Exploration | Poland | Divestment | Retail | | | | | | | | | |
| 2006 | Bosnia-Herce | Partial Priv. acq. (corsort IN | Retail | Oman | Concession | R&E | | | | | | | | | |
| 2007 | Italy | Acquisition | Refining | Croatia | Acquisition | Retail &wholesal | Czech Rep. | Alliance | Gas | | | | | | |

OIL started its foreign direct investment activity in 1995 through greenfield investments in petrol stations in Romania and Slovakia. The motivation to choose these locations was that these markets were undersupplied and characterized by high growth potential. The political motivation to invest in countries where Hungarian minorities live should be mentioned too. Meanwhile, the company joined to several international consortiums for crude oil exploration in Asia and Africa. In 1997, OIL renewed its joint venture agreement dated back to 1975 with an Austrian partner for wholesale oil trading in the region, partner that was bought out by OIL in 2004. The Austrian market is the most important "Western" market of OIL. Parallel with the above detailed internationalization activity OIL restructured itself. Through its restructuring process OIL had changed both its management style and its strategic direction. The state ownership gradually decreased[4], which resulted in a more dynamic and proactive behaviour. In 1999 simultaneously with the emergence of acquisition possibilities in the region, the ambitious strategy to become regional multinational was formulated. The role of the newly appointed leader with foreign business experience in formulating the new strategy was decisive. Parallel with this an expatriate manager was appointed to lead the financial operations of the company. The new strategy was to concentrate on refining and retailing activity. Consequently, the company divested its exploration business in most of the Asian and African countries. In 2000 the company realized a big success acquiring a decisive 36% stake in the Slovak refining, retailing and petrochemical leader with option for reaching a majority ownership after four years, which was achieved in 2004 through the takeover of 98.4% of the shares. The deal was one of the biggest takeovers on CEE market until that time. Through foreign acquisitions, several indirect investments in further international markets have been created. Following its corporate strategy, OIL continued the acquisition activity in the region. In 2001 OIL won the privatization tender for the Polish national oil company, privatization cancelled later by the local government. In 2002 the CEO left the company. The firms international expansion continued, however, the company reformulated its strategy as regards the exploration business seeking to participate in international consortiums for oil exploration. Consequently, a joint venture agreement with a Russian company for oil exploration and drilling was set down. In 2003 OIL realized its second big success acquiring 25+1% shares in the Croatian national oil company. In 2005 the company continued its international expansion acquiring the petrol station network of Shell from Romania. This was possible because the oil giant decided to withdraw its inefficient retail business from

Romania. In the end of 2005 OIL decided to sell its petrol stations from Poland because of the low market share achieved. In 2006 OIL won a privatization tender in Bosnia-Herzegovina in retail business and entered in a research and exploration concession in Oman strengthening its upstream portfolio. Just recently the company performed further acquisitions in Italy (refining) and Croatia (retail and wholesale) and formed a strategic alliance with a Czech company.

From the above one can draw the conclusion that the internationalization process of OIL was driven by the possibilities available on the market as well as the logistical considerations specific to the oil industry (location of pipelines). However, the entrepreneurial capability to become aware of the opportunities arising on the market and timing were decisive factors in this "acquisition battle" to achieve the winner position in the regional consolidation. The advantage of OIL was that it recognized in time the crucial importance of the interdependencies between different country markets on the regional oil industry in downstream sector and took immediate actions in this direction.

## Internationalization process of PILL

Established in 1901 PILL is the largest pharmaceutical manufacturer in Hungary and on the generic drug's market, important actor in the region as well. On the international arena, PILL's competitors are the generic drug producers originated in the region and some middle-sized generic producers from developed markets. The latter are very few and do not have brand names in the region. In global terms it is a medium-sized company.

PILL has been traditionally export oriented. In the period of WW II, the company established several subsidiary companies abroad and operated a worldwide network of representative agencies. In the state-socialist period, the company concentrated on Eastern European and Soviet markets. The 1990's brought along the loss of traditional Comecom[5] markets. The consistent restructuring and change process (upgrade of technology, organizational change) led by the same visionary leader since 1992, turned out to be a success. The company retained its status in the domestic market and regained its markets in the former Soviet Union, as well as in Eastern Europe. Moreover the company increased its exports to several Western European, Asian and US markets. The internationalization process of PILL is presented in Figure 4.

## Fig. 4. Internationalization process of PILL

| Date | Location | Mode | Business area | Location | Mode | Bus. area | Location | Mode | Bus. area | Location | Mode | Bus. area | Location | Mode | Bus. area |
|---|---|---|---|---|---|---|---|---|---|---|---|---|---|---|---|
| 1995- | CEE, CIS | indirect & direct export, rep. office, JV | Trade | US | strategic alliance | steroid API 's supply | | | | | | | | | |
| 1996 | Russia | JV (greenfield) | Land and infrastructure acquisition | EU15, Japan, US | Indirect inv. (acquisition of a trade company) | Trade | | | | | | | | | |
| 1998 | Romania | Sequential acquisition | Production | | | | | | | | | | | | |
| 1999 | Romania | Increasing control | Production | Russia | Buying out JV partner, Greenfield | Packaging & production | EU15 | indirect export | Trade | Germany | Licence-out | Trade | | | |
| 2000 | Germany | strategic alliance | Original research | Ucraine | Acquisition of a local wholesaler | Not operating (Packaging & production) | Japan | Licence-out | Trade and original API supply | USA | strategic alliance | steroid API's supply, trade | | | |
| 2001 | Russia | Acquisition | Trade | | | | | | | | | | | | |
| 2002 | Poland | Sequential priv. acquisition | Production | Poland | Indirect A | Production (veterinar) | USA | Strat. alliance cont. | Original final product trade (with profit sharing) | Japan | strategic alliance with profit sharing | API's supply, R&D | USA | strategic alliance | Dev. of discovery software |
| 2003 | Poland | Increasing control | Production | USA | strategic alliance | product development and trade | | | | | | | | | |
| 2004 | India | JV | Production | USA | strategic alliance | original research and trade | | | | | | | | | |
| 2005 | USA | strategic alliance | original research and trade | | | | | | | | | | | | |
| 2006 | USA | License-out (generic products) | Trade | Poland | Increase control | Production | Japan | Strat. alliance | Original research and trade | USA | strategic alliance | steroid API's supply | Romania | Indirect inv. via Ro subsidiar | Retail, wholesale |
| 2007 | Germany | JV(70%) | Biotechnology | Romania | Acquisition | Retail, wholesale | | | | | | | | | |

The expansion of its international commercial network in developed markets has been facilitated by the acquisition of the export-import foreign trade company (EXIM) that in the state-socialist period was the state owned export intermediary for drug producers from Hungary. In the CEE region commercial network has been built through the acquisition of small commercial firms. Further on, the internationalization of PILL has been marked by several supply agreements with developed multinational companies from US and Western Europe. R&D and marketing agreements with US and Japanese firms were formed. Later on the US market has become the most important export market of "PILL". The relationships with the US have been facilitated by social diaspora network relations as well.

The leader of the company has been working with PILL more than three decades in a number of R&D management positions having a chemical engineer background. During a period of six years he led the Mexican subsidiary of EXIM. Then became managing director for the same kind of subsidiary in UK. After four years he returned to PILL to lead the reorganization and privatization process and later on the foreign direct investment in the region as well.

The strategy to invest in foreign markets was formulated following the capital raise as a direct consequence of company privatization[6]. Presently, the company is majority foreign owned but there is no strategic investor between the owners. As a result of the dispersed structure of the ownership the company is management driven. The principal feature of the renewed strategy launched in 1998 after the Russian financial crisis was to invest in foreign production facilities in order to strengthen the market position and to gain the necessary critical mass key in the pharmaceutical industry. The hidden motive was to protect the company from a foreign strategic investor. The consecutive entries represented the implementation of the strategy to become a regional multinational company. Motives to choose the region as the main location of the investments were multiple. First of all, being a traditional exporter in Central and Eastern Europe (CEE) and in the Community of Independent States (CIS) the brand name of PILL was well known and appreciated in this region. An important advantage of PILL in these markets was its affordable-priced drugs as alternative to the very expensive drugs imported from developed markets. However, PILL's products are not the cheapest on the market. Local producers without GMP (Good Manufacturing Product) standard technology are cheaper. Location was also a consequence of the possibilities available on the market and affordable for a company based in a transformational country negatively affected by the economic disequilibrium. Therefore, the necessary critical mass could be acquired on these markets easier and more quickly than anywhere else. It is remarkable that in spite of the financial crisis from Russia PILL remained committed, moreover strengthened its position in CIS countries that proved to be a good strategy. One reason for this could be that PILL is used with unstable markets. Consequently, the willingness to take such kind of risk is higher than of competitors. On the other hand, one should take in consideration that the firm being a latecomer in the FDI arena was pushed towards unstable markets overlooked by firms from developed economies. For example, one of the important reasons that PILL outperformed a US company in the privatization tender in Poland was that it accepted the necessary state part-ownership for a longer period than its contender who was willing to do business on "real" market terms without state control. Having acquired and established these Eastern European companies PILL gained the necessary critical mass to become competitive in the region.

PILL is present in Indian market not just as exporter but also as a direct investor. It has been present on this market starting from 1969 through its equity shares (8.2%) in an Indian pharmaceutical company. In 2004 the company signed a contract with its Indian partner about the establishment of a new joint venture company (51% going to PILL) with production start in 2006. In this case the motivation of investment was efficiency seeking (to gain from law cost production possibilities) in order to sustain firm competitiveness.

The company formed several strategic alliances with US, EU and Japanese companies with the motivation to secure it's market for active pharmaceutical ingredients as well as to run collaborative projects on research and development. Just recently the company strengthened its position on the Romanian market acquiring local wholesalers and retailers throughout its local subsidiary (indirect investment) and entered in the biotechnological segment forming a joint venture company in Germany with a local partner.

We are able to observe some critical events and processes that have shaped the internationalization process of PILL. These are: the institutional change processes (e.g. privatization) in the home market and in the region (traditional export markets of PILL), the internal firm processes like restructuring and its own privatization, evolution of domestic performance, the network building processes at top management level.

## Reflections on the firms' internationalization process over time

The theoretical ground for this research is the general model of entrepreneurial internationalization process that probes internationalization process along time aiming to capture the whole dynamics of the process. One can say that it is an all-inclusive model focusing not just on the process of internationalization itself but also on the context.
The stories of the internationalization of the two companies analyzed herein shows that process data collected in real organizational context are often "messy" (Langley 1999, pp. 691) and difficult to analyse. At the present stage of data collection and analysis one was able to capture the dynamic profiles of internationalization (Jones and Coviello 2005) and some of the contextual factors that have influenced the process. We are far from having all the data needed to observe organizational reality and probably collecting more data will drive us to a more "shapeless data spaghetti" (Langley 1999, pp. 694) but we have not arrived yet to the stage of organizing data to observe the complex processes and the logic behind. However, this preliminary empirical study draws our attention to several important issues to be considered.

In common with the ground model of this research (i.e. EIPM) we have found that the process of internationalization is a multilayered, multidirectional phenomenon including actors and relationships on different levels. These levels are the external environment, the internal firm and the individual level. We have also found that the time dimension is important to be considered at all of these levels. The pace of the institutional transformation in different countries from the region at the environmental level, the transformation process at firm level, and the human-capital building process at the individual level are some of the examples that have been found to be important in our cases.

Asking about the motives of the business mode pattern, we have found that this was influenced by two parallel processes. One process has been the institutional transformation in the market (i.e. privatization). Companies entered foreign markets mainly through acquisition because of the second-wave privatization opportunities in the region. Another influencing process was the firm transformation process. In the course of restructuring of the acquired formerly state-owned companies, our case firms took advantage of their own experience of dealing with governmental bodies and knowledge of restructuring a "socialist" company that facilitated their tolerance for ambiguity and flexibility and consequently can be an explanatory factor of the entry mode choice.

Another example refers to the pace of the internationalization process. One of the case companies stressed on the fact that its competitive advantage in the region is attributed to the speed of their international expansion grounded in the decision-making. Searching for the explanation behind decision-making the 'normal' way of thinking is to go after the variable of human capital (for example west-trained managers) or organizational characteristics (organic structure). However, understanding the large picture of institutional transformation process and privatization one can give a totally different explanation. As a consequence of the gradual privatization process largely influenced by management lobby the companies arrived to a much dispersed ownership structure, thus managers have considerable autonomy in decisions, they could act quickly.

Thus, in order to describe and understand how the context affects the fingerprint pattern of internationalization we have to go beyond variables or "things" like tolerance for ambiguity, or management experience and educational background because that will lead us to a "weak" understanding of internationalization process. Instead we should drive our attention towards process-complexes to get to the "strong" understanding of internationalization process.

Based on research gaps identified in the literature, and the empirical phenomenon investigated herein a simplified model of internationalization process has been developed. This model is very general and has been developed not to be tested but to provide the framework for further analysis. Applying the results of the analysis along this general model, specific models can be created. These models can be further developed and tested on large samples.

**Fig. 5. Research model to analyze the internationalization process of formerly SOE's**

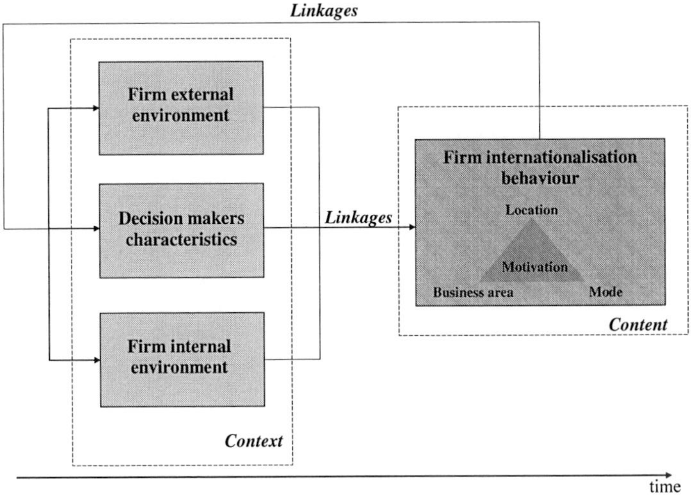


In common with the general model of entrepreneurial internationalization, the research model put forward the development of internationalization along time. In our case the context is depicted by process-complexes of the business environment and of the firm environment as well as the decision-makers characteristics. Chronological time (t) refers to the period of analysis. Using the temporal bracketing strategy (Langley 1999) the chronological time can be decomposed into three successive periods: before state-socialist system change, firm restructuring period, and the period after restructuring. These periods do not illustrate any phase in the sense of predictable sequence. They can be used to transform the eclectic data into series of more discrete but connected blocks (Langley 1999). The temporal bracketing strategy permits also to construct comparative units of analysis. The pattern of internationalization behaviour is indicated by the motivation, location and entry mode at the reference time. In order to handle the eclectic data that results from the empirical analysis of process-complexes one should use dynamic concept of events, decisions and actions when characterize the external and internal firm environment. At this point these categories are more or less vague. It is a further research task to identify them in somewhat more clear way but keeping their dynamism. However, as it has been stated there is a certain irony in the idea that researchers who aim to describe complex processes and collect a rich qualitative data in real organizations are so uncomfortable whit this richness that immediate try to reduce it (Langley 1999). The arrows in the figure indicate the direction of the influences between process-complexes we are interested in and the likelihood of the cyclical influence between firm evolution process and internationalization process.

## Limitations and future directions

By its nature process phenomena is complex, consequently process data tend to be eclectic and difficult to analyse (Langley 1999). We are confident of the many limitations that result from applying a process research design however we agree with Van de Ven and Poole that "...only research that adopts the processual perspective is suited for the study of processes." (Van de Ven and Poole 2005: 1390).

## Notes

[1] Details about these understandings are given in the theoretical section of the paper.

[2] Surprisingly if one try to search in JSTOR database using as key word „interpretative", narrowing the search to the title, only two articles are resulted.

[3] The expression was effectively created by scholastic philosophy to indicate an idea, an entity or a reality that cannot be included in a wider concept (http://en.wikipedia.org/wiki/Sui_generis).

[4] In the end of year 2005 the State ownership was 11,7%, however the company possess an option for max 10% of the State ownership enforceable in the next year.

[5] Council for Mutual Economic Assistance among socialist countries

[6] Right now PILL is the only independent Hungarian drug company. Acquisition of the majority stocks of the company by a foreign strategic investor depended on one vote! At present the government held owners own 25% of the company shares.

## References

Björkman, I. and Forsgren, M. (2000): Nordic International Business Research. A Review of Its Development, International Studies of Management and Organization, 30(1).

Chetty, S. and Blankenburg Holm, D. (2000): Internationalization of Small to Medium-sized Manufacturing Firms: a Network Approach. International Business Review, 9. 77-93.

Chia, R. and Langley, A. (2004): The First Organization Studies Summer Workshop: Theorizing Process in Organizational Research, call for papers, Organization Studies, 25(8).

Coviello, N. E. and Munro, H. (1997): Network Relationships and the Internationalization Process of Smaller Software Firms, International Business Review, Vol. 6, No. 4, 361-384.

Dunning, J. H. (1995): Reappraising the Eclectic Paradigm in an Age of Alliance Capitalism, Journal of International Business Studies, 26(3).

Eisenhardt, K. (1989): Building theories from case study research, Academy of Management Review. 14. 532-550

Forsgren, M. and Johanson, J. (1992): Managing Internationalization in Business Networks, in M. Forsgren, J. Johanson, (ed.) Managing Networks in International Business, Philadelphia and Amsterdam: Gordon and Breach pg. 1-15.

Hashai, N. and Almor, T. (2004): Gradually internationalizing 'born global' firms: an oxymoron?, International Business Review 13, pp. 465-483.

Hurmerinta-Peltomäki, L. (2003): Time and Internationalization. Theoretical Challenges Set by Rapid Internationalization, Journal of International Entrepreneurship, 1. 217-236.

Johanson J. and Mattsson, L-G. (1986): International Marketing and Internationalization Process – A Network Approach, in Paliwoda, S. and Turnbull, P. (eds.), Research in International Marketing, Croom Helm, London.

Johanson, J. and Mattsson, L-G. (1988): Internationalization in Industrial Systems – a Network approach, in N. Hood and J-E. Vahlne (eds.): Strategies in Global Competition, Croom-Helm, London, New York and Sydney, pp. 287-314.

Johanson, J. and Mattsson, L-G. (1992): Network Positions and Strategic Action - An Analytical Framework,. in: Axelsson, B./Easton, G. (eds.) Industrial Networks: A New View of Reality, Routledge, London, pp. 205-217.

Johanson, J. and Vahlne J-E. (1977): The Internationalization Process of the Firm-A Model of Knowledge Development and Increasing Foreign Market Commitments, Journal of International Business Studies, Vol. 8. No. 1.

Johanson J. and Vahlne J-E. (1990): The Mechanism of Internationalisation, International Marketing Review, Vol. 7 No. 4.

Jones, MV. (1999): The Internationalization of Small High Technology Firms. Journal of International Marketing 7(4): 15-41.

—. (2001): First Steps in Internationalisation: Concepts and Evidence from a Sample of Small High Technology Firms. Journal of International Management 7(3): 191-210.

Jones, M.V. and Coviello, N.E. (2002): A Time-Based Contingency Model of Entrepreneurial Internationalization Behaviour, Working Paper 2002/12, Haskayne School of Business

Jones, M.V. and Coviello, N.E. (2005): Internationalization: conceptualising an entrepreneurial process of behaviour in time, Journal of International Business Studies, 36(3): 284-303.

Kutschker, M et. al. (1997): International Evolution, International Episodes, and International Epochs – Implications for Managing Internationalization, Management International Review, 37 (2).

Langley, A. (1999): Strategies for theorizing from process data, Academy of Management Review, 24(4).

Luostarinen, R. et. al. (1994): Globalization and SME, Ministry of Trade and Industry: Helsinki

Malnight, Th. (1995): Globalization of an Ethnocentric Firm: An Evolutionary Perspective, Strategic Management Journal, 16. 119-141

Mathews, J. A. (2002): Dragon Multinational. A New Model for Global Growth, Oxford University Press, Oxford.

McDougall et. al. (2003): A Comparison of International and Domestic New Ventures. Journal of International Entrepreneurship, 1(1), 59-82.

McDougall P. and Oviatt, B (2003): Some fundamental issues in international entrepreneurship, July 2003 (http://www.usasbe.org/knowledge/whitepapers/mcdougall2003.pdf)

Oviatt, B. and McDougall, P. (1994): Toward a Theory of International Business Studies, Journal of International Business Studies, Vol. 25. Issue 1.

Pentland, B. (1999): Building process theory with narrative: from description to explanation. Academy of Management Review, 24(4).

Perrow, Ch. (1997). Szervezetszociológia (Complex Organisations: a critical essay), Osiris Kiadó, Budapest.

Reuber, A. and Fischer, E. (1997): The influence of the management team's international experience on internationalization behaviour, Journal of International Business Studies, 28(4).

Peng, M., Heath, P. S., (1996): The Growth of the Firm in Planned Economies in Transition: Institutions, Organizations, and Strategic Choice, Academy of Management Review, Vol. 21, Issue 2.

Peng, M. (2000): Business Strategies in Transition Economies, Sage Publications, Thousand Oaks, CA.

—. (2003): Institutional Transitions and Strategic Choices, Academy of Management Review, Vol. 28. No.2.

Reid, S. (1983): Firm Internationalization, Transaction Costs and Strategic Choice, International Marketing Review, Vol. 1. No. 2.

Sullivan, D. (1998): Cognitive Tendencies in International Business Research: Implications of a "Narrow Vision" Journal of International Business Studies Vol. 29, No. 4

Svetličič , M., and Jaklič A. (2003): Outward FDI by Transition Economies: Basic Features, Trends and Development Implications in Svetličič , M. Rojec, M. (eds.): Facilitating Transition by Internationalization: Outward Direct Investment from Central European Economies, Ashgate Publishing, Aldershot.

Szelényi (2004b): Kapitalizmusok, szocializmusok után (Forms of capitalism after forms of socialism), Egyenlítő, Társadalomkritikai és kulturális folyóirat, 2. sz

Turnbull, P. (1987): A Challange to the Stage Theory of the Internationalization Process in Reid, S. and Rosson, P. (eds.): Managing Export Entry and Expansion, Praeger, New York

Van de Ven, A. H. and Huber, G. P. (1990): Longitudinal field research methods for studying process of organizational change. Organization Science, 1: 213-219

Van de Ven, A.H. and Poole, M.S. (1995): Explaining Development and Change in Organizations, Academy of Management Review, 20(3): 510-540.

Van de Ven, A. and Egelman, R. (2004): Event- and outcome-driven explanations of entrepreneurship, Journal of Business Venturing, 19(3).

Van de Ven, A.H. and Poole, M.S. (2005): Alternative Approaches for Studying Organizational Change, Organization Studies, 26(9): 1377-1404.

Welch, L. and Luostarinen, R (1988): Internationalization: evolution of a concept. Journal of General Management, 14(2), 34-55.

Whitley, R. and Czabán L. (1998): Institutional Transformation and Enterprise Change in an Emergent Capitalist Economy: The Case of Hungary. Organization Studies Vol. 19, Issue 2.

Yin, R. K. (1984): Case Study Research Designs and Methods, Sage, Thousand Oaks, London.

# Co-opetition Opportunities in Lithuanian Alternative Telecommunication Market

Laura Šalčiuvienė, Regina Virvilaitė and Viltė Auruškevičienė


## Abstract

*"Co-opetition"*, a new approach to relationships between companies, is based on both competition and cooperation. This paper looks into the possibilities and benefits of co-opetition in the telecommunication industry. In the telecommunication infrastructure, business development needs high investment. Besides, alternative telecommunication service providers share only 7.6 per cent of the Lithuanian market. Therefore, small and medium companies in this market have limited possibilities for developing new services, competing with the major players and expanding their telecommunication business. Thus, the main objective of this study is twofold: a) to explore potential for the development of co-opetition relationship between small and medium alternative telecommunication service providers and b) to identify the area in which this relationship could create the highest value.

Research results indicated an important assumption for the development of co-opetition relations. Although Lithuanian alternative telecommunication service providers compete with each other, their attitude to co-opetition appears to be more positive in comparison to that of competition. The highest value for the telecommunication companies could be produced by co-opetition in the field of production (e.g., aggregating production capacity; outsourcing production to other companies; working on projects independently).

## Introduction

At the end of 2004, alternative telecommunication service providers comprised 5.65 per cent of the Lithuanian fixed telephone connection market. Though the greater part of alternative operators consists of small and medium-sized companies, their establishment made a significant impact on the situation in the national telecommunication market. For instance, the prices of international calls (the area that most alternative operators work in) have decreased ten times in the past two years, whereas the consumption of these services has been increasing much more rapidly than the whole telecommunication market.

Alternative telecommunication service providers have limited possibilities for independent development of a wider range of services, entering into serious competition with key market players or further developing their business. This by large is conditioned by the infrastructure of the telecommunication network that calls for high investment, which is beyond the capabilities of small and medium-sized companies. Alternative operators face similar problems in other countries too, though in some countries they do get some governmental attention.

Research on cooperation and competition is usually carried out from divergent theoretical perspectives. Dual and paradoxical relationships may develop where organizations cooperate in certain areas within the framework of a strategic alliance, yet tend to compete in other fields of activities (Bengtsson and Kock, 2000). The above phenomenon is called cooperation-competition, or *co-opetition.* Co-opetition involves two distinct logics of mutual interaction. On the one hand, competing interests lead to a certain level of hostility; on the other hand, attainment of common goals necessitates development of mutual trust and commitment.

The main objective of this study is twofold: a) to explore the potential for the development of co-opetition relationship between small and medium alternative telecommunication service providers and b) to identify the area in which such relationships could create the highest value.

This paper is structured as follows: it starts with some theoretical considerations that look into inter-organizational relationships from such perspectives as competition, cooperation and co-opetition. Subsequently the research design is presented and the results of the study conducted are discussed. The paper ends with some conclusions.

## Background

Competition and cooperation theories are traditionally considered as two distinct research areas. Researchers acknowledge the importance of maintaining a balance between competition and cooperation in the performance and survival of business organizations (Jorde and Teece, 1989). Nevertheless very few authors hold an opinion that organizations may successfully apply and benefit from the simultaneous application of both strategies (Bengtsson and Kock, 2000).

### Competition Attitude

For quite a while, the competition attitude was predominant in such management areas as strategic management (Porter, 1980), organizational economics (Williamson, 1985), and marketing management (Borden, 1964). Followers of this attitude hold that both horizontal and vertical interrelationships of organizations rely on the pursuit of individual benefit.

From the point of view of the horizontal interrelationships, the competitive attitude focuses on gaining a bigger profit, which is attainable by either occupying a more pre-eminent position in the industry (Porter, 1985), or by mobilizing and taking advantage of a company's core competences (Prahalad and Hamel, 1990), as this provides organizations a possibility to make better product offerings in comparison to the competition.

The attitude of vertical interrelationships points out value appropriation in the economic exchange. The neoclassic theory maintains that the competitive attitude views exchange as a discreet event, at which companies appropriate the created economic value based on the allocative efficiency principle. The above value allocation may take place in accordance to the instantaneous justice principle, as is proposed by the traditional marketing theory (Drucker 1954; Borden, 1964), or by the employment of the opportunistic behaviour, as it is suggested by the theory of transactional costs (Williamson, 1985).

### Cooperation Attitude

Cooperation attitude is an alternative that in part sprang out as a response to the competition attitude and focuses on the benefits of cooperation. Having originated in marketing management (Håkansson and Ostberg, 1976), this attitude later found place in the strategic management

(Contractor and Lorange, 1988; Hamel, Doz and Prahalad, 1989) and organizational economics (Hill, 1990) and covers quite an array of company interrelationships.

On the grounds of the cooperation attitude, the relationship marketing paradigm was developed (Borg, 1991). Drawing on the above paradigm, the interaction of market players is not based on single-use transactions. Conversely, interaction of the players develops into mutual long-lasting relationships that are considered a strategic property and a base for competitive leadership (Teece, Pisano and Schuen, 1997).

Economic benefit makes partners follow the norms of trustworthy behaviour (Griesinger, 1990). As a result, in comparison to the competition attitude, the cooperation attitude results in a considerable reduction of possibilities that may lead to opportunistic behaviour (Williamson, 1985).

## Co-Opetition Attitude

Raymond Noorda, the founder and CEO of *Novell,* developed the concept of co-opetition. Strategy theorists Brandenburger and Nalebuff further developed the co-opetition concept (1996). The new phenomenon was named *co-opetition* (**coo**peration + com**petition**).

The co-opetition attitude sprang out from the acknowledgement of the possibility that companies may be involved in mutual processes of value creation and sharing, or may have a structure of partly coherent interests and objectives, which provides grounds for a parallel coexistence of competition and cooperation. Creation of added value is the key stimulus for the development of co-opetition attitude.
The co-opetition attitude does not imply a complete match between partners' interests. A partial match of interests though calls for the assessment of fairness in the co-opetition relationship (Grandori and Neri, 1999). This attitude brings out some ambiguity that is caused by the lack of preconceived understanding as to each partner's benefits from the cooperation.

## Types of Interorganizational Attitudes

Dowling, Roering, Carlin and Wisnieski (1996) distinguished six types of interorganizational relationships (see Table 1).

**Table 1. Types of inter-organizational relationships**

| | | | |
|---|---|---|---|
| Vertical relationships | Hand's length exchange | Vertical multiple relationships, e.g.. IBM-Intel | Alliances of buyers and suppliers |
| Horizontal relationships | Traditional competitive market | Horizontal multiple relationships, e.g. Apple-IBM | Alliances of non-competing organisation, e.g. Siecor |
| | Competition | Co-opetition | Cooperation |

*Source*: Dowling et al., 1996

Both vertical and horizontal relationships may hold elements of competition/conflict and cooperation/harmony. Bengtsson and Kock (1999) propose that despite some similarities vertical and horizontal relationships are usually two distinct types of relationships, and it is quite obvious that trade-offs between cooperation and competition in vertical and horizontal relationships are of divergent origin.

Bengtsson and Kock (1999) propose that relationships between competitors are less studied than vertical relationships. Cooperation relationships between vertical players, i.e. buyers and suppliers, are much easier to comprehend, as the latter are based on the allocation of activities and resources between the members of a distribution chain. On the other hand, horizontal relationships are by far less formal and visible. Besides vertical relationships usually cover economic exchange (Easton and Araujo, 1992) that are rarely the case in the horizontal relationship, as the latter are usually associated with information and social exchange.

## Research Design

At the end of 2004, 23 companies in Lithuania provided fixed telephone services. Having eliminated the key fixed telephone service market player (*AB Lietuvos Telekomas*), the population of alternative telecommunication service providers comprised 22 organizations. To obtain representative results, it was decided to survey the total population.

Based on the theory of the key informant approach, which states that managers make the key providers of reliable and valid information (Tan and Litschert, 1994), data was collected from company managers. To make sure questionnaires were filled in by company mangers, interviews were carried out at the latter's workplace. Appointments with the respondents were made in advance. All survey participants were guaranteed confidentiality; besides they were ensured that research data would be processed and used only in a generalized form. Two service providers could not be reached either by phone or e-mail, which leads to a presumption that the latter do not carry out any activity. Accordingly research population and sample were reduced to 20 companies. Data collection took two weeks. Research went smoothly; all twenty prospective respondents consented to fill in a questionnaire.

As it has been noted in the introduction, the aim of his study is twofold: a) to explore potential for the development of co-opetition relationship between small and medium alternative telecommunication service providers and b) to identify the area in which this relationship could create the highest value.

Data collection was executed with the help of a specially developed questionnaire. The introductory part of the questionnaire comprised demographic questions, which were aimed at identifying whether provision of telecommunication services makes the respondent's primary activity, as well as the number of employees and the time-scope of operating in the market.

The main body of the questionnaire covered three question blocks. The first was aimed at determining the attitude of the alternative telecommunication service providers to competition and cooperation. The second block comprised questions that were developed for the identification of the value chain component that could possibly lead to the creation of the highest value. As to the third group of questions, the latter was designed to determine the possibly most critical and problematic stage of the cooperation process. Respondents were asked to evaluate their answers on a seven-point Likert-type summated ratings scale, where 1 stood for "strongly disagree" and 1 - "strongly agree".

## Results and Discussion

Research results were processed with the help of SPSS (Statistical Package for Social Sciences). The relationship between variables was assessed by means of Pearson correlation coefficient.

The analysis of the alternative telecommunication service providers' attitude to competition, cooperation, and co-opetition revealed that market players mainly support the co-opetition attitude (5.29); respondents also strongly support the idea of competition being the key performance driver (5.0). Respondents least supported the cooperation attitude (3.59) (see Figure 1).

**Figure 1. The attitude of alternative telecommunication service providers to competition and cooperation**

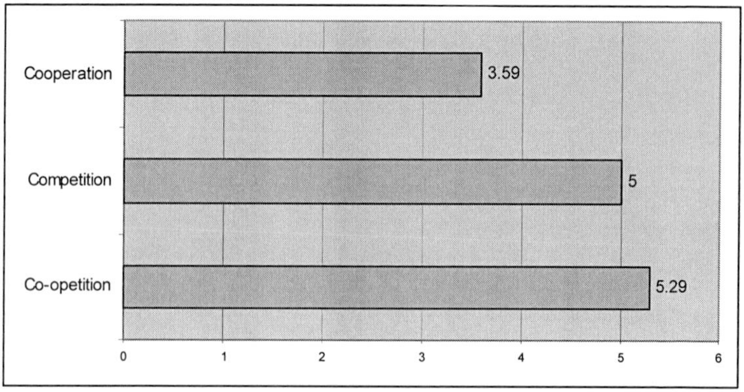


Analysis of the value chain component that bears highest utility level for cooperation demonstrated that alternative telecommunication service providers see greatest cooperation possibilities in the field of production, where cooperation may possibly be accomplished through joint use of production capacities by means of outsourcing or execution of certain projects, etc. (see Figure 2).

**Figure 2. Cooperation utility in different value chain components**

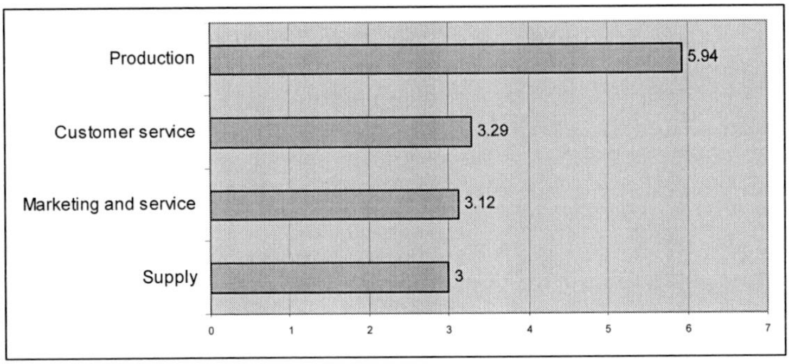


The most complicated stages of the cooperation process include goal coordination with cooperation partners (5.06), selection of the most appropriate cooperation form (4.65), and the development of the cooperation form project (4.41). As to the respondents' opinion, the less complicated stages of cooperation process included assessment of the company potential, development of cooperation strategy, search for a cooperation partner, and legal cooperation execution (see Figure 3).

**Figure 3. Assessment of cooperation process complexity**

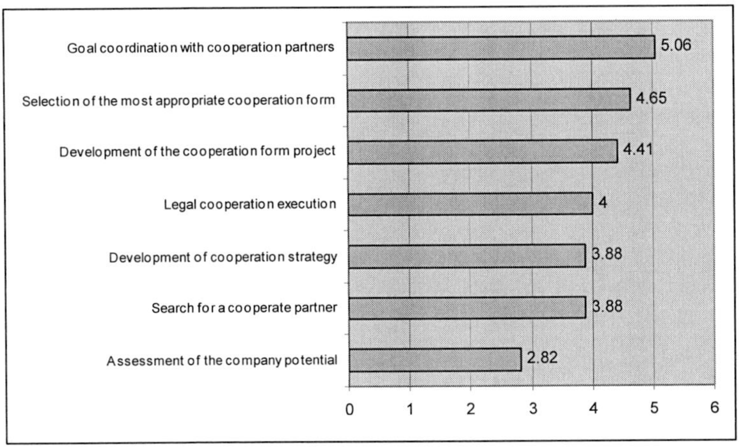

Analysis of correlation between the attitudes to cooperation and competition, and the perceived value of cooperation at different stages of value chain lead to the following findings:
1. There exists a positive relationship between the attitude to co-opetition and the perceived value of cooperation (r = 0,544).
2. There exists a positive relationship between a positive attitude to cooperation and perceived value of cooperation in the areas of marketing and sales (r = 0,536).
Research did not identify any other statistically significant relationships.

Analysis of the demographic characteristics of the respondents makes it possible to distinguish two distinct groups of alternative telecommunication service providers as to the above service delivery being primary activity or not. The greatest difference between the above-described companies comprises their attitudes to cooperation and competition. Alternative telecommunication service providers for whom provision of the above services constitutes the primary field of activity were found to be more supportive of co-opetition (5.67) rather than competition-based relationship (4.5). As to the companies for whom telecommunication service provision does not constitute the main field of activity, these seem to be more appreciative of competition-based relationship (6.2) rather than co-opetition (4.4). Cooperation-based relationships were assessed more or less equally by both groups (3.6).

A similar difference was also found in the comparison of the assessment of the overall utility of cooperation with other alternative telecommunication service providers as well as the key component of the value chain, in which cooperation would be most beneficial. Alternative telecommunication service providers for whom the above field of activity is the principal one seem to be of a higher opinion of the cooperation benefits (5.75); besides they see the highest cooperation potential in the production area (4.33). Other providers are of a lower opinion of the cooperation utility (4.0) and see the largest cooperation benefit in the customer service area (3.6).

Alternative telecommunication service providers for whom telecommunication service provision makes the principal field of activity among the most complicated cooperation process stages have named finding a match between cooperation aims with respective partners (4.92), selection of the most appropriate form of cooperation (4.83), and search for cooperation partners (4.42). Other providers assert that it is most difficult to prepare a cooperation project (5.8), match aims with cooperation partners (5.4), and legally establish cooperation (5.0).

## Conclusion

1. Vertical and horizontal relationships are in many ways divergent types of relationships, and trade-offs between cooperation and competition in each of these types of relationships is of a different origin and provides companies with varying benefits.

2. Research findings proved that Lithuanian alternative telecommunication service providers rank co-opetition higher than competition, which makes a highly relevant prerequisite for the development of cooperation, as a shift from dominant competing relationships to cooperation first and foremost necessitates a positive attitude to cooperation. Priority for cooperation was found to be given by companies who primarily specialize in the provision of telecommunication services. Other companies seem to believe that competition between companies is the key performance driver.

3. Research also demonstrated that cooperation between Lithuanian alternative telecommunication service providers may help them achieve better performance results, which makes it the key prerequisite of cooperation as well as a force that may induce companies change their interrelationship. Companies whose primary field of activity constitutes provision of telecommunication services tend to be more supportive of cooperation.

4. Given the company managers' assessment, cooperation is thought to be most useful in the field of production.

5. Analysis of the most likely serious problems that may occur in the cooperation process lead to the identification of the most critical stage, i.e. matching cooperation aims with those of a partner.

Research aim can be thought to be achieved, as research results proved that Lithuanian alternative telecommunication service providers do have prerequisites for developing cooperation relationship; besides the highest value was found to be created in the field of production.

## References

Bengtsson, M., Kock, S. (1999). Cooperation and competition in relationships between competitors in business networks. *Journal of Business & Industrial Marketing*, Vol. 14(3), 178-193.

Bengtsson, M., Kock, S. (2000). Coopetition in business networks - to cooperate and compete simultaneously. *Industrial Marketing Management*, Vol. 29(5), 411-426.

Borden, N. (1964). The concept of the marketing mix. *Journal of Advertising Research*, June, 2-7.

Borg, K. A. (1991). Problem shifts and market research: the role of network in business relationships. *Scandinavian Journal of Management*, Vol. 7, 285-295.

Brandenburger, A. M., Nalebuff, B. J. (1996). *Co-opetition*. New York: Doubleday.

Contractor, F. J., Lorange, P. (1988). *Cooperative strategies in international business*. Boston: Lexington Books.

Dowling, M. J., Roering, W. D., Carlin, B. A. and Wisnieski J. (1996). Multifaceted relationships under coopetition: description and theory. *Journal of Management Inquiry*, Vol. 5, 155-167.

Drucker, P. F. (1954). *The practice of management*. New York: Harper & Row.

Easton, G., Araujo, L. (1992). Non-economic exchange in industrial network. In B. Axelsson and G. Easton (Eds.), *Industrial Networks - A new view of reality*, London: Routledge.

Grandori, A., Neri, M. (1999). The fairness properties of interfirm networks. In A. Grandori (Ed.), *Inter-firm networks*. London: Routledge.

Griesinger, D. (1990). *The human side of economic organization*. Academy of Management Review.

Håkansson, H., Ostberg, C. (1976). Industrial marketing: An organizational problem? *Industrial Marketing Management*, Vol. 4.

Hamel, G., Doz Y., Prahalad, C. K. (1989). Collaborate with your competitors and win. *Harvard Business Review*, Vol. 67(1), 133-139.

Hill, C. W. L. (1990). Cooperation, opportunism and the invisible hands: Implications for transaction cost theory. *Academy of Management Review*, Vol. 15(3), 500-513.

Jorde, J. M., Teece, D. J. (1989). Competition and cooperation: striking the right balance. *California Management Review*, Vol. 31(3), 25-37.

Porter, M. E. (1980). *Competitive strategy. Techniques for analyzing industries and competitors*. New York: Free Press.

Prahalad, C. K., Hamel, G. (1990). The core competence of the corporation. *Harvard Business Review*, Vol. 90, 79-91.

Teece, D. J., Pisano, G. and Shuen, A. (1997). Dynamic capabilities and strategic management. *Strategic Management Journal*, Vol. 18(7), 509-533.

Williamson, O. E. (1985). *The economic institutions of capitalism*. New York: The Free Press.

# SECTION II:

# ADVERTISING

# IMPACT OF NUDITY IN ADVERTISEMENTS: COMPARISON OF THE FIRST RESULTS FROM SPAIN, FRANCE AND THE CZECH REPUBLIC

CHRISTIAN DIANOUX, ZDENEK LINHART AND JANA KETTNEROVÁ

## Abstract

Whilst recognizing that complaints about nudity vary between different countries and regions, it is important to understand what the impact of nudity is on consumers. The question of whether to maximize the impact of nudity through standardization or adaptation of advertisements has become the object of many researches. International comparisons of nudity impact are still rare. In this article we present the initial results of the first survey about the topic conducted amongst Czechs, French and Spanish. All the respondents were exposed to a journal folder containing a hidden advertisement with either a picture of a semi-naked woman, or a picture of the face of the same woman. Firstly, trials show that answers are influenced more by the gender of the respondents than by their nationality. Czech, French and Spanish women tend to react more negatively than men, when shown a picture containing an image of a woman's breast. Secondly, the answers of Czechs are less negative than those of the French and Spanish respondents. We consider that further research is therefore needed to provide more detailed answers about the relationships between such variables as product, cultural differences between countries, and attitudes to advertising in general.

## Introduction

Complaints about the sexual connotation of messages in advertising are becoming more and more frequent, but many researchers emphasise that this tendency is often generalised. Lombardot (2002) found this tendency in articles of authors like Hoyer and MacInnis (1997), Wells, Burnett and Moriaty (1998) or in a much older one by Sciglimpaglia, Belch and Cain (1978). Within each of these articles it was observed that "…a trend toward the increasing use of sex in advertising can hardly be disputed". These impressions seem to be more noticeable when media repeatedly speak about "scandalizing advertising". We can cite two very controversial pictures of a nude man (the "vice champion" of aikido, Samuel Debeker) where we can see his sex used in the launching of a perfume from Yves Saint Laurant (YSL), or more recently in February 2007, in the advertising of Dolce & Gabbana clothes collection, which had to be withdrawn from Spanish magazines after complaints from the Spanish women's institute (the advertising was then withdrawn from Italy and finally totally stopped worldwide). This particular advertisement showed a topless man wearing black glasses, who was holding a woman on the ground by her wrist. This woman was dressed in a black satin corset and high heels, and around the scene there were some men watching without any involvement in their faces. This scene invoked thoughts of collected rape.

Researchers counting the ratio of advertisements with sexual motives make these subjective impressions more relative. According to literature review carried out by Lombardot, it would seem that these feelings would essentially be due to more frequent and explicit sexual references, to the greater degree of nudity acceptable in advertising, or to the kind of studied review, and not only to the increasing ratio of advertising with a sexual connotation - as Kilbourne (2005) summarizes "Graphic sexual images seem more extreme, more pervasive and more perverse than before".

Whatever the tendency, the impact of this kind of communication varies substantially from one region to another. Thus, we can notice that, according to Piron and Young (cited by Lombardot 2002), nudity is used less in Germany than in the USA, because north Europeans are more used to certain kinds of nudity, causing it to lose some of its impact. Some advertisements can be judged indecent in USA, yet normal in Europe. The study of Nelson and Hye-Jin (2005), which relies on observations of advertisements published in Cosmopolitan magazine in seven countries (Brazil, China, France, India, South Korea, Thailand, and USA), also show large divergences between France and Thailand where advertisements have strong sexual content, and China where the sexual content is lower.

Despite greater awareness, and the question of standardization of such advertisements, there are few studies about this subject. The objective of this article is to contribute to best knowledge in this context from an experiment made in one country in the East, the West, and the South of Europe. For this, we will first define what is understood by "nudity", and we will make one statement on the main results of research made about this topic. This will permit us to define our research question. We then present the methodology used and the first results arising from this experiment. We will finish by outstanding points and principals related to main perspectives that we can forecast from complementary processing.

## Literature overview

Notion and impact of nudity are discussed to bring a research question.

### Notion of nudity

It is expected that talking about nudity in advertising also has a sexual context. "But, nudity is not necessary, neither sufficient, to make the stimuli considered as sexual" (Lombardot, 2002). The reactions of the Spanish and Italians to the Dolce & Gabbana advertisement mentioned above, where a non-sexual attribute was shown (totally dressed women and naked bodies of men), perfectly illustrates this point, as do Catholic churches which are filled with nude paintings.

Nevertheless, among the frequent characteristics giving the advertisement a sexual connotation, Reichert and Ramirez (2000) showed that the degree of clothing of the individuals was the characteristic most likely to produce this impression, as the very proximity of nudity implies sexual suggestions.

Among the direct link between nudity and sexual suggestions, we can observe that even the idea of nudity can vary significantly between different cultures and periods: spiritual tribes may consider an undressed woman as normal, however a fundamentalist Muslim will consider it as inadmissible and close to sanctions; within any one country, therefore, undressed bodies can be either tolerated or sanctioned against. As an example we cite the town council of Declambre, Lousiana (USA), which unanimously added underwear to the list of what must not be revealed under the State's indecent exposure law, threatening offenders with a $200 fine and the risk of up to six month in jail (BBC report, 2007-07). It should be emphasised in the end that clothes, which are accepted as normal today, were scandalous at the beginning of the 20th century. These different remarks illustrate the interest of studying the impact that nudity can have on an advertisement. But, what is known about this subject?

## Impact of nudity on the influence of an advertisement

The impact of nudity and sexual appeal has a positive role (Manceau & Tissier, 2006). Both nudity and sex appeal are confirming that displaying the positive role of nudity increases attention towards the advertisement and brand (Vezina & Paul, 1997; Geuens & De Pelsmacker 1998; Soley & Reid 1998). Studies notice, however, that results relative to its impact on attitude to the brand, and purchase advice, are contradictory (Severn *et al.* 1990; De Pelsmacker & Van Den Bergh 1996; Vezina & Paul 1997). This is probably coming about for several reasons, such as methodological problems (very few studies are based on experimental protocols, permitting verification of the influence of nudity the only variable), the studied context (using nudity for underwear is probably better received than for a car), and the profile of individuals, some of whom can take a central road, while what comes first into our mind is that one sexual element in the advertisement seems to attract the customer on the periphery (Reichert and al. 2001).

The approach proposed by McInnis, Noorman, and Jaworski (1991) can bring to mind some elements of the answer. For these authors, when the motivation to process information about the brand is low, the attention to the message is consequently also low. What is likely to catch the attention, are executional cues in the advertisement that an individual will notice, independent of the brand. Among these executional cues, sexual sources are likely to play this role. After this first stage of the process, and having had attention drawn to the advertisement, the individual next begins to increase its brand information processing within the advertisement.

This theoretical approach no longer conforms to the empirical results. Lombardot for example, from a review of literature inspired by the works of Jones, Stanaland, et Gelb (1998), talking about 23 research studies, shows that in spite of divergent results, a consensus seems to emerge on the fact that nudity increases arousal, interest, and attention (towards executional elements), and affects in a negative way the cognitive process of message treatment and understanding, and brand memorization. Such results show that there is still a lot of work to be carried out to better understand these mechanisms, and bring us to affirm that the measure of implication towards the product category is a fundamental minimum, even though this one doesn't permit us to focus on motivation, in its general sense.

Two other dimensions proposed by McInnis et al. (1991), opportunity and ability seem not to be influenced by the sexual character of the advertisement, and we will consider later in the methodology part how these elements can be considered.

Beyond the motivation - the determining factor, which brings the individual to process more or less information - other individual characteristics play a role in the attitude that the individual could have towards advertisements with sexual characteristics. We cite:

- age (Loroz, 2006- for instance emphasized the existing differences between Y generation and Baby boomers),
- gender (men would seem to have a positive attitude towards the presence of nude (or sexy) female models, and to have an opposite negative or neutral attitude towards the presence of nude (or sexy) male models, and is inversely for women, see Lombardot 2002),
- masculinity or femininity (especially about advertisements focused on an image or utilitarian aspect, see Chang, 2006).

## Research question

None of this, however, gives us much information about the differences that can exist between countries.

Ford, La Tour, and Clarke (2004) are clear that the perception of nudity in advertising varies in a significant way between the countries they studied (China, India, Singapore, USA). The qualitative study carried out by Lass et Hart (2004) in Germany, Italy and the UK comes as same in this sense, whilst pointing out that the gender and consumers' values also play an important role whatever the country.

It would therefore seem that practices can be relatively homogeneous in some cases. Dianoux, Kettnerová, and Linhart (2007) showed in a review based on the ten most-issued journals in the Czech Republic and in France, for the five main market segments (seniors, ladies, men, teenagers, businessmen), that no difference can be noticed in terms of quantity, and that the usage of nudity remains marginal in the two countries (see Table 1).

**Table 1: Comparison of the Content of French and Czech advertisements**

| (N=577 Advertisements except for (1) N=361 Advertisements) | France | Czech |
|---|---|---|
| Indoor Environment | 77% | 88%* |
| Female Presence (1) | 78% | 75% |
| Use of a celebrity (1) | 16% | 19% |
| Use of Nudity (1) | 3.4% | 2.9% |
| Information with at least 6 characteristics | 13% | 27%* |

* Significantly different at $p < .05$ (Chi² test)

Considering such homogeneous practices, the hypothesis that we are naturally brought to do is that practices are equivalent, and the efficiency of this executional cue seems to be similar in the two countries.

Considering these contradictory hypotheses, which seem to implicate an incidental approach due to the culture of the studied countries, we will try to verify if some differences exist between the two countries (Czech Republic and France) about the attitude towards the advertisement, and consequently also about the attitude towards the brand, based on the principle that the advertisement has an influence on the brand (Mitchell et Olson, 1981; Shimp, 1981).

To vary the study context, we will compare these results to those of Spain. This country has shown us its high sensibility towards the provocative advertisement, by its reaction to the Dolce & Gabbana clothes collection in February 2007 (mentioned in the introduction), which led to the cancellation of this European campaign.

## Methodology

The experiment is developed around the following four main principles: choice of media, support of sample, of advertisement, and organization of experimentation.

## Choice of media support

The advantage of the magazine advertising media is that it allows two fundamental elements, which are expected to influence the message processing (McInnis et al., 1991):

- the opportunity: according to Chaiken and Eagly (1976) "One strategy for controlling encoding speed is to use print media. Print enables consumers to process brand information at their own pace". They also found enhanced comprehension of a difficult message with print versus broadcast media (see also Andreoli and Worchel 1978; Wright 1981);
- the ability: Lang and Lanfear (1990) report research indicating that "both print and TV messages with (vs. without) narrative structures enhance comprehension and message recall".

## Choice of sample

The selection of a well-chosen sample of students has the major advantage of observing individuals from each country homogeneous enough and easy enough to compare. From another point of view, the usage of nudity in advertising targeted at young people is very common and facilitates the processing of results. Finally, from point of view of external validity, if we observe differences between countries in this kind of sample (generally consideration is more international), there is a high probability that we would observe the same phenomena, as well as more frequently cited phenomena, in other categories of individuals. The converse therefore is that, in the opposite case (no differences between groups), it is difficult to extrapolate the results.

## Choice of advertisement

There are many studies that consider the different attitudes, which could be generated when there was coherence between the product and the usage of nudity (e.g.: shower gel) or non-coherence (e.g.: car). We will focus here on the second option, which is in keeping with the logic of our research question, and permits us to examine the eventual differences between countries. The choice of the product was a mobile phone, which may be expected to interest the whole sample whatever the country and gender of the individuals, represents a product needed by most people, and with no direct or indirect link with nudity.

Regarding the brand, we have focussed on an international brand, operating in all three countries: Nokia. For the case of simplicity, we have taken an advertisement of the brand, to which we added either a picture of a topless lady or of her face only (see annex 1). Nudity could refer to a natural image (a child, an angel in the church, etc. …) or an erotic image.

We have focussed here on the erotic character, which is the most frequently studied and corresponds to our topic. Knowing in addition that several forms of nudity are possible, we have retained the higher level of the scale, which was proposed by Triandis (1995) that ranges from 0 = "no sexual appeal/fully clothed" to 4 = "nudity with bare bodies, wearing translucent underapparel or lingerie, poses where the model wears only a towel."

## Organization of Experimentation

The two experimental advertisements (topless or face) were inserted in a 12-page folder, which, whatever the country, contained:

-endpaper entitled "Campus" not necessitating a translation
-page 2: a ½ page advertisement for women's clothes (advertiser: YSL) and another ½ page advertisement for a car (advertiser: Smart)
-page 3 : an article on a scientific subject
-page 4: a ½ page advertisement for a drink (advertiser: Coca-Cola) and a ½ page article on the history of the brand name
**-page 5a**: a ½ page article offering architectural information concerning the sample region (Prague, Valence or Metz) and an experimental advertisement for Nokia on the other half of the page.
**-page 5b**: a full page experimental advertisement for Nokia
-page 6: information on Erasmus grants
-page 7: information on Erasmus grants
-page 8: information on possible activities to do in the sample region (Prague, Valence, or Metz)
-page 9: a full page advertisement on plane trips (advertiser: Air Europa)
-page 10: advertisements on various training courses
-page 11: an information page for students
-page 12: an advertisement for a film (Ice Age)

Thus, a total of 10 different advertisements (4 one quarter page advertisements, 3 half page advertisements, and 2 full page advertisements, plus the experimental advertisement).

Although the endpaper and the advertisements were totally identical in the three countries (except of course the texts, which were translated), the articles were talking about similar subjects but not totally identical because it was necessary to adapt the content to each country. The two folders were submitted to two samples of students in each of the three countries according the following experimentation plan:

| | Czech Republic | Spain | France | Total |
|---|---|---|---|---|
| Nokia advertisement with topless lady | 87 | 84 | 88 | 259 |
| Nokia advertisement with face of the lady | 92 | 85 | 78 | 255 |
| Total | 179 | 169 | 166 | 514 |

The delivery of the experimental journal folder was accompanied by the following comment: "We are testing a new shape of journals, which could become the journal for campus students. Before finalizing this shape, we would like your advice on its shape and content. We will give you a few minutes to have a look at it (10 minutes exactly). Then we will ask you some questions about it".

The experimentation proceeded as follows:

- after 10 minutes of reading the journal, students were requested to close the journal and answer the first part of questionnaire including particularly questions about memorization and the intention to buy
- When everybody had finished the answers of the first part, they were requested to open the folder once more, look attentively at the experimental advertisement, then to answer questions in the second part of questionnaire: the attention concerning the advertisement (Lombardot, 2005), affective reactions (Derbaix, 1995), attitude towards the advertisement (Falcy, 1997), trust in quality and attitude (like this Nokia mobile phone), and intention to buy. Then this questionnaire was concluded by questions measuring individual implications of respondents towards mobile phones (Kapefer et Laurent, 1986). In fact, in a high involvement situation, the efficiency of advertising depends mostly of arguments of the advertisement, so arguments are generally less important then the high involvement. In the low involvement situation, efficiency is mostly linked to the 'sympathy' felt towards the advertisement (developed for example by a sexy model) and to the broadcast frequency (Moser, 1998).

## First results

Although some complementary processing was indispensable to permit more detailed understanding of the differences between the countries, the first results have already given some answers to some parts of the questions. Among the three fundamental variables on which the advertisement is likely to have an effect: memorization, attitude toward the advertisement, and brand, it is interesting to note differences between countries concerning memorization and attitude towards the advertisement. This could be explained by the more particular attention of the French and Spanish towards the advertisement because of its sensual attractivity. We can observe in Table 2 that French people, who have best assisted memorization of the over promoted brand Nokia, are also those who consider the advertisement with the naked topless lady the most sensual. They have given more attention to the advertisement (with or without the picture of the topless lady). The observation of the spontaneous memorization also shows similar results even though non-significant. Conversely, with regards to the attitude towards the brand, we can notice no difference between the countries, whether the group of people were exposed to the advertisement showing the topless lady, or not.

**Table 2: Differences between countries concerning nudity in advertisement**

| | Naked woman | | | Face woman | | |
|---|---|---|---|---|---|---|
| Averages of scales | CR | France | Spain | CR | France | Spain |
| Q8b- Can you mark which brands of phones you have seen in the advertisement | 119 | 139 | 130 | 126 | 135 | 121 |
| | N=259 – pc= 0.041 | | | N=254 – pc=0.302 | | |
| Q10c- I have paid attention to this when reading the journal | 89 | 150 | 150 | 93 | 156 | 136 |
| | N= 259 - pc= 0.000 | | | N= 253 - pc= 0.000 | | |
| Q12h- This advertisement is sensual | 105 | 142 | 142 | 135 | 113 | 133 |
| | N=259 - pc= 0.001 | | | N= 255 – pc= 0.099 | | |
| Q6c- Spontaneous mention of Nokia as being a brand that was the object of an advertisement in the folder | 77% | 89% | 86% | 79% | 88% | 74% |
| | $Chi^2$=4,9 – df=2 –pc=0.086 | | | $Chi^2$=4,6 – df=2 – pc=0.097 | | |

Kruskall Wallis test except of Q6c $Chi^2$

Reading Table 2 more closely it is seen that differences between countries exist whatever the kind of advertisement, except with regard to assisted memorization. These results then bring us to think that it is not the stimuli variation used in the advertisement which provokes these differences, but, more fundamentally, the differences belonging to each nation. Table 3 confirms this argumentation by showing that, when we observe the scores of each advertisement in each of the three countries, the tendencies are exactly the same concerning the advertisement (we have only taken in the table the significant differences and a trust threshold of 95%).

**Table 3: The most significant items of country attitudes towards advertisement**

| | Czech Republic | | France | | Spain | |
|---|---|---|---|---|---|---|
| Averages of scales | Naked | Face | Naked | Face | Naked | Fac e |
| Q12b- this ad appeals more to feelings than to reason | 103 | 63 | 92 | 56 | 96 | 61 |
| | N= 166 – pc=0.000 | | N=151 – pc=0.000 | | N=158 – pc=0.000 | |
| Q12c- Information is satisfactory | 83 | 83 | 67 | 84 | 71 | 87 |
| | N=166 – pc=0.922 | | N=150 – pc=0.015 | | N=158 – pc=0.026 | |
| Q12d- advertisement is kind of unusual (CR), usual (SP, FR) | 101 | 65 | 84 | 67 | 102 | 53 |
| | N=166 – pc=0.000 | | N=152 – pc=0.017 | | N=158 – pc=0.000 | |
| Q12e- information seems to be objective | 72 | 94 | 67 | 86 | 69 | 89 |
| | N=166 – pc=0.002 | | N=151 – pc=0.008 | | N=158 – pc=0.005 | |
| Q12f- message is convincing | 74 | 92 | 69 | 84 | 69 | 89 |
| | N=166 – pc=0.014 | | N=152 – pc=0.032 | | N=158 – pc=0.004 | |
| Q12h- ad is sensual | 80 | 86 | 90 | 60 | 86 | 71 |
| | N=166 – pc=0.438 | | N=152 – pc=0.000 | | N=158 – pc=0.037 | |

Finally, it would appear that it might be rather the gender of the individual that influences the attitude towards the advertisement. Table 4 illustrates it perfectly, as many more men clearly prefer the advertisement with the topless lady and think her pleasant to look at, whilst we can notice exactly the opposite for the ladies.

**Table 4: The most significant items of attitudes on advertisement towards gender**

| | Men | | Women | |
|---|---|---|---|---|
| Averages of scales | Naked | Face | Naked | Face |
| Q12a- generally, I like this advertisement | 128 | 104 | 91 | 150 |
| | N=234 – pc=0.006 | | N=241 – pc=0.000 | |
| Q12g- this advertisement is nice to look at | 136 | 94 | 96 | 145 |
| | N=234 – pc=0.000 | | N=241 – pc=0.000 | |

## Conclusion

Maciejewski (2004) has shown that ladies clearly have a more negative attitude than men towards advertisements with sexy modelling women (from the kind of scale “It is right to use appeals involving sex when selling sunscreen”), and that this is independent of the philosophic opinions of the individuals. We can see here that it is not only the attitude of women to sexual messages that differs from men’s attitudes; there are other indicators, which also differ between the countries studied.

Beyond the fact that these results are worthy of deeper statistical investigations to detail relationships, four main limitations should be emphasised:

- The kind of product chosen here doesn’t naturally justify the use of nudity. What would happen in the case of a product more coherent with nudity?
- We only studied here the reactions to female nudity; it will be also interesting to study male nudity, which, with the exception of some rare studies, has never really been investigated, despite the fact that it seems to be growing more common in recent times. (Elliott and Elliott, 2005) ;
- The choice of known brand would be justified for the previous reasons, therefore we could repeat this kind of experimentation with a totally unknown brand and chosen differently in each country
- The selection of a sample of students may have erased the regional differences.

## References


Beetles, Andrea C., Harris, Lloyd C. (2005), Consumer Attitudes Towards Female Nudity in Advertising: An Empirical Study, *Marketing Theory*, December, Vol. 5, Issue 4, p397-432.

Chang Chingching (2006), Cultural Masculinity/Femininity Influences on Advertising Appeals, *Journal of Advertising Research*, September, 315-323.

Elliott Richard, Elliott Christine (2005), Idealized images of the male body in advertising: a reader-response exploration, *Journal of Marketing Communications*, Vol. 11, N° 1, 3-19.

Ford J.B., La Tour M.S., and Clarke I. (2004), A prescriptive essay concerning sex role portrayals in international advertising contexts, *American Business Review,* 22, 1, pp. 42-55

Kilbourne Jean (2005), What else does sex sell?, *International Journal of Advertising*, 24, 1, 119-122.

Lass Paushali, Hart Susan (2004), National Cultures, Values and Lifestyles Influencing Consumers' Perception towards Sexual Imagery in Alcohol Advertising: An Exploratory Study in the UK, Germany and Italy, *Journal of Marketing Management*, 2004, 20, 607-623

Lombardot Eric (2002), Nudité et publicité, l'utilisation de personnes nues en communication persuasive : un état de l'art, *Actes de la 7ème Journée de Recherche en Marketing de Bourgogne*, Dijon, 13 novembre, 196-215.

Loroz Peggy Sue (2006), The Generation Gap: A Baby Boomer vs. Gen Y Comparison of Religiosity, Consumer Values, and Advertising Appeal Effectiveness, *Advances in Consumer Research*, Volume 33, 308-309.

Lysonski *Steve (2005),* Sexism vs sexy: the conundrum, *International Journal of Advertising*, 24, 1, 116-119

Maciejewski Jeffrey J. (2004), Is the Use of Sexual and Fear Appeals Ethical? A Moral Evaluation By Generation Y College Students, *Journal of Current Issues and Research in Advertising*, Volume 26, Number 2, Fall, 97-105.

Maciejewski Jeffrey J. (2005), From Bikinis to Basal Cell Carcinoma: Advertising Practitioners' Moral Assessments of Advertising Content, *Journal of Current Issues and Research in Advertising*, Volume 27, Number 2, Fall, 107-115.

Maclnnis Deborah J., Moorman Christine, & Jaworski Bernard J. (1991), Enhancing and Measuring Consumers' Motivation, Opportunity, and Ability to Process Brand Information From Advertisements, *Journal of Marketing,* Vol. 55, October, 32-53

Mitchell Andrew A., Olson Jerry C. 1981), Are Product Attribute Beliefs the Only Mediator of Advertising Effects of Brand Attitude ?, *Journal of Marketing Research*, 28, august, 318-332.

Moser K. (1998), « Les modèles d'effet publicitaire », Recherche et Applications en Marketing, vol. 13, n° 1, pp. 25-35.

Nelson Michelle R., Hye-Jin Paek (2005), Cross-Cultural Differences in Sexual Advertising Content in a Transnational Women's Magazine, *Sex Roles*, Vol. 53, Nos. 5/6, September, 371-383

Orth Ulrich R., Holancova Denisa (2003), Consumer Response to Sex Role Portrayals in Advertisements, *Journal of Advertising*, 32, 4, 77-89.

Piron F. et Young M. (1996), Consumer Advertising in Germany and the United States : A Study of Sexual Explicitness and Cross-gender Contact, *Journal of Consumer Marketing*, vol. 8, pp. 211-223.

Reichert T. et Ramirez A. (2000), Defining Sexually Oriented Appeals in Advertising : A Grounded Theory Investigation, *Advances in Consumer Research*, vol. 27, pp. 267-273.

Sciglimpaglia D., Belch M.A., Cain R.F. (1978), Demographic and Cognitive Factors Influencing Viewers Evaluations of 'sexy' Advertisements, *Advances in Consumer Research*, vol. 6, pp. 62-65.

Shimp Terence A. (1981), Attitude toward the Ad as a Mediator of Consumer Brand Choice, *Journal of Advertising*, 10, 2, 9-15.

# Advertising in Central and Eastern Europe: A Case Study of Nestlé Television Advertising In Russia

Jorma Larimo and AiIa Pesonen

## Abstract

Advertising is one of the main tools firms employ for promotion. Although the transition in CEE countries started already in the early 1990s, the marketing strategies, especially the advertising strategies of Western companies have been analyzed very limitedly so far. The aim of the paper is to analyze advertising in Russia, focusing on the television advertising in the chocolate bar sector. In the analysis of advertising we will concentrate on the key features and the cultural values in the Russian television commercials. The study of television advertising is of our interest, since television advertising has the dominant role in CEE countries, especially in Russia. The cultural values in the commercials will be analyzed by employing Hofstede's (1980, 1991, 2001) research on cultural dimensions and the concepts of values identified by Pollay (1983). Since the research on cultural dimensions and values in advertising in the CEE and Russia is not very wide, the exploratory research approach, i.e. case methodology, was selected for the empirical part of the study. The analysis focused on twelve commercials by the case company, Nestlé, during the period 2000-2006 related to the brands *Nuts* - an international brand - and *Shok* - a local brand. The results gave support to the expectation of the existence of clever humor, which is typical to the Russian character. No celebrities were found. Regarding the *Shok* commercials, it was typical that the name of the product was written in Cyrillic. Three to eight appeals could be identified from the reviewed data. In total, 10 various appeals could be identified in at least one of the twelve commercials reviewed. The four key appeals from those presented by Pollay (1983) were revealed: distinctive, youth, relaxation, and enjoyment.

## Introduction

Advertising is one of the main tools firms employ for promotion. Therefore advertising research has been very extensive. During the last twenty-five years also the research focusing on international marketing has increased remarkably. In his assessment of international advertising literature between 1990 and 2002 Zou (2005) identified 180 articles in eleven leading international marketing journals. From those articles 122 had clear international focus. The clearly most common topic was the degree of standardization vs. adaptation in general, and additionally, which elements in the advertisements have been standardized and which adapted (34 articles, 27.8%). Other main topic areas were: consumer responses (26 articles), advertising content (18), social issues (17), and cultural values (14). Several studies focus on the behavior of U.S. or Western European firms and/or advertising in those countries. If some other country or countries, mainly emerging economies, have been included then the main focus has usually been China (see e.g. Taylor, 2005; Zou, 2005). Although the transition in CEE countries started already in the early 1990s, the marketing strategies, especially the advertising strategies of Western companies have been analyzed very limitedly so far. A literature search of international journal articles in research-oriented journals has resulted so far in 10 studies: Church (1992), Heyder, Musiol and Peters (1992), Andrews, Durvasula and Netemeyer (1994), Dianoux, Domanski and Herrmann (2000), Van Herpen, Pieters, Fidrmucove and Rosenboom (2000), Pelsmacker, Maison and Geuens (2002), Taylor, Bonner and Dolezal (2002), Dianoux, Kettnerova and Linhart (2006), Holak, Matveev and Havlena (2007), and Orth and Koenig (2007). Most of these studies focus on print advertising and on other CEE countries than Russia. Especially, television advertising in Russia has been studied extremely limitedly for the time being.

Before the transition period, the role of advertising in Russia was very limited and also the content of advertising was very different - much more product information focused – than that used in Western countries. However, after the transition period until the financial crisis of August 1998, for example, 90% of television advertising was either simply translated or in some way adapted for the Russian market, albeit produced entirely in the West (Omel′chenko and Bliudina, 2002). Since then the situation has changed, and advertising has increased significantly from the situation in the 1990s. In 2000, media advertising was less than EUR 1 billion, but in 2006 already ca. EUR 4.5 billion, and the estimate for the year 2007 is clearly over EUR 5 billion.

The aim of the paper is to analyze advertising in Russia focusing on the television advertising in the chocolate bar sector. In the analysis of advertising we will concentrate on the key features and the cultural values in the Russian television commercials. The study of television advertising is of our interest, since television advertising has the dominant role in CEE countries, especially in Russia. The cultural values in the commercials will be analyzed by employing Hofstede's (1980, 1991, 2001) research on cultural dimensions and the concepts of values identified by Pollay (1983). Since the research on cultural dimensions and values in advertising in the CEE and Russia is not very wide, the exploratory research approach, i.e. case methodology, has been selected for the empirical part of the study.

The structure of the paper is as follows: In section two, we shall briefly discuss some key issues concerning television advertising. In section three, the main concepts and development of advertising in Russia will be reviewed. Section four deals with cultural dimensions and values/appeals in advertising. Section five presents the case company and research methodology. Section six will analyze the selected television commercials, and section seven includes the summary and avenues for future research.

## International Television Advertising: General Issues

The advertising media selected for this study is television, which is an expensive but commonly used medium in attempting to reach broad national markets. In most developed countries, and increasingly also in emerging markets, the coverage is no problem. Therefore the contact price is much lower than the contact price of using several other media like print advertising. Furthermore, one of the great advantages in television advertising is the possibility to use speech, music and moving pictures. However, television is one of the most regulated communication media. Many countries have prohibited or set limitations for the advertising of several consumer products like cigarettes and alcohol other than beer. Furthermore, in some countries like in the Nordic countries, there are limits on the number of minutes that TV advertising is permitted to be sent. These countries also prohibit commercial breaks in TV programs.

Although from the producer's point of view, there are several advantages in television advertising, the results of several studies seem to indicate that television is the most irritating advertising media mainly because the commercials interrupt programs (see De Pelsmacker & Van den Bergh, 1998). For example, in a study made in the Netherlands (see Trendbox, 1995), 89% of the respondents explained that there is too much advertising on television. However, in addition to television, outdoor and radio advertising also scored very high on the statement "should be forbidden". Magazine and newspaper commercials scored much lower on this factor, but only because they scored high on "you can skip it".

Some key issues in the advertising research have been the impact of positive vs. negative context and emotional vs. rational advertising messages. General view seems to be that positive media context leads to more positive attitude towards the ad and to better recall and reaction than a negative context (see e.g. De Pelsmacker, Maison & Geuens, 2002). Usually irritation leads to negative attitudes towards the ad and recall of the product, therefore we shall discuss the causes of irritation towards the ads. De Pelsmacker and Van den Bergh (1998) present in their article a review of earlier research concerning irritation caused by television advertising. They analyze the impact of ad content, product category, repletion or frequent exposure, and consumer on the level of irritation.

Ad content: Emotional advertising in general influences ad-evoked feelings positively. More particularly, there is extensive evidence that warmth in advertising (creating a nice, friendly atmosphere, using warm characters) reduces irritation and other negative evoked feelings. De Mooij (2005), however, states that because the way people show their emotions are so different across cultures, the use of emotions in global marketing is not advisable. Also the use of humor seems to reduce irritation substantially, except when the humor is stupid or exaggerated (satire, sexually aggressive humor). Concerning eroticism the evidence is mixed. Some authors have found a negative effect on ad-evoked feelings, although men are less negatively affected than women, probably because erotic commercials are generally aimed at men. However, there are also results according to which erotic stimuli lead to positive feelings. The earlier results seem also to indicate that provocation leads to a negative ad-evoked feeling. Similarly, showing an uncomfortable situation or an unsympathetic character leads to irritation. Also fear appeals, especially physical ones, lead to increased irritation. The results by De Pelsmacker and Van den Bergh (1998) indicated that use of provocation and eroticism clearly increased irritation whereas fear appeals did not influence the level of irritation.

Information content: Most studies seem to conclude that informative commercials reduce ad-evoked irritation. However, repeating the main argument too often, and giving too much information in one advertisement, may lead to more irritation. Also comparative advertising seems to lead to more irritation. The results by De Pelsmacker and Van den Bergh (1998) indicated that irritation- reducing cues are objective (availability), important (safely, quality), or transformational (taste, nutritional value).

Advertising format: Presenting a situation that is perceived as false, exaggerated, unrealistic, incredible or over dramatized leads to irritation, but celebrity endorsement and expert appeals reduce irritation. All studies involving the use of music in advertising arrive at the same conclusion: the use of music reduces irritation. The results by De Pelsmacker and Van den Bergh (1998) supported earlier findings especially when the lyrics used were not about the product. The use of brand name jingles, on the other hand, increased irritation level. The level of irritation was also decreased by lively and dynamic commercials. The role of creativity and originality is unclear – some results indicate that original commercials do not lead to more positive ad-evoked feelings whereas some have found that originality increases likeability and even purchase intention. Perhaps surprisingly, the results by De Pelsmacker and Van den Bergh (1998) indicated that amateurish and very middle-of-the-road commercials were not more or less irritating than creative, professionally made ones. Finally, the effect of the length of advertising is inconclusive, but according to the results by De Pelsmacker and Van den Bergh (1998) did not affect the level of irritation.

Product category: Some products lead to more irritation than others when advertised. Several studies indicate that: female hygiene products, female underwear, laxatives, toothpaste and mouthwash, are amongst the most irritating product categories. De Pelsmacker and Van den Bergh (1998) had in their study five product categories: food, non-food, durables, services, and retail. Their results indicated that none of the emotional appeals studied was particularly or more suited to reduce irritation for a particular product category, only information content and formal characteristics seemed to be of any relevance. Because the focus in the empirical part of this study will be on chocolate bars we shall only refer that the results by De Pelsmacker and Van den Bergh (1998) indicated that for food products it is better to avoid informational motivation, price, performance as special offer argument, and action impulses. Furthermore, it seems to be good to use the argument of availability, a sign-off slogan, models, animals, long ads and creative execution.

Concerning the repetition or frequent exposure it seems that repetition or frequent exposure is mentioned by consumers as one of the main reasons for irritation in advertising. This view was clearly confirmed in the study by De Pelsmacker and Van den Berg (1998) independent of the executional strategy used in the ad.

Consumer: Some consumers are more irritated by advertising than others. Most studies come to the conclusion that men, youngsters, higher income and higher education and professional segments are generally more irritated than women, older people and lower income, lower education and professional segments.

One aspect of ads that seems to be important especially in television advertising is the use of humor. Perhaps partly based on the fact that more than 90 per cent of advertising practitioners have seen humor as an effective way to gain attention in Western countries, especially in the USA, a great share of television ads include humor (see e.g. Weinberger and Gulas, 1992). Related to the type of humor the review by Weinberger and Gulas (1992) indicated that "comic wit" had a negative impact whereas other types of humor positive impact on attitudes towards ads, but the results by De Pelsmacker and Van den Bergh (1998) indicated clearly that also satire had negative impact on the attitudes towards the reviewed ads. From different product types low involvement feeling products such as snack foods, beer, wine etc. are best suited for humorous ad treatments and whereas humor does not suit so well for high involvement feeling products (Weinberger & Gulas, 1992). Finally, some studies indicate that humorous ads are especially suited for better educated younger males, but the results are not conclusive (ibid).

After the review of advertising in Russia we shall discuss in more detail the national culture and dimensions of culture and the advertising appeals and the relationships between dimensions of culture and ad appeals.

## Development of Advertising in Russia

There was a lot of advertising, e.g. in St. Petersburg, before the Russian revolution in the 1910s (see West, 1998). But during the period from the revolution until the end of the 1980s, the amount of advertising was extremely low and the advertising was very different. This was because the local consumers were not accustomed to advertising, especially Western-style advertising. Advertising was seen as a form of propaganda to move merchandise that was unpopular and / or of poor quality, and the concepts and style used in Western commercials were uncommon and strange for most local people. Therefore advertising is a quite new commercial information and communication medium in Russia, and in its modem form, it has been essentially 'Western'. Prior to the financial crisis of August 1998, for example, 90% of television advertising was either simply translated or in some way adapted for the Russian market, albeit produced entirely in the West (Omel′chnko & Bliudina 2002).

Since the collapse of the Soviet Union, Russia has incorporated three major economic phenomena from 1991-1998. The first was privatization and increasing integration of the global capital markets. The second was the transition of Russia from central planning to market-oriented economies through the 'shock therapy' reform. The third was the rouble crisis, which took place in August 1998. As a consequence, Russian consumers were shaken by the fall in value of the rouble, economic instability, and price increases associated with the downfall of the local currency. When the importers of consumer goods and food products faced enormous problems, the local food producers enjoyed benefits because of the more expensive imports (BOEFIT, 1999).

The first period in Russian advertising history covers the years 1991-1996 when the markets generated a commercial culture that reflected a state of cultural confusion and the crisis of a unified culture. Americanism or Europeanism was noticeable. Many of the commercials appealed to a Russian male audience, businessmen and those with a high standard of living. Western technology was also emphasized in the advertising. The commercials revealed language mixing, code-switching and direct translations from English to Russian. Almost every advertised product had to be international, European, Scandinavian, and offer service in a foreign language or accent (Pesonen, 1997). The attitudes of local people seemed to be more favorable towards advertising in this period than in some Western countries, like in the USA (see e.g. Andrews, Durvasula & Netemeyer, 1994). A special feature of television advertising was, that in Russia as well as in other CEE countries, television ads were "bunched" together and shown after long intervals of uninterrupted programming or between programs. Furthermore, the number of available spots per day was limited compared to advertising possibilities in Western European countries (Church, 1992).

In 1992, a very popular slogan in Russia was *MMM - net problem* 'MMM - no problem'. The optimistic expression *net problem* is a direct translation from English (Boym, 1994; Grineberg & Petrushenko, 2004). This first Russian TV advertising campaign for MMM was remembered in Russian advertising history. It resulted in an enormous marketing success for the financial pyramid MMM, because instead of a Western lifestyle, it pictured a common Russian man (Lenia Golubkov) with some of the attributes of a folk-story 'smart fool'. He was involved in an activity that was perceived by viewers as a new type of marketing behavior. Unfortunately, the financial pyramid MMM collapsed, and hundreds of thousands of people lost their money (Boym, 1994; Grineberg & Petrushenko, 2002). The confidence of Russian consumers on local products at the beginning of the 1990s was very low (see e.g. Ettenson, 1993).

In the first period of Russian advertising, it was not marketing communication at all, but the magical attractions offered by promises of future happiness by appealing to 'Western' or 'the nostalgic pre-revolutionary native Russian capitalism' values. Communication seemed not to be aimed at actual sales. Many commercials did not advertise commodities for mass consumption, instead immaterial goods such as 'stock market seats' or 'patent protection' were offered. The advertising was experienced as either entertaining or annoying (Boym, 1994; Pesonen & Namsaraev, 1996).

It is only since 1998 that the real Russian advertising industry can be said to have taken off. The switch off of imports after the rouble crash proved an opportunity for Russian companies to respond to consumer demand with cheaper domestic products. The growing advertising industry was quickly transformed into a machine for the promotion of Russian and quasi-Russian products. According to Morris (2005), from 1999 onward, commercials for Russian products were more frequent and indicate that a new confidence in Russian products had been found in the consumer.

Prior to the financial crisis of August 1998, for example, 90% of television advertising was either simply translated or in some way adapted for the Russian market, albeit produced entirely in the West (Omel´chenko and Bliudina, 2002). Since then the situation has changed and the advertising has also increased significantly from the level in the 1990s. In the year

2000 media advertising was less than EUR 1 billion, but in 2006 it had already reached ca. EUR 4.5 billion, and the estimate for 2007 is clearly over EUR 5 billion (Typpö, 2007).

It can be said that in modern Russia, commercials have become an important part of the economic system. Since 2002, Video International and NTV-Media have held a dominant position selling advertising at the national level. Advertising agencies have raised their qualification and efficiency in marketing, sales of complex services and advertising, and sought to raise their qualification and efficiency through the optimization of their creative potential (AllNews, 2002).

The focus in the study will be on television advertising, because television advertising has the dominant role in CEE countries, especially in Russia. In the early 2000s the role of television advertising was somewhat less than 50% of all advertising (based on the value) and since then the role has risen to 60% in 2006. The growth rate of television advertising has been almost 30% during the last few years (Typpö, 2007). The popularity of television advertising is high because of the wide geographical coverage and low level of contact price. About 99% of Russian households own a television (ibid). Although Russian consumers rely more on print advertising than on television advertising, the costs of print advertising are much higher, especially per contact price. In newspaper advertising, the coverage is better than in magazine advertising, but a problem is often the quality of the newsprint (ibid). Problems in television advertising have been due to the increased costs of the advertising and a change in local legislation in 2006, which reduced the total time for advertising from the earlier 20% to 15%. Furthermore, it is not permitted to have more than 20% advertising in any given hour (ibid).

In a nationwide study made by the Public Opinion Foundation in March 2006, which included 100 residencies in 44 regions involving I 500 respondents, plus a sample of 600 respondents from Moscow, the views toward television advertising were reviewed (see Vovk, 2006). According to the results, more than half of the respondents (55%) have the opinion that television cannot exist without advertising. The attitudes toward advertising seem, however, to have become more critical than during the early years of transition. According to the results, almost two-thirds of the television reviewers react negatively to commercials - 51% of them switched the channel, 4% turned off the television, 7% watched the commercials with the sound turned off, and some 25% of the respondents do other things during the commercials. Only 11% of those surveyed said they really watch television commercials. Representatives of all age groups behaved relatively similarly. Half of the respondents informed that there were some television commercials they liked. The share of respondents who disliked television advertisements was in general 44%, higher in the older response group and lower among the younger group (30%). The overwhelming majority of respondents (91%) informed that television commercials were too long; only 8% informed that they had just the right duration. Again in the younger respondent group the latter view was somewhat more supported (11%).

## Cultural Values in Advertising

There are a lot of different ways to analyze culture and the impact of culture. Related to the culture, the most widely used framework for analysis are the dimensions of culture by Hofstede (1980, 1991, 2001). Researchers in marketing began to use Hofstede's model culture as a framework for testing cross-cultural differences in the 1990s, but for the time being there are still relatively few applications of his framework in the field of advertising (see e.g. Albers; 1994, Albers-Miller & Gelb 1996; De Mooij, 2005). The model is the output of an extensive study of work related values representing value system of the majority of the middle class. Hofstede's original study yielded a structure consisting of four dimensions on which societies differ: individualism (IDV), power distance (PDI), uncertainty avoidance (UAI), and masculinity (MAS). The data collection instrument used by Hofstede was developed by a multinational team in an effort to reduce cultural biases in the questionnaire (Hofstede, 1991, 2001). Partly based on the criticism about the great focus on Western cultures and cultural dimensions, and neglect of especially the Asian cultures, a fifth dimension, long-term orientation (LTO) was added (Hofstede 1991, 2001).

Individualism (IDV) indicates the degree to which individual decision making and actions are encouraged by society. This dimension reflects the way people live together. In a collectivistic society, the lower end of the individualism-collectivism continuum, individualistic behavior may be seen as selfish. Uncertainty avoidance (UAI) represents the degree to which society is unwilling to accept and cope with uncertainty. People use law, religion, and technology to address uncertainty. Power distance (PDI) indicates the degree to which power differences are accepted and sanctioned by society. Hofstede explains that the power distance index explains how different societies have addressed basic human inequalities in social status and prestige, wealth, and sources of power. In addition to measuring clearly defined sex roles, the masculinity dimension (MAS) indicates the degree to which traditional male values (assertiveness, performance, ambition, achievement, and materialism) are important to a society. The opposite end of this continuum has been labeled as femininity. Long-term orientation (LTO) stands for the fostering of virtues oriented towards future rewards, in particular, perseverance and thrift. Its opposite of this continuum, short-term orientation, stands for the fostering of virtues related to the past and present, in particular, respect for tradition, preservation of "face" and fulfilling social obligations.

In the empirical part of the study we are focusing on Russia. Table 1 includes the score values of selected countries along the above discussed five dimensions of culture by Hofstede. As it can be seen from the Table 1, Russia scores high along power distance and uncertainty avoidance indexes, but relatively low along individualism and masculinity indexes. The long-term orientation value for Russia is not included to the works by Hofstede. Thus, concerning the power distance Russia differs significantly from all other countries, especially from Austria. Along uncertainty avoidance the difference to the score value of France is not so great, but the difference to score of United Kingdom is significant. As may be expected along individualism the difference is greatest to the score value of United States (and United Kingdom) whereas the difference to Austria is not so great. Along masculinity dimension the score values of Finland and especially France are relatively close to those of Russia, but compared to the score value of Austria, the difference is very clear.

Russia is one of those countries for which Hofstede had more limited sample. Furthermore, there have been a lot of changes in the country. Therefore, Table 1 also includes results from some other studies where the dimensions by Hofstede have been used as basis. The score values for the dimensions received in the study by Bollinger (1994) differ more from the score values by Hofstede along individualism and power distance dimensions. Also the results by Naumov and Puffer (2000) differ quite a lot from the results by Hofstede. Only along the individualism dimension the results are very similar, along the three other dimensions the differences are great: uncertainty avoidance and power distance scores clearly lower than those by Hofstede and also by Bollinger, but masculinity scored higher. Furthermore, the study by Naumov and Puffer included also a score value along the fifth cultural dimension - long-term orientation. The value received is higher than for any other of the sample countries in Table 1. Thus, in the empirical part of the study we shall compare our results to those presented on the score values by Hofstede or those by Naumov and Puffer.

The study of values through appeals is common in cross-cultural research. Especially several cross-cultural researchers have included advertising appeals as part of their studies (Mueller 1987; Cheng & Schweizer 1996 Albers 1994, Albers-Miller & Gelb 1996; Khairullah & Khairullah 2002). One of the first to develop comprehensive lists of advertising appeals was Pollay (1983). The list was developed based on previous advertising literature and values researched in other disciplines. In total the list included 42 appeals. This list (see Table 2) has been later used e.g. in Albers (1994), Albers-Miller & Gelb (1996) and in modified form in e.g. Cheng & Schweizer (1996) and Khairullah & Khairullah (2002). It was decided to use the original list of appeals in this study because the original list by Pollay was linked to Hofstede's cultural dimensions (1980, 1991) in the study by Albers (1994), whereas the other studies do not link the modified versions so clearly to Hofstede's dimensions.

**Table 1: Country scores for selected countries ((H=Hofstede 1980, 2001; B=Bollinger, 1994; N & P=Naumov & Puffer, 2000)**

| | IDV | UAI | PDI | MAS | LTO |
|---|---|---|---|---|---|
| | | | | | |
| Austria | 55 | 70 | 11 | 79 | 31 |
| Finland | 63 | 59 | 33 | 26 | 44 |
| France | 71 | 86 | 68 | 43 | 39 |
| Germany | 67 | 65 | 35 | 66 | 31 |
| Hungary | 46 | 82 | 80 | 88 | 50 |
| Russia (H) | 39 | 95 | 93 | 36 | na. |
| Russia (B) | 26 | 92 | 76 | 28 | na. |
| Russia (N & P) | 41 | 68 | 40 | 55 | 59 |
| United Kingdom | 89 | 35 | 35 | 25 | 25 |
| USA | 91 | 46 | 40 | 62 | 29 |

The study of Albers (1994) included 11 countries - Brazil, Chile, Finland, France, India, Israel, Japan, Mexico, South Africa, Taiwan and United

States – and four product categories – office equipment, financial services, clothing, and travel services. The advertisements were taken mainly from local business magazines. Her results indicated clear differences between countries. The lowest average amounts of appeals, coded per ad, were found in Brazil (1.87), Mexico (2.82), and France (3.16), and the highest were found in India (9.16), Chile (15.53), and Finland (15.53). In the USA, the average number of appeals coded was 5.02. Thus, there existed very clear variation in the average number of appeals coded, and the differences were not clearly between Western and Eastern and/or between developed and developing/emerging countries.

The links between the appeals and Hofstede's five dimensions based on the original assumptions by Albers (1994) are presented in Table 2. As can be seen from the table, three of appeals were assumed to be positively and five negatively related to the individualism dimension; five of the appeals were positively related to the power distance dimension while five were negatively related; three appeals were positively related to the uncertainty avoidance dimension while five were negatively rated; five appeals were positively rated to the masculinity dimension while six were negatively rated, , and four appeals were positively rated to the long-term orientation dimensions. No appeals at all were expected to be negatively related to the last dimension. Related to twelve appeals even the research group to which Alberts and Alberts-Miller belonged could not reach total agreement. The twelve variables were: traditional, modern, technological, relaxation, wisdom, enjoyment, freedom, maturity, morality, sexuality, healthy, and neat. These appeals are presented with cursive in Table 2.

The links between the appeals and the five dimensions have bee researched empirically extremely limited degree. The empirical results in the study by Albers (1994) and Albers-Millar & Gelb (1996), for example, did not give significant support to all relationships expected based on the theory. The results in Albers (1994) indicated that freedom appeal, which was assumed to be positively related to individualism although it might have a negative relation to masculinity (=positive to feminism) and family appeal, seemed to have a positive, not a negative relationship with individualism. Furthermore, it may be that advertisers use some appeals across countries to do their products more salable. Therefore only very weak relationship between some appeals and cultural values could be found. These appeals were modern, technological, durable and productive which seemed to have been used as basic selling premises across cultures. Because of the very limited empirical testing of the relationships, the originally presented assumed relationships will be used as the starting point in this study.

The results by De Pelsmacker et al. (2002) indicated that in Poland emotional messages lead to more positive ad and brand responses in positive than in negative contexts – supporting the earlier findings in North America and West European countries (see Section 2 of the paper) and in negative contexts emotional messages lead to more negative responses than rational ads.

**Table 2: Pollay's 42 appeals (Pollay, 1983) and relationship with Hofstede's cultural dimensions (Albers, 1994; Albers-Miller & Gelb, 1996). ***

| ***Appeal*** | ***Description*** | |
|---|---|---|
| Distinctive | Rare, unique, unusual, scarce, infrequent, exclusive, tasteful, elegant, subtle, esoteric, handcrafted | **Individualism** |
| *Freedom* | Spontaneous, carefree, abandoned, indulgent, at liberty, uninhibited, passionate | |
| Independence | Self-sufficiency, self-reliance, autonomy, unattached, to do-it-yourself. to do your own thing, original, unconventional, singular, nonconformist | |
| Popular | Commonplace, customary, well-known, conventional, regular, usual, ordinary, normal, standard, typical, universal, general, everyday | **Collectivism** |
| Succorance | To receive expressions of love (all expressions except sexuality), gratitude, pats on the back, to feel deserving | |
| Family | Nurturance within the family, having a home, being at home, family privacy, companionship of siblings, kinship, getting married | |
| Community | Relating to community, state, national publics, public spiritedness, group unity, national identity, society, patriotism, civic and community organizations or other than social organizations | |
| Affiliation | To be accepted, liked by peers, colleagues, and community at large, to associate or gather with, to be social, to join, unite, or otherwise bond in friendship, fellowship, companionship, cooperation, reciprocity, to | |

| | | |
|---|---|---|
| | conform to social customs, have manners, social graces and decorum, tact and finesse | |
| Ornamental | Beautiful, decorative, ornate, adorned, embellished, detailed, designed, styled | **High power distance** |
| Dear | Expensive, rich, valuable, highly regarded, costly, extravagant, exorbitant, luxurious, priceless | |
| Vain | Having a socially desirable appearance, being beautiful, pretty, handsome, being fashionable, well-groomed, tailored, graceful, glamorous | |
| Status | Envy, social status or competitiveness, conceit, boasting, prestige, power, dominance, exhibitionism, pride in ownership, wealth (including the sudden wealth of prizes), trend-setting, to seek compliments | |
| *Healthy* | Fitness, vim, vigor, vitality, strength, heartiness, to be active, athletic, robust, peppy, free from disease, illness, infection, or addiction | |
| *Sexuality* | Erotic relations: holding hands, kissing, embracing between lovers, dating, romance, intense sensuality, feeling sexual, erotic behavior, lust, earthiness, indecency, attractiveness of clearly sexual nature | |
| Cheap | Economical, inexpensive, bargain, cut-rate, penny-pinching, discounted, at cost, undervalued, a good value | **Low power distance** |
| Humility | Unaffected, unassuming, unobtrusive, patient, fate-accepting, resigned, meek, plain-folk, down-to-earth | |
| *Wisdom* | Knowledge, education, awareness, intelligence, curiosity, satisfaction, comprehension, sagacity, expertise, judgment, experience | |
| *Morality* | Humane, just, fair, honest, ethical, reputable, principled, religious, devoted, spiritual | |
| Nurturance | To give gifts, especially sympathy, help love, charity, support, comfort, protection, nursing, consolation or otherwise care for the weak, disabled, inexperienced, tired, young, elderly, etc. | |

| | | |
|---|---|---|
| Safety | Security (from external threat), carefulness, caution, stability, absence of hazards, potential injury, or other risks, guarantees, warranties, manufacturers' reassurances | **High uncertainty avoidance** |
| Tamed | Docile, civilized, restrained, obedient, compliant, faithful, reliable, responsible, domesticated, sacrificing, self-denying | |
| *Neat* | Orderly, neat, precise, tidy, clean, spotless, unsoiled, sweet-smelling, bright, free from dirt, refuse, pests, vermin, stains and smells, sanitary | |
| Casual | Unkempt, disheveled, messy, disordered, untidy, rugged, rumpled, sloppy, casual, irregular, non-compulsive, imperfect | **Low uncertainty avoidance** |
| Adventure | Boldness, daring, bravery, courage, seeking adventure, thrills, or excitement | |
| Untamed | Primitive, untamed, fierce, course, rowdy, ribald, obscene, voracious, gluttonous, frenzied, uncontrolled, unreliable, corrupt, obscene, deceitful, savage | |
| Magic | Miracles, magic, mysticism, mystery, witchcraft, wizardry, superstitions, occult sciences, mythic characters, to mesmerize, astonish, bewitch, fill with wonder | |
| Youth | Being young or rejuvenated, children, kids, immature, underdeveloped, junior, adolescent | |
| Effective | Feasible, workable, useful, pragmatic, appropriate, functional, consistent, efficient, helpful, comfortable (clothes), tasty (food), strength, longevity of effect | **Masculinity** |
| Durable | Long-lasting, permanent, stable, enduring, strong, powerful, hearty, tough | |
| Convenient | Hendy, time-saving, quick, easy, suitable, accessible, versatile | |
| Security | Confident, secure, possessing dignity, self-worth, self-esteem, self-respect, peace of mind | |
| Productivity | References to achievement, accomplishment, ambition, success, careers, self-development, being skilled, accomplished, proficient, pulling your weight, contributing, doing your share | |
| *Relaxation* | Rest, retire, retreat, loaf, contentment, be at ease, be laid-back, vacations, holiday, to observe | |

| | | |
|---|---|---|
| *Enjoyment* | To have fun, laugh, be happy, celebrate, to enjoy games, parties, feasts and festivities, to participate | **Feminity** |
| Frail | Delicate, frail, dainty, sensitive, tender, susceptible, vulnerable, soft, genteel | |
| Natural | References to the elements, animals, vegetables, minerals, farming, unadulterated, purity (of product), organic, growth, nutritious | |
| Modesty | Being modest, naive, demure, innocent, inhibited, bashful, reserved, timid, coy, virtuous, pure, shy, virginal | |
| Plain | Unaffected, natural, prosaic, homespun, simple, artless, unpretentious | |
| *Traditional* | Classic, historical, antique, legendary, time-honored, long-standing, venerable, nostalgic | **LTO** |
| Maturity | Being adult, grown-up, middle-aged, senior, elderly, having associated insight, wisdom, mellowness, adjustment, references to aging, death, retirement, or age-related disabilities or compensations | |
| *Modern* | Contemporary, modern, new, improved, progressive, advanced introducing, announcing… | |
| *Technological* | Engineered, fabricated, formulated, manufactured, constructed, processed, resulting from science, invention, discovery, research, containing secret ingredients | |

*Lack of agreement about the hypothesized relationship between appeals with cursive and the cultural dimension.

Furthermore, the results by Dianoux, Domanski and Herrman (2000) indicated that in Poland advertising uses humorous, symbols, or the historic and literary past of the country with word plays and linguistic expressions with double meanings that are only understood by the Poles. In study based on a limited amount of in-depth interviews by Taylor, Bonner and Dolezal (2002) focusing on advertising in Czech Republic, the results indicated that direct, simple messages are desirable in Czech advertising. Furthermore, the informants consistently mentioned that appeals to family happiness, togetherness, and friendship are common and often desirable in Czech advertising. Finally, the results indicated that humor and clever creative approaches are a very important aspect of advertising in Czech Republic. The results in another study focusing on the similarities and differences in Czech and France print advertising by Dianoux, Kettnerova and Linhart (2006) indicated that the Czech ads differ significantly in their content and their form from the French ads. The results also indicated important differences in the cultural values found in the ads. All reviewed values were found more in the French than in the Czech ads independent whether the ads concerned international or local brands. The only exception was the use of erotic in the ads of international brands, which was higher in Czech ads, but the results did not indicate a statistically significant difference. Furthermore, Orth and Koenig (2007) found also between CEE countries clear differences in the impact emotions on advertising effectiveness and on attitudinal responses to positively and negatively framed ads. Unfortunately Russia was not included among the reviewed four CEE countries.

Van Herpen et al. (2000) analyze the information content of magazine advertising in market (Netherlands and the UK) and transition (Czech Republic and Russia) economies. Their results indicated more information cues in transition economies than in market economies and more feel elements in market economy ads than in transition economy ads whereas no significant difference was found in the amount of think elements between the two country groups. Of interest was the founding that the lowest amount of all think (arguments and problem solving) and feel (life style and pleasure) elements were found in Russian ads.

In a recent study by Holak et al. (2007) nostalgia in post-socialist Russia is discussed and they have examples of applications to advertising in Russia. They conclude that based on several reasons the use of nostalgia in advertising is and will be much more common in Russian advertising than in several other countries. As discussed earlier, no study was found where the use of ad values and links with Hofstede´s cultural dimensions in Russia would have been reviewed. Neither a greater amount of appeals have been included in any of ad studies focusing on Russia so far. Because Russia is more a high context culture than Czech Republic, related to the communication for the Russians posture, tone, facial expressions, silences and gestures are just as important bearers for the sense of things as words (Dianoux et al., 2006).

## Case Company and Research Methodology

Nestlé company has long traditions and the company is the world's leading manufacturer of food and beverages. The company is among the 40 largest non-financial companies in the world based on total assets and sales, and among 10 largest companies based on the number of employees in 2005 (United Nations, 2007). The company had ca. 246,000 employees in its 471 foreign affiliates around the world. The company has some 8,000 brands which include among others Nescafe instant coffee, Perrier water, and KitKat chocolate bars, which are produced and marketed around the world (See also Kommersant' 2007).

The Russian love for chocolate is a long-established phenomenon, and with a burgeoning middle class that now extends beyond metropolitan cities such as St Petersburg and Moscow, consumption figures are on the rise. There are more than 100 manufacturers of chocolate confectionery, many of which are domestic companies operating on a local basis. The Russian confectionary market is one of the largest in the world after the UK, Germany and the USA. In 2005, the market volume is estimated at EUR 6.8 billion. The business intelligence provider Euromonitor expects the Russian chocolate confectionery market to annually grow on average 14% in value and 5.4% in volume between 2006 and 2011; this compares with a 2-3% growth rate for the global chocolate market (Willmer 2007).

The chocolate sector can be divided into four major segments: 1) chocolate slabs, 2) boxed chocolates, 3) weighted (loose) chocolate sweets and 4) chocolate bars. The last segment is most popular among young consumers. The main chocolate segment has been chocolate plates where the volume growth has been around 34% during the last years. Chocolate bar segment has been relatively small, but the growth rate has been much higher than in the chocolate sector on average. This segment has been the most popular among young consumers.

Foreign producers entered the Russian confectionary market in the beginning of the 1990s when local production was of low quality, with a limited range of products, and unprepared for competition. The chocolate market has developed fastest of all confectionary markets. Mars started its local production and the company started already in early 1990s to launch aggressive advertising campaigns. Many Russians were eager to try the chocolate bar and viewed it as "a small piece of Western life".

Nestlé has operated in Russia since 1995. Nestlé endured Russia's currency crisis of the late 1990s, while several other foreign investors fled the country. Nestlé's main production assets are: Confectionery union Rossia, Nestlé Jukovskoe morojennoe, Altay, Kamskaya, Hladoproduct (in the Krasnodar region), Vologodky Zavod Detskogo Pitania and Svyatoi istochnik. The company manufactures drinks, ice cream, and confectionery. The company has continuously been among the top five companies in the Russian market since the mid-1990s. One key issue for the success of the company has been the ownership of the Rossiya-Shedraya Dusha brand - estimated as being the number one brand on the Russian chocolate market. Analysts state that 94% of Russians know this brand and 29% buy its products on a regular basis.

Some years ago (spring 2002) the Moscow based consultancy company, Market Advice, analyzed the chocolate markets and views of Russian consumers. The results indicated that Nestle was clearly the most popular chocolate manufacturer by over 22% of the respondents, whereas from the other foreign chocolate companies in the Russian market Stollwerck (Germany) received 6.6%, Cadbury 2.0% and Mars 1.7%. Especially Mars received surprisingly low voting results. Some local producers like Babaevskii, which was the number two with 16.4%, and Krasny Octyabr (=Red October), which was in the third place with 13.4% of the votes were clearly more popular than Mars. In 2005, the Norwegian company Orkla acquired the Russian chocolate company SladCo, and in 2006 it signed an agreement to buy more than 75 per cent of the shares of the CJSC Krupskaya Confectionery Company (Orkla, 2006).

Related to chocolate bars Mars has been the market leader before Nestlé and Cadbury. The leading chocolate bar brands have been: Bounty, KitKat, Milky Way, Nuts, Ritter Sport, Snickers, Twix, Babaevskii, Shok 'Shock'. All these brands are widely identified and recognized on the Russian market. From these brands KitKat, Nuts, and Shok belong to Nestlé.

As discussed earlier in the study, television advertising and the links between various advertising appeals have not been analyzed in more detail in the Russian environment. Since the aim of the study is also to analyze the development of television advertising, the case methodology was chosen to be applied in this study. We decided to investigate two products brands of the case company in more detail. The products selected are somewhat different and the commercials for them are targeted to the age groups of young people. In order to analyze the development of advertising, a period of seven years was selected (2000-2006). The time period was partly motivated by the case company's access to television commercials. The brands selected were Nuts and Shok. The former brand is also produced in other countries, and the origins of the brand are outside Russia, whereas the latter brand Shok is totally Russian and in is not available on other confectionery market where Nestlé operates. All the reviewed commercials ran minimum two-three months on the main television channels in Russia, i.e. Pervyj kanal, Rossiya, NTV, TNT, and STS.

The commercials were analyzed using content analysis. The content analysis method is a commonly used method in marketing, especially in the analysis of commercials. The analysis is made by a non-Russian, who is a specialist in Russian language and culture. Furthermore, the coder was familiar with the dimensions of culture presented by Hofstede and literature on advertising appeals. The commercials were coded as a dichotomous judgment: the appeal is used in the commercial or it is not used. This type of system is used also in the earlier studies (see e.g. Tse, Belk & Zou, 1989, and Albers, 1994). Because of the complex task of the coding, the coder did not view all of the appeals at the same time, but examined commercials separately for four to six related appeals at the same time.

The key features of the chocolate bar can be regarded: 1. People usually buy chocolate bars for enjoyment, to have energy, to cheer up, 2. People usually buy the product for themselves, more limitedly to somebody else, 3. The length of consumption is usually very short, 4. The visibility of the product is very limited, and 5. The price of the product is low.

Based on the Hofstede's dimensions, the score values for Russia indicated high power distance and uncertainty avoidance values and low individualism and masculinity values. Thus, we could expect appeals like popular, family, community, status, sex, safety, relaxation, and enjoyment to be possibly identified in the commercials. Furthermore, taking into account the target group - young people; the product – chocolate bar; and the advertising media – television; we could expect to find positive attitudes, humor and music in the commercials.

## Results of the Study

### Chocolate Bar Nuts

As a multinational company, Nestlé is well familiar with the cultural peculiarities of regional tastes. In the chocolate business generally, and in the war for chocolate bar consumers more specifically, the most important tactic is to understand the very specific tastes of the young target groups.

Chocolate bar commercials typically play up the fun or benefits associated with snacking by featuring themes like "don't let hunger happen to you" for Snickers, and "gimme a break" for KitKat.

The name of chocolate bar Nuts is written in Latin and it can be interpreted to denote its primary meaning in English – usually 'large hard-shelled seed' (coconuts, peanuts, hazel nuts etc.), Furthermore, Nuts can he also be understood by connoting its different metaphorical meanings, for instance, 'addict', 'whimsically eccentric person', 'head', 'toughness´, like in the phrases 'a football nut', 'to be off one's nut', or 'something is a tough/ hard nut to crack'. In Russia, the young generation knows English better than the older one, since English is studied at school and the contemporary urban popular culture is influenced by Anglo-American popular culture. So, it can be suggested that the product name Nuts itself appeals to a part of young people's psyche.

The slogan and discourse for Nuts commercials are in the Russian language, and the advertising message is targeted to a slightly older core group (12-24) than that of *Shok*. The Nuts campaigns were developed at the Lowe Adventa advertising agency. Their aim was to connect on a more emotional level with 12-24 year-old consumers and to stand out from the campaigns for older chocolate bars. The idea was to promote and ensure that Nuts is a delicious bar full of peanuts, creamy caramel and soft nougat covered in thick milk chocolate, Moreover, its premise was that Nuts was nutritious for brains, and not for the stomach (like Snickers). So, Nuts was positioned in terms of a young lifestyle rather than merely a spur of the moment purchase decision based on hunger. By linking humor and examples of' young people's lifestyles with eating Nuts, the suggestion from the campaign not only formed an emotional link with young adults, it also appealed to everyone in the 12 - 24 year-old age group traditionally making the bulk of the purchases.

The scenarios for commercials in 2000-2006 proceeded from representations of "peculiarities of national stereotypes washing dishes and watering flowers" to presenting characters in comical situations with a more adult-orientated message combined with issues of sex and gender.

In 2000 Nestlé launched a series of Nuts commercials with the slogan *Krepkij oreshek* 'a hard/tough nut', and the script was based on "national peculiarities", The commercials alluded to the humorous Russian films "Peculiarities of National Hunting" (1995) and "Peculiarities of National

Fishing" (1998) directed Alexander Rogozhkin. In these films, cultural differences play a crucial role in situations where the main characters are placed into other cultures.

In the national peculiarities of watering flowers commercial for Nuts, the main character is a young girl, 17-19 years old, dressed in a Western style, watering flowers with two water pistols. The commercial is stereotypically Western (Appendix, picture 1). In comparison, the national peculiarities of washing dishes commercial, features a young man trying to wash dishes but there is no water in the tap. Then he bites a bit of his bar of Nuts, and the water starts running. In both cases, Nuts represents something powerful that resolves difficult problems (hard nuts). Furthermore, in both commercials the main characters are posed in unusual Russian male/female roles. The girl is dressed in Western cowgirl-style clothes with pistols in hand, and the young man is washing dishes, which is not typical for a man in Russian culture. So, these national peculiarities, through the use of contrast and parody, aim to associate a basically Western chocolate bar with traditional Russian values.

In 2002, Lowe Adventa with the creative group of Nestlé started a new campaign for *Nuts* in the style of situation comedy. The slogan was *Zaryadi tvoi mozg* 'Load your brain' (Appendix, picture 2). The parody personages Mozg 'Brain' and Nuts, and characters Zheludok 'Stomack' and Belki 'Squirrels' were to be seen on the main Russian TV channels in 2002-2005 (Appendix, pictures 5-6). The story running through the commercials was that Nuts always helped Mozg 'Brain'. Humor and absurdity of situations make a spectator memorize the brand and its basic idea: *Nuts* is a reliable means to be friendly with Brain. The character Stomach alludes to other chocolate bars like Snickers and Mars, the slogan of which is based on the idea of snacking; the idea of other chocolate bars is embedded in a commercial from 2003. The clip begins with Mozg vacuuming, and three young men sitting on a couch. They are wearing brown T-shirts with the text on their chests reading *Shokoladnyi batonchik* 'Chocolate bar'. They symbolize other chocolate bars that do not help brain. At the end of 2005 a new campaign for *Nuts* started called *Nuts-o-maniya* 'Nuts -a- mania' with the slogan *'Orekh* -*éto uspekh* 'Nuts, Nuts - that is success' (Appendix, picture 5).

In 2006, Nuts helps Mozg to succeed in his affairs, and to succeed in a luxurious lifestyle. The series included commercials under the names Island, Kiss, Ball. The slogan is developed into the form *Nuts. Chtoby vse* v *zhizni poluchilos', zaryazhai mozgi*' 'Nuts. In order to be successful in everything in your life load your brain' (Appendix, picture 6).

The hero Mozg became a hugely popular and memorable character, which resonated with the target audience. The actors in the scenarios were Kirill Kanakhin (Mozg), Denis Solomovich (Nuts) and Pavel Kassinskij (Stomaek). The advertising was well liked and appreciated by the target audience. Moreover, the advertising was thought to be clever because the chocolate bar was integral to the spots without being overly hard sell.

At the preset stage of analysis, we presume that the 18-24 age group has come to represent an important demographic segment of the market. In conjunction with this, the campaigns had to maintain the *Nuts* profile among teenagers while increasing brand salience among young adults. So, in 2006 the commercial *Nuts Klubnichka,* 'Nuts-Strawberry′ was launched with the slogan *Zakroi glazki- otkroj rotik.* 'Shut your (small-) eyes, open your (small-) mouth' (Appendix, picture 7). The commercial itself had been gendered according to the target audience. There are several stereotypically male and female attributes, but the message primarily appeals to a male audience. Though the product is spiced with strawberries, which encourage the women to enjoy the Nuts bar, the verbal and visual images can be associated with a male audience. In the commercial, a group of young men and women are acting as funny male and attractive female squirrels. The male squirrels are sitting in a cabriolet, gesturing and listening to loud disco-music when they suddenly notice a roadster with attractive, overly feminine and sexually appealing young female squirrels in it waiting for the traffic lights to turn green. The young males are masculine, strong and active in trying to make contact with the young female squirrels in the car next to them.

It can be stated that the slogan for Nuts has been developed from 2000-2006 from 1) *Nuts – Krepkij oreshek* 'Nuts - a hard /tough nut' through 2) *Zaryadi tvoi mozg* 'Load your brain', 3) *Nuts - Orekh -éto uspekh* 'Nuts - it is a success' ,4) *Nuts. Chtoby vse* v *zhizni poluchilos', zaryazhai mozgi* 'Nuts. In order to be successful in everything in your life, load your brain' to 4) *Nuts - Klubnichka.* 'Nuts-Strawberry′ with the slogan *Zakroi glazki-Otkroj rotik* ′Shut your eyes. Open your mouth′.

The commercials for Nuts in 2000-2006 (see Appendix) emphasize a clever Russian humor, and the fact that Nuts is not like other chocolate bars. They also emphasize belonging to the young people's reference group, and suggest relaxation and enjoyment. Furthermore, in the commercials 2005 - 2006, it is possible to reveal sex and glamour appeals.

## Chocolate Bar Shok

The Shok chocolate bar was manufactured according to local tastes. It is a sub-brand of Nestlé´s trademark *Rossiya Shchedraya dusha* 'Rossiya - Generous soul' focusing on a teenage audience aged about 10 - 17 (Rossiya shokolad, 2007). The strategy and creative concept of the promotion were developed by the Lowe Adventa advertising agency. The designers use one language system and the cooperative model (Bhatia, 2000: 16, Kotin, 2005). The name *Shok* written in Cyrillic tries to outdo other chocolate bars - especially Mars' brands, including Bounty, Milky Way, M&M's, Mars, Snickers, Twix - in advertising to convince that the people who take *Shok* have better experiences. In increasing competitive intensity, which drives the ongoing search for differentiation, experience has become a new source of value: *Shok* delivers lifelike interactive and memorable experiences, and tries to involve the audience in an unfolding story. The scenarios for the commercials proceed from a fairy-tale-like setting through psychedelic transformation effects to realistic settings shot by candid camera.

The format of the chocolate bar, the original package design and the form of the chocolate, and communicative message intended only for teenagers, were based on an understanding of a modern Russian teenager psychology and the need for a "Russian" product on the chocolate bar market. The appeal *Shok - éto po nashemu* 'Shok - this in our way' acts as the slogan of the chocolate bar.

The key concept of the advertising message is Shock, which connotes the common and prominent phenomena in socio-economical discourses in Russia in the 1990s. The word applied to the chocolate bar has created an appropriate theme for scripting stories for new advertising campaigns. The economic crisis in 1998 led to many multinational corporations pulling out of Russia, or scaling down their levels of advertising. This was advantageous for domestic producers as the cost of advertising space was reduced. Advertisers began to tailor their campaigns to the domestic market; it was wholly logical that marketers would now extol the native virtues of Russian and so-called Russian products, and they became increasingly associated with propositions about Russian national identity.

The name *Shok* is one of the most important linguistic devices for impacting on viewers/readers and therefore has transferable meanings. *Shok* carries connotations of Russianness, Russian taste and quality, astonishment and the sudden disturbance of feelings, which are appealing due to the ideal target audience's expectations.

The first advertising campaign started in December 1996. At that time *Shok* was meant to be a Russian chocolate bar, but later the name was to be understood as an abbreviation derived from Sh.O.K 'Chocolate of the best quality'. In 1999 the slogan was changed to *Po-nashemu, éto shok. SH.O.K po-nashemu.* 'In our opinion, this is a shock. Sh.O.K in our way'

In the Shock commercials in 2000 - 2002 a shocking advertising concept was utilized. Examples of this kind of commercial are the Centaur and the Penguins (Appendix, pictures 8-9). The Centaur was shot in a stable. The main character is a teenage girl passing by a stall where a handsome young man is looking at her. The girl looks very flattered, but her delight changes to shock when she looks down at the feet of the young man and realizes that the young man is a centaur. Incidentally, it seems to be characteristic for *Shok* commercials that girls have minor roles. When they appear, it is in ways that reinforce the stereotypical image of women. Images suggest that girls are involved in different personal leisure spaces than those inhabited by boys. The centaur seems to appeal to girls interested in riding.

In the Penguins commercial, a teenage boy with curly hair and big eyeglasses is returning home from school. Entering the kitchen, he hears a strange noise, which comes from walking penguins. They have been in the kitchen and left behind an empty refrigerator. The boy is numb with shock. This is the concept of the slogan: *Shock is in our way.*

In 2003, Nestlé started a new brand-building campaign for *Shok.* The campaign was labeled 'shock therapy' (Appendix, picture 10). The first thing the viewer notices in this commercial is the group of three boys standing before an open door, and looking at a woman. She is apparently the mother of the boy, who is trying to see behind the back of the mother at the door. One of the boys has a football. It implies that the boys have come to ask him out to play football. Then the scene shifts inside the flat.

The boy was not given permission to join his friends, perhaps because he has not done his homework. The boy starts rapping and inviting people to join his campaign.

The concept of therapy implies that the chocolate bar is now something that is comparable with drugs. In the two campaign commercials in our data, consciously local/global images were used, symbolized by the prominence of teenage boys and the variation of the slogan: *Shok - terapiya po-nashemu.* 'Shok-therapy in our way'. The rap formula itself suggests certain feelings, conditions and actions. The boy's rapping creates an emotional ambience that draws addressees of his age into the commercial and evokes common feelings about boring everyday life. The boredom is wrapped in a musical folklore to provide stimuli for the body and mind. The function of the rap is to establish a bond of concern and sympathy with Russian teenage audiences, to which the message is directed. The music is appealing, since it is the most important leisure pursuit of young people.

The boy's rap performance, combined with his paralinguistic means and direct invitation to join the campaign, identify him to his audience - distinguishing him from others and the comparable commercials of which teens are aware. Thus, the *Shok* commercial delivers a lifelike interactive and memorable experience, and tries to involve the audience in an unfolding story: the chocolate bar has received a new added value since it is like a curative drug to help eliminate problems.

The *Shok* commercial *Z glazom* ′With an eye′ was broadcast in 2004. It begins with a picture of a group of three boys walking on the street. They go into a music store and start to select and pile up compact discs. One of the boys asks the salesperson to pass him a disc, the name of which he has forgotten. The boy tries to describe the label of the compact disc, or how it looks: *Nu, vot takoi* z *glazom.* 'Well, I mean the one with an eye'. The strange-looking salesman turns his back to the boys, bites a bit of Shok, and to the astonishment of the boy, the man transforms into a vision of a blue spirit or ghost rising up above the counter. In this context, the construction *z glazom* 'with an eye' may also connote to a 'bad eye', since the salesman has exceptionally striking eyes. The blue color of the spirit is worth noting: it motivates the impression of coolness. The boy is stunned, but his friend standing by him and eating the chocolate bar comments on the situation while laughing: *Uzhe vspomnil?* 'Do you already recall (the name)? 'The question in this context concerns the name of the disc. But it is also possible to imagine an implication to the brand-name Shok, since the final pictures focus on the slogan of the chocolate bar *Shok - éto po-nashemu.*

In 2004-2005, the format of the *Shok* commercials featured sequences taken by a hidden camera of everyday people caught in hoaxes. Two of this type of commercial were made, scenarios of which are shot in the same kind of setting. In one of this type of 'shocking' commercial, a teenage boy is disguised as a mannequin. While standing at a door to a shop, he starts to play a prank on passers-by. He tricks them when they enter the shop. The idea is that the reactions of the 'victims' make viewers laugh. At the end of the commercial, the slogan *Shok- éto po-nashemu* is voiced (Appendix, picture 11).

The second commercial in this series begins with a shot of a group of boys standing on the street facing a viewer. It is dark, and in the background shines the brand name *Shok* written in big colorful neon letters. After the opening shot, the commercials shift to focus on the boys carrying a panel, with which they block a doorway leaving the real door covered by the fake. The panel is painted to imitate a brick wall. Then the picture moves to ordinary Russian people who, opening the usual outdoor, get upset seeing the 'brick wall' instead of the usual doorway of the house. One of boys takes a bite of *Shok,* and the slogan *Shok - éto po-nashemu* ends the commercial. The commercial displays two opposite reactions: 'our' laugh and 'their' shock. Thus, the shock is caused by the teenagers who tend to be shocking. And the chocolate bar is an intensifying and overarching tool for a communicative message.

In 2005 Nestlé started a new advertising campaign for a chunky *Shok XXL* 'Shock XXL' (Appendix, picture 12). It is a new size of the teen favorite chocolate bar with peanuts. The chocolate bar is a 70 g bar size repacked milk chocolate with a heart in a colorful wrapper. The commercial was created by the Lowe Adventa advertising agency. It appeals to young men with an active lifestyle. It was shot at a basketball park in Moscow using new technology and stuntmen to create graphical monkey-like characters in part of the commercial. The slogan is modified into the form *Bol'shoj Shok sposoben na mnogoe, Bol'shoj Shok - éto po-nashemu!* 'Big Shok has a capacity for many things. Big Shok - in our way'. The intended shocking message is to the urban target audience, i.e. urban teenage boys. The last commercial for *Shok XXL* is supported by a fictional video game, Lara Croft; a Russian version of the English-speaking character and the heroine of the *Tomb Raider* series of video games, movies and comic books. The videogame is created by Lowe Adventa, Zenith Optimedia and EnterMedia.

Besides contributing added values to the chocolate bar and to the Russian consumer market, the 'shock' campaigns have intensified current formative practices in Russian culture and language. The slogan *Shok – éto po-nashemu* has become one of the most popular idioms in colloquial language. The familiar and newly coined term “shocking slayer” composes a particularly vivid snapshot of contemporary Russian values.

The Shok logo has been used to occupy a distinctive and desirable place in the minds of target teenagers. But at the same time, the consumer image of teenagers seemed to become more euphoric, and as a result advertising campaigns had to be changed to meet potential teenage aspirations. According to an all-Russian public opinion poll, young people value individualism and commercialism, which is assumed to be a normal reaction to the changing socio-political conditions in the country. Practically all the respondents surveyed said the values and goals of today's young people are very different from the ideals and goals of the young people of the 1970s and 1980s: "They all want to be millionaires". "Their main goal now is material well-being". "They want to live without financial problems". According to Pollay's (1983) and Hoftede's (1980, 1991, 2001) dimensions of cultural values, the Shok commercials in 2000-2002 emphasize belonging to the teenage group, differentiating Shok from its competitors, and suggesting that *Shok* will provide enjoyment, relaxation and miraculous effects.

The development of the slogan is as follows: 1) Sh.O.K 'Chocolate of the best quality', 2) *Shok - éto po nashemu* 'Shok - this in our way', 3) *Po-nashemu, éto shok. SH.O.K po-nashemu.* 'In our opinion, this is a shock. Sh.O.K in our way' 4) *Shok - terapiya po-nashemu.* 'Shok-therapy in our way', 5) Shok XXL. *Bol′shoj Shok sposoben na mnogoe. Bol′shoj Shok - éto po-nashemu!* 'Shock XXL. Big Shok has a capacity for many things. Big Shok - in our way'. The commercials related to the reviewed Shok chocolate bar can be found in the Appendix.

Table 3 summarizes the appeals found in the twelve commercials reviewed commercials. Three to eight appeals could be identified from the reviewed commercials. In total 10 various appeals could be identified in at least one of the six commercials reviewed commercials. The four key appeals from those by Pollay (1983) were: distinctive, youth, relaxation, and enjoyment. The commercials of *Shok* chocolate bar also contained appeals relating to community, adventure, and magic. The study by Albers (1994) included 11 countries, and the country samples indicated 1.83 to 3.16 appeals on average in Brazil, Mexico, and France; 5.02 in the USA; and even 15.38 in

Chile and 15.53 in Finland. Thus, the results of this study indicated an amount that was in the middle of those samples. The common existence of relaxation and enjoyment appeals in both commercials, and the community appeal in all three commercials related to *Shok*, was according to the expectations. But the other results were more against expectations. The greatest difference in the expectations and appeals found were perhaps among appeals related to the uncertainty avoidance dimension. The results of this study provide more support to the score values by Naumov and Puffer (2000) than those by Hofstede (2001), at least related to the uncertainty avoidance dimension of culture.

**Table 3**. Results of the study (for the ads see Appendix). **

| OFSTEDE'S DIMENSIONS | IDV | PDI | UAI | MAS | LTO | NUTS | | | | | | | SHOK | | | | |
|---|---|---|---|---|---|---|---|---|---|---|---|---|---|---|---|---|---|
| | | | | | | 2000-2001 | | 2002-2004 | | 2005-2006 | | | 2000-2002 | | 2003-2005 | | 2006 |
| | | | | | | 1 | 2 | 3 | 4 | 5 | 6 | 7 | 8 | 9 | 10 | 11 | 12 |
| Distinctive | + | | | | | | | x | x | x | x | x | x | x | x | x | x |
| *Freedom* | + | | | | | | | | | | | | | | | | |
| Independence | + | | | | | | | | | | | | | | | | |
| **Popular** | - | | | | | | | | | | | | | | | | |
| **Succorance** | - | | | | | | | | | | | | | | | | |
| **Family** | - | | | | | | | | | | | | | | | | |
| **Community** | - | | | | | | | | | | | | x | x | x | x | x |
| **Affiliation** | - | | | | | | | | | | | | | | | | |
| **Ornamental** | | + | | | | | | | | | | | | | | | |
| **Dear** | | + | | | | | | | | | | | | | | | |
| **Vain** | | + | | | | | | | | | | | | | | | |
| **Status** | | + | | | | | | | | | | | | | | | |
| ***Healthy*** | | + | | | | | | | | | | | | | | | |
| ***Sexuality*** | | + | | | | | | | | x | x | x | | | | | |
| Cheap | | - | | | | | | | | | | | | | | | |
| Humility | | - | | | | | | | | | | | | | | | |

| | | | | | | | | | | | | | | | | | |
|---|---|---|---|---|---|---|---|---|---|---|---|---|---|---|---|---|---|
| *Wisdom* | | - | | | | | | | | | | | | | | | |
| *Morality* | | - | | | | | | | | | | | | | | | |
| Nurturance | | - | | | | | | x | x | x | x | x | | | | | |
| **Safety** | | | + | | | | | | | | | | | | | | |
| **Tamed** | | | + | | | | | | | | | | | | | | |
| ***Neat*** | | | + | | | | | | | | | | | | | | |
| Casual | | | - | | | | | | | | | | | | | | |
| Adventure | | | - | | | | | | | | | | x | x | x | x | x |
| Untamed | | | - | | | | | | | | | | | | | | |
| Magic | | | - | | | | | | | | | | x | x | x | x | x |
| Youth | | | - | | | x | x | x | x | x | x | x | x | x | x | x | x |
| Effective | | | | + | | | | | | | | | | | | | |
| Durable | | | | + | | | | | | | | | | | | | |
| Convenient | | | | + | | | | | | | | | | | | | |
| Security | | | | + | | | | | | | | | | | | | |
| Productivity | | | | + | | | | | | | | | | | | | |
| ***Relaxation*** | | | | - | | x | x | x | x | x | x | x | x | x | x | x | x |
| ***Enjoyment*** | | | | - | | x | x | x | x | x | x | x | x | x | x | x | x |
| **Frail** | | | | - | | | | | | | | | | | | | |
| **Natural** | | | | - | | | | | | | | | | | | | |
| **Modesty** | | | | - | | | | | | | | | | | | | |

| | | | | | | | | | | | | | | | | | |
|---|---|---|---|---|---|---|---|---|---|---|---|---|---|---|---|---|---|
| **Plain** | | | | - | | | | | | | | | | | | | |
| *Traditional* | | | | | + | | | | | | | | x | x | | | |
| Mature | | | | | + | | | | | | | | | | | | |
| *Modern* | | | | | + | | | | | | | | | | | | |
| *Technological* | | | | | + | | | | | | | | | | | | |
| No appeals | | | | | - | | | | | | | | | | | | |

**Lack of agreement on the hypothesized relationship between appeals with cursive and the cultural dimension. Appeals expected to be identified based on scores of Russia on Hofstede's dimensions are bolded.

## Summary and Discussion

The aim of this study was to analyze television advertising in Russia, especially the use of different types of appeals in commercials by employing the list of 42 appeals by Pollay (1983) and relations with the five cultural dimensions by Hofstede (1980, 1991, 2001) as the framework. Since there have been a lot of changes in Russia and the score values for the cultural dimensions by Hofstede are very different in the study by Naumov and Puffer (2000), one goal in the study was to compare the results with both score values. An exploratory research approach was used to apply the framework to the analysis of twelve commercials by the case company, Nestlé, during the period 2000-2006. Television was selected as the advertising medium, because of its central role in Russian media. The advertised product was a chocolate bar and the brands selected were *Nuts* - an international brand - and *Shok* - a local brand.

According to the results in earlier studies (e.g. De Pelsmacker & Van den Bergh, 1998) irritation caused by television ads is common. The level of irritation can usually be lowered by using warm, humorous, lively and dynamic ads with music and creative execution.

Several of these recommendations were followed in the reviewed ads. Based on the dimensions by Hofstede (1980, 1991, 2001) the score values for Russia indicated high power distance, and uncertainty avoidance values, and low individualism, and masculinity values. Based on those score values, the existence of certain specific advertising appeals among the appeals by Pollay were those which could be expected.

Furthermore, taking into account the target group - young people - in the empirical part of the study, the product, i.e. the chocolate bar, and the advertising medium, the values relaxation, enjoyment, youth, and sound were according to the expectations and typical features in the commercials. The results gave support to the expectation of the existence of clever humor, which is typical to the Russian character. The sounds used in the commercials were global. No celebrities were found. Regarding the *Shok* commercials, it was typical that the name of the product was written in Cyrillic. Three to eight appeals could be identified from the reviewed data. In total, 10 various appeals could be identified in at least one of the twelve commercials reviewed. The four key appeals from those presented by Pollay (1983) were revealed: distinctive, youth, relaxation, and enjoyment. Concerning the commercials for the *Shok* chocolate bar, the appeals community, adventure, and magic were also identified. The study by Albers (1994) included 11 countries and the country samples indicated two to three appeals on average in Brazil, Mexico, and France, five in the USA, and even some 15 in Chile and Finland. Thus, the results of this study indicated an amount that was in the middle of those samples. The greatest difference in the expectations and appeals found were perhaps among appeals related to the uncertainty avoidance dimension. The results of this study provide more support to the score values by Naumov and Puffer (2000) than those by Hofstede (2001) for the four original cultural dimensions by Hofstede (1980).

The limitation of this study is that the study focused on a limited amount of commercials from one case company and all the 12 commercials selected were targeted at young people. Furthermore, the analysis was mainly made by one researcher familiar with Russian culture. So, one cannot make any generalizations. However, there are perspectives for future research. First, the data of the commercials could be expanded to other brands of the case company. Second, brands of other chocolate manufacturers (foreign and domestic) operating on the Russian market could also be included. Third, future studies could be focused on other fast moving consumer goods and other types of products. Fourth, future studies could be expanded to cover both television and print commercials and focus on comparative studies of advertising media. Fifth, research could be conducted by comparing television and/or print commercials for chocolate bars (and other consumer products) in Russia versus other CEE and/or West European countries. Sixth, this research did not focus on consumer attitudes and effectiveness of the ads. Thus, one interesting topic would also be the comparison of the various ads by Nestle combined with the attitude and effectiveness analysis of the ads by their competitors. Finally, Albers (1994) and Albers-Miller and Gelb (1996) could not connect clearly twelve of the original 42 appeals to any of the dimensions of culture by Hofstede (1980, 2001) and the latter one of those studies (more a summary of the first study) did not include the LTO dimension of culture. As the results of this study indicated four of the above referred twelve appeals (sex, relaxation, enjoyment, and traditional) could be identified from the reviewed 12 ads by Nestlé. Therefore further analysis of the relations between the all 42 appeals and all five dimensions of culture by Hofstede is clearly needed.

## References

Albers, N. (1994). *Relating Hofstede's Dimensions of Culture to International Variations in Print Advertisements: A Comparison of Appeals*. Ann Arbor. (Doctoral Dissertation at the University of Houston, USA)

Albers-Miller, N. & B. Gelb (1996). Business Advertising Appeals as a Mirror of Cultural Dimensions: A Study of Eleven Countries. *Journal of Advertising* 25(4), 69-82.

AllNews (2002), Home page. Retrieved [05.09.2002] from http://www.allnews.ru/economy/2002/03/15/tvad/

Andrews, J., S. Durvasula and R. Netemeyer (1994). Testing the corss-national applicability of U.S. and Russian advertising belief and attitude measures. *Journal of Advertising* 23(1), 71-82.

Bhatia, T. K. (2000), *Advertising in Rural India: Language, Marketing, Communication and Consumerism*. Tokyo, Tokyo University of Foreign Studies.

BOEFIT (1999), Russian Economy – *The Month in Review. Yearbook 1999*. Bank of Finland, Institute for Economics in Transition. Retrieved [03.02.2007] from http://www.bof.fi/bofit/fin/4ruec/ypdf/re1999.pdf.

Bollinger, D. (1994). The four cornerstones and three pillars in the "House of Russia" management system. *Journal of Management Development* 13(2), 49-54.

Boym, S. (1994). A Strange Hybrid. In *Boston Review*, February/March. Retrieved (24.4.2006) from http://bostonreview.net/BR19.1/boym.html.

Church, N. (1992). Advertising in the Eastern Bloc: current practices and anticipated avenues of development. *Journal of Global Marketing* 5(3), 109-129.

Cheng, H. & J. Schweitzer (1996). Cultural Values Reflected in Chinese and U.S. Television Commercials. *Journal of Advertising Research*, May-June, 27-45.

De Mooij, M. (2005). *Global Marketing and Advertising. Understanding Cultural Paradoxes*. Sage Publications 2nd edition.

De Pelsmacker, P. & J Van den Bergh (1998). Advertising Content and Irritation: A Study of 226 TV Commercials. *Journal of International Consumer Marketing* 10(4), 5-27.

De Pelsmacker, P.., D. Maison and M. Geuens (2002). Emotional and Rational Advertising Messages in Positive and Negative Polish Media Contexts. In "New Directions in International Advertising Research" ed. C. Taylor pp. 121-135, *Advances in International Marketing* Vol. 12. Elsevier, JAI Press.

Dianoux,C., T. Domanski and J.-L. Herrmann (2000). Comparative advertising in Central and Eastern Europe: The Case of Poland. *Proceedings of the 8th Annual Conference on Marketing Strategies for Central and Eastern Europe*, Vienna, Austria, December 2000, eds. P. Chadraba & R. Springer.

Dianoux, C. K. Kettnerova and Z. Linhart (2006). Advertising in Czech and French Magazines. *Journal of Euromarketing* 16(1/2), 139-152.

Ettenson, R. (1993). Brand Name and Country of Origin Effects in the Emerging Market Economies of Russia, Poland and Hungary. *International Marketing Review* 10(5), 14-36.

Grineberg, T. E. and M.V. Petrushenko (2002). *Reklama: kul'turnyi kontekst*. Moskva, RIP-Holding.

Heyder, H., K. Musiol and K. Peters (1992). Advertising in Europe – attitudes towards advertising in certain key East and West European countries. *Marketing and Research Today* 20(1), 58-68.

Hofstede, G (1980). *Culture's Consequences. International differences in work-related values*. Sage Publications: Beverly Hills, California.

—. (1991). *Culture's and oranizations: Software of the mind*. McGraw-Hill: London.

—. (2001). *Culture's Consequences. Comparing Values, Behaviors, Institutions, and Organizations Across Nations*. 2nd edition. Sage Publications: Thousand Oaks, California.

Holak, S., A. Matveev & W. Havlena (2007). Nostalgia in post-socialist Russia: Exploring applications to advertising strategy. *Journal of Business Research* 60, 649-655.

Khairullahd, D. & Z. Khairullah (2002). Dominant Cultural Values: Content Analysis of the U.S. and Indian Print Advertising. *Journal of Global Marketing* 16(1/2), 47-70.

Kotin, M. (2005), "*Paradoksal'naia desiatka*", retrieved [13.03.2007] from http://sovetnik.ru/konkurs /places/raso2/?id=171&type=view.

Kommersant'(2007). *Shveitsarskii kontsern Nestle perestroit svoi biznes v Rossii*. Retrieved (02.03.2007) from www.kommersant.ru/content.html.

Morris, J. (2005). The Empire Strikes Back: Projections of National Identity in Contemporary Russian Advertising. *The Russian Review* 64, 642-660.

Mueller, B. (1987). Reflections of Culture: An Analysis of Japanese and American Advertising Appeals. Journal of Advertising Research, June-July, 51-59.

Naumov, A. & S. Puffer (2000). Measuring Russian Culture using Hofstede's Dimensions. Applied Psychology 49(4), 709-718.

Omelchenko, E. & U. Bliudina (2002). On the Outside Looking In? The Place of Youth in Russia's New Media and Information Space. In "*Looking West? Cultural Globalization and Russian Youth Cultures*", eds. H. Pilkington, E. Omelchenko, M. Flynn, U. Bliudina & E. Starkova, pp. 21-49. Pensylvania State University Press: Pensylvania.

Orkla (2006). Orkla Strengthens Its Presence in the Russian Chocolate Market. Retrieved from http://www.orklafoods.com/eway/default.aspx?pid=272&trg=MainLeft -5664&MainLeft -5664=5590:16707:-:0:5667:7:::0:0.

Orth, U., H. Koenig & Z. Firbasove (2007). Cross-national differences in consumer response to the framing of advertising messages. An exploraty comparison from Central Europe. *European Journal of Marketing* 41(3/4), 327-348.

Pesonen, A. (1997). On Values in Russian Advertisements. In: Studia Slavic Finlandensia "*Ocenka y sovremennom russkom jazyke. Sbornik statej*" ed. N. Baschmakoff and E. Hellberg-Hirn, pp. 121-134. Helsinki, Venäjän ja Itä-Euroopan Instituutti

Pesonen, A. and V. Namsaraev (1996). Venäläinen mainosteksti (Russian advertising text). In "*Erikoiskielet ja käännösteoria. VAKKI-symposiumi XVI*, Vöyri 10.-11.2.1996. pp. 206-225. Vaasa, Vaasan ammattikielten tutkijaryhmän julkaisuja nr. 21.

Pollay, R. (1983). Measuring the Cultural Values Manifest in Advertising. In "*Current Issues and Research in Advertising*" eds. J. Leigh and C. Martin, pp. 71-92. Michigan University Press: Michigan.

Rossiia shokolad (2007), Home page, retrieved [15.03.2007] from http://www.rossiachoco.ru/products.asp?fuin=12.

Taylor, C. (2005). Moving International Advertising Research Forward. A New Research Agenda. *Journal of Advertising* 34(1), 7-16.

Taylor, C., P. Bonner and M. Dolezal (2002). Advertising in the Czech Republic: Czech Perceptions of Effective Advertising Clutter. In "New Directions in International Advertising Research" ed. C. Taylor pp. 137-149, *Advances in International Marketing* Vol. 12. Elsevier, JAI Press.

Trendbox (1995), Onderzoek naar reklame acceptatie en reklame irritatie. Internal report (project 15013). Amsterdam, Trendbox Market Research.

Tse, D., R. Belk and N. Zou (1989). Becoming a consumer society: A longitudinal and cross-cultural content analysis of print ads from Hong

Kong, the People´s Republic of China and Taiwan. *Journal of Consumer Research*, 15 (4), 457-472.

Typpö, A. (2007) Venäjä suitsii mainontaa. *Taloussanomat* 17.01.2007, p. 13-15.

United Nations (2007). *World Investment Report 2007. Transnational Corporations, Extractived Industries and Development*. Unctad: New York and Geneva.

Van Herpen, E., R. Pieters, J. Fidrmucove and P. Rosenboom (2000). The information content of magazine advertising in market and transition economies. *Journal of Consumer Policy* 23, 257-283.

Vovk, E. (2006). Population Poll, TV Advertising, 09.03.2006. Retrieved (12.03.2007) from http://bd.english.fom.ru/report/cat/az/T/ televidenie/ed061023.

Weinberger, M. & C. Gulas (1992). The Impact of Humor in Advertising: A Review. Journal of Advertising 21(4), 35-59.

West, S. (1998). The Material Promised Land: Advertising´s Modern Agenda in Late Imperial Russia. *The Russian Review* 57, 345-363.

Willmer, Karen (2007). Russia becomes a key market for Barry Callebaut. [03.02.2007] from http://www.confectionerynews.com/news/printNewsBis.asp?id=79864

Zou, S. (2005). Contributions to International Advertising Research. An Assessment of the Literature Between 1990 and 2002. *Journal of Advertising* 34(1), 99-110.

## Appendix: Commercials for Nuts and Shok

### Nuts 2000 – 2001

### Nuts 2002 -2004.

### Nuts 2005 – 2006

http://www.coloribus.com/paedia/reels/2006/7/18/504557/

## Shok 2000 – 2002

## Shok 2003 -2005

http://www.adme.ru/paedia/search/?q=%D1%88%D0%BE%D0%BA
http://www.sostav.ru/video/0/16/25/3/

## Shok 2006

http://www.reklam-film.ru/249.htm

# References

## Nuts

1. Commercials for ”Nuts” (Appendix, pictures 1-7) http://www.coloribus.com/paedia/reels/2006/7/18/504557/
2. Shokolad ”Nuts” http://www.showreel.ru/reels/636
3. Shokolad ”Nuts”, Krepkij oreshek. http://www.showreel.ru/reels/187
4. Nuts 2, Orech – eto uspech, http://www.showreel.ru/reels/3289
5. Nuts "Экзамен", Zarjadi mozgi, jesli oni jest, http://www.showreel.ru/reels/1242
6. Nuts "Клубничка", Zakroi glazki, otkroj rotikNuts, Orech – eto uspech, http://www.showreel.ru/reels/3288

## Shok

1. Commercials for “SHOK” (Appendix, pictures, 8-10), http://www.adme.ru/paedia/search/?q=%D1%88%D0%BE%D0%BA
2. Commercials for “SHOK” (Appendix, picture 11), http://www.sostav.ru/video/0/16/25/3/
3. Commercials for “SHOK” (Appendix, picture 12), http://www.reklam-film.ru/249.htm
4. Pingviny, http://adme.ru/paedia/search/?q=%D0%A8%D0%9E%D0%9A
5. Zvezdy na nebe, http://adme.ru/paedia/search/?q=%D0%A8%D0%9E%D0%9A
6.Konyushnya, http://adme.ru/paedia/search/?q=%D0%A8%D0%9E%D0%9A
7. My odin vo vselennoj, http://adme.ru/paedia/search/?q=%D0%A8%D0%9E%D0%9A
8. Glavnoe tolpani ne khodit´, http://adme.ru/paedia/search/?q=%D0%A8%D0%9E%D0%9A
9. Napryagi doma, v shole dostali, http://adme.ru/paedia/search/?q=%D0%A8%D0%9E%D0%9A
10. Shok- éto po-nashemu, http://www.sostav.ru/video/0/16/0/3/11. Shokolad Shok «Z glazom», http://www.showreel.ru/index.php?search_query=%D8%EE%EA&gid=search&eng=0
12. Shok XXL - Éto po-nashemu, http://www.showreel.ru/reels/3949http:/

# Time-Trend Patterns in Advertising Expenditure for Central, Eastern and Other European Countries

Vesna Zabkar and Katarina Kosmelj

## Abstract

As a general rule, the more developed an economy the more advertising plays a role of »oiling the economic engine«. The aim of our paper is to reveal different time-trend patterns in the ratio of advertising expenditure and gross domestic product for 28 Central, Eastern and other European countries in the 1994-2004 period. Two multidimensional statistical approaches: cluster analysis of time-varying data and multidimensional scaling, resulted in four clusters of CEE countries with similar trend patterns: awakening countries, stable countries, catching-up countries and the leading cluster. Results should assist in country segmentation and understanding of the advertising industry's dynamics in CEE.

## Introduction

The advertising industry is an important component of the economic activities of a certain country. In the 1980s, reliable data on total advertising expenditure in international advertising activities were lacking since measurements with any degree of accuracy were difficult from the statistical point of view (Advertising Statistics, 1985). In the 1990s data already became available through World Advertising Research Centre (WARC), ZenithOptimedia, Euromonitor and the World Association of Newspapers. The data is compared based on purchasing-power parities (PPPs), which should remove the distorting effects of exchange rate fluctuations and equalise the effective purchasing power of currencies.

European countries account for around one-quarter of the total global advertising spending (European Adspend Trends, 2005). European advertising expenditure rose steadily in the 1980s and early 1990s as a result of healthy economic growth and a higher level of liberalisation (Howard, 1998). As the economy and deregulation slowed down in the early 1990s, the growth rates were modest compared to the record growth seen in the mid-1980s. A peak in 2000 due to heavy investments by technology and new media firms was followed by a period of relative stagnation and decline. More recent years have brought about a relatively fragile economic recovery in the region that has been susceptible to the effects of higher oil prices and other factors impacting on consumer and business confidence (Macleod, 2006).

Advertising expenditure is connected to the development stage of an economy (Howard, 1998). Aggregate advertising expenditures differ among different countries with the following main factors being relevant (Jones, 2000): size of the buying population (number of inhabitants); economic development, and the extent of competitive activities in the branded products and services sector. For Central and Eastern European countries where competition for branded products is a more recent phenomenon, this ratio between total adverting expenditure and GDP is on average lower than for Western European countries. Leff and Farley (1980) argued that in developing markets a higher advertising intensity would help companies reinforce their competitive position. The transition to market-oriented economies in developing countries should be connected to the growth of modern marketing practices (Chan and Cui, 2004).

Our study is based on advertising expenditure and gross domestic product for 28 Central and Eastern European as well as Western European countries. The aim is to investigate different time-trend patterns in the ratio of advertising expenditure over GDP in Europe and mostly to identify countries with similar patterns over time. As a practical implication the study should reveal dynamics of advertising spending and assist in country segmentation for international marketing purposes.

This paper is divided into three sections. In the first section we lay the theoretical foundations for the paper and present the research question. Next, the methodology for classifying the countries into different groups is discussed. Finally, the country clusters thereby obtained are discussed, as are the limitations and directions for future research.

## Theory and Research Question

As a general rule, the more developed an economy the more advertising plays a role of »oiling the economic engine« (Jones, 2000). Growth in production capacities (greater possibilities of added value) leads to an increase of income per capita and enables higher levels of living. Advertising builds preferences and informs about the benefits of different brands. With fewer new customers entering the market, companies use advertising as an important weapon in the battle to increase their market shares (Turnbull and Doherty-Wilson, 1990).

Kshetri et al. (2007) focused their research on the impact of supply-side factors on company advertising spending: the level of economic development, foreign direct investment and an orientation towards democracy. They found that the drivers of advertising spending in the new EU countries are the income level and the inflow of foreign direct investment. However, no country-specific explanation is presented in their study.

The discussion of how national differences between different countries affect advertising expenditures is limited. Picard (2001) investigated the relationship between advertising expenditure and GDP for nine developed countries between 1989 and 1994. His important finding was that the relations between advertising expenditure and GDP differed across both countries and media. Advertising expenditure choices are affected by the nature of the economy, the degree of economic fluctuation, and national economic policies. A correlation analysis between advertising expenditure and GDP was applied. He found evidence of long-term relations between national economic performance and advertising as well as between national economic performance and consumer expenditures. Time trend patterns and similarities in patterns in advertising spending were not included in the study.

Much research into advertising spending has been developed in the area of the relative constancy of advertising spending, assuming the existence of a constant relationship between advertising spending and income. The original formulation of the principle of relative constancy (PRC) is attributed to McCombs (1972:10): 'The level of spending on mass media by consumers and advertisers is determined by the general state of the economy. Any change in the level of the economy causes parallel change in spending on mass media'. The statement was later empirically supported for the relationship between mass media spending and the general economy (McCombs and Eyal, 1980, McCombs and Nolan, 1992, Dupagne, 1994, 1997).

Yet the principle of relative constancy (PRC) has been criticised for being limited in its theoretical foundations. Lacy and Noh (1997) pointed to the absence of economic theory in the PRC research, along with the imprecision of the terms used and measurement problems. They argued that most articles about the principle of relative constancy have used empirical methods to test it without addressing the associated theoretical problems. Existing PRC studies have mostly focused on consumer spending instead of advertisers' spending. Advertisers' spending reflects the ability of the mass media to participate in the advertising market and reveals the economic mechanisms of the mass media much more than consumer spending (Chang and Chan-Olmsted, 2005).

In their study, Chang and Chan-Olmsted (2005) analyse the relative constancy of advertising spending across 70 nations over time (1991-2001). They focus on the relationship between advertising spending and GDP. They find that PRC seems to be more apparent in developed nations. In their dynamic analysis they test the time-trend proposition of PRC, whether advertising spending was constant over time and across the total set of included countries. However, time-trend patterns and similarities in patterns of advertising spending for different countries were not included in the study.

It is necessary to expand the analysis in order to better understand the dynamics of the advertising spending phenomena. Our study attempts to identify different time-trends patterns in advertising expenditures (AD) for several European countries for a longer time period. Our basic research question is the following:

*RQ: Which Central, Eastern and other European countries have similar time-trend patterns in the ratio of advertising expenditure to gross domestic product over time?*

## Methodology and Analysis

Our study examines advertising expenditure and gross domestic product data for 28 Central, Eastern and other European countries in the 1994-2004 period. The number of countries (28) and the 11-year period correspond to the largest data matrix for which the data were available (Euromonitor, 2006).

The original data is presented in local currency and current prices and are therefore not directly comparable over time and over countries. To harmonise the data, we considered advertising expenditures on a relative scale as the ratio of advertising expenditures (AD) to gross domestic product (GDP), which is an internationally recognized standard for measuring national economic activity. The derived variable represents the percentage of AD in GDP, denoted by AD/GDP %.

Advertising expenditure at the country level includes the aggregate value of advertising expenditure in the press (newspapers and magazines), television, radio, outdoor and cinema. Different European countries differ in their advertising expenditure components (Euromonitor, 2006): advertising agency commission, classified ads, discounts and production costs. Although there is no uniform view of aggregate advertising expenditure, it is vital for our analysis that the components of the expenditure remain in an aggregate number over the whole of the investigated period. We calculated the ratio AD/GDP % for each country; hence 28 time-series of length 11 were the inputs for our statistical analysis.

To meet our research objectives we applied two multivariate statistical approaches: cluster analysis and multivariate scaling. Several clustering methods and ordinal multidimensional scaling were used to identify different time patterns in AD/GDP % for the 28 countries under study. The analysis was performed using the programmes R 2.4 and SPSS 14.0.

## Results

The time series of interest for each country is the percentage of advertising expenditure relative to gross national product (AD/GDP %). These values range from 0.059% (for Russia in 1994) to 2.42% (for Cyprus in 2004), whereas the median is 0.759%.

The results obtained by different clustering methods identified four clusters; the results for different methods were identical except for Greece, which joined either Cluster 3 or Cluster 4. Ordinal multidimensional scaling visualized the clustering results in a two-dimensional space (see Figure 1).

**Figure 1: Two-dimensional scatter plot of countries obtained by ordinal multidimensional scaling.**

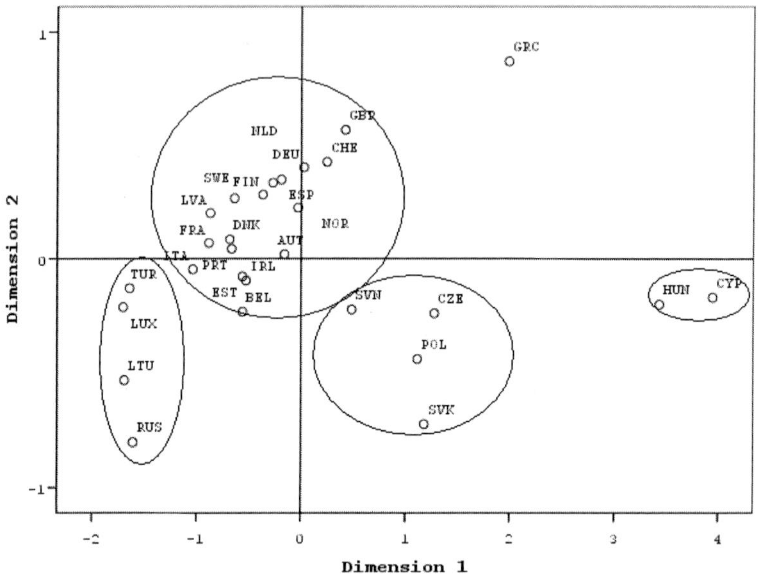


The clusters are allocated along the *x*-axis, 'Cluster 1' is on the left, followed by 'Cluster 2' and 'Cluster 3', 'Cluster 4' on the right, however Greece is allocated far-off. A simple linear regression of the time series within a particular cluster allowed for a meaningful explanation of the cluster's characteristics. The results are summarized in Table 1. The intercept is significantly different from zero for all four clusters; the slope is positive and significant in all clusters except in 'Cluster 2' where a non-significant slope was detected.

**Table 1: Results of the linear regression for clusters obtained by Ward's method.**

| Cluster | Members | Intercept | Slope | Comment |
|---|---|---|---|---|
| 1 | Lithuania, Luxembourg, Russia, Turkey | 0.293*** | 0.024*** | Very slow growth from a very low intercept. |
| 2 | Austria, Belgium, Denmark, Estonia, Finland, France, Germany, Ireland, Italy, Latvia+, Netherlands, Norway, Portugal, Spain, Sweden, Switzerland, United Kingdom | 0.745*** | 0.005 | No growth from a medium intercept. |
| 3 | Czech Republic, Greece++, Poland, Slovakia, Slovenia | 0.515*** | 0.099*** | Intensive growth from a low intercept. |
| 4 | Hungary, Cyprus | 0.998*** | 0.122*** | Very intensive growth from a high intercept. |

**Note: the intercept presents the predicted value for AD/GDP % in 1994, while the slope indicates the average change per year.**

**Legend:** *** $p<0.001$

+ Data for Latvia for 1998-2004

++ Data for Greece for 1996-2004

## Discussion

A deeper insight into time-trend patterns in advertising expenditures for the countries under study reveals several interesting issues. In 'Cluster 1' we observe a very low starting point (0.3%) and the ten-year growth of 0.2%; hence the percentage of AD in GDP increased from 0.3% in 1994 to 0.5% in 2004. The four countries (Lithuania, Luxembourg, Russia, and Turkey) can be characterised by a slow change from a very low starting point. This cluster incorporates the 'awakening countries'. Lithuania as a representative country of this segment seems to have low levels of advertising industry development (Manrai et al., 2001) and is classified as less attractive in its overall evaluation. Chang and Chan-Olmsted (2005) put these countries in the same group of countries that passed the time-trend[1] in their PRC analysis.

'Cluster 2' incorporates 17 countries where AD presents about 0.7% of GDP and is constant throughout the 1994-2004 period. The cluster members are the most developed European Union countries along with two Baltic countries. The main cluster characteristic is that PRC holds. This cluster consists of the 'stable countries'. This segment is in line with Chang and Chan-Olmsted's (2005) conclusion that PRC seems to be more apparent in developed nations. Latvia appears in this group of countries as a surprise since its advertising spending per capita does not exceed EUR 70, with advertising spending occurring predominantly in the print media. The reason could be attributed to the fact that earlier years saw extremely high growth in advertising spending (similarly to Estonia in Ilić, 2000), which were followed with more stability, whereas the data from the earlier period were excluded due to changes in the methodology.

In 'Cluster 3' we observe intensive growth from 0.5% in 1994 to 1.5% in 2004. These five countries (Czech Republic, Greece, Poland, Slovakia, and Slovenia) were candidates to join the European Union in the period under study, Greece joined the EU in 2001 and the others followed in 2004. The main characteristic of the cluster is 'intensive growth from a low starting point'. This cluster consists of 'catching-up countries'. These results are in line with Kshetri et al. (2007) where the marginal effect of income on advertising is significantly higher in new EU member countries than in old EU countries. The majority of these countries did not pass any test in the Chang and Chan-Olmsted (2005) study.

Advertising spending in Poland as a representative country in Cluster 3 experienced high growth in the examined period (Ilić, 1999). Large MNCs brought several new brands into the market and several Polish advertisers were stronger after privatization. New categories of advertisers developed in the financial sector (pension funds), insurance, telecommunications and automobile industry. Media development attributed more importance to TV (Malkowska-Szozda, 1999).

Greece experienced the deregulation of its TV and radio media and increased the penetration in retail and services sectors by international companies in the examined period. Advertising expenditure increased 75-fold from 1971 to 1989 and almost tripled as a percentage of GNP. It is important for our study that Greece has traditionally been influenced by the economic and business climate in Eastern Europe and has been a major trading partner of countries from there (Kouremenos and Avlanitis, 1995).

Cluster 4 has the highest starting point (1%) and the highest growth in the ten-year period (1.2 %). The two countries, Cyprus and Hungary, were very propulsive and had very intensive growth from the highest starting point. This cluster is the 'leading cluster'. Hungary as a representative of this cluster has, according to Manrai et al. (2001), the most developed advertising industry and is rated highly. Ilić (1998) pointed to an increasing share of electronic media in advertising spending as a consequence of the development of TV and radio as well as the media strategies of large MNCs and relative increases in the prices of print media advertising. In 1990-1994 Hungary was marked by a rise of free print media, Western-style advertising and marketing, and limited public relations. In spite of political developments, press, advertising and professional public relations practices seem to be taking hold in the business sector (Hiebert, 1994).

For international marketers, country segmentation can assist in marketing strategy decisions. Partitioning countries into homogeneous segments can be performed either on a single dimension or according to multiple economic, political and cultural criteria (Helsen et al., 1993).

The size of the buying population should determine the advertising activities of a specific country. Jones (2000) argued that advertisers seem to spend less to reach a smaller population and approach larger markets more aggressively, with a higher level of advertising spending. There should be significant heterogeneity of ad spending across the countries. Our clusters in this regard group countries of different size and buying population together (Lithuania & Russia in Cluster 1, Hungary and Cyprus in Cluster 4).

It seems that the countries in Clusters 3 and 4 are progressing in the direction of a higher level of media development, availability, fragmentation and, as a consequence, higher media costs per unit. In the more developed countries in Cluster 2, the higher media costs would also be attributed to the fact that they enable advertisers to reach buyers with a higher purchasing power and disposable income.

The extent of competitive activities among brands in the market should enable advertising activities in a specific country. Advertising should enable advertisers to communicate the uniqueness or other benefits of their brands to potential customers. The more competition there is in the market, the greater is the need for differentiation among brands and more demand for advertising space and time. These should lead to increased costs and advertising spending, intensive competition and, again, a higher ratio between advertising spending and GDP.

## Conclusion and Limitations of the Study

This study enquired into whether there are different time patterns of the AD/GDP ratio for 28 Central, Eastern and other European countries in the 1994-2004 period. The answer is affirmative. Further, we investigated which countries have similar patterns across time. Two multidimensional statistical approaches were used for this purpose: cluster analysis and multidimensional scaling, followed by a linear regression analysis of the time series within the clusters.

Cluster analysis was applied to partition countries into homogeneous segments. Such a classification can assist the international marketer in terms of entry and resource allocation (Helsen et al., 1993). There are many applications for which the country segments might be useful. In this paper, the suggestion of Manrai et al. (2001) about undertaking a longitudinal study to reveal patterns of shifts in country clusters was followed.

Certainly, in the development of the country clusters other variables besides advertising spending and gross domestic product can be included to make the analysis more elaborate and insightful. As Manrai et al. (2001) argued, for the international marketer there are several factors that need to be taken into account when deciding which markets to enter: economic, political, legal, competitive and technological environment, the marketing structure and support services.

In line with Cavusgil and Nevin (1981), further limitations of the study involve the reliance on aggregate data. Additional research is needed for an in-depth analysis of the advertising industries in the selected economies. This research analyses the longitudinal pattern of the development of advertising spending. However, it is not based on qualitative interpretive methods such as historical methods (Smith and Lux, 1993). A further investigation and exploratory data analysis of the reasons for homogeneous segments would be needed based on the structure of industrial and service sectors in the economy, structural differences related to changes in advertising expenditures over time, the relationship of foreign trade to advertising expenditure as well as the lagging influences of advertising expenditure on GDP.

## References

Advertising Statistics: Trends in Total Advertising Expenditures in 12 Countries, 1970-1983: Europe, Asia, Africa. *International Journal of Advertising*, Vol. 4 (3): 261-274.

Chang Byeng-Hee and Chan-Olmsted Sylvia M. (2005), "Relative Constancy of Advertising Spending. A Cross-National Examination of Advertising Expenditures and Their Determinants", *Gazette: the international Journal of Communication Studies*, Vol. 67 (4): 339-357.

Chan, T. S. and Cui, G. (2004), "Consumer attitudes toward marketing in a transitional economy: a replication and extension", *Journal of Consumer Marketing*, 21, 10-26.

Dupagne M. (1994), "Testing the relative constancy of mass media expenditures in the United Kingdom", *Journal of media economics,* 7 (3), 1-14.

Dupagne M. (1997), "A theoretical and methodological critique of the principle of relative constancy", *Communication theory,* 7 (1), 53-76.

Euromonitor. World Marketing Data and Statistics. www.euromonitor.com/womdas, 2006.

European Adspend trends (2005), *International Journal of Advertising*, 22, pp.149-152.

Helsen, K., Jedidi, K. & Desarbo, W. S. (1993), "A New Approach to Country Segmentation Utilizing Multinational Diffusion Patterns", *Journal of Marketing*, 57, 60-71.

Hiebert, R. E. (1994), "Advertising and public relations in transition from communism: The case of Hungary, 1989-1994", *Public Relations Review*, 20, 357-369.

Howard (1998), "Survey of European Advertising Expenditure 1980-1996", *International Journal of Advertising*, 17 (1): 115-124.

Ilić Miran (1998), "Prevlada globalnih podjetij", *Marketing magazin*, Ljubljana, 18, 207-208, 38-41.

—. (1999), "Velika rast bo upočasnjena", *Marketing magazin*, Ljubljana, 19, 217, 12-13.

—. (2000), "Čas velike rasti in čas umirjanja", *Marketing magazin*, Ljubljana, 20, 227, 18-19.

Jones John Philip, *International advertising: realities and myths.* Thousand Oaks (CA), London, New Delhi, Sage, 2000.

Kouremenos, A., Avlonitis, G. J. (1995), "The changing consumer in Greece", *International Journal of Research in Marketing*, 12, 435-448.

Kshetri, N., Williamson, N. C. & Schiopu, A. (2007), "Economics and politics of advertising: evidence from the enlarging European Union", *European Journal of Marketing*, 41, 349-366.

Lacy, S. and Noh, G. (1997), "Theory, economics, measurement, and the principle of relative constancy", *Journal of Media Economics*, 10, 3–16.

Leff, N. H. & Farley, J. U. (1980), "Advertising Expenditures in the Developing World", *Journal of International Business Studies*, 11, 64-79.

Macleod Colin (2006), "Global Adspend Prospects", *International Journal of Advertising*, 25 (3), 421-423.

Malkowska-Szozda Agata (1999), "Oglaševalski kolač raste, storitev zaostaja", *Marketing magazin,* Ljubljana, 19, 217, 14.

Manrai, L. A., Manrai, A. K. & Lascu, D.-N. (2001), "A country-cluster analysis of the distribution and promotion infrastructure in Central and Eastern Europe", *International Business Review*, 10, 517-549.

McCombs M.E. (1972), "Mass Media in the Marketplace", *Journalism Monographs* 24.

McCombs M.E., and C.H. Eyal (1980), "Spending on mass media", *Journal for Communications,* 30 (1), 153-8.

McCombs M.E., Nolan J.(1992), "The relative constancy approach to consumer spending for media", *Journal of Media Economics* 5 (3), 43-52.

Picard R.C. (2001), "Effects of recession on advertising expenditures: an Exploratory study of economic downturns in nine developed nations", *Journal of Media Economics*, 14, (1), 1-14.

Turnbull, P. W., Doherty-Wilson, L. (1990), "The Internationalisation of the Advertising Industry", *European Journal of Marketing*, 24, 1, 7-15.

# COUNTRY-OF-ORIGIN EFFECT AND COUNTRY IMAGE: STATE-OF-THE-ART AND RESEARCH NEEDS FOR CEE PRODUCTS AND COUNTRIES

KATRIN KUZMANY

## Abstract

A plethora of work has been published on the subject country-of-origin effect and country research. The present paper aims to give an overview over existing literature, identifying needs for research. Based on identified concepts and relationships, a model is then constructed and research hypotheses are formulated.

## Introduction

In an ever-changing marketplace, consumers are faced with a growing number of products from a plethora of producing countries (Graby, 1993). Globalization affects consumers and industrial buyers alike. A growing number of companies obtain goods from abroad or outsource parts of their production (Andersen and Chao, 2003).

These changes have been even more profound for companies within the European Union. On May 01, 2004 ten new countries joined the EU – Cyprus, Malta, Estonia, Lithuania, Latvia, Hungary, Czech Republic, Slovakia, Slovenia and Poland. The implementation of the Single European Market, most notably the free movement of goods and services, brings with it extensive changes for the Austrian corporate marketplace.

The enlargement of the European Union offers a multitude of prospects for Austrian companies, especially in connection with the five neighboring countries. Purchasing and production can be outsourced into these countries, resulting in a possibly substantial reduction of costs. However, possible effects of these decisions on product image have to be observed closely.

The present paper therefore aims at creating an insight into industrial buyers' perceptions of foreign goods and countries. A model, based on existing literature, will be then be created.

## Theoretical Background and State of the Field

Ever since the first mention of a possible influence of origin country on consumers' evaluations, an impressive amount of literature on the topic has been published. In 1962, Dichter stated that „[…] an understanding of world anthropology will be an important tool in international marketing" (Dichter, 1962). Three years later, in 1965, the first scientific study was published (Schooler, 1965), making Schooler one of the founders of this line of research.

Already in 1987 it was noted that the concept of country-of-origin might well be the most investigated aspect within the behavioral sciences – a statement still holding true today (Tan and Farley, 1987). More than 40 years of research have resulted in more than 750 publications (Papadopoulos and Heslop, 2002).

Although effect size varies across different product classes, consumers and research scenarios, existence of the effect of the country of origin on product evaluation is undisputed (Han and Terpstra, 1988, Heslop et al., 2004).

The following section aims at giving a systematic overview over existing literature dealing with the area of this paper.

## Country-of-Origin Effect

### Definition

Country-of-origin effect refers to the considerable influence of the image of a sourcing country on the buying process (Bruhn and Homburg, 2004). Sourcing country thus denominates the country of manufacture. Usually the sourcing country is indicated as "Made in …." or "Product of …" (Liefeld, 2004).

In order to further understand the effect's functioning, image, as understood in this paper, has to be defined. Kroeber-Riel define image as the picture somebody has of an object (Kroeber-Riel and Weinberg, 2003), with the objects being products, countries or companies (Kotler, 2003). Product image thus refers to the public's picture of a company and its products (Kotler, 2003).

As can be seen from this definition, image is based on personal assessment, not on real attributes. For the individual, this image represents the particular object, regardless of real circumstances (Jaffe and Nebenzahl, 1984). Within this paper, product image is conceived as stated by Nagashima: "The 'made in' image is the picture, the reputation, the stereotype businessmen and consumers attach to products of a specific country" (Nagashima, 1970).

Another concept of relevance is consumer attitudes. In order to avoid having to assess products anew, attitudes allow consumers to resort to existing patterns of thought (Kroeber-Riel and Weinberg, 2003, Kotler, 2003). These patterns have to be regarded as stable and only hard to change constructs (Bruhn and Homburg, 2004). On this persistence the importance of image research within marketing is based.

## How the effect works

Two forms of cues influencing product evaluations exist: intrinsic cues form part of the product. Smell, color or texture of a product are examples. Cues can however also be extrinsic and not form part of the physical product. Not only brand name or price but also country of origin fall into this category (Kochunny et al., 1993, Thakor and Prevel Katsanis, 1997).

Depending on the paradigm, two – cognitive and affective[i] (Liefeld, 1993) – or three – cognitive, affective and normative (Johansson, 1989, Obermiller and Spangenberg, 1989, Verlegh and Steenkamp, 1999, Weiss Richard and Kühn, 2004) – different types of effect are mentioned, as visualized in the figure below

**Figure 1: Direct and indirect influence of country information;**

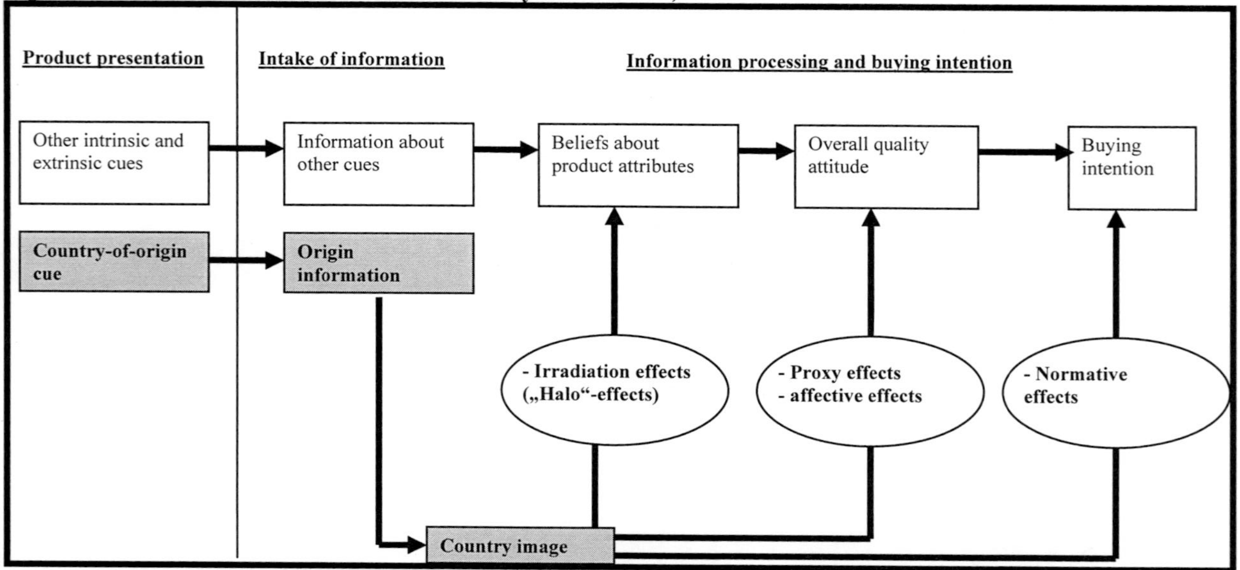


**Source: (Weiss Richard and Kühn, 2004)**

Cognitive processes allow the consumer to infer overall product quality from a single impression, facilitating and speeding up decision making (Kroeber-Riel and Weinberg, 2003). This cognitive effect explains the dominating influence of the origin country on product evaluation (Bilkey and Nes, 1982).

Within the area of cognitive effects, two different types of influence were discovered (Nebenzahl et al., 1997). If relevant cues, such as the country of origin, are used as an indicating variable,[ii] country image serves as a proxy for other product attitudes (Johansson, 1989). These subjective conclusions are called irradiation or halo effects (Kroeber-Riel and Weinberg, 2003, Trommsdorff, 2004, Bruhn and Homburg, 2004), with the influence caused by affections (Erickson et al., 1984). Under such an influence, it has to be assumed that the power of the effect has to decrease with increasing familiarity with the product (Johansson et al., 1985).

**Figure 2: Irradiation effects; source: simplified after (Han, 1989)**

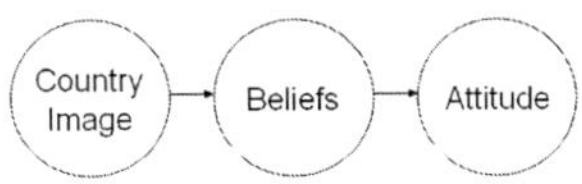


With proxy effects, also called summary constructs, information about a country is memorized. Upon evaluation of a new brand from the same country, a regress on the saved information occurs (Han, 1990). Further information processing is bypassed, as the proxy effect acts as a mental shortcut (Johansson, 1989).

Proxy effects are applied by more experienced consumers, as a certain degree of familiarity with a country's products is needed (Manrai et al., 1998). Several empirical studies were able to establish the existence of the proxy effect (Han, 1990, Kochunny et al., 1993, Mittal and Tsiros, 1995).

**Figure 3: Proxy-effects; source: simplified after (Han, 1989)**

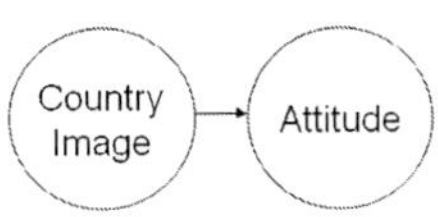

Affective processes stand independent of cognitive evaluations and form preferences or animosity based on emotional factors (Obermiller and Spangenberg, 1989). The disapproval of a product is not influenced by a positive or negative evaluation (Johansson and Nebenzahl, 1987). Affective evaluations can therefore contradict cognitive evaluations. An extreme example is the rejection of French products after the nuclear tests on the Mururoa-Atoll in 1995 (Edwards et al., 2006).

Although the majority of studies investigated cognitive processes, the affective component has been proven to be almost equally important (Li et al., 1994). Furthermore, this construct best explains the functioning of stereotypes, as which country-of-origin effect is mainly regarded (Johansson, 1989).

Normative Processes influence preference without altering product evaluation and/or emotional attitudes (Edwards et al., 2006, Obermiller and Spangenberg, 1989). If consumers model their behavior on a reference group's norms, the purchase of a good conflicting with these norms can inflict social sanctions. This process is especially relevant for highly visible products like cars and clothing (Weiss Richard and Kühn, 2004).

The influence of social norms on product evaluation has been investigated and confirmed both from a behavioral viewpoint (Johansson and Nebenzahl, 1987) as well as from a perceived social risk perspective (Witt and Rao, 1992, Chakra borty et al., 1996).

## Country-of-origin effects and industrial purchasing

The industrial or institutional buying process is defined as the purchase of a product or service by an organization, with the intent to further process, sell or use of the good within the organization (Kotler et al., 2003). Numerous differences between individual and industrial buying decisions exist however, qualifying a separate examination (Yu and Chen, 1993). For example, consumer buying decisions usually involve only a single person and are unstructured, while industrial purchase choices in general are highly standardized and involve a number of different people (Backhaus, 1997). Buying processes are usually either heavily formalized and documented (especially where large, cost-intensive acquisitions are concerned) or routine procedures (Cunningham and White, 1973, Kotler et al., 2003).

Although a plethora of work concerned with consumer buying behavior has been published, a lack of studies investigating the country-of-origin effect within industrial buying processes exists (Hakansson and Wootz, 1975b).[iii]

When choosing a supplier, origin country constitutes the most important characteristic, followed by company size, price and quality of the goods (Hakansson and Wootz, 1975b). Other studies were able to confirm this result (White and Cundiff, 1978, Lambert, 1981).

When breaking down the construct, country of design as well as country of assembly play an important role in decision making (Chetty et al., 1999). A closer investigation of the country evaluation yielded inconsistent results: while one study showed different evaluations of one and the same country, depending on whether it was used as CoD or CoA (Dzever and Quester, 1999), these results could not be reproduced (Quester et al., 2000).

When comparing industrial buyers and consumers, different product attributes had different ranks of importance (Ahmed and d'Astous, 1995). Companies ranked CoD before CoA and brand name, while consumers relied more on product warranties, brand name and sourcing country (with an equal importance of CoD and CoA) (Ahmed and d'Astous, 1995).
Industrial buyers show stereotypical behavior when ranking countries (Chasin and Jaffe, 1979, White, 1979, Kaynak and Kucukemiroglu, 1992, Güdüm and Kavas, 1996, Dzever and Quester, 1999), acting much the same as consumers.

When comparing different countries, in one particular case France and the US, similarities (a positive image of Western Germany) and differences (French respondents rate the UK better, while US industrial buyers prefer Japan) exist (Cattin et al., 1982). Also companies from New Zealand and Australia (Quester et al., 2000) as well as from Great Britain and France (Niffenegger et al., 1982) show differences when evaluating a third country.

In general, products from industrial countries were viewed as superior to those from transformation states, especially from central and eastern European countries (Kaynak and Kucukemiroglu, 1992, Ahmed and d'Astous, 1995).

The negative evaluation of a product was furthermore independent of actual experiences with the country concerned (White and Cundiff, 1978, Chasin and Jaffe, 1979), showing that familiarity has no influence on the effect for industrial buyers.

A preference for domestic products was found for industrial states (e.g. Canada (Heslop et al., 2004), USA (Chasin and Jaffe, 1979, White, 1979) and UK and France (Niffenegger et al., 1982)), but not for transition countries like India (Khanna, 1986).

Past research has made it clear that industrial buyers use country information to infer product quality. A country-of-origin effect for industrial buying processes therefore exists.

## Moderating variables

### Age

Numerous studies imply a change in cognitive procedures with increasing age.[iv] Older people tend to simplify cognitive processes (Schaefer, 1997b), suggesting an influence of age on the use of country information. The direction of this correlation is positive, as the influence increases with age. Previous work has however produced inconsistent results regarding existence, direction and size of influence.

A few studies were able to detect a distinct correlation between age and product evaluation (Schooler, 1971, Bannister and Saunders, 1978, Johansson et al., 1985, Wall et al., 1991), while others were at least able to prove a relation to some aspects of evaluation (Amine and Shin, 2002). Some studies were not able to show a correlation at all (Jaffe and Martinez, 1995).

The direction of the effect also remains unclear. Both a positive evaluation of countries and products with increasing age was shown (Smith, 1993, Dubois and Paternault, 1997, Ahmed and d'Astous, 2004) as well as with younger people (Hisrich et al., 1981, Wall and Heslop, 1986, Leonidou et al., 1998, Lundstrom et al., 1998, Ahmed and d'Astous, 2001).

Also a change in the number of information sources used over time is unclear. It has been shown that the significance and number of sources used when evaluating a foreign product increases with age (Leonidou et al., 1998). This would however imply a rising significance of the country-of-origin-cue. However, other studies only showed a low time expenditure for information search in older people (Chao and Gupta, 1995).

## Sex

Gender-related differences in information processing have been shown in the past (Meyers-Levy and Sternthal, 1991), with differences having both biological and sociological reasons (Darley and Smith, 1995). Amongst other things, judgment is influenced by interests, education (Wall et al., 1988) and knowledge (Meyers-Levy and Sternthal, 1991) associated with gender.

When processing information, women make use of more information and tend to consider all information available. Men on the other hand use easier accessible information, using them as heuristics (Meyers-Levy and Maheswaran, 1991, Darley and Smith, 1995).

These differences could have an influence on the use of the country-of-origin-cue. According to the theory, men make more use of the signal, as it is an easily accessible signal (Schaefer, 1997b). Different familiarity with products – originating from sociological differences – can determine perception and influence of the sourcing country on product evaluation.

While the scientific community agrees on an influence of gender on product evaluation, empirical examinations were unable to produce coherent results.

Some surveys were able to show clear distinctions between men and women when evaluating products (Bannister and Saunders, 1978, Wall et al., 1988). An apparent correlation exists between product interests (Tan and Farley, 1987) and frequently bought products respectively (Wall et al., 1988) and their evaluation. Furthermore women tend to rate those products they possess higher (Lawrence et al., 1992).

Other studies were at least able to show a connection between the evaluation of some aspects of certain products and respondents' gender (Wall et al., 1991), while no correlation was found in even other surveys (Jaffe and Martinez, 1995, Hisrich et al., 1981, Liefeld et al., 1996, Schaefer, 1997b, Insch and McBride, 2004a).

With regard to cognitive procedures women were shown – consistent with the theoretical doctrine – to make more use of all information sources available (Leonidou et al., 1998). Contrary to this position another study found an equal importance of the country-of-origin cue for both genders (Zain and Yasin, 1997).

Women tend to rate countries and products better when ranking them (Schooler, 1971, Johansson et al., 1985, Wall and Heslop, 1986, Wall et al., 1988). Only one study was able to refute this finding (Leonidou et al., 1998).

## Education

Consistent results can be found when investigating the correlation of education and the attitude towards foreign products. Several studies showed a positive relation between level of education and product evaluation, with higher educated respondents rating foreign products better (Anderson and Cunningham, 1972, Wall and Heslop, 1986, Wall et al., 1991, Jaffe and Martinez, 1995, Dubois and Paternault, 1997, Lundstrom et al., 1998) and domestic products being rated more critically respectively (Ahmed and d'Astous, 2004). Also, the attitude towards international trade (Hisrich et al., 1981) and foreign countries in general (Ahmed and d'Astous, 2001) improves with education.

The strength of the bias decreases with increasing levels of education (Schooler, 1971).

## Income

A comparatively small number of studies investigate a possible influence of income on country-of-origin effect. In general, a rising income entails a rising preference for foreign products (Wall and Heslop, 1986, Lundstrom et al., 1998). Respondents with lower income prefer domestic products (Bruning, 1997) or goods from transition economies (Ahmed and d'Astous, 2001).

Other studies could not however find a correlation between income and country-of-origin effect (Jaffe and Martinez, 1995, Dubois and Paternault, 1997).

### Familiarity

While the influence of familiarity on product evaluation is undisputed in theory, no consistent results could be produced. For example, one study showed a different use of country information for experts and novices (Maheswaran, 1994), with the product-country image dominating with novices (Ofir and Lehmann, 1986). Another study however refuted these results, showing an equal influence of sourcing country on respondents with high and low familiarity (Chiou, 2003). Furthermore, use of the cue decreases with rising expertise (Manrai et al., 1998, Ahmed et al., 2002, Moon, 2004) – only a very small country-of-origin effect could be demonstrated for well-known brands (Jo et al., 2003).

Still other studies showed a moderating effect of familiarity (Mittal and Tsiros, 1995), a finding that could not be reproduced (Akaah and Yaprak, 1993).

### Other Variables

In addition to the popular variables presented above, two other aspects are regarded as having an influence on the country-of-origin effect.
A study conducted in France showed a significant negative correlation of social status – using the indicators level of education, standard of living and number of cars in the household – and the attitude towards foreign products (Usunier, 1994).

Another survey measured socio-economic group based on the profession of the household's head (Schaefer, 1997b). Correlations were found with the product category (sparkling wines and beers). Members of higher socio-economic groups relied more on the origin country when evaluating sparkling wines, members of lower groups showed the same behavior when analyzing beer. A logical explanation could be a higher familiarity with the respective products, resulting in a utilization of the country cue by way of a proxy effect (Schaefer, 1997b).

## Country Image

### Definition

Countries possess distinct images, similar to brand images (Bannister and Saunders, 1978, Graby, 1993). The number of work published seems enormous, furthermore the demarcation to country-of-origin effect and product evaluation is complex as the terms are often used synonymously (Li et al., 1997).

For example, Nagashima defines country image as

> "[…] the picture, the reputation, the stereotype that businessmen and consumers attach to products of a specific country. This image is created by such variables as representative products, national characteristics, economic and political background, history and traditions." (Nagashima, 1970)

This explanation makes it clear that not country image but country-of-origin effect is meant. Some other authors also define this construct as the general impression of a specific country's product quality (Roth and Romeo, 1992, Thakor and Prevel Katsanis, 1997, Han, 1990).

Within the scope of this work however, country image is defined as consumers' perception of specific countries (Li et al., 1997). The description of Allred et al., based on an extensive literature review and expert interviews, shall be used:

> "Country image is the perception or impression that organizations and consumers have about a country. This impression or perception of a country is based on the country's economic condition, political structure, culture, conflict with other countries, labor conditions, and stand on environmental issues."(Allred et al., 1999)

Country image can also be described as the total of all descriptive and derived beliefs about a country (Martin and Eroglu, 1993).

While the definition by Allred et al. refers to the causes of country image, Martin and Eroglu bear on the type of opinion forming. Both definitions make clear that country image is influenced by various facets.

## Impact of country image

Country images are readily accessible for consumers, allowing a quick and easy inference of product quality (Papadopoulos and Heslop, 2000). These attitudes can be the result of direct experiences, for example a vacation, the outcome of external influences, like commercials or advertisements, or simply the effect of correct or false conclusions based on past experiences (e.g. product use) (Martin and Eroglu, 1993). Previous perceptions of strengths and weaknesses of a country, famous personalities, art and culture, geography and history also form country image (Roth and Romeo, 1992, Kotler and Gertner, 2002).

Similar to the functioning of country-of-origin effect, country image serves as a shortcut to opinion making. More attention is paid to information confirming existing attitudes as opinions about a country, an effect called confirmation bias (Kotler and Gertner, 2002).

## Country image and buying behavior

In empirical studies, country image was shown to have an impact on buying decision (Han and Terpstra, 1988, Lee et al., 2001, Parameswaran and Pisharodi, 2002). Consumers are in general more inclined to buy products originating from countries that are politically free, developed and close to their own culture (Wang and Lamb, 1980, Crawford and Lumpkin, 1993).

Coming from aforementioned globalization and outsourcing tendencies, a lot of products have more than one sourcing country. Country-of-origin effect is no longer a one-dimensional construct (Chao, 1993).

For example, a portable cassette player can be “Designed in Japan” but “Made in Malaysia”, with the parts originating from a third country. Country associations are therefore no longer tied to just one country (Chao, 1993). As a result, studies increasingly use different stimuli (Ahmed and d'Astous, 1995, Insch and McBride, 1998, Brodowsky, 1998). In most cases, the construct is broken down into the facets country of assembly or manufacture (CoA/CoM), country of design (CoD) and country of parts (CoP).

Country image thus can be seen as an intangible asset, influencing sales and market share positively (Kim and Chung, 1997, Kotler and Gertner, 2002). This effect occurs regardless of the country actively promoting its name like a brand or not – consumers make associations in any case (Kotler and Gertner, 2002)

## Cee-Research

In order to investigate the existing literature, the countries of Central and Eastern Europe have to be defined first. It is drawn upon the definition by the European Bank for Reconstruction and Development (EBRD), classifying the states into the following groups:

- *South Eastern Europe (SEE):*
  Albania
  Bosnia and Herzegovina
  Bulgaria
  Croatia
  Macedonia
  Rumania
  Serbia and Montenegro

- *Commonwealth of Independent States (CIS):*
  Armenia
  Azerbaijan
  Belarus
  Georgia
  Kazakhstan
  Kyrgyzstan
  Moldova
  Russia
  Tajikistan
  Ukraine
  Uzbekistan

- *Central and Eastern Europe and Baltic States (CEB):*
  Czech Republic
  Estonia
  Hungary
  Latvia
  Lithuania
  Poland
  Slovakia
  Slovenia

As has already been mentioned, the enlargement of the European Union by the CEB countries has brought with it profound changes for Austrian companies. As the Baltic States do not border on Austria, the present study will focus on the five countries Czech Republic, Hungary, Poland, Slovakia and Slovenia.

A total of 30 different studies were published using products from the countries selected for the present paper. The distribution is presented in table 2 (Schooler, 1971, Chasin and Jaffe, 1979, Kaynak and Cavusgil, 1983, Wall and Heslop, 1986, Wall et al., 1988, McCleary and Whitney, 1994, Liefeld et al., 1996, Schaefer, 1997b)

**Table 1: CEE-countries and studies; source: author's own**

| Country | Number of Studies | Country | Number of Studies |
|---|---|---|---|
| Czech Republic | 3 | Slovakia | 0 |
| Hungary | 14 | Slovenia | 1 |
| Poland | 12 | | |

Furthermore, the majority of studies were conducted in the 1990s or earlier. The applicability of the results on present circumstances is problematic, as the image of CEE-countries has been subject to dramatic changes within the last decade.

# Methodology

## Theoretical Framework, Development of Hypotheses

While the possible effect of origin country on product perception has been investigated in depth for consumer markets, only little is known about its influence on industrial purchasing processes. In detail, a three-fold need for research has been identified:

1. Both country image and product evaluation are a highly regarded field of research. Gaps do exist nevertheless regarding the perception of goods manufactured in Eastern Europe.
2. Moreover, the majority of studies were conducted in the USA. Austrian consumers – whether private or institutional – have hardly been investigated. Of all studies analyzed for this paper, only four were done in Austria (Crawford et al., 1987, Rawwas et al., 1996, Häubl and Elrod, 1999, Chao et al., 2005). Furthermore, few studies have been conducted in countries geographically close to Austria, like Germany. Applicability of these surveys to the Austrian market has to be questioned, as cultural differences and specific parameters (such as a joint historical past) exist.
3. Although a plethora of work deals with the effects of country-of-origin on consumer behavior, only a small amount of work is concerned with its effects on industrial buying behavior, which differs in many aspects from consumer behavior.

Based on the extensive literature review and the research needs mentioned above, the following model is proposed:

**Figure 4: Model; Source: author's design**

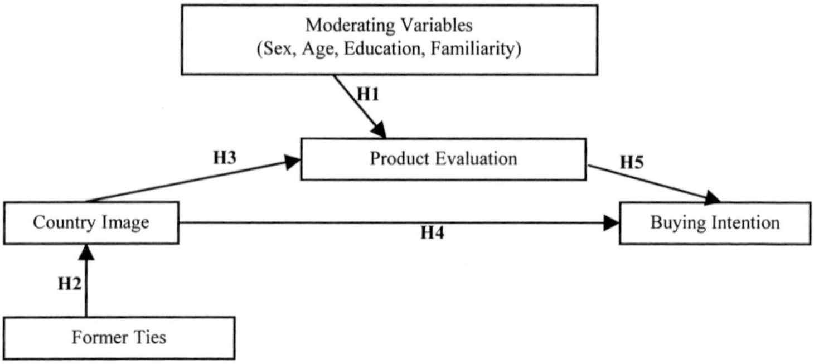


The following five research hypotheses are then formulated:

| | |
|---|---|
| Hypothesis 1 | Demographic variables of the buyer influence product evaluation. |
| Hypothesis 1a | Sex influences evaluation of foreign products. |
| Hypothesis 1b | Age influences evaluation of foreign products. |
| Hypothesis 1c | Education influences evaluation of foreign products. |
| Hypothesis 1d | Familiarity influences evaluation of foreign products. |
| Hypothesis 2 | Historic ties influence country image. |
| Hypothesis 3 | Country image influences product evaluation. |
| Hypothesis 4 | Country image influences buying intention. |
| Hypothesis 5 | Product evaluation influences buying intention. |

**Table 2: Research hypotheses**

## Study Design

As a result of the abundance of studies on country-of-origin effect, a multitude of methodological approaches exist. A number of these are unsuitable for the present research, such as conjoint analysis evaluating product alternatives (Churchill and Iacobucci, 2002, Ettenson, 1993, Klenosky et al., 1996, Knight and Calantone, 2000, Ahmed and d'Astous, 1996, Acharya and Elliott, 2003) or simple preference rankings

(Okechuku, 1994, d'Astous and Ahmed, 1999). Also the evaluation of advertisements are unsuitable for the present task (Chao, 1993, Agarwal and Sikri, 1996, Yun et al., 2002).

The method of choice when measuring images and attitudes is the semantic differential. This procedure allows the evaluation of a given item (in the present case, a country or a product) using two polar adjectives (Osgood et al., 1957). These attribute pairs are assessed using a rating scale (Hammann and Erichson, 1994). Computing mean values allows to construct image profiles (Tscheulin and Helmig, 2004). This procedure is especially suited for the task at hand, as affective-emotional and cognitive aspects of the items can be especially well captured (Tscheulin and Helmig, 2004).

For the present analysis, seven-item scales were used. Although some studies used scales with four items (Hastak and Hong, 1991, Jaffe and Martinez, 1995, Nebenzahl and Jaffe, 1996), scales with an uneven number of units are recommended, as respondents are otherwise forced to take sides when actually feeling neutral towards a question (Churchill and Iacobucci, 2002).

Furthermore it is argued that five or nine-item scales offer too little or too many alternatives respectively and are therefore not feasible (Osgood et al., 1957).

## Operationalization of the Constructs

### Country Image

Although country image is consistently regarded as a multi-dimensional construct (Roth and Romeo, 1992, Cattin et al., 1982, Han and Terpstra, 1988, Jaffe and Nebenzahl, 1984, Strutton et al., 1994), number and nature of dimensions vary substantially (Agarwal and Sikri, 1996).

In total, three dimension of country image could be identified (Martin and Eroglu, 1993) – political, economical and technological.

Martin and Eroglu developed a multi-item scale for measurement of country image, which is to be used in this study. The instrument is comprised of a total of 14 items – five measuring the political, five the economical and four the technical dimension (Martin and Eroglu, 1993).

In order to ensure methodological equivalence, a translate/re-translate procedure was employed (Green and White, 1976).

## Product Evaluation

In order to be applicable to a great number of products, the dimensions used to measure this multi-dimensional construct have to be adequately abstract (Agarwal and Sikri, 1996). Earlier studies within the area of industrial buying favored two product categories as stimuli: tools and machine parts on the one hand (Li et al., 1997, Zain and Yasin, 1997), and telecommunication devices on the other hand (White, 1979, Wall and Heslop, 1986).

In order to ensure comparability across sectors, company size etc., the use of precise products or even product categories is not feasible. Rather the very conceptual statement “products from this country” allows for all respondents to make associations. The use of such unspecific notations has been used often and successfully within the field of industrial buying (Cattin et al., 1982, Chasin and Jaffe, 1979, Baker and Abou-Ismail, 1993) as well as consumer research (Bannister and Saunders, 1978, Chasin and Jaffe, 1979, Liefeld et al., 1996) and has been shown to have no influence on effect size (Liefeld, 1993).

Owing to this unspecific product definition, a number of constructs could not be used, as they were constructed for and using specific products.[vi]

Product evaluation is measured using items first constructed by Insch/McBride (Insch and McBride, 1998). A total of 16 items measures the different quality aspects. Furthermore, the items allow for testing the multiple facets country of design, country of parts, country of manufacture and country of assembly. These elements have already been used in further studies (Insch and McBride, 2004b).

These items were also translated using the translate/back-translate procedure.

## Buying Intention

Buying intention is regarded as a mediator between attitude and actual buying behavior (Kroeber-Riel and Weinberg, 2003). As an observation of actual buying behavior is feasible only in a very limited number of cases, analysis of buying intention is used as a proxy (Kim and Pysarchik, 2000).

Buying intention is measured using a seven-item scale, ranging from 'Would definitely buy' to, 'Would definitely not buy' (Peris et al., 1993, Chinen et al., 2000, Brodowsky et al., 2004).

## Moderating Variables

Sex: Gender is measured as a dichotomous variable

Age: To allow for a metric scaling, age is surveyed using an open question.

Education: Using four categories, education is measured on a nominal scale, with respondents stating their highest completed level of education:

- Mandatory school
- Apprenticeship/upper vocational school
- Higher level
- University
- Not specified

Familiarity: Respondents are asked to indicate which of the five countries they have dealt with before within the scope of their profession.

## Data Collection

Based on the nature of the tests employed and making assumptions on α, β and effect size, ideal sample size was computed. In general it is understood that effect sizes in the social sciences are low. Values above $f = 0.50$ are only seldom encountered and can not be presumed (Cohen, 1988). Using earlier studies, effect size was computed as a benchmark (Liefeld, 1993). A total of six surveys were analyzed (Hakansson and Wootz, 1975b, Ettenson et al., 1988, Hong and Wyer, 1989). On average, country-of-origin effect was medium, therefore the effect size was set at 0.25 (values of 0.10 are regarded as low, values above 0.50 are viewed as high). An ideal sample size of 255 responses was thus computed.

Data was then collected using computer aided telephone interviews in week 35, 2006. A total of 273 questionnaires were completed.

In order to keep the extent of questions asked manageable for respondents, only one country per questionnaire was used as a cue.

## Summary, Outlook

The present paper aims to give an insight into the existing literature on country-of-origin effect and country image. Furthermore, three distinct areas with need for research are identified. These subjects – country image and product perception for goods emanating from central and eastern European countries, studied from an industrial buying point of view and investigated in Austria – are then brought together in a model.

In a next step, the model and the proposed hypotheses will be tested, in order to find underlying relationships.

## Notes

[i] For a general functioning of cognitive and affective structures, (Zajonc and Markus, 1982) provide an excellent overview

[ii] In much a same manner price works as a surrogate, see (Rao and Monroe, 1989)

[iii] For an extensive overview over existing literature on the topic see (Andersen and Chao, 2003)

[iv] A detailed introduction is provided by (Cole and Balasubramanian, 1993) and (Birren and Fisher, 1995)

[v] A total of eight studies from former Czechoslovakia should be mentioned as well

[vi] For example, see (Chetty et al., 1999)

## References

Acharya, C. & Elliott, G. (2003) Consumer ethnocentrism, perceived product quality and choice - an empirical investigation. Journal of International Consumer Marketing, 15, 87-114.

Agarwal, S. & Sikri, S. (1996) Country image: consumer evaluation of product category extensions. International Marketing Review, 13, 23-39.

Ahmed, S. A. & D'astous, A. (1995) Comparison of country-of-origin effects on household and organizational buyers' product perceptions. European Journal of Marketing, 29, 35-51.

Ahmed, S. A. & D'astous, A. (1996) Country-of-origin and brand effects: a multi-dimensional and multi-attribute study. Journal of International Consumer Marketing, 9, 93-115.

Ahmed, S. A. & D'astous, A. (2001) Canadian consumers' perceptions of products made in newly industrializing East Asian countries. International Journal of Commerce and Management, 11, 54-81.

Ahmed, S. A. & D'astous, A. (2004) Perceptions of countries as producers of consumer goods: A T-shirt study in China. Journal of Fashion Marketing and Management, 8, 187-200.

Ahmed, Z. U., Johnson, J. P., Ling, C. P., Fang, T. W. & Hui, A. K. (2002) Country-of-origin and brand effects on consumers' evaluation of cruise lines. International Marketing Review, 19, 279-302.

Akaah, I. P. & Yaprak, A. (1993) Assessing the influence of country of origin on product evaluations: an application of conjoint methodology. Journal of International Consumer Marketing, 5, 39-53.

Allred, A., Chakraborty, G. & Miller, S. J. (1999) Measuring images of developing countries: a scale development study. Journal of Euro-Marketing, 8, 29-51.

Amine, L. S. & Shin, S.-H. (2002) A comparison of consumer nationality as a determinant of COO preferences. Multinational Business Review, 10, 45-53.

Andersen, P. H. & Chao, P. (2003) Country-of-Origin effects in global industrial sourcing: toward an integrated framework. Management International Review, 43, 339-360.

Anderson, W. T. & Cunningham, W. H. (1972) Gauging foreign product promotion. Journal of Advertising Research, 12, 29-34.

Backhaus, K. (1997) Industriegütermarketing, Wiesbaden.

Baker, M. J. & Abou-Ismail, F. (1993) Organizational buying behaviour in the gulf. International Marketing Review, 10, 42-60.

Bannister, J. P. & Saunders, J. A. (1978) UK consumers' attitudes towards imports: the measurement of national stereotype image. European Journal of Marketing, 12, 562-570.

Bilkey, W. J. & Nes, E. (1982) Country-of-origin effects on product evaluations. Journal of International Business Studies, Spring/Summer, 89-99.

Birren, J. E. & FisheR, L. M. (1995) Aging and the speed of behaviour: possible consequences for psychological functioning. Annual Review of Psychology, 46, 329-353.

Brodowsky, G. H. (1998) The effects of country of design and country of assembly on evaluative beliefs about automobiles and attitudes toward buying them. Journal of International Consumer Marketing, 10, 85-113.

Brodowsky, G. H., Tan, J. & Meilich, O. (2004) Managing country-of-origin choices: competitive advantages and opportunities. International Business Review, 13, 729-748.

Bruhn, M. & Homburg, C. H. (2004) Gabler Lexikon Marketing, Wiesbaden.

Bruning, E. R. (1997) Country of origin, national loyalty and product choice. International Marketing Review, 14, 59-74.

Cattin, P., Jolibert, A. P. & Lohnes, C. (1982) A cross-cultural study of "made in" concepts. Journal of International Business Studies, Winter, 131-141.

Chakraborty, G., Allred, A. & Bristol, T. (1996) Exploring consumers' evaluations of counterfeits: the roles of country of origin and ethnocentrism. Advances in Consumer Research, 23, 379-384.

Chao, P. (1993) Partitioning country of origin effects: consumer evaluations of a hybrid product. Journal of International Business Studies, 24, 291-306.

Chao, P. & Gupta, P. B. (1995) Information search and efficiency of consumer choices of new cars: country-of-origin. International Marketing Review, 12, 47-59.

Chao, P., Wührer, G. & Werani, T. (2005) Celebrity and foreign brand name as moderators of country-of-origin effects. International Journal of Advertising, 24, 173-192.

Chasin, J. B. & Jaffe, E. D. (1979) Industrial buyer attitudes toward goods made in Eastern Europe. International Marketing Review, 12, 74-81.

Chetty, S., Dzever, S. & Quester, P. (1999) Country of origin perception and industrial purchase decision-making in New Zealand. European Journal of Purchasing & Supply Management, 5, 185-196.

Chinen, K., Jun, M. & Hampton, G. M. (2000) Product quality, market presence, and buying behavior: aggregate images of foreign products in the U.S. Multinational Business Review, 8, 29-38.

Chiou, J.-S. (2003) The impact of CoO on pretrial and posttrial product evaluation. Psychology & Marketing, 20, 935-954.

Churchill, G. A. J. & Iacobucci, D. (2002) Marketing Research. Methodological Foundations, Mason.

Cohen, J. (1988) Statistical Power Analysis for the Behavioral Sciences, New Jersey.

Cole, C. A. & Balasubramanian, S. K. (1993) Age differences in consumers' search for information: public policy implications. Journal of Consumer Research, 20, 157-169.

Crawford, J. C., Garland, B. C. & Schweiger, G. (1987) Austrian, German and Swiss product quality perceptions of foreign goods. Werbeforschung & Praxis, 2, 29-34.

Crawford, J. C. & Lumpkin, J. R. (1993) Environmental influences on country-of-origin bias. IN PAPADOPOULOS, N. & HESLOP, L. (Eds.) Product-Country Images. New York.

Cunningham, M. T. & White, J. G. (1973) The determinants of choice of supplier. European Journal of Marketing, 7, 189-202.

D'astous, A. & Ahmed, S. A. (1999) The importance of country images in the formation of consumer product perceptions. International Marketing Review, 16, 108-125.

Darley, W. K. & Smith, R. E. (1995) Gender differences in information processing strategies: an empirical test of the selectivity model in advertising response. Journal of Advertising, 29, 41-56.

Dichter, E. (1962) The World Customer. Harvard Business Review, 40, 113-122.

Dubois, B. & Paternault, C. (1997) Does luxury have a home country? An investigation of country images in Europe. Marketing and Research Today, May, 79-85.

Dzever, S. & Quester, P. (1999) Country-of-origin effects on purchasing agents' product perceptions: an Australian perspective. Industrial Marketing Management, 28, 165-175.

Edwards, R., Gut, A.-M. & Mavondo, F. (2006) Buyer animosity in business to business markets: evidence from the French nuclear tests. Industrial Marketing Management, XX, XX-XX.

Erickson, G. M., Johansson, J. K. & Chao, P. (1984) Image variables in multi-attribute product evaluations: Country-of-Origin Effects. Journal of Consumer Research, 11, 694-699.

Ettenson, R. (1993) Brand Name and country of origin effects in the emerging market economies of Russia, Poland and Hungary. International Marketing Review, 10, 14-36.

Ettenson, R., Wagner, J. & Gaeth, G. (1988) Evaluating the effect of country of origin and "made in the USA" campaign: a conjoint approach. Journal of Retailing, 64, 85-100.

Graby, F. (1993) Countries as corporate entities in international markets. In Paternault, C. & Heslop, L. (Eds.) Product-Country Images. New York.

Green, R. T. & White, P. D. (1976) Methodological considerations in cross-national consumer research. Journal of International Business Studies, 7, 81-87.

Güdüm, A. G. & Kavas, A. (1996) Turkish industrial purchasing managers' perceptions of foreign nad national industrial suppliers. European Journal of Marketing, 30, 10-21.

Hakansson, H. & Wootz, B. (1975b) Supplier Selection in an International Environment - an experimental study. Journal of Marketing Research, XIII, 46-51.

Hammann, P. & Erichson, B. (1994) Marktforschung, Stuttgart.

Han, C. M. (1989) Country image: halo or summary construct? Journal of Marketing Research, 26, 222-229.

—. (1990) Testing the role of country image in consumer choice behaviour. European Journal of Marketing, 24, 24-40.

Han, C. M. & Terpstra, V. (1988) Country-of-origin effects for uni-national and bi-national products. Journal of International Business Studies, 19, 235-255.

Hastak, M. & Hong, S.-T. (1991) Country-of-origin effects on product quality judgments: an information integration perspective. Psychology & Marketing, 8, 129-143.

Häubl, G. & Elrod, T. (1999) The impact of congruity between brand name and country of production on consumers' product quality judgments. International Journal of Research in Marketing, 16, 199-215.

Heslop, L., Papadopoulos, N., Dowdles, M., Wall, M. & Campeau, D. (2004) Who controls the purse strings? A study of consumers' and retail buyers' reactions in an America's FTA enfironment. Journal of Business Research, 57, 1177-1188.

Hisrich, R. D., Peters, M. P. & Weinstein, A. K. (1981) East-West trade: the view from the US. Journal of International Business Studies, Winter, 109-121.

Hong, S.-T. & Wyer, R. S. J. (1989) Effects of country of origin and product-attribute information on product evaluation: an information processing perspective. Journal of Consumer Research, 16, 175-187.

Insch, G. S. & Mcbride, J. B. (1998) Decomposing the country-of-origin construct: an empirical test of country of design, country of parts and country of assembly. Journal of International Consumer Marketing, 10, 69-91.

Insch, G. S. & Mcbride, J. B. (2004a) The impact of country-of-origin cues on consumer perceptions of product quality. Journal of Business Research, 57, 256-265.

Insch, G. S. & Mcbride, J. B. (2004b) The impact of country-of-origin cues on consumer perceptions of product quality: a binational test of the decomposed country-of-origin construct. Journal of Business Research, 57, 256-265.

Jaffe, E. D. & Martinez, C. R. (1995) Mexican Consumer attitudes towards domestic and foreign made products. Journal of International Consumer Marketing, 7, 7-27.

Jaffe, E. D. & Nebenzahl, I. D. (1984) Alternative Questionnaire Formats for Country Image Studies. Journal of Marketing Research, 21, 463-471.

Jo, M.-S., Nakamoto, K. & Nelson, J. E. (2003) The shielding effects of brand image against lower quality countries-of-origin in global manufacturing. Journal of Business Research, 56, 637-646.

Johansson, J. K. (1989) Determinants and effects of the use of "made in" labels. International Marketing Review, 6, 47-58.

Johansson, J. K., Douglas, S. P. & Nonaka, I. (1985) Assessing the impact of country of origin on product evaluations: a new methodological perspective. Journal of Marketing Research, 22, 388-396.

Johansson, J. K. & Nebenzahl, I. D. (1987) Country-of-origin, social norms and behavioral intentions. Advances in International Marketing, 2, 65-79.

Kaynak, E. & Cavusgil, S. T. (1983) Consumer attitudes towards products of foreign origin: to they vary across product classes. International Journal of Advertising, 2, 147-157.

Kaynak, E. & Kucukemiroglu, O. (1992) Consumer perceptions of foreign products; an analysis of product-country images and ethnocentrism. European Journal of Marketing, 26, 36-55.

Khanna, S. R. (1986) Asian companies and the country stereotype paradox: an empirical study. Columbia Journal of World Business, Summer 1986, 29-38.

Kim, C. K. & Chung, J. Y. (1997) Brand popularity and country image in global competition: managerial implications. Journal of International Business Studies, 28, 361-386.

Kim, S. & Pysarchik, D. T. (2000) Predicting purchase intentions for uni-national and bi-national products. International Journal of Retail & Distribution Management, 28, 280-291.

Klenosky, D. B., Benet, S. B. & Chadraba, P. (1996) Assessing Czech consumers' reactions to western marketing practices: a conjoint approach. Journal of Business Research, 36, 189-198.

Knight, G. A. & Calantone, R. J. (2000) A flexible model of consumer country-of-origin perceptions. A cross-cultural investigation. International Marketing Review, 17, 127-145.

Kochunny, C. M., Babakus, E., Berl, R. & Marks, W. (1993) Schematic representation of country image: ist effects on product evaluations. Journal of International Consumer Marketing, 5, 5-25.

Kotler, P. (2003) Marketing Management. International edition, New Jersey.

Kotler, P., Armstrong, G., Saunders, J. & Wong, V. (2003) Grundlagen des Marketing, München.

Kotler, P. & Gertner, D. (2002) Country as brand, product, and beyond: a place marketing and brand management perspective. Journal of Brand Management, 9, 249-261.

Kroeber-Riel, W. & Weinberg, P. (2003) Konsumentenverhalten, München.

Lambert, D. R. (1981) Price as a quality cue in industrial buying. Academy of Marketing Science, Summer, 227-238.

Lawrence, C., Marr, N. E. & Prendergast, G. P. (1992) Country-of-origin stereotyping: a case study in the New Zealand motor vehicle industry. European Journal of Marketing, 26, 37-51.

Lee, C. W., Suh, Y. & Moon, B.-J. (2001) Product-country images: the roles of country-of-origin and country-of-target in consumers' prototype product evaluations. Journal of International Consumer Marketing, 13, 47-62.

Leonidou, L. C., Hadjimarcou, J., Kaleka, A. & Stamenova, G. T. (1998) Bulgarian consumers' perceptions of products made in Asia Pacific. International Marketing Review, 16, 126-142.

Li, W.-K., Monroe, K. B. & Chan, D. K.-S. (1994) The effects of origin, brand, and price information: a cognitive-affective model of buying intentions. Advances in Consumer Research, 21, 449-457.

Li, Z. G., Fu, S. & Murray, L. W. (1997) Country and product images: the perceptions of consumers in the People's Republic of China. Journal of International Consumer Marketing, 10, 115-137.

Liefeld, J. P. (1993) Experiments on country-of-origin effects: review and meta-analysis of effect size. In Papadopoulos, N. & Heslop, L. (Eds.) Product-Country Images. New York.

Liefeld, J. P. (2004) Consumer knowledge and use of country-of-origin information at the point of purchase. Journal of Consumer Behaviour, 4, 85-96.

Liefeld, J. P., Heslop, L., Papadopoulos, N. & Wall, M. (1996) Dutch consumer use of intrinsic, country-of-origin, and price cues in product evaluation and choice. Journal of International Consumer Marketing, 9, 57-81.

Lundstrom, W. J., Lee, O. W. & White, S. (1998) Factors influencing Taiwanese consumer preference for foreign-made White Goods: USA vs. Japan. Asia Pacific Journal of Marketing and Logistics, 10, 5-29.

Maheswaran, D. (1994) Country of origin as a stereotype: effects of consumer expertise and attribute strength on product evaluations. Journal of Consumer Research, 21, 354-365.

Manrai, L. A., Lascu, D.-N. & Manrai, A. K. (1998) Interactive effects of country of origin and product category on product evaluations. International Business Review, 7, 591-615.

Martin, I. M. & Eroglu, S. (1993) Measuring a multi-dimensional Construct: Country Image. Journal of Business Research, 28, 191-210.

Mccleary, K. W. & Whitney, D. L. (1994) Projecting Western consumer attitudes toward travel to six Eastern European countries. Journal of International Consumer Marketing, 6, 239-256.

Meyers-Levy, J. & Maheswaran, D. (1991) Exploring differences in males' and females' processing strategies. Journal of Consumer Research, 18, 63-70.

Meyers-Levy, J. & Sternthal, B. (1991) Gender differences in the use of message cues and judgments. Journal of Marketing Research, 28, 84-96.

Mittal, V. & Tsiros, M. (1995) Does country of origin transfer between brands? Advances in Consumer Research, 22, 292-296.

Moon, B.-J. (2004) Effects of consumer ethnocentrism and product knowledge on consumers' utilization of country-of-origin information. Advances in Consumer Research, 31, 667-673.

Nagashima, A. (1970) A comparison of Japanese and US attitudes toward foreign products. Journal of Marketing, 34, 68-74.

Nebenzahl, I. D. & Jaffe, E. D. (1996) Measuring the joint effect of brand and country image in consumer evaluation of global products. International Marketing Review, 13, 5-22.

Nebenzahl, I. D., Jaffe, E. D. & Lambert, S. I. (1997) Towards a Theory of Country Image Effect on Product Evaluation. Management International Review, 37, 27-49.

Niffenegger, P., White, J. & Marmet, G. (1982) How European retailers view American imported products: results of a product image survey. Academy of Marketing Science, 10, 281-291.

Obermiller, C. & Spangenberg, E. (1989) Exploring the effects of CoO labels: An information processing framework. Advances in Consumer Research, 16, 454-459.

Ofir, C. & Lehmann, D. R. (1986) Measuring images of foreign products. Columbia Journal of World Business, Summer, 105-108.

Okechuku, C. (1994) The importance of product country of origin: a conjoint analysis of the United States, Canada, Germany and The Netherlands. European Journal of Marketing, 28, 5-19.

Osgood, C. E., Suci, G. J. & Tannenbaum, P. H. (1957) The measurement of meaning, Urbana.

Papadopoulos, N. & Heslop, L. (2000) Countries as brands. Ivey Business Journal, 65, 30-36.

Papadopoulos, N. & Heslop, L. (2002) Country Equity and country Branding: problems and prospects. Journal of Brand Management, 9, 294-314.

Parameswaran, R. & PisharodI, R. M. (2002) Assimilation effects in country image research. International Marketing Review, 19, 259-278.

Peris, S. M., Newman, K., Bigne, E. & Chansarkar, B. (1993) Aspects of Anglo-Spanish perceptions and product preferences arising from 'country of origin' image. International Journal of Advertising, 12, 131-142.

Quester, P., Dzever, S. & Chetty, S. (2000) Country-of-origin effects on purchasing agents' product perceptions: an international perspective. Journal of Business and Industrial Marketing, 15, 479-490.

Rao, A. R. & Monroe, K. B. (1989) The effect of price, brand name, and store name on buyers' perceptions of product quality: an integrative review. Journal of Marketing Research, 26, 351-357.

Rawwas, M. Y. A., Rajendran, K. N. & Wührer, G. (1996) The influence of worldmindedness and nationalism on consumer evaluation of domestic and foreign products. International Marketing Review, 13, 20-38.

Roth, M. S. & Romeo, J. B. (1992) Matching product category and country image perceptions: a framework for managing country-of-origin effects. Journal of International Business Studies, 23, 477-497.

Schaefer, A. (1997b) Do demographics have an impact on country of origin-effects? Journal of Marketing Management, 13, 813-834.

Schooler, R. D. (1965) Product Bias in the Central American Common Market. Journal of Marketing Research, II, 394-397.

Schooler, R. D. (1971) Bias phenomena attendant to the marketing of foreign goods in the U.S. Journal of International Business Studies, 2, 71-80.

Smith, W. R. J. (1993) Country-of-origin bias: a regional labelling solution. International Marketing Review, 10, 4-12.

Strutton, D., Pelton, L. E. & Lumpkin, J. R. (1994) Internal and external country of origin stereotypes in the global marketplace: effects and implications for the domestic promotion of U.S. automobiles. Journal of Global Marketing, 7, 61-77.

Tan, C. T. & Farley, J. U. (1987) The impact of cultural patterns on cognition and intention in Singapore. Journal of Consumer Research, 13, 540-544.

Thakor, M. V. & Prevel Katsanis, L. (1997) A model of brand and country effects on quality dimensions: issues and implications. Journal of International Consumer Marketing, 9, 79-100.

Trommsdorff, V. (2004) Konsumentenverhalten, Stuttgart.

Tscheulin, D. K. & Helmig, B. (Eds.) (2004) Gabler Lexikon Marktforschung, Wiesbaden.

Usunier, J.-C. (1994) Social status and country-of-origin preferences. Journal of Marketing Management, 10, 765-783.

Verlegh, P. W. J. & Steenkamp, J.-B. E. M. (1999) A review and meta-analysis of country-of-origin research. Journal of Economic Psychology, 20, 521-546.

Wall, M. & Heslop, L. (1986) Consumer Attitudes Toward Canadian-Made Versus Imported Products. Academy of Marketing Science, 14, 27-36.

Wall, M., Heslop, L. & Hofstra, G. (1988) Male and female viewpoints of countries as products of consumer goods. Journal of International Consumer Marketing, 1, 1-25.

Wall, M., Liefeld, J. P. & Heslop, L. (1991) Impact of Country-of-origin cues on consumer judgments in multi-cue situation: a covariance analysis. Academy of Marketing Science, 19, 105-113.

Wang, C.-K. & Lamb, C. W. J. (1980) Foreign environmental factors influencing american consumers' predispositions toward european products. Academy of Marketing Science, 8, 345-356.

Weiss Richard, M. & Kühn, R. (2004) Country-of-Origin-Effekte. Bedeutung und Implikationen für das Internationale Marketing. IN Zentes, J., Morschett, D. & Schramm-Klein, H. (Eds.) Außenhandel. Marketingstrategien und Managementkonzepte. Wiesbaden.

White, P. D. (1979) Attitudes of US purchasing managers toward industrial products manufactured in selected Western European Nations. Journal of International Business Studies, 10, 81-90.

White, P. D. & Cundiff, E. W. (1978) Assessing the quality of industrial products. Journal of Marketing, January, 80-86.

Witt, J. & Rao, C. P. (1992) The impact of global sourcing on consumers: Country-of-origin effects on perceived risk. Journal of Global Marketing, 6, 105-128.

Yu, C.-M. J. & Chen, C.-N. (1993) A research note on country-of-origin in industrial settings. In Papadopoulos, N. & Heslop, L. (Eds.) Product-Country Images. New York.

Yun, T., Lee, W.-N. & Sego, T. (2002) Direct and indirect use of country of origin cues for hybrid and non-hybrid products. New Directions in International Advertising Research, 12, 195-214.

Zain, O. M. & Yasin, N. M. (1997) The importance of Country-of-Origin information and perceived product quality in Uzbekistan. International Journal of Retail & Distribution Management, 25, 138-145.

Zajonc, R. B. & Markus, H. (1982) Affective and cognitive factors in preferences. Journal of Consumer Research, 9, 123-131.

# SOME ISSUES ABOUT PRINT ADS IN FRANCE AND CZECH REPUBLIC

CHRISTIAN DIANOUX AND ZDENEK LINHART

## Abstract

This article presents the principal results of two researches which can be found with more details in Dianoux, Kettnerová, Linhart (2006, 2007). The first research examines the differences between print ads in two European countries, a recent central country (Czech Republic) and an old western country (France). The second research checks if the most important difference observed between the two countries (the size of the ads) can be explained only for economic reasons or by consumer differences between the two countries.

The results do not show any clue consistence with the literature in the following experimental conditions: a well known brand which communicates towards young target in two different European countries (Czech Republic, France). Almost no difference between full page and half page ads were found within each country about memorization and attitude toward brand, though many differences were found between the countries. Advertisers will find it useful, because they can save money as larger ads don't have a bigger impact than smaller ones in that specific case.

**Key words:** ad-size, magazine, attention, memorization, attitudes, beliefs, intentions, Czech Republic, France, cross-cultural advertising, adaptation, standardization.

## Introduction

Recently, Al-Olayan and Karande (2000) noted that the largest number of studies exploring the cross-cultural differences between advertisements concentrated mostly on just a few countries: USA (with a range of 40 out of 59 studies in the meta analysis of Abernathy and Franke, 1996), the

Western European countries (France, Sweden, Great Britain, etc), and the leading countries in Asia (Japan and Korea). On the other hand, countries such as those from the former Soviet bloc have had very few studies despite their increased economical importance and their integration into the European Union. In fact, the entrance of seven of these countries (Czech Republic, Estonia, Hungary, Lithuania, Poland, Slovakia, and Slovenia) into the EU in May, 2004, now allows advertisers to develop communication strategies with at least the plan of regulations (notably those dealing with misleading publicity and comparative advertising), which will enable them to benefit from homogenous constraints.

The first objective is based on the understanding of the politics of the advertisers' communication in two different EU countries: a new and old members (Czech Republic and France), because “Which approach is adopted by practitioners is, however, still a matter for some speculation, since the writers have confined themselves to giving only anecdotal examples in support of their arguments” (Whitelock and Chung, 1989).

The second objective is to verify if the main difference we have seen in the analysis content between the two countries (the size of ads) is really pertinent.

Firstly, we will see the comparative research at the international level and what we know about the two countries which helped us to formulate our working hypothesis (§.1). Secondly, we will present the obtained results (§.2). Finally, we will conclude by revealing the principal tendencies observed, the managerial recommendations that emerge, and will indicate the limits of this work from which several research perspectives arise. These results are a digest of two papers published in Journal of Euro marketing and presented in 9th Vaasa Conference on International Business, for more details about the methodology and the results; see Dianoux, Kettnerová, and Linhart (2006, 2007).

## Review of the Literature and the Hypothesis

### International Communication

The debate on the standardization of the politics of multinational communication enterprises was born several decades ago with the positions, notably, of Elinder (1965) and Fatt (1967), who alleged that the evolution of societies brings about a bigger and bigger convergence level between countries and has a tendency to eliminate cultural barriers in permitting the emergence of standardized international communication. Roostals (1963) noted that even if standardization of advertising developed logically, the diversity of the languages in Western Europe, as well as the media and the rules, made things even more difficult. Others, like Buzzels (1968), commented that, on the other hand, in most cases the many differences between the local markets encouraged a vision of an adaptation of communications.

In fact, even if the standardization was favourable to achieve the economic ladder (Levitt, 1983), a certain local adaptation was necessary and seemed, in most cases, economically the most pertinent point of view (Auelch and Hoff, 1986), and was stated by the famous expression, “Think global, act local” (Wind and Douglas, 1986). Other authors have also shown that the general debate on the standardization was futile because this question was notably contingent on the existence of homogeneous international segments and that in this case it justified itself but not in the other (Baalbaki and Malhotra, 1993).

Adding to the debate, numerous studies and been led to analyse the practices of enterprises and have shown that the practice of total standardisation was rare, with most cases having a tendency to adapt the communication. This adaptation always had to be considered unified. According to Harris (1994), after a study on the practice of multination Americans and Europeans in the European Union, there exists, in reality, a very large spectrum of practices from the adaptation of total standardisation. This spectrum can be considered as a sort of continuum in which all the states were represented:

-a visual, text or simply a claim adaptation,
-an adaptation with no value, limited, moderate or high value,
-an adaptation that varied according to the markets.

Finally, if the total adaptation is the exception, so is the pure standardisation, even if there has been a strong tendency during the last 40 years to move towards standardisation, because even though it is still not effective, it permits the economic ladder to envision significances and to diffuse an identifying position around the world (Agrawal, 1995).

In such a context, the study of the differences between countries from the analysis of the contents of the advertisements is most interesting. This is so because, besides the consumer study and what the enterprises claim to practice, the analysis of the contents permits one to give objective indications on the actual practices of the advertisers. Even though this approach is not moving in the sense that was recommended by Taylor (2002) who affirmed that the academic research on international publicity produced too many content analyses and not enough experiments: "what we need is experimental research in which the impact of specific executional variables is isolated", it is not far from the end. For us, the analysis of the contents is not an end in itself but a first step permitting an orientation towards future investigation of the elements of execution of experimental testing. Before looking at the comparison of the efficiency of this or that element of execution between two or more countries, it seems more important to us that we should, firstly, define the limits of the advertisers' practices and, secondly, provide orientation for future research.

## Differences between the Czech Republic and France

If, as already stated, the majority of the comparative studies were based on the advertising styles, they concerned essentially the comparisons between the Americans and Asians, or the Americans and Europeans. The comparisons concerning European countries are fewer (Walliser and Moreau, 2000), and those concerning the comparisons of Eastern and Western Europe are fewer still. However, even the small number of studies on this subject allows us to point out the following characteristics:

-In France, the diverse publicities are preferred to the informative publicities (Mandel, 1991) which tend to orientate the creation towards messages mostly centred on a global image of a product rather than on the explanation of facts (Hall and Hall, 1990; Walliser and Moreau, 2000), with ads that are emotional (Zandpour, Chang and Catalano, 1992) and rich messages with subtle hints and non verbal expressions (Fleury, 1990), are dominant. In Poland, publicity uses humorous symbols or the historic and literary past of the country with word plays and linguistic expressions with double meanings that are only understood by the Poles (Dianoux, Domanski, and Herrmann, 2000; Domanski, Dianoux and Herrmann, 2003).

-By contrast, Vida and Fairhurst (1999) did not find a strong ethnocentricity in Poland, the Czech Republic, Hungary and Estonia, in comparison with the western European countries;

-The study of Kaynac and Kara (2001), even though dealing mostly with Asia, shows that the creative strategies emphasizing family values were more obvious in the countries where there was a strong family image;

-According to Grapard (1997), even if the solid communal bases between the European countries on the geographic and social-political plans leave us to assume that there are many similarities, actually many differences subsist, notably between the East and the West. This is because of the tendencies of the consumers situated in clarified levels, affinities and diverse cultural influences, distinct expressions in their languages, rapid and brusque reforms and economic performances which haven't yet converged.

Parallel to these studies, which were focused on the consumer behaviour, are numerous differences mentioned in management manuals that can equally be pointed out. It is, for example, preferable to avoid the seriousness and aloofness that characterize the French in business relations; the Czechs tend to weave personal relationships into their business relationships with their partners. Misunderstandings with the Czechs are possible. Those who find themselves in the upper cultures of the Russians, where the posture, the tone, facial expressions, silences and gestures are just as important bearers of the sense of things as the words, will notice the great contrast provided by the lower cultures of the Germans who express themselves essentially by the spoken word. In the same line of thinking, general studies emphasize thoughts like those of Todd (1990, quoted by Demorgon, 1996): "The Western European family community, which expresses more strongly than anywhere else its values, must affirm to the East an absolute, divine authority and salvation for everyone." A study on professional values by Hoefstede (Table1) shows the significant differences between the two principal countries concerning two dimensions (the distance between power and the fear of uncertainty), suggesting the idea that the Czechs would be more inclined than the French to accept a stranger and less inclined to accept the differences between the status and the dependence on a leader.

**Table 1. Hofstede's Country scores**

| | Power distance | Individualism | Masculinity | Uncertainty avoidance |
|---|---|---|---|---|
| France | 68 | 71 | 43 | 86 |
| Czech Republic | 35 | 60 | 45 | 60 |
| Germany | 35 | 67 | 66 | 65 |
| Poland | 50 | 60 | 70 | 50 |
| Austria | 11 | 55 | 79 | 70 |
| Russia | 95 | 47 | 40 | 75 |

Source : http://www.centreurope.org/france/france-in-figures/hofstede-analysis-france.htm

Bearing in mind the numerous marked differences between the Czech and French consumers, and despite the tendency noted in standardized multinational communication (Laroche, Kirpalani, and Darmon, 1999), it seemed probable that the advertisers, voluntarily or not, had a natural tendency to adapt their communications to the two countries. We must, therefore, find this tendency in the contents of the publicity and the hypotheses of the following basis must be demonstrated: the Czech ads differed substantially in their content, form and their medium of discourse from the French ads.

## The Effect of Attention and Memorization

Among the first to try and determine the impact that a print advertisement format could have, together with the characteristics to which the reader is attentive (size, colour, number of words, prominence to branding, etc), Diamond (1968) showed that an advertisement's size declined according to the following hierarchy: double-page, single-page, horizontal half-page, and vertical half-page. With the same perspective, Finn (1988) showed that the principal characteristics of a print ad influencing attention was linked to size and positioning (ad size, cover position, front or back, right or left page) and to size - pictorial characteristics- (colour and illustration size).

In the business to business sector (B2B), we can observe the same effects. For Hansens and Weitz (1980), the size of the ad is strongly correlative to the fact of having seen the ad (0.78) and to the fact of having read it almost entirely (0.71). Naccarato and Neuendorf (1988) believe the same, affirming that among the variables that seem to have a universal positive effect is the size of the ad itself.

Besides these different factors it is also possible that the facts automatically linked to the size of the ad play a part. In the study carried out by Pieters and Wedel (2004) which shows that contrary to what a large number of papers confirm (e.g. Rossiter and Percy 1997: "the bigger the picture, the better"), the size of the text also plays a decisive role. While the increase in the number of images does not attract attention regarding the ad, the increase in the surface devoted to the text increases attention (an increase of 1% of the surface increases attention by 0.85%). Whatever the surface devoted to the image or the text we can postulate that these two characteristics are automatically linked to the size of the ad, the bigger the ad size the bigger the size of the image or the text will be, everything else remains constant.

In the light of these different facts, we can advance our first hypothesis:

> **Hypothesis 1-** a bigger ad will have a bigger impact on attention and memorization than a smaller ad.

However this attention is sensitive to change according to the country. Indeed, as previously mentioned, because of media costs, advertisers who are compelled by their budgets tend to use small formats in countries where press media cost is higher and bigger formats in countries where the cost is less. Consequently it is possible that the classic format of one page attracts more reader attention in countries used to smaller formats. Therefore our hypothesis:

> **Hypothesis 1a-** An advertisement on one page will have more impact on the reader used to ads of an inferior size than readers used to this kind of ad size.

## The Effect of Beliefs, Attitudes, and Intentions

In parallel to these studies it is also interesting to note that advertisement size can also have an effect on attitudes and behaviour. Edell and Staelin (1983), based on an alternative model of the hierarchy of the effects, suggest not only a direct effect of attention on the understanding but also on the attitudes. Many papers illustrate this relationship. For Kirmani (1990) the size of an ad can serve as an indicator to the amount of money a company devotes to its advertising. Thus ad size is much more than a simple tool to attract attention, according to the author relying on the attribution theory, it also allows consumers to make inferences by linking together the company's capacity to make the financial efforts (as long as the company is not considered as manipulative) to its capacity of proposing a product of quality which is somewhat successful. Similarly Homer (1995) showed that the size of an ad has a positive effect on the perception of the product quality and the intention of purchasing.

These results would seem to be similar to those of Percy and Rossiter (1983) who showed that between three image sizes used in an ad, it is the ad whose image is bigger that opens onto a better attitude (from a multi-attribute compensatory model). Indeed it can be presupposed that all the elements included in the ad (image, texts, brand name, etc) vary in the same way as the size of the ad, everything else remains constant. This allows us to assert the following hypothesis:

> **Hypothesis 2-** A large ad will have more positive impact on intention, attitudes, and beliefs (notably concerning quality) than a small ad.

However this attitude is subject to much change according to the country for two principal reasons. Firstly, Herpen and al. (2000) and also Dianoux, Kettnerová, and Linhart (2006) show how different the informative ad content is between countries, and secondly probably because of preferences. It is possible that a link automatically exists between the size of the ad and its level of information, knowing that the bigger the ad size, the higher the possibility of information content. Furthermore the link highlighting the firm's capacity to offer quality products will be made if the size of the ad largely exceeds that which is generally carried out in the country, where:

> **Hypothesis 2a-** A full-page ad will have more impact on readers used to ads of an inferior size than to the readers used to unchanged formats.

# Results

## Comparison of Ad Contents in Czech and French Journals

### *Structure of ads in journals*

Of all of product categories used, the most significant differences occurred in the categories of computers, automobiles and books (see Table 2). We observed that in the other categories there was not a very clear difference between the Czech and French reviews.

**Table 2: Total number of different advertisings taken from 20 magazines (base 577)**

| Product Category | Czech Reviews | French Reviews | Total |
|---|---|---|---|
| Food and Cleaning Products | 5,2% | 6,0% | 5,5% |
| Cosmetics, Health and Hygiene | 19,7% | 23,9% | 21,7% |
| Clothing-Textiles | 10,7% | 12,3% | 11,4% |
| Computers, Hifi-sound-image-Telephones | 10% | 1,5% | 6,1% |
| Automobile, Motorcycles | 3,9% | 8,2% | 5,9% |
| Books, Magazines, DVDs | 10,4% | 5,2% | 8,0% |
| Other products | 6,8% | 12,0% | 9,2% |
| Banks and Insurance | 4,2% | 6,7% | 5,4% |
| Telecommunications | 4,5% | 6,3% | 5,4% |
| Other services | 24,6% | 18,1% | 21,5% |
| | 100% | 100% | 100% |

Note: These figures do not take into account the size of the publicities

As for the fact that we found brands, which were more or less known in the two countries, no difference was observed ($Chi^2$=0,42 ; p.c.=0,52), with 32% of the brands being the object of an ad in a Czech magazine were known in France, against 30% for the opposite cases.

Concerning the position of the name brand (high, low or in the middle of the ad), there was no difference, except the fact that in France the brand is repeated in different places in the ad, which was not the case in the Czech Republic. If such a difference appears odd, it is sufficient to study the dimensions of the ads for a better understanding, since the fundamental difference rests, without doubt, on this point: the Czech ads have a tendency to repeat the formats, which are clearly inferior to those observed in France. This explains the fact that we can often repeat the brand name.

**Table 3: Dimensions of ads**

| (N=577) | Less than one page | One page or more | Total |
|---|---|---|---|
| Czech Republic | 53,7% | 46,3% | 100% |
| France | 15,3% | 84,7% | 100% |
| | 35,9% | 64,1% | 100% |

The dependence is very significant. Chi² = 92,11, ddl = 1, p.c. = 0,00

This economic research is easy to understand when we look at the tariffs used by the Czech media. In fact, if the average tariffs used in France were largely greater (6.860 euros in the Czech Republic per normal page in four colours vs. 26.721 euros in France), they were significantly lower than those that led the Cost Per Thousand (CPM) with 135 vs. 58 because of the low distribution of magazines. This is a problem inherent in countries with a low population even if the numbers of the Czech readers are proportionally greater (the number of French readers per review is 4 times greater, even though the French population is 6 times greater).

Indeed whatever the total price[1], it could be interesting to increase the size of the ad if it is largely offset by an increase in the campaign efficiency and we could assume that for the advertiser who distances himself from the general trend of the country concerned with bigger ads, it might be largely offset by the effects of the campaign. In this respect, « the goal becomes to find the level of media spending which maximizes the return on investment » (Danaher and Rust, 1994). Therefore the main issue here is to determine in which proportion the increase of spending is reasonable in comparison to the effect (in term of memorization or attitude toward the ad or the brand) one would hope to get from the ad.

### *Content of ads in journals*

In respect to the differences according to the contents of the Czech and French ads, we can similarly observe significant differences illustrated in Table 4.

**Table 4: Comparison of French and Czech Ad Contents**

| (N=577) | USA[1] | UK[1] | France[1] | | France | Czech |
|---|---|---|---|---|---|---|
| Black and white | 6% | 11% | 13% | | 2% | 5%* |
| Comparison | 10% | 5% | 1% | | 2% | 4%* |
| Minority race | 7% | 5% | 7% | | 7% | 7% |
| Elderly person | 3% | 2% | 1% | | 11% | 3%* |
| Children | 16% | 4% | 6% | | 16% | 9%* |
| Photograph | 72-82%[2] | 74-68%[2] | 48-60%[2] | | 80% | 85% |
| Product shown | 57-41%[2] | 60-49%[2] | 49-37%[2] | | 77% | 75% |
| Price shown | 16-6%[2] | 24-8%[2] | 16-15%[2] | | 21% | 31%* |
| Description | 68-43%[2] | 67-42%[2] | 72-39%[2] | | 52% | 55% |
| Symbolic | 10-6%[2] | 16-23%[2] | 37-20%[2] | | 36% | 44%* |

1. The data in the first three columns come from the study of Cutler, Javalgi and Erramilli (1992), and are given an illustrated title.
2. The first number corresponds to the durable product category, the second to the non durable.
*- when the difference is at least 95% significant (Khi$^2$ test)

Apart from the racial minority characteristics, considering the photography, product presentation and description of the products, the ads presented in the Czech reviews had, in a significant way, tendency to differ from those presented in the French reviews. Taking into account only international brands (known in both the Czech Republic and France) didn't change the results, except in the children category (no significant difference between the two countries).

It seems that, in general, the advertisers adapt the contents of their communications to the local context.

We have equally indicated the results obtained by Cutler, Javalgi, Erramilli (1992) within the framework of a comparative study between the USA, Great Britain and France (note that the study also concerns India and Korea, which aren't discussed here). The important differences appear between the two studies, France illustrates one of the principal problems, which was encountered when comparisons between the content studies were made: the selection of magazines and ads. In their study, Cutler, Javalgi, Erramilli (1992) only used three magazine categories (women, business, general interest) with the same types, as closely as possible, in the other countries. They excluded ads concerning fashion clothing and all ads not having a one page format. On our part, we believe that the selection carried out by the authors leads to a poor appreciation of the advertising tendencies in a given country because the exclusions lead to an "imperialist" analysis, accentuating the tendencies of the native country of the researchers. As an example, if we had used only one-page or more ads in this study, we would have rejected the majority of the Czech ads and would have had partially false results.

## Ad Size Perception of Czech and French Consumers

We have seen that one of the most important differences between Czech and French ads is the size. So, we have carried out an experiment (a comparison of the memorization and attitudes toward half and full size ads for the well known brand Nokia within each country) to verify if there are differences between Czech and French consumers about their ad size perception according to the above hypotheses.

### *Memorization and Attention*

Table 5 shows no difference in memorisation of Nokia brand from the ad, which respondents could find in an experimental journal folder either with the size of full page or half page.

**Table 5: Spontaneous memorization about the brand name advertised**

| | No answer | Wrong answer (any other brand) | Wrong and right answer (Nokia and other brand) | Right answer (Nokia quoted) |
|---|---|---|---|---|
| Half page | 17% | 5% | 3% | 75% |
| Full page | 16% | 2% | 4% | 78% |

Chi²= 3,7 – ddl= 3 – p.=0.290

If there is no difference between the size of the ads in general, we have to check firstly if there is no hidden country effect on the ad size. No significant differences were found. Because of restrictions shown by $Chi^2$ only "No answer" and "Right answer" options were taken into account. "Wrong answer" and "Wrong and right answer" were excluded from processing, because both of them had an insufficient number of answers and it seemed inappropriate to mix these respondents with "No answer" or "Right answer".

**Table 6: Spontaneous memorization about the brand name advertised**

| | No answer | | Right answer (Nokia quoted) | |
|---|---|---|---|---|
| | CR | France | CR | France |
| Half-page | 23% | 8% | 77% | 92% |
| Full page | 20% | 14% | 80% | 86% |

With respectively (two-sided Fisher Test) p.= 0.71 (CR) p.= 0.30 (France)

Secondly, further data processing was made to prove the possible significance of other variables (first of all the five facets of involvement toward the product defined by Laurent and Kapferer) without reaching any significant relationships. The result and framework of the experimentation is evidently confirming that there is no difference between half and full page ads. Memorisation of promoted brand name was also not influenced by the tested ad size whatever the involvement toward the mobile phone.

No significant difference in attention related to the studied ad country by country was found on the three items measured (attention toward the ad, concentration on the ad, watching the ad) by respondents who received half or full page ad. However, we have found some differences between the two countries. Czechs tend to have lower attention to Nokia ad than French (Table 5). The ad size has not influenced this difference. The attention of Czechs towards the ad was generally lower without regard to its size.

**Table 7: Attention toward the ad by countries**

| Mean Rank Mann Whitney test | Country | Half-size | | Full size | |
|---|---|---|---|---|---|
| | | Mean Rank | p. | Mean Rank | p. |
| You have paid no attention to this ad | CR | 108,16 | 0.005 | 108,78 | 0.000 |
| | France | 121,16 | | 144,72 | |
| You haven't concentrated on this ad | CR | 121,08 | 0.837 | 115,01 | 0.006 |
| | France | 122,31 | | 150,33 | |
| You haven't watched this ad | CR | 91,72 | 0.000 | 91,73 | 0.000 |
| | France | 139,08 | | 167,56 | |

These different results of this experimentation deny both hypotheses 1 and 1a. Both of them must be rejected.

## Attitudes

No real significant difference (p.<0.05) was found in attitude toward the ad, and belief, attitude and intention toward the promoted brand (see table 8). Respondents who were exposed to the half page or full page ad of Nokia in the experimental journal folder presented a relative homogeneity in their answers whatever the country.

**Table 8: The influence of ad size on attitudes, beliefs, and intentions country by country**

| Mean Rank Mann Whitney test | Country | Half size Mean rank | Full size Mean rank | p. |
|---|---|---|---|---|
| Generally, I like this ad | Czech Republic | 89 | 90 | 0.831 |
| | France | 87 | 81 | 0.437 |
| This Nokia phone seems to have high quality | Czech Republic | 90 | 90 | 0.952 |
| | France | 82 | 84 | 0.791 |
| I like this Nokia phone very much | Czech Republic | 86 | 94 | 0.314 |
| | France | 81 | 86 | 0.497 |
| I would like to have a Nokia phone like this one | Czech Republic | 88 | 92 | 0.573 |
| | France | 79 | 87 | 0.268 |

So, it seems that our second hypothesis should be rejected also. Size of ad can't influence attitude. This is valid for both the ad and brand attitudes. Intentions and beliefs of individuals who are exposed to the full page ad or the half page ad are also the same. Globally, the country of origin doesn't change the results.

It is interesting to note, however, that significant differences were found in comparison of answers between countries independently of the ad size (Table 9).

It seems that differences between countries are connected with specific features of their respective markets. Indeed initial beliefs can strongly influence final purchase independently of the ad impact. Table 10 shows relevant data confirming this expectation through summarized answers "I would probably buy the Samsung phone" which is a brand, which was not promoted in the experimental journal folder.

**Table 9: The influence of country on attitudes, beliefs, and intentions for full and half size**

| Mean Rank Mann Whitney test | Country | Half-size | | Full size | |
|---|---|---|---|---|---|
| | | Mean Rank | p. | Mean Rank | p. |
| Generally, I like this ad | CR | 142 | 0.002 | 158 | 0.001 |
| | France | 125 | | 129 | |
| This Nokia phone seems to have high quality | CR | 114 | 0.244 | 126 | 0.367 |
| | France | 125 | | 142 | |
| I like this Nokia phone very much | CR | 118 | 0.090 | 142 | 0.368 |
| | France | 115 | | 133 | |
| I would like to have a Nokia phone like this one | CR | 126 | 0.009 | 145 | 0.228 |
| | France | 104 | | 126 | |
| How probable is that you will select the Nokia brand when buying a new mobile phone? | CR | 144 | 0.000 | 156 | 0.001 |
| | France | 86 | | 114 | |

**Table 10: Brand purchase intentions – Samsung**

| Mean Rank Mann Whitney test | CR n=88/91 | France n=74/90 | p. |
|---|---|---|---|
| Half page | 100 | 160 | 0.000 |
| Full page | 100 | 167 | 0.000 |

It can be concluded from these results that significant differences are between countries only in the case of purchase intentions of Nokia and Samsung brand: Czechs prefer Nokia phones, and French Samsung phones independently of the ad. Ad size doesn't matter because group exposed either to half page or full page Nokia ads are showing same tendencies.

## Conclusion

We strongly ascertain that there is a large number of differences between France and the Czech Republic in the point of creative advertising, whatever the structural plan (formats are smaller in the Czech Republic), or in terms of contents (the price is more often mentioned in the Czech Republic, and children and older persons are used less). Our hypothesis is therefore largely supported by the collected data and we can conclude that the advertisers have the tendency to adapt the contents of their communication in function with the Czech or French context.

From the methodological point of view, this study shows the importance of taking into account a statistically sufficient (large) publicity sample from each country, in order to avoid the methodological choices chosen by Cutler, Javalgi, Erramilli (1992). We hope to have a representative perception of the communication forms used in a given country. In this sense, it is important to pay attention to the following issues:

- To use a large category of magazines covering different segments of the population and then post information such as "X % of the persons in the ads are older persons" (Cutler, Javalgi and Erramilli, 1992) logically would not make great sense when the selected magazines are not targeting the senior segment;
- Selecting identical magazines in different countries is interesting because it permits a homogenous target but it also generates a greater problem of concentrating on groups which could be marginal in the studied countries. If we wish to have a representative sample, it seems preferable to keep magazines in separate categories in relation to their respective level;
- Similarly, to exclude certain publicities can generate important biases (except, of course, those which can be qualified as short ads and not publicities, communicating precise products: offer or request for employment, real estate sales, etc.). Also, being limited to one page formats risks, according to the country, a creation of important distortions such as has been the case between the Czech Republic and France. This confirms the comments of Avery and Franke (1996) within the framework of their meta-analysis.

This first tour of the horizon of the universe of the Czech and French advertising has permitted us to have a global view of the practices of the advertisers in the two countries and the perception of the consumers. Each time, knowing that the idea of "what is practiced is what is effective," doesn't always exactly reveal that what is practiced. This conforms with the suggestion[2] of Harris and Attour (2003) that there are basic characteristics that permit advertising to be as efficient in France as in the Czech Republic, notably those in which we have observed the most differences between the two countries, such as the communication on the functional attributes, the images, and the price.

## Notes

[1] Please note that they also exclude adverts with the requests for employment or for real estate. We also excluded them because they aren't true ads proposing permanent products.

[2] The authors propose that instead of looking for the winning tools of a complete adaptation or a total standardization (which is, without doubt, a fantasy), it would be better to try to understand the benefits taken from the standardized forms applied.

## References


Abernethy Avery M., Franke George R. (1996), The Information Content of Advertising A Meta-Analysis, *Journal of Advertising*, 25, 2, 1-17.

Abernethy, A. M. & D. N. Laband (2002), The Customer Pulling Power of Different Sized Yellow Pages Advertisements, *Journal of Advertising Research,* 42:3, 66-72.

Abernethy, A. M. & D. N. Laband (2004), The Impact of Trademarks and Advertisement Size on Yellow Page Call Rates, *Journal of Advertising Research*, 44:1,

Agrawal Madhu (1995), Review of a 40-year Debate in International Advertising, *International Marketing Review*, 12, 1, 26-48.

Albers-Miller Nancy, Gelb Betsy (1996), Business Advertising Appeals as a Mirror of Cultural Dimensions: A Study of Eleven Countries, *Journal of Advertising*, 25, 4, 57-70.

Al-Olayan Fahad, Karande Kiran (2000), A Content Analysis of Magazine Advertisements from the United States and the Arab World, *Journal of Advertising*, 29, 3, Fall, 69-82.

Baalbaki Imad B., Malhotra N. K. (1993), Marketing Management Bases for International Marketing Segmentation: An Alternative Look at the Standardization/Customization Debate, *International Marketing Review*, 10, 1, 19-44.

Bollinger Daniel et Hofstede Geert (1987), *Les différences culturelles dans le management. Comment chaque pays gère-t-il ses hommes ?,* Paris, Les Editions d'Organisation, 268 p.

Burtt, H. E. (1938), Psychology of Advertising, *Cambridge, MA: Houghton Mifflin Company, The Riverside Press.*

Buzzel Robert D. (1968), Can You Standardize International Marketing?, *Harvard Business Review*, 46, November/December, 103-113.

Cutler Bob, Javalgi Rajshekhar, Erramilli Krishna (1992), The Visual Components of Print Advertising: A Five-country Cross-Cultural Analysis, *European Journal of Marketing*, 26, 4, 7-20

Danaher, P. J. & R. T. Rust (1994), Determining the Optimal Level of Media Spending, *Journal of Advertising Research*, January/February, 28-34.

Demorgon Jacques (1996), *Complexité des cultures et de l'interculturel*, Paris, Anthropos, 319 p.

Diamond, D. S. (1968), A Quantitative Approach to Magazine Advertisement Format Selection, *Journal of Marketing Research*, 5, November, 376-86

Dianoux Christian, Kettnerová, Jana, & Linhart Zdenek (2006), Advertising in Czech and French Magazines, *Journal of Euromarketing*, 16:1/2, 139-152.

Dianoux Christian, Linhart Zdenek, Kettnerová Jana (2007), The effect of the Print Ad Size in Three Different European Countries: Czech Republic, France, and Spain, *9th Vaasa Conference on International Business*, University of Vaasa, Vaasa, Finland, August 19-21.

Dianoux Christian, Tomasz Domanski, & Jean-Luc Herrmann (2000), Comparative advertising in central and Eastern Europe: the case of Poland, *Proceedings of the 8th Annual Conference on Marketing Strategies for Central and Eastern Europe*, Vienna, Austria, december, Edited by P. Chadraba et R. Springer, 59-71.

Domański Tomasz, Dianoux Christian, Herrmann Jean-Luc (2003), Reklama porównawcza w świetle prawa, *Marketing y Rynek*, 2, 2-6.

Domański Tomasz, Dianoux Christian, Herrmann Jean-Luc (2003), Wpływ reklamy porównawczej na zachowania konsumentów, *Marketing y Rynek*, 3, 2-6.

Durvasula, S., Lysonski, S. & U. C. Mehta (1999), A Cross-Cultural Comparison Of Cognitive Responses, Beliefs, and Attitudes Toward Advertising In General In Two Asian Countries, *The Journal of Marketing Management,* Winter, 48-59

Edell, J. A. & R. Staelin (1983), The Information Processing of Pictures in Print Advertisements, *Journal of Consumer Research.* 10, June, 45-61.

Elinder Erik (1965), How International Can European Advertising be? *Journal of Marketing*, 29, April, 7-11.

Falcy, S. (1997), Les processus d'influence publicitaire: un essai de modélisation intégrant implication vis-à-vis de la publicité, caractéristiques psychologiques et publicitaires, Thèse, *Université Pierre Mendès-France de Grenoble*, ESA.

Fatt Arthur C. (1967), The Danger of Local International Advertising, *Journal of Marketing*, 31, 1, 60-62.

Ferguson, L.W. (1935), The Importance of the Mechanical Features of an Advertisement, *Journal of Applied Psychology*, 19:5, 521-526.

Finn, A. (1988), Print Ad Recognition Readership Scores: An Information Processing Perspective, *Journal of Marketing Research,* 25,, May, 168-77

Fleury Pascal (1990), Au-delà des particularismes. Quels fonds universels ?, *Intercultures*, 8, déc.- janvier, 119-130.

Grapard U. (1997), Theoretical Issues of Gender in the Transition from Socialist Regimes, *Journal of Economic Issues*, 31, 3, 665-685.

Gudykunst W. B., Ting-Toomey S. (1998), *Culture and Interpersonal Communication*, Sage.

Hall Edward T. (1976), *Beyond Culture*, New-York, Anchor Press/Doubleday, traduit en français, *Au-delà de la culture*, Paris, Ed. du Seuil.

Hall Edward T., Hall Milred R. (1990), *Guide du comportement dans les affaires internationales*, Paris, Ed. du Seuil, 261 p.

Han, J. K. (1992), Involvement and Advertisement Size Effects on Information Processing, *Advances in Consumer Research*, 19, 762-769.

Harris Greg (1994), International Advertising Standardization: What Do the Multinationals Actually Standardize?, *Journal of International Marketing*, 2, 4, 13-30.

Harris Greg, Attour Suleiman (2003), The International Advertising Practices of Multinational Companies: A Content Analysis Study, *European Journal of Marketing*, 37, 1/2, 154- 169.

Hendon, D. W. (1973), How Mechanical Factors Affect Ad Perception, *Journal of Advertising Research*, 13, August, 39-45.

Herpen van, E., Pieters, R., Fidrmucova, J & P. Roosenboom (2000), The Information Content of Magazine Advertising in Market and Transition Economies, *Journal of Consumer Policy*, 23:3, September, 257-283.

Hoeken Hans, Van Den Brandt Corine, Crijns Rogier, Dominguez Nuria, Hendriks Berna, Planken Brigitte, Starren Marianne (2003), International Advertising in Western Europe: Should Differences in Uncertainty Avoidance be Considered when Advertising in Belgium, France, The Netherlands and Spain?, *The Journal of Business Communication*, 40, 3, July, 195-218.

Hofstede Geert (1991), *Cultures and Organisations, Software of the mind, Intercultural Cooperation and its importance for Survival*, McGraw-

Hill, traduit en français : *Vivre dans un monde multiculturel, comprendre nos programmations mentales,* Les Editions d'Organisation, 1994.

Homer, P. M. (1995), Ad Size as an Indicator of Perceived Advertising Costs and Effort : The Effects on Memory and Perceptions, *Journal of Advertising*, 24:4, Winter, 1-12.

Kapferer, J. N. & G. Laurent (1986), Consumer involvement profiles: a new practical approach to consumer involvement, *Journal of Advertising Research*, 25:6, 48-56.

Kaynac Erdener, Kara Ali (2001), An Examination of the Relationship among Consumer Lifestyles, Ethnocentrism, Knowledge Structures, Attitudes and Behavioural Tendencies: a Comparative Study in two CIS States, *International Journal of Advertising*, 20, 4, 455-482.

Kirmani, A. (1990), The Effect of Perceived Advertising Costs on Brand Perceptions, *Journal of Consumer Research*, 17, September, 160-171.

Koudelova, R. & J. Whitelock (2001), A Cross-ultural Analysis of Television Advertising in the U.K and the Czech Republic, *International Marketing Review*, 18:3, 286-300.

Laroche Michel, Kirpalani V. H., Darmon René (1999), Determinants of the Control of International Advertising by Headquarters of Multinational Corporations, *Canadian Journal of Administrative Sciences*, 16, 4, 273-290.

Leogn E. K. F., Huang X., et Stanners P. J. (1998), Comparing the Effectiveness of the Web Site with Traditional Media, *Journal of Advertising Research*, 38, September/October, 44-51.

Levitt Theodore (1983), The Globalizations of Markets, *Harvard Business Review*, 61, May/June, 92-102.

Linton Ralph (1945), *The cultural background of personality*, traduit en français par Andrée Lyotard, Le fondement culturel de la personnalité, Paris, Dunod, 1965.

Manrai Lalita, Lascu Dana-Nicoleta, Manrai Ajay, Babb Harold (2001), A Cross-Cultural Comparison of Style in Eastern European Emerging Markets, *International Marketing Review*, 18, 3, 270-286.

Marcoux Jean-Sébastien (1995), L'influence de l'origine de fabrication de produits sur les préférences des consommateurs polonais, *11ème Congrès de l'Association Française de Marketing*, Reims, ESC, 73-95.

McCullough Lynette (1993), Leisure Themes in International Advertising : A Content Analysis, *Journal of Leisure Research*, 25, 4, 380-388.

Mehta, A. (2000), Advertising Attitudes and Advertising Effectiveness, *Journal of Advertising Research*, May-June, 67-72.

Mendel Dorothea (1991), Comparaison des cultures allemande et française et implications marketing, *Recherche et Applications en Marketing*, 6, 3, 31-75.

Moriarty Sandra, Duncan Thomas (1990), Global Advertising : Issues and Practices, *Current Issues and Research in Advertising*, 13, 2, 313-341.

Muehling, D. D. (1987), An Investigation of Factors Underlying Attitude-Toward-Advertising-in-General, *Journal of Advertising,* 16:1, 32-40.

Naccarato, J. L. & K. A. Neuendorf (1998), Content Analysis as a Predictive Methodology: Recall, Readership, and Evaluations of Business-to-Business Print Advertising, *Journal of Advertising Research*, May, 19-33.

Nasierowski W. (1996), Emerging Patterns of Reformations in Central Europe: the Czech Republic, Hungary, and Poland, *Journal of East-West Business*, 1, 143-171.

Okazaki Shintaro (2004), Does Culture Matter?: Identifying Cross-national Dimensions in Japanese Multinationals' Product-based Websites, *Electronic Markets*, 14, 1, 58-69.

Percy L. & J. R. Rossiter (1983), Effects of Picture Size and Color on Brand Attitude Responses in Print Advertising, *Advances in Consumer Research*, 17-20.

Pieters, R. & M. Wedel (2004), Attention Capture and Transfer in Advertising: Brand, Pictorial, and Text-Size Effects, *Journal of Marketing,* 68, April, 36–50.

Quelch John A., Hoff E.J. (1986), Customizing Global Marketing, *Harvard Business Review*, 64, May/June, 59-68.

Raju P. S. (1995), Consumer Behavior in Global Markets: the ABCD Paradigm and its Application to Eastern Europe and the Third World, *Journal of Consumer Marketing*, 12, 5, 37-56.

Resnik Alan, Stern Bruce L. (1977), An Analysis of Information Content in Television Advertising, *Journal of Marketing*, January, 50-53.

Roostals Ilmar (1963), Standardization of Advertising for Western Europe, *Journal of Marketing*, October, 15-20.

Solberg Carl Arthur (2002), The Perennial Issue of Adaptation or Standardization of International Marketing Communication: Organizational Contengencies and Performance, *Journal of International Marketing*, 10, 3, 1-21.

Taylor Charles R. (2002), What Is Wrong with International Advertising Research?, *Journal of Advertising Research*, Nov.-Dec., 48-54.

Vida Irena, Fairhurst Ann (1999), Factors Underlying the Phenomenon of Consumer Ethnocentricity: Evidence from Four Central European

Countries, *International Review of Retail, Distribution and Consumer Research*, 9, 4, October, 321-337.

Walliser Björn et Moreau Fabienne (2000), Comparaison du style français et allemand de la publicité télévisée, *Décisions Marketing*, 19, janvier-avril, 75-84.

Whitelock J., Chung D. (1989), Cross-Cultural Advertising : An Empirical Study, International Journal of Advertising, 8, 291-310.

Wind Yoram, Douglas S.P. (1986), The Myth of Globalization, *Journal of Consumer Marketing*, 3, Spring, 23-26.

Zandpour Fred, Chang Cypress, Catalano Joelle (1992), Stories, Symbols, and Straitght Talk : a Comparative Analysis of French, Taiwanese, and U.S. TV Commercials, *Journal of Advertising Research*, january-february, 32, 1, 25-38.

Zandpour Fred, Harich Katrin (1996), Think and Feel Country Clusters: A New Approach to International Advertising Standardization, *International Journal of Advertising*, 15, 4, 325-345.

# WHAT WORKS BEST? THE IMPORTANCE OF AD CHARACTERISTICS IN ANTISMOKING ADVERTISING TO ADOLESCENTS

IRENA VIDA AND DOMEN BAJDE

## Abstract

The negative health effects of smoking have been well documented. Considerable effort has been extended to avert the most vulnerable groups, such as the adolescents, from smoking. This paper aims to enrich the knowledge of anti smoking advertising by focusing on the impact antismoking advertising has on the adolescent segment. The research survey is set in Slovenia where smoking among adolescents has been exceedingly problematic. We aim to examine the role of antismoking ad characteristics, in particular, the effect they have on the adolescents' attitude toward antismoking ads. The range of ad characteristics examined includes three dimensions: (1) message intensity, (2) message valence, and (3) type of appeal. The data was generated in three Slovene high schools, surveying 480 adolescents aged between 14 and 19.

## Introduction

Cigarette smoking has been repeatedly exposed as damaging to health, causing unnecessary deaths, decreasing the quality of life, increasing public health costs and causing significant losses in productivity (Andrews et al., 2004). As a result, considerable effort has been spent to avert the public from smoking. In particular, the most vulnerable groups, such as the adolescents, have repeatedly been cautioned against smoking (Smith and Stutts, 2003). Whereas, antismoking advertising has played a significant role in these attempts (Wakefield et al., 2003), our understanding of antismoking advertising remains very restricted. This paper aims to develop knowledge regarding antismoking advertising by focusing on the adolescents' attitudes towards antismoking ads. The research survey is set in Slovenia where the elected segment and its engagement with smoking have proved exceedingly problematic. For instance, according to the National Institute for Health Safety (IVZ, 2004), 15 percent of preventable deaths in Slovenia can be attributed to smoking. What is more, during the past decade the number of teenage smokers has increased significantly (CINDI, 2005). The European School Survey Project on Alcohol and other Drugs reports a shocking increase in smoking among the 15- and 16-year old group. The percentage of smokers in this age group has soared from the initial 16.4% in 1994 up to 25.7% in 1999 (ESPAD, 2003). Evidently, the existing efforts to discourage smoking have largely proven ineffective with the Slovene teenage segment. This empirical study offers some insights into the workings of antismoking advertising, thus, attempting to contribute toward an increase in the effectiveness of the antismoking campaigns aimed at the adolescent segment.

## Theory and Hypothesis

There are several gaps in the literature addressing the role of antismoking ad characteristics, such as the type of appeal used, or the valence and the intensity of the appeal. After conducting an extensive study, Pechmann and colleagues (2003) conclude that ads depicting social disapproval of smoking are more effective than those highlighting the long-terms health risks, or the shrewdness of tobacco marketing. In opposition, Goldman and Stanton (1998) find that exposing tobacco industry's marketing tactics in advertising to be most effective. Smith and Stutts (2003) conclude that while long-term health appeals can be effective with female adolescents, the male participants respond much better to short-term cosmetic appeals such as bad breath, yellow teeth and bad skin. Other antismoking appeals, such as promoting the dangers of passive smoking and communicating non-health disadvantages of smoking have been largely neglected by existing research. Similar inconsistencies and gaps can also be found in the literature delving into the role of appeal intensity (strong vs. moderate advertisement appeals) and appeal valence (positive vs. negative advertisement appeals). For instance, strong appeals arousing fear have been found very effective. On the other hand, an excessively intensive antismoking message has been shown to provoke undesired defiance from the audience (Wolburg, 2004). It is very likely that intensive appeals will produce negative attitudes toward antismoking ads and fail to be accepted by the audience.

Similar reservations also apply to the literature investigating the role of appeal valence. Antismoking advertising can either stress the benefits of avoiding tobacco (positive valence), or focus on the losses incurred by smokers (negative valence). It has been suggested that the effectiveness of positively/negatively framed advertising is hard to predict as it is moderated by a number of factors (Robberson and Rogers, 1988; Maheswaran and Meyers-Levy, 1990). Negative messages (e.g., health threats of smoking) are believed to be superior when addressing a highly involved audience, or audiences with lower processing ability, and when promoting behavior with an uncertain outcome, or addressing health issues. Conversely, positive messages have been found superior in situations of low-involvement, low-processing ability, and with appeals to self-esteem. The literature offers little advice as to what works best with antismoking advertising to adolescents. Due to the methodological limitations, our study does not measure antismoking advertising effectiveness directly. Instead we focus on attitudes toward different antismoking ads as mediators of ad effectiveness. Attitudes toward advertising have been shown to largely determine the overall effectiveness of advertising (Mehta, 2000). In particular, attitudes toward a specific advertisements were found to be an important mediator of advertising effectiveness both in terms of the impacting the ads have on the audiences' cognition and in terms of the impact they have on behavioral intentions (Lutz and Belch, 1983). As a result, a through study of attitudes toward antismoking advertisements can produce a number of valuable implications for antismoking advertisers.

Against this theoretical background a number of hypotheses were formulated. In accordance with the data presented earlier on adolescent smoking situation in Slovenia (CINDI, 2005; ESPAD, 2003), it is expected that:

H1a: More than 25% of the teenage participants engage in smoking.
H1b: The proportion of teenage smokers increases with age.

The second set of hypothesis is related to the differences between teenage smokers and non-smokers regarding their attitudes towards smoking and their attitudes towards various types of antismoking advertisements. The smokers are expected to hold a more positive attitude toward smoking, and they are also expected to react differently to antismoking appeals (Wolburg, 2004).

H2: Teenage smokers exhibit a more positive attitude toward smoking in comparison to their non-smoking peers.

H3: When exposed to advertisement appeals, teenage smokers and nonsmokers differ in their attitudes towards the ad.

The concluding hypothesis tackles the differences in the attitudes towards antismoking ads employing varying appeals. Whereas, the existing literature fails to consistently confirm the prominence of a certain type of appeal, the majority of the existing findings do find a difference in appeal effectiveness (e.g., Goldman and Stanton, 1998; Smith and Stutts', 2003).

H4: There will be significantly difference in the respondents' attitudes towards the ads across four selected types of advertisement appeals.

## Methods

Our study explores the adolescents' attitudes towards smoking, their intentions to smoke, and how different antismoking appeals produce varying attitudes toward advertising. The range of advertisement appeal characteristics examined here includes: (1) appeal intensity, (2) appeal valence, and (3) type of appeal. As a part of a large cross-cultural project on antismoking advertising (Reardon et al., 2006), sixteen distinct print ads with matching visuals and headlines were developed to facilitate a 2x2x4 experimental design. The data was generated in three high schools; surveying 480 adolescents aged 14 to 19. The questionnaire included various constructs whereby some of the item measures were taken from the literature and some of them were developed specifically for this project. The following constructs were used in this study: a 7-item scale measuring *attitudes toward smoking*, a 9-item scale measuring the *attitudes toward a particular antismoking ad*, a 3-item scale measuring the *intent to smoke*, a classificatory question (smoker or non-smoker), and demographics. All items were translated into Slovene and back into English independently by two bilingual natives.

The multi-item scales were first tested for unidimensionality of measures and their reliability by conducting an exploratory factor analysis (the principal component method) and examining the internal consistency (coefficient alpha). The three-item scale for measuring the intent to smoke proved very reliable, thus, all 3 items were retained (alpha = 0.908). Conversely, only 4 of the 9 items measuring the attitudes toward particular antismoking ads were retained (alpha = 0.839). The scale measuring attitudes toward smoking yielded two strong dimensions: the rational dimension (eigenvalue of 3.12; alpha 0.77), and the hedonic dimension (eigenvalue of 0.954; alpha 0.78). As a result, our initial construct (i.e., attitude toward smoking) was broken into two attitude constructs: (1) the teenager's beliefs regarding the (ir)rationality of smoking (4 items), and (2) their perceptions regarding the appeal of smoking (2 items). Together, the two factors account for 67.9 percent of total variance. The average age of our respondents was 16.46 years (SD= 1.11) with students from the first through the fourth year students being somewhat equally represented. 56.3% of the respondents were male 43.7% female.

## Results

Our data analyses clearly support **Hypothesis 1a.** 33.3 percent of the teenage participants categorized themselves as smokers. The percentage of smokers clearly exceeds 25% ($p = 0.000$); hence, it is significantly higher than the percentage of teenage smokers reported by ESPAD in 1999. Although due to the methodological and sample differences the two sets of data cannot be compared directly, the data clearly confirms the efflorescence of smoking among teenagers. The percentage of smokers steadily increases with age. In the 14-16 year old group the percentage of those who smoke is 28%. With the "17 or above" age group this percentage increases to 38.6%. As a result, Hypothesis 1b is also confirmed ($\chi^2$ test: $p = 0.020$). Next, the attitudes toward smoking scores were analyzed. On average, the adolescents exhibit a negative attitude toward smoking, describing it as bad, unwise, harmful, unappealing, dangerous, and unpleasant. Nevertheless, the attitudes are considerably less negative in the smoker group than they are with nonsmokers. Smokers perceive smoking as somewhat less irrational (t = -4.13, $p = 0.000$) and by far more appealing (t = -13.23, $p = 0.000$) than do nonsmokers. Consequently, the data strongly confirms **Hypothesis 2.**

The respondents were exposed to antismoking ads of varying valence and intensity. Both the valence and the intensity of ads have been found to influence the respondents' attitudes toward a particular ad. Positively framed ads resulted in more favorable attitudes toward ads than negatively framed ads (t = -1.99, $p = 0.048$), while strong appeals produce more favorable attitudes toward the ad than do moderate ones (t = 2.27, $p = 0.024$). However, as demonstrated later, the all respondents do not necessarily share the described preferences for certain antismoking appeals. Our data confirms **Hypothesis 3**, stating that adolescent smokers form different attitudes toward antismoking ads than do nonsmoking adolescents. The attitude score was significantly lower with the smoker group than with the nonsmokers (t = -3.67, $p = 0.000$). It has also been found that the difference in attitudes between the two groups varies according to ad appeal intensity. The discord in attitudes between adolescent smokers and nonsmokers is especially striking in the case of respondents exposed to high intensity appeals (t = - 3.99, $p$ = 0.000). Whereas nonsmokers report a positive attitude toward intensive antismoking ads, with the smoker group high intensity appeals resulted in very negative attitudes. These findings correspond to Wolburg's (2004) conclusion that high intensity appeals produce undesirable effects with smokers.

The study also employed 4 distinct appeal types: (1) health appeals (health threats/benefits), (2) other-centered appeals (positive/negative impact on bystanders), (3) social approval appeals (acceptance/disapproval of others), and (4) well-being appeals (impact on own well-being). 120 adolescents were exposed to each type of antismoking appeal. A One-way ANOVA test was conducted to test the differences in ad attitude scores across the four appeal types. The results do indicate that the adolescents' attitudes toward ads differ according to the type of appeal, but the differences are not statistically significant ($p$ = 0.080). As a result, **Hypothesis 4** cannot be confirmed.

## Conclusion

The results of the study offer several implications for public policy. First, the results indicate a disturbing popularity of smoking among adolescents. The high number of high school smokers further stresses the need to actively engage in antismoking campaigns. Smoking is particularly widespread among the older adolescents (i.e., the above 17 age group). Our data also shows that adolescents respond differently to antismoking advertising. There are significant differences in the attitudes toward smoking between smokers and nonsmokers. It is the perceptions of pleasantness and the appeal of smoking that differ most significantly across the two groups. As a result, antismoking advertising targeting adolescent smokers will do well to aim at reducing the perceived hedonic, and social benefits of smoking, and/or at increasing the perceived hedonic/social costs of smoking. While strong antismoking appeals produce very favorable results with the nonsmoker group, smokers perceive them less favorably. Our results suggest that highly intensive antismoking appeals are less appropriate when targeting smokers. On the other hand, positive appeals proved superior to negative appeals with both adolescent groups. Advertisers need to devise appeals that draw on the benefits attained when refusing to smoke (e.g., health benefits, social benefits, increased quality of life).

Beyond doubt, much additional work is required to achieve a comprehensive understanding of the workings of antismoking advertising. In this paper we aimed to produce a much-needed contribution toward a systematic study of the ad characteristics and their impact on attitude toward antismoking advertising. Such an approach unavoidably results in several limitations. For one, the limited sample size proved detrimental in testing the hypotheses concerning the differences in the four selected appeal types. A more extensive survey would have a greater chance of success in teasing out these differences. In addition, the constructs measured in the study (i.e., reported attitudes and intensions) are only a crude indicator of actual behavior. As a result, this study only represents a rudimentary initial step toward a better understanding of antismoking advertising.

## References

Andrews, J. Craig, Richard G. Netemeyer, Scot Burton, D. Paul Moberg and Ann Christiansen. 2004. Understanding Adolescent Intentions to Smoke: An Examination of Relationships Among Social Influence, Prior Trial Behavior, and Antitobacco Campaign Advertising. *Journal of Marketing* 68: 110--123.

CINDI. 2005. 2001 Research Report: Preventable Disease Risk Factors Afflicting Slovene Adults. http://www.cindi-slovenija.net

Craig, C. S. and Douglas, S. P. (1999). *International Marketing Research.* New York, NY: John Wiley & Sons, LTD.

ESPAD. 2003. 1994-1999 Research Report: The European School Survey Project on Alcohol and other Drugs. http://www.espad.org

Goldman, Lisa K. and Stanton A. Glantz. 1998. Evaluation of Antismoking Advertising Campaigns. *Journal of the American Medical Association* 279(10): 772--777.

IVZ. 2004. Health Protection Institute. http://www.ivz.si.

Lutz, Richard J., McKenzie, Scott B. and George E. Belch. 1983. Attitude Toward the Ad as a Mediator of Advertising Effectiveness: Determinants and Consequences. *Advances in Consumer Research*, 10 (1): 532--539.

Maheswaran, D. and Joan Myers-Levy. 1990. The Influence of Message Framing and Issue Involvement. *Journal of Marketing Research* 27 (August): 361--367.

Mehta, Abhilasha. 2000. Advertising Attitudes and Advertising Effectiveness. *Journal of Advertising Research*, 40 (3): 67--72.

Pechmann, Cornelia, Guangzhi Zhao, Marvin E. Goldberg and Ellen Thomas Reibling. 2003. What to Convey in Antismoking Advertisements for Adolescents: The Use of Protection Motivation Theory to Identify Effective Message Themes. *Journal of Marketing* 67: 1-18.

Reardon, J., Miller, C., Faubert, B.,Vida, I. and Rubyna, L. (2006). "Antismoking Messages for the International Teenage Segment: The Effectiveness of Message Valence and Intensity across Different Cultures", *Journal of International Marketing*, 14 (3), 115--138.

Robberson, Margaret R. and Ronald W. Rogers. 1988. Beyond Fear Appeals: Negative and Positive Persuasive Appeals to Health and Self-Esteem. *Journal of Applied Social Psychology* 18(3): 277--287.

Smith, Karen and Mary Ann Stutts. 2003. Effects of Short-Term Cosmetic Versus Long-Term Health Fear Appeals in Anti-Smoking Advertisements on the Smoking Behaviour of Adolescents. *Journal of Consumer Behaviour* 3(2): 157--177.

Wakefield, Melanie, Brian Flay, Mark Nichter and Gary Giovino. 2003. Effects of Anti-Smoking Advertising on Youth Smoking: A Review. *Journal of Health Communication* 8: 229--247.

Wolburg, Joyce M. 2004. The Need for New Anti-smoking Advertising Strategies That Do Not Provoke Smoker Defiance. *Journal of Consumer Marketing* 21(3): 173--174.

# TRADE FAIRS EXHIBITORS COMMUNICATION EXCELLENCE

PIOTR KWIATEK, GRZEGORZ LESZCZYNSKI, AND MAREK ZIELINSKI

## Abstract

The role of trade fairs has shifted from selling to establishing and fostering communication. The change in operators strategy from exhibitor-centric to visitor-centric view can be also observed. The intense competition for time and attention of visitors has made us to pose the question: are communication behaviors of exhibitors adjusted to visitors' preferences? In our research we simultaneously learn preferences of visitors and behaviors of exhibitors. The results show that the process of serving visitors meets their preferences on its beginning. But when it comes to communication after trade fairs exhibitors behavior is different and does not fulfill visitors' needs.

## Evolution of Trade Fairs Role

Fairs were organized in European cities for centuries. Polish cities have a history of fairs and trade similar to Europe. In the 12th century, every Polish village, which obtained city rights, had its own fair which was the basis of its economic existence. Since the turn of the 18th and 19th centuries, the idea of organizing industrial exhibitions became a great passion of the French, then the English and finally the rest of Europe and the rest of the civilized world. The first modern fairs (also called "introductory fairs") took place in 1894 in Leipzig. Since that time, all major trade fairs in Europe were organized according to that standard – in Poznań in 1921. Today at least seven Polish cities organize international trade fairs, but the leading position undoubtedly belongs to Poznań International Fair (Kuca and Mruk, 2006). Due to the statistics conducted by Polish Fairs Corporation there were over 230 fairs events in Poland in

2005 where 27.630 companies were present. The expositions were attended by more than 915 000 visitors[1].

Trade fairs are events that bring together, in a single location, a group of suppliers, distributors, and related services that set up physical exhibits of their products and services from given industries or disciplines (Black, 1998).

There are two visible quality tendencies in trade fairs evolution – the role of fairs changes from trading into communicative one as well as the orientation – from exhibitor- to visitor-oriented. A sign of the first tendency is the assumption that the fairs do not have to generate the sale but they can be of use to create and develop customers' relationships. The focus of companies, which operate in business-to-business markets on communicative role of fairs make them more a relationship tool. It is at the same time a very important premise to study communicative behaviour of fairs participants. Studying these behaviours is justified not only from the relationship marketing perspective but also from the perspective of an economy based on knowledge (as the communication itself is the source of knowledge). In Poland the historical conditions caused that communicative values are being noticed just recently[2]. The research among Polish exhibitors in 2004 point at significance of exhibitions in their marketing actions, which more and more frequently are considered a direct marketing scene. The exhibitors assign them two substantial roles: trade fairs are the perfect opportunity for professionals to discuss problems of the sector and new trends and they have a considerable impact on purchase decisions - much more considerable, then it was five years earlier[3].

The other tendency is visible among the trade fair organizers in countries of Western Europe, the USA and on the fairs in the Far East. The belief that it is not the number of exhibitors but the number and kind of visitors that determine success of fairs, grows in strength. Providing an appropriate number and quality of visitors is becoming a priority for the fair operator[4]. This tendency is also appearing among leading trade fairs operators in Poland.

Therefore the inquiry: how much exhibitors' strategy is visitor-oriented, is justified. Whether exhibitors take visitors' preferences into consideration when planning their fairs participation or not? This question is appropriate in view of conclusions given by Ph. Kreindler i G. Rajguru, which show that few products and services suppliers ask themselves a question what in fact a customer expects from a seller who is attending them. In their research they revealed the gap between the skills that the company expects its employees to have and the skills that the customer expects from the company workers (Kreindler, Rajguru, 2006).

Empirically verified answers to the inquiry about the adaptation of exhibitors to visitors' preferences may show to what extent companies participating in trade fairs, right down into evolution trends coming about in fair branches.

## Literature Review

Taking into consideration the role of fairs in business-to-business relations, the review of the existing marketing literature shows little interest in trade shows and trade show literature shows very few empirical studies. The majority of the studies are "how to" articles or, at best, conceptual works (Hansen, 1996).

Philip Kolter, in his concept of marketing-oriented management of companies, used mostly experiences of the US economy (Kotler, 1994). They are, however, different from European counterparts, where trade fairs and exhibitions have always had great importance. Trade fairs play a prominent role in countries like Germany, the UK, France and even Poland. This is one of the most important reasons why there is so little said about trade fairs in English literature – the marketing started in North America, whereas trade fairs did not (Kuca and Mruk, 2006).

In marketing, trade fairs are mostly approached from the exhibitors' point of view – their targets, decisions and trade fairs participation evaluation, and, most of all, techniques of sale (Bonoma, 1983, Kerin and Cron, 1987,). A big role of trade fairs on the field of business-to-business marketing is stressed concurrently (Parasuaraman, 1981, O'Hara, 1993). A less frequently considered option is a chance to use expiations for the sale purposes as well as communicative ones (Cavanaugh, 1976, Hansen, 1996,). It is believed that the aim of trade fairs is to satisfy two groups: exhibitors leading through promoting of their products to increase in sales and visitors who would buy promoted goods on the condition that they were positively impressed during the trade fairs (Thomas, 1995). Focusing on the sale as the effect of fair participation is understandable – it is measurable and it allows evaluation of the effectiveness of the enterprise easily. The communicative effect of fairs is much more difficult to capture and probably that is the reason of the gap in marketing literature.

Another research domain is dragging the attention to visitors' aims or their comparison with the aims of exhibitors. Studies of K. Hansen (Hansen 1996) and J. Blyth (Blyth, 1999) led to the conclusion that there is a divergence in perceiving trade fairs events. Another research focused on relations between the exhibitor and visitor during the fairs show the difference in behaviour of the exhibitors and visitors (Rosson and Seringhaus, 1995). Unfortunately, the three-level model proposed by the authors of this research was created on the basis of secondary source analysis and has not been empirically tested.

Taking for granted quoted results of studies that fairs are a tool of creating and establishing the relationships between companies and their employees, it is worth extending the research domain comprising not only general aims and participants' needs but also to go one level back and focus on the interaction on the stand which takes place within direct communication of a exhibitor and visitor.

## A Process of Serving the Customer

The relationship between exhibitors and visitors is created within a process, which as most observations at industrial exhibitions, consists of three stages – contact before reaching the stand, a visit at a place and relationship continuance after leaving. Relations are created then during the interactions, which can appear on each of the mentioned stages. Comprehension of these relations needs an interaction approach (Hakansson, 1982), considered as studies that focus on exchange processes and relationship formation between organizations. It aims at a more thorough understanding of interaction, its forms and development processes over time (Moller, 1994). Therefore aspects of interpersonal communication must be taken into consideration in researching exchange processes from an interaction perspective. Interpersonal communication is a substantial part of the interaction process and can therefore be regarded as a processual element of relationships and networks. Relationships and networks are essentially formed by interpersonal communication processes, which, in turn, are affected by their contextual and structural factors. Relationships and networks, therefore, cannot be understood without having knowledge of the communication processes occurring within them, and communication processes can be understood only if the situational factors (contextual and structural characteristics) are considered (Olkkonen et al., 2000).

It can be assumed that the course of communication process between the exhibitor and visitor should be adapted to the preferences of a visitor. At the same time, process of trade fairs attendance should be considered in a context of actions before, during and after the exhibition. Based on the Service-Dominant Logic (Lusch and Vargo, 2004) this service can be considered in the context of a service performed on the behalf of the visitor. Its quality can be described in accordance with attainments of service marketing. From this point of view, the quality means perceived quality of service as the difference between customers' expectations and their perceptions of the service they have actually received (Grönroos, 1984, Parasuraman et al., 1985). The adjustment of service process to visitors' needs can be described in five dimensions: tangibles, reliability, responsiveness, assurance, and empathy (Parasuraman et al., 1988). In the case of trade fairs these dimensions can be defined as follows:

- tangibles – a stand together with the exposition and the location of the stand in the fairs hall; the location where the relation takes place,
- reliability – the ability to serve the visitor efficiently,
- responsiveness – staff availability at the stand, staff interpersonal skills,
- assurance –ability of the staff to solve visitors' problems,
- empathy – the atmosphere, visitor's individual treatment.

## Trade Fairs as Research Field

The relationships between business partners are a significant study domain in business-to-business marketing. However, one is faced with certain restrictions in conducting research on these relations. The restrictions are due to the difficulty in observing a single process of creating and developing the relationship. The main problem is not to get to know the opinion of seller and buyer on the relation between one another but on the character of the relation itself. In the business-to-business market these relations are based on interpersonal communication. It can be studied on many arenas, for example during formal business negotiations, telephone discussions, e-mail or fax correspondence analysis (Olkkonen et al. 2000). None of these approaches, however, gives such opportunities of the research as the ones that are possible during trade fairs. The pros of conducting the research in fairs location are as follows: similar conditions of many interaction simultaneously and the opportunity to observe the creation of the relation at different stages – from the first contact with potential customers to the contact with permanent customer. The possibility to comprise within the research (in one place and time) a big part of companies of the same branch (due to appropriate fairs selection) is of great importance. All these pros advocate conducting the research on business relations during the fairs. Doing such a research needs the understanding of the role of the fairs.

## Conceptual Framework of the Research

Seeking the answer to the question about exhibitors' communicative adjustment to the visitors' preferences led to designing the research which aim was to state to what extent the adjustment appears. For the evaluation of communicative actions of exhibitors a benchmark must be established. A lack of ideal trade fair communication model inclines to accept, on the basis of a customer (i.e. visitor) orientation paradigm, that exhibitors' actions should be evaluated in relation to visitors' expectations. The authors' concept of Exhibitor Communication Excellence is based on the assumption, i.e. the better exhibitor's communication fulfils the visitors' expectations, the more excellent the process of communication. This evaluation should be done in service quality five dimensions. However, considering the focus on interpersonal communication it was decided to put secondary treatment of material process of services. Justification of this approach is the belief that when selling a tangible product in the business-to-business arena, the vendor often finds that the services provided in conjunction with the product are considered more important by the customer than the product itself (Cann, 1998).

When formulating the hypothesis dealing with exhibitors' communication adaptation to visitors' preferences it can carry a notion that it should be present in all these dimensions. The paradigm of customer orientation in conditions of intense competition for time and attention of visitors (which is common at fairs) advocates it. In the paper only a part of the research project is presented regarding to responsiveness. In this area it was assumed that the customer service after approaching the stand is compliant with his expectations. There are five hypotheses due to it:

H1. Time of starting the service after a visitor has approached does meets visitor's preference

H2. Exhibitor's behaviour after a visitor has approached the stand adjusts to visitors' expectations
H3. In case when the service process cannot be continued exhibitor acts in the way expected by visitors
H4. Exhibitor adjusts to visitor's preferences in sustaining the contact after the event by:
a) Proposing the contact
b) Aligning means of contact

Verification of the hypotheses was based on the Exhibitor Communication Excellence conception presented above. In our research we adopted a new approach to simultaneously learn preferences of visitors and behaviours of exhibitors. So far, trade fair research has not covered the interaction between the two groups. Representative visitor survey and comprehensive systematic direct observation of exhibitors provided us with rich scientific material.

## Research Methodology

The aim of the research was to identify and evaluate the course of contact action between a visitor and an exhibitor before the fairs, the service during fairs and the contact after the event. The aim of the research among visitors was to identify their communicative preferences in following areas:

- visitors' service,
- availability of the staff,
- communicative skills of the staff,
- abilities to solve visitors' problems and general atmosphere at a stand.

In our model we verify the hypotheses on comparison between the groups.

MEBLE (Fair of Furniture, Accessories and Furnishing) organized in May 2006 by Poznań International Fairs were taken in the research and within these fairs a group of 67 exhibitors offering beds and house furniture. In the exhibitors' research a mystery visitor method was used – a modification of mystery shopper. Adaptation consisted in establishing the paths of the researchers and taking into consideration behaviour specifics of the visitor in relation to an exhibitor. Each stand taken into the research was visited by three trained mystery visitors. Each mystery visitor behaved according to the same scenario and watched the same behaviours of the staff noting them after the visit in a special questionnaire/ survey. Thus a visit was our unit of analysis, not an exhibitor.

Simultaneously (the same day, same hours and the same market-halls) there was a research carried out among 244 visitors, which makes the results representative for exhibitions guests of that day (N=6000, E=4,4%, Z=1,96). Due to the lack of visitors' list, which could make it possible to do the lottery drawing to the sample, every *n* person entering the hall where were the stands covering the research.

## Results

In this section we present the results obtained while testing the proposed hypotheses.

### Hypothesis 1

Time of starting a conversation in exhibitors' research in Mystery Visitor method was measured with a stopper. The results were grouped and combined in table 2 according to visitors' expectations.

**Table 1: Behaviours and expectations of fairs participants due to starting the conversation**

| 1.1.1 time | Group | |
|---|---|---|
| | Visitor (n=242) | Mystery Visitor (n=190) |
| less than 3 minutes | 60.3% | 90.5% |
| 3-5 minutes | 7.5% | 2.7% |
| more than 5 minutes | 25.6% | 6.8%** |
| Time does not matter* | 6.6% | - |

* not taken into consideration in a comparative analysis.

** according to established procedure in the Mystery Visitor method the visitor left the stand if he/she had to wait for more than 5 minutes

The comparison of preferences of visitors and reactions of exhibitors shows significant differences ($\chi^2$=75,575, *df*=4, p<0,001). It could incline rejecting the h1. However, it should be stressed that the differences is positive in meaning. Declared waiting time of professional visitors appeared to be much longer than tested exhibitors' reaction.

## Hypothesis 2

Visitors' preference in a domain of initial waiting after approaching the stand was tested by one question with the possibility of multiple answer (6 item multiresponse).

**Table 2: Behaviours and expectations of trade fairs participants during the first contact at a stand**

| Name | Pct of Cases for Visitor (n=244) | Pct of Cases for Mystery Visitor (n=181) |
|---|---|---|
| Being a specialist | 53.7 | 80.7 |
| Calling a specialist | 30.7 | 12.2 |
| Pointing a specialist | 16.0 | 7.2 |
| Treat offer | 6.1 | 1.1 |
| Passing informational papers /catalogues about a company | 29.1 | 34.3 |
| Noting visitor's data | 10.7 | 0.6 |
| No expectations/ No reaction | 0.0 | 3.3 |

The results show that the attendance staff behaviour exceeds visitors' expectations, as the visitors do not expect the first person met at the stand to be a specialist. In this context the attention is called by the lack of noting the data of the visitor by the exhibitor personnel. Omitting this element can make a contact after the fairs difficult or even impossible.

In order to compare both groups, an index was created to reflect interdependence of given responses (e.g. "calling a staff member" and "treat offer"). On the basis of statistic analysis independence of the results of both groups ($\chi^2$=104,287, *df*=29, p<0,001) was stated. Thus, hypothesis h2 was rejected.

## Hypothesis 3

In the case of most 'mysterious visits' a moment of attendance occurred. Mystery Visitors could not have been attended only in 14 cases. Five of the exhibitors gave the reason of waiting; they also informed what the approximated waiting time would be and offered waiting for the specialist. The others apart from the refusal of attendance gave neither the reason for lack of attendance nor the time of waiting. They did not make offers of any kind (e.g. re-visit, waiting for a specialist).

Figure 1 presents visitors' expectations due to exhibitors' behaviours in case the attendance is impossible. Most frequently visitors pointed the offer of waiting (35.1% of indications). Visitors seem to present greater interest in being given exact (33.5% indications) than approximate (22.7%) time of waiting. The intention of hearing the reason of lack of attendance was declared by 14% of fairs guests. This, in fact, helps us support the proposition that professional visitor might possess bigger time budget than expected.

**Figure 1: Visitors' expectations when the start of specialist attendance at the stand is impossible**

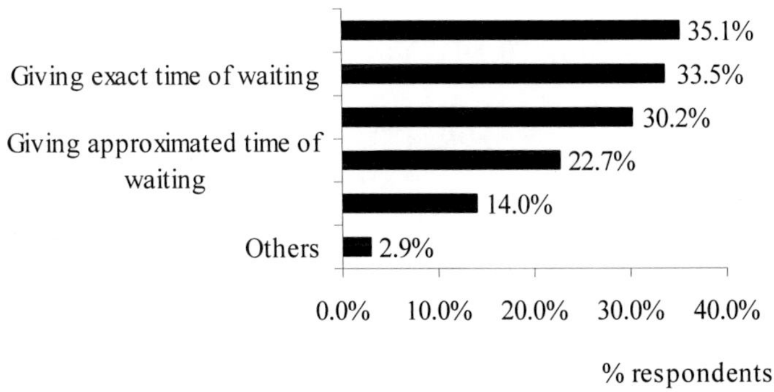


As there were only 14 cases of attendance lack among exhibitors the authors quit studying the statistic dependencies and further verification of this hypothesis. However, the observation of these situations incline to designing a research among visitors who leave the stand unattended – their impressions, opinions and inclinations to undertake co-operation with the exhibitor, who was not able to provide the attendance.

## Hypothesis 4a

Important elements of trade fairs communicative process are actions after the end of the exhibition (follow-up). The contact after the event is expected 91.4% of professional visitors (table 3). Meanwhile, a little more than a half of exhibitors within a mystery visitor study (54.8%) offered that.

**Table 3: Expectations and behaviours of fairs participants in a contact domain after the event**

| Expecting / offering the contact | Group | |
|---|---|---|
| | Visitor (n=244) | Mystery Visitor (n=166) |
| Yes | 91.4% | 54.8% |
| No | 8.6% | 45.2% |

No contact initiative in case of almost a half of the exhibitors may suggest that they do not put to much attention to the actions after fairs. Meanwhile, professional visitors treat it to be a significant element of fairs attendance (service). Statistic analysis showed significant divergence between the groups ($\chi^2$=73,694, df=1, p<0,001). Therefore, h4a was not accepted.

## Hypothesis 4b

As mentioned above the contact after trade show was expected by most of the visitors. Most of them preferred exhibitors' personnel to offer it and establish it during at least two weeks after trade fairs by electronic mail. During each of the mystery visits, exhibitors were asked to sustain the contact by e-mail. After three weeks the e-mail boxes were checked (table 4).

Almost all exhibitors did not follow up the contact established during the trade fairs though most of their visitors expected it. Statistic analysis showed significant divergence between the groups at the level ($\chi^2$=254,642, *df*=1, *p*<0,001). Therefore h4b was rejected, which shows that exhibitors did not meet visitors' preferences in the field of after trade fairs communication.

**Table 4: Visitors' expectations of after trade fairs contact and exhibitors' behavior**

| Expecting / sending an e-mail after trade fairs | Group | |
|---|---|---|
| | Visitor (n=244) | Mystery Visitor (n=166) |
| Yes | 74,6% | 1,8% |
| No | 25,4% | 98,2% |

## Discussion

Professional visitors come to trade fairs for certain reasons and their time is believed to be limited. After approaching the stand they want to start the conversation with the specialist, not with auxiliary staff. On the exhibitor's side namely there is a difficulty in matching the number of technical staff with the number of visiting guests. The solution is to prepare a reception desk, which is to manage attendance of the visitors especially in times when the specialists are occupied. Hypothesis h2 was rejected and the comparison of results of both research shows that exhibitors plainly exceeded expectations of visitors in the field of actions undertaken at the beginning of the contact at the stand. The results reached in the first field indicate that the exhibitors attended the visitors efficiently after their approaching the stand.

The visitors' expectations level is not surprising (with exception to the identified group of potentially invulnerable to the waiting time). Their professional character makes them well prepared to the fair visit. Authors' former studies show that merely one third of professional visitors come to fairs without a visit plan (Kwiatek and Zieliński, 2006). Visitors try to meet chosen exhibitors and are willing to wait for the appointment. They also allow the first person they met at a stand to not possess professional knowledge. However, they expect that this person would be able to manage the motion of visitors and would point or call a specialist with whom they could carry on further conversation. They expect that the first-contact staff would offer waiting for the meeting or rearrange the date of it.

Every third visitor expects brochures and leaflets about a company and products in the very beginning of the visit at the stand. In Polish fair guidebooks it is suggested that an exhibitor should send brochures after the fair event to the interested visitors. The results of a mystery visitor study show, however, that in one-third of cases the leaflets were obtained during conversation.

Probably exhibitors are aware of the significance of the first impression they can make on visitors, therefore most of the conversations simply aim to give answers to questions. Exhibitors can fear that a customer, who is not attended immediately, will never come back so there are actions taken to answer any questions instantly.

However, we cannot give high marks for exhibitors due to divergence of the visitors' expectations and exhibitors' actions in the field of registering the guests at stands. Such an action was taken only in 1.6% mystery visitors' cases. Expectation of registration was declared by 10.7% of visitors. Registration of data at the beginning of conversation is a prerequisite for the "after-exhibition" contact, which is expected by 91.4% of visitors. They come to trade fairs less to buy and more to distinguish latest advances, update information about the market and meet their partners[5]. Therefore they can expect that when a contact has been established during the trade fair it would be continued after the event has ended. They can also presume that noting the guest data is a sign of respect and putting attention to their visit.

A rejection of h4a may indicate that exhibitors forget that participation in the exhibition is a process, which is not exclusively limited to the communication and contact with a customer at a stand. Exhibitors do not offer to propose a sustaining contact while it is what customers expect. The need to develop trade fair contact after the event comes from the fair trade evolution into communicative role. Trade fairs are just a beginning or a stage of the process and certainly not its end.

The extent of the gap between exhibitors' actions to visitors' preferences are reflected in the results of h4b test. There is a significant disproportion in meeting the visitors' expectations concerning the attendance during and after exhibition. Observed exhibitors' inclination of putting too little attention to "after-show" contacts is proved by results of published studies according to which 80% of exhibitors conducts no follow-up actions in promised way (Seringhaus and Rosson, 1995). Meanwhile they are reckoned to be key features influencing the efficiency of fair participation (Saschi and Parretty, 1992).

## Implication for Further Research

One may wonder whether a noted decrease of adjustment is not a result of the construction of mystery visitors' role. It was of a trade character – combined with the will of single purchase of products. Perhaps when it was revealed by the staff, the level of interest in sustaining a contact dropped. Verification of such a statement needs further research in which mystery visitors should act as a user of the product and have more technical character. Another element, which is worth verifying in future studies, is defining whether pursuing time of attendance of a customer determines the quality of service. The subject of the research could also be intriguingly low interest in references in observed conversations and visitors' expectations. It may be due to the specifics of furniture branch in Poland.

In further research it is worth taking into consideration that testing by using mystery visitor method presents huge difficulties in finding and selecting people conducting the observation. In a business-to-business setting, they must be specialists in exact domain and at the same time they should have an ability to watch and notice important elements of service process. A big diligence is needed to plan a scenario of visits. Due to the fact that fairs are dynamic environment a lot of situations that may occur during the test must be taken into consideration.

## Manager Implications

The presented results show unequal spread of exhibitor's staff efforts in serving visitors. Fairs are an attendance process, which consists of mutually linked stages. In the initial phase actions exceed visitors' expectations, however, in the final one they are hardly fulfilled. The weakness of tested exhibitors is mostly a lack of initiative to sustain the contact. Taking into consideration the importance of fairs as a tool of prospecting, it is an unacceptable action. Levelling presented disproportion would influence the increase of efficiency of the actions undertaken by managers.

## Notes

[1] Data of Polish Fairs Corporation, www.polfair.com.pl
[2] During socialist economy the fairs were the opportunity to enter into relations but most of all to sign international contracts. In official announcements the indicator of a success of exact fairs was the value of all signed contracts.
[3] A research among 300 Polish exhibitors Pentor Research International, Trade fairs and exhibitions have been changing their image, Polish Trade Fairs Organization, Poznan 2005, http://www.polfair.com.pl/pentor_dobre_en.htm
[4] A symptom of visitor orientation can be an example of Euromedlab Fairs (in Amsterdam). A pre-registration, which was conducted before the fairs, guarantees the buyers being freed of fair charge. Organisers of fairs in Hausewares in Chicago provides the buyers who registered earlier not only with a free entry but also a free lunch during the visit on the fair premises. Paris Batimat Fairs consist mostly of conferences and seminars for the visitors.
[5] Exhibitions / Fairs Visitor Survey Repoart, Centrex, 2004, s. 8

## References

Black R., The Trade Shows Industry: Management and Marketing Career Opportunities, Trade Show Bureau, East Orleans, 1986

Blyth J.., *Visitor and exhibitor expectations and outcomes at trade exhibitions*, Marketing Intelligence & Planning 17/2 (1999), 100-108

Bonoma T. V., *Get more of your trade shows*, Harvard Business Review, January-February 1983, 75-84

Cann C.W., Eight steps to building a business-to-business relationship, Journal Of Business & Industrial Marketing, Vol. 13 no. 4/5 1998, pp. 393-405

Cavanaugh S., *Setting Objectives and Evaluating the Effectiveness of Trade Show Exhibits*, Journal of Marketing, October 1976, 100-103

Consumer perceptions of service quality. Journal of Retailing, 64 (1), 1988 Spring, 12-40

Grönroos C., A service quality model and its marketing implications. Journal of the Academy of Marketing Science, 24 (1), 1984, Winter, pp. 36 – 44.

Hansen K., *The dual motives of participants at international trade shows*, International Marketing Review, Vol 13, No. 2, 1996, 39-53

International Marketing and Purchasing of Industrial Goods. An Interaction Approach, Hakansson, H. (Ed.) John Wiley & Sons, Chichester 1982

Kerin R.A., Cron W.L., *Assessing Trade Show Functions and Performance: An exploratory Study*, Journal of Marketing, Vol. 51 (July 1987), 87-94

Kotler Ph., Marketing Management. Analysis, Planning, Implementation and Control, Prentice-Hall 1994

Kreindler Ph, Rajguru G., What B2B Customers Really Expect?, Harvard Business Review, April 2006.

Lusch R.F., Vargo S.L., Evolving to a New Dominant Logic for Marketing, Journal of Marketing 68(1) 2004, pp. 1-17

Kwiatek P., Zielinski M., Wpływ doświadczenia na preferencje komunikacyjne na rynku business to business (The Influence of Experience on Communication Preferences in B2B Context), Handel Wewnętrzny, październik 2006

O'Hara B.S., Evaluating the effectiveness of trade shows: a personal selling perspective, Journal of Personal Selling and Sales Management, Vol. 13, No.3, 1993, pp. 67-78

Olkkonen R., Tikkanen H., Alajoutsijarvi K., The role of communication in business relationships and networks, Management Decision 38/6, 2000, pp. 403-409

Parasuaraman A., The relative importance of industrial promotion tools, Industrial Marketing Management, Vol. 10, 1981, pp.277-81.

Parasuraman A., Zeithaml V.A., Berry L.L., A conceptual model of service quality and its implications for future research. Journal of Marketing, 49, 1985 Fall, 41-50.

Parasuraman A., Zeithaml V.A., Berry L.L., SERVQUAL: a multiple-item scale for measuring

Research Traditions in Marketing, Laurent, G. et al. (Eds), Kluwer Academic Publishers, London.

Saschi C. M., Parretty J., Do trade shows provide value? Industrial Marketing Management, 1992, s. 255

Seringhaus R., Rosson P., *Visitor and exhibitor interaction at industrial trade fairs,* Journal of Business Research 32, 1995, 81-90

Thomas M.J., Gower Handbook of Marketing, Gower Publishing 1995, p. 609

Trade Fairs Marketing, A.Kuca, H.Mruk (Ed.), Polish Trade Fairs Corporation, Poznan 2006, pp.9-11

# SECTION III:

# FINANCE AND BANKING

# FOREIGN BANKS IN CENTRAL EUROPE: DO THEY CONTRIBUTE TO ECONOMIC DEVELOPMENT?

PETER R. HAISS, KATHARINA STEINER AND MARKUS ELLER

## Abstract

This paper contributes to the finance-growth debate by reviewing the relationship between financial sector foreign direct investment and economic growth and development. The positive view of the finance-led growth hypothesis normally focuses on more open and liberalized financial systems. Banking markets in Central European transition economies are an extreme case of openness, as they are majority-held foreign. Does this spur economic growth? We contribute to the development literature by discussing through what kind of transmission channels foreign owned banks may have an impact on economic development and growth in transition economies.

## Introduction

In former socialist countries, financial sectors were characterised by state-owned monobank systems that caused inefficient resource allocation and thus large amounts of non-performing loans. Capital was scarce and overall productivity low. The inflow of foreign capital and in particular of Foreign Direct Investment (FDI) was seen as a key component for a solution to these problems (Sergi, 2004).

Various studies have attempted to provide theoretical and empirical answers to the question of the overall impact of general FDI on the host economy (e.g. Borensztein, De Gregorio and Lee, 1998; Mencinger, 2003; Dimelis and Louri, 2004; Rojec and Damijan, 2004), but results are mixed. We suggest that FDI effects on economic development might differ depending on the target industry, making a difference between real sector companies and financial firms. Financial sector foreign direct investment (FSFDI) into EU-Accession countries and (now) New EU Member states in Central and Eastern Europe (CEE) sharply rose in the second half of the 90s (Mišun and Tomšík, 2002; see figure 1). With an average of about 20% over 1999-2003, FSFDI accounted for a major fraction of total FDI in CEE, with foreign banks as major acquirers (OECD, 2004). Recent trends show a decline in primary FSFDI in CEE because privatization is ending in most Accession countries (besides Romania) and a shift in FSFDI further east and southeast. Secondary transactions – i.e. consolidation among (frequently foreign) bank owners - may bring about another round of financial sector mergers and acquisitions (M&A) in CEE, spurred by the UniCredit/BA-CA/HVB-consolidation.

**Figure 1: Total financial M&A from abroad and Economic Growth in 10 EU-Accession (CEE) countries1 (EUR mn), 1994-20022**

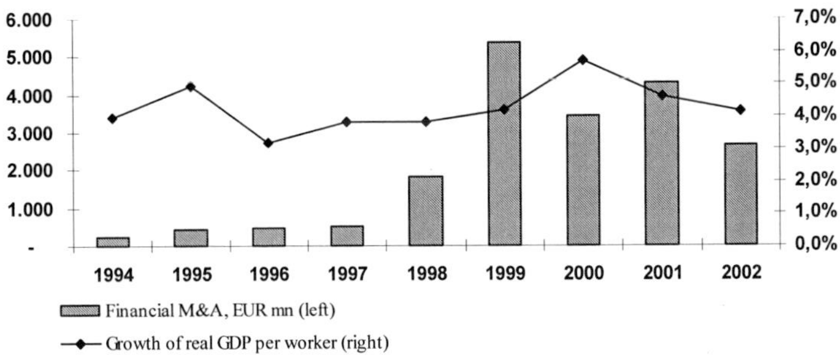


According to Breyer (2004), the share of total bank assets controlled by foreign owners accounted for around 70% in CEE in 2004. Since this is a very high level, possible consequences of foreign bank entry on financial sector development are increasingly discussed (e.g. Goldberg, 2004; Claessens, Demirgüç-Kunt and Huizinga, 2001) and the issue arises if this could have triggered growth in the host countries. Only recently, a few studies started to shift the focus from implications of foreign bank entry on financial sector development to implications on economic development and growth (e.g. Mehl and Winkler, 2003). The literature on foreign direct investment (FDI) in other industries is more familiar with analyzing direct links from foreign ownership to economic development (e.g. Mencinger, 2003).

We close this gap in research by investigating the impact of financial sector foreign direct investment (FSFDI) and in particular foreign bank entry on economic development and growth[3] in transition economies. Figure 2 provides preliminary evidence that growth in FSFDI is correlated to economic growth in CEE. Differences in development among CEE countries are reflected in the broad dispersion of FSFDI inflows.

**Figure 2: Economic Growth vs. FSFDI change in 10 EU-Accession (CEE) countries4, 1997-2003**

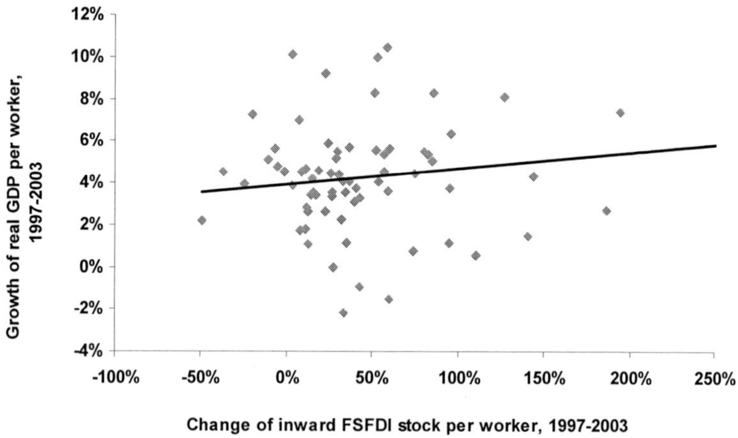


We contribute to the development literature by discussing through what kind of transmission channels foreign owned banks may have an impact on economic development. What are the opportunities for host economies? What challenges for host nations exist in order to promote rather positive effects? To tackle these issues we review theoretical literature and empirical studies on foreign bank entry as well as on the links between financial development and economic growth[5]. As the entry of foreign banks via FDI into CEE transition markets has been rapid, remarkable, and massive (Vessel, 2003), we collect descriptive evidence and put emphasis on these countries. The issue equally applies to other emerging markets: does FSFDI contribute to economic growth? We find that FSFDI is related to financial sector development as well as general economic development and growth, but the strength of the link varies.

The rest of the paper progresses in the following way. First, we explore how the financial sector is linked to economic development. Next, we discuss particular efficiency-driving characteristics of foreign owned banks in transition economies such as their strategic approaches and risk management. The following chapters analyze possible transmission channels and spill-over effects from foreign owned banks to economic development, such as efficiency spillovers, lending practices of foreign owned banks and further signal effects. A summary concludes.

## Relationship between Financial Sector and Economic Development

Financial intermediaries play an essential role in the economy because they mobilize savings and allocate and redistribute capital for investment. Well-working financial intermediaries will put effort in reducing the transaction costs involved, which leads to greater efficiency (Levine, 1997, 891). According to King and Levine (1993), efficiency, overall cost of financial services as well as depth and breadth of intermediation have an impact on economic growth. This finding assumes a positive link from the financial sector to economic growth. The "finance - economic development" link may follow five patterns, as Blum et al (2002, 7) put it: a leading role of the financial sector (supply-leading approach), a demand-following, a bi-directional link, negative causality from finance to economic growth and no link. The direction of the causality link may change with the level of economic development and seems less robust with more recent data (Rousseau and Wachtel, 2005). Patrick (1966) points out that the financial sector plays a supply-leading role in underdeveloped markets. Cross-country studies such as Beck, Levine and Loyaza (2000)[6] generally seem to support this supply-leading link. Time-series studies and regional studies like in Al-Tamimi, Al-Awad and Charif (2001) provide mixed evidence.

## Characteristics of Foreign Owned Banks in Emerging Markets

Bonin, Hasan and Wachtel (2005) analyzed a sample of 67 banks from six CEE countries and point out that foreign owned banks operating in emerging markets have been more efficient with regard to costs and profits than domestic banks, whereas the opposite is true in the case of mature markets. What may be the reasons? The following issues may provide some answers.[7]

## Strategic Issues

As foreign institutions enter emerging markets their strategic interests will vary according to their home-market or global activities. Most investors in CEE emerging banking markets have long-term profit interests as these markets offer the potential for strong business volume growth across the various client groups, including retail banking (BIS, 2004; Vessel, 2001).[8] Such "going local" strategies may help local financial market development e.g. by the implementation of products new to the host market (Gallego, Herrero, Luna, 2004). In case of an acquired bank, the integration into a multinational or even global financial organization leads to a migration of strategic decisions to the foreign headquarters whereas day-to-day responsibilities remain at the local level (BIS, 2004, 10). Close ties to the parental institution also derive from the access to parental resources, which might be a stable funding base in times of crisis. Possible negative impacts might occur as shocks from the groups' home market may be imported to the host market (BIS, 2004). Apart from such possible negative consequences, strategic reorientation has an impact on efficiency – may it be through the integration into the foreign bank and further specialisation or diversification among products.

## Risk Management Issues

Acquired banks usually receive a capital injection from the new owner (Papi and Revoltella, 2003, 157), so the ability of the target to bear risk and grant fresh credit rises. Particularly foreign owned banks have great interest in implementing sound policies and risk management as they have the capacity to implement group-wide risk assessment techniques (BIS, 2004, 15). An important issue is loan quality. According to Sergi and Matousek (2005), foreign owned banks play an important role in reducing the share of non-performing loans that was and still is high particularly in former state owned banks. Table 2 provides some evidence for selected countries. Papi and Revoltella (2003, 175) support this view and argue that the clearing of risky credit-portfolios requires majority interest by the foreign bank and takes time due to restructuration needs. The transfer of technology and know-how to the acquired bank is necessary to adapt to international practices and standards. Economies of scope due to risk-diversification contribute to greater efficiency in risk management.

**Table 1: Non-performing loans (NPL) to total bank loans (in percent)**

| | BUL | CZ | EE | HU | LV | LT** | PL** | SK | SL |
|---|---|---|---|---|---|---|---|---|---|
| 2000 | 17.3 | 19.9 | 1.0 | 3.0 | 4.6 | 11.3 | 15.5 | 13.7 | 6.5 |
| 2001 | 13.1 | 13.7 | 1.3 | 2.7 | 2.8 | 8.3 | 18.6 | 12.3 | 7.0 |
| 2002 | 8.6 | 10.6 | 0.8 | 2.9 | 2.0 | 6.5 | 22.0 | 9.2 | 7.0 |
| 2003 | 7.3 | 4.9 | 0.4 | 2.6 | 1.4 | 3.0 | 22.2 | 6.4 | 6.5 |
| 2004 | 7.1 | 4.1 | 0.3 | 2.7 | 1.1 | 2.3 | 15.5 | 5.4 | 5.7 |

(**) 30-day NPL classification; (***) 60-day NPL classification[1]

## Operational Efficiency

Foreign owned banks will have a great interest in implementing internal group-standards. As Li (2005, 40) points out, standardization across borders may be difficult to achieve. Drawing on U.S. experience, Goldberg (2004, 6) argues that foreign owned banks are likely to have more efficient credit allocation as well as sound monitoring and thus less risk; their operating costs are lower. On the other hand, foreign entrants might have to bear higher information costs, as they usually do not have local know-how to such an extent as domestic owned banks. Green, Murinde and Nikolov (2004) point out that foreign and domestic owned financial organizations are not really different with regard to economies of scale and scope. Papi and Revoltella (2003) make an interesting point arguing that for "cost efficiency a majority interest of at least 70 percent in the host bank capital is necessary" (Papi and Revoltella, 2003, 177). Only after a period of experimental learning in the new market and time for restructuration and upgrading of technology in case of acquisitions, cost efficiency can be realized (Papi and Revoltella, 2003, 177).

The previous issues have shown some evidence on higher efficiency of foreign owned banks. How is efficiency in financial intermediation linked to economic development? Most of the discussion on efficiency argues that efficiency gains in the whole sector are induced by changes in the competitive structure of the banking industry. The aim of the following sections is to identify channels through which foreign ownership in banking may affect economic development.

## Transmission Channels from FSFDI to Economic Development

### Transmission channel I: Intermediation / Efficiency

First, foreign ownership may drive down banks´ interest rate margins, thus lower companies cost of borrowing, which should facilitate investment. Foreign owners may have a direct impact on efficiency gains in loan portfolio management of the affiliate and thus external finance for investment by corporations and households. Better risk management, lower operating costs and the like allow for more efficient capital allocation. Foreign banks are able to set narrower interest margins and offer their services and products at lower prices. Local as well as regional competition among banks will increase (Drakos, 2003). These changes in the competitive structure of the banking industry may induce efficiency gains in the whole sector as argued by most of the discussion on efficiency (Goldberg, 2004, 5). Koivu (2004) found evidence that increasing financial sector efficiency measured by interest margins has growth enhancing effects on economies in transition. She applied cross-country and time-series regressions on nine CEE countries over a period of 1995-2002.

According to Eschenbach and Francois (2004), financial sector competition triggered by foreign banks is closely linked to economic growth in emerging market economies. Their cross-country regression analysis covered 130 countries, including most of the transition countries over a time period of 1990-1999. Higher sector efficiency induced by higher financial sector competition should result in an overall reduction of transaction costs. Greenfield investors represent new competitors per se, whereas acquisitions foster competition due to new market policies implemented by foreign owners, restructuring and the rollout of group risk systems and corporate governance practices. In case domestic banks are able to cope with foreign contenders, competition with foreign banks might improve the efficiency of the domestic banking system, according to Claessens, Demirgüç-Kunt and Huizinga (2001). Banks will need to refocus their business and specialize on (other) new target groups (e.g. SMEs) what will lead to higher costs for domestic banks. They might succeed by offering services more closely tailored to the needs of the local population and not by trying to compete on price with foreign competitors, which are mostly backed by large financial groups. Or, they might be crowded out as foreign owners "cherry pick" and only riskier target groups remain. Periods of severe instability in the financial sector might follow (IADB, 2005, 133; Papi and Revoltella, 2003, 176). Empirical evidence on knowledge spillovers to local enterprises is weak, according to the ECB (2001, 209). It is rather a long-run phenomenon.

While on the one hand competition will increase, on the other hand particularly cross-border mergers and acquisitions contribute to an increase of concentration in the financial systems of emerging market economies (BIS, 2004, 21). This might be a simple effect of transition reflecting the deepening of host country financial sectors that demand host country supervisors to monitor this development. Foreign bank entry also exposes local markets to regional (if not global) competition. External shocks may have an impact on the activities of foreign owned banks in the host market, e.g. through the reduction of foreign operations. The recent diversification of Spanish banks away from a previous concentration on Latin America by acquiring banks in Italy and the UK could be interpreted this way.

All in all, these issues point out that foreign owned banks may create an environment where the entire financial system is forced to become more efficient, with interest rate margins and thus lending rates under severe downward pressure. This is important for the investment climate, economic growth and development (Rossi, Schwaiger and Winkler 2004, 77).

## Transmission Channel II: Intermediation / Volume

Well-capitalised foreign owners may provide a higher volume of credit to the host countries′ companies. In CEE and other emerging markets, bank lending is the most common method of external financing and thus important for investment. Credit to the private sector remains relatively low, although it is most important for investment activities. Wachtel (2003, 44) points out that "deeper financial intermediation may be a significant causal factor in economic growth [..]". But, "[..] one cannot infer that every expansion of intermediary activity will be beneficial" (Wachtel, 2003, 44). As foreign owned banks hold increasingly high shares in banking assets in emerging market economies, it is crucial to look at the role that foreign owned banks play in credit allocation.

De Haas and Van Lelyveld (2002, 27) found evidence that local credit by foreign owned banks to domestic credit as well as to GDP rose in the 90s, with the only exception of Slovenia. The Slovenian financial market was opened to foreign institutions in 1998. The increasing number of foreign market entries to CEE is reflected in these numbers, too[1]. In contrast, Engerer and Schrooten (2004) find no empirical evidence for eight CEE countries over the period of 1995-2002 on a clear impact of foreign bank entry on financial depth in terms of credit volume. In general, the impact of foreign bank entry on credit supply depends on the form of market entry. In case of an acquisition, the existing client base is acquired. Restructuring may shift the focus to different target groups and requires a cleaning of non-performing loans (Naaborg et al, 2003). In case a new subsidiary is established, the number of financial intermediaries increases. Competition is going to rise in both cases. Better risk assessment allows foreign owned banks to finance higher risk/return projects. They have the ability to provide fresh money to the financial host-market because foreign owned banks are backed by their parent companies. These issues on foreign bank entry affect a foreign banks' behaviour in the host market. All in all, the impact of foreign bank lending on capital accumulation, consequently on investment and economic development, depends on their lending practices to different target groups (the private and the public sector) and on their reaction in times of economic downturn.

## Impact of lending practices on the private and the public sector

Credit supply to different target-groups has various impacts on economic development. Lending the private sector is necessary to further support private investment, whereas providing finance to an efficient state and thus improve infrastructure efficiency can be a major way to reasonably foster economic growth during transition (Fink, Haiss and Vuksic, 2004). Bol, De Haas and De Haan (2003, 15) argue that foreign financial institutions are more involved in lending to the private sector than domestic banks in CEE. The rising involvement of foreign banks in private sector credit may have a positive impact on investment activities. According to Papi and Revoltella (2003, 159), foreign bank lending is mostly directed to subsidiaries of multinational corporations because the assessment of information coming from the local private sector is often too difficult due to missing transparency or even lack of information. Mehl and Winkler (2003, 17) find anecdotal evidence for South-Eastern Europe that foreign owned banks "cherry picked" the best borrowers particularly those from their own country of origin. The economy might grow below potential if this is the case. But foreign banks can also be primarily involved in retail banking, such as most Austrian banks in CEE (Breyer, 2004) and contribute to extending credit to the private sector compared to domestic banks. They seem to have replaced domestic banks as creditors. Credit to the private sector is on the rise from a comparatively low level according to Naaborg, Scholtens and De Haan et al (2003).

Credit to the public sector exceeds credit to the private sector in foreign owned as well as domestic banks in CEE (Bonin, Hasan and Wachtel, 2005, 2172). According to Fink, Haiss and Vuksic (2004, 20) who applied panel data and cross-section regressions on a sample of nine CEE and 18 developed countries (1996-2000), domestic credit, which includes private credit as well as credit to central and local governments, was more important for growth than private credit. Koivu (2004) supports these results applying a fixed effects regression analysis on 25 transition countries. These results are different from most theoretical literature because the above mentioned estimations use data on domestic credit. The specific characteristics in the accession countries account for these results (Fink, Haiss et al, 2004, 22). The results suggest that credit to the public sector may be growth enhancing as well. The financing of budget and current account deficits (Breyer, 2004, 73) can create a certain mutual dependency of the public and the financial sector increasing the interest of foreign banks in an efficient, sound, regulated and stable financial sector in order to mitigate country risk and promote economic development.

The effects of foreign owned bank lending are unevenly distributed among firms showing differences in e.g. size. Foreign bank entry therefore affects lending to SMEs and overall industrial structures particularly in industries that are dependent on bank finance. Small local businesses mostly rely on relationship lending (IADB, 2005, 136). In many developing and transition economies, banks are highly involved in relationship lending. In other words, already established companies owned by related individuals may receive funding even if they are operating inefficient whereas potentially highly profitable but young projects may face problems in search for funding. This entrepreneurial activity is important for economic development in transition economies. Foreign owned institutions often "do not serve" relationship lending due to a lack in the transparency of information. Interestingly, young enterprises that were established after the early transition period profited more from foreign bank entry (Giannetti and Ongena, 2005). Giannetti and Ongena (2005) focused on lending practices of foreign owned banks in a sample of 14 CEE countries over a period of 1993 to 2002. In contrast, one of Vanasschee's (2004, 20) results showed that financial integration positively affected the external financing situation of older and more mature firms. A possible explanation is that information for such firms is easier available than for new ventures. Foreign owned banks have information disadvantages as they face large information asymmetries vis-à-vis SMEs in emerging and transition economies. The use of soft information in lending decisions requires a decentralized organization because it is difficult to pass soft information within a bank. Decision making is often not that much decentralized because of a lack of local expertise or local personnel may be considered untrustworthy. Therefore, SMEs may profit to a lesser extent from financial integration than large and established companies. This does not necessarily imply a negative impact on SMEs. The application of international standards by foreign owned banks may enhance allocational efficiency, contribute to institution building over the long run and enhance overall stability as well as sustainable economic development, i.e. support SMEs investment environment positively.

According to Bruckbauer and Perrin (2004, 37), the offering of structural funds by the EU to the CEE member states were seen as a potential tool for stepping up lending to SMEs as banks had an opportunity to co-finance loans from these funds. For example in the Czech Republic, banks provided information for SMEs on how to qualify for the structural funds and they conducted pre- and co-financing.

All in all, foreign banks are more involved in lending to the private sector than domestic banks. Foreign lending stimulates firm growth in sales, assets and leverage via investment activities (Giannetti and Ongena, 2005). Countries experienced higher growth rates in case they had higher investment to GDP ratios. Among other reasons, efficient allocation of resources contributes to differences in growth (Wachtel, 2001, 339).

**Lending practices, sector stability and economic development**

Growing credit-supply is not enough to guarantee a positive impact on investment activities and thus economic development. Fast credit growth can also be a warning signal indicating a potential financial crisis (Mehl and Winkler, 2003). A lending boom may for example reflect an accumulation of bad loans such as in the Czech Republic at the end of the 90s when private sector credit to GDP attained relatively high levels. In addition to that, countries can experience high rates of savings and investment, but have poor economic growth such as in the case of the former Soviet Union. Saving rates as well as investment rates used to be high, but machinery and equipment were scarce. What was the reason? Capital was simply not allocated in an efficient way (Wachtel, 2001, 338). These examples show that quality of lending as well as efficient credit allocation seems to be significantly more important for economic performance than mere lending volumes (Giannetti and Ongena, 2005). Financial markets were mostly opened in CEE in hope for fast improvement in the quality of the financial system (De Haas and Van Lelyveld, 2002). Empirical evidence on the possible stabilizing influence of foreign ownership is provided by Engerer and Schrooten (2000) who analyzed eight CEE countries over a period of 1995 to 2002. Their results as well as evidence provided by the IADB (2005) emphasize several advantages of foreign owned banks in this regard. Foreign parent companies might act as a lender of last resort to their local units and related private institutions. Furthermore, foreign owned banks are less exposed to local default risk due to the higher degree of global (risk) diversification and their often long-term interest. In addition to that, they argue that less volatile deposits and higher loan quality of foreign owned banks compared to domestic banks add to it. Mathieson and Roldos (2001) argue in support of more stable lending sources, too. Better disclosure, accounting and reporting practices as well as stronger prudential supervision are crucial for positive impacts of foreign bank entry on lending practices as well as financial sector stability.

De Haas and Van Lelyveld (2002, 27) argue that there is at least no evidence of a persistent decrease in foreign credit during adverse economic times. They outline that recessions and crisis may lead to a temporary decrease in cross-border credit, which is then offset by foreign subsidiaries' credit. In addition, the presence of foreign banks within borders may encourage domestic depositors to keep their money within the domestic financial system in times of economic or financial distress because foreign banks are often recognized as being healthier and more efficient than domestic ones (Goldberg, 2004; Levine, 1996). In a macroeconomic point of view, this "flight to quality" may be better than capital flight out of the country.

Foreign owners may also have lower exit costs, depending on the organizational form of market entry. They may be more sensitive to shocks in the host country and cut back on local operations rapidly (IADB, 2005, 134). This argument is in favour of procyclical lending practices of foreign subsidiaries (e.g. Goldberg, 2004). If lending becomes overly procyclical due to foreign banks behaviour, credit swings might affect financial sector stability strongly. Goldberg (2004) points out that foreign banks as procyclical lenders do not appear to magnify the boom-boost cycles in emerging markets. If foreign owned banks are inclined to contribute to the overall soundness of the local financial market, financial crisis risks should decline and greater stability may foster economic development.

## Transmission Channel III: Institution Building & Corporate Governance

From the perspective of most CEE host countries, financial markets were opened to foreign investors in hope of fast improvement in the quality of banking and the whole the financial system (De Haas and Van Lelyveld, 2002), such as in the case of Hungary. Already in 1987 with the establishment of a two-tier banking system, foreign banks were encouraged to enter the Hungarian market, anticipating that they could improve the performance of domestic banks (Sabi, 1995, 180)[1]. It was generally assumed by host governments, that they were not only operating more efficiently but would also introduce higher, international standards to the respective market

Acquired banks are usually subject to strategic reorientation and receive a capital injection, which allows for the upgrading of technologies, know-how und operational practices. Credit policies are usually being adapted to group-wide and thus international standards. This seems of particular importance as banks in CEE were burdened with large amounts of bad loans. The government cleaned the banks' loan portfolios before or during privatization to make them more attractive for potential investors. Foreign banks are less involved in connected lending, as they need to stick to international standards and comply with internal group-wide rules, which contribute to a reduction in bad loans. Giannetti and Ongena (2005) applied panel data estimations based on data from 14 CEE countries over the period of 1993 to 2005. The results showed that firms established in early transition received less lending from foreign owned banks. According to them, this may suggest that foreign banks might be able to mitigate problems of related lending as these firms mostly had worse corporate governance, had less dispersed ownership, and benefited from favours of politicians. In which way these firms nevertheless contribute to economic growth shall not be discussed, however, the implementation of sound and international standards is crucial for stable economic development. Better loan portfolio and risk management can contribute to financial stability, which is important for economic development[1] (King and Levine, 1993). In order to finance public and private investment and expenditure, there is a need for a stable and efficient banking system (Uiboupin, 2004, 11). The implementation of sound financial practices in the affiliates may contribute to sound and more stable financial systems. But what about spillovers to domestic banks?

FDI literature highlights the importance of spillover effects (Uiboupin, 2000, 11). Nevertheless, know-how and technology transfer within the same branch is seen as a problem (Hunya, 2002). It might be less problematic to transfer know-how to other industries that do not represent competitors to the (foreign) investor. Mutual gains for both industries are rather possible. In case of the financial industry, the implementation of stricter credit requirements will create the need for companies seeking external finance to adapt to these standards – mostly international standards. To put it differently, resources might be allocated to more profitable businesses that themselves stick to international accounting standards, auditing practices, sound corporate governance and the like. This holds truth for companies seeking external finance. But over the long run, all industries might be affected which might contribute to stable economic development. Again, a certain initial level of social capabilities and absorptive capacity of domestic companies as well as infrastructure in support of an improvement in corporate standards is needed. In that case, a crowding-out effect of investment can be avoided. Of course, this does not only hold true for foreign banks, but also for domestic banks adapting their standards to the international level in the process of restructuration. The particular role of the financial sector as an intermediator within an economy will encourage such spillovers on the economic infrastructure including regulation, legislation, supervision and the like (Bonin and Wachtel, 2002). As foreign banks enter emerging markets, the introduction of products or services being new to the market is faster and innovation might even be accelerated through FSFDI (Wachtel, 2001). This creates the need for supervisors to adapt the legal environment to these developments. In case regulations for new services are not in place or are not accurately and fast enough adapted, abuse can occur which would harm the financial sector and the whole economy (Bonin and Wachtel, 2002). Foreign banks might even be inclined to introduce new products to evade existing legislation, particularly in case of weak financial systems (Goldberg, 2004, 14). Therefore, local supervisors have to upgrade their knowledge and further adapt regulations in order to secure financial sector stability. Foreign banks seeking to mitigate their own risk act as a catalyst for regulatory changes and implementation of international standards (BIS, 2004, 14). In this way, foreign banks can contribute to institutional quality, which is determined by the absence of corruption, red tape, or political violence (Faria and Mauro, 2004, 3).

An interesting aspect in this context concerns the origins of the legal system. Legal systems (e.g. English common law vs. Continental European civil law) have different approaches to e.g. creditor-debtor relationships which are important for the stability and performance of the financial system and thus for economic development (La Porta, Lopez-de-Silanes and Shleifer, 2002). In case, foreign parental organizations have different backgrounds with regard to the legal system they come from, does and if yes, how may this have an impact on the above discussed transmission channel via institutional building? For space considerations, we will not elaborate this notion further here, but it seems of interest to raise this question.

Institutional upgrading not only within the financial industry is basic for stable economic development of domestic industries. Foreign banks might contribute to economic development in two ways as presented in this chapter. First, by a direct impact on the improvement of loan portfolio quality. The reduction in bad loans and thus channelling of credit to profitable businesses that does not represent risk, or by not complying to international standards or by means of too low levels of standards. Second, by indirectly contributing to improvements in accounting standards, auditing practices and the like – in other words spillovers - on and improvement in overall corporate governance in any industry (seeking external finance) as well as infrastructure (i.e. regulations and supervision).

## Transmission Channel IV: Signal Effects

Foreign owned banks may strive to gain higher market share through product innovation and by offering a variety of new financial services, such as asset management services. New market segments are being developed. Rising national income together with pension reforms may add to the demand for and implementation of tradable securities as well for private investors (BIS, 2004, 13). Product innovation and the need of local risk-management to hedge risks locally foster capital market development. In consequence, corporate investors may chose from a greater range of finance possibilities that may spur investment and economic growth.

Furthermore, additional non-financial portfolio investment as well as non-financial FDI might be drawn in, which in turn influence economic growth (Durham, 2003; Reisen and Soto, 2001). If investors that are rather regarded as rather cautious and risk averse (a usual perception of banks) enter and invest into a certain market, this initial move may pull in followers from other industries.

## Challenges for Host-Countries

At the macroeconomic level, a transparent and effective legal and supervisory environment is necessary to allow sound financial market development and efficient implementation of sound credit policies at firm-level. At the beginning of the transformation both the institutional and legislative frameworks in CEE were underdeveloped (Sergi, 2005). Therefore, problems occurred right after the opening of financial markets. Too soft initial licensing conditions for banks lead to the entry of many small and risky banks that were sometimes involved in fraudulent activities (Fink et al, 2004, 7). Foreign owned banks might also be inclined to introduce new products to evade existing legislation, particularly in case of weak financial systems (Goldberg, 2004, 14). Therefore, local supervisors have to upgrade their knowledge and further adapt regulations in order to secure financial sector stability. Foreign owned banks seeking to mitigate their own risk act as a catalyst for regulatory changes and implementation of international standards (BIS, 2004, 14). Due to the increasing complexity as banks expand operations to several markets, greater cooperation among home and host country supervisors is needed (BIS, 2004, 25)[1]. Consequently, improvements in accounting standards and auditing practices usually follow (BIS, 2004, 13). All industries may profit from higher standards and transparency in the long run because these basics are part of transparent competition and stable economic growth. The legal and regulatory environment influences growth e.g. via sector stability (La Porta et al, 1998; Wachtel, 2003, 45). Financial deepening can only be growth promoting together with a sound legal and regulatory environment and hard budget constraints. Foreign owned banks play a proactive role as they can improve overall corporate governance and thereby improve economic development.

## Conclusion

The finance-growth literature maintains that the financial sector can contribute to economic growth. The followers of foreign direct investment

(FDI) argue that FDI can be a major growth trigger. What about financial sector foreign direct investment (FSFDI)? We combine these separate streams of literature by investigating the impact of FSFDI on economic growth, particularly in EU-Accession countries from Central and Eastern Europe (CEE). This issue equally applies to other emerging markets: does FSFDI contribute to economic growth?

In reviewing the literature, we first identify special characteristics of foreign owned banks, such as better risk-management techniques, and discuss research results on how foreign owned banks have an impact on financial sector development. We find some positive but preliminary evidence. We contribute to the literature by identifying the following possible transmission channels between FSFDI, financial sector development and economic growth: financial market development; intermediation/price; intermediation/volume; institution building and corporate governance; capital market development; attraction of further capital inflows. Technology and know-how spillover within foreign owned banks operating in the host market are the basis for direct and indirect transmission channels to financial sector development. Concerning spillover effects on domestic institutions within the whole financial sector, ambiguous results exist. Data availability also limits the ability to identify possible long-term effects in the transition economies of CEE. The specific mechanisms of the transmission channels between FSFDI and economic growth are not clearly explored yet. Despite this fact, consensus exists on the importance of the legal and supervisory environment as well as further cross-border cooperation of supervisors. Their improvement is and will continue to be one of the most important challenges for host financial markets in transition economies.

It seems evident that most transmission channels are linked to financial sector development. The key point is that previous studies on foreign bank entry do not particularly emphasize the possible importance of the latter for economic development. This issue is of great importance to host nations as it raises the question whether possible benefits of foreign bank entry spillover on overall economic development and justify the costs of attracting further foreign investors in the financial sector (Goldberg, 2004). As the financial sector has particular impacts on all other industries and thus economic growth and development, this issue needs further detailed research.

## Notes

[1] CEE 10 include Bulgaria (BG), Croatia (HR), Czech Republic (CZ), Estonia (EE), Hungary (HU), Latvia (LV), Lithuania (LT), Poland (PL), Slovenia (SL), Slovakia (SK).
[2] Source: Baudino, Caviglia, Dorucci et al (2004); AMECO (2005); own calculations.
[3] For seminal research on the finance-growth-nexus see King and Levine (1993), for the law-and-finance-view see La Porta, Lopez-de-Silanes and Shleifer (2002).
[4] Source: AMECO:(2005); Hunya and Stankovsky (2005); own calculations.
[2] Economic development refers to more than economic growth which is being used to quantify economic development in most studies: development of the private sector, economic stability, increasing income etc. Therefore, we talk about economic development.
[3] For details see Blum et al (2002).
[7] We make no distinction between forms of investment of FSFDI as it is difficult to distinguish the effects of foreign bank entry on host economies by mode of entry due to limited data availability and the dominance of acquisitions in the course of privatisations in CEE (Mišun and Tomšík 2002, 40). Therefore we have to concentrate on acquisitions.
[8] For details see BIS (2004).

## References


Al-Tamimi, Hussenin / Al-Awad, Mouawiya / Charif, H. (2001): Finance and growth: evidence from some Arab countries, *Journal of Transnational Management Development* 7/2, 3-18.

AMECO (2005): annual macroeconomic database of the European Comission's Directorate General for Economic and Financial Affairs (DG ECFIN), April 2005.

Baudino, P. / Caviglia, G. / Dorrucci, E. / Pineau, G. (2004): Financial FDI to the EU accession countries, *European Central Bank paper*, http://www.bis.org/publ/cgfs22ecb.pdf.

Beck, Thorsten / Levine, Ross / Loayza, Norman (2000): Financial intermediation and growth: causality and causes, *Journal of Monetary Economics* 46, 31-77.

BIS (2004): Foreign direct investment in the financial sector of emerging market economies, Report submitted by the Committee on the Global Financial System, Bank for International Settlement, March 2004, http://www.bis.org/publ/cgfs22.pdf.

Blum, David / Federmair, Klaus / Fink, Gerhard / Haiss, Peter (2002): The Financial-Real Sector Nexus: Theory and Empirical Evidence, *EI Working Paper* 43, http://fgr.wu-wien.ac.at/institut/ef/wplist.html.

Bol, Hanneke / De Haas, Ralph / De Haan, Jakob (2003): How Important are Foreign Banks in the Financial Development of European Transition Countries?, *CESifo Working Paper Series* 2003, http://ssrn.com/abstract=484944.

Bonin, John / Hasan, Iftekhar / Wachtel, Paul (2005): Privatisation matters: Bank efficiency in transition countries, *Journal of Banking & Finance* 29, 2155-2178.

Bonin, John / Wachtel, Paul (2002): Financial sector development in transition economies: Lessons from the first decade, *BOFIT Discussion Papers* 9, Bank of Finland, Institute for Economies in Transition.

Borensztein, E. / De Gregorio, J. / Lee, J.-W. (1998): How does foreign direct investment affect economic growth?, *Journal of International Economics* 45, 115-135.

Breyer, Peter (2004): Central and Eastern Europe – The Growth Market for Austrian Banks, *Monetary Policy & The Economy* 3, 63-88, http://www.oenb.at/en/img/mop_20043_analyses5_tcm16-21311.pdf.

Bruckbauer, Stefan / Gardó, Sándor (2004): Banking in CEE, *BaCa Xplicit Extrareport*, April 2004, http://economicresearch-.ba-ca.com

Claessens, Stijn / Demirgüç-Kunt, Asli / Huizinga, Harry (2001): How Does Foreign Entry Affect Domestic Banking Markets?, *Journal of Banking and Finance* 25/5, 891-991.

De Haas, Ralph T.A. / Van Lelyveld, Iman (2002): Foreign Bank Penetration and Private Sector Credit in Central and Eastern Europe, *De Netherlandsche Bank Staff Reports* 91, http://papers.ssrn.com/sol3/results.cfm.

Demirgüç-Kunt, Asli / Maksimovic, Vojislav (2002): Funding growth in bank-based and market-based financial systems: evidence from firm-level data, *Journal of Financial Economics* 65, 337-363.

Dimelis, S. / Louri, H. (2004): Foreign Direct Investment and Technology Spillovers: Which Firms Really Benefit? Review of World Economics 140/2, 230-253.

Drakos, Kostas (2003): Assessing the success of reform in transition banking 10 years later: an interest margins analysis, *Journal of Policy Modelling* 25, 309-17.

Durham, Benson (2003): Foreign Portfolio Investment, Foreign Bank Lending and Economic Growth, *The Federal Reserve Bank - International Finance Discussion Papers* 757.

Engerer, Hella / Schrooten, Mechthild (2004): Do foreign banks improve financial performance? Evidence from EU accession countries, *Research Notes DIW Berlin* 1, 1-19, http://www.diw.de/deutsch/produkte/publikationen/.

Eschenbach, Felix / Francois, Joseph / Schulknecht, Ludger (2000): Financial Sector Openness and Economic Growth, in Claessens, S./ Jansen, M. (ed.), *The Internationalization of Financial Services*, Kluwer Law International, 103-115.

Faria, André / Mauro, Paolo (2004): Institutions and External Capital Structure of Countries, *IMF Working Paper* 04/236.

Fink, Gerhard / Haiss, Peter / Vuksiç, Goran (2004): Changing Importance of Financial Sectors for Growth from Transition to Cohesion and European Integration, *EuropeInstitute Working Paper* No. 58, http://fgr.wu-wien.ac.at/institut/ef/wp/WP58.pdf.

Gallego, Sonsoles / Herrero, Alicia / Luna Crista (2004): Investing in the financial sector of emerging countries: potential risks and how to manage them, FDI in the financial sector of emerging market economies, BIS Committee on the Global Financial System, March 2004, http://www.bis.org/publ/cgfs22bdel.pdf.

Giannetti, Mariassunta / Ongena, Steven (2005): Financial Integration and Entrepreneurial Activity: Evidence from Foreign Bank Entry in Emerging Markets, *SSRN Working Paper Series*, http://papers.ssrn.com/sol3/paper.cfm?abstract_id=669421.

Goldberg, Linda (2004): Financial-Sector Foreign Direct Investment and Host Countries: New and Old Lessons, *Federal Reserve Bank of New York Staff Repor* 183, April 2004, http://www.newyorkfed.org/research/staff_reports/sr183.pdf

Green, Christopher / Murinde, Victor / Nikolov, Ivaylo (2004): The efficiency of foreign and domestic banks in Central and Eastern Europe: Evidence on economies of scale and scope, *Journal of emerging market finance* 3/2, http://emf.sagepub.com/cgi/reprint/3/2/175.

Hunya, Gábor (2002): Recent impacts of foreign direct investment on growth and restructuring in Central European transition countries, WIIW, no. 284, May 2002.

Hunya, Gábor / Stankovsky, Jan (2005): Foreign Direct Investment in Central and Eastern Europe with Special Attention to Austrian FDI Activities in this Region, *WIIW-WIFO Database.*

IMF (1993): Balance of Payments Manual 5, Washington D.C., 1993.

—. (2005): *Global Financial Stability Report, Sept. 2005*, http://www.imf.org.

Inter American Development Bank (2005): *Unlocking Credit: The Quest for Deep and Stable Bank Lending*, http://www.iadb.org/res/ipes/2005/index.efm.

King, Robert G. / Levine, Ross (1993): Finance and growth: Schumpeter might be right, *Quarterly Journal of Economics* 108/8, 717–37.

Koivu, Tuuli (2004): Banking sector development and economic growth in transition countries, in Balling, Morten / Lierman, Frank / Mullineux, Andy (ed.), *Financial Markets in Central and Eastern Europe*, London, 47-60.

La Porta, R. / Lopez-de-Silanes, F. / Shleifer, A. (2002): Government ownership of banks, *Journal of Finance* 57/1, 265-301.

La Porta, R. / Lopez-de-Silanes, F. / Shleifer, A. / Vishny, R. (1998) 'Law and finance', *Journal of Political Economy*, 106/6, 1113–55.

Levine, Ross (1996): Foreign Banks, Financial Development and Economic Growth, in Barfield (edit.), *International Financial Markets: Harmonisation Versus Competition*, Washington, AEI Press: 224-254.

—. (1997): Financial development and economic growth: Views and agenda, *Journal of Economic Literature* 35/2, 688–726.

Mathieson, D. / Roldos, J. (2001): The role of foreign banks in emerging markets, in R. Litan, P. Masson, Pomerleano, The role of foreign banks in emerging markets, The Brookings Institution, Washington D.C., 15-55.

Mehl, Arnaud / Winkler, Adalbert (2003): *The finance-growth nexus and financial sector environment: new evidence from Southeast Europe*, paper presented at the Ninth Dubrovnik Economic Conference on "Banking and the Financial Sector in Transition and Emerging Market Economies", Croatian National Bank, June 2003, http://www.hnb.hr/dub-konf/9-konferencija-radovi/mehl-winkler.pdf.

Mencinger, Jože (2003): Does Foreign Direct Investment Always Enhance Economic Growth?, *Kyklos* 56/4, 493-510.

Mišun, Jan / Tomšík, Vladimír (2002): Does Foreign Direct Investment Crowd in or Crowd out Domestic Investment?, *Eastern European Economics* 40/2, 38-56.

Naaborg, Ilko / Scholtens, Bert / De Haan, Jakob et al (2003): How important are foreign banks in the financial development of European Transition Countries, *CESifo Working Paper Series* 1100, 2003.

OECD (2004): *International Direct Investment Statistics Yearbook 1992-2003*, 2004 Edition, OECD, Paris.

Papi, Luca / Revoltella, Debora (2003): Foreign direct investment in the banking sector: experiences and lessons from CEECs, in Colombe, Emilio / Driffill, John (ed.), The role of financial markets in the transition process, Physica Verlag, 155-178.

Patrick, H. T. (1966): Financial Development and Economic Growth in Underdeveloped Countries, *Economic Development and Cultural Change* 15, 174-189.

Reisen, Helmut / Soto, Marcel (2001): Which types of capital inflows foster developing-country growth?, *International Finance* 4, 1-14.

Rojec, Matija / Damijan, Joe (2004): Foreign Direct Investment and the Catching-up Process in New EU Member States: Is There a Flying Geese Pattern, wiiw Research Reports No. 310, The Vienna Institute for International Economic Studies (wiiw), Vienna, October; OeNB Jubiläumsfonds-Project No. 9958.

Roldos, Jorge (2001): FDI in emerging markets banking systems, paper presented at the OECD Global Forum on International Investment, Mexico City, 26-27 November, 2001.

Rossi, Stefania / Schwaiger, Markus / Winkler, Gerhard (2004): Banking Efficiency in Central and Eastern Europe, OenB: *Financial Stability Report* 8 /12, 77-91.

Rousseau, Peter / Wachtel, Paul (2005): Economic Growth and Financial Depth: Is the relation extinct already? Paper presented at the UNU/WIDER Conference on Financial Sector Development, July 2005, Helsinki.

Sabi, Manijeh (1995): Comparative analysis of foreign and domestic bank operations in Hungary, *Journal of Comparative Economics* 22/0017, 179-188.

Sergi, Bruno (2004): Understanding the „EU-factor“: the Balkans regions as recipients of FDI and industries, *South-East Europe Review* 7/4, 7-20.

Sergi, Bruno / Matoušek, Roman (2005): Management of Non-Performing Loans in Eastern Europe, *Journal of East-West Business* 11/1/2, 141-166.

Uiboupin, Janek (2004): Effects of foreign banks entry on bank performance in the CEE countries, *Tartu University Press* 569.

Vanassche, Ellen (2004): The impact of international financial integration on industry growth, paper presented at the 2004 SUERF Colloqium, Madrid..

Vessel, Vello (2003): FDI into banking sectors of some EC candidate countries: comparative empirical evidence, *Proceedings of the University of Vaasa*.

Wachtel, Paul (2001): Growth and Finance, What do we know and how do we know it?, *International Finance* 4/3, 335-362.

—. (2003): How much do we really know about growth and finance?, *Federal Reserve Bank of Atlanta-Economic Review* 1/2003, 33-46.

# THE QUALITATIVE BENEFITS OF FOREIGN BANKS' ENTRY: ESTONIAN EXPERIENCE

MART SÕRG

## Abstract

Reconstruction of the Estonian banking system started twenty years ago. Estonia built up for the market economy a banking oriented financial sector, which is centred around commercial banks. During the two decades, less than ten banks remained from more than 50 licensed commercial banks, the rest were not able to continue independently, they merged, or have failed. The negative result of this type of development was also the excessive concentration of banking.

The banking sector in Estonia during the transition period was opened to the invasion of foreign banks due to the openness of the economy and excessive risks taken. Two banking crises, selected quickly the very limited number of prosperous banks, and the major commercial banks went into the ownership of Scandinavian banks.

The qualitative effects of foreign banks' entry into the Estonian banking market where intensification of the overall competition in the banking market and the transfer of various know-how from foreign banks. Better liquidity risk management techniques, information systems, credit policy, and personnel policy transfer from foreign banks was highly evaluated by the Estonian domestic banks. These directions are noticeable also by quantitative analyses of banking market development.

The takeover of main commercial banks by the large Swedish and Finnish banks was an important factor in the gradual increase of the social orientation of Estonian banks. However, the ideas of social responsibility of enterprises are especially popular in Scandinavia. In our paper, we analyse Estonian banks' practices of supporting socio-political development of Estonia.

## Introduction

Reforms in the Estonian banking sector started in 1988, three years before restoring the political independence in August 1991.

In addition to the transition to market economy, Estonia had one more aim in reconstructing its banking system – to restore financial independence, and the result was that Estonia became a pioneer in the reformation of banking system in former USSR.

During the two decades, less than ten banks remained from more than 50 licensed commercial banks, the rest were not able to continue independently, they merged or have failed. The bad result of this kind of development was also the excessive concentration of banking. Market share of the biggest bank is over 50 per cent.

The main roots of the first banking crisis in Estonia came from the deep crisis of the whole economy; poor banks risk management and weak supervision from the side of the central bank. Reasons of the second banking crisis was a pitfall in the Tallinn Stock Exchange in autumn 1997 and a financial crisis in Russia, an important Estonian trading partner, in autumn 1998. The most notable similarity of both crises was that banks with poor risk management and control levels suffered in more difficult troubles and a remarkable share of the population either lost their entire savings or lost part of their savings exchange value.

The banking sector in Estonia during the transition period was opened to the invasion of foreign banks due to the openness of the economy and excessive risks taken. Two banking crises, selected quickly the very limited number of prosperous banks, and the major commercial banks went into the ownership of Scandinavian banks.
The qualitative effects of foreign banks' entry into the Estonian banking market where intensification the overall competition in banking market and transfer of various know-how from foreign banks. Better liquidity risk management techniques, information systems, credit policy and personnel policy transfers from foreign banks were highly evaluated by the Estonian domestic banks. These directions are noticeable also by quantitative analyses of banking market development.

The negative experiences of people and entrepreneurs with the financial sector force the financial institutions to make efforts to improve their reputation and trustworthiness. As the transition economies have difficulties with improving the social sphere because of financial constraints, participation in social programs is useful in order to improve the reputation. Thus one can argue that for the Estonian financial sector, supporting social development is one of the ways to improve its low image. Such spending profits from being visible, is useful not only to the society, but also to bank's owners themselves.

The takeover of main commercial banks by the large Swedish and Finnish banks was an important factor in the gradual increase of the social orientation of Estonian banks, however the ideas of social responsibility of enterprises are especially popular in Scandinavia. In our paper we analyze profitability indicators of Estonian banks' and their practices of supporting socio-political development of Estonia.

## Development of the Banking Internationalization in Estonia

Introduction of the market economy in transition countries took place simultaneously with structural and legal reforms. Reforms of banking systems and the creation of workable financial markets are among the biggest institutional changes of these states.

Financial sector reforms for transition countries were not an easy task for high speed of changes and for effects of economic and financial crises in this period. Therefore, the risk management experience of the staff of banks was short and the banking regulations were in a forming stage.

Reforms in the Estonia banking sector started in 1988, three years before restoring the political independence in August 1991.

The first period of development of new banking in Estonia can be named as a "wild" banking period and it ended with the first banking crisis. The Crisis started in autumn 1992 and decreased the number of operating banks twice. The second period can be called as a "naïve-optimistic" banking period and was interrupted by second banking crisis in 1998. It led to the mergers of certain banks, the coming of foreign banks into Estonia as the strategic investors for Estonian banks and the bankruptcy of three smaller banks. After the second banking crisis in Estonia operated only 5 banks and one branch office of a foreign bank and the market share of the biggest bank was over 50% by assets. The “modern” banking period in Estonia started after the second banking crisis.

The main roots of the first crisis came from the deep crisis of the whole economy, poor bank management, and weak supervision from the side of central bank. Reasons of the second banking crisis was a pitfall in the Tallinn Stock Exchange in autumn 1997 and a financial crisis in Russia, an important Estonian trading partner, in autumn 1998. The most notable similarity of both crises was that the banks with poor risk management and control levels suffered in more difficult troubles.

Banking crises initiated the Bank of Estonia to improve the banking regulation and supervision. Estonian Parliament (Riigikogu) passed several new acts concerning the financial sector. Credit Institutions acts were passed in 1994 and in 1999. Since January 2002 financial sector supervision establishments are merged into one Financial Supervision Authority.

The essential difference of the banking crisis in 1998–1999 from the previous one was the fact that the Swedish banks, SE Banken and Swedbank were involved in saving the two major banks of Estonia, the Hansabank and the Union Bank of Estonia. Those banks had just merged with weaker banks and now their share in the banking market of Estonia was respectively, 50% and 30%. They had also been evaluated by international rating agencies. As they were not able to carry on business independently any longer, the owners and managers had to look for strategic investors. The troubles had lowered the price of shares, so the international bank found it the right time to come to help. The small banks of Estonia also looked desperately for partners, but as their market share was small and they did not own international ratings, they were not able to draw international interest. Empirical results from 15 emerging markets (Roldos; 2001; 15) show that each crisis of the banking system leads to a further increase in participation and control by foreign banks in the domestic banking sector. During the crisis it is necessary to intervene to further capitalize banks or to sell unsuccessful banks. Foreign banks are the only ones with resources to do so.

Before the currency reform in 1992, the Bank of Estonia did not allow any foreign share in Estonian commercial banks. But the new regulations of the issuance of banking licences after the currency reform did not impose such restrictions. Therefore on 26 August 1992 Ameerika-Balti Ühispank

(American Bank of the Baltics), whose sole proprietor was an USA businessman, received a licence as well as INKO Balti Pank (INKO Baltic Bank) on 29 September 1994, which was the subsidiary bank of the Ukrainian INKO Bank. But the Board of BOE did not approve all applications. For example, the representatives of the Austrian Doonau Bank had to return barehanded. In September 1994 Merita Bank established a branch in Tallinn. As the first two banks, created on the basis of foreign capital, did not find their place in Estonia and had lost their licences by now, then the branch of Merita-Nordbanken (now Nordea) after a long period of quiet growth has began to apply an expansion strategy and wishes to increase its market share in Estonia.

In spite of some unsuccessful foreign banks, the "open doors" policy of BOE was undoubtedly an accurate strategy, because the positive aspects of the coming of foreign banks balance up the possible negative ones. The policy of the central bank of India, that allows only 20% of foreign capital shares in an Indian bank, is a warning example. The Economist stated in its January copy this year that one of the main reasons for the poor situation in Indian banking is untrustworthiness to foreign banks (India's ..., 2001).

Experts are on the opinion that in transition countries it is necessary to allow the foreign capital to enter the banking sector. Thus the journal "Business Central Europe" criticized Hungary for protectionism. Hungary has decided to sell after refining the balance of Postabank, which is in difficulties, to a strategic investor, a local bank OTP. The market share of the merged bank would form 50% of the banking market in Hungary. The journal calls it a wrong direction and considers that the correct decision would have been a sale of the bank to a foreign strategic investor (Serényi, 2000/2001).

The major foreign banks have always been waiting for a suitable moment to come to Estonia. Schleswig-Holsten Landesbank, based on the German capital, started a bit too early and met in autumn 1997 the resistance of the management of Eesti Investeerimispank to the wish to acquire 60% of the shares of the Estonian bank. The resistance was justified by the necessity to continue the activities as an investment bank and not to turn to a retail bank. But this idea was not realized. In June 2000 Optiva Pank, which was established by the merger of Eesti Investeerimispank and Forekspank, and had received financial injections from the central bank, was acquired in favourable conditions by Sampo Finance Ltd, a joint company owned by the Finnish banking and insurance company Sampo-Leonia and the Estonian Kaleva Mutual Insurance Company. The new owners turned Optiva Pank to Sampo Pank that offers both insurance and banking retail services.

The foreign banks got an opportunity to acquire shares in Estonian banks because the local banks turned to quoted companies. Hansapank was the first one to reach the foreign stock exchanges in 1994. The banks also faced a need to raise foreign capital in connection with the schedule of the growth of share capital and equity capital prescribed by the central bank. By the end of 1995, foreigners (foreign banks ownership formed 29.2% and 5.7% were the clients of foreign banks) held 35% of the share capital of Estonian banks.

The Swedish major banks (Swedbank and SEB) managed to wait their time. They bought from the stock exchange the cheapened shares of the Estonian major banks and in 1998 they were able to acquire without resistance an essential share of the share capital of Hansapank and Eesti Ühispank that were facing financial difficulties.

The question why the Nordic banks are especially active in the Baltics has its own logic. The Baltic region is geographically ideal for Nordic banks in their expansion spree. Decisive action can be observed in Estonia, which banking sector is the most advanced Baltic State as far as the banking sector is concerned (Tiusanen & Jumpponen, 2000).

Banking research in Lithuania and Romania also showed that the main reason for foreign banks' entry into Lithuanian and Romanian banking market has been due to a realization of their strategy of searching for new business opportunities (Dubauskas, 2002; Florescu, 2002).

By the end of 1998, the share capital of Eesti Ühispank and Hansapank were on the hands of foreign credit institutions respectively 68.4% and 64.9% and the foreign share in the share capital of Estonian banks had increased to 55.8%. By the end of 2006, 94.4% of the shares of Estonian commercial banks were in the ownership of non-residents (Figure 1).

**Figure 1: Shareholders structure of Estonian Commercial Banks (end of the year*, %)**

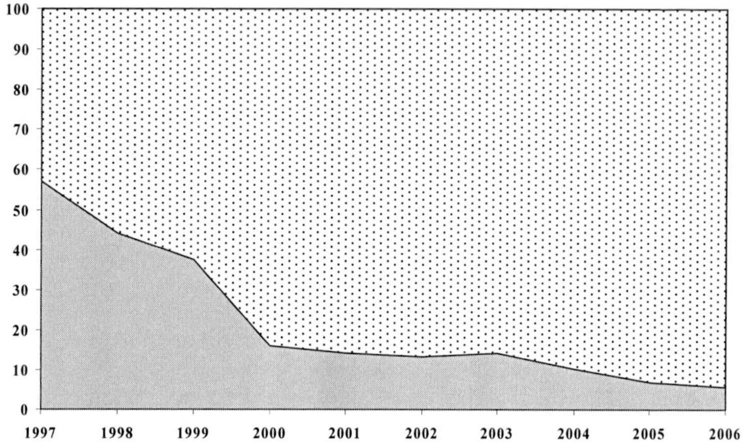


* October 1th 1997
Source: Data of Bank of Estonia.

Foreign banks came to other transition countries the same way as to Estonia – when the local banks were in difficulties. For example, the analysis of the Croatian banking proves that during the period of the third banking crises (1999–2000) the share of private capital in the banking sector increased to 90%, most of it was a foreign share (Barisitz, 2000).

At the end of 1996 there was a survey made of the main banks, which had invested in CEE countries (Konopielko, 1999). The survey showed that the main motivation for entry in CEE banking market according to factor's level of importance (1 – not important at all; 2 – not important; 3 – important; 4 – very important) was the following: the first rank got supporting client base (3.46 points) and the second was looking for new business opportunities (3.32 points) (Table 1).

**Table 1: Prevailing Elements of Entry Strategies* and Country Characteristics**

| | Poland | Czech Republic | Hungary |
|---|---|---|---|
| Reason for entry | Follow client | Follow client | Search for new opportunities |
| Method | Subsidiary | Branch | Take-over |
| Activity | Corporate financing | Corporate financing | Corporate financing |
| Branching | Underbranched | Overbranched | Overbranched |
| Profit growth expectation | Yes | Yes | Yes |
| Period of investment return** | 3.12 years | 3 years | 2,5 years |

* Table lists highest rated or dominant answers for each question in the survey.

The mentioned survey showed that the entry strategies were different for different transition countries. Table 1 shows that in the Czech Republic and in Poland the preferred entry strategies were similar. For the Hungarian banking sector, as the most mature, it is necessary to adopt a more aggressive strategy, characterized by the willingness to search for new business as well as an expectation of a relatively short period of investment return.

Most of the Estonian banks had quite ambitious growth strategies. Growth was achieved by introducing new ideas, by cheaper service or by cheaply acquiring competitors during banking crises. Already the researchers analyzing the Finnish banking crisis at the beginning of 1990s discovered the fact that a banking sector that grows faster than the overall economy will in the long run end up in a banking crisis. The economists analyzing the Japanese banking crisis came up with two reasons for this: deregulation and excess power of the banking sector. These were the reasons why they did not pay very much attention on risk management and regulative measures (Kanaya and Woo, 2001). Apparently, this was also the case in Estonia: rapid growth in several years led to excess capacity of banking and also to underestimation of risk management in 1997. The banking crisis in 1998 brought the banking back to the ground from the clouds (Table 2), when number of operating banks decreased twice and sector was suffering.

The banking crisis in 1998 started a new growth period. Joining the EU in 2004 even accelerated growth of the loan portfolio, which was in 2006 near twice as large as in 2004. It was a good basis for growth profits of the banks. During three last year profits of the banks near tripled.

**Table 2: Development of Banking in Estonia**

| Year | Number of operating banks* | Totally by the end of the year, bill EEK (€ 1 = EEK 15,6) | | | Banks assets, % of GDP | Loan portfolio, % of the assets |
|---|---|---|---|---|---|---|
| | | assets | loan portfolio | profit | | |
| 1992 | 41 | 5.2 | 2.1 | 0.09 | 36.4 | 40.4 |
| 1993 | 22 | 6.4 | 2.7 | 0.25 | 28.0 | 42.9 |
| 1994 | 24 | 10.4 | 4.5 | 0.04 | 33.2 | 43.6 |
| 1995 | 18 | 15.5 | 7.1 | 0.29 | 36.0 | 45.9 |
| 1996 | 13 | 22.9 | 12.3 | 0.51 | 41.0 | 53.7 |
| 1997 | 11 | 40.6 | 21.3 | 0.96 | 59.2 | 52.5 |
| 1998 | 6 | 41.0 | 23.9 | –0.50 | 52.6 | 58.3 |
| 1999 | 7 | 47.1 | 26.7 | 0.67 | 57.6 | 56.7 |
| 2000 | 7 | 57.8 | 34.3 | 0.61 | 60.5 | 59.2 |
| 2001 | 7 | 68.4 | 40.7 | 1.68 | 63.2 | 59.5 |
| 2002 | 7 | 81.7 | 50.0 | 1.15 | 67.3 | 61.2 |
| 2003 | 7 | 98.8 | 69.2 | 1.32 | 72.6 | 70.0 |
| 2004 | 9 | 133.6 | 92.6 | 2.46 | 94.2 | 69.3 |
| 2005 | 13 | 185.1 | 125.5 | 3.11 | 105.5 | 67.8 |
| 2006 | 14 | 239.5 | 177.7 | 3.63 | 115.6 | 74.2 |

* incl. branches of foreign banks
Source: Eesti Pank.

We agree with opinion of ECB that the rapid growth of credit to the private sector observed in a number of countries in the region could pose risk to both macroeconomic and financial stability. Macroeconomic risks relate, in particular, to an overheating economy and an associated worsening of the current account. (ECB Monthly Bulletin, 2006). And really in Estonia current account deficit is over 10% comparing with GDP and GDP growth in 2006 was 11, 4%.

# Development of Profitability Estonian Banks after entry of Foreign Capital

While reconstructing their banking systems to adjust them to a market economy, some transition countries like Estonia have preferred commercial banking. The main purpose of commercial banks' shareholders and executive management is to increase the value of the company, which requires both a quick rise in the capacity of financial services and a high level of profitability of the business activities.

The managements of banks must therefore ensure high profitability of banks in order for their banks to remain competitive despite any unforeseeable developments in the market. Thus, they eagerly grasp at any profit opportunities.

In spite of the large amount of empirical literature devoted to banking efficiency on all continents (Molyneux *et al.*, 1996;Berger and Humphrey, 1997; Dietsch and Lozano-Vivas, 2000; Goddart *et al.*, 2001), there are only a few studies that measure banking efficiency in transition economies. A likely reason for this deficit may be the relative lack of banking data in these countries, with long periods of data missing.

The most extensively studied developing countries are in Asia, where markets of Thailand (Leightner and Knox Lovell, 1998), Korea (Gilbert and Wilson, 1998), Singapore (Rezvanian and Mehdian, 2002), Pakistan (Hardy and Bonaccorsi di Patti, 2001), India (Bhattacharyya et al., 1997), and Turkey (Isik and Hassan, 2002) were analysed. Some studies investigate a number of countries in Central and Eastern Europe and the Commonwealth of Independent States (Grigorian and Manole, 2002; Tomova *et al.*, 2003; Uiboupin, 2005), Hungary (Hasan and Marton, 2003), Croatia (Kraft and Tirtiroglu, 1998), Poland (Opiela, 2001; Havrylchyk, 2003), and Ukraine (Mertens and Urga, 2001) and Baltics (Hansson and Tombak, 1996) were studied. After 1998, the profits in Estonian banking sector have stabilized (Table 3). In 2006 in euro area banks average cost-income ratio was 60,4% and ROE 19,6% (ECB, 2007: S30).

**Table 3: Key Efficiency Ratios in Estonian Banking (%)**

| | Solo banks | | | | | | |
|---|---|---|---|---|---|---|---|
| | 2000 | 2001 | 2002 | 2003 | 2004 | 2005 | 2006 |
| Cost to income ratio | 72,5 | 52,4 | 61,6 | 53,0 | 45,8 | 45,6 | 46,6 |
| Return on assets | 1,2 | 2,7 | 1,6 | 1,7 | 2,1 | 2,0 | 1,7 |
| Equity multipler | 7,4 | 7,5 | 7,3 | 7,9 | 8,8 | 9,9 | 10,7 |
| Return on equity | 8,0 | 20,7 | 14,7 | 14,1 | 20,0 | 21,0 | 19,8 |
| Net interest margin | 4,3 | 3,9 | 3,6 | 2,9 | 2,4 | 2,0 | 2,2 |
| Spread | 4,1 | 3,7 | 3,4 | 2,8 | 2,3 | 1,9 | 2,1 |

Source: Eesti Pank. Financial Stability Review.

Research has shown that the increase in the degree of concentration in the European banking sector is negatively related to competition (Bikker and Groenveld, 2000). Lower competition is linked to higher profitability. As banking concentration in Estonia is very high (see Figure 3) it is helping bigger banks to increase their profits.

Banks' profit growth has also been supported by the continuous expansion of loan portfolio and the rise in key interest rates. As most of the loans in Estonia have been granted with a Floating interest rate, banks' interest income on interest-earning assets has increased by 1 percentage point, year-on-year, to 4.9% on an aggregate basis. The interest paid on interest-bearing liabilities has increased by only 0.7 percentage points to 2.7%. The impact of the changes in key interest rates, however, has been reduced by the decreased share of deposits (as it is a cheaper resource than external financing) in banks' funding.

Besides the growing incomes, the profitability of the banking sector has also been fostered by the so far relatively low risk costs. Although the share and volume of the net write-downs of claims has continued to increase, banks' total net write-downs of claims did not exceed 0.1% of assets as an annual average. In case of banking groups the share of write-downs is somewhat higher (0.26%) (Eesti Pank. Financial Stability Review, May 2007).

As regards the future profitability of banks, the further rise in key interest rates would probably facilitate the continuing growth of the net interest margin. However, this would occur at a slower pace, should the growth of loan portfolios still exceed that of deposits. In that case, the share of the more expensive external funds in banks' liabilities would increase.

# Development of Socio-Political Orientation of Estonian Banks

Reconstructing the Estonian banking sector began in 1988, when the first commercial banks were founded. The development of the banking sector during near the past 20 years has been stormy and has undergone crises in which a remarkable share of the population either lost their savings in their entirety or lost part of their savings exchange value.

Such developments after the crisis period have made the population suspicious of the banking sector. This is indicated by the large share of demand deposits of banks' deposits in Estonia. From Figure 2 we see that credibility of banks started to decrease during the second banking crisis in years 1998–1999 when the share of demand deposits grew and stabilized on the level a bit higher of 60%. Surely demand deposits share it is too high taking into account Estonian stable economic policy and development.

**Figure 2: Structure of Deposits of Individuals in Commercial Banks (%, end of year)**

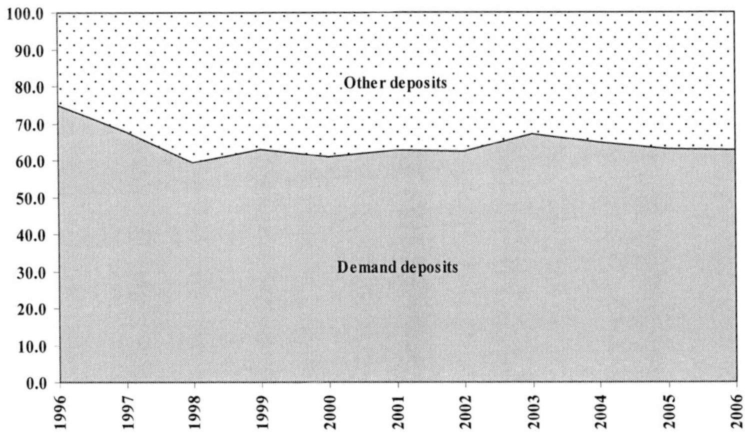


Source: Eesti Pank, author's calculations.

The negative experiences of people and entrepreneurs with the banking sector forced commercial banks to make efforts to improve their reputation and trustworthiness. As the transition countries have difficulties with improving the social sphere because of financial constraints, participation in social programs is useful in order to improve the reputation. For example, social protection expenditure in Estonia amounted to 16–17% of GDP in 1995–1999, and in 2000 and 2001, it decreased to 15.6% and 14.8% of GDP, respectively. Social protection expenditure in the EU countries on average accounted for 27.3% of GDP in 2000, ranging from 14.1% in Ireland to 32.3% in Sweden (Püss and Viies 2003, p. 257). Corrected data of 2001 show that in 2001 social expenditure in Estonia amounted only 13,1% of GDP (Estonian Human Development Report 2006 2007, p. 112).

Thus one can argue that for the Estonian commercial banks, supporting social development is one of the ways to improve its low image. One example, SEB Eesti Ühispank is the first in Estonia to offer its customers a possibility to personally design the picture of their credit cards. The bank has developed a simple and convenient photo-shop environment on the Internet for printing one's picture on the credit card (visit the website at www.seb.ee/pildikaart). Such spending, we might add, profits from being visible, not only to others, but also to themselves. Of course, the SEB Eesti Ühispank picture bank card costs for customer more than ordinary card.

All market participants must go along with this, in order to not lose clients to competitors in an extremely concentrated market. As can be seen from Figure 3, the market share of the two largest commercial banks in Estonia was 77.6% by the end of the year 2006, whereas had given up some of their market share to smaller market participants.

Here Estonia is not an exception. In research of a highly concentrated banking sector in the Netherlands retail banks aim is to distinguish themselves from their competition by maintaining or creating a different image. Through this diverging behaviour they try to attract different market and/or customer segments (Boonstra and Groenveld 2006).

**Figure 3: Market Shares of Banks According to Total Assets at the End of 2006 (end of 2000 in brackets)**

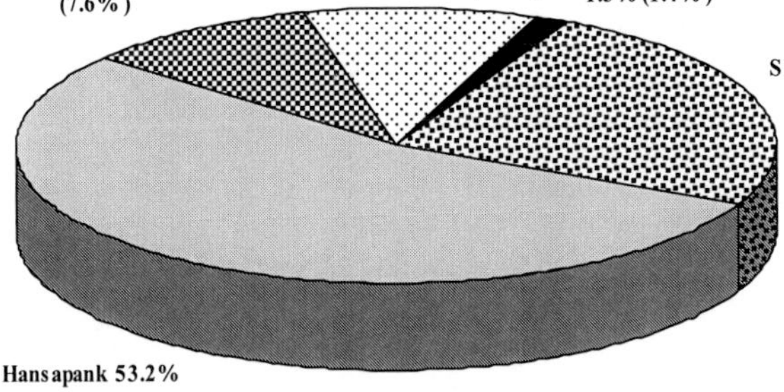


Source: Eesti Pank, author's calculations.

It is necessary to distinguish between moral, political, and legal responsibility. Moral responsibility may be related only to consciousness; its extreme expression is Dostoevski's statement: "Everybody is guilty of everything" (Responsibility 1972).

The takeover of the two largest commercial banks (Hansapank and Eesti Ühispank) by the large Swedish banks, Swedbank and SEB, has surely been a factor in the gradual increase of social orientation of Estonian banks. The ideas of social responsibility are known to be especially popular in Sweden, certainly affecting also the banks' policies. After the takeover of Hansapank and Eesti Ühispank, representatives of the Swedish side were appointed to their councils and directives were issued from Sweden on the need to pay more attention to supporting the social development.

In the new Millennium while other countries fell into a period of stagnation, Scandinavia showed robust growth, moved up into the leading group of innovative counties, maintained its welfare state (Becker, 2007). He sees, that one of the cornerstones of it is the comparatively low social inequality and poverty and the corporatism, which makes it possible to coordinate economic and social objectives.

The banks that own the third and fourth largest commercial banks in Estonia (Nordea Pank, Sampo Pank) are of Finnish origin. In Finland, like in Sweden, the emphasis on social development is especially strong. This explains well why Nordea Pank and Sampo Pank are unwilling to lag behind the leaders with their social programs.

To achieve the rapid growth of assets, it is necessary to ensure that the number of clients as well as their financial assets in the bank increases. To win new clients from competing banks is neither easy nor cheap, however. Thus, the appropriate method to get more clients is to look for new ones by offering various benefits and investment opportunities.

One method to get new clients and tie them strongly to the bank is to grant student loans. The conditions for this type of loan are the most favourable ones offered by Estonian banks. The maximum annual amount of the government-guaranteed loan is 25,000 kroons (ca € 1280) and the fixed interest rate is 5%. This is granted for the whole period of post-secondary education, with either two sureties or with real estate as collateral. Because government-guaranteed loans are not granted to distant education and self-financed students, banks have on their own initiative and risks started to grant student loans for them, too. To the end of 2006 student loans formed in Estonia totally EEK 3.2 bil., and they grew 73.5% comparing with 2000.

In addition to finding new clients, an important component of growth strategies of financial institutions is also offering the products that could attract the clients to save more. This is an explanation for why the share of banks in other financial intermediaries was so high.

By now, banks have lowered the interest rate paid on demand deposits to 0.20–0.25% per year. Also some periods their interest rates of the time deposits were below the inflation rate. Because the main motive for saving is precautionary motive in Estonia (see also Figure 2), banks are not afraid of outflow of deposits. Growth of deposits, however, is ensured only by the addition of new motives for saving. Such motives can be e.g. financially insuring of the future against accidents or old age. It is therefore not surprising that in addition to ordinary investment opportunities, banks offer also pension insurance in the form of either an insurance certificate or an insurance fund. The latter kind is especially beneficial for the banks, as it ensures them stable, very long-term risk-free resource for financial investments. Because payments from the pension funds to future pensioners will be paid out not on the basis of the sum actually paid, but its present value, the fund can use the money without risk, because the possible loss and costs of administering the fund reduce the amount paid out as pensions.

The above analysis shows that the Estonian financial sector has several motives for supporting social development, which ultimately can be reduced to the intention to improve their image and facilitate the growth of profits.

As the Estonian financial sector is centered around banks, the Estonian commercial banks naturally also have a central role in supporting the socio-economic development. They do so by offering novel saving schemes, various benefits for the less-insured client groups, and sponsorship. The costs of running and advertising such programs are remarkable. For example, according to the annual report of Sampo Pank for 2005, its consolidated group communication and data processing expenses were EEK 52.5 mln., and advertising expenses EEK 23.9 mln. That the amounts are significant can be seen from comparison with their 2005 year profits, which was EEK 172.2 million (AS Sampo Pank … 2006, p. 11).

The most significant part of social responsibility of the financial sector seems to be the participation of banks in the introduction of Estonian three-pillar pension system. Discussion of the pension reform in Estonia started already at the beginning of the 90s, as it was clear that in the future, government pension could not ensure the sufficient standard of living for most pensioners. The rise in the overall dependency ratio is mainly due to rise in the old age dependency ratio (defined as the ratio of those people older than 64 to those of working age), which is projected to continue to increase from the current level of about 26% to a level close to 55% by 2050 (ECB 2006, p. 50). Thus, on September 12, 2001, Estonia approved the Funded Pensions Act, which became the basis for the three-pillar pension system. Share of old age population on Estonia is twice higher than in the world (Table 4).

**Table 4: Share of More than 65 Years in Population and Place in the World in 2005**

| Country | Place among world countries | More than 65 years old people share (%) |
|---|---|---|
| Japan | 1 | 20 |
| Italy | 2 | 19 |
| Germany | 3 | 18 |
| Belgium | 7 | 17 |
| Spane | 8 | 17 |
| EU–25 | 12 | 16 |
| France | 12 | 16 |
| England | 17 | 16 |
| Estonia | 17 | 16 |
| Denmark | 26 | 15 |
| Netherlands | 33 | 14 |
| Russia | 34 | 13 |
| USA | 44 | 12 |
| World | 91 | 7 |

Source: Pison, 2006.

The theoretical framework of the three pillars is adopted internationally mainly in order to enable convenient description and international comparisons of pension systems. The first pillar (Pillar I, national pension) is financed according to the principle of pay-as-you-go, i.e. payments to people at the pension age are financed from taxes of the working generation. Pillar II is a pre-funded private capital-based mandatory pension. Pillar III is voluntary pre-funded pension, which is meant mainly for people who wish for the future a standard of living higher than that offered by the state. The third pillar of the pension system is like an agreement between people and the state that if the person takes care of her own future, the state demands less in taxes from him or her. So far, almost all responsibility for the pensions has been borne by the state, whereas now, people themselves have to assume part of it.

Administration of state-supported mandatory pension funds is a profitable business. Because of the favourable opportunity for business, six Estonian financial institutions are fighting for a good position in the pension market – Hansapank, Eesti Ühispank, Seesam, Sampo Pank, LHV and ERGO, who have altogether brought to market 16 pension funds. Because administration fees of pension funds will be a stable source of income, the pre-funded pensions are important for the fund manager.

Business newspaper Äripäev calculated that when 25 years old worker will join the pension system II Pillar and when his salary is 10 000 kroons per month, then he will pay to the foundation until his pension age 978 510 kroons from which 30–40% will get foundation in form of servicing fees (Tuul, 2007). Already started discussion that it is necessary to cut fees rates because Estonian fees are the highest in Europe. For example, funds servicing fees in Estonia are from 1/3 to 2/3 over average levels in Europe say Estonian Financial Supervision Authority (Linnamäe and Uusen, 2007).

Voluntary pension insurance (Pillar III) is offered by five Estonian life insurance companies and four voluntary pension funds are also growing. Most of the market participants have several different products – there are altogether some twenty possibilities to choose from.

Pillar II of the pension system was launched in May 2002 in Estonia. Advertising campaigns by banks and insurance companies brought more than 200 thousand entrants (for those older than 18 years, joining was not mandatory), which exceeded even the most optimistic forecasts. In one year, the Pillar II funds had accumulated EEK 530.5 million. At the end of October 2006, the number of subscribers to the second pillar of the pension system amounted to approximately 517,000 persons, i.e. about 64% of the labour force. The total volume of the second pillar's funds increased by 58% (by 2.4 billion kroons) within the past year and stood at 8.6 billion kroons at the end of April 2007.

Pillar III funds, although they were launched already in 2001, have accumulated less resources however they only involve people with higher than average incomes. The number of subscribes to the third pillar reached nearly 100,000 persons by October 2006, comprising approximately 12.3% of the labour force. The year-on year growth of the third pillar funds was 75%, i.e. 251 million kroons (in September 2005, it was 140% and 195,6 million kroons, respectively. There is limited number of such enough rich people in Estonia at present, but their sharc will increase in the future. Thus, this pension scheme has also good perspectives for the banks.

If compared with an average household, then the welfare level of older people and big families has shown a declining trend. The government has identified the increasing inequality as a serious problem and has, thus, granted several benefits for the groups in the risk of poverty. Child benefit as well as benefits in the form of free public transport for both minors and pensioners could serve here as an example. The banks have an incentive to provide similar kind of benefits in order to promote their reputation, and they do so, quite often. For example a small bank Eesti Krediidipank (look Figure 3) in his Annual Report writes: for several years (from 1996) Krediidipank has focused its attention on expanding the opportunities for supporting families with many children, and making society aware of the problems related to big families and the Estonian demographic situation. For Krediidipank, this is an opportunity to take social responsibility for the society's less well-off members (Krediidipank 2007, p. 15).

Most of the banks have set lower prices for transactions made by senior and junior clients. The price list for private customers of SEB Eesti Ühispank is brought in Table 5. Some benefits are also applied to the customers in the student age (18–25). The price list for seniors applies to the customers who are at least 60 years old. In addition, lower fees are applied to the older and handicapped people in opening privatization voucher accounts and to the young people in formalizing housing loans.

**Table 5: Prices of More Important Bank Services of SEB Eesti Ühispank by Client Groups**

| | Usual customer | Senior customer (60 years and older) | Junior clients (younger than 18 years) | Student age clients (18–25 years old) | New clients to the end of quarter |
|---|---|---|---|---|---|
| Cash transactions fees (over the counter) | 12 | 12 | 12 | 12 | 6 |
| Transactions via electronic services | 3 | free of charge | free of charge | free of charge | free of charge |
| Cash withdrawal (over the counter) | 0.25%, min. EEK 20 | 0.25%, EEK 1000 free of charge | 0.20%, EEK 1000 free of charge | 0.25%, min. EEK 20 | min. EEK 10 |
| VISA Elektron monthly fee | 15 | free of charge | 15 | 10 | 10 |
| VISA Elektron prolongation | 30 | free of charge | free of charge | free of charge | free of charge |

Source: http://www.seb.ee.

The benefits offered by the banks and other financial institutions to the young and older people have, along with humanitarian goals, a more pragmatic benefit for the banks as well. These clients make transactions very rarely and higher transaction fees would probably scare them away and, thus, support more intensive using of cash. This, in turn, means the withdrawal of deposits form the banks.

The benefits for juniors seem to be even higher than for older people. This may be due to the fact that the bank is afraid to loose a potential life-long client. The saving and intensity of transactions of older people is, however, expected to decline and thus the attention is drawn more towards younger people.

The banks are, in addition to the benefits, involved in providing direct sponsorship. This makes them visible and respectable. The homepage of Hansapank lists the sponsoring principles, which state "Hansapank is a company that due to its size feels certain responsibility for the society. Our goal is to support Estonia's development" (http://www.hansa.ee). Appendix 1 includes the sponsoring principles of Hansapank. Main fields sponsored by Hansapank are education, culture and sports.

The goals and principles of education sponsoring by Hansapank are brought here as an example:

Human resources, an educated population and new ideas are key words that we emphasise in speaking of Estonia's opportunities to stand out among other developed countries. As the rest of society, educated people are also the most valuable resource for Hansapank, as an employer.

It is for that reason that we think of the future and support youth with various stipends, the provision of favourable student loans, education loans or master's loans and the organization of conferences.

Since 1999 we issue, in co-operation with Tallinn Technical University, annual stipends to support masters and doctoral studies at the university. As of 2000, we will also support the ten most successful students at the Estonian Information Technology College with annual stipend bearing the Hansapank name.

They have also made a contribution through the publishing of economics-related high school textbooks and workbooks, which will appear through the Junior Achievement Fund.

Other banks and financial institutions have followed the example of Estonian leading bank by trying to be on the list of sponsors of popular cultural events, as well as by supporting the fields like education and health that are acknowledged as the priorities in the society. For example SEB Eesti Ühispank has issued the Basketball card for basketball is very popular in Estonia. The Basketball card with benefits for a sports fan was prepared in co-operation with SEB Eesti Ühispank and the Basketball Association. Besides the traditional debit card functions, the card provides several sports-related benefits. A card application may be sent to the bank from Internet address (HTTP://www.seb.ee/korvpall).

## Conclusions

Reconstructing the Estonian banking sector began in 1988, when the first commercial banks were founded. The development of the banking sector during the past near twenty years has been stormy and has undergone crises in which a remarkable share of the population either lost their savings in their entirety or lost part of their savings exchange value. Such developments have after the crisis period made the population suspicious of the banking sector.

The negative experiences of people and entrepreneurs with the banking sector forced commercial banks to make efforts to improve their reputation and trustworthiness. As the transition countries have difficulties with improving the social sphere because of financial constraints, participation in social programs is useful in order to improve the reputation.

Thus one can argue that for the Estonian commercial banks, supporting social development is one of the ways to improve its low image. Such spending, we might add, profits from being visible, not only to others, but also to themselves.

The takeover of the two largest commercial banks (Hansapank and Eesti Ühispank) by the large Swedish banks, Swedbank and SEB, has surely been a factor in the gradual increase of social orientation of Estonian banks. The ideas of social responsibility are known to be especially popular in Sweden, certainly affecting also the banks' policies. After the takeover of Hansapank and SEB Eesti Ühispank, representatives of the Swedish side were appointed to their councils and directives were issued from Sweden on the need to pay more attention to supporting the social development.

Estonian commercial banks are the main owners of leasing and life insurance companies and investment funds. Such control of commercial banks over the Estonian financial sector means that the social orientation of banks will be carried over to their subsidiary financial institutions and the securities exchange, forming their policy.

One method to get new clients and tie them strongly to the bank is to grant student loans. The conditions for this type of loan are the most favourable ones offered by Estonian banks.

The most significant part of social responsibility of the financial sector seems to be the participation of banks in the introduction of Estonian three-pillar pension system. Discussion of the pension reform in Estonia started already at the beginning of the 90s, as it was clear that in the future, government pension could not ensure the sufficient standard of living for most pensioners.

Administration of state-supported mandatory pension funds is a profitable business. Because of the favourable opportunity for business, six Estonian financial institutions are fighting for a good position in the pension market – Hansapank, Eesti Ühispank, Seesam, Sampo Pank, LHV and ERGO, who have altogether brought to market 15 pension funds.

Most of the banks have set lower prices for transactions made by senior and junior clients. The benefits offered by the banks and other financial institutions to the young and older people have, along with humanitarian goals, a more pragmatic benefit for the banks as well. These clients make transactions very rarely and higher transaction fees would probably scare them away and, thus, support more intensive using of cash. This, in turn, means the withdrawal of deposits form the banks.

The banks are, in addition to the benefits, involved in providing direct sponsorship. This makes them visible and respectable.

Other smaller banks and financial institutions have followed the example of Estonian leading banks by trying to be on the list of sponsors of popular cultural events, as well as by supporting the fields like education and health that are acknowledged as the priorities in the society.

Professor Hans Blommestein found that society expects that banks take on increased gatekeeper responsibilities in the new business landscape. This means that banks are expected to play a central and active gatekeeper's role to monitor the behaviour of their clients and other counter-parties (Blommestein, 2006). Our research showed that Estonian banks very well understand their new role and responsibilities in the changed business environment.

## References

AS Sampo Pank Annual Report 2005 (2006). Sampo Pank, 66 p.

Barisitz Stephan (2000) The Development of the Croatian Banking Sector Since Independence, Focus on Transition, Oesterreichische Nationalbank, No 2, pp. 96–122.

Becker, U. (2007) The Scandinavian Model: Still an Example for Europe? Internationale Politik und Gesellschaft, nr. 4, pp. 41–57.

Berger, A. and D. Humphrey (1997).Efficiency of financial institutions: International survey and directions for future research // European Journal of Operational Research 98, pp.175–212.

Bhattacharyya, A. and C. A. K. Lovell, P. Sahay (1997). The impact of liberalization on the productive efficiency of Indian commercial banks // European Journal of Operational Research 98, pp. 332–345.

Bikker, J. A. and J. M. Groenveld (2002).Competition and Concentration in the EU Banking Industry. Kredit und Kapital, 33, pp. 62–98.

Blommestein, H. J. (2006). Visions about the Future of Banking. SUERF Studies, No. 2.

Boonstra, W. and J. M. Groenveld (2006). Competition in a highly concentrated banking sector. – Competition

Dietsch, M and A. Lozano-Vivas. (2000). How the environment determines bank efficiency: a comparison between French and Spanish industries //Journal of Banking and Finance. No. 24, pp. 185–200.

Dubauskas, G. (2002) Motivation of Foreign Banks' Entry into the Emerging Economies: The Case of Lithuania. – Working Papers TTUWPE No 02/69, Tallinn.

ECB (2006). Demographic change in the euro area: Projections and consequences. European Central bank. Monthly Bulletin. October 2006, PP. 49-64.

—. (2007). Financial Stability Review. June 2007.

ECB Monthly Bulletin (2006). Financial Development in Central, Eastern and South-Eastern Europe. November, pp. 93–104.

Eesti Pank (2007). Financial Stability Review. May 2007.

Estonian Human Development report 2006 (2007). Public Understanding Foundation, Tallinn.

Florescu, G. (2002) Foreign Banks Entry into Romania. – Working Paper TTUWPE No 02/71, Tallinn.

Gilbert, R. A. and P. W. Wilson. (1998). Effects of deregulations on the productivity of Korean Banks // Journal of Economics and Business, 1998. No. 50, pp. 133–155.

Goddard, J. A. and P. Molyneux, J. O. S. Wilson (2001). European banking. New York: Wiley.

Grigorian, D. A. and V. Manole (2002).Determinants of commercial bank performance in transition: an application of data envelopment analysis // IMF Working paper, No. 02/146.

Hansson, A. H. and Tombak, T. (1996) Banking Crises in the Baltic States: Causes, Solutions and Lessons. – Stockholm School of Economic, Working Paper No 112, 33 p.

Hardy, D. C. and E. Bonaccorsi di Patti. (2001). Bank reform and bank efficiency in Pakistan // IMF Working paper, No. 01/138.

Hasan, I. and K. Marton (2003). Development and efficiency of the banking sector in a transitional economy: Hungarian experience // Journal of Banking and Finance.

Havrylchyk, O. (2003). Effeciency of the Polish banking industry: foreign versus national banks // Paper for 24th SUERF Colloquim, Tallinn, 27 p. (mimeo).

http://www.epbe.ee

http://www.hansa.ee

http://www.seb.ee

India's Banks. Living Dead (2001) *The Economist*, January 6th–12th, p. 67.

Isik, I. and M. K. Hassan (2002). Technical, scale and allocative efficiencies of Turkish banking industry. Journal of Banking and Finance. No. 26, pp. 719–766.

Kanaya, A. and D. Woo (2001) The japanese Banking Crises of the 1990s: Sources and Lessons. – Essays in International economics. No. 222. New Jersey, Printeton University, June.

Koford, K. and A. E. Tschoegl (1997) Problem of Bank Lending in Bulgaria: Information Assymetry and Institutional Learning.

Konopielko, L. (1999) Foreign Banks' Entry into Central and East European Markets: Motives and Activities, *Post-Communist Economies*, Vol. 11, No. 4, pp. 463–485.

Kraft, E., and D. Tirtiroglu (1998). Bank Efficiency in Croatia: A Stochastic-Frontier Analysis // Journal of Comparative Economics. No. 26, pp. 282–300.

Krediidipank (2007). Consolidated Public Annual Report 2006. Eesti Krediidipank, Tallinn, 68 p.

Leightner, J. E. and C. A. Knox Lovell (1998). The impact of financial libaralization on the performance of Thai Banks. Journal of Economics and Business. No. 50, pp. 115–131.

Linnamäe, L. and K. Uusen (2007). Pensionirahast võtavad endale suurima ampsu LHV fondid. – Postimees, 31. oktoober 2007.

Mertens, A. and G. Urga. (2001). Efficiency, scale and scope economies in the Ukrainan banking sector in 1998 // Emerging Markets Review. No. (2)3, pp. 292–308.

Molyneux, P., Y. Altunbas and E. Gardener. Efficiency in European Banking. – John Wiley & Sons Ltd., 345 p.

Opiela, T. P. (2001) Assessing the efficiency of Polish commercial banks. Materialy I Studia, National Bank of Poland.

Pison, G. (2006). The population of the world (2005). Population & Societies. July/August, No. 414, pp. 1–8.

Püss, T. and M. Viies (2003). Impact of Socio-Demigraphic Changes on the Convergence. Reports-papers of the XI scientific and educational conference (Tartu-Värska, June 26–28, 2003). Berlin-Tallinn, pp. 257–264.

Responsibility. International Encyclopedia of Social Sciences (1972). Vol. 13 and 14. Edit. David L. Sills. The MacMillan Company & The Free Press. New York.

Rezvanian, R. and S. Mehdian (2002). An examination of cost structure and production performance of commercial banks in Singapore // Journal of Banking & Finance. No. 26, pp. 79–98.

Roldos, J. (2001). FDI in Emerging Markets Banking System. In OECD Global Forum on International Investment: New Horizons and Challenges for Foreign Direct Investment in the 21st Century. Mexico City, November, pp. 1–19.

Serényi P. (2000/2001) Wrong Direction, *Business Central Europe*, December 2000/January 2001, pp. 31–32.

Tiusanen, T. and J. Jumpponen (2000) The Baltic States in the 21st Century. Western Investors in Estonia, Latvia and Lithuania, *Studies in Industrial Engineering and Management*, Lappemranta University of Technology, No 11.

Tomova, M., N. Nenovsky and T. Naneva (2003). The Efficiency of the Banking Sector in CEE – Inequality and Convergence to the EU // Paper for 24th SUERF Colloquim. Tallinn, 28 p. (mimeo).

Tuul, H. (2007). Teine pensionisammas Euroopa kalleim. Äripäev, 27. aprill 2007.

Uiboupin, J. (2005). Foreign Banks in Central and Eastern European Markets: Their Entry and Influence on the Banking Sector // Doctoral Thesis, Tartu: Tartu University Press, 190 p.

# Appendix 1. Sponsoring principles of Hansapank

**We carry social responsibility**

Hansabank is a company that due to its size feels certain responsibility for the society. Our goal is to support Estonia`s development:

- we conduct our business activities so as to support Estonian economic growth and contribute to higher living standards with the means available to us
- we contribute to the debate about the development trends in the society
- we support the development of the society through sponsorship

**Vitality and innovation - the principles we support**

In our development strategy, we have prioritised vital and innovative development. Therefore, in our sponsoring activities, we prefer co-operation projects that are consistent, original and promote the development of the society.

**Education, culture, social sphere find more support**

Hansabank does not allocate money subjectively based on momentary impressions. We have firm preferences in the areas the society needs most. We support children, young people and education, big families, culture, and sports.

Source: http://www.hansa.ee

# INSTITUTIONAL BUYING BEHAVIOR – THE CASE OF DRUG PURCHASE OF HOSPITALS IN HUNGARY

ZSUZSANNA SZALKAI AND MÁRIA VÁGÁSI

## Abstract

This paper focuses on the drug purchasing decision of hospitals in Hungary as a special field of institutional buying behaviour. After a concise and contrastive review of the theoretical background, the specificities of drug purchasing are discussed and some results of an empirical research are presented. Results concern especially information sources, motivation of drug selection and expectations of hospitals toward pharmaceutical suppliers and products. These results are interpreted as factors influencing marketing and customer relationship policy of pharmaceutical producers and wholesalers toward hospitals.

## Introduction

The analysis of the drug purchasing decision of hospitals is an important topic for the different stakeholders of the health sector (government, insurance companies, hospital managers, medical practitioners, patient associations, patients, etc.) and the pharmaceutical market (pharmaceutical firms, distributors and retailers). The description of a specific institutional buying behavior is of interest for the marketing discipline as well. The general models of the buying behavior of organizations describe common characteristics, but there are essential differences between business organizations and institutions, and due to the great variety of the formers, between the different types of institutions as well. Buying behavior differs at public and private institutions, respectively. Our paper analyses the drug purchasing decision of public hospitals in Hungary.

The health sector in Hungary has not (yet) been privatized at the same extent than in developed countries, and the overwhelming majority of hospitals belongs to the group of institutional buyers controlled directly by government or local authorities especially trough their budget. At the same time, pharmaceutical industry and distribution have been privatized and are controlled by (big) international firms. Before the transition to market economy the pharmaceutical industry in Hungary belonged to the most developed and competitive national sectors, consequently its attractiveness for foreign investors was undoubtedly high. Now government property is marginal and government intervention is carried out through control over the pharmaceutical market, involving public procurement law for hospitals, price negotiation with pharmaceutical firms and distributors and cost reimbursement in the framework of national health insurance system.

The buying behaviour of public hospitals may vary by countries or regions, according to the intensity of regulation, or due to the differences in their health insurance systems and to traditions, in all probability. There are differences even in the different European countries as well. It is no doubt, that the Hungarian case might have more similarities with the cases of the countries of transition economy than with other ones, but we have not carried out any systematic comparative analysis. Anyway, specific conditions of Central and Eastern European countries require particular market knowledge from international suppliers.

The pharmaceutical market is globally expanding and the market of hospitals plays a privileged role for the pharmaceutical industry. Hospitals are not only users of specific hospital drugs, they buy and generate demand for different generic and ethical medicines, related to their treatments, prescriptions and opinion leaders role. Nevertheless, the strategic role of the hospital sector is rather due to experiments for pharmaceutical innovations. A better understanding of the decision making process at hospitals may allow pharmaceutical companies to set up appropriate promotional strategies and customer relationship policy toward hospitals.

## Theoretical Background

### Institutional Buying Behavior V.S. Business Organizations' Buying

Institutional buying behavior (IBB) shows special features comparing to that of profit-seeking companies. Marketing literature (Kotler; 2003, Hutt and Speh, 1992; and others) points out that institutions are characterized by low budget, high public control, and excessive bureaucracy. In their purchase decisions they put emphasis on price advantage and require suppliers to submit bids. Political sensitivity and non-economic criteria are additional features. However, their markets are important ones, consequently many suppliers are ready to accept special requirements and to develop adapted policy and marketing tools for these markets.

Institutional buyers are similar to governments in terms of regulation: important decisions are regulated by law, while institutions which operate privately are rather similar to profit-making firms. Table 1 presents similarities and differences in these organizational behaviors (OBB).

**Table 1: Similarities and differences in the OBB of industrial and institutional buyers**

| ***Similarities*** |
|---|
| Importance of the buying center |
| Complexity of decision-making |
| ***Differences*** |
| Number of members in the buying center |
| Buying objectives |
| Type of purchased products |
| Perceived risk |
| Formal buying committee |
| Bidding system – centralized and public procurement |
| Price negotiations |

Source: Szalkai (2002), based on Reeder-Brierty-Reeder (1991)

According to Reeder et al. (1991), a greater number of influencers are involved in the buying center when the organization is a nonprofit institution or a governmental agency (in a modified rebuy situation the average number of persons: 2.58, in a new task situation: 2.70), than for example in a manufacturing firm (1.90 and 2.20). Buying centers of nonprofit institutions and government units have to fulfil requirements of high visibility, and to be accountable for their decisions to the public sector. We can find differences in the buying objectives as well: nonprofit organizations are concerned with budgetary constrains, purchasing at a lowest possible price is in most cases necessary. Institutions are usually driven by community needs, while firms are profit orientated. Among the risks perceived by the buyer, economic risk is of first importance in institutional buying. Products are generally more similar to the consumer goods in a sense that institutions' main activity is not production. Hence, concerning the classification of goods in business market (entering goods, foundation goods, and facilitating goods) institutional buyers hardly buy entering goods: raw materials, component materials, etc. Considering the variability of products, institutions, more often than industry, purchase unique or seldom purchased items (Heinritz et al, 1991). In some cases buying center appears as a more formalized group, called buying committee. In the committee concept a wider range of experiences is applied to the decision-making process, decisions are made more scientifically, and the level of pressure in the buyer-seller relationship is lower (Hutt et al., 1992). This statement coincides with the empirical findings of Laios et al. (1994), namely, institutions set up interdepartmental evaluation committees to administer the bidding process. Asking for and evaluating bids take up most of the time of the organizational buying process. For institutions centralized procurement is sometimes not optional but obligatory. In the aim of the legal competition institutions are required to purchase through the bidding system. At last, price negotiations are general features of OBB, but because of the price-sensitiveness of institutions, it is more emphasized is this case. Table 2 summarizes the characteristics of institutions, which lead to the characteristics of the institutional buying behavior.

**Table 2: Characteristics of institutions and their buying behavior**

| **Characteristics of institutions** | **Characteristics of IBB** |
|---|---|
| Low budget<br>Community need<br>Governmental regulations on procurement | Transparency and accountability<br>More influencers in the buying center<br>Formulating buying committee<br>Formal bid evaluation<br>Price has a major role in evaluation<br>Use of centralized and public procurement<br>Decision often made by non-expert |

Scanning the literature of OBB we cannot find any model created to institutions as buyers. According to a comprehensive study of Sheth (1996), "business-to-business marketing seems to be still in search of a good theory". From the great number of models dealing with OBB, we have chosen Sheth's integrative model of industrial buyer behavior (1973) for further investigation of the topic. This model (see Fig. 1) reflects the psychological aspects of buyer's behavior. The expectations of the individuals in the buying center about the procurement differs due to the different individual backgrounds, information sources, active search, perceptual distortion, and satisfaction with past purchases. These key elements make this model adaptable also to institutions as buyers.

## Basic Specificities of the Drug Purchase Behavior of Hospitals

In the OBB literature a fewer number of empirical researches reports about institutions than about industrial firms. Articles related to the buying behavior of hospitals as example for institutions, usually investigate purchases of capital item, medical devices (Laczniak, 1979; Laios et al., 1994; Moon et al., 2002). The drug consumption of hospitals is rather in the focus of medical journals (Journal of American Medical Associations, American Journal of Health-System Pharmacy, Krankenhauspharmazie, etc.). This observation points out, that drug purchase of hospitals is a very complex topic and offers different research opportunities. Nevertheless, drugs as products raise some problematic issues we will discuss later in this paper.

### Specific Roles of Hospitals

Hospitals play a special role in the pharmaceutical market that can be identified by the following characteristics:

(1) Hospitals play a key role in the drug development process by taking part in the clinical trials of new drugs and in other tests.

(2) Hospitals are considered to be the place of the introduction stage of drugs' life cycle, so the success of a new drug in the total pharmaceutical market will be greatly affected by the sales toward hospitals.

(3) Pharmaceutical sales in pharmacies are often induced by the hospitals in the case of ethical drugs, since family practitioners prescribe the brand, which was taken by the patient during his/her therapy in the hospital.

(4) Prescription behavior of physicians working for a hospital and having special surgery hours is greatly influenced by the drug preference of the given hospital.

**Figure 1: Integrative Model of Industrial Buyer Behavior**
Source: Sheth (1973)

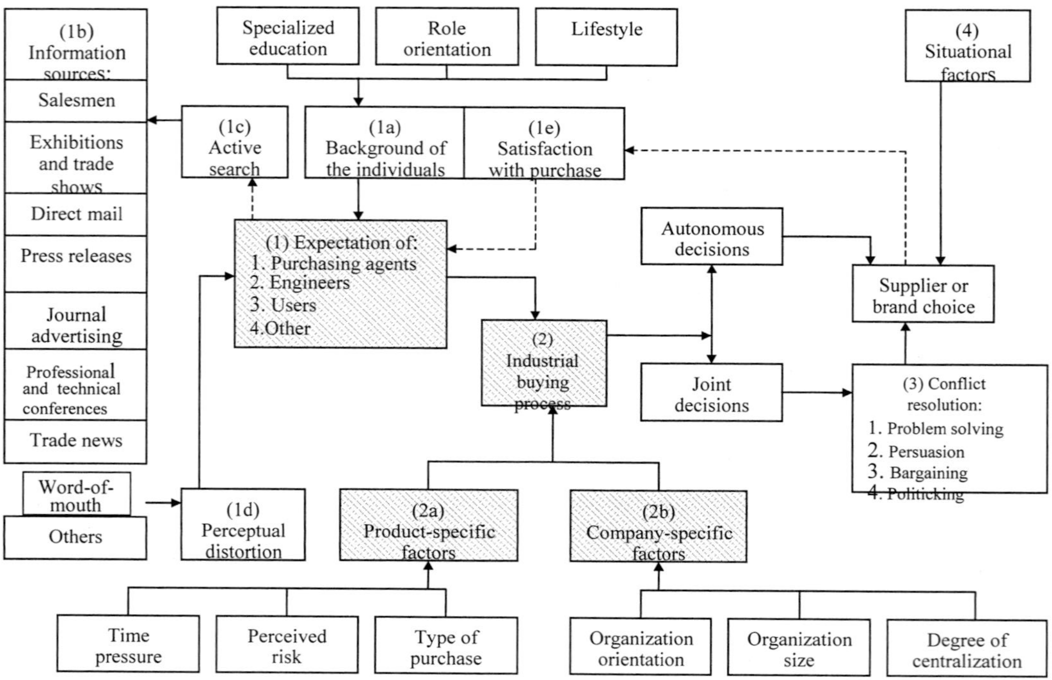

(5) Since the opinion leaders work in hospitals, these hospitals participate in the image building of a medicine or a pharmaceutical producer/brand.

(6) Post-marketing studies (analysis of new medicines launched into the market, for example in order to reveal incidental side effects) take place also in the hospitals whereby the awareness of the brand can be sustainable and it may increase the sales.

## Actors of the Pharmaceutical Market of Hospitals

The direct participants of the hospital market are recapitulated in Fig. 2. The hospital is represented by the buying center whose members is selected depending on the organization specific factors, buying situations, and personal characteristics, among others. A market research report written in France underlines that the hospital sector is a privileged place of experiments for pharmaceutical innovations as well as for the initial education of medical practitioners, and suggests that one box of medicines sold to hospital brings about sales of 10 boxes in the town. It defines these roles as a "source effect" and as a "bringing about effect" of sales to hospitals on the ambulatory sales (Eurostaf, 2003).

**Fig. 2: Buyer-seller relationships in the hospital market**

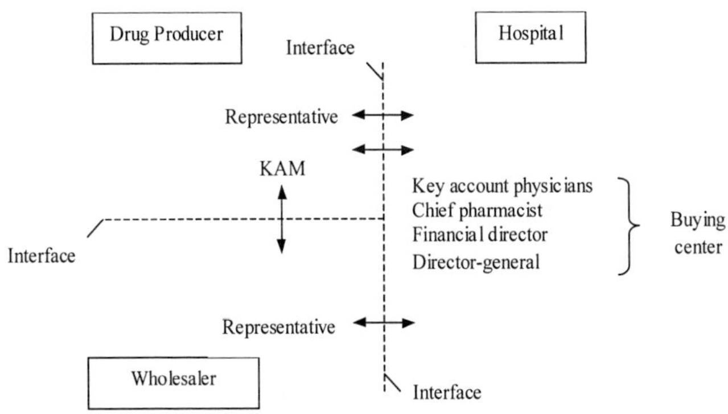


Source: Szalkai (2004)

For the further analysis of the drug purchase of the Hungarian hospitals, we have to underline two main specificities. On the one hand, buying behavior differs according to their status e.g. they are privately owned institutions or directly controlled by government or other authorities. The latter institutions are submitted to a greater administrative control. On the other hand, drugs are specific products: their commercialization, prescription and use are submitted to particular regulation.

## Drug Purchasing Decision of Hospitals in Hungary

### General Characteristics

In Hungary, similarly to other countries, the drug purchase of hospitals represents a relatively small part of the pharmaceutical market. Approximately 15% of the total pharmaceutical sales go to hospitals, this ratio seems to be constant in the last 10 years. This part is lower than in France for instance, where it represents 18% (an amount of 3,6 billion EUR in 2002) of the total pharmaceutical sales in contrast with 15% at the middle of 90's. Analyzing the Hungarian statistical data of sales from previous years, top selling medicines in hospitals are mostly original/innovative products. This latter is similar to the French case, however, in relation to Hungary, the profit gained from innovative products in the French pharmaceutical market of hospitals is particularly high (Eurostaf, 2003).

The drugs are mostly (80%) purchased from wholesalers and not directly from producers. Similarly, wholesalers are the major drug suppliers in The Netherlands, Slovakia, Slovenia, Great Britain, Finland, Sweden, and Norway, while the direct supply from producers is typical in France, Austria, Germany, Spain, Belgium, and in Greece (Amman, 2003). In Hungary, four wholesaling companies cover more than 80% of the hospital market.

Differences between sales realized by wholesalers in pharmacies and in hospitals, respectively, can be identified as follows (Szabó, 2001):

- The range of drugs sold to hospitals is wider than the range sold to pharmacies.
- The average price of drugs sold to hospitals is higher than the average price of drugs sold to pharmacies.

- ➢ The shipping cost for hospitals is lower than for pharmacies.
- ➢ Hospitals have lower buying power than pharmacies have.
- ➢ It is difficult to forecast sales to hospitals on long term.

The rate of the drug expenditures within the hospital's budget is 12,1%, which is much higher than in other European countries (Amman, 2003). In Sweden (0,73), Norway (1,56), and in Finland (1,6) these expenditures are around 1% of the total budget. This high value of Hungary is followed by the data of Greece (9,6), Slovenia (8,96) and Slovakia (8,55), but it does not reach 10% even in these countries. The third group of countries: Belgium (6,22), Spain (5,14), Austria (4,25), Germany (4,07), The Netherlands (3,86), Switzerland (3,83), Great Britain (3,6), Denmark (3,23), and France (3,22) falls within these two extreme values. These differences are due to the different reimbursement systems and the different definitions of drugs. There is no unique definition for drug, so the number of products – considered to be drugs – is of a wide range. For example in Hungary many products are considered to be drugs, which are not in the drug category in other countries.

The definition of the category *drug or medicine* is not unanimous, is rather contradictory in the practice of the different hospitals. In some hospitals, medical gases for example, are also called drugs while in other hospitals they are considered as other products. Drugs are extremely heterogeneous products, it is almost impossible to define product groups that have the same procurement method. Due partly to this fact, the application of public procurement regulation in practice is problematic. In Hungary the procurement of drugs is submitted to the public procurement law. The minimum value of goods to purchase according to public procurement is determined by the budget law in force. During our research, the determined minimal amount was 18 million HUF (approx. 72.000 EUR). An annual drug budget of a small hospital (where the number of beds is less then 500) is around 100 million HUF (400.000 EUR).

The relationships with the suppliers are affected by the applied purchase method. So, suppliers have to identify these methods in hospitals in order to make a reasonable offer. In Hungary, hospitals may satisfy their need of drug in five different ways, by

- centralized public procurement
- public procurement

- shipping contracts
- non-regular procurement (price discounts)
- delivery of 'gratis drugs' – free delivery of drugs by firms

In the practice of hospitals the above-mentioned methods are usually combined. The category 'gratis drugs' means drugs, which go to hospitals from the pharmaceutical manufacturers for free. The amount of these drugs represents and means a hidden part of the pharmaceutical market, but it is considered as indispensable for the normal daily operations of the Hungarian hospitals.

For the evaluation of bids, the following factors are usually evaluated with different weights: service quality (safety and flexibility); the amount and duration of price discount; payment period; rate of price change; producer's discount (rabatt); availability of preliminary stock in hand. The evaluation procedure shows, that a remarkable proportion of factors is in relation with the financial conditions of the purchase. Hungarian hospitals are not alone in Europe to have problems with the application of public procurement. A study made in a university hospital in Serbia points out, that "the drug tender is a resource-consuming, laborious, and risky job. Aggregation of individual tenders, on a national level and/or regional ones, is probably the best choice for hospitals in transition countries at this time." (Milanovic et al., 2004).

We have to note two additional organizational factors of the IBB. The first one is the role of the Committee of Drug Therapy. It has an important influence on the drug purchase because it has the right to define products and brands to choose. The Committee is composed from the director of physicians, the chief pharmacist, and other leading physicians and experts. They are responsible for the modern, cost-effective drug therapy, as well as for its control processes. The second one is the hospital's overall management approach to the drug expenditures. There are different methods available for the hospitals to make the drug purchase as cost-effective as possible. In some hospitals the amount of money the departments may spend on drugs is limited. Another solution for cost saving is offered by the opportunities of formulary management. Different kinds of lists are used in order to encourage the physicians to choose the most cost-effective therapy. Such lists are: the list of essential drugs, the list of substitution, and the list of gratis drugs. The chief pharmacist is in charge to compose the list of substitution and the list of gratis drugs. The

Committee of Drug Therapy is responsible for developing the list of essential drugs. The number of hospitals in Europe that use this kind of list is increasing (Amman, 2003). The most sophisticated technique is perhaps the use of therapeutic guidelines. Unfortunately, there are different barriers to the usage of these methods, and the most important among them is the resistance of physicians.

## Results of an Empirical Research

The need of an empirical research on the drug buying behavior of Hungarian hospitals has been arisen in the framework of another research topic. We have examined factors of competitiveness of the pharmaceutical industry. The role of hospitals inside the pharmaceutical market has proved to be an important but not enough explored field.

### Research Objectives and Methodology

The research has intended to reveal: What special factors influence drug purchase decision of hospitals, with special attention to main requirements toward pharmaceutical suppliers and products? How product attributes – especially those of innovative and generic products, respectively – influence the choice of decision makers and affect competitive strategy of pharmaceutical producers in the drug market? How regulation of public procurements influences competitive strategies of suppliers in this market? How the drug demand of hospitals is satisfied in this special condition?

As an exploratory research, interviews with chief pharmacists, physicians and pharmaceutical experts have been initiated. The objectives of these interviews were to reveal the factors influencing the drug purchase of hospitals, purchasing methods, organizational factors of the purchase, the buying center, provisions of hospital's management toward financial constraints concerning the drug choice and other different factors of the buying decision.

In the framework of the survey data have been collected from the chief pharmacists in charge of purchasing and one physician at each of the 152 public hospitals in Hungary. The survey was conducted in November and December 2002. The overall response rate is 42,8 % (65) for chief pharmacists and 28,3% (43) for opinion leader physicians. The response rates may be considered representative to geographical, ownership, and hospital size variables.

Two different questionnaires were made up for the chief pharmacists and for the physicians, respectively. Chief pharmacists were asked about drug supplier choice, the hospital's drug purchase method, the application of public procurement model for drugs, relationship with drug suppliers, among others. Physicians were asked about their product choice, attitude about generic drugs, source of information about new drugs, etc. We limited the citation of the asked questions according to the topic of this paper.

## Characteristics of the Buying Process

The results of the survey will be presented below according to the core parts of the Sheth's model (Fig. 1): the characteristics of the buying process; the expectations of the chief pharmacist, and the physician as participants in the buying center; product specific factors in the field of interior administrative regulations will be put in focus.

As the characteristics of the buying process, it was found that hospitals set up different restrictions aimed at decreasing drug expenditures. In most of the cases (in 49 hospitals out of 65 hospitals) financial limits were defined in order to regulate the spending of the different departments, respectively. In 41 hospitals (out of the 65 respondents) a list of essential drugs is used, with minimum 20 and maximum 1050 different brands and with minimum 110 and maximum 600 different active substances on it. The practice of hospitals is very heterogeneous in relation to these lists in spite of the fact, that every hospital in Hungary has the same variety of drugs to choose from.

We examined the practice of hospitals in the use of the public procurement method for drugs. Only the half of the surveyed hospitals has used the public procurement and the other half rejected to use it. The chief pharmacists were asked to rank the listed reasons of rejection into order of importance. The most important reason of rejection was that (1) the hospital may obtain better conditions in drug purchase by using other purchasing methods, like purchasing directly from the manufacturer. The further reasons was ranked as follows: (2) the amount of consumption of the different specific groups of drugs does not justify the general use of public procurement, (3) long term planning (needed for the application of the public procurement method) is difficult for the drug consumption of the hospital, (4) the procedure of public procurement is expensive, (5) The weak liquidity of the hospital's budget does not allow the use of public procurement. A clear correlation can be noticed between the use of public procurement and the size of the hospital. A bigger hospital uses public procurement for drug purchase most probably than a small one. We have collected information about the groups of drugs usually purchased by public procurement as well. It was found that public procurement used to the different types of drugs depends on the individual practice, most of the hospitals have used this purchasing method for all the drugs they need.

## Expectations toward Suppliers and Products

According to the responses of the chief pharmacists, financial factors – price and discounts – are the most convincing for the drug procurement. The influencing effect of the producers' promotion on drug procurement has brought the most heterogeneous results; the same number of respondent indicated this factor as important, or not important and less important factor. Price, price discounts, and the physician's opinion are the most determining factors of the purchase (Fig. 3).

**Fig. 3: Importance of the different influencing factors of drug purchase according to the chief pharmacists (on a 1-5 scale)**

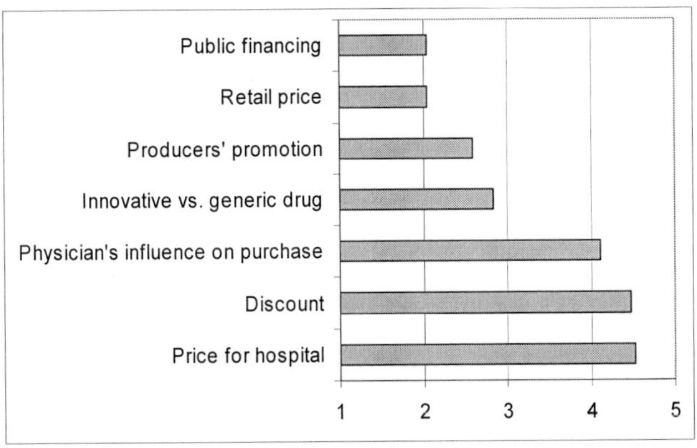


The chief pharmacists were asked to evaluate the relationship with the major drug supplier (in most of the cases they are wholesalers). The results are shown in Fig. 4. More than a half of the respondents gave the mark 5 (on a scale from 1 to 5, where the 5 mark means the most adequate characteristic) for the variables of trust and stability in the relationship. The role of former experiences with the supplier and the continuity of the relationship were also significant characteristics of the relationship. The respondents gave very distinct opinions about the role of personal bonds in the relationship. Many pharmacists have evaluated this factor rather not typical at all than typical. The modus were around 3. Concerning the total satisfaction, most of the respondents are satisfied with the drug suppliers. Trust and stability are the most relevant characteristics of the relationship with the major supplier.

**Fig. 4: Evaluation of the relationship with the major supplier by the chief pharmacist (on a 1-5 scale)**

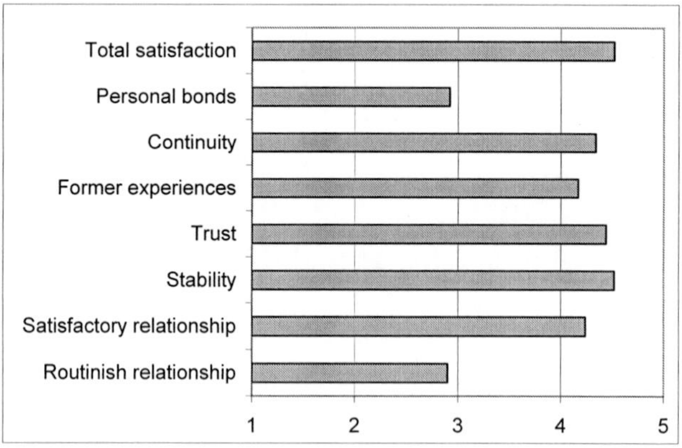


Pharmacists and physicians were asked about the information sources they use about new drugs. Questions were set up for innovative and generic drugs separately, because we have assumed that the innovativeness of the drug results differences in the importance of the different information sources. Results of the survey have proved the very important role of manufacturer's representatives in both cases. Manufacturer's representatives are the most important information sources about new drugs for pharmacists, but for physicians literature precedes them a little bit, while conferences are almost equally important. For generic drugs it is not surprising that after manufacturer's representatives direct mail came up to the second place both for pharmacists and physicians while literature and conference is more important for chief pharmacists than for physicians.

**Table 3: Information source of new innovative drugs**

| Pharmacist (number of mention) | | Physician (number of mention) | |
|---|---|---|---|
| Producer's representative | 61 | Producer's representative | 32 |
| Literature | 45 | Literature | 33 |
| Conference | 34 | Conference | 22 |
| Direct mail | 31 | Direct mail | 13 |
| Wholesaler's representative | 8 | Pharmacist | 8 |
| Physician | 3 | Colleagues | 6 |
| Internet | 2 | Drug database | 1 |
| Postgraduate course | 1 | | |
| Electronic database | 1 | | |

**Table 4: Information source of new generic drugs**

| Pharmacist (number of mention) | | Physician (number of mention) | |
|---|---|---|---|
| Producer's representative | 61 | Producer's representative | 37 |
| Literature | 33 | Literature | 10 |
| Conference | 23 | Conference | 9 |
| Direct mail | 40 | Direct mail | 18 |
| Wholesaler's representative | 7 | Pharmacist | 15 |
| Physician | 1 | Colleagues | 3 |
| Internet | 1 | Drug database | 1 |
| Electronic database | 1 | | |

The number of respondents for the questions about the information sources was 65 in case of pharmacists and was 43 in case of physicians.

According to their answers, most of the physicians (36 out of 43) are willing to try out new drugs because they have read about it in the literature. The majority of the respondents (23 physicians out of 43) have found it mostly motivating if the drug has new therapeutic advantage over the existing ones. On average (2,95) physicians evaluated least of all the producers' representatives in the motivation. So, according to the respondents, the literature is the most important motivating factor for try-out new drugs (see Fig. 5). Younger physicians marked the experience of colleagues and conferences more important than older ones did.

**Fig. 5: Sources of motivation to try out new drugs (on a 1-5 scale)**

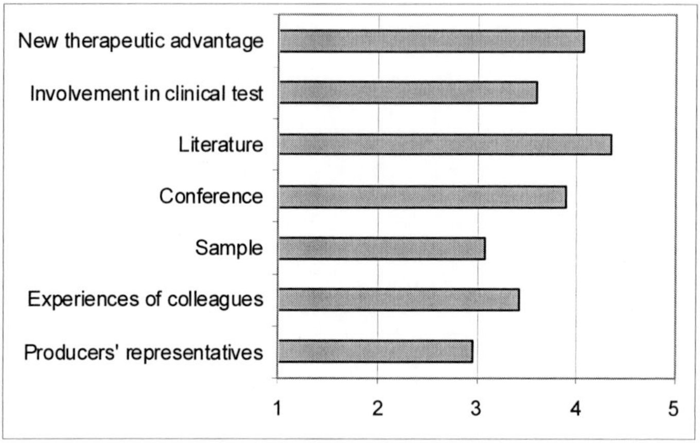


According to the research results, the higher effectiveness of a new drug is the primary factor for applying a new drug in the therapy (Fig. 6), while the manufacturer reputation is of the latest one. 24 out of 34 respondent physicians think that producer's reputation is moderately important or preferably not important when he/she opted to try a new drug. So, effectiveness is the most important factor for regular use of a new drug followed by fewer side effect, own experiences, and gentile care.

**Fig. 6: Motivations of the regular use of new drugs (on a 1-5 scale)**

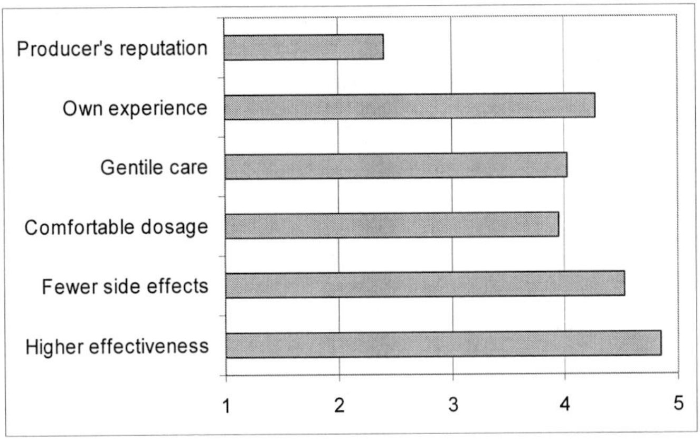


## Product Specific Factors

Physician's behavior toward generic and innovative products has been already tackled in the previous paragraph. We have also examined the practice of physicians regarding the shifting from innovative to generic drug, because their behavior is often considered as a barrier to the use of cheaper drugs. During the year before the research 34 physicians out of 43 changed the previously used innovative drug to a generic one (at least once). The first reason for changing therapy to a generic drug was its lowest price.

A very interesting question of the research was the attitude of physicians about generic drugs. Their most important requirement toward generics is related to effectiveness: they should be as effective as the original innovative one. This result coincides with the rank of motivations of regular usage of a new drug (see Fig. 6). Results show, that the attitude of physicians toward generics does not influence the choice of generics instead of innovative products. 36 physicians have had special surgery hours among the 41 respondents. 22 out of the 36 have changed the therapy in his/her ambulatory practice and replaced innovative medicines used in the hospital by generic ones. They mentioned the weak financial conditions of the patient and the lower price of the generic product as motivation of this behavior.

As an additional problem we have tried to reveal the rate of gratis drugs in the Hungarian hospitals. According to the responses, the average rate of gratis drugs in hospitals was found about 18% of the total drug consumption.

**Fig. 7: Therapeutic categories of gratis drugs**

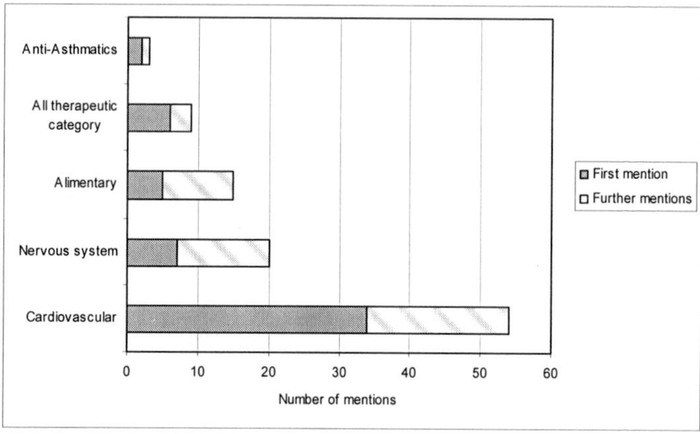


The therapeutic composition of these drugs is shown in Fig. 7. The therapeutic categories of gratis drugs are influenced by the hospital's profile. Fig. 7 shows that pharmaceutical firms prefer to give gratis drug to hospitals for long-term (life-long) therapies.

## Conclusion

The main objective of our paper was to present the drug buying behavior of Hungarian hospitals based on the marketing models of organizations, with focus on institutions. Additional elements to these models have been specified according to features related to public institutions, government buying, and other specific characteristics related to hospital and product in general, and in Hungary especially. This topic has not yet been examined in Hungary, so the paper reports about a set of original information related to this specific segment of the pharmaceutical market, and can be of interest for stakeholders both of the buyers and sellers side. (The research has not been sponsored by any actor of the health sector or the pharmaceutical market.)

The expending pharmaceutical market continues to benefit from the increasing expenditures of the health sector including public hospitals spending on pharmaceutical products. In Hungary, 15 percent of the pharmaceutical sales is realized in the hospital sector. The involvement of users in product innovation is a corner stone of the successful new product development and in this regard, hospitals offer a not substitutable opportunity to pharmaceutical firms. On the other side, submitted to budget pressure hospital management does not stop seeking for cost effective solutions for all of its services and purchases including drug purchase (such as bulk-buying organizations, direct purchase from manufacturer, substitution lists, etc.). In the majority of European countries governments make efforts to control even distributor mark-ups as an important factor of final prices of reimbursable medicines.

At the beginning of the 21$^{st}$ century, pharmaceuticals firms face a number of different challenges in their environment and in their industry, respectively: globalization, information technology, increasing competition, shortening product life-cycle, increasing R&D expenditures, health care reforms, intensifying regulation, high distribution costs, the competition of generic products, etc. On average, 12 years pass from the invention of a molecule to the market launch of a new product. The part of distribution costs may reach 25-35 percent of final prices. Pharmaceutical companies mainly market their products through contact between their sales force and healthcare providers. However, due to the nature of its products, the pharmaceutical industry has been subject to heavier marketing and advertising restrictions than most other industries and has remained focused on the purchasers and providers of healthcare, rather than the consumers. The need for a sophisticated marketing knowledge and for shifting to more appropriate strategies is of decisive importance.

The segmentation of this market and also the promotion is becoming more sophisticated. Pharmaceuticals firms spend a lot on promotion and about the 60 percent of expenditures are used for promotion toward medical practitioners, while among other partners' hospitals and their chief pharmacists are also considered as very important ones. Manufacturer's representatives continue to play the most important role in promotion. Marketing of pharmaceuticals is becoming a multidimensional activity; firms have to combine different tools such as key account management, marketing of services, and political marketing. They have to identify opinion leaders and to supply not only products, but also different services as well to medical practitioners, patients, different organizations, and society. They need to intensify lobbying toward political decision makers for subventions to the health insurance system or to the launch of a new medicine. As the customer relationship marketing effects directly the drug purchasing decision, it is indispensable to identify decision makers, expectations of the members of buying centers, and their attitudes. Our research has justified the privileged role of hospitals for the pharmaceutical market in Hungary. Customer relationship management is becoming a valuable tool in marketing in the Hungarian pharmaceutical market as well.

## References

Amman, S. (2003): Krankenhausapotheken in Europa – Ergebnis einer Umfrage der EAHP im Jahr 2000. *Krankenhauspharmazie*. 24. Jahrgang Nr. 3. pp. 77-86

Eurostaf (2003) : Les mutations du marché pharmaceutique hospitalière en France. Etude de marché.

—. (2003) : Distribution des médicaments en Europe. Etude de marché.

Heinritz, S., Farrell, P.V., Giunipero, L., and Kolchin, M. (1991): Purchasing: Principles and Applications. 8th ed., Prentice Hall

Hutt, M. D., and Speh, Th. W. (1992): Business Marketing Management – A Strategic View of Industrial and Organizational Markets. The Dryden Press

Kotler, P. (2003): Marketing Management. Analyzing, planning, implementing and controlling. Prentice Hall

Laczniak, G. R. (1979): An Empirical Study of Hospital Buying. *Industrial Marketing Management.* 8 pp. 57-62.

Laios, L, and Xideas, E. (1994): An Empirical Investigation of Institutional and Industrial Purchasing Structure. *European Journal of Marketing*. Vol. 28 No. 4, pp. 20-38

Milanovic, D. R., Pavlovic, R., Folic, M., and Jankovic, S. M. (2004): Public drug procurement: the lessons from a drug tender in a teaching hospital of a transition country. *European Journal of Clinical Pharmacology*. 60 pp. 149-153

Moon, J., and Tikoo, S. (2002): Buying decision approaches of organizational buyers and users. *Journal of Business Research*. 55 pp. 293-299

Reeder, R. R., Brierty, E. G., and Reeder, B. H. (1991): Industrial Marketing – Analysis, Planning, and Control. Prentice-Hall Inc.

Sheth, J. N. (1973): A Model of Industrial Buyer Behavior. *Journal of Marketing*. Vol. 37 pp. 50-56

—. (1996): Organizational buying behavior: past performance and future expectations. *Journal of Business and Industrial Marketing*. Vol. 11 No. 3/4 pp.7-24

Szabó, F. (2001): A gyógyszer-nagykereskedelem kialakulása, helyzete és lehetséges irányai II. rész. (The evolution, situation, and future development of pharmaceutical wholesale trade Part II.) *Gyógyszerészet*. augusztus pp. 431-440.

Szalkai Zs. (2002): Investigation on Organizational Markets through the Organizational Buying Behavior focusing on Institutional Buyers. *2nd International Conference for Young Researchers*. Gödöllő, pp. 321

Szalkai, Zs. (2004): A gyógyszeripari versenyképesség vizsgálata, különös tekintettel a kórházi piac szerepére. PhD Disszertáció. (Competitiveness of the Pharmaceutical Industry with a special focus on the Role of the Hospital Market of Pharmaceutical products. PhD Thesis, directed by Vágási, M.)

Vágási, M., Jankó, Á., and Szalkai, Zs. (2003): Sustainable Customer Relationship. In Corporate Sustainability. Proceedings of the *5th Summer Academy on Technology Studies*. Deutschslandberg, Austria pp. 289-302.

Vanderveer, R. (2001): The new micromarketing: Looking at the practice as an account to be managed, rather than the doctor as a target to be hit. International Journal of Medical Marketing. Vol 2,3 200-205.

# PHENOMENON OF DOUBLE JEOPARDY ON FINANCIAL SERVICES MARKET IN POLAND

SŁAWOMIR SMYCZEK

## Abstract

This paper examines the phenomenon of double jeopardy on the financial services market in Poland. Today, the market of financial services is one of the fastest growing and the most dynamic sectors of Polish economy. Foreign investments foster competition, extend market offers and contribute to the modern development of distribution systems, etc. Intense promotional activities conducted by foreign institutions lead to the less rational consumer behaviour where consumers tend to choose those financial institutions and services that, from an economic point of view, ensure them maximum advantage. Consumers, however, are more frequently influenced by many subjective factors, which results in a situation where they prefer definite financial institutions and services to others and remain more loyal to them. Thus, it can be concluded that phenomenon of double jeopardy is present on the market of financial services in Poland. This phenomenon is demonstrated through the fact that buyers of less important brands are less loyal to them than those who tend to buy more popular brands. This means that less popular brands are simultaneously less favoured by consumers. This principle also works the opposite way i.e. more popular brands on the market are given preference over others in consumer purchases.

## Introduction

Since the beginning of the transformational process of the Polish economy, the market of financial services has been the fastest growing and the most dynamic sector of the economy, which has undergone significant changes since 1989. These changes comprised:

- structural and ownership changes – several state monopolies have been replaced with a diversified entity structure on the banking and insurance market,
- support of the monetary policy through the internal exchange of Polish złoty, maintenance of a relatively stable Polish złoty exchange rate against other currencies and absorption of surplus funds on the market,
- active involvement of banks in the process of privatization and creation of the capital market,
- assumption of the burden connected with financial restructuring of companies,
- reforms of the National Insurance initiated in 1999,
- visible improvement of financial services,
- disappearance of clear-cut differences between banking, insurance and other financial institutions.

The system changes on the market of financial services spurred by political transformations gave rise to infrastructural changes as well as changes in the consumer behaviour. Consumers became independent market players, limited in their choices only by their own financial resources and abilities. Today, their decisions are made according to their own system of values, which means that consumers themselves decide whether to use definite financial services and or not, and if so, which institution to choose, when to buy a given service, etc. Consequently, a question arises whether consumers behave rationally in their market decisions by choosing those institutions and services that ensure them maximum advantage from the economic point of view. Or maybe there are many other subjective factors thanks to which consumers favour certain services and institutions over others and remain more loyal to them? In other words, is the phenomenon of double jeopardy present on the market of financial services?

## Nature and Character of Double Jeopardy Phenomenon

The phenomenon of double jeopardy was observed during different evaluations of the consumer brand loyalty and assessments of the consumer satisfaction with products of a particular company, in a situation where consumers make a choice between products that are similar but enjoy different popularity among buyers. Double jeopardy is a theoretically justified regular phenomenon existing on markets whose operation is based on competition. It is demonstrated through the fact that customers of smaller companies (brands) tend to be less attached to them than customers of bigger firms. This phenomenon was mentioned for the first time by W. McPhee (W. McPhee, 1963).

Double jeopardy is not a common subject of empirical research, and therefore it still remains an unexplored area. In over 50 articles published worldwide, the issue is discussed in a limited way and appears as a supplement to other major subjects such as consumer loyalty and satisfaction or the consumer behaviour. The most literature data on the phenomenon of double jeopardy refer to multiply purchases (fast-moving consumer goods) which comprise over 40 various and frequently-bought product categories, including breakfast cereal, washing powder, petrol (A.S.C. Ehrenberg, G.J. Goodhardt, 1988). Double jeopardy has also been observed with respect to media, newspapers, TV stations and regular TV serials (T.P. Barwise, 1986 and T.P. Barwise, G.J. Goodhardt, A.S.C. Ehrenberg, M.A. Collins, 1998). Moreover, it has been identified in multiple car purchases (R.A. Colombo and D.E. Morrison, 1989) and in the operations of the industrial market, which is confirmed by the data on the number of contracts for oil purchase between airlines and petrochemical companies at different airports (M.D. Uncles, A.S.C. Ehrenberg, 1990). The phenomenon of double jeopardy is also present in distribution channels, e.g. in the case of multiple purchases of ready-made goods in small or big supermarkets (K.A. Keng, N.R. Wrigley, R. Dunn, 1984).

In spite of an increasing number of empirical data and better theoretical explanations of double jeopardy, the phenomenon is not widely known among theoreticians and pragmatists. Little is said about it in the scientific literature. Nevertheless, the identification and explanation of double jeopardy seem indispensable in order to diagnose certain regularities existing on a given market and to learn about the consumer behaviour. Pragmatists should be aware of the existence of this phenomenon as a basis for undertaking strategic and tactical activities with respect to building programs of market share retention and extension.

The occurrence of double jeopardy in so many various situations and with respect to different aspects of brand preferences and brand loyalty might imply the existence of one common and underlying reason. Otherwise some temporary explanations should be put forward, for example: more popular brands have better advertising or else have a wider range of distribution on many markets – both these factors may contribute to the growth in the number of consumers and to the enhancement of their loyalty, but can they be generally referred to all markets? They would not explain, for instance, the occurrence of double jeopardy in different distribution channels, and therefore some other theoretical explanations would be required. On the other hand, one small set of probabilistic arguments shows that double jeopardy tends to occur when two rival products differ in popularity (e.g. market share) unless there are other more influential specific factors (M. Lambkin, G. Foxal, F. van Raaij, B. Heilbrunn, 2001). This conclusion is common both for the primary explanation by W. McPhee, as well as later concepts.

The theoretical explanation of double jeopardy proposed by W.N. McPhee was based on the asymmetry relating to people's knowledge of or contacts with products that are similar in nature, but different in popularity.

W. McPhee (W. McPhee, 1963) explained the phenomenon on the basis of a town with two restaurants only: one more and one less popular. According to his assumption, people who know both restaurants find their quality of service identical (e.g. food, service, price, access). However, if the people were asked about their restaurant preferences, the phenomenon of double jeopardy would undoubtedly occur. The reason for this would lie in the fact that among many people who know the popular restaurant there are plenty of those do not know the less popular one, and consequently they cannot answer the question which restaurant they prefer. On the other hand, most people who know the less popular restaurant also know the other, more popular one. Therefore, their opinions are divided - it is equally probable that they would indicate the first or the second restaurant as their favourite one since it was assumed that both restaurants had the same quality of service for people who know both of them. Consequently, among many people who know the popular restaurant, the majority will consider it as their favourite, whereas among few people who know the other restaurant, only 50% will find it more attractive. This is a classic example of the double jeopardy phenomenon.

Similar arguments can be provided with respect to the consumer behaviour. Fewer consumers make less frequent visits to the less popular restaurant because almost every second time they decide to eat at the more popular one (which they find equally good). However, a majority of patrons of the popular restaurant choose it because they are unaware of the existence of the other place. For the double jeopardy to occur, it must be assumed that both restaurants differ from each other only in terms of the number of customers' visits and in terms of their popularity, in other words, how well they are known and how often they are frequented (S.P. Raj, 1985).

The question arises why the two restaurants of the same service quality do not enjoy the same popularity? Such a phenomenon is common on markets based on competition – particular brands may be similar but have different market share as a result of present or past marketing activities. Hence, the less popular restaurant is facing a marketing challenge. In order to increase its turnover without losing its character, service quality, price level, etc., the restaurant must not only become better-known but also must gain and maintain the same recognition among its consumers as the more popular restaurant.

While making some preliminary predictions about the range, occurrence and development of the phenomenon of double jeopardy among competitive brands, stochastic models of the consumer behaviour were created, including the most popular, so-called, intuitive model w(1-b) and the Dirichlet model (M. Lambkin, G. Foxal, F. van Raaij, B. Heilbrunn, 2001). These models predict the appearance of double jeopardy on the basis of differences in popularity between particular brands (i.e. market share) without using any information about the market position of a product, promotional activities or any other factors.

The simplest model assumes that all consumers are identical. Each of them buys a given product twice a year and every time chooses one out of two brands: A or B, with a constant probability 0.7 and 0.3. Following this, a comparison should be made between the annual number of buyers of a particular brand and the frequency of particular brand purchases. In order to identify the number of consumers who buy brand A at least once a year, it is necessary to define the number of consumers who do not buy the brand at all. Since the probability of not buying brand A in a given purchase situation is 1 – 0.7 = 0.3, the probability of not buying brand A during every purchase is 0.32 = 0.09. The sales of brand A per capita amounts to 1.4 (i.e. 0.7 x 2). Hence, the average frequency rate of buying brand A by one consumer is 1.4/0.91 = 1.54. Proper calculations for brand B reveal that 51% of consumers buy brand B 1.18 times a year on average with its sales per capita at the level of 0.6.

**Table 1: The "intuitive" model of the double jeopardy phenomenon – brand A and B**

| No. | Brand | Purchase probability | Sales per capita | % of buyers purchasing at least once | Average purchase per brand buyer |
|---|---|---|---|---|---|
| 1. | **A** | 0.7 | 1.4 | 91 | 1.54 |
| 2. | **B** | 0.3 | 0.6 | 51 | 1.18 |

Source: M. Lambkin, G. Foxall, F. van Raaij, B. Heilbrunn, 2001

This is an example of the double jeopardy phenomenon where, in comparison with brand A, a less popular brand B has a smaller number of less frequently buying consumers.

The second model explaining the occurrence of double jeopardy on the market takes into consideration the heterogeneity of the consumer behaviour. Therefore, it can be regarded as more realistic compared to the previous one. In literature this model is referred to as w(1-b) and it compares bx (the proportion of customers buying brand X at least once during the analysed period) and wx (the average frequency rate of buying the brand within this period) with respective values by and wy for brand Y. According to this model, wx(1-bx) = wy(1-by) = wo, where wo is a constant (estimated as an average value w(1-b) for all considered brands). A predicted value wx for a given bx equals wo/(1-bx). Hence, the lower value b, the lower w, which points to the existence of the double jeopardy phenomenon.
This model was worked out by means of algebric transformations from two assumptions of independence:

- buying different brands is an independent process among particular consumers e.g. the proportion of households buying brand X during the analysed period is $b_x$, no matter if they also buy brand Y,
- brands do not differ from each other in terms of the average frequency rate of buying products from a particular category of products as a whole, i.e. consumers buy any possible brand (A.S.C. Ehrenberg, A.J. Bound, 1990).

In approximation, both these assumptions work in reality, hence the conclusion that model w(1-b) should also follow the suit.

The third, Dirichlet model also takes into regard the heterogeneity of the consumer behaviour, yet it is more flexible and comprises a wider range of situations compared to model w(1-b). Here, the assumptions which were used in model w(1-b) are more elastic. Moreover, each brand not only has its b and w (with the direction development of double jeopardy), but also many other collective features of the consumer behaviour e.g. the range of buyers 100% attached to a brand (G.J. Goodhardt, A.S.C. Ehrenberg, C. Chatfield, 1984).

According to this model, the time when a buyer makes a purchase and the brand that he/she chooses, are generally of irregular character and can be treated as a "random process" at some definite probabilities. Such a situation is likely to arise even when particular consumers have various and pre-defined reasons for their behaviour.

From the technical point of view, the Dirichlet model uses four distributions of probability to define more accurately the ways in which particular customers make their purchases. Two of them allow for the evaluation of the buying frequency rate, where purchases made in a given category of products by each buyer are formulated according to Poisson distribution, whereas long-term average purchase indicators among particular consumers are expressed by means of Gamma distribution. The two other distributions refer to brand selection. Purchases of particular brands made by each consumer are formulated according to the multidimensional distribution, whereas the distribution of such probabilities among consumers is expressed by means of Beta multivariable distribution referred to as the Dirichlet model. This model relates to the market which:

- is stable – without any changes between the analysed periods,
- is not segmented – the distribution of particular brands is independent (J.E. Mosimann, 1984).

The Dirichlet model has only three parameters of product categories. One of them reflects the market size, whereas the two others show differences between customers in terms of the buying frequency rate and brand selection (i.e. the general frequency at which consumers change brands in a given category of products). All the three parameters can be assessed on the basis of market penetration with a given product category, the average frequency rate of buying the category products as well as the frequency of buying each or any brand during a selected basic period. The procedure calls for complicated calculations but special computer programs may be helpful in dealing with the problem (M.D. Uncles, 1989).

The nature of the Dirichlet model is revealed through the fact that once the three required parameters have been assessed, the only indispensable information specific for a brand must be looked for in the market share of particular brands. It must be remembered, however, that in real terms, most buyers of a given brand often reach for other competitive names over a long period of time i.e. time comprising several purchases of a certain product category. To provide some examples, consumers of a certain brand of instant coffee tend to buy coffee in general (any brand) at the average frequency of nine times a year, which is three times as frequently as the average number of purchases of this particular brand. This regularity is based on some observation as well as the Dirichlet model.

Moreover, the phenomenon of double jeopardy does not result from the fact that buyers of smaller brands tend to use few products from a particular category in general. On the contrary, consumers of less popular brands would be able to buy more of them without being forced to use a given product category more often. They could, however, reverse the direction of double jeopardy by buying more products of one particular brand and fewer of other brands. In general, consumers choose more than one brand within certain period of time i.e. they tend to vary in their brand selection, even in very stable conditions with no special promotional campaigns, etc. The research conducted on many industrial markets confirms the predictions of the theory according to which a great majority of consumers rarely reach for each separate brand. In such circumstances, the phenomenon of double jeopardy exists with reference to smaller and less popular brands.

To sum up, the phenomenon of double jeopardy is revealed not only through consumer attitudes, as it was primarily suggested by McPhee, but also through the consumer behaviour. In other words, less popular brands with a small market share are bought less frequently than big brands. In this case, the phenomenon of double jeopardy is demonstrated exclusively through the consumer behaviour. Additionally, consumers who rarely choose “their” brand say they like the brand less than those who buy it more often. Since a small brand has a greater proportion of less-frequently buying consumers, their attitudes to the brand are less positive compared to attitudes expressed by buyers of more popular brands. In this case, the double jeopardy phenomenon is visible through consumer attitudes.

## Phenomenon of Double Jeopardy on the Market of Financial Services and Empirical Research

The Polish market of financial services is dominated by banking and insurance sectors where the rivalry for clients is especially fierce. Therefore, the problem of double jeopardy on these markets is gaining more significance. Despite the broad knowledge of the consumer behaviour and attitudes through which double jeopardy is demonstrated, theoreticians as well as managers of financial institutions are not commonly familiar with principles behind the phenomenon. In fact, such knowledge would help them better understand the nature of the consumer behaviour and provide them with a sound foundation for strategic and tactical marketing decisions in financial institutions.[1]

## Characteristics of Double Jeopardy Phenomenon in Polish Banking Sector

In order to identify the phenomenon of double jeopardy in the banking sector, it is necessary to define the size of particular brands (banks). It must be mentioned, however, that there is no universal indicator that could synthetically determine the "size" of a given financial institution.

The share of a financial institution in the total assets of the banking sector greatly determines its position in the whole banking system. In Poland, the first position in terms of total assets is occupied by PKO BP, whereas the second and the third one by PeKaO S.A. and BPH respectively. Other banks of high total assets value include Citibank, BRE Bank, ING Bank Śląski S.A., Kredyt Bank and Bank Zachodni WBK

**Table 2. Banks of the biggest total assets in Poland (in mln zł)**

| Position | | BANK | Total assets in million Polish złoty | |
|---|---|---|---|---|
| 2004 | 2003 | | 2003 | 2004 |
| 1 | 1 | PKO BP | 84,568 | 88,763 |
| 2 | 2 | PeKaO S.A. | 63,013 | 59,334 |
| 3 | 3 | BPH | 48,379 | 53,857 |
| 4 | 6 | ING Bank Śląski | 28,917 | 34,968 |
| 5 | 4 | Bank Handlowy (Citibank Polska) | 34,035 | 33,948 |
| 6 | 5 | BRE Bank | 30,532 | 32,722 |
| 7 | 7 | BZ WBK | 24,169 | 27,583 |
| 8 | 8 | Kredyt Bank | 23,893 | 21,671 |
| 9 | 9 | Bank Millenium | 20,833 | 20,440 |
| 10 | 11 | Raiffeisen Bank Polska | 8,782 | 11,243 |
| 11 | 15 | GE Money Bank | 6,979 | 8,012 |
| 12 | 12 | Bank Gospodarstwa Krajowego | 7,955 | 11,081 |
| 13 | 13 | Bank Ochrony Środowiska | 5,917 | 6,944 |
| 14 | - | Bank Polskiej Spółdzielczości | 4,807 | 5,967 |
| 15 | 14 | Fortis Bank | 4,586 | 5,384 |
| 16 | 16 | Nordea Bank Polska | 4,049 | 5,113 |
| 17 | 17 | Lukas Bank | 3,970 | 4,728 |
| 18 | 20 | ABN Amro Bank | 3,388 | 4,673 |
| 19 | 21 | Getin Bank | 3,096 | 4,586 |
| 20 | 18 | Rabobank Polska | 3,657 | 4,155 |

Source: Own elaboration based on Supplement: *Najlepsze banki 2005*, Gazeta bankowa 4-10 July 2005.

The size and the importance of a bank on the Polish market largely depend on the development of its units, its branches and agencies. Although the number of clients per one bank unit has been declining in Poland for some years (from 9.2tho in 1998 to 7tho in 2000, and to approximately 3tho in 2004), it is still much higher compared to West-European countries. To provide some examples, in Germany the index stands at 2,025 consumers per one single bank unit, in Portugal at 1,938, and in Austria at 1,509. These shortfalls are partly compensated for by longer opening hours of branches and agencies which, on working days serve their clients 2-3 hours on average longer than their equivalent bank units in more developed EU states. Moreover, in Poland some bank branches are also open on Saturdays.[2]

In terms of the number of bank units in Poland, the leading position belongs to PKO BP and PeKaO S.A., with PKO BP being the leader with 1.200 bank units.

**Figure 1: Banks with the biggest number of units in Poland**

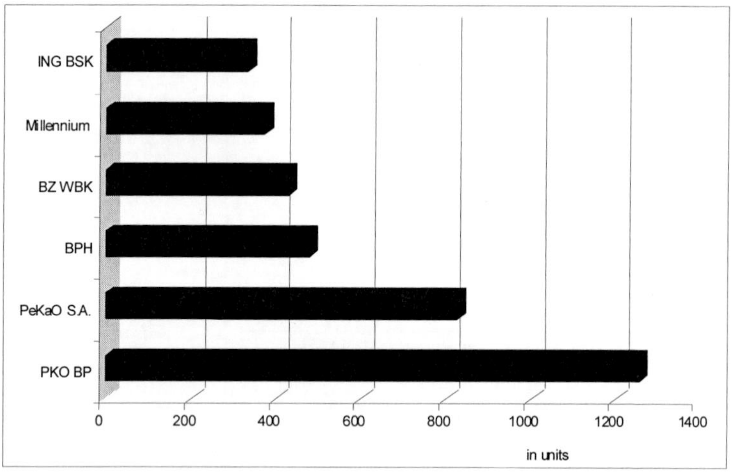


Source: (P. Włodarczyk, 2004)

With reference to the above-presented observation, it can be concluded that PKO BP, PeKaO S.A. and BPH constitute the group of the biggest banks operating on the Polish market. Other positions in this hierarchy differ depending on adopted criteria.

While identifying the phenomenon of double jeopardy in the banking sector, it must be remembered that in terms of the buying behaviour, this phenomenon is mainly revealed through the consumers' stronger tendency for using services of bigger banks, and slighter one for services offered by smaller institutions. However, it should be emphasised that banks' offer is very rich and can satisfy a variety of consumers' financial needs. The most popular services include: bank accounts – for settlements and other transactions, deposits – for the allocation of free financial funds, loans and other credit facilities – for taking financial commitments. Therefore, the analysis of double jeopardy on the market of banking services ought to be made with reference to various banking services used by consumers.

In Poland PKO BP bank is an unquestionable leader in terms of personal bank accounts used by individual clients (about 35%). A considerable share in this market is also claimed by PeKaO S.A. (16%) and BZ WBK (9%).

**Figure 2: Banks and their market share in terms of personal bank accounts in Poland in 2004**

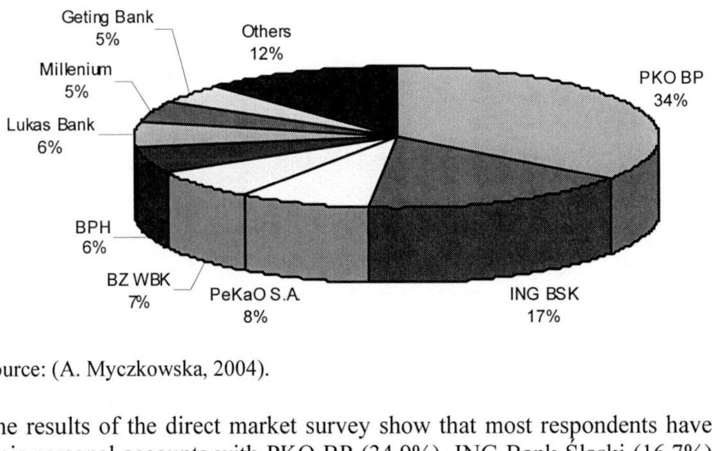


Source: (A. Myczkowska, 2004).

The results of the direct market survey show that most respondents have their personal accounts with PKO BP (34.9%), ING Bank Śląski (16.7%) and PeKaO S.A. (8.2%).

**Figure 3: Use of personal bank accounts by respondents in different banks**

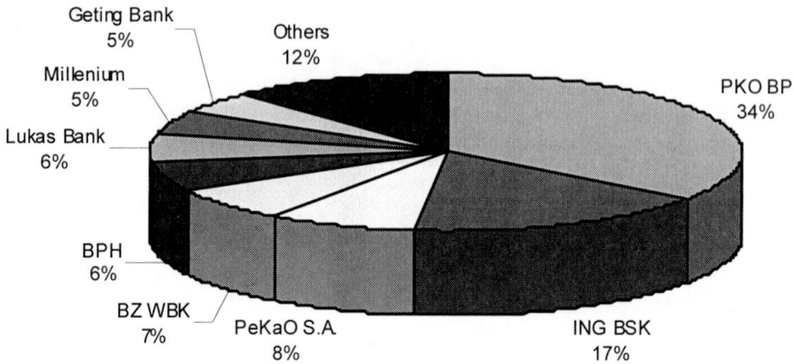


The results overlap, to a great extent, with the market share of particular banks in terms of personal bank accounts across the whole country. In many regions, ING Bank Śląski constitutes an exceptional case, with its big market share and the second position in the rating. However, this case cannot be univocally declared an exception to the phenomenon of double jeopardy on the market of financial services. It is worth emphasising that the Silesian voivodship is the main area of the bank's activity, and its regional strength as well as significance are demonstrated through numerous bank branches and cash dispensers. A similar situation can be observed with regard to Getin Bank, whose distant 21st position on the national scale, is not confirmed in the studied region where it is much favoured by consumers.

Deposits are another very important service in the banking offer including various term deposits (in different currencies), savings accounts, deposit certificates, etc. A majority of Silesian consumers allocate their surplus money in deposits offered by PKO BP (27.3%), PeKaO S.A. (18.9%) and ING Bank Śląski (18.2%).

**Figure 4: Use of deposit services by respondents in particular banks**

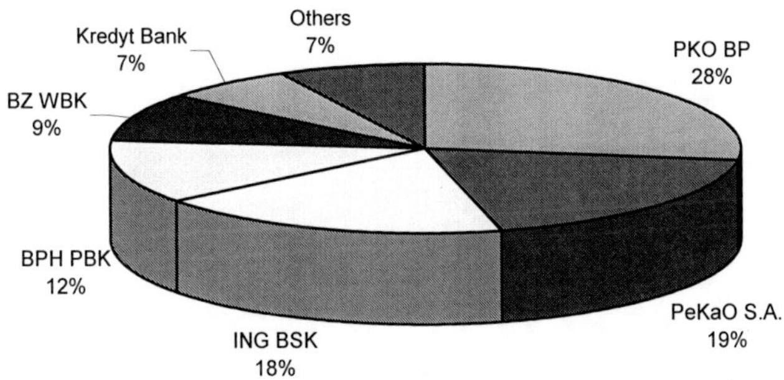


The third group of banking services comprises facilities which enable customers to take financial commitments such as cash loans, special purpose loans, credit lines, etc. Like in the previous cases, the dominant position in this group is held by PKO BP (19.8%), ING Bank Śląski (15.4%) and PeKaO S.A. (14.9%). It is noteworthy that many consumers use credit facilities provided by a small local bank - Getin Bank (11.6%).

**Figure 5: Use of credit facilities services by respondents in different banks**

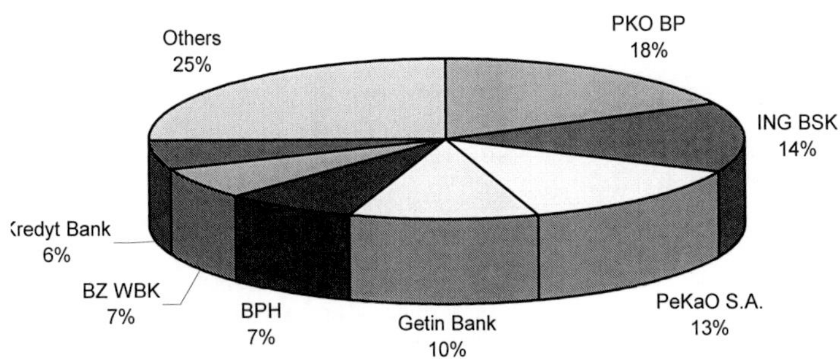

Taking into consideration the banks' shares in the market of deposits and consumer credits, the situation on the Polish market is similar to the one in Silesia. The leading market position belongs to PKO BP, with 29% shares on the deposit market and 22% on the credit facilities market.

**Figure 6: Banks' share in market of deposits in Poland**

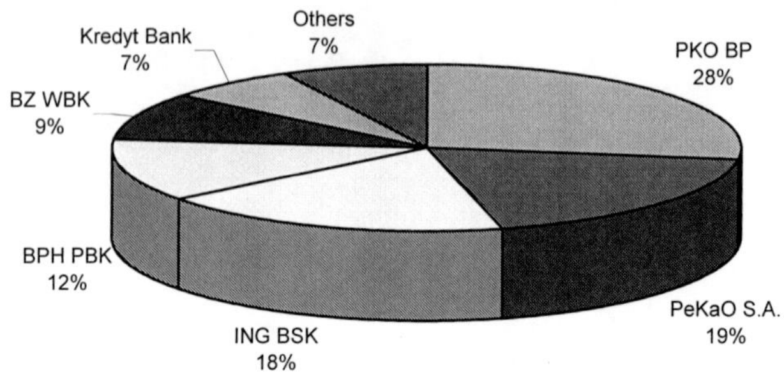


Source: (G. Gadomski, 2004).

**Figure 7: Banks' share the market of consumer credits in Poland**

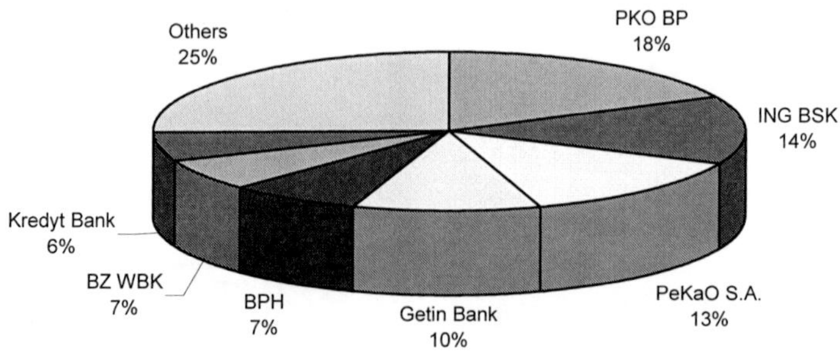


Source: (G. Gadomski, 2004).

While analysing the consumer buying behaviour on the market of financial services, it can be observed that big institutions such as Bank Handlowy in Warsaw, being part of Citi Corporation, as well as BRE Bank were mentioned by a small number of respondents. However, this case cannot be considered as an exception to the studied phenomenon as, despite the banks' fifth and sixth ranking position in terms of their size and range, the banks are mainly focused on corporate rather than individual clients.

The phenomenon of double jeopardy is not only revealed through the consumer behaviour but also through consumer attitudes towards definite bank names. According to respondents' opinions, PKO BP is the best bank operating in Poland, followed by: PeKaO S.A., BPH, ING BSK and BZ WBK.

**Figure 8: The best banks - respondents' ratings**

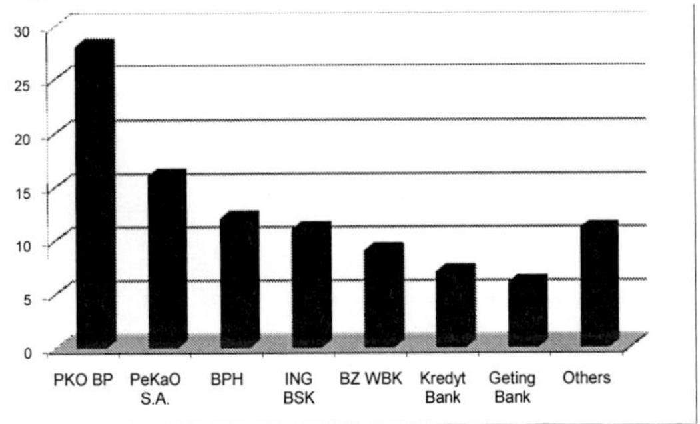


The bank rating created by respondents indicates that the double jeopardy phenomenon on the analysed market is also present in consumer attitudes.

This thesis is additionally supported by the data on respondents' satisfaction with banks whose services they use. The research results show that the most satisfied consumers are clients of big banks such as PeKaO S.A. (74.9%), PKO BP (71.3%) and ING BSK (70.6%). Taking into account the smallest institutions i.e. cooperative banks, it can be concluded that about 63% of consumers are satisfied with services provided by these institutions. This is evidence of some deviation from the general direction of the double jeopardy phenomenon since the level of satisfaction with services of these banks is higher than in the case of BPH (61.7%), being a much bigger institution. The most negative opinions (as many as 23.4%) of all institutions were expressed towards savings and loan associations.

However, it is noteworthy that a very numerous group of respondents expressed their satisfaction with (42.5%) or delight in services offered by these institutions (4.3%).

With reference to the above-presented data, a conclusion may be drawn that consumers are rather satisfied with services provided by banks operating on the Polish market. The highest notes, however, are obtained by the biggest commercial banks and small cooperative banks, which is an exception to the principle of the double jeopardy phenomenon.

Consumer attitudes to banks largely depend on consumer confidence in a particular financial institution. The results of the direct market survey show that consumers are relatively confident in banks whose services they use. The biggest banks enjoy the greatest public confidence, especially PKO BP (the average on a five-point scale is 3.67 at the standard deviation of 0.934), PeKaO S.A. (3.64, standard deviation 0.843) and ING Bank Śląski (3.36, standard deviation 0.944). As many as 69.1% of PKO BP clients have trust in their bank, including 13.4% of those who trust it very much. PeKaO S.A. enjoys confidence of 66.7% of its clients, whereas ING BSK of 64%. A slightly less confidence is put in cooperative banks - 59.7%. Savings and loan associations are trusted only by 28.4% of respondents and distrusted by 23%. A very big group of clients cannot define their attitude towards these institutions (nearly 50%).

It can be concluded that consumers have great confidence in banks operating on the Polish market, which is particularly important, as these are institutions of public trust. The loss of confidence in one of the banks cannot bring satisfaction to competitors as this state of affairs can be reflected in consumers' attitudes to the whole sector.

The great satisfaction and confidence do not mean, however, that consumers will use services of a given financial institution in the future. Nevertheless, these features can be contributory factors in reinforcing the consumer loyalty (S. Smyczek, I. Sowa, 2005). Thus, it is vital to recognize consumers' intentions as for their further cooperation with banks. The study results show that PKO BP has the biggest group of loyal clients (almost 80% of them want to cooperate with "their" bank in future). The other banks that have also been able to build a sound base of loyal consumers are represented by: ING BSK (76.3%) and cooperative banks (72%).

It can be stated that the deviation from the phenomenon of double jeopardy is confirmed through consumer attitudes towards banks. The explanation of this phenomenon should not be looked for in intensive marketing activities, but in consumers' access to banks. Cooperative banks, for example, are located in small towns where competition in the banking sector is very small or non-existent. Hence, consumers are "doomed" to use services of one definite cooperative bank.

This observation leads us to the conclusion that the phenomenon of double jeopardy on the market of financial services appears both in the area of the buying behaviour and consumer attitudes on the market. Clients of bigger banks are more frequent users of their services and better evaluate the functioning of such banks. Moreover, they have more trust in these institutions and, more importantly, they are more attached to them (loyal) in the practical activity.

## Phenomenon of Double Jeopardy and Insurance Sector

The research into double jeopardy so far reveals the occurrence of the phenomenon during the assessment of consumers' attachment to or predilection for a brand (their preference), in a situation where consumers make a choice between products that are similar in nature, but different in popularity.

The market of insurance services displays significant similarities in the offer of particular insurance companies because each institution of this specific market can provide only one definite range of services i.e. life insurance, property insurance and other personal and pension insurance policies. Therefore, the phenomenon of double jeopardy should be analysed in such a context.

**Figure 9: The biggest life insurance companies in Poland in terms of volume of gross insurance premium**

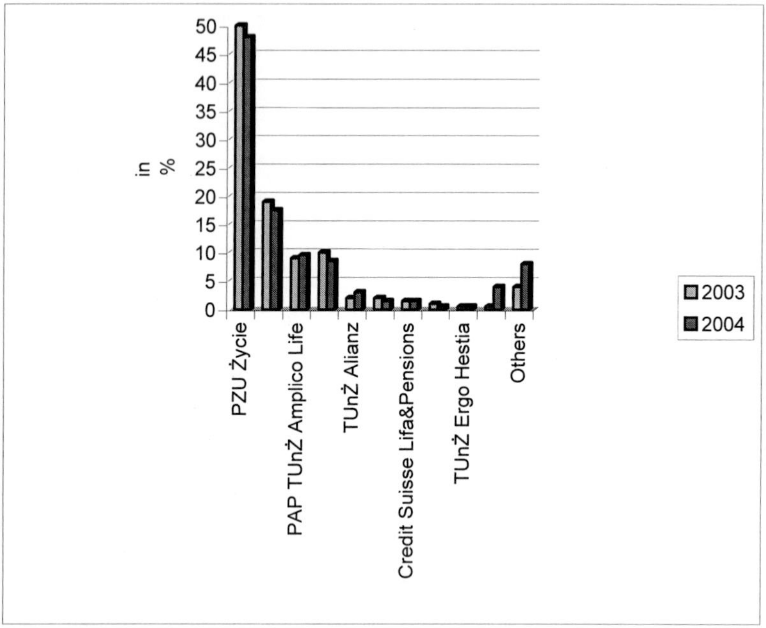


Source: (M. Dygas, 2004)

The four biggest insurance companies dominate the insurance market. However, while making the analysis of the premium volume per each company (chart 14), it is noteworthy that the market share of the leaders is gradually declining whilst the other smaller companies are gaining more and more market significance (mainly the companies with foreign capital). According to market analysts, the competition between these institutions also arises from their ambitions connected with their prestige and role on the international market. Thanks to this internal rivalry, the companies may faster catch up with "the big three" whose members (CU, Amplico, NN) also compete with each other, thus shortening their distance towards the market leader – PZU Życie (KNUiFE, 2004). The alignment of the smaller companies with the market leaders is quite possible, which is clearly demonstrated through the growth rate and consumer attitudes. This, in turn, may be evidence of the double jeopardy phenomenon.

On the basis of the secondary sources and direct survey analyses, life insurance companies have also the biggest client base, which ensures them a considerable share in the market. To provide some examples, Poles are the most frequent holders of life insurance policies offered by PZU Życie (nearly 50%). Significant market shares are also claimed by Commercial Union (about 16%) and Amplico Life (12%).

**Figure 10: Market share of life insurance companies on Polish insurance market**

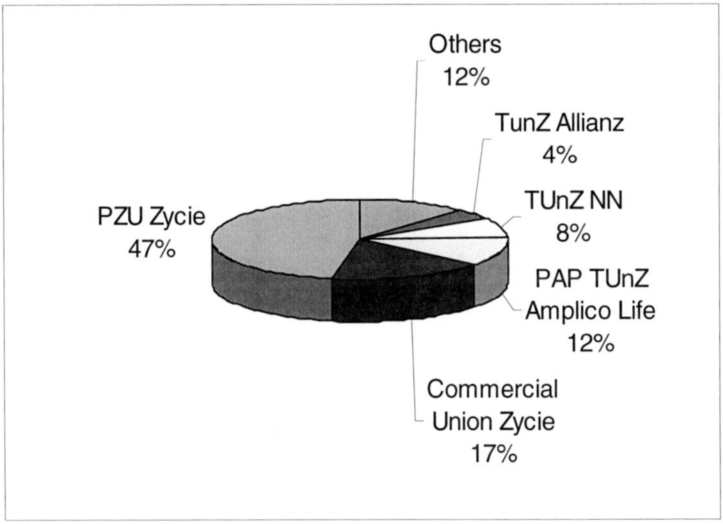


The research confirms that market is dominated by PZU Życie with its leading position in the volume of sold insurance policies – over 40% of respondents are members of the company. The policies offered by Commercial Union (17.3%) also enjoy great popularity among members of the focus group. It is worth emphasising that TUnŻ Nationale Nederlanden has a very big market share many regions compared with Warsaw (12.9%), which is undoubtedly a consequence of the company's references to its affiliation with ING Bank Śląski in its selling strategy.

**Figure 11: Use of life insurance policies offered by different insurance companies**

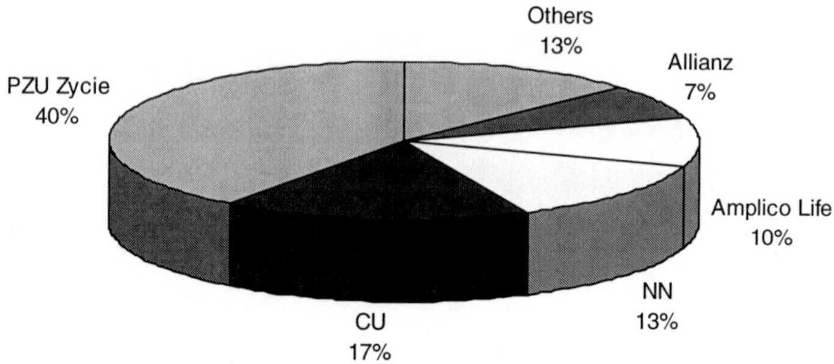


Bearing in mind the above-presented observation, it can be concluded that the phenomenon of double jeopardy exists on the insurance market with respect to the consumer behaviour. However, in order to properly define this phenomenon, it is necessary to describe consumer attitudes towards companies offering insurance services. According to respondents, PZU Życie is the best life insurance company operating in Poland, and is followed by: NN, CU, Amplico Life and Allianz.

**Figure 12: The best life insurance company in Poland - respondents' ratings**

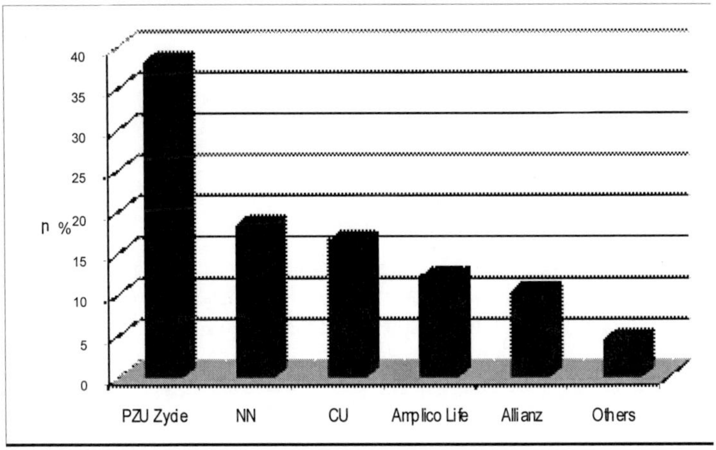


The presented data may be evidence of the phenomenon of double jeopardy on the studied market also with respect to consumer attitudes.

This thesis is additionally supported by the data on consumers' satisfaction with services provided by their insurance companies. The most satisfied consumer groups are represented by clients of PZU Życie (54.2%), CU (51.7%) and Amplico Life (48.3%), in other words, companies which are the biggest institutions offering life insurance.

The direct market survey also shows that consumers have relatively much confidence in insurance companies active on the Polish market, especially the biggest ones, including PZU Życie 51.5%, CU 49.2% and NN 43.5%. It is noteworthy that PZU Życie has the greatest number of distrustful clients in its portfolio. By way of contrast, 20.3% of respondents on average declare lack of confidence in major foreign institutions, which, however, does not change the direction of the development of double jeopardy.

A relatively high level of consumer satisfaction with services of insurance companies and significant confidence in these institutions are clearly reflected in the consumers' strong intention of further cooperation with these companies in the future. The research results show that PZU Życie has the greatest number of loyal clients on the Polish market (77.1%) with only 11.5% of disloyal ones. Other insurance companies which can boast many loyal clients in their portfolio are represented by: NN (70.3%) and CU (68.9%).

With reference to the above-presented figures it can be observed that the research results confirm the existence of the double jeopardy phenomenon on the life insurance market also in the sphere of consumer attitudes. The clients of major insurance companies are more satisfied with their services, have greater confidence in them and stay loyal to these institutions.

While analysing the phenomenon of double jeopardy on the market of property insurance, it is necessary to identify institutions that offer these types of service on the Polish market and to determine their size and range. With respect to the volume of gross insurance premiums, PZU S.A. is the market leader.

**Figure 13: The biggest property and other personal insurance companies in Poland in terms of gross premium volume**

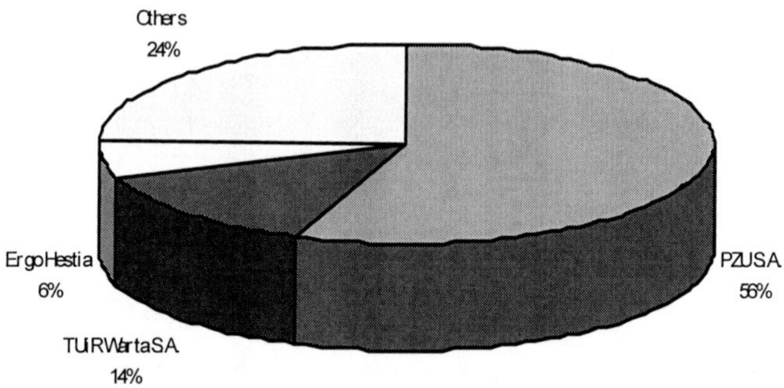


Source: (B. Pietrzak, Z. Polański, B. Woźniak, 2004)

It should be emphasised that since the beginning of the transformational process of the Polish economy until 1990, PZU S.A. and Warta S.A. sustained some loss in their market share. A significant share was claimed by Polisa S.A. (in 1998 as many as 4.1%), yet in 1999 the company went bankrupt. The dynamic development has been maintained by Ergo Hestia

S.A. (former Hestia Insurance) whose market share accounted for 6.29% in 2003. Allianz insurance company has come next in the ranking with its market share of 3.72%. Since 2000, PZU S.A. has managed to regain its market share in spite of many controversies around the privatization of the company. In 2001 it claimed almost 60% of the market.

The direct survey indicates that consumers prefer to use services of the biggest insurance companies. In terms of the volume of sold insurance policies, the leading position is occupied by PZU S.A. - almost 44% of respondents are members of the company. The insurance policies offered by Warta S.A. (27.8%) are also very popular with members of the focus group. Two other companies: Allianz and ergo Hestia have similar shares in the market (7.8% and 7.1% respectively).

**Figure 14: Use of property insurance policies in different companies**

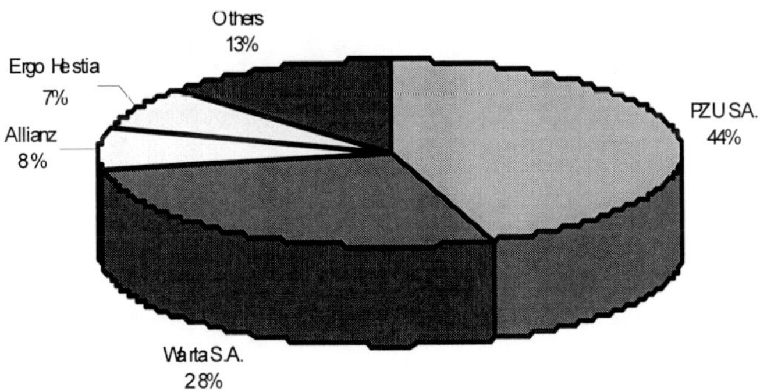


Taking into consideration the above-presented figures, it can be observed that the phenomenon of double jeopardy is demonstrated through the consumer behaviour on the market of property insurance. Nonetheless, some deviation from this trend is visible in the case of Allianz company which is more popular with individual consumers than Ergo Hestia, although the latter occupies the third position in terms of its gross premium volume. Such a deviation can be a consequence of Allianz's intensified marketing activities.

In order to identify the phenomenon of double jeopardy on the property insurance market, it is vital to determine consumer attitudes towards companies offering this type of service.

The research results reveal that the position of the best insurance company in Poland is held by PZU S.A, followed by: Warta S.A., Ergo Hestia, Allianz.

**Figure 15: The best property insurance company in Poland - respondents' ratings**

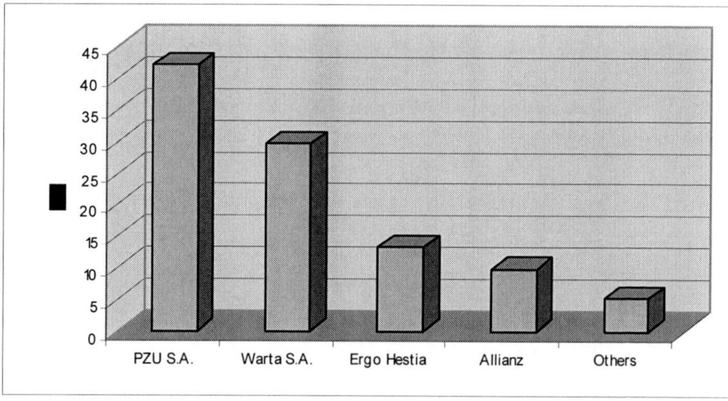


In addition, the research shows that individual clients are more satisfied with services provided by bigger companies that those who use services of less popular institutions. With the market average of 39.5%, as many as 51.2% of PZU S.A. clients express their satisfaction with the company. 48.7% of consumers are satisfied with Warta S.A., 48.2% with Ergo Hestia and 46.9% with Allianz.

According to the survey, consumers' confidence in insurance companies active on the Polish market is relatively high. In respondents' opinions the most trustworthy companies are represented by PZU S.A. – 56.7% (the number of clients who trust this institution exceeds the number of those who are satisfied with its services), Ergo Hestia – 47,9%, Warta S.A. – 46,3% and Allianz – 42,8%.

The high level of consumer satisfaction and confidence is reflected in the consumer loyalty. On the basis of the research data, almost 64% of PZU S.A. clients declare their attachment to this institution. Other companies can also pride themselves on a significant number of loyal clients in their portfolio: Warta S.A. with 55.3% and Ergo Hestia with 47.9%.

Taking into consideration the above-presented results, it can be observed that the phenomenon of double jeopardy is present on the property and other personal insurance market also with respect to the consumer behaviour. Clients of major insurance companies are more satisfied with their services, have more confidence in them and stay loyal to these institutions.

Pension funds constitute the third market of the insurance sector, which has been gaining more importance on the Polish market within the last few years. In 1999, 21 institutions referred to as Open Pension Funds (OFE) entered the market with the offer of the pension insurance. The funds included the following companies: AIG OFE, Bankowy OFE, CU OFE BPH CU WBK, OFE Dom, OFE Allianz Polska, OFE Credit Suisse LP, OFE Ego, OFE Epoka, OFE Kredyt Banku, OFE NN Polska, OFE PBK Orzeł, OFE Pocztylion, OFE Polsat, OFE Pionier, OFE PZU Złota Jesień, OFE rodzina, OFE Sampo, OFE Skarbiec-Emerytura, OFE Zurich, OFE EGO, PeKaO OFE, Winterthur OFE. In the first year of the pension funds' operation over 11mln Poles had to choose the fund that could manage their financial resources. Given the fact that these institutions were in the initial stage of their operation, the phenomenon of double jeopardy seemed to be non-existent. However, it turned out that a majority of funds that were established by big financial institutions enjoyed much greater popularity among consumers than others, and at the end of December 1999 the biggest net assets were in the possession of OFE Commercial Union, OFE ING Nationale Nederlanden and OFE PZU.

The analysis of changes in the portfolio value of the funds in the first years of their operation allows for the formulation of the hypothesis about the phenomenon of double jeopardy on the market of pension funds. Bigger institutions have gained much greater significance, whereas the smaller ones have been operating on a much narrower scale. Moreover, some of the institutions, including OFE Pionier, OFE Rodzina or OFE Epoka, have been acquired by other financial institutions (with the exception of OFE Skarbiec-Emerytura). The company's value of the net assets has grown considerably within the last two years, which, however, was not a consequence of special marketing activities, but of the company's takeover of another fund.

**Table 3: Net assets volume of the biggest Open Pension Funds in 1999 (after one year of their operation) and 2004**

| No | Open Pension Fund | Value in million Polish złoty in 1999 | Value in million Polish złoty in 2004 |
|---|---|---|---|
| 1. | Commercial Union | 630.6 | 12,102.4 |
| 2. | ING Nationale Nederlanden | 439.6 | 9,586.6 |
| 3. | PZU | 332.4 | 5,995.4 |
| 4. | AIG | 164.3 | 3,667.2 |
| 5. | Bankowy | 73.1 | 1,303.4 |
| 6. | Sampo | 66.8 | 1,284.6 |
| 7. | Skarbiec-Emerytura | 58.6 | 1,585.6 |
| 8. | Credit Suisse LP | 46.1 | 1,061.8 |
| 9. | Ergo Hestia | 31.6 | 855.1 |
| 10. | PeKaO | 31.4 | 695.0 |

The thesis regarding the double jeopardy phenomenon is confirmed by the number of clients who decided to join a definite pension fund. According to collected data, the largest client portfolios are in the hands of the biggest pension funds: OFE Commercial Union, ING NN OFE and OFE PZU.

**Table 4: The number of members of the biggest open pension funds (in 2004)**

| No according to the pension fund size | Open Pension Fund | Number of members | Change in relation to the previous year |
|---|---|---|---|
| 1. | Commercial Union | 2,538,721 | 103.9 |
| 2. | ING Nationale Nederlanden | 1,944,795 | 112.4 |
| 3. | PZU | 1,852,048 | 105.7 |
| 4. | AIG | 923,133 | 109.8 |
| 5. | Skarbiec-Emerytura | 618,228 | 164.1 |
| 6. | Bankowy | 393,667 | 101.0 |

| | | | |
|---|---|---|---|
| 7. | Sampo | 490,868 | 108.6 |
| 8. | Credit Suisse LP | 394,258 | 113.8 |
| 9. | Ergo Hestia | 361,219 | 150.9 |
| 10. | PeKaO | 292,294 | 100.1 |

With reference to the figures it can be concluded that the direction of the double jeopardy phenomenon has been continued despite a slight difference in the number of members of Bankowy OFE and OFE Sampo.

The analysis of the phenomenon of double jeopardy on the pension insurance market calls for the definition of consumer attitudes towards institutions offering this type of service. The results of the opinion poll show that OFE Commercial Union is considered the best insurance company in Poland. Further on the list are: ING NN OFE and OFE PZU.

**Figure 16: The best pension fund in Poland – respondents' ratings**

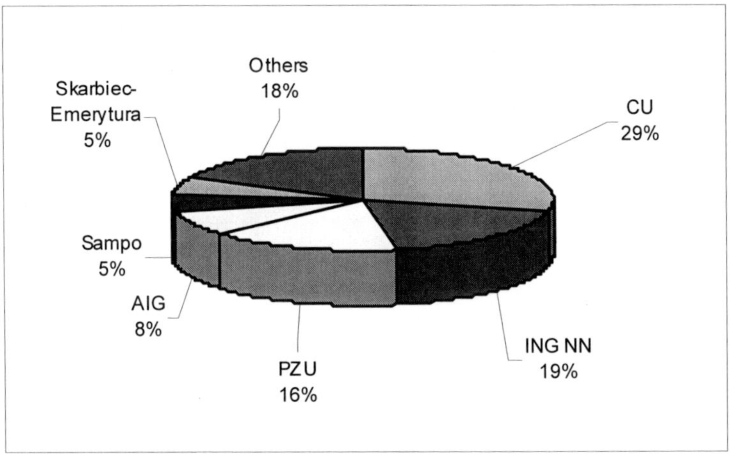


According to the survey results, consumers have more confidence in bigger pension funds. Although the level of trust in this type of institutions is relatively low (34% on average – this can be explained by the fact that these are rather new and not very popular institutions on the market. Furthermore, so far consumers have not had the opportunity to check the real effects of their market choices), a group of the most trustworthy institutions on the Polish market is represented by OFE CU – 42.3%, OFE ING NN – 40.9% and OFE PZU – 40.0%

Despite this low level of trust in pension funds, most members of the biggest institutions have the intention of continuing the cooperation with "their" company. It is noteworthy that up till now nearly 1.5mln Poles (about 13%) have changed one fund in favour of another. The market research shows that 83.3% of OFE CU clients declare their attachment to this institution. OFE ING NN and OFE PZU can also boast a large number of loyal clients in their portfolios (81.2% and 78.9% respectively).

To sum up, double jeopardy is a common phenomenon on the market of pension funds and also refers to attitudes presented by consumers. Clients of major pension funds better assess their institutions, have more trust in them and stay loyal to their pension funds.

## Conclusion

Taking everything into consideration, the phenomenon of double jeopardy is a widespread feature on the Polish market of financial services, especially banking and insurance services. With regard to the consumer behaviour, this phenomenon is revealed through the consumers' greater tendency for using services of big banks and insurance companies and a slighter one for services provided by small financial institutions. The market research shows that the direction of the double jeopardy phenomenon is maintained in both sectors, with some small deviations being a consequence of marketing activities.

The phenomenon of double jeopardy is visible not only in the consumer behaviour, but also in consumers' attitudes towards particular financial institutions, which is confirmed by research data. Clients of bigger banks and insurance companies better evaluate their functioning, have more confidence in these institutions and are more loyal to them, which is important in the practical activity. Some deviation from this trend can be observed in the case of cooperative banks, which, despite their small size, have managed to build a very big portfolio of loyal, confident and satisfied clients. The explanation of this deviation should not be looked to for in intensive marketing activities but in consumers' access to these banks, as they are located in small towns where competition in the banking sector is very small or non-existent.

In conclusion, it should be emphasised that the knowledge of the phenomenon of double jeopardy should provide pragmatists with a new view on their markets and market operations. Managers should consider the phenomenon of double jeopardy as something regular. Moreover, they should remember that no immediate remedial measures must be taken if a given financial institution has a lower level of multiply sales compared to other similar institutions. First, it is necessary for them to determine if this low multiply use index is typical of institutions of this size. The phenomenon of double jeopardy should be taken into consideration in a tactical planning and in the assessment of its effects as well as in the development of long-term strategies for brands. Otherwise, the ignorance of the phenomenon will inevitably end in failure. The experience shows that despite being faced with the phenomenon of double jeopardy, managers can successfully come up with a variety of financial services and develop dynamic marketing policies.

## Notes

[1] The direct study conducted in Poland by means of the direct interview method in September 2005. The focus group comprised 1,200 randomly selected respondents.
[2] www. zbp.pl/doc/komentarz.pdf

## References

Barwise T.P. (1986), *Repeat-viewing of prime-time US programs*, Journal of Advertising Research No. 28.

Berwise T.P., Ehrenberg A.S.C. (1998), *Television and Its Audience*, Sage Publications Inc., Newbury Park.

Colombo R.A., Morrison D.E. (1989), *A brand switching model with implications for marketing strategies*, Marketing Science No. 8.

Dygas M. (2004), *Ubezpieczenia na życie*, Gazeta Ubezpieczeniowa No 1.

Ehrenberg A.S.C, Bound A.J. (1990), *Prediction and predictability" a case discussion*, London Business School, CMaC Working Paper, London.

Ehrenberg A.S.C., Goodhardt G.J. (1988), *The double jeopardy effect for UK daily papers*, London Business School, CmaC Working Paper, London.

Gadomski G. (2004), *Ranking – Najlepsze banki*, Bank No 1.

Goodhardt G.J., Ehrenberg A.S.C., Chatfield C. (1984), *The Dirichlet: a comprehensive model of buying behaviour*, Journal of Royal Statistcal Society No. 147.

Keng Kau A., Ehrenberg A.S.C. (1984), *Paterns of Store-choice*, Journal of Marketing Research No. 21.

Lambkin M., Foxal G., van Raaij F., Heilbrunn B. (2001), *Zachowanie konsumenta. Koncepcje i badania europejskie*, PWN, Warszawa.

McPhee W.N. (1963), *Formal Theories of Mass Behavior*, Free Press, New York.

Mosimann J.E. (1984), *Size and shape analisis*, in S. Kotza, N.L. Johnsona (eds): *Encyclopedia of the Statistical Sciences*, John Wiley, New York.

Myczkowska A. (2004), *Przybywa kont internetowych*, Rzeczpospolita.

*Najlepsze banki 2005*, Gazeta bankowa 4-10 July 2005.

Pietrzak B., Polański Z., Woźniak B. (2004), *System finansowy w Polsce*, PWN, Warszawa.

Raj S.P. (1985), *Striking a balance between brand popularity and brand loyalty*, Journal of Marketing No. 49.

Smyczek S., Sowa I. (2005), *Konsument na rynku – zachowania, modele, aplikacje*, DIFIN, Warszawa.

*Sytuacja na polskim rynku ubezpieczeń*, Dodatek Ubezpieczeniowy KNUiFE, Ogma No 3/2004.

Uncles M.D. (19890, *BUYER: Software for Dirichlet*, London Business School: CMaC Working Paper, London.

Uncles M.D., Ehrenberg A.S.C. (1990), *Aviation fuel contracts in Europe*, International Journal of Research in Marketing.

Włodarczyk P. (2004), R*anking banków na przyjazny bank*, Newsweek.

# SPILLOVER EFFECTS IN SLOVAKIA

SONIA FERENČIKOVÁ
AND MARTINA FIFEKOVÁ

## Abstract[1]

This paper examines the indirect effects of foreign direct investment, commonly referred to as spillovers, in Slovakia. It provides a theoretical framework of this phenomenon, reviews existing literature on the topic, presents some examples of Slovak companies over the last decade regarding spillovers, and describes qualitative research of spillovers in the Slovak automotive industry. The results show that spillovers are present only through backward linkage, which is related to the technology transfer from foreign customer to domestic supplier.

## Introduction

Foreign direct investment takes place in an environment, which is day-by-day more policy distorted. Following the advice of international trade and development agencies, governments move from creating a more liberal and stable environment to providing enormous public subventions and using all measures possible to attract the inward investment. The foreign investor is expected then to bring employment, capital, and technology, as well as increase the productivity and competitiveness of domestic companies. The theoretical arguments explaining how the technology will spill over to domestic firms seems to be reasonable. The only trouble is that the evidence, which could prove the existence of such spillovers is somewhat missing. If willing to conclude that policymakers use subventions to gain effects, which are generally taken for granted, but actually may not even exist, we would need deeper research, especially in Central and Eastern Europe.

The objective of this paper is therefore to provide a theoretical and practical understanding of the indirect effects of foreign direct investment (commonly referred to as spillovers effects) taking into consideration a wide range of theoretical and empirical literature on this topic. In the theoretical part we will analyze the content and forms of spillovers, identify their scope, impacts on the host economies, and factors influencing their existence. After a short investigation of the empirical evidence, we will provide some examples of the effects from foreign direct investment in Slovakia and present results of research on spillovers in the automotive industry.

## Theoretical Framework

The inflow of foreign direct investment (FDI) has both positive and negative effects on the host economy. Thus governments are taking actions to attract FDI and offer substantial public subventions presumably to gain one of the positive effects:

- creation of jobs
- transfer of skills and knowledge
- technological transfer
- structural changes
- export growth
- regional development
- creation of clusters

The positive effects can generally be divided into two groups-with direct and indirect influences on the economy. Foreign companies have proven to be more productive than the local ones and increase their productivity, which is referred to as the direct effect of FDI. More important for the economy, though more difficult to measure and observe, are the indirect effects, commonly referred to as spillovers. Spillovers are positive economical externalities emanating from FDI, which are generated involuntarily, cannot be adequately reflected in a market pricing, and therefore have no cost for those profiting from them. Spillovers from FDI take place when the entry or presence of a foreign company increases productivity of domestic firms in the same sector, or even in other sectors of the host economy and the corporation does not fully internalise the value of those benefits. Spillovers arise because multinational corporations in general bring with them some kind of technological advantage- a firm specific asset, like superior marketing, management or production techniques, which enables them to compete successfully abroad. Since this technological advantage usually has the characteristics of a public good, there is a scope for positive externalities, which domestic firms can benefit from.

The theoretical literature identifies four **channels** through which the host country can boost its productivity via spillovers: imitation, skills acquisition, competition and enhanced export propensity (Blomstrőm, Kokko 1998).

| **DRIVER** | **SOURCES OF PRODUCTIVITY GAIN** |
|---|---|
| Imitation | • Adoption of new production methods<br>• Adoption of new management practices |
| Competition | • Reduction in X-inefficiency<br>• Faster adoption of new technology |
| Human Capital | • Increased productivity of complementary labor<br>• Tacit knowledge |
| Exports | • Scale economies<br>• Exposure to technology frontier |

Source: Görg, H. – Greenaway, D.: Foreign Direct Investment and Intra-Industry Spillovers: A Review of the Literature. GEP, Leverhulme Centre for Research on Globalisation and Economic Policy, Research Paper 2001/37

Many authors consider *imitation* the most important transmission mechanism for new products and processes. Simple manufacture and production processes are easier to be imitated than the more complex ones, so the scope of imitation clearly depends on the product/process complexity. We cannot expect all processes to be dissipated by imitation, however, any improvement of local technology deriving from imitation can result in a productivity spillover and can be beneficial to local firms.

Technology transfer can occur also through *acquisition of human capital*. Multinationals demand usually relatively skilled labor in the host country and invest in this labor through training. It is not possible to fully protect such investment in human capital, because of the movement of labor to other firms, or to start new firms. Both these movements can generate productivity spillovers via two mechanisms. First, a direct spillover to complementary workers, as skilled labor working alongside unskilled labor tends to raise the productivity of the latter. Second, workers that move carry with them knowledge of new technology, new management techniques and consequently can become direct agents of technology transfer. (Gőrg, Greenaway 2001)

*Competition* as another transmission mechanism of spillovers is debatable. If the multinational company does not have a monopoly status in the host market, it produces in direct competition with domestic firms in the same sector. These are therefore under pressure to produce more effectively and increase their competitiveness. Such struggle to survive can indeed lead to productivity gains, but not as a result of technology or knowledge dissipation from the foreign company, thus is controversial to be called a spillover.

An indirect source of spillovers can also be via *market access, or export knowledge*, which basically means the possibility for domestic companies to learn from multinationals how to export. When investing abroad, multinational companies generally already have information about foreign markets and are armed with export knowledge, which domestic firms can gain through collaboration or more likely imitation. If they learn how to penetrate export markets, they can increase their productivity exploiting scale economies.

As described in many studies[2], different **types of spillovers** have been generated, both intrasectoral (horizontal) and intersectoral (vertical). If local firms benefit from the presence of multinational companies in their sector, it is referred to as *horizontal spillovers*. To the extend that domestic firms compete with the multinationals, these try to avoid the spillovers effect in the same sector and prevent their specific assets from leaking. They can achieve this via formal protection of their intellectual property, trade secrecy, paying higher wages to prevent labor movements to local firms, or they simply try to locate in countries or industries where domestic firms have limited imitative capacities. (Smarzynska Javorcik 2003)

On the other hand, foreign companies have no incentives to prevent spillovers in downstream, or upstream sectors, increasing the productivity of their suppliers or customers. This phenomenon is called *vertical spillovers* and can take place between foreign and domestic firms active in different sectors through two mechanism-via backward and forward linkages. Backward linkage is related to spillovers from foreign customer to domestic supplier through direct knowledge transfer, higher requirements regarding products and services, or increased demand enabling domestic firms to exploit the economies of scale. Many case studies show examples of foreign firms offering technical assistance or employees trainings to their local suppliers and helping them with searching for other customers, buying materials, or quality control. The broader the relationship is, the bigger the scope for potential spillovers effects.

Spillovers through forward linkage occur when the domestic firms become productive due to access to new, better, or cheaper inputs produced by a multinational.

The basic difference between the horizontal and vertical spillovers is that from the multinational point of view, the horizontal spillovers are involuntary and unwanted, leaking to domestic competitors, while the vertical are voluntary and wanted, usually being passed to domestic suppliers.

The presence of a multinational in the economy can also have **negative effects** on domestic firms. In this case it is debatable again, whether we can consider these effects spillovers, since we defined them as positive externalities from foreign firms to domestic. If we define spillovers as all the effects that the multinationals have on domestic firms, then we find the whole spectrum of positive and negative effects, not just in the area of productivity. The most important would be the so-called crowding-out effect- a result of *negative horizontal spillovers.*

As Gőrg and Strobl (2004) argue, multinationals producing at lower marginal costs than domestic firms will most likely increase their output and attract demand away from these firms. Having the demand decreased, the domestic companies will have to cut their production, which if having fixed costs of production, will raise their average cost. Quite usual is also that foreign companies offer higher wages to their employees, which leads to higher wage demand in the whole economy and creates pressure on domestic firms to increase their wages as well if not willing to lose employees. This, of course, increases firm's average costs as well. The phenomenon is called wage spillovers, and derives from the competitive pressures in the sector. If the domestic company cannot survive such pressure, it is crowded out by its competitor.

Negative horizontal spillovers occur if the domestic firm is crowded out by a foreign competitor in the same sector/industry. If the domestic supplier is crowded out by foreign suppliers, and the negative effect influences a different sector, it is referred to as negative vertical spillovers.

A logical question would be now, whether the final effect of a multinational on domestic companies is positive or negative. The answer depends on a lot of factors and is subject of many present research papers.

The incidence of spillovers is influenced by various **host industry and host country characteristics**, such as the technological gap between host and home economy and between foreign and domestic companies, absorptive capacity of indigenous firms and economy, educational level of the local labor force, nationality of investors, form and structure of foreign affiliate, and many others. It seems clear that host country and host industry characteristics determine the impact of FDI and therefore systematic differences between countries and industries should be expected. There is strong evidence pointing to the potential for significant spillovers benefits from FDI, but also ample evidence indicating that spillovers do not occur automatically. Whether these potential spillovers will be realised or not depends on the ability and motivation of local firms to engage in investment and learning to absorb foreign knowledge and skills.[3]

The existence of spillovers was not accepted because of theoretical arguments pointing to some possible externalities occurring from the presence of FDI, but thanks to case studies dating back to the late 1960s. Since then many authors researched the effects of FDI on the economy and particularly on domestic companies.

The **existing literature** nowadays is of three kinds. First, already mentioned *case studies*, which include specific country examples, offer relevant information about the channels of spillovers, but are difficult to be generalized. Then, there is a plethora of *industry level studies*, most of which show a positive correlation between the presence of a multinational and productivity increase of domestic firms. Their downside is that it is not fully possible to establish the direction of causality, so actually the positive association might be a result of foreign companies locating in high productivity industries instead of productivity spillovers. Another explanation for increasing productivity in a certain industry is already mentioned crowding out effect- when more productive foreign companies force the less productive domestic firms out of industry, so the overall productivity increases. ( Smarzinska- Javorcik 2003) These studies are therefore not recommended to be used for measuring spillovers and all the positive results from such studies should be treated with caution.

Finally, there is also research based on *firm-level panel data*, which appear to be the most appropriate to determine the true existence of spillovers, however, most of them failed to prove them, or found only negative spillovers effects of multinationals on domestic firms in the same sector. Taking into consideration a wide range of papers using appropriate data and methodology, we have to conclude that the evidence of spillovers is surprisingly very weak.

This knowledge gets us to our research aimed at searching for spillovers in Slovak companies, trying to prove their existence, mainly by qualitative research. First some examples of Slovak firms will be presented, and then the first results of more concrete research of technology spillovers on both horizontal and vertical level in the automotive industry.

## Spillovers in Slovakia- Lessons from the Last Decades

The major entry mode for foreign investors in Slovakia has been the entry into existing companies in privatization or post-privatization era – at the beginning the typical entry mode was the creation of a joint venture with a local parent company. It was driven either by local conditions and the relationships toward foreign investors or by the legal limitations of the share of foreign capital in so-called strategic enterprises. Later, at the end of the 90's and after the year 2000, we have witnessed growing number of brownfield and especially greenfield operations in Slovakia.

There is no doubt that the entry of foreign investor causes significant and direct change in the acquired companies or in the joint venture where foreign investor is one of partner companies. These changes usually start with massive restructuring including changes in product or service lines, technology improvement, lay-offs and the follow-up training of remaining labor force, development of management, and transfer of management knowledge and the improved productivity.

The indirect changes and spillovers we have witnessed most frequently in Slovakia include:

## Change in the Local Parent Company of a Joint Venture with Foreign Partner

Many domestic parent companies were state-owned at the time of the establishment of the joint venture. Managers in the domestic parent expected the above-mentioned positive effects to spread eventually from the joint venture to the parent or to their own domestic daughter companies, but these expectations were rarely met.

Many joint ventures in Slovakia were established at the beginning of the 1990's. Since that time, all the Slovak parent companies have gone through privatization. Later, some of them faced serious financial problems and some of them went bankrupt. It is very interesting to watch this development and to realize that joint ventures in transition can have a very unusual nature with a very limited power and influence of the local parent company, no matter what its real share in the joint venture is. On the other hand, some of them have gone successfully through the process of transformation and restructuring and were privatized by their own management.

Generally stated, several cases of companies we studied show that FDI had only a limited impact on the local parent companies. The extent of the change in the Slovak parent can be the result of several factors and spillovers:

* *"Unintentional learning"*—spreading of managerial attitudes, business discipline, corporate ethics, new corporate cultures, and work practices. This effect is undeniable, but indirect and hard to measure. Many joint ventures in Slovakia were located on the same site as their Slovak parent companies (for example, the Slovak parent might contribute buildings from the former large production facility to the joint venture), which should theoretically make this kind of change and spillover very easy. This type of transfer is facilitated by labor force movements. Because of the higher or high salaries and wages in the FDI-invested companies, however, the movement of labor force from the joint venture to the original parent company is usually very low. Moreover, some of the practices in the joint venture are simply not applicable to other local companies (e.g., KAIZEN system at Volkswagen).
* *Intentional learning from the activity of its own joint venture.* Some Slovak parent companies literally copied the marketing methods and partially also managerial methods of their foreign partner in their own

company including the ways of decisions, investment policy, and human resource management. If the question is how this was possible without the movement of the labor force or management, the answer could be found in the meetings of supervisory board of joint ventures and unofficial information flow between parent companies and their joint ventures that was easy due to geographical location on the same site. The intentional learning could also be related to the wages: if Slovak parent companies do not follow the pattern of the joint venture, the best people from them had the tendency to leave and to work for a joint venture where the wages were usually moderately higher.

* *Becoming a supplier of it's own joint venture.* When the parent company becomes a supplier to it's joint venture, their linkage has become direct through the quality and delivery requirements of the joint venture, but also indirect, through adapting to the "modus vivendi" of the FDI company in terms of entrepreneurial ethics and attitudes towards business partners.

* *Becoming a supplier of the corporate network of foreign parent company.* Again, we have noticed more of such cases in Slovakia: one of the cases is for example Tatramat - the parent company of the previous Whirlpool-Tatramat joint venture. It has not only supplied its own joint venture in Slovakia, but it has also established a joint venture with an Italian company to supply Whirlpool-Europe network with components.

* *Internationalization* - the above mentioned case could be also used as an example when the presence of foreign investors drives a local company to internationalize its operations and to create another international alliance either abroad or home.

* *Becoming a direct competitor of its own joint venture.* No company enters any joint venture with this immediate target, but we found such examples in Slovakia. Although competitive pressure can lead to dynamic efficiency gains in the future, at the beginning especially local parent companies understood it as betrayal.

* *Receiving dividends or cash for shares after the buy-out by foreign partner.* It may help in solving immediate problems in cash-starved Slovak companies, but there is no evidence to show that it can cause significant long-term change.

None of these impacts are generally common among all the joint ventures in Slovakia, with the exception of "unintentional learning". The impact of FDI on the local parent company is different in each case. However, based on approximately one decade of experience, certain conclusions could be drawn. Many companies we studied show that FDI has, paradoxically, a limited impact on the local parent, even though all of them entered joint ventures with the explicit intention of improving the performance of the parent firm. In our opinion, there are three main reasons for this. The first one is objective, and lies mostly in an inheritance from the previous system: most factories have obsolete technologies and limited means for their renewal, i.e. they are not able to cooperate and keep pace with foreign companies, especially with the MNC (e.g., to enter their supplier networks with quality products or simply to learn from them). The next two are: (1) a very complicated process of privatization and transformation of local companies resulting in changes in ownership structures and management, and (2) high and unfulfilled expectations from the partnership and the ensuing jealousy and rivalry of local managers. If the combination of all these factors is present in the Slovak parent company, the FDI has almost no impact on it. If at least one is missing, the change and resulting spillovers are possible. Paradoxically, we find that the potential for change in the local parent depends to a much greater extent more on the attitudes of its management than on the presence of foreign partner. The deepest changes could be noticed in such Slovak parent companies that were later privatized by their own management, i.e. where the active management had decision/making power and could actively influence its company.

Nevertheless, with the end of a privatization process and clearer ownership structures, we expect a more rational approach among local managers towards the creation of strategic alliances with foreign investors. Their decision will not depend on state bureaucracy and approvals as at the beginning of transition. We suppose that they will create more resource- and especially learning-oriented alliances, and that they will prefer to cooperate with more comparable, medium-sized companies. In such cases, from the point of view of Slovak companies, the danger of take-over is not as high as with a large MNC, and at the same time, the chances that the foreign partnership will result in changes in the parent are much higher.

## Change in the Local and National Business Environment

In comparison to the transfer of change to the parent companies, **the transfer of change into local environments has been easier to measure and more significant**. This part deals with the influence of all foreign investors- those in the joint ventures, acquirers, and those who created a fully new enterprise – a greenfield operation.

* *Influence on labor force and employment.* In spite of the decline in employment in some joint ventures and acquired companies at the beginning of their operations, the companies with FDI are important employers (for example Volkswagen, Siemens, foreign retailers rank among the biggest Slovak employers) who make significant investments in human capital. In all the FDI-companies we studied or interviewed, the wages are higher (sometimes as much as two times) than the local or national average. However, skill and knowledge transfer is not high because of the limited movement of managers and workers from companies with FDI and generally, low flexibility of Slovak labor force. If the labor force is leaving the FDI-invested companies, the majority of cases are that they start working at another FDI-invested company. Sometimes, managers leave for a Slovak company or build their own, especially in the case when the foreign investor cannot fulfill their carrier expectations or dictate too high working pace. However, the most frequent is the case when the management leaving the former employer ends at other FDI-invested companies.

* *Influence on local suppliers.* In some cases the companies with FDI are mainly supplied from the global network of their foreign parent companies, but in other cases the number of local suppliers has grown, meaning that local companies have successfully adapted to the quality requirements and entrepreneurial and cooperative principles of their partners. This learning process is significant, but it is limited by the number of companies involved in the supplier's network. The biggest foreign investor to Slovakia, Volkswagen even created a special program for its potential suppliers in which VW taught the participating companies how to comply with its standards.

* *Increase of competition.* This change is limited because the socialist idea of the division of production was based on monopolies: each factory had a different production program. This system remains intact in many ways: foreign investors often enter monopoly productions and have not directly increased domestic competition. However, since these companies import the goods from their global supplier, there is increased competition for the domestic suppliers and local producers. Increase of the competition for local companies is highly visible in retail sector and in retail supplier sector, especially after the entry of global or regional multinational companies – big retailers, such as Tesco, Metro, Billa etc. on the Slovak market.

* *Development of entrepreneurship and new businesses.* This effect is possible if the local managers or workers employed in FDI companies create their own companies on the basis of their experience. Due to the

necessity to have certain starting capital, this is not a usual case, however some cases were reported, especially when it comes to trading companies that are not so capital-intensive.

* *Supply on the domestic market.* The companies with FDI usually manufacture and place high-quality products on the Slovak market. In some cases, their quality may be lower than the quality of original local suppliers (private labels), but they contribute to the bigger assortment offered to Slovak customers and to wider choice for them in terms of price.

* *Export growth.* The quality of products, together with the use of distribution networks of foreign parent companies, has also led to higher exports on foreign markets. Export growth is often considered to be the proof of increased competitiveness and successful transition to market-oriented companies.

As seen from the latest rankings of the biggest Slovak companies, FDI-invested companies play an important role in Slovakia in quantitative terms and are, or belong to the biggest employers, to companies with highest turnover and profits. Contrary to the situation in developed countries, most of them do not contribute to the development of the entrepreneurial sector and to the growth of competition in Slovakia. The reason for this paradox can be found in the former monopolistic and artificially created industry structure and the ensuing high capital barriers to entry. The next paradox is the big influence of foreign investors on the quality of the labor force and its limited movement from FDI-invested companies to the domestic sector. The reason could be found in the existence of a dual labor market (high salaries in FDI-invested companies) and the limited possibility for relocating (shortage of flats, slow development of home mortgages). The influence on local suppliers is also still limited, mostly because of the fact that the local companies are not yet able to meet quality and quantity requirements among large MNCs. In order to adjust (and sometimes to survive), local companies will be pressed to cooperate with foreign partners in the future to a much larger extent. One of the examples is growing car assembly sector in Slovakia and its impact on local suppliers. Local suppliers in car industry have become the target segment of our short study that was supposed to get the first information about spillovers in this industry.

## In Search for Spillovers in the Automotive Industry

Slovakia's car industry is one of the most important sectors in the economy, accounting for some twenty percent of the exports and about one fourth of Slovakia's total industrial production. With a large amount of inward investment over the past few years, Slovakia is predicted to become the world's number one car producer per capita in 2006. Considerable number of huge foreign investors (Volkswagen, PSA Peugeot Citroen, Hyundai) and domestic producers acting in a highly competitive environment of an important industry could be in our opinion a good base for spillovers. The purpose of our study was therefore twofold. First, we decided to use qualitative research in form of questionnaires to see whether there is actually any potential for spillover effects in the automotive industry. Second, by shedding light on the possible channels of spillovers in the industry, we aimed at creating a broader base for further research extended to all sector of Slovak economy.

As we explained in the theoretical framework, spillovers can be both horizontal and vertical, with the latter being objectively more probable since foreign companies have no incentives to prevent spillovers in downstream, or upstream sector, increasing the productivity of their suppliers or customers but at the same time try to avoid the spillovers effect towards domestic competitors in the same sector. By this reason we decided to look first of all at the empirical evidence of vertical spillovers.

Due to the nature of the automotive industry in Slovakia, where domestic companies mostly act as suppliers to foreign car producers, we searched spillovers only through backward linkage, which is related to spillovers from foreign customer to domestic supplier, and considered three possible channels: direct knowledge transfer, higher requirements regarding products and services and movement of employees.

### Direct Transfer of Knowledge from the Foreign Customer

Direct transfer of knowledge is determined mainly by the quality of relationship between supplier and customer and their *communication*. Out of fifteen researched domestic suppliers[4], only one company stated the communication with their clients is formal and not very frequent, seven consider their communication both formal and informal frequent, and other seven very frequent. Still the *transfer of technology* from client to the supplying company was in ten cases rare and in five infrequent. None of the companies experienced intensive technology transfer from their customers.

More common than the direct transfer of technology was the indirect transfer in form of technological assistance. Nine domestic companies were frequently supplied by *technical specifications of orders* and six occasionally. Eight companies learned to *develop new products/services* by virtue of their relationship with clients to some extent, four learned significantly, and only three firms stated they did not learn anything in this area. Seven companies declared they have been able *to improve their marketing approach/strategy* as a consequence of the relationship with their clients considerably and eight managed this to some extent. There was no company, which would not improve their marketing/strategy when having foreign customers.

## Pressure for Product and Services Quality Increase Due To Higher Requirements from Foreign Customer

Eleven companies stated that their clients closely *monitor the quality of products* provided and check nearly 100% of the shipments, three said that more than 50% of shipments are inspected and only one company had a client, who inspected less than 50% of shipment, which clearly shows that there is existing pressure for quality management and production improvements. Eight companies have upgraded significantly (and seven companies to certain extent) their *technology base* and improved their *products/services quality* as a consequence of the relationship with foreign clients.

## Trainings and Movement of Employees

Foreign firms *offered secondments for domestic staff, or shared personnel* with only four domestic companies. The rest almost never experienced such situation, so this channel for vertical spillovers can be considered probably very rare.

## Overall Improvement

Expecting vertical spillovers through at least one of the above-mentioned channels, we wanted to know whether the product/service improvements also led to *higher prospects for gaining new customers and exporting.*

Five companies thought they would for sure find new customers for their products, eight saw this very probable, and only one company improbable. We gained similar answers asking about exporting perspectives. Three companies saw their export prospects as excellent, nine considered them good, and three neutral. We might conclude that the technological improvements led to higher possibility for finding new clients and exporting the production abroad.

Foreign investors in the automotive industry have a strong ability to pull a number of foreign suppliers with them, which then compete in the domestic market with domestic suppliers and create an environment for **horizontal spillovers**. These take place in case local firms benefit from the presence of multinational companies in the same sector.

In the theoretical framework we identified four main channels through which the host country can boost its productivity via horizontal spillovers: imitation, competition, skills acquisition (through human capital) and enhanced export propensity.

## Imitation

The scope of imitation as the first possible channel for spillovers is determined on one hand by the product/process complexity and on the other by quality of relations between competitors. Two researched companies stated that there is no *possibility to improve their production/managerial processes by imitating* foreign competitors, six thought it was partly possible and only one found the possibilities considerable. As for the *relations/communication* between domestic and foreign competitors, only three companies have friendly relationships with their foreign competitors, eight have neutral and two companies stated their relations are rare. Accordingly, the extent of cooperation was very low. Two companies did not experience a *cooperation in the area of knowledge sharing/management* at all, eight very rarely and four companies cooperate in this area only sometimes. Looking at *joint investment in the infrastructure*, the picture is even worse. With one exception, none of the companies ever cooperated with competitors in such field.

## Competitive Pressure

The competitive pressure, defined as *the pressure to use the existing technology more effectively*, is according to all the companies very high. With two exceptions, the same applies for the *pressure to innovate and improve the products and services offered.*

## Human Capital

Horizontal spillovers can take place also thanks to movement of labor from foreign companies to domestic. To see, whether such movement takes place, we approached a sample of 18 foreign companies in the same industry and found out that *manual workers* usually move to other foreign companies in five cases, to domestic companies in two cases and for the rest, firms stated they had minimal fluctuation. As for the *management,* in seven firms managers leave mainly to other foreign firms, in three to domestic firms and the rest again had minimal fluctuation. Even though there are examples of employees moving from multinationals to domestic firms, such cases are as presented above somewhat rare.

## Export Spillovers

The possibilities for domestic companies to *learn from multinationals how to export* are again low. Nine companies do not cooperate in the area of export promotion at all, four of them very rarely and two sometimes.

Next to the positive spillovers, we described also the negative externalities in the form of crowd-out effect and so called wage spillovers. These take place if the domestic firms are pushed to increase their wages in order to not lose their employees. According to our research this situation did not appear as a real threat since majority of companies questioned felt such pressure only to a certain extent.

# Conclusion

The inflow of foreign direct investment has both positive and negative effects on the host economy, which can be generally divided in two groups- with direct and indirect influence on the economy. More important are the indirect effects, commonly referred to as spillovers, which occur if the entry or presence of foreign companies increases productivity of domestic firms. In case local firms benefit from the presence of multinational in the same sector, it is referred to as horizontal spillovers. These can take place through four main channels: imitation, acquisition of human capital, competition and export knowledge. In case local firm benefits from the presence of a multinational in upstream or downstream sector, it is called vertical spillovers. The main channels for these types of spillovers are direct knowledge transfer, higher requirements regarding products and services, or increased demand enabling domestic firms to exploit the economies of scale.

This paper analysed both types of spillovers in the Slovakia's automotive industry and the findings can be summarized as follows.

Considering vertical spillovers, even though communication between local suppliers and foreign clients was quite frequent, the direct transfer of technology did not appear. On the other hand the indirect transfer of technology in the form of technical assistance proved to be one of the possible spillover channels with domestic companies learning how to develop new product/services and to improve their marketing approach or strategies. Higher requirements from foreign customers also led to significant technology and product improvements. Spillovers due to the movement of employees were rare, but the overall picture of vertical spillovers remains optimistic as companies stated their prospects for gaining new customers and exporting their products abroad are improving. Much weaker is the evidence of horizontal spillovers. The possibilities for imitating are low, relationships between local and foreign competitors do not lead to any significant cooperation, employees from foreign companies leave mainly to other foreign firms, and the potential to learn about exporting is weak. The only channel for horizontal spillovers is the debatable competitive pressure, which is pushing domestic firms to use existing technology more effectively, innovate and improve their products. Negative externalities in the form of wage spillovers did not prove to be present either.

Results of this research are in line with other empirical studies, which did not prove the existence of horizontal spillovers. They are far from complete, but can help us understand the complicated nature of spillovers and channels through which they can take place. Further research should be aimed at searching for other possible ways for spillovers to occur and extend the sample to all the industries in Slovakia.

## Notes

[1] This paper was partly funded by the research grant VEGA 1/2638/05- Strategies of Multinational corporations in CEE markets: last decade trends, expected developments and possible implications for the economic policy in target countries.

[2] See, for example. Belderbos 2001, Saggi 2002, or Smarzinska Javorcik 2003

[3] The Economics of International Investment Perspectives, OECD 2002

[4] Each company researched had at least one main foreign customer.

## References

Aitken, B.J. - Harrison, A. E.: Are There Spillovers From Foreign Direct Investment? Evidence from Panel Data for Venezuela. mimeo, MIT and the World Bank, 1991

Blalock, G.- Technology from Foreign Direct Investment: Strategic Transfer through Supply Chains. Mimeo, Haas School of Business, University of California, Berkeley 2001

Balasubramanyam, V. N. - Salisu, M.: Foreign Direct Investment and Globalisation. Regionalism and Globalisation, London, Routledge 2001

Barrios, S. - Strobl, E.: Foreign Direct Investment and Productivity Spillovers: Evidence from the Spanish Experience. mimeo, CORE Catholic University of Louvain-la-Neuve 2001

Barrios, S. - Görg, H. - Strobl, E.: Multinational Enterprises and New Trade Theory: Evidence for the Convergence Hypothesis. CEPR Discussion Paper DP2827, 2001a

Barrios, S. - Görg, H. - Strobl, E.: Explaining Firms' Export Behaviour: The Role of R&D and Spillovers". GEP Research Paper 01/27, University of Nottingham, 2001b

Barry, F. - Görg, H. - Strobl, E.: Foreign Direct Investment and Wages in Domestic Firms: Productivity Spillovers vs Labour-Market Crowding Out. mimeo, University College Dublin and University of Nottingham 2001

Belderbos, R. - Capannelli, G. - Fukao, K.: Backward vertical linkages of foreign manufacturing affiliates: Evidence from Japanese multinationals. World Development, 2001, 29(1)

Bhagwati, J.: Free Trade Today. Princeton, Princeton University Press 2001

Blalock, G.:.. Technology from Foreign Direct Investment: Strategic Transfer through Supply Chains. Mimeo, Haas School of Business, University of California, Berkeley 2001.

Blomström, M.: Foreign Investment and Productive Efficiency: The Case of Mexico. Journal of Industrial Economics, 1986, Vol. 35

Blomström, M. – Kokko, A.: How Foreign Investment Affects Host Countries. Washington, D.C., World Bank 1997

Blomström, M. – Kokko, A.: Multinational Corporations and Spillovers. Journal of Economic Surveys, 1998, Vol. 12

Blomström, M.- Kokko, A - Zejan, M.: Foreign Direct Investment. Firm and Host Country Strategies, London: Macmillan 2000

Blomström, M. – Persson, H.: Foreign Investment and Spillover Efficiency in an Underdeveloped Economy: Evidence from the Mexican Manufacturing Industry. World Development, 1983, Vol. 11,

Blomström, M. - Sjöholm, F.: Technology Transfer and Spillovers: Does Local Participation with Multinationals Matter. European Economic Review, 1999, Vol. 43, pp. 915-923

Blomström, M. - Wolff, E., N.: Multinational Corporations and Productive Convergence in Mexico. In Baumol, W. - Nelson, R. J. - Wolff, E. N.: (eds.): Convergence of Productivity: Cross National Studies and Historical Evidence.Oxford: Oxford University Press, 1994, pp. 263-283

Caves, R. E.: Multinational Enterprise and Economic Analysis. Second Edition. Cambridge: Cambridge University Press 1996

Cohen W.M. - Levinthal, D. A.: Absorptive capacity: a new perspective on learning and innovation. Administrative Science Quarterly, 1990, Vol. 35

Damijan, J. P. - Majcen, B. - Knell, M. - Matija Rojec, M.: The Role of FDI, Absorptive Capacity and Trade in Transferring Technology to Transition Countries: Evidence from Firm Panel Data for Eight Transition Countries. Mimeo, UN Economic Commission for Europe, Geneva, 2001

Damijan, J. P. - Knell, M. - Majcen, B. - Rojec, M.: Technology Transfer through FDI in TOP 10 Transition Countires: How Important are direct Effects, Horizontal and Vertical Spillovers? Ljubljana, Institute for Economic Research. Working Paper No. 17, 2003

Davidson, C. - Matusz, S.: Globalization and Labour Market Adjustment: How Fast and at What Cost? Oxford Review of Economic Policy, 2000, Vol. 16

Djankov, S. - Hoekman, B.: Foreign Investment and Productivity Growth in Czech Enterprises. World Bank Economic Review, 2000, Vol. 14

Driffield, N.: The Impact on Domestic Productivity of Inward Investment in the UK. Manchester School, 2001, Vol. 69, pp. 103-119.

Dutrénit, G. – Martínez, J.: Knowledge Spillovers, Absorptive Capacity and Economic Performance of the SMEs. Economic and Management of Technological Change., Universidad Autónoma Metropolitana-Xochimilco 2004

Ferenčíková, S.: Foreign direct investment as a factor of change: case of Slovakia. Teaching the Dinosaurs to dance: Organizational Change in Transition Economies. Chapter 17. Edited by Daniel Denison. Lawrence Earlbaum Publishers, Inc. USA, 2001, p. 445 – 481

Ferenčíková, S.: Aliancie a ľudské zdroje v medzinárodnom podnikaní, KON-PRESS Trnava, 2002

Girma, S. – Greenaway, D. - Richard Kneller, R.: Exports and Productivity. forthcoming as GEP Research Paper, University of Nottingham 2002

Girma, S. – Wakelin, K.: Regional Underdevelopment: Is FDI the Solution? A Semiparametric Analysis. GEP Research Paper 01/11, University of Nottingham 2001

Glass, A. and K. Saggi, K.: Multinational Firms and Technology Transfer. Ohio State University Working Paper 97-04, 1998

Görg, H. – Greenaway, D.: Foreign Direct Investment and Intra-Industry Spillovers: A Review of the Literature. GEP, Leverhulme Centre for Research on Globalisation and Economic Policy, Research Paper 2001/37

Görg, H. - Strobl, E.: Multinational Companies and Productivity Spillovers: A Meta-analysis. Economic Journal, 2001, Vol. 111, pp. F723-F739

Görg. H. - Strobl, E.: Multinational Companies, Technology Spillovers, and Plant Survival. Berlin, German Institute for Economic Research, DIW Berlin 2003

Greenaway, D. – Sousa, N. - Wakelin, K.: Do Indigenous Firms Learn to Export from Multinationals?", mimeo, University of Nottingham 2002

Haddad, M. - Harrison, A.: Are there Positive Spillovers from Direct Foreign Investment? Evidence from Panel Data for Morocco. mimeo, Harvard University and the World Bank 1991

Harris, R. - Robinson, C.: Spillovers from Foreign Ownership in the United Kingdom: Estimates for UK Manufacturing Using the ARD, mimeo, University of Durham and University of Portsmouth 2001

Kathuria, V.: Productivity Spillovers from Technology Transfer to Indian Manufacturing Firms. Journal of International Development, 2000, Vol. 12,

Knell, M. - Radosevic, S.: .. „FDI, technology transfer and growth in economic theory". In: G. Hunya ed.. *Integration Through Foreign*

*Direct Investment. Making Central European Industries Competitive*. Vienna: WIIW 2000,

Kinoshita, Y.: R&D and Technology Spillovers through FDI: Innovation and Absorptive Capacity". CEPR Discussion Paper DP2775, 2001

Kokko, A.: Technology, Market Characteristics, and Spillovers. Journal of Development Economics, 1994, Vol. 43,

—. Productivity Spillovers from Competition between Local Firms and Foreign Affiliates. Journal of International Development, 1996, Vol. 8

—. Export-Led Growth in East Asia. Mimeo, Stockholm School of Economics, 2001

Konings, J.: The Effects of Foreign Direct Investment on Domestic Firms: Evidence from Firm Level Panel Data in Emerging Economies". CEPR Discussion Paper DP2586, 2001

Krugman, P. R.: Geography and Trade. Cambridge, MA: MIT Press 1991.

Kugler, M.: The Diffusion of Externalities from Foreign Direct Investment: The Sectoral Pattern of Technological Spillovers. Mimeo, University of Southampton 2001

Lipsey, R.E. - Sjöholm, F.: Foreign Direct Investment and Wages in Indonesian Manufacturing. NBER Working Paper 2001

Markusen, J. R. -. Venables, A. J.:. Foreign direct investment as a catalyst for industrial development. European Economic Review, 1999, 43(1999

Moran, T.: Parental Supervision: the new paradigm for foreign direct investment and development. Institute for International Economics, Washington, DC 2001

Saggi, K.:.Backward Linkages under Foreign Direct Investment. Mimeo,Southern Methodist University 2002

Schoors, K. - van der Tol, B.:. The productivity effect of foreign ownership on domestic firms in Hungary. Mimeo, University of Gent 2001

Sjöholm, F.: Technology Gap, Competition and Spillovers from Direct Foreign Investment: Evidence from Establishment Data. Journal of Development Studies, 1999a, Vol. 36

Smarzinska-Javorcik, B.: Does Foreign Direct Investment Increase the Productivity of Domestic Firms? In Search of Spillovers through Backward Linkages. The world Bank 2003

Szarková, M.: Psychológia pre manažérov a podnikateľov. Bratislava, Sprint 2004, s. 45 – 55

—. Personálny manažment pre prax. Bratislava, Karprint 2002, s. 84 - 92

# BANKING TRANSITION PROGRESS, FOREIGN BANK MARKET ENTRY AND ECONOMIC DEVELOPMENT: THE CASE OF SERBIA

GERHARD FINK, PETER R. HAISS AND MINA VON VARENDORFF

## Abstract

In Serbia and other South Eastern European Countries (SEE) financial sector transition started late. In Central and Eastern Europe (CEE), better developed financial systems already translate into faster growth through channelling savings into productive investments. What are the lessons from progress in the CEE financial sector for South Eastern Europe, in particular Serbia? We provide an overview of banking reform in transition countries, draw lessons in financial sector reform for policy makers, bank supervision and market participants, and compare and apply the evidence from bank restructuring in CEE to the current situation in Serbia and Montenegro.

## Introduction

Theoretical studies and empirical evidence have shown that countries with better developed financial systems enjoy faster and more stable long-run growth. Well developed banking systems and financial markets have a significant positive impact on total factor productivity, which translates into higher long-run growth. Financial sector development levels differ between the candidate and new EU Member States from Central and Eastern Europe (CEE) on the one hand and South Eastern Europe (SEE) on the other. The goal of the paper is threefold: (1) to provide an overview of banking reform in transition countries (2) draw lessons for laggards in financial sector reform and (3) compare and apply the evidence from bank restructuring in transition countries to the current situation in Serbia and Montenegro.

The experiences of transition countries showed that faster reform and development of financial sector can lead to improved economic performance, as measured by GDP growth. Reform policies should first concentrate on ensuring basic property rights and creating a sound legal infrastructure. Banking reform should go hand in hand with enterprise reform. Via financial sector foreign direct investment (FSFDI), hard budget constraints can be imposed on banks, and appropriate incentives for lending on a commercial basis can be created. Investors need to be carefully screened on their intentions and capabilities. Foreign banks are able to bring in modern banking technology. Their entry increases competition in the banking sector and reduces the potential for political infringement on bank lending. Foreign direct investment in banking represents a long-term commitment and may reduce the chances of financial crisis. Successful reform of the financial sector in CEE countries is supporting sustainable economic growth. This involves diverse roles of the sector in mobilizing and reallocating savings, facilitating trading of risk, and, through the operation of both banks and capital markets, strengthening corporate governance in the enterprise sector.

In comparison with CEE transition economies, financial sector reform has started late in the South Eastern European Countries (SEE; Penev and Rojec, 2004). The establishment of a working financial sector has been delayed or jeopardized by a number of adverse developments like war, political instability, hyperinflation, and pyramid schemes in the late 1990's. The financial sector in all countries of the region is dominated by commercial banks. Privatization of the banking sector has advanced during the last years and foreign ownership has gradually increased, although at an unequal pace among SEE countries. New lending has primarily been directed towards households and less to the corporate sector. But the banking sector is still relatively small and fragile. Credit worthiness of individual borrowers hampers long-term lending, and non-performing loans are still high.

Serbia is a country at the early stage of its transition (Ristić, 2004). After ten years of isolation, the economy of the country collapsed, infrastructure was nearly destroyed and poverty increased. The payment and settlement system in Serbia was inefficient, and the banking sector was weak and not competitive. The new Government of Serbia and Montenegro assumed power in October 2000 and adopted a comprehensive reform agenda. In 2001 and 2002 major steps were taken in cleaning up the republic's banking sector and to strengthen banking supervision by introducing new laws on banks, non-banks and the central bank. The new management of the National Bank of Serbia (NBS) carried out a comprehensive assessment of the banking sector and drew up a bank restructuring and privatization strategy. The banks were classified according to the credit rating and the insolvent banks were liquidated. Measures were taken to encourage new foreign exchange savings. Entry of foreign banks into the market increased confidence in the banking sector and brought rapid improvements in many areas of the banking business.

The main contribution of this paper is to show the significance of banking sector reform in transition countries on their way to market economies. We focus on South Eastern European countries with emphasis on Serbia, which is still at the early stages of transition. Our paper uses a comparative theoretical framework. This enables us to compare previous reform measures in transition economies with measures in South East Europe and Serbia, in particular.

The paper is organized as follows: Section two explains the necessary reform steps in the light of the experiences of new EU Member States. Next we analyze the process of banking reform in South East European countries, and finally the Serbian banking reform in the period between 2000 and 2004. A summary concludes this article.

## Outcome, Process and Lessons from Banking Reform in CEE

The development of a financial system, including banking reform, is one of the most important challenges facing Central and South East European countries during the transition from centrally planned to market economy. The creation of a full-fledged financial system is an integral and important part of the transformation strategy. In a market economy, the financial sector has a special role, as it mobilizes resources and allocates them to those investments that are capable of generating the highest returns on capital. The better the financial sector can perform this role, the better the economy will perform in the long term. A sound financial sector improves the screening of fund-seekers and the monitoring of the recipients of funds, which improves allocation of resources. It encourages the mobilization of savings by providing attractive instruments and savings vehicles. This may also increase the savings rate. In the medium term, economies of scale in financial institutions lower costs of project evaluation and origination, and facilitate the monitoring of projects through corporate governance. Financial intermediaries provide opportunities for risk management and liquidity. They promote development of markets and instruments with attractive characteristics that enable risk sharing (Levine 1998, Wachtel 2001; Bonin and Wachtel, 2003). After 15 years of economic transition, it is possible to draw some useful lessons for next-wave countries. The most important first step for the creation of a full-fledged financial system is a reform of the banking sector and the respective regulatory and supervisory framework. The basic elements of the reform process of banking sectors include (EU Commission, 2004a):

- *Balance sheet restructuring* - Clearing the bad debt off bank balance sheets is one of the first necessary steps. Cleaning bank portfolios without changing the framework within which banks operate will not lead banks to behave as market-based entities and the bad debt problem could quickly appear again. The costs of loss-making state-owned firms should be made explicit in the state budget and not be imposed on the banking sector. In this way further losses would be discouraged. From an economic point of view, a properly executed bank restructuring operation is cheaper than the continuation of providing loans from state-owned banks to loss-making enterprises. The benefits include more efficient allocation of resources and strengthening of the structural conditions for effective monetary control (Bonin and Wachtel, 2003).
- *Recapitalization of the banks* – It is a key element of their rehabilitation. Governments need to decide to what extent they will compensate banks for their lost assets. There are several techniques, like providing a capital transfer from the budget directly to the banks, assigning interest-paying state bonds of a reasonable maturity of at least 5 years to the banks (Fink et al, 1998; OECD 1993).
- *Improvement of bank management* – This implies improved regulations and effective supervision. Regulation and supervision of the financial system play a central role in determining quality and stability of services. Without the requisite development of lending expertise, supervisory and regulatory skills and monitoring mechanisms, growth in financial depth and intermediation may hamper instead of support economic growth (Rousseau and Wachtel, 2005). Banking regulation and supervision are typically aimed at the protection of depositors from the potentially opportunistic behaviour of the owners and managers of banks. They promote trust of potential depositors in the financial system.

- *Financial sector environment* - Important elements of the financial sector environment include clear and universally applied accounting standards and auditing practices, and a legal framework for debtor-creditor relationships. Countries with better creditor rights, more rigorous enforcement and better accounting information tend to have more highly developed financial intermediaries (La Porta et al, 1998). These environmental characteristics provide more reliable information for decision making by intermediaries and bolster confidence in financial contracting (Holden and Prokopenko 2001; Wachtel 2001)
- *Privatization and foreign ownership* - The quickest way to bring the necessary management changes is to give the bank independence from the government through foreign direct investment (FDI) in the banking sector. There are several strategies to privatise banks: outright trade sales, sale by voucher, initial public offerings. Privatisation of state-owned banks together with opening of banking institutions to foreign investors improves the performance of banking sectors in transition countries. Bonin, Hasan and Wachtel (2005) indicate that foreign-owned banks are most efficient and government-owned banks are least efficient. Foreign banks bring with them stability and rapid improvements because of their know-how in marketing, risk management and information technology (OECD 1993, Kraft 2004).

## Still Low Level of Financial Intermediation in CEE

There is a broad agreement that the financial sector of many transition countries has converged towards a universal bank-based system with substantial foreign ownership. Financial markets of New Member States are still small in both absolute and relative terms (Breuss, Fink and Haiss, 2004). While total domestic financial intermediation (measured as sum of stock market capitalization, bonds outstanding and credit granted by monetary financial institutions in 2003) relative to GDP is about 260 per cent in the Euro zone and in the EU, it is about 110 per cent of GDP in the New Member States (NM-10) and especially low in the Baltics with 70 per cent of GDP. While in the Euro zone and the EU, aggregate bank assets are slightly above 200 per cent of GDP, the ratio is about 70 per cent for the New Member States, ranging from 36 per cent in Lithuania to 90 per cent in the Czech Republic. In the Euro zone and the EU, domestic credit granted by monetary financial institutions (mainly banks) is slightly above 100 per cent of GDP and again at about half of that level in the New Member States (Table 1). The lending structure still differs from the EU-

15, as most lending in transition economies goes to government, non-bank financial institutions or short-term capital for enterprises (EU Commission, 2004a). Housing finance is virtually absent or at an early stage of development. The concentration in the NM-10-banking sector is high. Net interest margins are above the EU average, what can be interpreted as an indicator of poor efficiency.

**Table 1: Relative Size of Financial Sector (in per cent of GDP, 2003)[1]**

| 2003, in % of GDP | Czech Republic | Slovak Republic | Hungary | Poland | Slovenia | Estonia |
|---|---|---|---|---|---|---|
| Domestic shares | 26% | 4% | 20% | 16% | 23% | 40% |
| Domestic Bonds | 60% | 38% | 62% | 38% | 47% | 4% |
| Domestic credit | 51% | 45% | 55% | 35% | 49% | 59% |
| Total financial intermediation* | 137% | 86% | 137% | 89% | 120% | 103% |
| | | | | | | |
| Bank assets** | 90% | 77% | 64% | 48% | 84% | 28% |
| **2003, in % of GDP** | **Latvia** | **Lithuania** | **Bulgaria** | **Romania** | **Turkey** | **Croatia** |
| Domestic shares | 10% | 17% | 3% | 6% | 25% | 19% |
| Domestic Bonds | 12% | 16% | 30% | 10% | 49% | 19% |
| Domestic credit | 46% | 23% | 30% | 14% | 52% | 65% |
| Total financial intermediation* | 68% | 57% | 63% | 30% | 126% | 103% |
| | | | | | | |
| Bank assets** | 86% | 36% | 46% | 26% | 54% | 101% |

* total domestic financial intermediation, ** total domestic and foreign bank assets

In per capita of GDP

| 2003 | USA | JPN | EUR-12 | EU-15 | EU-25 | CEE-5 |
|---|---|---|---|---|---|---|
| Domestic shares | 116% | 57% | 54% | 67% | 65% | ? |
| Domestic bonds | 146% | 157% | 92% | 88% | 86% | ? |
| Domestic credit | 80% | 283% | 105% | 111% | 108% | ? |
| Total financial intermediation** | 343% | 516% | 251% | 266% | 259% | ? |
| Bank assets*** | 85% | 304% | 19% | 211% | 205% | ? |

| 2003 | BALTIC-3 | CEE-8 | CEE-10 | NM-10 | ENL-14 |
|---|---|---|---|---|---|
| Domestic shares | 20% | 29% | 17% | 19% | 20% |
| Domestic bonds | 12% | 45% | 40% | 45% | 43% |
| Domestic credit | 38% | 43% | 40% | 47% | 46% |
| Total financial intermediation** | 71% | 106% | 97% | 112% | 109% |
| Bank assets*** | 60% | 64% | 59% | 71% | 64% |

*** total domestic and foreign bank assets

Note: domestic credit and bank assets for Japan as of 2002; bonds issued by financial institutions are not included in corporate bonds.

Data Source: BIS (2004), ECB (2003, 2004b) for data on domestic bonds for CEE-countries, FIBV (2003), IFS (2004)

While New Member States' financial markets are small relative to the size of the respective economies, this of course is also the case in absolute terms (Breuss, Fink and Haiss, 2004). Total domestic financial intermediation (measured as sum of stock market capitalization, bonds outstanding and credit granted by monetary financial institutions in 2001) of the New Member States amounts to 1.7 per cent of the EUR-12 Euro zone and to 1.2 per cent of the EU-15. Total bank assets (including foreign assets) and private credit amount to 2.4 per cent and 2.1 per cent of the Euro zone, respectively. Capital markets are even smaller, with stock market capitalization and bond volume outstanding of 1.4 per cent and 1.6

per cent of the Euro zone. The financial sector is characterized by a limited number of financial instruments compared to the most developed countries and, in particular, the capital market segment for long term finance is illiquid or absent (Bonin and Wachtel, 2003). In addition, non-bank financial intermediaries such as life insurance companies and private pension funds are still in embryo (EU Commission 2004a).

In several New Member States, credit constraints limit the growth of small and medium size enterprises (SME). The main issues are: lack of implementation or experience with bankruptcy laws; the length of court proceedings and other deficiencies in the judicial process; and the absence of a properly functioning land registry that make it difficult to establish ownership over land and thus use property as collateral in loans; venture capital markets in the New Member States suffer from rather narrow and weak stock markets that limit investors' exit opportunities (EU Commission, 2003a and 2003b; Bonin and Wachtel, 2003). The modest depth of financial intermediation thus still is a constraint to effectiveness of interest rate and credit channels (Backé and Thimann, 2004; ECB, 2004a). However, deficiencies are being levelled out by both regulatory and market improvements, many of which are positively influenced by the prominent role of foreign banks in CEE.

## Foreign Ownership as a Solution to Bad Debt in CEE

After 1990, the new state owned commercial banks started life with an inherited overhang of troubled assets (the "stock problem"; Fink et al, 1998; Breuss, Fink and Haiss, 2004). This "old" bad debt resulted in first-round bank recapitalizations. Due to the lack of efficient banking reform, a wave of new bad debt had to be swallowed first by the banks and later on by the respective taxpayers via several waves of further recapitalizations (the "flow problem"). The process of cleansing the accounts of the politically sensitive state-owned enterprises and of the banking system brought hidden liabilities of the public sector to the surface.1 Average annualized net fiscal cost of bank restructuring (direct fiscal costs minus sales proceeds of state banks) was above 1.5 per cent of average 1995-2002 GDP in the Czech Republic and Turkey, in the 1-1.5 per cent-range in Croatia and Romania, in the 0.5-1 per cent range in Bulgaria, Hungary, Lithuania and Slovakia and below 0.5 per cent in Latvia and Slovenia (Sherif, 2003).

Figure 1: Non-Performing Loans in Per Cent of Total Loads (2002)

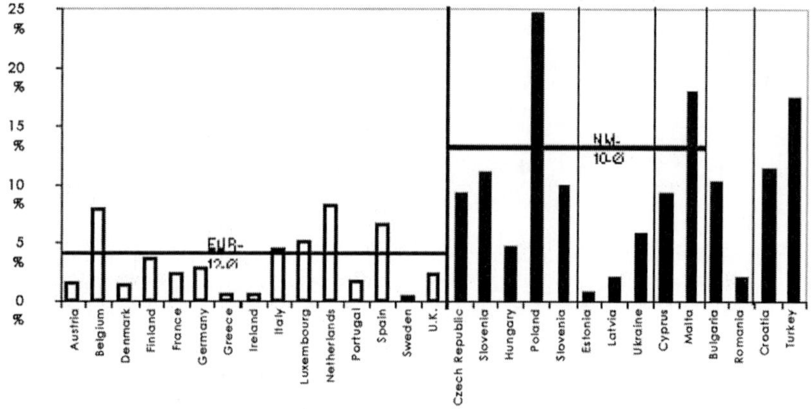


Non-performing loans accounted for 13.6 per cent of total loans in the New Member States in 2001. Only the Baltic countries reached a low level of 3.6 per cent comparable with the EU-15 level. On the negative side, Poland stood out with a reported level of 25 and 18 per cent of non-performing loans in 2002. However, a change of the hitherto tighter classification standards for "non-performing" loans in Poland might bring that reported level down to about half, which is comparable to the other New Member States from Central Europe (Breyer, 2004:14).

More stringent lending policies by foreign-owned banks helped to reduce bad debt levels. On average roughly 70 per cent of the banking market in the New Member States is under control of foreign banks – way above the 16 per cent foreign bank assets in the Euro zone. In Estonia, Lithuania, Malta and Slovakia (and also Croatia) local banks are essentially owned by foreign banks. In the Czech Republic, Hungary, Poland and Croatia the share of foreign owners is around 80 per cent (Backé and Thimann, 2004; Buch, Kleinert and Zajc, 2003), with Slovenia as notable exception. Two thirds of the Baltic bank assets are in Swedish hands. Greek and Italian banks are most active in South-Eastern Europe (Bastian, 2003). Austrian and German banks are strongly involved in the neighbouring CEE5-markets (Czech Republic, Slovakia, Hungary, Poland, and Slovenia; Breyer, 2004). Hand in hand with the high involvement of major banking groups from neighbor countries goes a high level of market concentration. The top five banks, often foreign, account for more than 60% of aggregate bank assets in new EU Member States against about 40% in the Euro12-zone (Breuss, Fink and Haiss, 2004; Bruckbauer, 2004).

These foreign banks so far substitute for domestic financial supervision in CEE (Wagner and Iakova, 2001), which still needs to be improved in most New Member States (European Commission, 2003a). Bonin, Hasan and Wachtel (2005) and Fries and Taci (2005) find that foreign-owned banks are more cost-efficient than domestic banks in transition economies. Besides providing stability and bringing "fresh money", credit risk management techniques and improved corporate governance to these markets (Buch, Kleinert and Zajc, 2002), the strong involvement of foreign banks in CEE markets, mainly from the European Union, also implies a growing integration of these financial markets into the "old" EU-15 financial markets. Theory and empirical findings (e.g. Beale et al, 2004; Gianneti et al, 2002) suggest that integration of financial markets contributes to economic growth, which should equally apply to the transition economies.

**Figure 2: Foreign Share in Total Bank Assets (2002)**

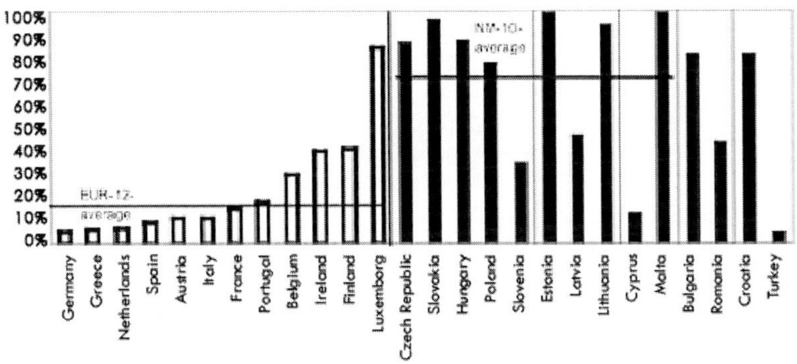


Source: Breuss, Fink and Haiss, 2004

Despite the strong foreign involvement and general success in transforming banking markets, there still are some weak spots with regard to product availability and the market setting. Missing pieces and gaps in the New Member States include entrepreneurial finance, bond markets, leasing, housing finance, institutional investors and non-bank financial intermediaries and supervisory structures (Bonin and Wachtel, 2003). The degree of availability and terms of consumer finance, most importantly mortgage finance, make these services accessible only to a small fraction of the population (Saccomanni, 2003).

On the positive side it has to be mentioned that in most New Member States growth is especially strong in those hitherto neglected financial segments, especially driven by foreign banks expanding their reach. Compound annual growth for the CEECs' banking sector till 2013 is forecast at about 14 per cent, and at 18 per cent in the retail banking sector (Di Maggio, Romanowski and Walter 2003; Perrin and Bruckbauer, 2004).1 The major factors behind these forecasts are per capita income doubling within a decade, rising financial product usage, and GDP growth (Perrin and Bruckbauer, 2004:38; Bruckbauer, 2004:6). Hitherto underdeveloped customer and product groups are increasingly targeted, especially retail banking with a share of the overall market of 36 per cent in the CEECs compared to 55 per cent in the EU in 2001 (Di Maggio, Romanowski and Walter 2003). Overall, competition has strengthened in CEE banking as evidenced by a shift in bank portfolios from government securities to private sector lending (Iakova and Wagner 2002) and by shrinking interest rate margins (Perrin and Bruckbauer, 2004) which are conducive to investment and economic growth. Bank market structures have reached levels conducive to economic growth in CEE. The following section will analyze whether this is also the case in SEE.

## Reform Process in South East Europe

In the South East European countries (SEE), financial sector reform has started late in comparison with the Central and Eastern European transition economies (CEE). For a prolonged period, the SEE financial sectors were characterised by insufficient restructuring of state-owned banks and poor governance, lax regulation on licensing new private banks and connected lending, lack of lending expertise, inadequate banking supervision and a poor institutional and legal environment (Cocozza et al, 2002; Popović, 2004; Stubos and Tsikripis, 2004). The reasons for that delay were a number of circumstances which jeopardized reforms, like war and political instability in Bosnia and Herzegovina, Serbia and Montenegro, and hyperinflation in Serbia and pyramid schemes in the late 1990s in the former Yugoslav Republic of Macedonia and in Albania (Bastian, 2003; Cocozza et al, 2002; Petkovski and Bishev, 2004). Only recently some macroeconomic stability has been reached in these countries (European

Commission 2004a; Mamatzakis, Staikouras and Koutsomanoli-Filliaki, 2005; Popović, 2004; Ristić, 2004).

**Tble 2: Characteristics of the banking sector in South East Europe (2003)**

| | Number of banks | Total banking sector assets | State owner-Ship | Foreign owner-ship | Concen-tration: 3 largest banks | Loan-to-deposit ratio | Net interest spread |
|---|---|---|---|---|---|---|---|
| | | % of GDP | % of total capital | % of total capital | assets in % of total | % | % |
| Albania | 16(1) | 50,2 | 4,4 | 95,6(2) | 68,5 | 81,9 | 5,9 |
| Bosnia and Herzegovina (BiH) | 37 | 58 | 10 | 70 | - | 79,8 | 6,8 |
| Former Yugoslav Republic of Macedonia (fYRoM) | 22 | 41,2 | 13 | 48 | 66 | 87 | 8 |
| Serbia and Montenegro (SCG) | 57 | 43,7 | 36,9 | 26,8 | 33 | 74 | 12,7 |
| *Serbia* | 47 | 46 | 37,5 | 26,3 | 30 | 71,4 | 13,2 |
| *Montenegro* | 10 | 32,3 | 25 | 36,2 | 59 | 95,6 | 8,9 |
| SEE | 132 | 48,3 | 16,1 | 60,1 | 41,8 | 80,7 | 8,4 |
| NMS-8(3) | 217 | 64 | - | - | - | 111 | 2,6 |

(1): 2004; (2): 2004 figure, after privatization of the Savings bank (3): NMS-8: EU New Member States from Central and Eastern Europe (Czech Republic, Slovakia, Slovenia, Poland, Hungary, Latvia, Lithuania, Estonia) Source: European Commission 2004a: 25.

*Privatization* of the state-owned banks and opening of banking institutions to foreign investors in SEE started slowly compared to CEE, but gained some momentum since 1998 (Penev and Rojec, 2004; Stubos and Tsikripis, 2004). The European Bank of Reconstruction and Development (EBRD) played a pivotal role in this respect in SEE (Bastian, 2003). By the beginning of 2004, state ownership in Albania, Bosnia and Herzegovina and FYR Macedonia was below 15% of total capital (EU Commission, 2004a). In most of SEE, foreign banks now dominate. In 2004, the main financial institution in Albania, Savings Bank, holding to 60% of total deposits was privatised and sold to a foreign bank. In Montenegro, public ownership decreased from 43% of share capital in 2001 to 23% in 2003. As described in more detail below, Serbia started reforms only after the fall of Slobodan Milosevic in 2000. A total of 25 banks were put into liquidation, among them four of the largest banks holding 57% of aggregate bank assets (Gardó, 2005). Privatisation of the state-owned Serbian banks has been relatively slow (European Commission 2004a).

With the exception of Serbia and Montenegro, SEE banking markets are characterised by rather high concentration levels (see Table 2), a phenomenon also observed for CEE banking markets. Mamatzakis, Staikouras and Koutsomanoli-Fillipaki (2005) analyze the concentration-competition link and provide evidence that a non-collusive behaviour among banks is in operation in the SEE banking industry and that the market is characterized by intensifying competition. Kraft (2004) argues that banking systems characterized by 5-10 rather strong foreign-owned banks may be more competitive than large numbers of small banks seen in SEE in the previous decade.

Changes in the structure and ownership and the clean-up of the banks' balance sheets have kept total banking sector assets rather stagnant in the region. With 46% of GDP in 2003, they are still even below the 64% level of the new EU Member States from CEE (Table 2). Deposits are similarly low at about 34% of GDP in SEE compared to about 45% of GDP in CEE (2003, see table 3; European Commission 2004a). Deposit rises (in fYRoM1 and BiH mainly 1999 to 2001) reflect growing confidence in the banking system after foreign banks entered.1 Serbia's deposit ratio amounted to 25% of GDP in 2003, reflecting late reforms, and Montenegro had the lowest deposit ratio with 15% of GDP.

**Table 3: Money and deposits in South East Europe in percent of GDP**

| | Broad money (M3) | | | Deposits | | |
|---|---|---|---|---|---|---|
| | 1999 | 2001 | 2003 | 1999 | 2001 | 2003 |
| **Albania** | 61.7 | 64.5 | 60.2 | 44.6 | 44.9 | 43.4 |
| **BiH** | 25.9 | 44.9 | 48.4 | 18.1 | 30.3 | 43.0 |
| **fYRoM** | 18.0 | 25.8 | 31.3 | 13.5 | 25.8 | 25.7 |
| **SCG** | | 16.3 | 23.6 | | 17.7 | 24.2 |
| **Serbia** | | 18.1 | 23.3 | | 18.1 | 25.2 |
| **Montenegro** | | | 26.8 | | 14.1 | 15.3 |
| **SEE** | 26.4 | 37.9 | 40.8 | 19.1 | 29.7 | 34.1 |
| **NMS-8** | 46.1 | 50.5 | 51.5 | | 44.2 | 44.5 |

Source: EU Commission 2004a: 27

With a ratio of *domestic credit* relative to GDP at 23% in 2003, the SEE region was considerably below the 47% credit ratio of the new EU Member States from CEE (see tables 1 and 4) and way below the 110% level for the "old" EU-15 (Mehl and Winkler, 2003). The last years brought some structural improvements in SEE. Private sector credit as a share of total domestic credit strongly rose during the last years in SEE, while public sector credit decreased relative to GDP (table 4; Cottarelli, Dell'Ariccia and Vladkova-Hollar, 2005; EU Commission, 2004a). Serbia is at the lower end of the SEE peers in credit intermediation, reflecting income levels and remaining below potential. SEE credit growth has generally been driven by a rise in consumer lending (Kraft, 2004). The possibility for banks to increase their lending operations to the corporate sector has been limited by the credit quality of private enterprises and unsatisfactory legal and institutional frameworks for a prolonged period (EU Commission, 2004a).

**Table 4: Lending activity of the banking sector in South East Europe**

| | Credit to private sector | | | | Credit to public sector | | | | Total domestic credit | | | |
|---|---|---|---|---|---|---|---|---|---|---|---|---|
| | % of GDP | | | Growth rate(1) | % of GDP | | | Growth rate(1) | % of GDP | | | Growth rate(1) |
| | **2001** | **2002** | **2003** | **2003** | **2001** | **2002** | **2003** | **2003** | **2001** | **2002** | **2003** | **2003** |
| **Albania** | 5.6 | 6.8 | 7.8 | 26.0 | 28.2 | 26.1 | 27.7 | 16.6 | 33.9 | 33.0 | 35.6 | 18.5 |
| **BiH** | 15.7 | 24.2 | 31.7 | 37.1 | 3.5 | 3.6 | 2.6 | -24.4 | 19.2 | 27.6 | 34.3 | 30.1 |
| **fYRoM** | 17.6 | 17.7 | 19.5 | 14.9 | 3.6 | 3.7 | 2.8 | -21.1 | 21.2 | 21.4 | 22.4 | 9.1 |
| **SCG** | | 16.3 | 15.7 | 14.1 | | 2.7 | 2.6 | 14.1 | | 19.0 | 18.3 | 14.1 |
| **Serbia** | 34.0 | 16.9 | 15.3 | 12.2 | 4.1 | 2.9 | 2.6 | 12.2 | 38.1 | 19.8 | 18.0 | 12.2 |
| **Montenegro** | | 7.8 | 12.2 | 32.8 | | 2.4 | 2.4 | 32.8 | | 10.2 | 14.6 | 32.8 |
| **SEE** | 9.7 | 16.3 | 18.7 | 23.1 | 8.8 | 9.1 | 8.9 | -3.7 | 18.6 | 25.3 | 27.7 | 17.9 |
| **NMS-8** | 31.9 | 31.5 | 33.6 | 4.9 | 10.6 | 12.8 | 13.9 | 6.8 | 42.6 | 44.3 | 47.5 | 5.5 |

1): in national currency; NMS-8 in EUR; Source: EU Commission 2004a: 29

While average loan portfolio quality improved in the SEE region recently, a closer look at country data reveals a quite uneven development (see table 5). Serbia and fYRoM still report levels way above the average of both the SEE and CEE regions (Stubos and Tsikirpis, 2004:5). Correspondingly, banks´ ROE is still negative in Serbia, with two state-owned banks accounting for over 60% of losses, while several other banks (mostly foreign) banks were making a profit. The high degree of risk in bank liquidity and non-banking items on banks' balance sheets is also reflected in high capital adequacy ratios in SEE (see table 4). The smaller and local banks have a higher ratio compared to the foreign owned banks. The regional average accounts for 27,5% in 2003 compared to 14% of the new EU Member States from CEE in 2002. However, the average capital adequacy ratio has been decreasing due to better management of credit risks recently (European Commission 2004a).

Although there are recent signs of improvement on both the deposit and lending sides, we conclude from the literature reviewed here that the contribution of the financial sector to SEE growth so far was limited. The overall fragility of the banking system was not conducive to economic take-off in SEE for an extended time (Cocozza et al 2002:4). Due to the low level of development, the financial sector in SEE could not support economic growth directly through intermediation over a prolonged period. The unfavourable situation in the banking sector in SEE also posed a serious obstacle to inflows of foreign direct investment (FDI) into the region in the 1990s (Penev and Rujec, 2004:82), thus hampering GDP growth indirectly as well. As the presence of foreign ownership in the banking sector has only increased recently, positive effects of foreign ownership have not yet reached its full scope in SEE (EU Commission, 2004a). Recent policies focused on alleviating the bottlenecks to financial intermediation, most importantly providing stable macroeconomic conditions and a sound legal and supervisory environment, should contribute to financial development in South-East Europe (Mehl and Winkler 2003). Serbia has made first steps into that direction, as discussed in more depth the following.

**Table 5: Bank soundness indicators in South-East Europe**

| | Capital adequacy (2003) | Non-performing loans in %of total loans* | | | | ROE in % (profitability) (2003) |
|---|---|---|---|---|---|---|
| | | (2000) | (2001) | (2002) | (2003) | |
| **Albania** | 18,5 | 42,6 | 6,9 | 5,6 | 4,6 | 19,5 |
| **Bih** | 18,8 | 15,8 | 20,7 | 11,4 | 8,3 | 6,4 |
| **fYRoM** | 25,8 | 46,5 | 44,4 | 35,7 | 34,9 | 2,28 |
| **Serbia and Montenegro** | n.a. | 27,8 | 24,4 | 28,5 | 23,8 | -4,8 |
| **Serbia*** | 31,3 | 13,7 | 12,6 | 24,3 | 21,8 | -1,2 |
| **Montenegro*** | 39,3 | n.a. | 14,8 | 11,9 | 7,4 | 6,3 |
| **SEE unweighted average** | 28,7 | 33,2 | 19,9 | 17,8 | 15,4 | 6,7 |

## Bank Reform in Serbia – Status and Open Issues

The recent political history, the former workers′ self-management system and the diaspora of guest workers differentiates the legacy countries of the former SRF Yugoslavia from other European transition economies. These facets have repercussions to the economic and financial system in Serbia. In order to delineate growth implications from financial sector reform, it thus makes sense to take a closer look at the specifics of financial development in Serbia.

On the political side, a major territorial issue is worth clarifying. While Serbia and Montenegro have formed a state union in February 2003 and are a single legal person in international law in succession of the SFR Yugoslavia, the National Bank of Serbia continues to operate on the territory of Serbia (Dvorsky, 2004). Banking licences for Montenegro are a concern of the Central Bank of Montenegro, which introduced the Deutsche Mark as republic's legal currency and withdrew the dinar from circulation in 2000 (Barisitz, 2003; Bastian, 2003). More recently, Montenegro has announced to hold a referendum on dissolving the union with Serbia and transforming into a loose alliance in 2006 (Gardó, Pudschedl and Saravanja, 2005; Jansson, 2005a). This highly sensitive territorial issue has repercussions into bank operating licenses, FDI, investor sentiment and financial market and economic prospects at large (Bastian, 2003; Jansson, 2005a). We will concentrate mainly on Serbia from 2000 on in the following, while tying in related aspects.[1]

## Initial Reform Measures and Bank Restructuring in Serbia

Compared to other planned economies, the "workers′ self-management-system" based on "associated labor" in former Yugoslavia brought about somewhat different banking structures (Cocozza, 2002). In a massive form of "connected lending", this workers′ self management system led to enterprise-owned banks granting loans mostly to finance owner firms′ investment projects under soft budget constraints at low interest rates (Barisitz, 2003). While resembling several characteristics of a market oriented, two-tier banking system, "the main function of a bank was not to make profit by undertaking calculated risk, but to extend as much credit possible to enterprises at the lowest possible interest rate" (Petkovski and Bishev, 2004:22). Credit ceilings and selective credits at preferential rates were used for public control of these banks.

In 1970s and 1980s a number of banks took up foreign currency credits under sovereign guarantee on international financial markets and financed those owner-enterprises projects that were supported by political authorities. Another source of foreign exchange was generated from tourism earnings and guest worker remittances (i.e. from people working abroad; Barisitz, 2003). The foreign exchange accounts and credits accounted for two-thirds of Yugoslav banks' liabilities. Most of these deposits were re-deposited with the National Bank of Yugoslavia (NBY), but were used to service government debt in foreign currency. After the major hyperinflation of 1993-94, about 90% of all bank loans were estimated as bad. The balance sheets of banks were dominated by non-performing and unprofitable loans. The households' foreign currency accounts were confiscated by the state. The authorities that were obliged to repay the banks' liabilities to the foreign creditors failed to fulfil their obligations.

The political turnaround in late 2000 and the related easing of the economic isolation market the beginning of banking sector reform in Serbia (Gardó, 2005). Credit expanded strongly in 2000 as a result of accumulation of structural problems and external effects (economic isolation and the Kosovo war caused a contraction of GDP by abut 20% in 1999), with inflation reaching 113.5% (Barisitz, 2003). Public confidence in the banking sector could hardly dwindle further, having been expropriated twice by hyperinflation and freezing of foreign currency deposits. Large enterprises remained unreformed, were financed by inter-enterprise arrears and barter arrangements and accrued heavy losses. Credit institutions were largely insolvent and saddled with negative capital (Barisitz, 2003). On the deposit side, the conversion of DEM to the Euro in the euro zone led to a general rise in bank deposits Serbia at about the same time (Bastian, 2004). This shift from cash to deposits provided some resources to banks for expanding their loans (Cottarelli, Dell´Arriccia and Vladkova-Hollar, 2005).

The new democratic authorities of Serbia that assumed power in October 2000 and adopted a comprehensive reform agenda (Penev and Rojec, 2004; Ristić, 2004; EU Commission, 2004a). The authorities have strengthened banking supervision by introducing new laws on banks, non-banks and the central bank (Gardó, 2005).[1] In the first half of 2001 the new management of the National Bank of Serbia (NBS) carried out a comprehensive assessment of the banking sector and drew up a bank restructuring strategy. This NBS assessment listed the following deficiencies of Yugoslav banking (NBS Supervision Department 2001, 2002, 2003; Begovic, Zivkovic and Mijatovic 2001):

- High level of contaminated bad assets and low level of real interest-bearing assets, which resulted directly in low profitability
- Low level of real reserve for potential loss provisions
- Real undercapitalisation and inability of capital and reserves to absorb undertaken risks
- Insolvency of the largest banks accounting for the majority of total bank assets
- High liquidity
- Non-existence of adequate internal control and audit
- Inadequate risk management system

Real sector reform also suffers from a special legacy. The principle of voluntary privatisation of socially owned firms adopted in 1997 ("Marcović law") gave preference to insider privatisation via management and employee buyout and led to growing links between politics and business and the prevalence of management and employee buyouts of small and medium sized enterprises (Barisitz, 2003; Ristic, 2004; Sergi, 2004). New privatisation legislation was adopted in 2001 and subsequently reformed several times. Privatisation of state and socially owned enterprises was made compulsory, with at least 70% of shares to be sold via public tender and auction procedures. Accusations were made that this enabled individuals to legalize money acquired from cooperation with former authorities (Ristic, 2004). In several cases, the level of indebtedness, redundancies and poor condition of infrastructure discouraged potential investors (Penev and Rojec, 2004). Deep-rooted corporate governance problems such as unclear ownership and dominance of insiders are still common (Barisitz, 2003). This is a pending issue for the financial sector to contribute to economic growth, as socially owned enterprises still play an important role as owners of Serbian banks.

The *process of bank restructuring* itself was carried out in several phases (NBS Supervision Department 2001; Barisitz, 2003; Gardó, 2005):

- Classification of the credit rating of banks into four categories
- Liquidation of insolvent banks
- Regulations governing credit rating of banks were adjusted to international standards
- Formulation of privatisation strategies for of state-owned banks
- Capital requirements for commercial banks were raised
- Measures for encouraging new foreign exchange savings were taken
- The National Bank of Serbia established the Central Credit Registry (CCR) in order to enable banks to obtain higher-quality information on potential borrowers
- The former Bureau for Settlement and Payment Transfers (Zavodi za obracun i placanja – ZOP) was transformed and the former payment system was replaced by a bank-based settlement system.

Amidst severe fiscal and budgetary constraints the restructuring strategy was to only recapitalize and restructure banks if it could be expected to create viable institutions with decent prospects (Barisitz, 2003). The National Bank of Serbia (NBS) accordingly classified all banks into A, B, C and D categories. Categories A and B contained sound banks, with good capital base, as well as banks which have certain problems in their operations in terms of insufficient liquidity, but with real chance of "self-rehabilitation" in a short-term. Category C contained banks that were, due to insolvency, put under administration of the Federal Agency for Deposit

Insurance, Bank Rehabilitation, Bankruptcy and Liquidation, with the aim of their rehabilitation. Category D contained banks that were undergoing bankruptcy and liquidation and didn't come under the competence of the National Bank of Serbia, but under the competence of the Commercial Court. Five banks were left unclassified: four sound but undercapitalized banks that were given a deadline for recapitalization and one bank that was placed under administration of the NBS. At end June 2001 of a total of 71 banks in Serbia, 29 (accounting for 13% of total assets of the banking sector) were assessed to be healthy i.e. in a group A, 16 were judged to be solvent but undercapitalized i.e. in a group B, 7 credit institutions (accounting for over 60% of total assets) were comprised in a group C and 19 banks were found to be insolvent i.e. were put in group D (NBS Supervision Department 2001, Barisitz 2003).

**Figure 3 : Financial Intermediation in Serbia**

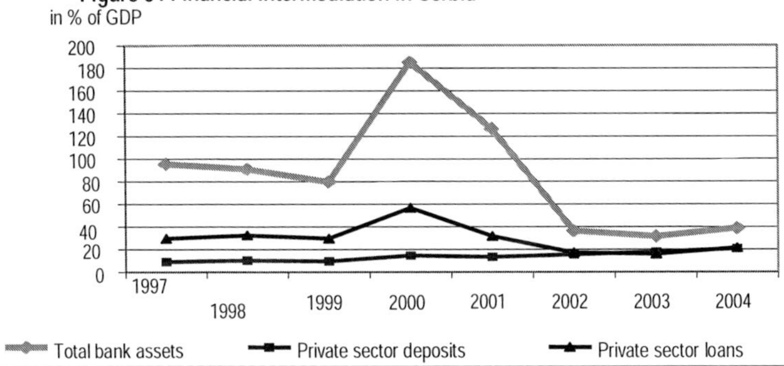


Source: Gardó (2005)

In late 2001, the authorities reached an important debt restructuring agreement with the Paris Club, which provided for a 66% reduction of the country's liabilities to the group of sovereign creditors (some USD 4,5 billion). Also in 2001, 23 smaller banks out of a total of 84 had lost their licenses (these accounted for about 10% of the banking sector's total assets; NBS Supervision Department, 2001). At the beginning of 2002, the four largest banks (Jugobanka, Beobanka, Beogradska Banka and Investbanka), accounting for 57% of total banking assets and for about two-thirds of outstanding commercial credit to the non-financial sector, were closed.1 The state also acquired significant interests in sixteen other ailing banks in 2001/2002 via debt-equity swaps (Gardó, 2005).

In conjunction with measures to solve the bad debt problem in 2001 and 2002, these massive bank closures led to a sharp contraction of bank loans to the private sector of 16% of GDP in 2003 (Gardó, 2005). The total liquidation cost of these four banks amounted to about 1% of GDP. The determined intervention of the authorities helped to improve public confidence (Barisitz, 2003).

## First Signs of Improvement in Serbian Banks

By liquidating the banks with negative capital, the aggregate capital structure of Serbian banks improved (NBS Supervision Department 2001). By the end of 2001, 49 banks had operating licenses issued by the National Bank of Yugoslavia, of which 19 were so-called "transformed banks" and 30 "newly-established banks"1. The two categories of banks differed significantly, both regarding balance sheet size and structure, and capital quality. The "transformed banks" were socially-owned, carried negative capital on their books and had a share in aggregate bank assets of total FRY banks of 90%, including the four large ones that were liquidated. In their balance sheets they had obligations and claims relating to the refinanced loans (Paris Club, London Club, etc) with a share exceeding 40% and obligations related to blocked household foreign savings and claims from the FRY on the same grounds (over 20%), which means that over 60% of their balance sheet total was frozen, i.e. it did not generate interest income.

The "newly-established" banks had significantly lower balance sheet totals – only 10% of aggregate bank assets, and a very different loan tenure structure (about 94% below one year). They were founded by fictitious payments towards the initial capital, performing recapitalization through subsequent issues of shares and, in such a way, artificially increasing their capital, which made them attractive to new depositors (NBS Supervision Department 2001).

Aggregate data from reclassified balance sheets as of 2001 indicate that total assets amounted to YUD 291,460.1 million, down by over YUD 400 mn or by 59% (at the end of 2000 the balance sheet total amounted to YUD 704,349.5 mn). Excluding the banks which had their licenses revoked by the National bank of Serbia in 2001, the aggregate balance sheet total would have been YUD 223,947.4 mn, 30% above the 2001 level. Total assets of banks that existed in both periods under observation rose by 24%, excluding banks newly-established in 2001. The data point to the first successes in the banking sector reform in 2001. The number of medium sized banks with total assets ranged from YUD 1000 to 5000 million rose, while the number of small banks with below YUD 1000 million in total assets declined (NBS Supervision Department 2003). This is a sign that confidence is returning to the banking sector (EBRD, 2004:170).

## Recent Developments and Data on Serbian Banks

Much of the more recent data on banking reform in Serbia reflects the fact that Serbia started reforms late. As mentioned before, Serbia is at the lower end of the peers in aggregate credit intermediation, in credit to the private sector, in deposits relative to GDP, in the share of foreign banks in total assets, profitability, and average loan quality (see tables 2 to 5). Lack of collateral and difficult claim enforcement keep lending cautious. Short-term lending prevails. Bank concentration is comparatively low (with the three largest banks accounting for 30% of total assets in 2003), and half of these banks have market shares below the 1% level (Gardó, 2005). Taking a look at developments over time allows us to draw a more rosy picture (see table 6).

While arguably still over-banked, the number of banks in Serbia was cut down to 43 at the end of 2004, about one third of the 1995 peak level (EBRD, 2004) and is supposed to go down to 35 by the end of 2005 (Jansson, 2005b). Based on the underlying fundaments during prevalent up to 2002, Cottarelli, Dell´Ariccia and Vladkova-Hollar (2005) saw a limited scope for further large increases in real credit growth. In 2004, reviving private consumption and strong investment activity boosted credit demand especially for loans to households (+126%), with corporate loans growing by 43% and access to credit by private enterprises still somewhat limited (Gardó, 2005; EBRD, 2004). Though from a low base, the National Bank of Serbia is ready to step in with the usual measures (raising of minimum reserve requirements, minimum down payments for loan applicants, credit risk provisions and the like) to avoid overheating loan growth (Gardó, 2005). The establishment of the Central Credit Registry (CCR) in mid-2002 should also help in this respect. Shrinking interest rate spreads reflect the more competitive banking scene. Both private sector deposits and loans are on the rise, with the share of short-term loans (47%) and foreign-currency loans (23%) to the private sector going down in 2004 (Gardó, 2005). Banking concentration (47% for the largest five banks) showed an upward trend in 2004 and will further go up via foreign bank entry in the ongoing privatization process.

**Table 6: Banking- sector related indicators for Serbia**

| | | | | | | | | |
|---|---|---|---|---|---|---|---|---|
| Number of Banks | 106 | 104 | 75 | 81 | 54 | 50 | 47 | 43 |
| Return on Assets (ROA) | n.a. | n.a. | n.a. | -6,2 | -3,6 | 8,7 | 0,3 | n.a. |
| Return on Equity (ROE) | n.a. | n.a. | n.a. | -78,5 | -26,0 | -34,5 | 1,2 | n.a. |
| Capital adequacy ratio (%) | n.a. | n.a. | n.a. | 0,7 | 21,9 | 30,6 | 31,3 | n.a. |
| non-performing assets (in % of total classified assets) | n.a. | n.a. | n.a. | 13,7 | 12,6 | 24,3 | 21,8 | n.a. |
| Spread between lending and deposit rates | 52,7 | 44,2 | 42,1 | 71,614,7 | 28,4 | 16,5 | 12,1 | 11,0 |
| Private sector deposits (in % of GDP) | 9,2 | 10,4 | 9,7 | 61,6 | 13,4 | 15,5 | 17,7 | 20,7 |
| Private sector FX deposits (in % of total classified assets) | 34,8 | 42,5 | 35,7 | 94,4 | 60,1 | 56,9 | 62,1 | 67,4 |
| Private sector short-term deposits (in % of private sector deposits) | 98,1 | 96,1 | 90,2 | 54,5 | 96,7 | 98,4 | 97,4 | 94,4 |
| Corporate loans (in % of GDP) | 27,9 | 31,0 | 28,3 | 56,6 | 29,7 | 15,2 | 13,2 | 16,2 |
| Private sector loans (in %of GDP) | 29,7 | 32,5 | 29,6 | 81,2 | 31,7 | 17,2 | 16,0 | 21,5 |
| Private sector FX loans (in & of private sector loans) | 56,9 | 58,7 | 55,0 | 27,5 | 75,2 | 41,7 | 29,8 | 23,2 |
| Private sector short-term loans (in % of private sector loans) | 42,5 | 43,6 | 45,6 | 385,0 | 28,2 | 49,8 | 52,9 | 47,1 |
| Private sector loans to private sector deposits (in %) | 323,0 | 313,6 | 305,6 | 185,2 | 37,3 | 114,4 | 90,3 | 104,1 |
| Total bank assets in % of GDP | 95,6 | 91,2 | 79,8 | n.a. | 126,7 | 36,4 | 31,5 | 38,8 |
| Concentration ratio (C%- total assets, in %) | n.a. | n.a. | n.a. | 90,9 | n.a. | 46,6 | 39,5 | 47,3 |

| | | | | | | | | |
|---|---|---|---|---|---|---|---|---|
| Market share of state-owned and socially owned banks (total assets, in %) | 89,8 | 90 | 89 | n.a. | 65,5 | 49,4 | 34,1 | n.a. |
| Market share of forreign-owned banks (total assets, in %) | n.a. | n.a. | n.a. | n.a. | 13,2 | 27 | 38,4 | n.a. |
| Market share of foreign-owned banks (capital, in %) | n.a. | n.a. | n.a. | n.a. | 15,7 | 19,4 | 26,3 | n.a. |

Source: Gardo (2005:8); data excludes Kosovo and Montenegro

The high level of non-performing loans combines the intertwined issues of enterprise reform and banking restructuring (Cocozza et al, 2002:19). Banking reform must go hand in hand with reforming the real sector, the latter still operating under soft budget constraints (Gardó 2005:11). Given that the banking sector is still partly burdened with the unresolved problem of claims on heavily indebted companies, a strategic decision concerning non-performing loans in the portfolios of banks will have to be made as this blocks privatization of both banks and indebted companies and may cause additional delays (EU Commission, 2004b: 26). Continuing banking reform and privatization and ensuring sufficient budgetary resources for restructuring and recapitalisation of the banking system is among the short-term priorities identified in the European Partnership with Serbia and Montenegro (EU Commission. 2004c: 9).

## Privatization Via FDI in the Serbian Banking Sector

Foreign ownership and participation in the banking sector generally form a crucial part of bank privatization in transition countries (Bonin, Hasan and Wachtel, 2005). Specific to Serbia is the desperate need to re-establish public confidence to banks. In a population that was expropriated consecutively by hyperinflation, bank closures and freezing of foreign currency deposits, and that suffered from being shut off economically from most of the rest of the world (Barisitz, 2003), strong signals are necessary to re-establish confidence in the banking system. While Serbia started late with full-fledged bank privatization, both the visible support of the EBRD encouraging foreign bank entry and the arrival of foreign banks provided such strong signals to the economy and investors at large and helped to restore confidence (Bastian, 2003).

On the one hand, new licences for foreign-owned banks were issued (European Commission, 2004a)1 and, after initial delay, bank privatization is proceeding step by step (Hunya, 2004). Most banks were privatized via tender offers with large participation of foreign banks (Penev and Rujec, 2004:82).1 The European Bank for Reconstruction and Development (EBRD) invested about EUR 2.6 million in Volksbank Belgrade, becoming the owner of 15 percent of the bank's shares, with Austria's Volksbank Group as owner of the majority 85-percent block of shares. In November 2004 Bank Austria Creditanstalt represented by its subsidiary HVB Bank Serbia, bought Serbian Eskimbanka which took place number 12 in Serbian banking market (BA-CA, 2004). It acquired 98,3% of its shares offering 3.688,59 dinar a share. The balance sheet amount of both banks together accounts for EUR 320 million. This acquisition improved the market position of BA-CA in Serbia by making it number 5 in Serbian banking market (BA-CA, 2005). The first bank privatization tender for Jubanka, fifth largest bank in Serbia, was launched in spring 2004. Eight of eleven banks entered the second round of tender sale, including Alpha Bank, Bank Austria Creditanstalt, Erste Bank, General Electric Europe Capital, Nova Ljubljanska Banka, OTP Bank, Societe Generale and Unicredito. In January 2005, the Greek Alpha Bank won the Jubanka tender, acquiring 89% of its capital, while Piraeus Bank purchased Belgrade-based Atlas Bank. Austrian-owned Erste Bank acquired Novosadska Banka (with a current market share of 5%) in May 2005, Slovenian-based Ljubljanska banka acquired Continental banka (Jansson, 2005b). OTP Bank, the largest Hungarian bank, is taking part in tender for purchase of 99,89% of Niska banka shares. Delta Banka, Serbia's second largest bank by assets, has been acquired by Banca Intesa, Italy's biggest bank (The Banker, 2005). So the markets share of foreign banks will markedly go up from the 2003 level of 38.4% towards level common in CEE markets. While so far growth was rather driven by private consumption and foreign direct investment in Serbia than by domestic financial intermediation, the strong presence of foreign banks is likely to change that. Besides provision of financial services at market standards, foreign banks as visible signals of change play a special role in framing expectations by market participants (Vives, 1996). Finding a solution to the highly sensitive territorial issues and overcoming the legacy of self management system still impeding enterprise restructuring will be imperative for banks being able to their potential in bringing about healthy economic growth in Serbia.

## Summary And Conclusion

This article discusses how and if the banking sector in transition economies can influence economic growth with a specific emphasis on financial sector reform in Serbia. We draw lessons from banking reform in Central and Eastern Europe (CEE), discuss ongoing banking reforms in South Eastern Europe (SEE) and in Serbia in particular and provide data on various financial sector aspects in these countries and in comparison to the European Union.

In South East European countries, economic and bank transition started later than in CEE because of political circumstances. Serbia is at a rather earlier stage of transition, even compared to other South East European countries (European Commission, 2004b, 2004c). The fact that the European Commission (2005) recently confirmed sufficient progress to open negotiations on a Stabilisation and Association Agreement provided a signal of growing institutional stability and EU involvement to foreign and domestic investors in Serbian banks and enterprises at large. So did the recent EBRD annual meeting in Belgrade and the massive roll-in of foreign banks. Such signals strengthen investor confidence and thus help markets to grow. The "EU-factor" (Sergi, 2004:15) alone will not be enough to enable the financial sector to contribute to economic growth. The financial sector can only provide positive growth triggers if the real sector also follows market rules and if state frameworks allow for good investment opportunities (European Commission. 2004a). In Serbia, restructuring of some big industries is still pending, with the real economy still showing some hybrid facets of strong state involvement.

Continuing banking reform and privatization and ensuring sufficient budgetary resources for redundancy and restructuring costs of the banking system is among the short-term priorities identified in the European Partnership with Serbia and Montenegro. As evident from the experience in CEE, financial development is not growth-supportive when the institutional and legal framework given to market participants is not appropriate. Unsound banking intermediation has a direct impact on economic growth as such behaviour perpetuates economic stagnation and inefficient use of resources. Unsound financial sectors in SEE also indirectly hamper economic growth, as they pose serious obstacles to inflows of foreign direct investment which in turn would contribute to economic growth. When financial institutions are subject to poor governance and incentive structures, finance can hardly promote growth.

Instead of supporting growth, granting bad loans back to companies of their owners, for example, leads to resource misallocation, reduced private sector confidence and results in lower investment and growth. Policies thus should continue to focus on alleviating the bottlenecks to financial intermediation by guaranteeing stable macroeconomic conditions and a sound institutional legal and supervisory environment. The involvement of foreign banks is found to be a major factor for stabilizing the banking sector and making it fit to support economic growth.

Serbia is still over-banked, with financial intermediation strongly on the rise from a very low base recently. With rising foreign involvement by reliable banks with a long-term commitment, confidence returned to the banking sector. This is further supported by the fact that these banks focus on establishing a regional network, with the implication not to abandon their regional strategy should local difficulties arise. Access to capital for the private corporate sector remains still limited and the level of non-performing loans is still high in Serbia. The first necessary steps have already been taken, but it requires persistent commitment and strong support to achieve lasting reform. Lending growth must not be accompanied by a return to dubious lending practices. Expectations on finances′ contributions to growth have not yet fully been met in Serbia, as financial development in a proper sense may have just started.

Continuing reform will attract foreign investors, improve the overall business environment, encourage investments and bring back the confidence of the population. The relationship with international organizations will continue to play a crucial role in the assessment of the stability and progress in Serbia and will be a precondition to further integration into the EU. In most of Central and Eastern Europe, the financial architecture has converged to a bank-based system with substantial foreign ownership. There are encouraging signs that financial development in Serbia may follow the successful path of Central and Eastern Europe, but the banking sector cannot get too far ahead of the rest of the economy.

## Notes

[i] CEE-5 includes Poland, the Czech Republic, Slovakia, Hungary and Slovenia; CEE-8 includes CEE-5 plus the three Baltic countries Estonia, Latvia, Lithuania; CEE-10 is CEE plus Bulgaria and Romania; NM-10 refers to the 10 new Member States of the European Union, comprised of CEE-8 plus Cyprus and Malta. ENL-14 is NM-10 plus Bulgaria, Romania, Croatia and Turkey.

[ii] In the Czech case, taking the Consolidation Agency activity into account drove general government deficit up from 3.9 per cent of GDP to 6.7 per cent of GDP in 2002, with total holdings of bad assets amounting to about 15 per cent of GDP (European Commission 2003a: 15f).

[iii] Rapid growth of consumer credit is a widespread phenomenon in both CEE and SEE; see Kraft (2004). Cottarelli, Dell'Ariccia and Vladkova-Hollar (2005) analyze credit growth in CEE with regard to the likely convergence to "normal" credit/GDP-levels of countries with similar fundamentals.

[iv] Former Yugoslav Republic of Macedonia (fYRoM); Bosnia i Herzegovina (BiH)

[v] The use of different indicators for financial depth is motivated by the importance to measure the state of development in various segments of the markets, following Beale et al. (2004:4).

[vi] For financial sector reform in the Kosovo and in Montenegro, see Gardó (2005), European Commission (2004a), and Popovic (2004); for Macedonia, see Petkovski and Bishev (2004). For a review of earlier financial market development in Serbia and Montenegro, see Barisitz (2003).

[vii] For an overview of related regulatory reforms, see Mamatzakis, Stakouras and Koutsomanoli-Fillipaki (2005) or Dvorsky (2004). An in-depth description is provided by Gardó (2005).

[viii] The reason for that was that the fiscal resources for rehabilitation of these banks were not available - estimated at around USD 3,8 billion – accounting for more than the state-guaranteed obligations to London and Paris Club creditors and frozen foreign currency deposits in the early 1990s (Barisitz 2003).

[ix] The category of "transformed" banks includes the banks which were founded in the period before 1989 and transformed, according to the provisions of the 1989 Law on Banks and Other Financial Organizations, into joint-stock companies by a mere transformation of previously existing funds and not by cash payments into their initial capital. "Newly-established" banks are the banks founded as joint-stock companies according to the 1989 Law on Banks (NBS Supervision Department 2001).

[x] The National Bank of Serbia issued seven new licenses for foreign-owned banks from late 2000 to 2002 (European-Commission. 2004a; Barisitz, 2003): Micro Finance Banka (owned by German and Dutch banks, the EBRD and IFC), Alfa Banka (Russian ownership), HVB Banka Serbia (Austria), National Bank of Greece (a private Greek credit institution), Raiffeisenbank Jugoslavia (Austria), Delta Banka (Cyprus) and Zepter Banka (Switzerland). Societe Generale (France) had already been licensed to operate in Yugoslavia in early 1990s.

[xi] Previous, though rather unsuccessful, privatisation of socially and state-owned enterprises were conducted via insider privatisation and mass voucher privatisation; see Ristić (2004) or Penev and Rojec (2004) for a review.

## References

Backé, P. and Thimann, Ch. (2004) `The Acceding Countrie's Strategies Towards ERM II and the Adoption of the Euro: Analytical Review, *ECB Occasional Paper* No. 10, http://www.ecb.int

Barisitz, S. (2003) `On the Catching-Up route – The Development of Banking in Serbia and Montenegro since 2000`, *Focus on Transition* 1/2003: 89-216, Oesterreichische Nationalbank, http://www.oenb.at/de/img/ftr_20031_tcm14-1668.pdf

Barro, R.J. (1991) ′Economic growth in a cross-section of countries′, *Quarterly Journal of Economics*, 106(2): 407-443.

Bastian, J. (2003) ′Banking on Southeast Europe: Financial Sector Reform amidst Regional Economic Volatility′, *Journal of Southeast European and Black Sea Studies* 3(1): 81-107.

Beale, L., Ferrando, A., Hördahl, P., Krylova, E. and Monnet, C. (2004) ′Measuring Financial Integration in the Euro Area, *ECB Occasional Paper* no. 14, April, http://www.ecb.int/pub/pdf/scopes/ecbocp14.pdf

Begovic, Boris, Zivkovic, Bosko and Mijatovic, Bosko (2001), Finansijsko stanje banaka u SR Jugoslaviji, *Ekonomski Anali,* 19-22, 54-57

Benhabib, J. and Spiegel, M. (2000) 'The role of financial development in growth and investment', *Journal of Economic Growth*, 5: 341–60.

BIS (2004): *Securities Statistics,* table 14A, 14B, 16A and 16B, Bank for International Settlements, www.bis.org/statistics/secstats.htm

Bonin, J. and Wachtel, P. (2003) `Financial Sector Development in Transition Economies: Lessons from the First Decade`, *Financial Markets, Institutions & Instruments* 12(1): 1-66.

Bonin, J., Hasan, I., and Wachtel, P. (2005) ′Bank performance, efficiency and ownership in transition countries′, *Journal of Banking & Finance* 29(1): 31-53.

Breuss, F., Fink, G. and Haiss, P. (2004): How well prepared are the New Member States for the European Union, *Journal of Policy Modeling* 26: 769-791.

Breyer, P. (2004) `Central and Eastern Europe – The Growth Market for Austrian Banks, *Monetary Policy & The Economy* Q3/2004: 63-89, Oesterreichische Nationalbank, http://www.oenb.at

Bruckbauer, S. (2004) ′CEE Banking Market after EU Accession′, *Xplicit,* Banking in CEE, April: 4-12, Bank Austria Creditanstalt, http://economicresearch-e.ba-ca.com

Buch, C.M., Kleinert, J. & P. Zajc, (2003) `Foreign Bank Ownership: A Bonus or Threat for Financial Stability?` *SUERF Studies* 2003/4, 45-83.

BA-CA (2004) 'HVB Bank Serbia and Montenegro.a.d., http://www.ba-ca.com/de/1650.html

—. (2005) `*CEE Report* 4/ 2004: Business information on Central and Eastern Europe,` http://economicresearch-e.ba-ca.com

Cocozza, E., Fabbrini, A., Gisolo, E., Gresti, M. and Micucci, G. (2002) 'The Banking and Financial Sector in the Countries of South-Eastern Europe, *Banca d'Italia Working Paper*, http://www.bancaditalia.it

Cottarelli, C., Dell'Ariccia, G. and Vladkova-Hollar, I. (2005) 'Early Birds, late risers, and sleeping beauties: Bank credit growth to the private sector in Central and Eastern Europe and in the Balkans, *Journal of Banking & Finance* 29(1): 83-104.

Di Maggio, F., Romanowski, P. & Walter, C., (2003) `Eastern European Banking Matures`. *The McKinsey Quarterly* 2/2003.

Dvorsky, S. (2004) 'Central Bank Indepencence in Southeastern Europe with a View to Future EU Accession, *Focus on European Economic Integration* 2/04: 50-75, http://www.oenb.at

EBRD (2004): *Transition Report 2004*, London.

ECB (2003): *Bond markets and long-term interest rates in European Union accession countries*, 2003 edition, 6 October, European Central Bank, www.ecb.int/pub/pdf/other/bondmarketacc2003en.pdf

—. (2004a) `The Acceding Countries' Economies on the Threshold of European Union`, *ECB Monthly Bulletin*, European Central Bank, February, Frankfurt: 45-56.

—. (2004b): Bond markets and long-term interest rates in non-euro area member states of the European Union and in Accession Countries, 2004 edition, 24 November, European Central Bank, www.ecb.int/pub/pdf/other/bondmarketnoneumember_accctr2004en.pdf

European Commission (2003a) `Progress towards meeting economic criteria for accession: the assessment from the 2003 comprehensive monitoring reports and regular report`, *Enlargement Papers No. 19*, November 2003.

—. (2003b) `*Communication from the Commission to the Council and the European Parliament*: Access to finance of small and medium-sized enterprises`, Brussels, December 2003, Com (2003) 713 final.

—. (2004a) `The Western Balkans in transition`, *Enlargement Papers* No. 23, http://europa.eu.int/comm/economy_finance/publications/enlargement_papers/2004/elp23en.pdf

—. (2004b) ´Serbia and Montenegro Stabilisation and Association Report 2004, *Commission Staff Working Paper* COM (2004) 206 final / SEC(2004) 376 March 30, http://europe.eu.int/comm/external_relations/see/sap/rep3/cfr_s-m.htm

—. (2004c) ´Proposal for Council decision on the principles, priorities and conditions contained in the European Partnership with Serbia and Montenegro including Kosovo as defined by the U.N. Security Council Resolution 1244 of 10 June 1999, COM(2004), http://europe.eu.int/comm/external_relations/see/sap/rep3/cfr_s-m.htm

—. (2005) ´Serbia and Montenegro: Commission confirms sufficient progress to open negotiations on a Stabilisation and Association Agreement, IP/05/421 – Brussels, 12 April 2005, http://europa.eu.int/comm/external_relations/see/news/2005/ip05_421.thm

FIBV (2003): Time Series 1990-2003 of Market Capitalization of shares of domestic companies, World Federation of Exchanges, 22 June 2004, www.fibv.com/WFE/home.asp?menu=325&document=2288

Fink, G., Haiss, P., Orlowski, L. and Salvatore, D. (1998): Central European Banks and Stock Exchanges: Capacity-building and Institutional Development, *European Management Journal* 16(4): 431-446.

Fries, S. and Taci, A. (2005) ´Cost efficiency of banks in transition: Evidence from 289 banks in 15 post-communist countries, *Journal of Banking & Finance* 29(1): 55-81.

Gardó, S. (2005) ´ Serbia and Montenegro – Coming to terms with the past´, *Xplicit*, Banking in Serbia and Montenegro, May 2005: 4-19, Bank Austria Creditanstalt, http://economicresearch-e.ba-ca.com

Gardó, S. Pudschel, W. and Saravanja, G. (2005) ´Legacy of the past overshadows the road to the EU, *Xplicit*, South-Eastern Europe – On the right track, May 2005: 4-5, Bank Austria Creditanstalt, http://economicresearch-e.ba-ca.com

Giannetti, M., Guiso, L., Jappelli, T., Padula, M. and Pagano, M. (2002) ´Financial Market Integration, Corporate Financing and Economic Growth, *Economic Papers* No. 179, http://europa.eu.int/comm/economy_finance/publications/economic_papers/2002/ecp179en.pdf

Holden, P. and Prokopenko, V. (2001), Financial Development and Poverty Alleviation:

Issues and Policy Implications for Developing and Transition Countries, *IMF Working Paper* No 01/160, 11-30

Hunya, G. (2004): Foreign Direct Investment in South East Europe in 2003-2004, Study commissioned by the Investment Compact for South East Europe, OECD, WIIW, Vienna, June 2004, http://www.investmentcompact.org/pdf/Min2004FDIinSEE.pdf.

Iakova, D. and Wagner, N. (2002), *Financial Sector Evolution: Challenges in Supporting Mcroeconomic Stability and Sustainable Growth,* Into the EU – Policy Frameworks in Central Europe, IMF, 35-95

IFS (2004): International Financial Statistics, International Monetary Fund, www.imfstatistics.org

Jansson, E. (2005a) 'Serbia – Confident times`, *The Banker* 155(951, May): 118-120.

—. (2005b) 'Serbia – Takeover trend', *The Banker* 155(951, May): 122-123.

Kraft, E. (2004): Banking Reform in Southeast Europe: Accomplishments and Challenges, Paper presented at the OeNB Conference on European Economic Integration, Nov. 28-30, 2004, Vienna, http://www.oenb.at/en/img/ceei_paper_kraft_tcm16-22784.pdf

La Porta, R., Lopez-de-Silanes, F., Shleifer, A. and Vishny, R. (1998), 'Law and finance,' *Journal of Political Economy* 106(6): 1113-55.

Levine, R. (1998), The Legal Environment, Banks, and Long-Run Economic Growth, *Journal of Money, Credit and Banking* 30: 610-621

Mamatzakis, E., Staikouras, C and Koutsomanoli-Fillipaki, N. (2005) 'Competition and concentration in the banking sector of the South Eastern European region', *Emerging Markets Review* 6(2): 192-209

Mehl, A. and Winkler, A. (2003) `The finance-growth nexus and financial sector environment: New evidence from Southeast Europe`, paper presented at The Ninth Dubrovnik Economic Conference on "Banking and the Financial Sector in Transition and Emerging Market Economies, organized by the Croatian National Bank, June, http://www.hnb.hr/dub-konf/9-konferencija-radovi/mehl-winkler.pdf

NBS Supervision Department (2001), *Banking Sector in FRY*

—. (2002), *Banking Sector in FRY*

—. (2003), *Banking Sector in FRY*

OECD (1993), `*Transformation of the Banking System: Portfolio Restructuring, Privatisation and the Payment System*`, Paris, Organization for Economic Cooperation and Development.

Penev, S. and Rojec, M. (2004) 'Foreign direct investment and the investment climate in South-East Europe', *Economic Annals* no. 163, Oct. 2004 – Dec. 2004: 71-92, http://www.ekof.bg.ac.yu/visitors/Annals/163.htm

Perrin, L. and S. Bruckbauer (2004) 'Banking in CEE Post-EU accession', *Xplicit*, CEE – from Transition to Convergence, July 2004: 34-41, Bank Austria Creditanstalt, http://economicreseach-e.ba-ca.com

Petkovski, M. and Bishev, G. (2004) 'Understanding Reforms in Macedonia, Global Development Network Southeast Europe (GDN-SEE), http://www.wiiw.ac.at/balkan/files/GDN_UnderstandingREform_Macedonia.pdf

Popović, S. (2004) 'The role of the capital market in the transition of the Montenegrin economy', *South-East Europe Review* 7(4): 69-78, http://www.boeckler.de/pdf/SEER_2004_Popivic.pdf

Ristić, Z. (2004) 'Privatisation and foreign direct investment in Serbia', *South-East Europe Review* 7(4): 121-136, http://www.boeckler.de/pdf/SEER_2004_Ristic.pdf

Rousseau, P. and Wachtel, P. (2005) 'Economic Growth and Financial Depth: Is the relationship extinct already? Paper presented at the UNU / WIDER Conference on Financial Sector Development for Growth and Poverty Reduction, July, Helsinki

Saccomanni, F. (2003) `Ensuring Financial Stability: Global and European Perspectives`, *SUERF Studies* 2003/4: 25-44.

Sergi, B. (2004) 'Understanding the 'EU-factor': the Balkans regions as recipients of FDI and industries, *South-East Europe Review* 7(4): 7-20, http://www.boeckler.de/pdf/SEER_2004_Sergi.pdf.

Sherif, K. (2003) `Direct Fiscal Costs of Restructuring in Transition Countries. Paper, presented at the "East-West Conference 2003`, Oesterreichische Nationalbank (OeNB) and Joint Vienna Institute, Nov. 4, 2003, Vienna, http://www.ksherif.com/pages152503/index.htm.

Stubos, G. and Tsikripis, I. (2004) 'Banking Sector Developments in South-eastern Europe, Global Development Network Southeast Europe (GDN-SEE), http://www.wiiw.ac.at/balkan/files/GDN_EU_IBEU_Stubos_BankingSectorSEE.pdf

The Banker (2005) 'Intesa extends its CEE network with Serbian acquisition', *The Banker* 155 (949, March): 13

Vives, X. (1996) 'Social learning and rational expectations, *European Economic Review* 40(3-5): 589-601

Wachtel, P. (2001), 'Growth and Finance: What Do We Know and How Do We Know It?', *International Finance* 4:3, 335-362.

—. (2003), 'How much do we really know about growth and finance?' *Federal Reserve Bank of Atlanta Economic Review* 88:33-47

Wagner, N. and Iakova, D. (2001) `Financial Sector Evolution in the Central European Economies: Challenges in Supporting Macroeconomic Stability and Sustainable Growth`, *IMF Working Paper* No. 01/141, September 2001.

# CONSUMER ATTITUDES TO THE PHENOMENON OF MONEY LAUNDERING

SŁAWOMIR SMYCZEK

## Abstract

The inclusion of Poland into the European Union combined with liberalization of commodity and service turnover as well as a free flow of technology, people and, above all, capital have had a stimulating effect on the development of the economy in these countries. Nevertheless, all these factors also create opportunities for various businesses to conduct some criminal activity and related to it money laundering. The development of the phenomenon of money laundering is mainly facilitated by differences existing between legal and financial systems of particular countries and international standards, as well as by achievements of the scientific and technological revolution. Money laundering can pose a serious threat not only to the functioning of the whole market and companies but also households and individual customers. Therefore, the author of the paper undertakes an analysis of the phenomenon of money laundering, its nature and evolution as well as makes an attempt to identify and characterize attitudes of Polish consumers towards money laundering. In the paper, a special focus is put on determination of a degree of understanding the phenomenon by consumers and on their knowledge of the range of the phenomenon and methods of its prevention.

## Introduction

The inclusion of Poland and other CEE countries into the European Union combined with liberalization of commodity and service turnover as well as a free flow of technology, people and, above all, capital have had a stimulating effect on the development of the economy in these countries. Nevertheless, all these factors also create opportunities for various businesses to conduct some criminal activity and related to it money laundering. The development of the phenomenon of money laundering is mainly facilitated by differences existing between legal and financial systems of particular CEE countries and international standards, as well as by achievements of the scientific and technological revolution. The commonness of a fast and efficient information transfer combined with an unlimited possibility of global traveling brings about a situation where money laundering assumes new and more refined forms. Therefore, the harmfulness of the phenomenon can neither be treated as a one-facet problem nor considered in isolation from other elements of an economic and financial pathology. Money laundering can pose a serious threat not only to the functioning of the whole market and companies but also households and individual customers. Therefore, the author of the paper undertakes an analysis of the phenomenon of money laundering, its nature and evolution as well as makes an attempt to identify and characterize attitudes of Polish consumers towards money laundering. In the paper, a special focus is put on determination of a degree of understanding the phenomenon by consumers and on their knowledge of the range of the phenomenon and methods of its prevention. Additionally, the author identifies a degree of acceptance of the phenomenon by individual consumers.

## Money laundering – Evolution and Characteristics

Money laundering appeared for the first time in the twenties of the previous century in the United States of America. The phenomenon did not appear in the course of the evolution of crimes and transgressions of economic nature, but occurred as a new type of criminal activity, which evolved together with the development of modern organized crime. High proceeds from illegal business and criminal operations, as well as threats following the investigation process against Alphonse Capone[1] forced the elites of the criminal world to legalize illicit funds (Bartosiak, 2003). The eighty-year-old history of money laundering, the history of an invasive character, can be divided into two stages of development. The first stage is characterized by the use of simple methods of funds legalization.[2] In the second stage of its development, money laundering evolved into specialized international criminal activity organized in a regular business defined as "full-time criminals" (Lerbell, 1978).

The main direction of the phenomenon evolution has been influenced by existing correlations between:

a) the process of transformation of small local criminal groups into organizations of a regional range, as well as the transposition of some of the groups into organizations of a distinct organizational structure,

b) fast-developing professional methods of activity of criminal groups,
c) new fields and areas of interest of criminal circles and new possibilities provided by ongoing geopolitical changes,
d) achievements of the scientific-technical revolution.

The legalization of big sums of money has become a necessity for members of criminal groups, as it is the "laundered" money that can ensure the "consumption of fruits" of criminal activity and guarantees its further development. Illegal funds come from two main sources of criminal activities:

1) traditional activities,
2) activities which evolved with new trends, as a consequence of system transformations of Central and Eastern Europe countries and a new process of international integration within the European Europe.

Traditional offences and crimes that constitute a source of illegal funds comprise:

- all types of drug crimes,
- tax frauds,
- customs crimes,
- arms trading, especially nuclear materials,
- organized prostitution including children prostitution and procurements,
- international terrorism and contract murders,
- extortions and ransoms,
- trading children, women and life body organs,
- forgery of money, securities and personal documents,
- theft, smuggling and fencing stolen arts, antiques and luxury items,
- illegal transfer of people over international borders,
- production and trading of illegal software and counterfeited CDs and DVDs.

The second group of crimes that have been evoked by geopolitical changes comprises:

1) Activities directly related to business and financial operations in the field of privatization being part of a system transformation of CEE countries.
2) Frauds connected with a structural policy, particularly the embezzlement of the EU funds (Jasiński, 2002).

The process of money laundering consists in the introduction of means of payment, securities or other currencies of unknown origin into the legal circulation (Pracki, 1995). The executive activities may differentiate depending on the country where the money is laundered and on the profile of criminal activity. Nevertheless, these activities are always subjected to goals that can guarantee effective legalization of financial means:

1) hiding a real source of funds and identity of their owner,
2) constant supervision and necessary safety of illegal money in the process of its legalization.
3) legalization of illegal proceeds through their introduction into the official financial system.

The process of money laundering has been based on a three-stage model (Gilmore, 1999) for the sake of a precise description of stages, characteristic features and rules of the process functioning. Thanks to this, it is possible to define the areas of operational activities of money laundering, and, above all, to expose the weak points of the mechanism whereby the probability of identifying suspicious financial operations is bigger.

**Table 1: Stages and main objectives of the process of money laundering**

| Stages of the process | Main objectives of the stages of a classic process of money laundering |
|---|---|
| Placement | Disposal of illegal money through:<br>- purchase of luxury items or real estate<br>- purchase of financial instruments<br>- different forms of deposits with financial institutions |
| Layering | Separation of illegal money from the source of its origin through:<br>- purchase of short-term deposits,<br>- very frequent financial operations ,<br>- artificial extension of the duration of financial transactions. |
| Integration | The introduction of illegal money into the legal circulation through assimilation of the illegal and legal funds. |

Source: Wąsowski and Wąsowski, 2001 and Bilmore, 1999

The revealed and examined cases of the legalization of illicit funds show that the process of money laundering can be conducted with the omission of particular stages (due to: lack of possibility of purchasing financial assets: shares, bonds, banker's and traveler's cheques and/ or use of deposit services provided by banks and deposit institutions "…exceptional attractiveness of deposit institutions for criminal groups as a result of a wide range of services which give "launderers" a possibility to hide deposits and legitimize incomes, in other words, to launder money through the second and third stage), the stages may exist simultaneously or else they may overlap (Gilmore, 1999). Nevertheless, the executive activities always demonstrate the following features:

1) Complex forms of operational activities.
2) The use of a perfect camouflage.
3) Character of participants of the process.
4) The main objective of the operation.
5) A cross-border strategy of the operation.

In view of the growing importance of globalization of the world economy, the cross-border character of the process of money laundering is gaining still more significance. The international character of money laundering is presented in Table 2.

**Table 2: Characteristic features of the process of money laundering**

| No | Characteristics of crime defined as a business |
|---|---|
| 1. | **Complex forms of operational activities** are characterized by high adaptability to a dynamic changes occurring in the environment and by high flexibility of functioning, which is developed through the use of the most recent technological and scientific achievements. All this is reinforced by extremely strict internal discipline within criminal organizations. |
| 2. | **The use of a perfect camouflage** - refined appearances of a legal operation. |
| 3. | **The character of the process participants**. These are not "people from a social margin" but "high-class specialists in banking and law whose activities are supported by state legislators. |
| 4. | **The main objective of the operation**; a cut-throat pursuit to maximize profits. |
| 5. | **A cross-border strategy of the operation** pursued within the international criminal operation enables launderers to use all types of loopholes in order to facilitate the concealment of illegal funds and their origin. |

Source: Lernell, 1978 and Jasiński, 2002

The high adaptability of the process participants to new geopolitical conditions and their ability to use scientific and technological achievements contributes to the development of natural mechanisms which facilitate further evolution of money laundering.

In order to precisely define the nature of particular stages of the process and the existing relations between them, the model has been presented in a block diagram as in Figure 1.

**Figure 1: The classic process of money laundering**

**Sources of origin of financial means**
Traditional crimes of primary nature.
Crimes being a consequence of new trends in organized criminal activity.

↓ Anonymous entities participating in transactions.
Anonymous character of transactions.
Cash handling.

**Financial means appropriated for legalization**
Means of payment, securities

**Preparation of financial means**
The purifying or refining of money.
Transfer of money to the place of its allocation

↓ The evasion of declarations or registration required for account deposits.

**Placement**
Disposal of funds gained from criminal activity

Blending legal and illegal money.
Deposits made into both fictitious and existing bank accounts.
Purchase of financial instruments.
Purchase of luxury items.
Money transfers.
Smurfing.
Purchase of foreign currencies.

↓

Entering a system of financial disguise of money origin

**Layering**
Hiding the source and the owner of financial means.

The general rule of a fast money transfer.
SWIFT Society for Worldwide Interbank Financial Telecommunications.
EFT Electronic Funds Transfer.
Traditional ways of money transfers.
Purchase of financial assets such as shares, bonds, traveler's or cashier's cheques
Electronic transfers between accounts.
Simulation of a cash withdrawal.
Establishment of fictitious firms.
Purchase of companies in insolvency.

↓ Return of clean money to the owner

**Integration**
Providing evidence of a legal character of financial means.

Transactions in tax havens.
Credit-deposit operations.
Purchase of expensive and luxury items.
Commercial transactions with foreign countries
Repayment of loans.

Source: Gilmore, 1999

The process of money laundering is directly preceded by activities that aim at the adjustment of the money denomination to the most favourable value defined by one of the two procedures of further conduct:

1) The provision of funds to the place where attempts are made to introduce the funds into the banking system.
2) Placement – the first stage of the classic model of money laundering.

The provision consists in the transfer of illegal money from the place of illicit income to the place of money laundering. These are often tax havens where the focus is put on discretion and anonymity, regulations allow for cash deposits and the money exchange is not subject to monitoring. The provision is most frequently made through:

1) A physical transfer of money.
2) The change of money into luxury items that are most frequently sold at cut prices after transportation.

The main objective of activities undertaken within the first stage of money laundering, referred to as placement, is the introduction of means of payment into the financial system by virtue of three types of operations:
1) Physical deposits into accounts (transaction structuring).
2) Deposits made into accounts through smurfing (smurfing).
3) Blending legal and illegal money (blending).

Physical deposits made into accounts (a proper definition of transaction structuring) consist in making various financial operations at the stage of placement. Deposits are made into all types of accounts, including fictitious accounts of non-existent companies, organizations and natural persons. This method, however, is restricted by the obligation to identify the ordering party of an operation and to register transactions over the equivalent value of 15,000 euros. In order to evade the obligation, combined transactions are used, where series of deposits below a certain regulatory cash limit are made into definite accounts. Thus, the accumulated funds are wired into collective accounts (Kowalski, 2001).

"Smurfing" is a form of a physical deposit and constitutes one of the safest, the most developed and the best organized technique of money laundering. It is also the most difficult to divulge, but at the same time very laborious and time-consuming. The method is used on all continents, especially in Asia and Europe. "Smurfing" involves splitting and distributing illicit money among "smurfs" who either pay the money into bank accounts below some limit sum or buy traveler's cheques.

"Blending", in other words mixing illicit money with legal funds, constitutes the oldest and the simplest method of money laundering at the placement stage. The blending of financial means is performed within three methods:
1) Supporting criminal activity.
2) Company takeovers.
3) Cooperation defined by terms and provisions stipulated in the agreement between the management of a company and leaders of a criminal group.

The method of blending illicit funds with legal proceeds of service companies, where cash flow (turnover) is very big and its volume is hard to estimate by law enforcement agencies, is defined as "supporting criminal activity". If a company belongs to a criminal organization, it serves an extra function of an official place of employment for members of such an organization. The history of money laundering has witnessed cases where contracts were signed between owners of companies and organizers of the process of money laundering. Such indicative data as high turnovers and due settlement of VAT and income taxes have made the procedure extremely safe. Only sudden appearance of big volume turnovers, which are incompatible with the company's size and potential, and an in-depth analysis of the company's business activity may raise some suspicions which are, however, extremely difficult to confirm (Czajkowski, 2002).

The main objective of undertaken activities within the second stage of money laundering, referred to as layering, is the separation of funds from a source of their origin. This is achieved through various fast-banking operations. The duration and number of performed transactions are subjective and launderers must be absolutely sure that the establishment of a real source of money origin is not feasible. In order to achieve this, the following methods are employed:

1. Fast transfers with the use of electronic tools:
    a) SWIFT (Society for Worldwide Interbank Financial Telecommunication),
    b) EFT (Electronic Funds Transfer) and traditional methods of money transfer.
2. The purchase of financial assets and the change of their form.
3. Setting up fictitious companies - even for one financial transaction.

Very fast performance of electronic orders and easy access to SWIFT and EFT make these tools perfect for layering interdepartmental, inter-bank and international operations with a simultaneous change of their name and owner (Wójcik, 2002).

Another method of money laundering at the stage of layering involves the purchase of financial assets that could not be bought in the previous stage. In this case the separation of illicit funds from their source occurs at the moment of purchase or during the change of a deposit form. Every restructuring of invested capital poses a threat of capital loss or its value change. The process of money laundering also employs a method that involves setting up fictitious companies or saving insolvent businesses whose accounts are used to conduct previously discussed activities (Zadworny, 2002).

The main objective of activities at the stage of integration is to legitimize both the criminals' wealth and their high incomes. This is achieved through the introduction of both illegal and legal money into the joint circulation by means of the following methods:

1) Purchase and sale of luxury items and tangibles.
2) Repayment of loans.
3) Saving companies in bankruptcy.
4) Foreign trade transactions and transactions using transfer prices.
5) Credit-deposit activity (Gilmore, 1999).

The mechanism of money laundering through the purchase and sale of luxury items and tangible assets below the market price works in the following way: the payment of financial liabilities resulted from the purchase is effected from two sources:

- the legal source with respect to the official price defined by the purchase-sale agreement.
- the illegal source, with respect to the difference between the market price and the prices stipulated in the agreement (Fijałek, 2001).

The sale legalizes and justifies the profit. The method engages all kinds of real estate agencies as well as companies involved in selling means of transport, even without their knowledge of the game which they are part of. The repayment of loans with illicit funds is another method of money laundering at the stage of integration. The means obtained from the loan are proved legal, whereas the repayment is effected with funds from secret sources. The method is extremely effective and difficult to reveal, particularly when institutions applying for a loan are managed or controlled by criminal groups.

Another technique of money laundering at the integration stage consists in the introduction of financial means from a criminal activity into an insolvent company with an apparent intention of saving it. The procedure is facilitated by some attitudes of managers who are in charge of an insolvent company or its assets. They usually do not scrutinize the origin of saving funds, or else deliberately enable their legalization (Zadworny, 2002).

Some other methods of money laundering at the integration stage comprise international commercial transactions, which use:

- Double sources of import financing.
- Manipulative changes of prices of imported goods.

- Deliberate and planned lack of correspondence of a declared value and volume of imported goods to the market price and volume of goods delivered by the exporter (Matusz, 2002).

Such actions allow for the manipulation of customs duties whose lowered value is a decisive factor during the identification of suspicious transactions.

The technique of a double source of financing involves the introduction of illegal money into the circulation at the stage of payment for imported goods. This is performed by means of two sources of money:

1) The legal source, used to pay for imported goods at reduced prices according to invoices.
2) The illegal source, used to pay the difference resulted from a real value of imported goods and the legal payment (Kęsicka, 1993).

The method of transfer price manipulation is based on a deliberate change of the price value and most frequently constitutes one of the elements of wider-range criminal activities. The planned change of transfer prices and the use of differences in particular areas of taxation, which are obligatory for both importers and exporters, lead to the development of informal financial relations between institutions participating in the process. The relations are of informal and mutual character, and their existence is known exclusively to the authors of the process. All this ensures an increase of the value of illegitimate money transfer by means of higher and lower taxation within:

1) Mutual provision of fictitious services.
2) Fictitious complaints concerning quality of a product or service.
3) Licence fees (Matusz, 2002).

The credit-deposit method of funds legalization at the stage of integration involves the use of illicit money as long-term deposits or low-interest loans. Illegal money deposited mainly with foreign banks in the form of long-term deposits constitutes a perfect security or a source of repayment of a loan granted mostly in a home country. The second element of the strategy comprises granting long-term and low-interest loans either by institutions participating in money laundering or directly by criminal groups. The borrowers are companies which have been denied credit facilities by other banks due to lack of credibility with respect to sources of loan repayment and to their financial and economic standing.

Money laundering is a process comprising a series of financial activities undertaken by the same "work group" and for the same reasons, expressed through repeated correlations and producing definite socio-economic results. The authors of the process are top specialists in banking and vast areas of law who aim at creating more effective and better concealed methods of money legalization. Hence, it can be presumed that there exist other, so-far undiscovered methods reaching beyond the popular techniques of money laundering.

## Research Methods

In order to define customer attitudes to the phenomenon of money laundering, a survey was conducted by means of a structured questionnaire. The questionnaire was prepared with following problems:
1. Determination of the scope of definition of money laundering presented in colloquial terms.
2. Determination of factual knowledge of money laundering and understanding the phenomenon as well as methods of money laundering prevention by the test group representatives.
3. Definition of the role and significance of different information sources in creating the respondents' general opinion.
4. Establishment of a degree of acceptance of the economic-financial pathology.

The variety of views presented by respondents is a result of their own hierarchy of values and goals prioritized according to individually perceived utility.

After preparation of the questionnaire, the measurements were submitted to the evaluation of three experts – marketing and statistic professors – in terms of wording/meaning and consistency.

The research was carried out on a sample of respondents (students, as future businessmen responsible for identifying and eliminating phenomenon of money laundering in business enlivenment) selected by means of a quota – sample method which is based on the assumption that the test group represents all features (quotas) which are considered important and interesting from the researchers' point of view (Blackwell, Miniard, Engel 2001). The assumed quotas included type of university (type of education: economist, humanist and technical) and gender. The respondents' quotas were selected on the basis of an already known structure of the examined population of Silesian students. The structure of the sample group and that of the examined population in were identical. The direct survey comprised 600 respondents, who were questioned by trained inquirers at the end of April and beginning of May 2007. After collection, all questionnaires were subject to screening and verification in terms of information completeness, correctness and reliability. This helped to reveal arithmetic mistakes, record inaccuracies, as well as logical and systematic errors, i.e. errors that distort data in a biased way (e.g. contradictory answers to questionnaire questions, etc.). The questionnaire verification ensured and enhanced credibility of the data through the exclusion of erroneously completed questionnaires. As a result, 574 questionnaires were approved for further analyses

## The Characteristics of Students' Attitudes towards the Introduction of Financial Means of Illegal and Unknown Origin into Financial Circulation

### The concept of money laundering and the direct studies

On the basis of the conducted study, it can be concluded that the majority of respondents (88.30%) consider money laundering to be a process of creating appearance of legal introduction of funds from illegal or undisclosed sources into the financial circulation (Table 3). 11.70 % of the test group members do not agree with such an opinion, including 7.17% of those for whom money laundering is tantamount to illegal introduction of financial means from banking systems. 3.40% of respondents maintain that money laundering occurs when members of some organized criminal group receive remuneration for execution of unlawful commissions. 0.38% of respondents associate the process of money laundering with black economy transactions which are identified and taken over by the General Inspector for Treasury. Finally, 0.38% of respondents is not familiar with the concept of money laundering or refers the process to some other activities not mentioned above.

**Table 3. Structure of respondents' opinions with respect to character of money laundering (in %)**

| The scope of the definition of money laundering | Result |
|---|---|
| Illegal withdrawal of financial means from banking systems | 7.17 |
| Making appearance of a legal origin of money obtained from a criminal activity | 88.30 |
| "Black economy" transactions identified and suspended by the General Inspector for Treasury | 0.38 |
| Remuneration for members of criminal groups for execution of unlawful commissions | 3.40 |
| I do not know what money laundering consists in | 0.38 |
| A process connected with other activities not mentioned above | 0.38 |

In terms of a practical use of the obtained results, it is interesting to note that opinions on legalization of financial means vary depending on academic environments (Figure 2). Such differentiation has been illustrated through the aggregation of respondents' answers into two more general categories:

1. Money laundering consists in making appearance of a legal origin of funds obtained from criminal activities, a definition provided in the second out of six possible answers.
2. Other possible answers.

The differentiation has had a considerable impact on the results of Pearson chi-square independence test. The test statistics value $\chi^2$ falls within the critical limit (the test statistics value $\chi^2 = 8.49$, with a critical value $\chi^2 = 5.99$), which rejects the hypothesis $H_0$ about the independence of the examined features. Hence, it can be concluded that the type of university has great influence on the degree of familiarity with money laundering and on understanding the phenomenon.

**Figure 2. Aggregated opinions on character of money laundering with respect to type of studies**

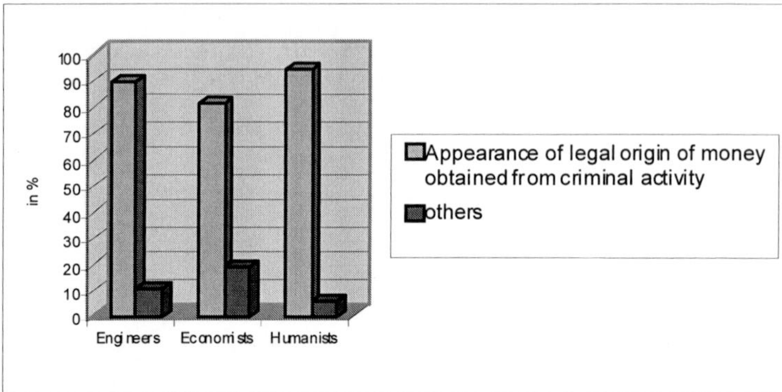


Such factors as students' age, gender and mode of studies (full-time, part-time) as well as a stage of the studying process (the first, the last year of studies) do not affect students' perception of the phenomenon of money laundering. The chi-square test results do not provide any grounds for the thesis that any of the mentioned features has important influence on familiarity with the process of funds legalization.

As many as 94.34% respondents expressed the conviction that money laundering was a global process. It is noteworthy that only 0.75% of students considered it to be a local phenomenon. The remaining group of 4.91% respondents claimed that money laundering was conducted within certain world regions. The opinions concerning the geographical extent of money laundering presented by particular academic environments demonstrated coherence and cohesion of opinions formulated by the students and the test group members.

**Figure 3. Geographical extent of money laundering according to respondents**

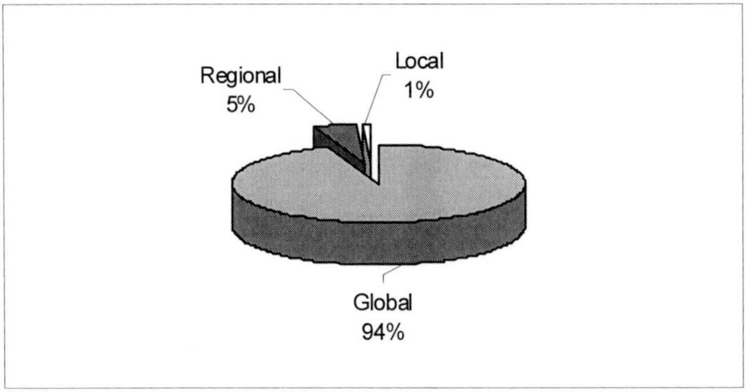


The study results provide grounds for the conclusion that 84.90% to 93.59% of the test group members considered money laundering to be a very great or a great threat to individual financial systems in global, national and regional terms. Surprisingly, there were a relatively big percentage of people who did not have a definite opinion on that: with 6.42% of those who referred to money laundering as a global phenomenon, 4.15% who considered it in regional terms and 1.89% who assessed it with respect to particular states. The remaining group of respondents expressed the conviction that money laundering posed either a negligible or a minor threat on a global, regional and national scale, with 8.68%, 10.95% and 4.53% of answers respectively. Within this field of analysis a special focus should be put on respondents' gender. This feature was greatly differentiated (Figure 4), which had a considerable effect on the result of the Pearson chi-square independence test. Hence, it can be concluded that the gender has a great influence on the determination of a threat level with regard to national financial systems on a global scale. In this case the value of the chi-square test dramatically approached the critical value (the test statistics value $\chi^2 = 9.43$ with the critical value $\chi^2 = 9.49$ on a global scale and $\chi^2 = 6.95$ with the critical value $\chi^2 = 9.49$ on a regional scale).

**Figure 4. Differences in opinions on threat from money laundering to national financial systems**

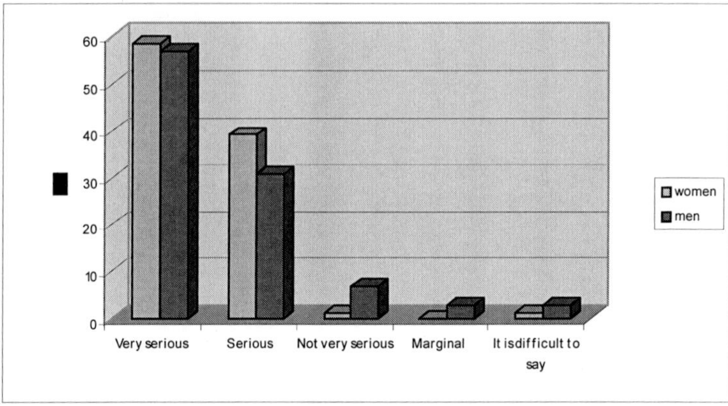


It seems interesting that most people who could not recall concrete cases of money laundering claimed that legalization of financial means posed a very serious, both global and regional, threat.

The answer "serious" was given as second with respect to the global and regional threat. In case of respondents who declared to have heard about money laundering, these proportions were reverse. Here, the chi-square statistics value is close to the critical value, which does not mean that this correlation is important from the statistical point of view (the test statistics value $\chi^2 = 6.67$ with the critical value $\chi^2 = 7.81$ *in a* global scale and $\chi^2 = 6.51$ with the critical value $\chi^2 = 7.81$ in a regional scale).

The presented differences in views on the regional and global threat do not apply to opinions concerning the national (state) threat, whichin both cases, was regarded as "very serious".

**Table 4: Determination of degree of threat with respect to financial systems on global, regional and local scale (in %)**

| Threat to financial systems | Globe | Region | State |
|---|---|---|---|
| Very serious | 41.13 | 35.09 | 57.74 |
| Serious | 43.77 | 49.81 | 35.85 |
| I do not know | 6.42 | 4.15 | 1.89 |
| Not very serious | 6.42 | 9.06 | 3.40 |
| Marginal | 2.26 | 1.89 | 1.13 |

## Cases of Money Laundering Process in Respondents' Opinions

47.92% of respondents declared to have heard about a particular case of money laundering. By contrast, 4.53% of the test group members did not hear about activities aiming at legalization of financial means. The pie chart below presents a strikingly big percentage of "I do not remember" answers, which may also prove that respondents did not attach importance to this sort of information and quickly forgot it. This group comprised as many as 47.55% of the test group members.

The following quality features have a considerable influence on the process of acquiring and remembering information about concrete cases of money laundering: type of studies ($\chi^2$= 13.01 - Figure 5) and respondents' gender ($\chi^2$ = 19.56 6).

The differences in opinions with respect to the gender showed that men declared a greater ability to acquire and remember this type of information. 62.5% of men claimed to have heard of such information. By contrast, 61.50% of women denied hearing about a particular case of money laundering.

**Figure 5. Differences in opinions expressed by students representing different universities with respect to contact with information about concrete case of money laundering**

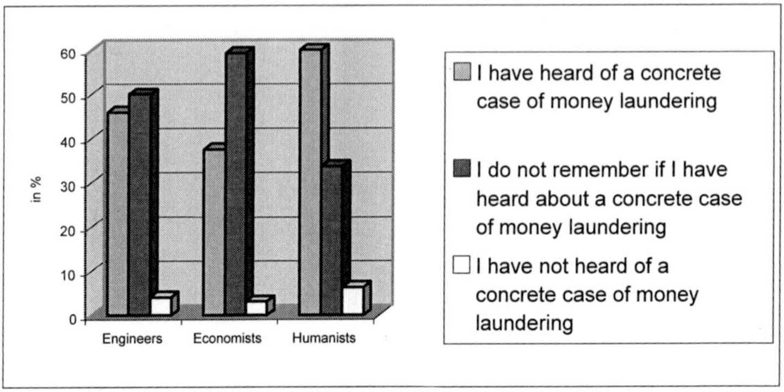


This differentiation becomes more complex while analyzing the influence exerted by a particular type of university or course of studies on students' ability to acquire and remember information about money laundering. In the case of two types of studies: engineering and economics, the answers: I do not remember, or I have not had any contact with such information were dominant. With respect to the volume of answers there was a noticeable difference between these two schools, with 62.51% for the University of Economics and 54.05% for the Polytechnic. A completely different situation was observed among humanists where majority of students, as many as 60%, declared their contact with information about money laundering, 33.68% did not remember hearing about concrete cases of money laundering and 6.32% did not have any contact with such information. Respondents who heard about cases of money laundering pointed out the most spectacular economic-political scandals in the country.

The aggregation of different cases of money laundering allowed for distinction of two more general categories. Within the first category, 7.93% of respondents pointed out cases in which formal state institutions such as Parliamentary Commissions and the Public Prosecutor's Office made allegations of money laundering. The second category comprised cases where the problem of funds legalization came up in the context of conveyed information. This opinion was expressed by 8.67% of students.

The aggregation of fields of informal business and criminal operations based on respondents' answers (Figure 6) helped to distinguish two areas of organised criminal activity:

"Dirty criminal activity" - popular one, often being a subject of films involving drugs, kidnapping and contract murders.

"Clean criminal activity" - defined as white-collar crimes, invisible activities followed by top specialists employing the latest scientific and technological tools.

**Figure 6. Areas of organised criminal operations according to respondents**

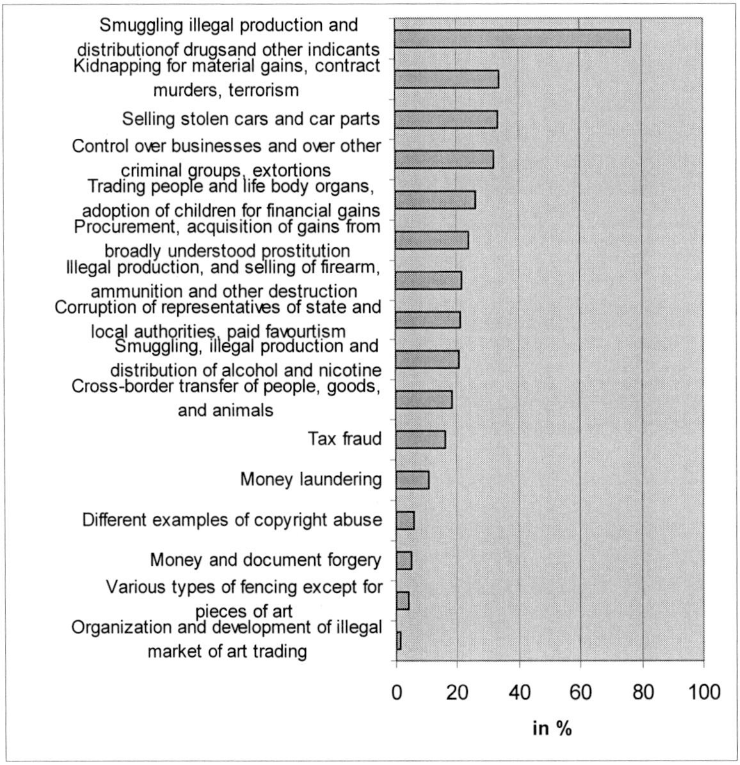


The rating proposed by respondents was dominated by the first group of crimes with the overwhelming opinion - 76.98% that creation and management of drug market is one of the interest areas of organised criminal operation. The list of other crimes with half as many indications - 34.34%, was opened by murders, contract kidnapping and terrorism. Crimes of a financial character were classified only in the second part of the list, whereas tax fraud, considered in broader terms, was pointed out by 15.47% of respondents.

With respect to the influence of quality features on the way of defining smuggling, illegal production and distribution of drugs and other intoxicants, it turned out that only one quality feature-namely the type of university, was important for the definition of this area of interest and activity of criminal groups. The differentiation in opinions was characterised by huge diversity in the structure of expressed opinions between students who either indicated or who omitted smuggling, illegal production and distribution of drugs and other intoxicants as an area of interest and activity of criminal groups.

**Figure 7: Smuggling, illegal production and distribution of drugs and other intoxicants recognised as area of interest of criminal groups**

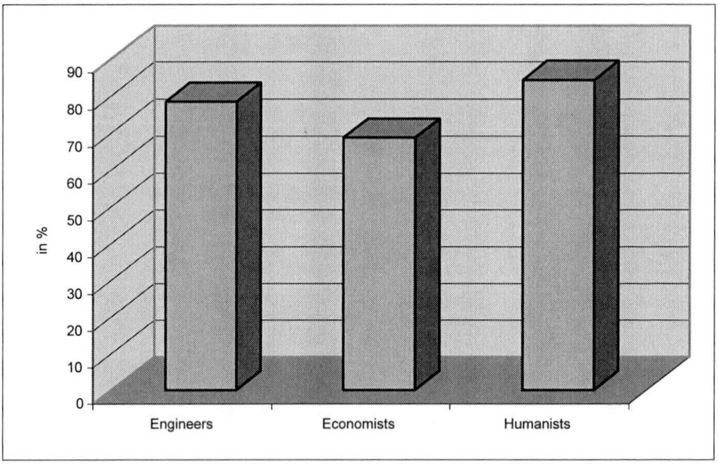


## Events Connected with the Prevention of The Process of Money Laundering in Respondents' Opinions

The definition of funds legalization and the determination of respondents' familiarity with events related to money laundering constitute two out of five elements of the whole picture of the phenomenon. The third element of this picture refers to presentation of strategic assumptions of money laundering prevention and to introduction of local as well as international initiatives in this respect. According to the results of the study, 53.96% of respondents related money laundering prevention to such operational activities as identification of transactions and, if possible, their suspension. 46.04% of test group members did not agree with such an opinion, including 21.51% of those who claimed that prevention was based on the interception of illicit funds by the Central Investigation Office. Moreover, 17.36% of students did not know what money laundering prevention consisted in, whereas 3.77% associated the process with a deliberate transfer of dirty money to the National Bank of Poland, and 1.89% of students connected the prevention with a transfer of illicit funds to commercial banks accompanied by notification of the procedure submitted to the National Bank of Poland. The remaining group of students, 1.51%, related prevention strategies to some other activities.

**Table 5: Respondents' opinions with respect to money laundering prevention (in %)**

| The scope of the definition of money laundering prevention | Result |
|---|---|
| Identification of transactions and, if possible, their suspension | 53.96% |
| Interception of illicit funds by the Central Investigation Office | 21.51% |
| I do not know what money laundering prevention consists in | 17.36% |
| Deliberate transfer of dirty money to the National Bank of Poland | 3.77% |
| Transfer of dirty money to commercial banks with a simultaneous notification of the procedure to the National Bank of Poland | 1.89% |
| Other operational activities not mentioned above | 1.51% |

In order to arrive at a proper interpretation of the results for their further practical use, it was necessary to make some aggregation of the expressed opinions into two more general categories:

1. Money laundering prevention consists in identification of suspicious

transactions and, if possible, suspension of such transactions.

2. Other activities indicated within proposed answers.

61.05% of the Silesian University students and 48.65% to 51.04% students of the two remaining schools shared the opinion that money laundering prevention was related to identification, and if possible, suspension of suspicious transactions. The majority of students at the Polytechnic associated money laundering prevention with all other operation activities except for identification and suspension of suspicious transactions (51.35%). Most students of the University of Economics (51.04%) declared that money laundering prevention was based on identification, and possible suspension of suspicious transactions.

**Figure 8: Differences in opinions with respect to strategies of money laundering prevention according to type of studies**

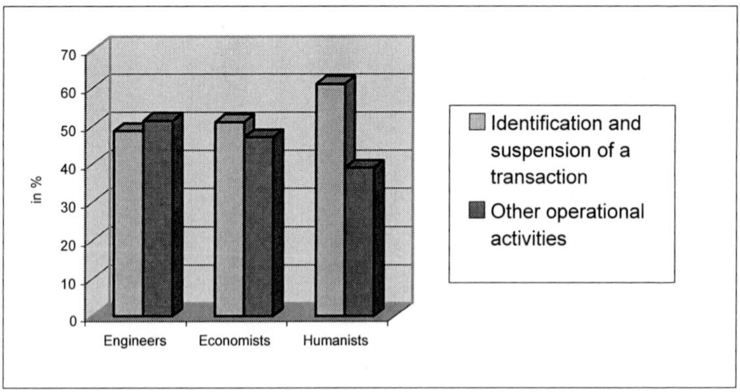


## THE ROLE AND QUALITY OF INFORMATION IN THE PROCESS OF MONEY LAUNDERING RECOGNITION ACCORDING TO RESPONDENTS

The classification of information sources allowed for a statistical distinction of two categories of media:

1. Media that was pointed out by 70% of respondents.
2. Other media that was indicated by less that 70% of respondents.

Within the first category, an analysis was carried out with respect to five quality features and the chi-square test of independence in order to determine if any of the features affects respondents' preferences for particular sources of information.

Within the second category a distinction was made between two groups that differed in terms of number of respondents indicating particular sources of information:

a) media of indirect significance in the system of message conveyance:

- radio – 50.39%
- the Internet – 45.67%
- friends and colleagues – 33.86%

b) media closing the list:

- books – 7.87%
- other sources of information – 6.30%

The structure of the second group is illustrated in Figure 9.

**Figure 9: Variety of sources of information about cases of money laundering**

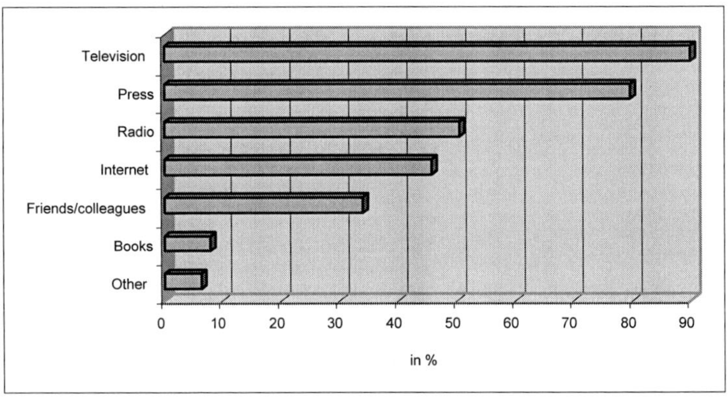


It is noteworthy that proportions of the assessment of press, radio and TV information were almost identical: TV – 86.79%, radio -85.28% and press – 84.15%

## Characteristics of Students' Attitudes Towards Economic and Financial Pathologies

In order to characterise motives of ethically justified decisions with regard to financial events (but directly relating to people), respondents were asked to share reflections on accidental finding of 100 PLN (around 25 EURO). The results are presented in Table 6.

**Table 6: Reflections declared by respondents on finding 100 PLN (in %)**

| Reflections | Result |
|---|---|
| Thanks to the accidental money the purchase of a desired object has become more realistic | 46.42 |
| I have a feeling of internal contradiction: I gained 100 PLN at the cost of another person who disapproved of this behaviour as a possible manner of conduct | 32.08 |
| I am worried that somebody has lost, maybe their last 100 PLN this month | 11.70 |
| I have doubts if circumstances of acquiring the money can guarantee full anonymity | 4.91 |
| Other reflections, and if possible, please describe them | 4.91 |

The presented opinions were dominated by two contradictory reflections. The first opinion was shared by students (46.42%) who opted for their individual interpretation of utility, where the acquisition of some money belonging to another person enabled them the purchase of a desired object. An extremely different view (32.08%) was held by students who claimed that their duty towards individually perceived utility was of prior importance. Respondents who sympathised with the money loser accounted only for 11.08%.

With reference to the statement that "the first million in business should be stolen" 19.25% of students gave a positive answer, including 4. 53% of "Yes" and 14.72% of "Supposedly yes" answers. The majority of respondents were against the statement (69.81%), with 42.26% of "Not" and 27.55% of "Supposedly not" answers. 10.94% of respondents were unable to give a precise opinion on the issue. Figure 11 illustrates the structure of presented views.

**Figures 11: Differences in opinions on statement that the first million in business should be stolen**

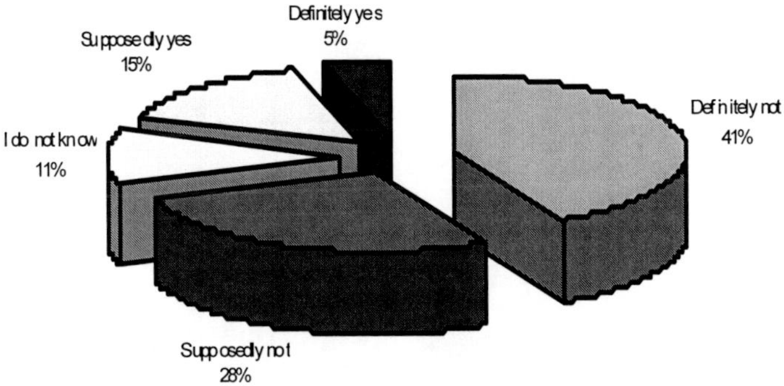


**Figure 12: Presents a hierarchy and types of justifications of opinions with respect to stealing the first million within conducted business operation**

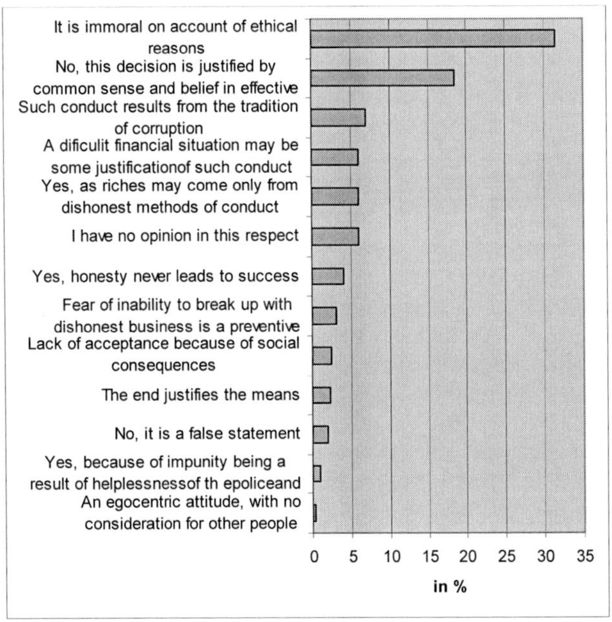

The final element of the research was connected with determination of a degree of acceptance or rejection of the Roman adage "Pecunia non olet" - money does not smell. The structure of the opinions is illustrated in Figure 13.

**Figure 13: Different degrees of acceptance of adage "Pecunia Non Olet"**

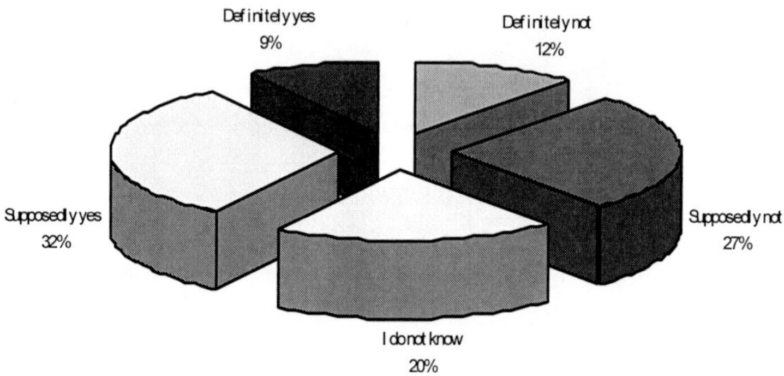


The aggregation of the results into three more general categories produced two groups of opposite views with equal percentage share. The students who accepted the adage accounted for 41.13%, whereas those who rejected it accounted for 38.87%. There was a relatively big share of students who were not able to express any opinion in this regard (20.00%), which may have been caused by lack of knowledge on circumstances of the adage development or unfamiliarity with "Pecunia non olet".

The hierarchy and justifications, either accepting or rejecting the adage, are illustrated in Figure 14.

Among justifications which accounted for more than 10%, two opinions implied rejection of the adage, including: 16.60% of students shared the conviction that conforming one's behaviour to the adage "Pecunia non olet" was immoral and 14.34% of respondents claimed that only dirty money smelt, and one opinion (13.58%) accepted it as one of the elements of the ethical code: money has magical power, whatever its origin.

It is noteworthy that the structure of opinions expressed by both atheists and Catholics was similar with respect to:
1. the degree of acceptance of the adage “Pecunia non olet”,
2. the degree of acceptance of the statement that the first million in business should be stolen,
3. the reflection on finding 100 PLN.
These correlations are presented in Figures 15.

Both in the group of Catholics and atheists, the biggest percentage share was accounted for by respondents who indicated the answer “Supposedly yes” or “Supposedly not”, with a small dominance of students accepting the adage “Pecunia non olet”. With respect to very definite opinions (“yes” or “no”), in the group of Catholics the majority of respondents were against the statement, whereas in the group of atheists most opinions were in favour of the statement.

The gradual character of the assessments and the order of their appearance were almost identical. Majority of students did not approve of behaviour that conformed to the statement that the first million in business should be stolen. Surprisingly, there was a big group of students who were unable to present any opinion in this respect. However, with regard to reflections on finding 100zł (Figure 19), a practical use of the opportunity took precedence over other choices.

The obtained results provide solid grounds for the thesis that majority of students have an individually elaborated system of values and codes of conduct. Both the Catholics and the atheists either accepted or rejected the adage “Pecunia non olet” in a way that was not representative of their religious views. An identical correlation with respect to the structure of presented views was observed in the remaining studies concerning reflections on finding 100 PLN and acceptance or rejection of the statement that the first million in business should be stolen.

**Figure 14: Differences in students' opinions with respect to either acceptance or rejection of adage "Pecunia Non Olet"**
(in %)

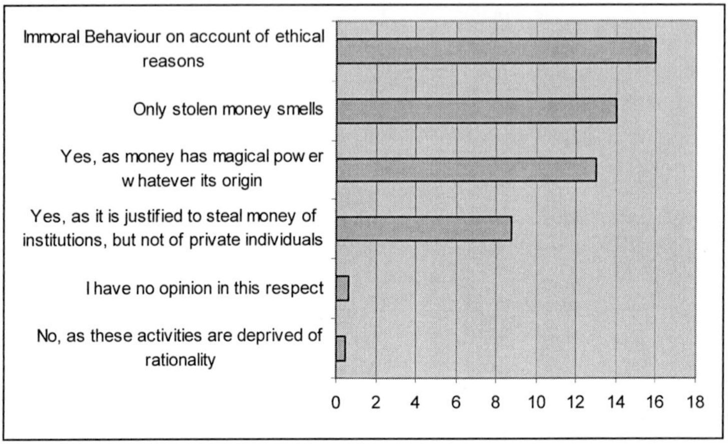


**Figure 15: Differences in opinions concerning acceptance of economic and financial pathologies among students of diverse religious views**

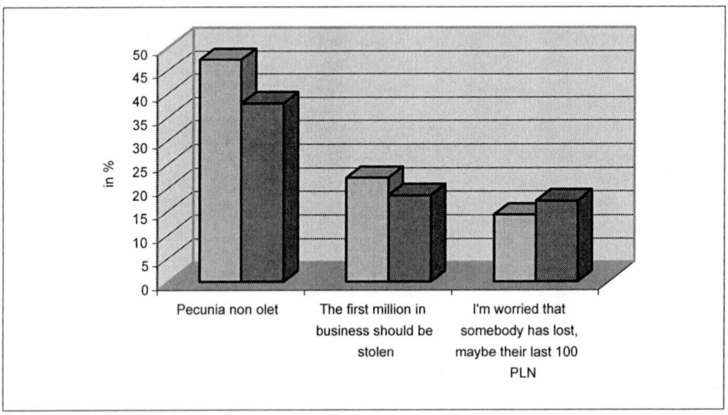

## Conclusion

The process of money laundering is of strategic importance to organised criminal groups that constitute informal economic power of the contemporary world. Money laundering enables "legal consumption" of enormous sums of money that come from illegal and undisclosed sources. The character of the process with respect to its tendencies for:
a) achievement of the climax of money legalization from any stage of the process,
b) perfectly elaborated self-regulation in terms of intensity of the phenomenon occurrence,
c) stability in relations with the closest environment, has contributed to great adaptability of the process. Consequently, it harmonizes with every environment and functions in:
a) developed countries where the society is the main consumer of the drug business,
b) structures of the European international integration,
c) states under system transformations,
d) totalitarian and pauperised states.

The economic and political transformations in the CEE have obliged Polish authorities to take preventive measures, which seem revolutionary for the Polish penal law at the turn of the 20$^{th}$ and 21$^{st}$ centuries. The strategy of money laundering prevention has been mainly concentrated on the formation of proper behaviour of people who are most exposed to unconscious participation in the process of money legalization on account of their professional responsibilities. Graduates of schools of higher education are potential employees of financial institutions, and in this context the presented results may constitute one of key elements influencing the current knowledge of Poles' attitudes to the process of money laundering.

The results provide grounds for the definition of an organized crime as gigantic potential of unlimited technical and financial possibilities, aimed at dominating and subduing the public life mainly by drug business and development of traditional organised crimes, such as contract murders and contract kidnapping, terrorism and intimidations and extortions. According to respondents, the main operational activities of the process of money laundering are connected with issuance of counterfeited invoices, with smuggling and with exchange of financial means in banks and exchange bureaus. With respect to the definition of interest areas of organised crime and classification of money legalization methods, respondents did not mention the newly developed areas directly related to the international integration within the European Union. In view of threats to the stability of financial systems, over 75% of respondents were convinced that money laundering was dangerous or very dangerous to financial systems.

The study results have brought out two very interesting types of information, which refer to the number of people who heard about money laundering-related cases, and those who heard about initiatives and activities connected with prevention of money laundering.

47.92% of respondents claimed to have heard about money laundering, whereas 14.34% admitted that they had heard about preventive measures. It can be observed that the opinions are strongly influenced by the ongoing debate on connections of political elites with the criminal world. Taking into consideration the study results in terms of sources, quality and importance of information, it can be concluded that respondents obtain their knowledge from two sources: radio and television. In spite of positive opinions about radio, television and the press regarded as "credible" or "rather credible" sources of information, respondents critically referred to the broad media coverage of financial and economic pathologies.

Majority of students (69.81%) did not approve of the opinion that "the first million in business should be stolen". 32.08% of respondents justified their decision by considering this behaviour immoral without reference to the ethical imperative. Another group of respondents (18.87%) was convinced of effectiveness of the honest behaviour based on common sense. The opinions concerning the Roman adage "Pecunia non olet" - money does not smell, seem very interesting with respect to further use of the study results in the development of educational programs on money laundering. However, the balance between opinions in favour of the adage (41.13%) and against it (38.87%) calls for some considerations. These opinions are complemented by the following justifications:
a) immoral behaviour on account of ethical reasons – 16.60%,
b) only stolen money smells – 14.34%,
c) money has magical power whatever its source and origin – 13.58%,
d) illegal money can be accepted only in a difficult situation – 9.06%.

A personal approach to the events assessed on the basis of religious beliefs constitutes an important element in the general picture of Poles' attitudes to the phenomenon of money laundering and pathologies of economic-financial character. The assessments were similar, no matter how the events were interpreted by Catholics or atheists.

One of the main objectives of the study was to present its pragmatic character and to provide some possibilities of a practical use of the research into the phenomenon of money laundering. Thanks to this, the study results can be used in: further research into the problem of Poles' attitudes towards introduction of illegal and secret money into the public circulation, education of university and secondary school students acquiring banking and financial knowledge, auxiliary materials for people in charge of development of school and university educational programs with respect to strategies of presentation of a real influence of economic-financial pathologies, including money laundering, on proper functioning of national and international systems, suggestions for people responsible for teaching the subject of business ethics at schools or universities and training-educational materials for personnel of financial institutions.

## Notes

[1] Al. Capone, the founder of a modern criminal organization whose activity involved corruption of politicians and police representatives, extortions, illegal gambling, and management of brothels. The gigantic annul proceeds of 60 mln dollars of that time (at present it equals about 2 billion dollars) were gained through illegal alcohol trafficking in the whole area of the State of Illinois. Al Capone was sentenced to 10 years in prison for evading tax on winnings gained in an illegal casino.

[2] Al. Capone bought a chain of city laundries and introduced illegal money into the legal circulation through fictitious proceeds from fictitious services.

## References

Bartosiak, A., (2003). Zakazany owoc lepiej smakuje, *Rzeczpospolita*, No. 14.

Bojarski, J., (2001). *Przestępstwa związane z działalnością banków*. Toruń: TONiK.

Czajkowski, M., (2002) Brudny pieniądz musi smerfować, *Gazeta Wyborcza*, No. 75

Engel J.F., Blackwell R.D., Mirniard P.W. (1986). *Consumer Behavior*, New York: The Dryden Press

Fijałek, K., (2001). Kamienice. Gangsterzy inwestują w krakowskie nieruchomości, *Gazeta Wyborcza*, No. 247

Gilmore, W.G., (1999). *Brudne pieniądze: metody przeciwdziałaniu brudnych pieniędzy*. Warszawa: Polskie Wydawnictwo Ekonomiczne

Jackson, J., ed. (2004). *Zarys historii Europy*, XX wiek. Warszawa: Świat Książki

Jasiński, W., (2002). Nie puszcza brudu, *Rzeczpospolita*, No. 17

Kęsicka, K., (1993) Pieniądze w pralni, *Gazeta Wyborcza*, No. 91

Kościelniak, P., (1999). Technika wyprzedza policję, *Rzeczpospolita*, No. 18

—. (1996). Pranie elektronicznych pieniędzy, *Rzeczpospolita*, No. 25

Kowalski, M., (2001). Wielka pralnia, *Gazeta Wyborcza*, No. 228

Lerbell, L., (1978). *Współczesne Zagadnienia Polityki Kryminalnej*. Problemy kryminologiczne penelogiczne. Warszawa: Wydawnictwo Prawnicze

Matusz, J., (2002). Cypryjskie interesy, *Rzeczpospolita*, No. 19

Niklewicz, K., (2002) Raport o podatkowych rajach. Pralnia Luksemburg?, *Gazeta Wyborcza*, No. 19

Pracki, H., (1995). *Obrót gospodarczy pod ochroną, przepisy prawne, komentarze*. Warszawa: INFOR.

Wąsowski, K., Wąsowski, W., (2001). *Pranie brudnych pieniędzy, poradnik dla bankowców*. Warszawa: Biblioteka Menedżera i Bankowca.

Wotava, M., (2000). *Podatkowe raje*. Kraków: Małopolska Oficyna Wydawnicza Korona.

Wójcik, J., (1997). Problem, który narasta, *Rzeczpospolita*, No. 14

Wójcik, J.W., (2002). Zachować czujność , *Rzeczpospolita*, No. 20.

Zadworny, A., (2002). Jak ganag inwestował, *Gazeta Wyborcza*, No. 67

# SECTION IV:

# HUMAN RELATIONSHIP MANAGEMENT

# INTERCULTURAL COMPETENCES FOR ENHANCED BUSINESS RELATIONS WITH LITHUANIAN COMPANIES. A FRANCO-GERMAN STUDY

CHRISTOPHE MORACE, ALISON GOURVÈS-HAYWARD AND MARIO GLOWIK

## Abstract

This article builds on our previous research, which shows that intercultural competences are necessary to develop and maintain long-term international relationships. Using the data from semi-structured interviews, we demonstrate and analyse the intercultural management competences shown by both French and German managers doing business with small and medium businesses in Lithuania. The interpersonal competences, which emerged strongly from these interviews are presented and categorized using Byram's intercultural communicative competence model (ICC), which combines attitudes, knowledge, skills and critical cultural awareness. These findings are then further analysed in terms of intercultural management competences using the cultural dimensions that are well established in the literature and Demorgon's multiperspectivist theory. This three-tiered analysis will both provide a framework for future work in the field and recommendations for enhanced business relations with Lithuanian companies.

## Introduction

It is now well established in the management literature, that intercultural skills are necessary to conduct business in an international context (Hofstede 1993; Trompenaars, 1998; Chevrier, 2000; Adler 2002). Many studies of multinational enterprises (MNEs) show that managers and employees develop and apply intercultural skills in daily business situations. These studies stress that MNE staff are highly aware of the importance of such skills and of the need for appropriate recruitment policies and training programmes.

Unfortunately, there is a paucity of literature analysing intercultural skills in small and middle enterprises (SMEs) (Morace & Schulze, 2005, 2006). The few existing studies call for more research on the subject, for several reasons. Firstly, SMEs account for the vast majority of European and indeed world business. Secondly, SMEs, like MNEs, face fierce international competition but do not seem to have enough intercultural resources to compete. Finally, they have fewer employees with the specialized skills of MNE-staff and do not generally pay so much attention to intercultural skills in the business process, including recruitment and training of their staff.

In the present article, we start from the general premise, as demonstrated in our previous research, that SMEs in Western Europe need intercultural competences to do business with countries of Eastern Europe (Gourvès-Hayward & Morace, 2005; Morace & Schulze, 2005, 2006). Our present objective is to discover and analyse the specific intercultural competences that are needed to do business with Lithuanian companies. SMEs in Western countries have had limited experience with newcomers and particularly with small countries like the Baltic States and Lithuania. Our former research (Glowik & Morace, 2006) has shown that SMEs in France and Germany are willing to do business with Lithuanian companies but they face challenges and difficulties that may be linked to intercultural competences.

In the following, we present the intercultural skills that emerge from business relations between Lithuanian companies and SMEs located in Brittany (France) and Saarland (Germany). We will first introduce our theoretical framework, which includes a definition of intercultural competences, cultural models for management and Jacques Demorgon's multiperspectivist theory. Secondly, we will present our methodology, including data collection and presentation of semi-structured interviews conducted in SMEs in Brittany and in Saarland. Thirdly, the results, which emerged from the interviews, in terms of intercultural competences, will be presented and categorized using Byram's intercultural communicative competence model. Finally, these findings are further analysed in terms of intercultural management competences using the cultural dimensions that are well established in the literature and Demorgon's multiperspectivist theory. This three-tiered analysis will both provide a theoretical framework for future work in the field and recommendations for enhanced business relations with Lithuanian companies.

## Theoretical Framework

As our main objective is to discover which intercultural competences French and German SMEs use in management situations with Lithuanian companies, a theoretical framework is needed to identify, categorize and analyze intercultural management competences, as opposed to general intercultural competences. In the following section, we propose such a theoretical framework based on the definitions of intercultural competences in the literature and on three combined cultural models (Byram's ICC, cultural dimensions and Demorgon's multiperspectivist theory).

## Definition of Intercultural Competence

In order to clarify our position, we first propose a broad definition of intercultural competences, based on the definitions[1] provided by Landis & Bennett (2004), Meier (2006), and Knapp & Knapp-Pottoff (1990), in Barmeyer (2000), who are all widely known in the field of intercultural management. If we stress the points these three definitions have in common, it seems that an intercultural competence is seen as an ability to act and/or communicate in a pragmatic way in a concrete situation, including not only individuals but groups from different cultures. This definition of intercultural competence presupposes the ability to act effectively in every concrete *situation* but to act effectively by adapting to different cultural *contexts*. By combining these three definitions, we can define intercultural competence as *the ability to interact appropriately in different cultural situations and contexts*.

However, in spite of these common points, the three definitions selected also have many differences, which we highlight in the following. Such differences in the definitions, perhaps intercultural themselves, show the diversity and the complexity of the notion of intercultural competences. There seem to be different possibilities to analyze, to understand, to relate to contexts and to gain knowledge about foreign cultures. Intercultural competences emerge as a learning skill based on cognitive, emotional and behavioural processes. The definitions show that there are different cognitive processes of analyzing, interpreting and understanding the outside world, which operates on several levels of cultural awareness.

Attitudes may also play a role in facilitating interaction and effective communication in a particular situation. Different aspects of the business context also need to be taken into account, in order for intercultural management competences to be developed. The definitions selected show particular or more general conceptions of intercultural management. For instance, should intercultural competences applied to management concern only different missions in a company, such as human resources and marketing or a "professional context" or even a much broader context? If we take business aspects like "efficiency", "productivity" and "goal orientation" into account, it is clear that a business strategy will go beyond marketing and human resources. As intercultural management integrates different environments and countries it may also be concerned with ethical aspects, including values like respect for minorities and "diversity".

After analysing these definitions, we can conclude that in spite of their complementarities, none of them is complete and can show *what* intercultural management competences really are precisely, *how* they can be identified, observed, analysed and explained, or *how* they can be related to practical business situations and adopted by managers. As a consequence, it seems important to adopt an appropriate theoretical framework, such as Demorgon's multiperspectivist theory, which takes the complexity of intercultural situations and contexts into consideration. One or several cultural models for management are also needed in order to show which intercultural competences emerge from business situations, as our task will be (1) to identify, observe and analyse skills in international business situations, (2) to explain to what extent these skilled are intercultural, (3) to give (if possible) advice to implement these intercultural skills in another context.

## Cultural Models for Management

*Dimensional models for intercultural management*: Trompenaars (1998) considers that culture is the way in which a group of people solves problems. As each group of people regularly solves its problems in a common way, this way disappears from consciousness and becomes a "basic assumption" or an "underlying premise". If we assume that different groups of people solve their problems in different ways, basic assumptions, underlying premises and values may vary from one culture to another. Hofstede (2001) suggests that cultures vary in essential patterns of thinking, feeling and acting. At the most concrete level, cultures may vary in terms of dress, food and greeting habits but it seems that it is not these concrete aspects that are the source of intercultural difficulties, especially in business. The greatest intercultural problems arise from more implicit aspects or underlying patterns of culture called "cultural dimensions". Hofstede (2001, 2005) defines dimensions as "an aspect of a phenomenon that can be measured". These dimensions allow comparisons between cultures and some of them are especially applied to business activities. Osland and Bird (2003) present 22 dimensions, Berry (2004) reduces these dimensions to 6 main dimensions (Diversity, Equality, Conformity, Wealth, Space and Time) and Adler retains 3 main dimensions (relationship to time, space and other people (Adler 2002). The intercultural management literature uses "dimensional models" (Hofstede 2005) as sets of dimensions used in order to describe a phenomenon. These dimensions make it possible to identify and categorize cultural differences but they cannot explain the cultural behaviour of individuals and the organisation and strategies of companies. The widely used "dimensions models" in the management literature therefore need to be completed with further models.

## Multiperspectivist Theory

Demorgon's multiperspectivist theory, which analyses the complexity of cognitive, emotional and behavioral processes in a given intercultural situation, was chosen as an analytical framework for our research. This theory is based on an epistemology (Demorgon, 2004b), which integrates the different perspectives provided by such diverse disciplines as biology, physics, history, sociology and psychology (Demorgon, 2002). It was first developed in 1993, in order to analyze the interaction between a Franco-German group of action researchers, including one of the authors of this article. As we will show below, it provides an appropriate research model and analytical tool to analyze intercultural situations of management.

### Creation of Culture through Pre-adaptive Opposites

For Demorgon, the concept of culture is connected to the way human beings constantly adapt to their environment, attempting to establish a long and stable relationship between their inner world (cognition, emotions, behavior) and the outer world (other people/ environment). According to Demorgon, culture – as a closing and opening system – is a chain of human activities, which are continually involved in a production process. Culture is therefore a human construct, which is deeply rooted, in a specific context and a "singular" (unique) situation, resulting from both diachronic and synchronic processes.

Demorgon explains the synchronic production of culture through two concepts called "action process" and "pre-adaptive antagonisms" ("antagonismes pré-adaptatifs"). In accordance with the principle of co-evolution, the human being can only survive if s/he both complies with the environment and transforms it at the same time. This antagonism between action and situation is given in every society and in every culture. Demorgon describes this first antagonism between situation and action as co-evolution. Antagonisms can be termed as pre-adaptive or (complementary) opposites because they are pre-established before every action. These opposites are adaptive and complementary because each action will change the situation, but the situation will have a retroactive effect on the action itself.

Each (intercultural) situation offers many possibilities for what Demorgon terms "oscillation" between two or more opposites. Oscillation denotes the human ability to choose different gradations between "adapting the situation appropriately" (assimilation) and "adapting appropriately *to* the situation" (accommodation). Antagonisms can be pictured on a virtual line between two or more poles representing the whole range of behavior as "potential oscillation". Cultural orientation limits the possibilities to a smaller range of "habitual oscillation". Each individual has the possibility to develop his or her "habitual oscillation" and to transform it into "potential oscillation" through informed action. Thus, as Demorgon & Molz (1996) point out, the cultural dimensions posited by Hall or Hofstede could be described as binary adaptive antagonisms, which will not only reflect cultural tendencies but will also be adapted according to the individual situation.

According to this theory, each individual has the possibility of acting in accordance with his or her own culture or, on the other hand, with another culture. The minimum requirements for oscillation to take place are motivation, the necessary knowledge about the foreign culture and the time to adapt to the new situation. If there is no time available to gain adapted knowledge, s/he will react to a new situation with his or her own culturally biased knowledge. In a given situation, culture will provide the pre-adaptive opposites that are more appropriate to the situation. However, Demorgon stresses the fact that culture will not impose only one specific action but a range of possible actions on an adaptive axis of these pre-adaptive opposites. In every situation influenced by culture, the individual has the possibility to choose or to oscillate.

## Six Perspectives for Cultural Analysis

Every synchronic intercultural situation is embedded in a specific context, which can be described from the following perspectives at the origin or as products of culture (Demorgon 2004). The *field* (religious, political, economic or technological) and the *levels* (individual, corporate and/or national) where cultural interactions take place should be taken into consideration. These different *fields* and *levels* are interesting to enable us to differentiate between different aspects of an intercultural situation and to identify the focus of our informants. For instance, for cultural reasons, French managers tend to privilege the economic and technological *field* and ignore the religious *field*, which is considered to be a private matter (Adler 2002), whereas German companies tend to underestimate the influence of the political *field* in business (Morace 1997). Furthermore, a distinction should be made between what is dependent on *self-organization* (or dealing with uncertainty) and what is dependent on the *strategy* of the different actors. A company needs a *strategy* which can be either culturally influenced or not, but its members must also be open to unpredictable factors or changes, to which they have to adapt in a *synchronic* way. Finally, it is also important to analyze *synchronic* intercultural situations from the *diachronic* or time perspective. Demorgon explains that, through the repetition of synchronic oscillations over centuries, a specific new culture or new cultures in general are produced diachronically.

## Multiperspectivist Theory as a Pragmatic Tool

Jacques Demorgon's theory and methodology provide a useful pragmatic tool, which enables us to work on different levels. Firstly, it describes the process of cultural interaction and production of culture in a given situation. Secondly, it facilitates consciousness-raising for cultural awareness and provides some orientation, knowledge, problem solving and decision-making tools for practitioners and researchers. Finally, it makes it possible to observe and analyze negotiation, cooperation and teamwork in a situation of intercultural communication and management. His methodology draws on the different cultural dimensions provided in the intercultural literature (high vs. low context, long vs. short power distance etc.) but it goes far beyond a purely comparative-descriptive approach that remains partial and therefore possibly biased.

## Methodology, Data Collection and Presentation

In order to use a research paradigm that corresponds to our research questions and to the needs of both informants and researchers, we used an exploratory approach. This was based on qualitative content analysis of interviews describing singular professional situations and practices. Rae & Carswell (2000) recommend this methodology in order to "identify and analyse" intercultural skills, especially with entrepreneurs and informants working in SMEs. Other researchers also give priority to analyzing professional practices in SMEs using a narrative and interpretative framework based on content analysis (Cope 2003, Erikson 2003, Rogoff et al. 2004). Pavlenko & Lantolf (2000) point out that the narrative genre is gaining increasing stature as a rich, meaningful, data source which may bring to the surface aspects of human activity not always captured by more traditional research. This paradigm and methodology make it possible to focus on the singularity of real, situated, hands-on intercultural situations where intercultural competences may emerge.

## Exploratory and Interpretative Methodology

In terms of methodology, we analysed the experience of the managers interviewed using a method based on the production of categories identified through analytical categories and indicators, in the tradition of Grounded Theory (Glaser & Strauss, 1967; Corbin & Strauss 1998). More specifically, we used Müller's interpretative method for content analysis of intercultural contexts (1995). Müller recommends the reconstruction of an extract of social reality through qualitative (semi-structured) interviews. The analysis of interview transcriptions is based on reflective interpretation by the informants themselves (Müller 1995). The first stage, A, concerns the construction of an "extract of social reality". Müller (1995) understands "social reality" as the description (in their own words and after the events) of experiences interviewees have had and of what they have learned for further action in the future. This learning experience constitutes an "episode". The construction of the social reality that interviewees interpret in a reflective way constitutes stage B, called the constitution of the episode in the situation itself. The transcription of each narrated episode constitutes stage C. In the final stage, D, it is then possible to identify intercultural competences which may be used to make recommendations for effective action in an intercultural context.

## Data Collection and Analysis

### Data and Interviews

In Stage, A, our data corresponds to an extract of "the social reality" of managers involved in international activities. In this first stage, the context of companies and the situation of the managers interviewed whose statements will be later on analysed and interpreted are described. The companies were selected in Brittany and in Saarland according to the criteria set up by Wöhe (1986). For each company, these criteria include the sector of activity, the type of production, the type of product, the size of the company (capital, number of employees, turn over and export rate) corporate name, the date of creation, distribution networks and channels. We organized our sample in the following way. In both countries, SMEs specialized in the production, import and export of machine tools were identified. In Germany they had between 15 and 500 employees with a turnover of between 6 and 50 million euros, while in France they had between 3 and 250 employees and a turnover of between 3 and 32 million euros. Contacts were provided by the Chambers of Commerce in the respective countries. In Germany, 53 SMEs were selected, 43 companies were questioned and 9 qualitative interviews were conducted. In Brittany, 31 enterprises were questioned and 8 qualitative interviews were conducted. These numbers reflect both regional trends and international figures which place Germany as Lithuania's second most important trade partner after Russia whereas France is in seventh place (Glowik & Morace, 2006). In both countries, interviews took an average of 90 minutes (by telephone or in situ). The interviewees were Company Directors or Export or Production Managers and were all men between 35 and 65 years of age, again a reflection of the current situation in German and French SMEs in the industrial sector. All of them were directly involved in international affairs and the export activities of their company.

### Analysis of Interviews

The contents of the 9 German and 8 French interviews represent Stage B, the constitution of the episode describing the situation, that is to say the description of the international activities by the managers themselves. The main objective of the interviews consisted in identifying the international activities of the managers. As they were semi-structured interviews, the following questions were asked: What was the purpose of the international strategy of the company? Which problems did the company encounter and how did it solve them? What about the results and success of the company?

## Data Presentation

Stage C – is based on a narrative analysis of a verbatim transcription of the interviews. The interpersonal competences, which emerged strongly from these interviews are presented and categorized using Byram's intercultural communicative competence model (ICC) which combines attitudes, knowledge, skills and critical cultural awareness. Once our data has been categorized according to the intercultural communicative competences demonstrated, they are further analysed using both the cultural dimensions present in the literature and Demorgon's perspectives.

### Five Saviors

The five *savoirs* model was developed by Byram, Zarate and others (Byram & Zarate 1994; Byram 1997; Byram, Gribkova & Starkey 2002) as guidelines for the skills and competences aimed at in the teaching of language and culture. They were adopted by the Common European Framework of Reference for Language and Culture teaching (Kelly, Elliott & Fant, 2001), interestingly retaining the French terminology. Byram et al built on the tradition of communicative foreign language teaching and focus specifically on informed communication and interaction with the other, across cultural boundaries. Their work on ICC (Intercultural Communicative Competence) can be extended beyond language and culture teaching to provide a framework for identifying ICC in other contexts (Morace & Gourvès-Hayward, 2007). The five *savoirs* are defined as follows:

***Savoir-être (attitudes and values)****:* Ability to see yourself as someone from another culture might see you, to question what you previously took for granted, and to accept the validity of different cultural attitudes and values. Attitudes of curiosity and openness.
***Savoirs (Knowledge)****:* Knowledge of the social organisation, institutions, products and practices and expectations of one's own and other cultures. Knowledge of both the visible and invisible signs of beliefs, behaviours,

values and assumptions which are learned by groups of people from different cultural backgrounds

***Savoir-faire & savoir apprendre*** *(skills of discovery and interaction): Ability* to acquire and demonstrate cultural knowledge and to operate knowledge, attitudes and skills.

***Savoir-comprendre (skills of interpreting and relating)****:* Ability to interpret ideas, documents or events from one's own or another culture and to relate them to one's own and other's social identity.

***Savoir s'engager (critical cultural awareness)****:* Ability to evaluate products, processes and practices of your own and other cultures with an open-mind in order to proceed on the basis of new perspectives
(Gourvès-Hayward, Kennedy & Sudershan, 2007; LOLIPOP 2007)

The intercultural skills identified by this model can be summed up as the ability to decentre, to stand back from what is taken for granted, to feel at ease with the unfamiliar and to put one's own values into a broader perspective. Both declarative and procedural knowledge about one's own and the other culture and awareness of one's own values, beliefs and behaviours and of those of members of other cultures need to be acquired in order to operate these skills effectively. Attitudes of tolerance and openness towards difference; adaptability, flexibility and sensitivity to verbal and non-verbal communication between members of different cultures, along with the ability to preserve one's own identity are also deemed necessary. These *savoirs* provide us with the analytical categories recommended by Müller (1995) and allow us to identify the intercultural competences demonstrated by our informants. This information will then be contextualized by the use of Demorgon's multisperspectivist model, in order to take the business, national and international environment into account.

## Results: Intercultural Competences

### Intercultural Competences for Business with Lithuania

In Stage D, we observe how intercultural competences are operated in practical business situations. The aim of this section is, firstly to show that intercultural competences emerged from the analysis of the interviews of both French and German companies who state that they have been doing successful business in Lithuania for at least 3 years. Secondly, possible differences in the results of French and German companies will be analysed. In the following, the results are presented in relation to Byram et al's attitudes, knowledge, skills and critical cultural awareness.

***Attitudes****:* Both French and German interviewees pay a lot of attention to their attitudes towards Lithuania. They show a real interest in the country and in its people and are willing to demonstrate to their Lithuanian partners that they want to build up a deep and long term relationship in the business and the private sphere:

> "Cooperation is very good, in the private sphere and in business. It is very important to set up a personal relationship and to build trust in the long term. People in Lithuania are distrustful and are afraid they won't get paid for example. We have to give them the feeling that they are very important for us." (IG-2).

Both Germans and French businessmen avoid a parochial (Adler 2002) approach to doing business with Lithuania and clearly express the idea that there is no one best way of doing business there. They have learned a lot about the changes in Lithuania and appreciate the improvement achieved in the country over the years in terms of living and working standards, quality of products and services, quality management and productivity.

> "Each time I have been there during the last few years in order to analyse the market, I noticed how fast the country was changing in terms of technology, for example". (IF-9)

The informants try to analyse the country from the viewpoint of the Lithuanians and take an interest in the specificities of the Lithuanian market. They are happy to see that their Lithuanian partners appreciate their respective countries:

> "Lithuania is a small country. This country appreciates France. We want to do more business there and it's really possible to do a lot of things there with a niche product." (IF-2);

> "German products are very well accepted (…)." (IG -5)

They show a deep respect for the mentality of Lithuanian people and admiration for their willingness to catch up with Western economies. They argue that they encounter success because they are able to establish personal relationships with their agent or with their direct customers. This is the reason why they are sometimes unhappy that their Lithuanian partners distrust them or when they do not understand why they do not seem to share the same positive attitude or curiosity:

> "Lithuanians are very hospitable, very open-minded, the Managing Director and his sales managers spoke German perfectly but no confidence was built, probably because of too different price ideas." (IG-1)

Finally, it is important to point out that German and French companies show positive attitudes of curiosity and interest in the Lithuanian companies and at the same time lay the foundations for improving their knowledge, skills and critical culture awareness of Lithuania.

***Knowledge***: German and French companies dealing successfully with Lithuanian have gained thorough knowledge about the country in general, its market and its cultural specificities. First of all, they make a clear distinction between the Baltic States in general and Lithuania:

> "The French tend, from a French perspective, to see the Baltic States as a block which is not the case. Actually, we are dealing with three different countries. This has in turn an impact on the way we organized our distribution network. Our agent in Lithuania is German because there are many people there who have a German origin. In Lithuania, we organized a network of direct sales with Lithuanians who speak Russian and Lithuanian. In Estonia, our agent is a Finn. When somebody wants to do business there, he (sic) has to consider these specific aspects."(IF-3).

French and German managers see the advantages of the Lithuanian economy with their skilled workers who are highly motivated and who want to do well and improve. At the same time, they see difficulties with infrastructures, finances, productivity and quality of the products. As a consequence, they anticipate some adaptation in terms of R&D, production, marketing/sales and finances. Before starting their business, they are aware of the fact that they have to acquire some overall knowledge about infrastructure and logistics in general including road, railways, airport and harbour facilities, which do not correspond to Western standards. They search for thorough information about the country including history and recent developments in Lithuanian society. They know a lot about changes in Lithuania since the country separated from the Soviet Union, went its own way and joined the EU. As they know that they have to adapt their products to the market they carry out market studies: *"We did some market research in order to evaluate the business opportunities which are the basis for the business plan."* (IG-8). In terms of production, they have in-depth knowledge of technology, quality and production costs:

> "Particularly the "after- production run" costs are difficult to calculate for us. I think the future is more and more determined by technically sophisticated manufacturing processes. In Germany almost nothing has moved during the last 15 years regarding the real wage costs (there was no increase). But in Germany there is a much better infrastructure and we have access to the latest technologies, which is not the case in the Baltic area. For our product, however, this is very important." (IG-9)

They also know that they have to compensate for the differences in productivity:

> "In the working process, we know that we will have to employ four skilled workers for one single operation in Lithuania whereas only one can carry out the same operation in Germany. As we need skilled workers for our products, we know that it is just an illusion to believe that a good skilled worker in Lithuania will just earn one Euro per hour"(IG-3).

The managers who took part in the interviews have a good understanding of the country in general, its market, including different sectors of activities and products, and detailed knowledge of the organization and working processes in the companies.

***Skills of interpreting and relating**:* Besides an interest in and in-depth knowledge of the business culture in Lithuania, the informants are able to analyse and apply their knowledge consciously, using either general frames of knowledge or specific information acquired through theory or practice. These skills enable them to know what they can achieve in Lithuania and how to do it. Over time, our informants, both German and French were able to interpret their experience and to relate it to business practices in general or with specific working styles, including business meetings and negotiation skills. As far as business practices in general are concerned, French and German companies have developed the ability to relate their business experience in Lithuania to aspects of a transition economy, the resurgence of Russian influence, cultural aspects in Eastern Europe as well as to market, products and distribution networks. As an example, we can see from the following quotation that a French company does not really complain about the Lithuanian company's wish to have a transaction secured with outdated terms of payment. The French manager is able to relate the wish for outdated terms of payment to a lack of experience with the terms of payment within the European Union. He does not distrust or reject the Lithuanian partner but explains through a historical, political and economical context a demand of the company in an economy which is still in transition and therefore out of touch with modern business reality in Europe:

> "They used to have a very Soviet approach to business which was very administrative and not sales driven at all. This has changed over the years, they are more customer-oriented now. But, as far as finance is concerned, their conception of business is not up to date yet. They are inclined to ask for secured terms of payment, which are no longer used in the EU, things like documentary credits or letters of credit or things like that. Nowadays, in the UE, we use credit insurance or just a guarantee from the bank. In this respect, they still have to improve". (IF-7)

French and German managers state that business practices in general are less production-oriented and more and more sales driven and relate this development to the past:

> "They had limited international experience, but things have changed, they improved their marketing and sales approach. In former days they had a very empirical approach to business, saying things like: 'I have products, who would like to buy them?' Now they come to international fairs and sales exhibitions where they put their products on display. (…) In the past they had a Soviet approach 'We have no more products on the shelves because we have no more products in the factory'. Now, they have adopted a fully integrated marketing action, including international fairs, a customer-oriented and sales approach."(IF-8)

Focusing more specifically on exports, the informants stress the importance of finding the appropriate distribution network, depending on the market and the product. They are aware that using different networks will have different impacts on the way to conduct and to see business in Lithuania and that it is therefore impossible to make generalized assessments about business in Lithuania.

> "If you sell machine tools, you lose the contact with your customer shortly after you have performed the sales of one single machine tool because it will last ten years. But if you sell food products for example, you have permanent contact with the customer. Selling machine tools (…) you may access the market through direct sales because you have roughly ten customers over there. As soon as you have sold three machine tools, you can work directly with the customer if you have the mobility and the

mentality to do it. But if you sell consumables, you need an agent. (…) Therefore it is impossible to give general guidelines to do business."(IF-4)

Besides general skills, the interviewees interpret and relate their experience in Lithuania to specific working styles, including business meetings and negotiation skills. They notice that the way to do business is formal. The decision-making process including more people than in France and Germany may take more time. This seems to be due to a more step-by-step, linear and sometimes theoretical approach. The French managers particularly noticed that preparing and conducting meetings in a formal way (including an agenda, detailed written information and a precise schedule) was important do business. *"The working atmosphere is normal and pleasant as long as you took the time to prepare the meeting and to set up a clear agenda."* (IF-6) Some of them even draw a comparison between Lithuanians and Germans:

"Working with Lithuanians is a bit like working with Germans. There is rigour and time for reflection. They take the time to set up a problem… it's not like in Poland. The workforce is highly skilled, full of common sense and takes the time for reflection." (IF-3)

***Skills of discovering and interaction**:* Beside positive attitudes towards Lithuania, in-depth knowledge of the country and the skills of interpreting their business experience and relating it to general frames of reference, the informants have developed a real ability to work with their Lithuanian partners. They have learned through their own experience to use their personal relationships to facilitate their discovering and interacting skills. Many of the *savoirs* quoted above are the results of the discovering and interaction skills, which are enhanced by the wish of Lithuanians to develop personal relationships with their foreign partners. Lithuanian agents especially play an important role in the learning process of the French and German managers:

"As soon as you find a new customer, you have to pay a visit to him/her. They [Lithuanians] are very keen on personal contact (…). In this country, unless you are a multinational company, especially in this market, you need an agent there. And if you want him to do a good job, you often have to go out for dinner and for a drink with him. This belongs to the reminiscence of the old days…. It's true, you have to know people very well there and it's actually the nice part of business. If I had to give at least one piece of advice to SMEs: find a good agent there and build up a very close relationship with him/her."(IF-2)

Agents give their partners, and especially French export managers, the possibility of understanding the country better and play the role of intercultural mediators:

> "We have had a business relationship with Lithuania for 7 or 8 years now. We have an agent in each country. We have had good relationships but I would like to make a big difference between Estonia and Lithuania. Estonians remind me very strongly of Finns. They are silent and hardly speak to us. We flew to Estonia for the first time after a three year long business relationship. They gave us a good, but short reception of 30 minutes after business relationship of 3 years. Can you imagine the long trip we had done! At least, they accompanied us to the door. It works much better with Lithuanians. They are Slavs, they are nice and they are not reluctant to spend more time with us. We had lunch together and we went together for coffee afterwards, just for the fun of it. Anyway, we had been warned by our agent."(IF-1)

Through their close relationship with the Lithuanians and close cooperation in long term technical projects in the country itself, German companies have found that complete delocalisation is not possible and that sometimes relocation is needed.

> "The whole concept should make sense: costs for production, skilled workers, technical equipment and the infrastructure should be adapted. We have had a bad experience with one of the major aspects, which is quality. If we have to employ too many people on quality control, then outsourcing doesn't make sense. Besides this, we run the risk that our know-how could be transferred to local companies". (IG-8)

***Critical cultural awareness (savoir s'engager)***: Close relationships with agents in Lithuania or through technical cooperation on a daily basis in long term projects in the country itself give the Germans and the French the opportunity to check how far their cooperation can go. Their own experience makes it possible for them to address issues in a very critical way, as they can compare official sources with the reality in the field:

> "The statistics about wage costs say nothing. There are wages per hour like € 2 mentioned for example for the Baltic States. This also might be true for some very remote areas where I have to go by Jeep several km to reach my factory. However, a production plant with a relatively developed infrastructure, for example with airport connections, the wages per hour are then 600 to 800 percent higher than mentioned in the official statistics."(IG-6)

Even if they notice some discrepancies between official statements and some doubtful practices in everyday business life, some interviewees have been supporting business in Lithuania for a long time. As a consequence, Lithuanian businesses have been able to develop a real trusting relationship with them over the years.

> "The reasons for our good business relationship go back to the time where we brought them a market. In the past, they were able to produce but they were not able to sell (…). They found in us a reliable partner: we bought their product and sold it in Western Europe. We guaranteed everything including delivery and payment. In fact we went far beyond sales, we provided them with a full service" (IF-2)

The majority of the interviewees have been involved in business with Lithuania for a long time. Based on the positive attitudes quoted above, they have been able to support their Lithuanian colleagues with very close cooperation. After many years of cooperation, they are still willing to work on a long term basis and to provide some know how transfer in order to develop synergies in future:

> "I could go up the wall when I hear opinions why the business has failed with the partners from Lithuania. You really cannot expect it to work if you simply hand over a technical drawing and tell them: please produce this, but of course much cheaper than us. It is necessary to connect these suppliers to their own processes. An established partnership, which is close and based on confidence, provides a big advantage in the long run. It is inevitable that know-how is transferred. Of course one day they will have the same expertise as we have."(IG-4)

As we can see, both German and French interviewees were able to stand back and consciously analyse their relationship with Lithuanian companies regarding business opportunities and limits. At the same time many of them showed how they have been deeply involved in this business for many years.

## French and German Managers - Different Intercultural Competences

Even if the French and German managers demonstrated similar skills in their approach to the Lithuanian market, it appears that these skills may sometimes be different because of the respective cultural background of the managers. For instance, it seems that some French companies faced language problems.

> "We will have to recruit more staff, at least one or two people next year. They should be able to speak English and German; and when I mean 'to be able to speak English and German' I mean, they should really be able to negotiate in these languages."(IF-1)

The difficulty of negotiating in English or German with their Lithuanian partners illustrates the problem many French SMEs face with negotiation in foreign languages in general. In some cases, the French managers took the opportunity to negotiate in German:

> "(…) You shouldn't speak Russian there, it's bad taste and you won't gain trust. You may speak English but German is very appreciated and I negotiate in German very often."(IF-7)

> "I was quite embarrassed because I don't speak German… and my agent speaks Lithuanian there. So, sometimes we talked in English as well, but back home it was a real problem when I tried to contact the customers again. I have the overall impression that everybody there speaks German. So they had to speak Lithuanian with the agent, but I should have spoken German."(IF-5)

On the other hand, the German interviewees are very satisfied to have the opportunity to use their mother tongue in many circumstances but feel very comfortable with English as well.

As far as working styles are concerned, French managers had to adapt to the formal way of doing business. They had to get used to intensive meeting preparation including detailed agendas and schedules. In terms of time management, they felt some contradiction, due to the fact that they needed a lot of time for personal relationships but could not understand why the decision-making process, which included more people than in France, should take so much time. So they needed time for personal relationships and felt quite close to Lithuanians in this respect but felt impatient with the duration of the decision-making process. On the other hand, the Germans managers appreciated the warm and positive atmosphere in Lithuania but they give the impression of being able to do without it. They are themselves quite used to a longer decision-making process and just think it could be a bit more efficient in Lithuania. The following example illustrates how a French businessman wants to boost the decision-making process through personal relationships, which is not always the case with the Lithuanians who have been influenced by American business practices:

> "There is a difference between our two customers. We have a very direct and close relationship with our small customer. I invite him in the restaurant and we go out for a drink in the evening. This doesn't work with the staff of a multinational company. Maybe they do have to respect some internal rules. I tried to invite them several times to a restaurant but it didn't work." (IF-6)

The German interviewees find it hard to tolerate delays in payment, which they perceive as a common practice in Lithuania. They react to this by setting up procedures that they expect the Lithuanians to respect. On the other hand, the French informants, who seem to tolerate these delays more readily, try to use personal relationships to obtain payment. As a conclusion, because of their positive attitudes and their in-depth knowledge of Lithuania, successful French and German companies show specific competences in their export or engineering business with Lithuania. Besides this, they are able to stand back, to analyse their situation consciously. They are able to put their experience into perspective. However, they are quite reluctant to generalize from their experience and to give general advice, which is in fact an intercultural skill in itself. In other words, they remain convinced that learning by doing is the only way to acquire intercultural competences (Morace & Gourvès-Hayward, forthcoming).

## Discussion – Intercultural Management Competences

In the following paragraph, some answers to the question: "*Which intercultural competences emerge from business relationships with Lithuanian managers? A French and German perspective*" will be provided. In the results section some intercultural competences were categorized, using Byram's five *savoirs*. These findings will be now analysed using the cultural dimensions that are widely used in the management literature and Demorgon's model, in order to highlight the management aspects of the intercultural competences we have identified.

The categorization and analysis of the interviews reveal several cultural dimensions that are specific to management situations. Both the German and French managers describe situations including monochrony vs. polychrony and low vs. high context (Hall 1990, 2003a, 2003b), person vs. task orientation (Trompenaars 1998) or long-term orientation (Hofstede

1993, 2001, 2005). However they are often situated at opposite ends of the scale. For instance, the Germans, who are often classified as monochronic, find the Lithuanians polychronic, whereas the polychronic French state that the Lithuanians are monochronic. This is partly due to the communication context. Low-context Germans expect more written information and more formal meetings, with more detailed agendas and short decision-making processes. On the other hand, the French are slightly overwhelmed by such formality in business meetings and negotiation and expect more personal contact in the business relationship. Task-oriented Germans (Trompenaars 1998) oscillate towards the Lithuanians who are – from their perspective – more person-oriented. The person-oriented French, however, see the Lithuanians as more task-oriented than themselves. This shows that both the Germans and the French need to oscillate and to adapt but in the opposite direction. As far as time is concerned, both the French and the German managers agree to get involved in long term orientation because they realize it is necessary for adaptation and because they are committed to a long-term business strategy.

The dimensional model has helped us to identify the need for intercultural competences. Cultural dimensions can be easily categorized and analysed for business situations, but they are not sufficient to describe, to understand, analyse and explain the broader contexts in which they take place. In order to analyse and explain intercultural competences, oscillations and decentring, we also need a synchronic approach and a diachronic approach. To address this issue, the categorized intercultural competences presented in the results are now analysed using the six perspectives of Demorgon's multiperspectivist model: (1) *synchrony*, (2) *diachrony*, (3) *fields*, (4) *levels*, (5) *self-organisation* and (6) *strategy*. To start with the (1) *perspective of synchrony*, it is clear that the managers interviewed oscillate between pre-adaptive antagonisms such as cultural dimensions in management (as shown above). Both the German and the French managers adapted to dimensions like short term vs. long term orientation, task vs. person orientation, monochrony vs. polychrony and low vs. high context. Using Byram's categories, it is possible to observe that their positive **attitudes** towards Lithuanians and their skills of **discovery and interaction** enable them to set up business relationships with their partners by adapting to their cultural dimensions in daily *situations*. They are able to oscillate in the situation (moving from a task to a more person-oriented relation for the Germans and the other way around for the French) and to adapt to a new form of business. In the situation, they demonstrate decentring and avoid parochialism while they attempt to see the business reality from the viewpoint of the Lithuanians. As they bring positive attitudes to the table, they accept and adapt to different living and working standards, quality of products and services, quality management and productivity.

It is important to stress that the informants are able to adapt and learn in a given business situation. However, these informants do not display only positive **attitudes** and **interaction skills**. As well as positive attitudes and **skills of discovery and interaction**, they show competences in terms of **knowledge** and **critical cultural awareness**, as they have been using their **skills of interpretation and relating** over a long period of time. According to Demorgon's (2) perspective of *diachrony*, our informants have been able to interpret and relate their daily activities, adaptation and oscillation to a broader context, because they have gathered thorough knowledge (through information or/and experience) over many years of cooperation. The diachronic perspective explains how successful companies have acquired knowledge about the country in general, its market and its cultural specificities. They were able to observe the country and changes in terms of living and working standards as well as the development (from production to sales driven) of business practices. For instance, they were able to relate the working style including business meetings and negotiation skills to the formalism of the decision-making processes.

Using Demorgon's theory, it is interesting to observe that managers explain business practices in the situation (synchrony) or in the long term (diachrony) not only in the (3) *field* of economy. They relate business practices and knowledge acquired through their own experience to a broader context including the historical and political fields of a transition economy. Using Demorgon's (4) *levels*, we see that the managers interviewed developed intercultural management skills at the national, company and individual level. As shown above, they gained knowledge about the country as a whole. They searched for thorough information about the country, including history and recent developments in Lithuanian society. Besides this, they decided to acquire knowledge about the infrastructure and logistics including roads, railways airport and harbour facilities which, they have noted, do not correspond to Western standards at the moment. At the company level, they considered many aspects of technology, production and quality. They adapted their R&D, production, marketing/sales and finance practices. As we saw above, they used their skills of discovery and interaction to build up personal business relationships at the individual level. Being able to cope with challenges in daily situations in different fields and levels of the Lithuanian context testifies to the (5) self-organisation of the German and French managers. They are able to act, react and adapt in many business situations and show resilience and determination. This is of course a result of their long-term (6) *strategy*. The main feature of their strategy was their involvement in Lithuanian business for a long time. The French and German managers considered very rewarding that fact that they consciously decided to get involved in Lithuanian business and to support Lithuanian companies even before the time of the transition economy. Their strategy can be analysed as the successful combination of attitudes, knowledge and skills. They consciously show a positive attitude to their partners in the country at an individual level. They acquire knowledge in different fields and sectors of activity of Lithuanian society. They show in-depth knowledge of the organization and working processes in the companies in Lithuania and in their own country. The interviewees interpret and relate their knowledge and experience in Lithuania to specific working styles, including business meetings and negotiation skills. They have developed real skills from working with their Lithuanian partners and are able to stand back and analyse their success critically.

Combining Demorgon's perspectives, with Byram's typology and the cultural dimensions from the management literature, three different types of intercultural management competences seem to emerge. Managers with the first type of competences (Proficient) use their skills of discovery and interaction in business situations. They have good communication and negotiation skills. They show oscillation, adaptation and reactivity, using their skills of interpreting and relating. They are able to interpret the situations they face, relating theory to practice. They can combine in-depth knowledge in all fields and on all levels of Lithuanian society with their own experience. They have very positive attitudes towards the country, its companies and its people and have the capacity of reflective practitioners to stand back from their actions. Their long-term commitment to supporting their Lithuanian partners has allowed them to acquire sophisticated critical cultural awareness. The interviews reveal at least three cultural dimensions. Besides this, the managers are able to explain these cultural dimensions, in their own words, to find a link between these cultural dimensions and a broader context. As they are aware of these dimensions, they can use them for business purposes.

Managers with the second type of competences (Intermediate) find it more difficult to use their skills of discovery and interaction in business situations because they lack experience. Therefore their communication skills and their limited negotiation experience do not give them the opportunity to oscillate and adapt and it is difficult for them to interpret the daily business situations they face. They focus especially on the economic field and neglect the historical and political fields. They concentrate their efforts at the company and individual and forget the country level. If they have gained some knowledge and practice on all levels, it is not obvious that their skills of interpreting and relating make it possible for them to find a link between their daily business practices in the situation and a broader context. Even if their attitudes are positive to neutral, they do not show much critical cultural awareness- their involvement is not long enough and they have a more or less medium term strategy. The interviews reveal some (between 1 and 3) cultural dimensions but the managers are rarely aware of these dimensions and of how to use them in business situations.

Managers with the third type of competences (Novice) have little access to Lithuanians as agents or as direct partners. They cannot really interpret and relate their little experience to any broader context because they lack experience and have almost no knowledge about the country, its companies and people. They show neutral to sometimes negative attitudes towards Lithuania and are not able to show any critical cultural awareness. This is partly due to their lack of strategy for this market, as they prefer to short term business. No cultural dimensions can be identified from their interviews.

These three types of intercultural management competences correspond to three intercultural business behaviour profiles. The first profile concerns companies with direct access to the market, long-lasting business relationships (between 5 and 25 years) and a high export rate (above 15%). These companies consider they have successful business cooperation with Lithuania, which they explain by their long-term support of their Lithuanian partners. Our analysis confirms that they also demonstrate proficient intercultural skills, including critical cultural awareness. The second profile concerns companies who work more with agents. Their business relationship has existed for between 3 and 5 years and their export rate is between 5 and 15%. These companies want to improve their business with Lithuania. Their intercultural skills are still in progress, or intermediate. Companies with the third profile have little access to the market, either with or without an agent. They have had their first experiences and have an export rate of up to 5%. Most of the time they acknowledge that they are only interested in short term business and that they do not intend to develop a strategy for Lithuania. They do not show any visible cultural skills. These companies partly answered our questionnaire but did not take part in our interviews.

## Conclusion

Our main objective was to demonstrate that managers and entrepreneurs of SMEs in France and Germany need intercultural management competences to conduct business with Lithuanian companies. We identified intercultural competences using an exploratory methodology, semi-structured interviews and content analysis. These intercultural competences were categorised using Byram's intercultural competence scale and then analysed using the cultural dimensions from intercultural management research. The synchronic categorization with Byram's model was completed by the multiperspectivist theory of Jacques Demorgon which makes it possible to explain intercultural management competences in a broader context adding, diachrony, levels, fields, self-organisation and strategy to the variable of synchrony. The use of these three models allowed us to identify three specific intercultural management competences (Proficient, Intermediate and Novice) and combine them with three intercultural business behaviour profiles. These results illustrate and confirm intuitive evidence that managers with long-term effective business relationships with Lithuania display high levels of intercultural competence, whereas those with little or no involvement also show fewer intercultural skills.

The results obtained from the successful managers lead us to develop Stage D where we list some recommendations to enhance business with Lithuanian partners. The informants recommend that prospective partners develop a real interest in the society, its culture, history, market and its business particularities. Based on this positive attitude, they recommend acquiring in-depth knowledge about Lithuania, bearing in mind that this country is still a transition economy. This makes it necessary to learn about specific details of the organization and working processes in the companies. They especially recommend that companies who have not started doing business with Lithuania obtain information by thorough market research but also that they recruit agents who know the country very well. They warn managers and entrepreneurs against relying blindly on official statistics and information which does not correspond to the market situation. In their opinion, newcomers should take the time to stand back in order to analyse their action from a critical viewpoint. For this purpose a close and informal relationship to consultants, agents and partners is essential.

Our recommendations for the Novice group would be to weigh up the pros and cons of developing a long-term business strategy for the Lithuanian market. If this commitment appears worthwhile for them it should be accompanied with relevant intercultural awareness, skills and knowledge. They should concentrate particularly on improving their s*avoir-être, or attitudes and values*. The Intermediate group has already made progress in terms of s*avoir-être* and appears ready to acquire more knowledge and skills. This could be achieved both by peer learning with representatives from the Proficient group and appropriate intercultural training programmes which integrate the insights acquired by the Proficient group (Morace & Schultz 2006). As far as the Proficient group is concerned, their intercultural competences, and by extension their international business success, could be still further improved by learning to transfer their knowledge and skills to younger or less experienced managers. This *savoir s'engager* or *critical cultural awareness* could be an integral part of a consulting package for Lithuanian, German and French partners, thus enhancing business relations which already build on knowledge transfer, as well as sales and production.

## Notes

[1] Capacité d'un individu à analyser et comprendre les situations de contact entre personnes et groupes de cultures différentes, et à les gérer et valoriser dans un contexte professionnel.» (Meier 2004)

> "In general terms, intercultural competence is the ability to communicate effectively in cross-cultural situations and to relate appropriately in a variety of cultural contexts. Developing this kind of competence is usually a primary goal of diversity initiatives in organizations, where it is assumed to contribute to effective recruitment and retention of members of underrepresented groups, management of diverse workforce, productivity of multicultural teams, marketing across cultures, and the development of a climate of respect for diversity in the organization."(Bennett 2004)
>
> „Es geht im wesentlichen um einen Komplex von analytisch-strategischen Fähigkeiten, die das Interpretations- und Handlungsspektrum des betreffenden Individuums in interpersonaler Interaktion mit Mitgliedern anderer Kulturen erweitern. In diese analytisch-strategischen Fähigkeiten sind Wissen über andere Kulturen generell, die Veränderung von

Einstellungen und eine Sensibilität (awareness) gegenüber kulturbedingter Andersartigkeit integriert." (Knapp/Knapp-Potthoff, 1990 in Barmeyer 2000)

## References

Adler, N. J. (2002). International dimensions of organizational behavior (4th ed.). Cincinnati: South-Western.

Barmeyer, C.I. (2000). Interkulturelles Management und Lernstile. Studierende und Führungskräfte in Frankreich, Deutschland und Quebec. Deutsch-Französische Studien zur Industriegesellschaft. Vol. 25, CIRAC: Paris.

Byram, M. (1995). Intercultural competence and mobility in multinational contexts: A European view. Clevedon, Avon: Multilingual Matters.

—. (1997). Teaching and assessing intercultural communicative competence. Clevedon, Avon: Multilingual Matters.

Byram, M, Gribkova, B & Starkey, H (eds). (2002). Developing the Intercultural Dimension in Language Teaching: a practical introduction for teachers. Council of Europe, Language Policy Division.

Byram, M. & Zarate, G. (1994). Definitions, objectives and assessment of socio-cultural competence. Strasbourg: Council of Europe.

Chevrier, S. (2000). Le management des équipes interculturelles. Paris:Puf, 211.p

Cope, J. (2003). Entrepreneurial learning and critical reflexion: Discontinuous events as triggers for 'higher-level-learning' Management learning, Vol. 34, p. 429-450.

Corbin, J. & Strauss, A. (1998).Basics of qualitative research. Techniques and procedures for developing grounded theory. Thousand Oaks, London, New Delhi: Sage, 310 p.

Demorgon, J. (2000). L'interculturation du monde. Paris: Anthropos Economica.

—. (2002). L'histoire interculturelle des sociétés (2nd ed.). Paris: Anthropos Economica.

—. (2004a). Complexité des cultures et de l'interculturel. Contre les pensées uniques. (3rd ed.). Paris: Anthropos Economica.

—. (2004b). Une épistémologie sans frontière – Complexité des antagonismes de la nature à l'histoire. Paris : Synergies, p. 77–109.

—. (2005a). Critique de l'Interculturel. L'horizon de la sociologie. Paris: Anthropos Economica.

—. (2005b). Intercultural exchanges target and source- codes, adaptation, history. Keynote speech at the SIETAR Europa Congress, Nice, France 2005. Retrieved from the net at http://www.sietar-europa.org/congress2005.

Demorgon, J. et al. (2003). Dynamiques interculturelles pour l'Europe. Paris: Anthropos Economica.

Demorgon, J. & Molz, M. (1996). Bedingungen und Auswirkungen der Analyse von Kultur(en) und interkulturellen Interaktionen. Psychologie interkulturellen Handelns, p. 43–86.

Erikson, T. (2003). Towards a taxonomy of entrepreneurial learning experiences among potential entrepreneurs. Journal of Small Business and Enterprise Development, 2003, Vol. 10, N°1, p. 106-112.

Glaser, B. & Strauss, A. (1967) The discovery of grounded theory: Strategies for qualitative research. London: Wiedenfeld and Nicholson.

Glowik, M.& Morace. C. (2006). Doing business with new EU member states: A comparative empirical analysis of German and French medium-sized enterprises and their business experiences in the Baltic States. Proceedings of the 14th Annual Conference on Marketing and Business Strategies for Central & Eastern Europe. Vienna University of Economics and Business Administration.

Gourvès-Hayward, A. Kennedy, F. & Sudershan, A. (2007). The Intercultural dimension in LOLIPOP. How interculturally competent are you? Paper given at the SIETAR EUROPA annual conference, East, West, North & South: Culture's Impact on Economy, Religion, Ecology, Politics. Sofia, Bulgaria, 25-29 April.

Gourvès-Hayward, A. & Morace, C. (2005). Intercultural Management : third place, third space, from conflict to consensus. Conference. International Academy for Intercultural Research, Kent (USA).

Hall, E. T. & Hall M. R. (1990). Understanding cultural differences. Yarmouth, Maine: Intercultural Press.

Hall, E. T. (2003a). The vocabulary of culture. In: G. Redding, & B.W. Stening (eds.) Cross-cultural management. Volume 1: The theory of culture (p. 113 –139). Cheltenham: Edward Elgar Publishing Limited.

Hall, E. T. & Hall, M. (2003b). Key concepts. Underlying structures of culture. In: D. C. Thomas (Ed.), Readings and cases in international management. A cross-cultural perspective (p. 151–162). Thousand Oaks, London, New Delhi: Sage Publications.

Hofstede, G. (1993). Intercultural conflict and synergy in Europe. In D. J. Hickson (Ed.), Management in Western Europe: Society, culture and organization in twelve nations. Berlin, New York: de Gruyter.

—. (2001). Culture's consequences: Comparing values, behaviors, institutions and organizations across nations (2nd ed.). Thousand Oaks: Sage.

Hofstede, G. & Hofstede, G. J. (2005). Cultures and organizations. Software of the mind (2nd ed.). New York: McGraw-Hill.

Kelly, M., Elliott, L.& Fant, L (eds) (2001). Third Level, Third Space. Bern; Berlin; Bruxelles; Frankfurt am Main; New York; Oxford; Wien: Lang (Transversales, Vol. 2).

Knapp, K. & Knapp-Potthoff, A. (1990). Interkulturelle Kommunikation. Zeitschrift für Fremdsprachenforschung. p. 62-93.

Landis, D., Bennett, J.M. & Bennett, M.J. (2004). Handbook of Intercultural Training. Sage Publications : Thousand Oaks, London, New Delhi (3rd ed).

LOLIPOP (2007). Language On- line Portfolio Project. http://lolipop.computing.dcu.ie

Meier, O. (2006). Management interculturel. Stratégie. Organisation. Performance. Dunod: Paris (2nd ed).

Morace, C. & Schulze, H. (2006). L'apprentissage interculturel des PME/PMI. Expériences d'entrepreneurs en Bretagne et en Basse-Saxe. Communication CIFEPME (Congrès international francophone en entrepreneuriat et PME), Fribourg.

Morace, C. & Schulze, H. (2005). Quelles compétences interculturelles pour les PME/PMI en Europe? L'exemple d'entrepreneurs en Bretagne et en Basse-Saxe. In: J. Klusmeyer, U. Meyerholt & P. Wengelowski (eds.), Beratung – Evaluation – Transfer, (Vol. 3), (p. 73–90). Oldenburg: BIS-Verlag.

Morace, C. & Gourvès-Hayward, A. (2007). Comment favoriser l'apprentissage de la complexité par l'expérience interculturelle? Une approche inter-établissements, interdisciplinaire et interculturelle. Proceedings of the 35th UPLEGESS Conference: Les Langues au Coeur de la Transversalité, comment répondre au défis de la complexité, Grenoble Ecole de Management, 30 May-1 June, 2007.

Morace, C. & Gourvès-Hayward, A. (forthcoming) Learning by Doing or Learning to Do? Intercultural Management Competences for the manager of the future.

Müller B.D (1995). Sekundärerfahrung und Fremdverstehen. In: J. Bolten (ed.): Cross-Culture – Interkulturelles Verstehen in der Wirtschaft. Schriftenreihe interkulturelle Wirtschaftskommunikation. (Vol.1), Berlin, p.43-59.

Osland, J.S. & Bird, A. (2003). Beyond sophisticated stereotyping: Cultural sensemaking in context. In: D. C. Thomas (Ed.), Readings and cases in international management. A cross-cultural perspective (p.58–71). Thousand Oaks, London, New Delhi: Sage Publications.

Pavlenko, A. & Lantolf, J.P. (2000). Second language learning as participation and the (re)construction of selves. In: J.P. Lantolf, (ed.) Sociocultural theory and second language learning. Oxford: Oxford University Press.

Rogoff, E.G.; Myung-Soo, L. & Dong-Churl, S. (2004).“Why done it?” Attributions by entrepreneurs and experts of the factors that cause and impede small businesss Success. Journal of Small Business Management, 2004, Vol. 42, N°4, p. 364-376.

Trompenaars, F. (1998). Riding the waves of culture. New York. McGraw-Hill.

Wöhe, G. (1986) Einführung in die Allgemeine Betriebswirtschaftslehre. Munich: Gabler. (16th.ed.)

# DEALING WITH DIFFERENT STAKEHOLDERS IN RUSSIA: EXPERIENCES OF FINNISH COMPANIES

ASTA SALMI

## Abstract

A key success factor for companies in foreign markets is to know how to deal with different stakeholders. In transition countries dealing with the administration in particular calls for attention to different ethical considerations. We know still very little about how managers tackle these issues in practice. This study aims at analyzing how different stakeholders in the Russian business context are approached and how Finnish companies tackle the local norms for behaviour in their stakeholder relations. This study is based on reviewing earlier studies in the area. It reports empirical findings from interview and survey studies of Finnish managers doing business the Russian markets (Pekkanen & Salmi, 2006 and Ruoho & Salmi, 2007). The approach of analyzing business taking place between a country of low corruption and a country of high corruption is especially revealing as it exemplifies a situation where the managers are continuously making decisions on how to behave when cultural and social norms are fundamentally different and when two sets of ethics collide. The key conclusion is that the pressures coming from the stakeholders and administration, in particular, in the host country are very different from the home country, and the companies need to find special ways to deal with these norms. Often, locals are used as middlemen when dealing with the pressures, but still, foreigners remain easily outside the inner circles of influence.

## Introduction

A key success factor for companies in foreign markets is to know how to deal with different stakeholders. In some contexts (e.g. transition countries) dealing with the administration in particular is important, and moreover, may call for different ethical norms. Today, ethical behaviour in business is increasingly discussed by managers, policy makers, and researchers, but we still know little about the practices as comes to ethical decision making. This paper analyzes business taking place between a country of low corruption (Finland) and a country of high corruption (Russia). It is therefore especially revealing as it exemplifies a situation where the managers are continuously making decisions on how to behave when cultural and social norms are fundamentally different and when two sets of ethics collide.

This study aims at analyzing how different stakeholders in the Russian business context are approached and how Finnish companies tackle the local norms for behaviour in their stakeholder relations. In particular, the study analyzes what kind of state corruption foreign companies actually encounter in transition economies and how managers perceive corruption and react to it.

This paper is based on reviewing earlier empirical studies in the area that report findings concerning Finnish managers dealing with the Russian markets. Firstly, a survey study (Pekkanen & Salmi, 2006) on enterprise-state relations is investigated. Secondly, the paper reports an interview study (Ruoho and Salmi, 2007) of Finnish SMEs and their ethical considerations in the Russian markets. Most studies of ethics focus on large companies (MNCs), and the SMEs have received relatively little attention so far, especially as comes to the international and global dimensions in ethical considerations (Moore and Spence, 2006).

A specific feature relating to ethical behavior is the question of corruption. While studies on the causes and consequences of corruption abound (Shleifer and Vishny 1993; Tanzi, 1995, 1998; Tirole 1996; DiRienzo et al. 2007) and there are suggestions for strategies to cope with it (Doh et al. 2003), we know little of *how managers tackle the issues in practice*. Reasons for this are obvious: it is difficult to discuss illegal behavior. However, openness is of critical importance, since transparency of rules, processes and laws are important ways to reduce corruption (Tanzi, 1998). We aim to fill the knowledge gap by analyzing how corruption is seen and tackled by foreign companies in their relations with different stakeholders in a highly corrupt business context.

The paper is structured as follows. It firstly reviews the literature on responsible business of SMEs and corruption in Russia in particular, in order to provide the theoretical basis of our analysis. The next sections discuss first the methods and then the results of two Finnish studies. The first one is an empirical survey of Finnish companies conducted in 2005 (Pekkanen and Salmi, 2006). This survey reports perceptions of 35 companies on corruption in Russian administration. It shows, among other things, that foreign companies are more corrupt in a corrupt country, thus the norms of the host country play a role in ethical behavior. The second study goes into deeper analysis of these findings by face-to-face interviews to see how ethics and corruption are tackled in practice. It reports how Finnish SMEs perceive ethical business behavior and corruption in contemporary Russia and how they tackle it. The conclusions focus on the role of Russians as middlemen and on the difficult task of operating at the border between business contexts with very different ethical norms.

## Literature Review: Ethical Behaviour and Stakeholders

### Transition and Ethics

The sudden and dramatic collapse of the Soviet Union and the subsequent transition process to a market economy has been difficult. During this process the absence and inconsistency of laws and regulations has lead to rent-seeking, corruption, and outright theft. There is ample evidence claiming that transition economies are characterized by extensive corruption (as shown by, for example, Transparency International). More than a decade into the simultaneous political and economic transitions in the former Soviet Union and Eastern Europe, dynamic market economies have been created and states have been reshaped, but the boundaries between the state and the economy remain murky (World Bank 2000, xiii).

In transition economies it seems to be especially important to differentiate between two types of contacts, namely, those with other managers and those with officials (Peng & Luo 2000), which brings public-private relations into focus. Corruption relating to the interaction between foreign enterprises and local administrations has received little attention, and yet such research could clearly yield important insights for Western governments, companies, and managers. It seems that among different stakeholders, the relations to administration are of special character.

As comes to SMEs in particular, the potential unethical behavior has special meaning. Corruption and illegal payments involve both the individual and the firm: business people take (real) personal risks for (potential) organizational benefits, either through company loyalty or personal interest. (Usunier 2000) Thus the company risks being implicated in a scandal and individuals risk being implicated, indicted, and imprisoned – and in fact, both parties of the business relation are involved. (Salmi, 2000) So, in pragmatic terms, the individual is dealing with both personal and corporate norms – how these norms are created in transition economies is one of the fundamental managerial and research issues of today.

Recently, corruption has been discussed more openly as a result of studies and publications by, for example, Transparency International. Both the Corruption Perception Index (CPI) and the Bribe Payers Index (BPI) (www.transparency.org/surveys/index.html) have acquired a certain reputation. The CPI ranks countries in terms of the degree to which corruption is perceived to exist among public officials and politicians. Published annually since 1995, the index has become the leading indicator of corruption worldwide. The composite index uses both surveys of business people and assessments by country analysts. The goal of the CPI is to provide data on widely-held perceptions of corruption within countries. The CPI shows that the level of corruption is highest in transition and developing countries, but that there is also corruption in market economies. Russia has had a high ranking in the index over several years as a corrupt economy (ranked at 143rd among 179 countries in the most recent index for 2007), while Finland has consistently been in the first or second place, that is, has been the least corrupt country).

The other side of the coin, of course, is the payer of the bribe. Transparency International's Bribe Payers Index, a relative newcomer to the scene, has been carried out for 1999 and 2002. The BPI ranks leading exporting countries by the degree to which their corporations are perceived as paying bribes abroad to senior public officials. Thus, it measures the 'supply' side of bribery in the key emerging (i.e., transition and developing) economies. The BPI of 2002 was conducted in 15 emerging economies, including Hungary, Poland and Russia from Eastern Europe. The questions concerned nineteen exporting countries (including Sweden, but not Finland). It found that, Australian, Swedish, and Swiss companies were the least likely to pay or offer bribes in emerging economies, while Russian companies were the most likely to do so.

In this study we empirically analyze foreign company corruption in one transition economy, namely Russia, and, in particular, managerial perceptions of enterprise-state corruption between Finnish companies and the Russian administrative environment. Thus we link the corruption practices found in Russia, which has a high ranking on the Corruption Perceptions Index, with the perceptions of managers from Finland, which has had one of the lowest scores on the CPI over the years. The contrasting of two business environments at opposite ends of the corruption spectrum provides an interesting research setting: Finnish companies here represent Western countries and Russia is an illustrative case of a transition economy. As Russia is an important and large economy, we expect the results to be of interest to international companies worldwide.

## Studies on Corruption

Until the 1980s, scholarly research on corruption was largely confined to the fields of sociology, political science, history, public administration, and criminal law (Abed and Gupta 2002, 1). Since then, economists have become interested in the subject, largely on account of the clear link between corruption on the one hand and economic performance and development on the other (Bardhan 1997; Shleifer and Vishny 1993). The accelerating trends of globalization, world economic integration, and liberalization have forced scholars and governments alike to address the issue of international corruption. Economists have generally highlighted the adverse impact of corruption on economic performance while providing some insights into its origins, manifestations, and possible remedies (Abed and Davoodi 2002, 490). Nevertheless, relatively few studies have managed to examine the causes of corruption or find practical ways of dealing with them.

The literature on corruption is relatively new, and different schools of thought have yet to emerge. Researchers are, however, beginning to agree on the negative impact of corruption on economic progress. The study of corruption by international organizations, such as the World Bank (WB), the European Bank of Reconstruction and Development (EBRD), and the International Monetary Fund (IMF); and nongovernmental organizations, such as Transparency International, and Freedom House as well as multilateral action on the part of the European Union (EU), the Organization for Economic Cooperation and Development (OECD) and the United Nations (UN), are of profound importance. These institutions publish valuable working papers, surveys, and recommendations, and shape the emerging research tradition on corruption (for discussion see e.g

DeVel & Csonka 2002; Corruption and Good Governance 1997; Pacini, Swingen & Rogers 2002).

In 2000, the World Bank published a study called "Anticorruption in Transition – A Contribution to the Policy Debate" (World Bank 2000). This report was the first comprehensive study of the corruption faced by the business community in the transition economies of Central and Eastern Europe and the former Soviet Union. It was based on an extensive "Business Environment and Enterprise Performance Survey" (BEEPS) of over 4,000 firms in twenty two transition economies. This was a fundamental study that identified the varied nature of corruption and was the first to identify and compare different patterns of the problem across transition economies and to develop anticorruption strategies and reform models.

Two "Anticorruption in Transition" studies by World Bank (2000, 2004) form the basis for the interview study reported here, as they identify the different types of corruption and their variation between the transition economies. Another central work is the study by Hellman et al. (2002): "Far From Home", which focuses on the corruption of foreign investors in transition economies.

If we look at views regarding the frequency of corruption on the one hand and the actual level or incidence of corruption on the other, we find that there is a self-fulfilling equilibrium of corruption. If the view that "everybody is corrupt" circulates as the result of information or disinformation it creates an atmosphere of corruption; people who believe they are living in a climate of corruption become corrupt themselves (see Bardhan 1997, 1334). Moreover, the reputations of individuals and the groups they are part of (their collective reputation) are interlinked, and the bad reputation of a previous generation may explain the persistence of perceptions on corruption (Tirole 1996). These aspects highlight the difficulties in measuring corruption and adapting to it.

It is difficult to define corruption. Two definitions may be given as examples: "the intentional non-compliance with the arm's-length principle aimed at deriving some advantage for oneself or for related individuals from this principle" (Tanzi 1995, 167), and "the use of public office for private advantage, the latter understood not only in a pecuniary sense but also in terms of status and influence" (Palmier 1983, quoted in Ledeneva 1998, 42). The term corruption comes from the Latin verb to break, *rumpere*, thus implying that something is broken (Tanzi 1995). It may be a moral or social code of conduct or an administrative rule that has been broken. For the latter, there are several requirements: firstly, the rule that is broken should be precise and transparent; secondly, the official who breaks it must derive some recognizable benefit for himself or some relevant person/group; and, finally, the benefit derived must be a direct quid pro quo from the 'corrupt' act. (*ibid.* p. 168).

There are three specific types of corruption; state capture, administrative corruption, and public procurement kickbacks. *State capture* refers to the actions of individuals, groups, or firms in both the public and private sectors designed to influence the *formation* of laws, regulations, decrees, and other government policies to their own advantage by means of the non-transparent and illicit provision of private benefits to public officials (World Bank 2000, 1). *Administrative corruption* refers to the creation of intentional distortions in the prescribed *implementation* of laws, rules, and regulations by providing advantages to state or non-state actors as a result of the non-transparent and illicit provision of private gains to public officials (World Bank 2000, 2). *Public procurement kickbacks* are defined as illicit private payments to public officials in order to secure public procurement contracts (Hellman et al. 2002, 6). This is a form of "grand" corruption that takes place in large-scale government contracts and privatization deals. State capture and public procurement kickbacks are types of corruption that are utilized strategically by foreign companies for economic benefit. Administrative corruption is a different issue, as it is not economically beneficial or strategic to the company. It is an extortion imposed by government officials. As such, it works as an additional tax.

The origins of corruption in transition economies are found to be related to the legacy of communism, the rewriting of legislation, the redistribution of wealth, institutional voids, and international trends. Moreover, social norms explain different behavior in different countries. For instance, it is widely recognized that in developing countries gift-exchange is an accepted social norm in business transactions (Bardhan 1997). Scholars analyzing personal relations have struggled to differentiate personal relations from bribery and corruption (*guanxi* in China and *blat* in Russia) (Ledeneva 1998; Lovet et al. 1999; Xin & Pearce 1996). For example, a distinction has been made between *guanxi* and bribery. The former means relationship building while the latter is simply an illicit transaction. More specifically, the following three qualities help define an act of bribery: 1) a gain-and-loss calculation dominates the act of bribery, 2) bribery is for an immediate and specific purpose, and 3) there is no emotional content or affection involved in bribery. (Lovett et al. 1999) It should therefore be stressed that the maintenance and use of personal relations and, for example, gift-giving, is not necessarily the same as bribery and corruption, but may simply be symbols of friendship.

In conclusion, the developments within business studies and socio-economic investigations have drawn attention to the difficulty in drawing a line between bribes and gifts as well as to the differences in business norms found in different countries. The latter reveal the complicated situation in which managers often find themselves when dealing with foreign administrators and business partners.

## Ethics in Finnish-Russian Business – Analyzing Corruption

Studies of ethics in the Russian-Finnish context are scarce. Business ethics and corporate social responsibility of Finnish companies, managers and entrepreneurs have been studied relatively little, examples being the studies by Kujala (2001, 2004), Grünbaum (1997) and Panapanaan et al. (2003). Russian managers, companies and business environment instead have been studied more in terms of business ethics (see e.g. Beekun et. al. 2005; Jaffe and Tsimerman, 2006; Ahmed, et al., 2003; Puffer and McCarthy, 1995; and Puffer, 1996). Studying business ethics in the Russian context is, however, challenging due to the constant change of the country. Further, there is great ambiguity in Russia of acceptable codes of behavior in a capitalistic market economy (Ahmed et al., 2003). It is thus important to have updated and current information on the developments in the Russian business community.

The cultural heritage regarding bribes is noticeably different in Finland and Russia. In Russia, it may be difficult for foreigners to make the distinction between bribes and normal business gifts; small gifts are more common in Russian business culture than in Finnish business culture (Haapaniemi et al. 2003, 108). What constitutes a bribe in Finland may well be considered a legitimate business gift in Russia. In order to know the difference, one needs experience and first-hand knowledge of local business customs. Hirvensalo et al. (2000, 50) propose a concept of *the skill of social bargaining,* referring to "the personal capacity of an economic actor (usually a local manager) to use negotiation and persuasion to influence key actors in a company's context and thereby solve daily problems". In some cases it is hard to draw the line between social bargaining and playing along with corrupt bureaucrats. There seems to be a "grey zone" between legal and illegal actions (ibid, 56).

This paper reviews two studies providing empirical data on corrupt practices, or perceptions of corruption by Finnish companies in the Russian markets. Before reviewing the studies, the methods used are discussed next.

## A Note of Methods

Corruption and ethics are issues that are very difficult to study and for which collection of reliable data is not easy. The two studies to be discussed here were based on two different types of data collection. In the first (Pekkanen & Salmi, 2006), an internet survey was used as a method of data collection, while the second (Ruoho & Salmi, 2007) is based on face-to-face interviews with the managers. In both cases the underlying reasons for the methodological choices was the need for confidentiality. In both studies, anonymity of the respondents was stressed, but different means for it were used.

An important limitation of this paper and of both of the reviewed studies is that the viewpoint is largely that of Finnish entrepreneurs. Had we interviewed Russian parties as well, many of the dilemmas that seem incomprehensible from a Finnish point of view could have gotten an explanation from the other side.

The perception of corruption depends on how well informed one is about local business culture and on one's social bargaining skills (Hirvensalo et al. 2000). A first-hand knowledge of Russian business culture is important as a respondent's familiarity with local practices might influence his or her view on the role and significance of corruption. Therefore, when reporting the study methodologies we also show the extent to which the respondents were aware of the Russian context.

### Study of Enterprise-State Relations

A self-administered internet survey was chosen as the method of data collection for confidentiality reasons. Respondents may answer more honestly with electronic surveys than with paper surveys or interviews (http://colostate.edu/references/research /survey/com3c1.cfm). The need for a large sample, and considerations of time and cost were other reasons for using this method. Closed-end questions were utilized. It was especially important to make answering as easy a process as possible, as people are generally reluctant to discuss corruption openly. The formulation of the questions also allows one to compare the results with previous studies – this means also that the questions were in English. An open-end field was included, enabling the respondents to include any additional information they deemed necessary. A relatively low response rate was expected due to the illicit nature of corruption. The survey was conducted in such a way that the respondents would remain totally anonymous in the hope that this would facilitate open and honest responses.

The survey was targeted at members of the Finnish – Russian Chamber of Commerce and to the people involved in Russian business. They were contacted via e-mail and urged to answer a short web-based questionnaire. The preliminary list contained 540 email addresses, of which 360 were in practice reachable. There were several problems in the data collection and some responses were lost in the process. The response rate was 10 %, as 35 usable replies were received.

Most of the respondents represented companies that were wholly Finnish-owned. More specifically: 57 % were wholly owned Finnish companies, 14 % joint ventures with Russian and Finnish partners, 11 % Russian wholly owned companies and 17 % other. The respondents' knowledge of local business culture was investigated by asking about their visits to Russia. Figure 1 shows that the respondents were well informed about Russian business culture. 51 % percent lived or had lived in Russia, and one respondent was a native Russian. Only 11 % (four respondents) can be classified as having a weak knowledge of Russian business culture. All but one of the respondents represented foreign (that is, non-Russian) nationalities.

**Figure 1: Respondents' knowledge of Russian business culture (n=35) in the study by Pekkanen & Salmi, 2006.**

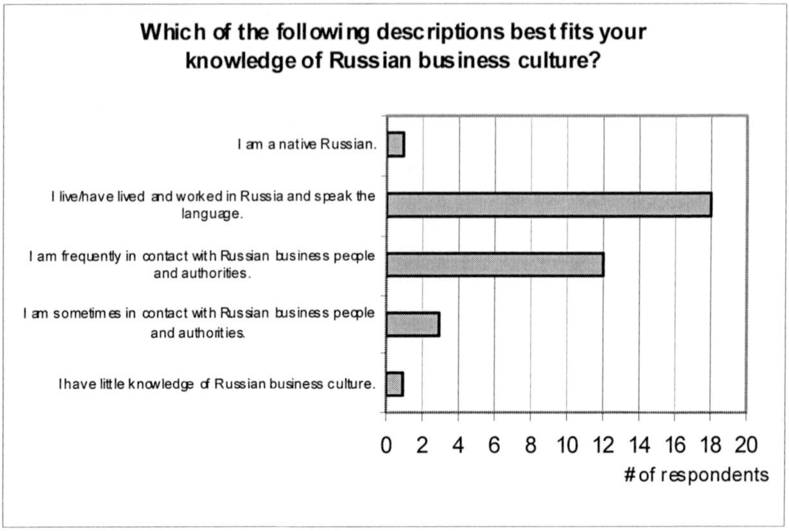


## Study on SME's Operations

For this study, qualitative research and interviewing were chosen for three main reasons. Firstly, the topic, especially from the point of view of SMEs, is relatively new and there is no established theory. Secondly, the aim was to study motives and reasons for different behaviors rather than frequencies. Qualitative research goes beyond the measurement of observable behavior and seeks to understand the meaning and beliefs of the underlying action (Marschan-Piekkari and Welch (2004). Thirdly, business ethics and corruption are delicate issues that call for openness and confidentiality, which was seen to be achieved in face-to-face-contact. Most of the interviewees seemed honest and relaxed, and many were surprisingly open. Further, anonymity for the respondents in the final report was guaranteed, which is the common practice when doing research on sensitive issues (Kuula 2006, 75).

In total, 12 respondents in Southern Finland were interviewed for the study. The interviews were conducted in 2006. They were conducted in Finnish, which is the native tongue of both the interviewer (Ruoho) and the interviewees. The interviews lasted ½-2 ½ hours, on average one hour. The interviews were tape recorded, transcribed, and analyzed in Finnish, and they have been translated into English in the reporting phase. The approach of an open-ended discussion with only a broad topical area to guide the interviews was chosen. This paper reports the results concerning in particular corruption and the way the companies were tackling it.

11 of the respondents were company people, mainly CEOs, and one respondent consulted Finnish SMEs doing business in Russia. The interviewees had a relatively long background in Russian business, ranging from ca. 10 to 40 years. They all visit Russia relatively often (from several times a year to several times a month), and some of them had earlier been living in Russia longer periods.

## Results

### Enterprise-State Relations or Dealing with the Administration

The research questions of the study by Pekkanen and Salmi (2006) were firstly, what kind of enterprise-state corruption foreign companies encounter in transition economies and, secondly, how managers perceive corruption and react to it. The focus was on administrative corruption.

The earlier literature shows that *international anti-corruption initiatives* have had surprisingly few positive effects; they do not seem to reduce either the level of corruption or perceptions of corruption. As far as *host-country factors* (transition economies) are concerned, it appears that national-level anticorruption programs are ineffective, and that legislative reform has a weak influence in reducing the level of strategic corruption. Although the literature provides no evidence for suggesting that legislation, in itself, is not equally binding for both foreign and domestic companies, it is suspected that the implementation of legislation is unjust, and that the administrative environment of transition economies discriminates against foreign companies. *Home-country factors* were analyzed by resorting to the CPI index. A correlation has been found between the CPI and BPI indices, indicating that companies from countries with low levels of corruption behave less corruptly in transition economies, than companies from countries with higher domestic (home-country) corruption levels.

In the following key findings on various propositions are given. The low number of responses did not allow for using any advanced analytical methods. Instead, the distribution of responses is discussed.

Proposition 1. *Foreign companies engage in more corruption in transition economies than in their home country.*

The literature suggests that companies engage in more corruption in markets that are more corrupt. This relatively straightforward assumption was tested by asking the respondents whether they believed Finnish companies engaged in more corruption in Russia than in their own country. When asked, "Do you believe Finnish companies engage in more corruption in Russia than in Finland?" 86 % of the respondents (30/35) replied affirmatively. This was as expected. Companies engage in more corruption in markets that are more corrupt, and transition economies are typically more corrupt than the home countries of foreign companies. Moreover, Finland is a much less corrupt country than Russia.

Proposition 2. *International anti-corruption initiatives have not markedly reduced foreign company corruption in transition economies*

The literature (Hellman et al. 2002; Steves and Rousso 2003) argues that international anti-corruption initiatives have had little if any effect in restraining the corrupt activities of foreign companies when doing business in transition economies. This proposition concerned attempts to reduce corruption and stated that *International anti-corruption initiatives do not markedly reduce foreign company corruption in transition economies*. The respondents were asked, "In your opinion, what impact has the OECD Anti-Bribery Convention of 1997 had on Finnish companies operating in Russia?" As expected, most of the respondents were either not familiar with the Convention ( 22 out of 34 responses or 65 %), or deemed it had had no impact ( 11 out of 34 responses or 32%) (see Figure 4). Not surprisingly, no-one felt that the Convention had increased corruption in Finnish companies, but more importantly, only one respondent out of thirty-four was of the opinion that the Convention had reduced corruption in Finnish companies. Hence, it is clear that this – internationally most important – initiative has not affected corruption.

One may argue that the Convention has had so little impact on reducing Finnish company corruption, because its stipulations are not strict enough to affect the already low level of corrupt activity of Finnish companies.

Even if this were the case, the lack of knowledge of the Convention implies that international anti-corruption initiatives are of little, if any, interest to business people. Several studies (Hellman et al. 2002; Steves and Rousso 2003) have argued that the effect of international anti-corruption initiatives is miniscule in restraining the corrupt activities of foreign companies operating in transition economies. Companies appear to have a cynical approach to corruption and do not seem to believe the situation will improve. The comment of one respondent on corruption illustrates this view, *"This is the common practice around here and has been for several hundred years."*

Proposition 3. *Transition economy authorities discriminate against foreign companies.*

This proposition concerns the impact of host-country factors on corruption levels. It was expected that authorities follow the (new) rules very strictly when foreign companies are concerned; thus the implementation of legislation binds foreign companies more than domestic companies. Transition economy authorities and public officials may take advantage of foreign companies by, for example, extracting illegal rents from them to a larger extent than from their own domestic companies.

The respondents were asked the following question: "In your opinion, do Russian authorities and public officials treat Finnish and Russian companies in an equal way?" 56 % (19 out of 34) replied, "No, they treat Russian companies better", while 18 % (6 out of 34) were of the opposite view, namely, that Finnish companies were treated better. 26 % (9 out of 34) considered that Russian and Finnish companies were treated the same way (See Figure 2).

Over half of the respondents thought that the Russian authorities favored Russian companies or discriminated against Finnish companies. Extracting illegal rents and payments from foreign companies seems to be easy and profitable. This provides evidence supporting the proposition, and suggests that the authorities may use legislative formal rules as an excuse for rent lifting – informal practices and payments help to overcome any problems relating to formal legislation.

**Figure 2: The treatment of companies by the authorities. Source: Pekkanen & Salmi 2006.**

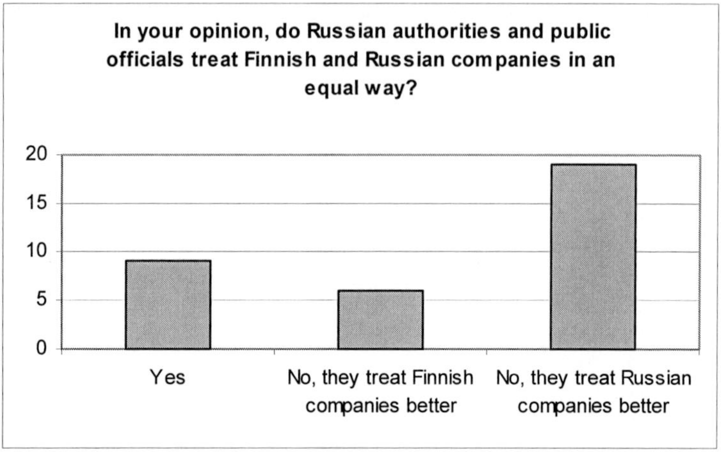


Proposition 4. *Foreign companies do not view corruption in transition economies as economically beneficial*

Although foreign companies appear to engage in corruption on a large scale, and although some corruption may even be necessary, it was hypothesized that they do not see corruption as beneficial *per se.* Companies realize the overall cost of corruption, but engage in it, as it would not be economically beneficial to refrain from doing so, when other companies seem to be involved in corrupt practices. This proposition thus concerns the strategic stance that companies adopt with regard to corruption. The respondents were asked, "In your opinion, would it be economically beneficial for Finnish companies operating in Russia to engage in more corruption?" Over two thirds of the respondents (68 %, or 23 out of 34) thought that it would *not* be economically beneficial for Finnish companies to engage in more corruption.

The results suggest that Finnish companies do not, in general, see corruption as being economically beneficial or even acceptable. However, the literature on this subject suggests that corruption may be a strategic choice and tool for a company, which often brings economic benefits.

Hence, the results do not necessarily mean that Finnish companies do not engage in corruption in Russia and don't see it as being beneficial. It may mean instead that the companies believe that they are engaging in the right amount of corruption - so that more or less corruption would be less beneficial. A certain level of corruption may be beneficial. Some corruption, whether it be called business gifts, "greasing the wheels", or just administrative corruption, may be justified in some situations and cultures. Or, as one of the respondents commented, *"When in Rome, do as the Romans do."*

Furthermore, information specific to Finnish companies' experiences with corruption in Russia was collected. In order to study the different contexts in which foreign companies encounter administrative corruption in Russia, one question concerned how frequently extra payments were made for certain services or in certain situations. These included the following: to access public utilities, obtain licenses, when dealing with tax or customs officials/issues, to gain orders, when dealing with the courts, or to influence laws. These purposes were adapted from the earlier BEEPS study (2002), which analyzed the business environment of local companies in transition economies. (http://info.worldbank.org/governance/beeps2002/). Consequently, the following question was posed: "In your opinion, how often do Finnish firms operating in Russia need to make extra, unofficial payments to public officials for any of the following?"

Q1: To get connected to public services (electricity, telephone)
Q2: To obtain licenses and permits
Q3: To deal with taxes and tax collection
Q4: When dealing with customs/imports to Russia
Q5: To gain government contracts
Q6: When dealing with the courts
Q7: To influence the content of new laws, decrees, or regulations?

Question 5 refers to public procurement kickbacks, whilst questions 6 and 7 involve state capture, with the other issues representing administrative corruption. The results are presented in Figure 3. It seems that extra payments were most common when companies needed to get licences and permits, deal with customs issues, or win, or at least seek to win, government contracts. According to the responses, it appears that payments are never or seldom used in situations involving dealing with the courts or influencing new laws and regulations.

**Figure 3: Unofficial payments for different purposes (n = 35). Source: Pekkanen & Salmi, 2006.**

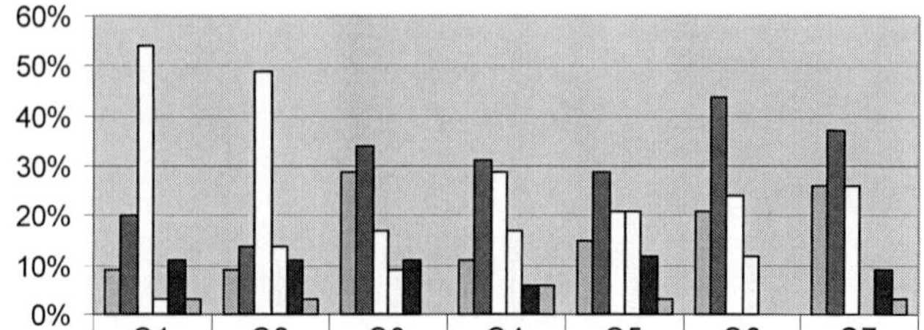


| | Q1 | Q2 | Q3 | Q4 | Q5 | Q6 | Q7 |
|---|---|---|---|---|---|---|---|
| Never | 9% | 9% | 29% | 11% | 15% | 21% | 26% |
| Seldom | 20% | 14% | 34% | 31% | 29% | 44% | 37% |
| Sometimes | 54% | 49% | 17% | 29% | 21% | 24% | 26% |
| Frequently | 3% | 14% | 9% | 17% | 21% | 12% | 0% |
| Most of time | 11% | 11% | 11% | 6% | 12% | 0% | 9% |

Never Seldom Sometimes Frequently Most of time Always

## Ethical Behaviour of SMEs

There are both managerial and research needs to analyze how SMEs tackle corruption and manage different ethical codes in international business. Both the home country and the host country features seem to affect the interaction between companies, and therefore, it is particularly challenging for companies to operate in a business context where the ethical rules are much different from the ones prevailing in the home country. Therefore, it is worth investigating what kind of pressures and from which stakeholders are put on the foreign companies as comes to the ethical decision-making and actions.

On this basis the study by Ruoho and Salmi (2007) pose the following research questions: What kinds of pressures affect SME's ethical behavior? And, what are the ways, in practice, that SMEs adopt to cope with different ethical pressures, and in particular, how do they deal with corruption?

One aim of the interviews was to find out, what kind of pressures the interviewees had felt in Russia that made them to change their behavior in an ethical sense, especially in terms of corruption. Every interviewee came up with at least one example of the pressures and most had several examples. Based on the answers, the *pressures are classified here into five categories*: pressures from the authorities, pressures deriving from the regulative environment, from influential persons, from the partners' and from the employees.

All respondents had felt at least some pressures and persuasion suggesting that they should modify their behavior towards the local practices. The respondents mentioned specifically *the pressures coming from the authorities*. Abuse of authoritative power and small-scale corruption Brovkin (2003) seem to be the norm in Russia and the core of the problems with the officials. The bribes asked for are not big (tobacco, chocolate or small sums of money). Refusing to pay these may lead to uncertainty concerning the timeline for handling e.g. the documents and licenses, as well as the verdict. It is difficult not to be exposed to the pressures set by the authorities when doing business in a foreign country and across the borders.

The Finnish entrepreneurs are constantly searching for the balance, since it is impossible to follow the norms of both countries if the norms are in contradiction with each other. *Pressures coming from partners, employees and outsiders* were seen to be more random and varying. By the choice of these contact persons one could either decrease or increase the pressures. The influence from the partners' and employees' side were generally more friendly by nature and thus left more room for own consideration.

The interviewees tended to distinguish between 'small' or 'obligatory' corruption and 'large" or 'criminal' corruption. A couple of companies had very clear and explicit policies on all kinds of corruption, which they had implemented also in practice. Most of the interviewees had more situational approach to bribing, which however does not mean that they would support corruption. On the contrary, the interviewees perceived corruption as a highly unfortunate feature in Russian business environment and felt awkward taking part in it. Still, several of them mentioned more or less explicitly that in their opinion their companies' operations in Russia would have halted, had they taken a very strict zero-corruption policy. Thus by adopting the institutionalized practices, the organizations gained better survival prospects (Meyer and Rowan, 1977). One of the main functions of small bribes was speeding up the otherwise stagnant treatments of various issues and fading out the ambiguity on the end result (thus informal payments skirt the imperfections, which explains partly the perceived high corruption rate as argued by Hellman, Jones and Kauffman, 2000) The few companies who had strict policies concerning bribing had also gained benefits by refusing to pay bribes: gradually the authorities ceased to asking bribes and there was no fear of getting caught about anything.

The reason for adapting to the local practices concerning 'small' corruption was not only the perceived impossibility to operate without bribing. Many companies made notions like, "*We can't take there different set of norms*" and "*It's their country*", "*It has been so since the times of Dostoyevsky and already many thousand years back from that, it's a cultural thing",* implying that in their opinion, one should not export one's own concepts of ethicality as the only correct ones. Thus many of the respondents thought that up to some limit the habitants in their own country had the right to determine the local norms. Generally the interviewees seemed to be culturally sensitive, and regarded that it was important to have a wider international perspective on business ethics. This sensitivity and fairly relativistic approach might be a result of the very close and personal contacts that the persons working in the SMEs have with the foreign environment. It is challenging to decide to take measures that are unknown in the host culture, if one knows that one has to push through and implement these practices oneself.

In general, the small bribes were used when dealing with the authorities. Concerning these, the interviewees had an approach that reminds discourse ethics, the idea of which is that because it is impossible to justify norms rationally, the norms should be created on day-to-day and situational basis to ethical problems, and that solving of ethical problems should start with real-life experiences rather than from belief systems. (Crane and Matten, 2004, 99). According to Puffer (1996, 208) the situation often guides the behavior for the Russians, so by taking a situational stance the Finnish respondents take a step towards adopting the Russian business mentality.

Everyone seemed to be totally unanimous on that 'large' or 'criminal' corruption was excluded. When defining the absolute ethical principles, several respondents mentioned that 'criminal corruption', 'corruption' or 'criminal acts' were not accepted. While small bribes to authorities and unofficial bonuses were occasionally mentioned, no respondents admitted paying large sums in order to get a deal or to persuade people to act in the company's favor. Furthermore, no one told about paying bribes without some one asking for them first. Small bribing is usually directed towards states officials, but sometimes the initiative for it comes from partners, employees or other stakeholders.

The trusted Russian employees are highly valued in Finnish companies, probably partly due to their cultural knowledge and background and their capability (and maybe also willingness) to handle the problematic situations that might be ethically difficult for the Finns. However, the world is not black-and-white and excessive reliance on stereotypical thinking is dangerous: if the company appoints a Russian to take care of certain issues, it does not necessarily mean that these would be handled unethically or against the moral of the Finnish partner. Variation in the perceptions may be a question of generations too. Naumov and Puffer (2000) found a large attitudinal gap in Russia between different generations; the older generations are more impacted by the Soviet times whereas younger generations have grown up in the transition period. Thus it might be that latter is more impacted by the Western business culture, which would also suggest a change in the future.
The common feature of using Russian employees as middlemen and dividing work between the Finns and the Russians, is partly based on each partners' competences.

A typical arrangement seems to be that those issues, which are ethically or culturally difficult for the Finns, are taken care of by the Russians. As one interviewee says: *"In most cases they have in the firms this...how would you call it...an errand boy or a Russian that takes care of these awkward issues so that the company won't get into trouble."* These Russians may be employed by the company or its Russian partner company.

There seem to be several reasons for using Russians as middlemen in ethical dilemmas. The Russian employees may take care of visits to Russian offices, because they can manage the situations better. As one interviewee noted, *"It is useless for us two Finns to go to any Russian offices. The doors open only to these Russians who speak their own language, own cultural language, with the help of which they then handle these things. In their own way."* Indeed, the notion of the 'cultural language' seems to come close to the concept of 'social bargaining skills' as specified by Hirvensalo et al. (2001), i.e. skills that are needed to get things arranged. As the following quotation shows, the division of work between the partners seems to be based on competences: who gets the things done. In addition, the division is due to the Finnish side's reluctance to be part of ethically questionable activities.

There seems in fact to be a contradiction: on the one hand corruption in relation to authorities is regarded as very undesirable, and on the other, they are not entirely denying the partner to use corruption. There thus seems to be an (unwilling) recognition that the local environment may still require this kind of measures. There thus seem to be dual pressures facing the entrepreneurs.

Indeed, by letting the Russians take care of, for example, relations with authorities, the Finnish entrepreneurs respond to both pressures: the inner moral pressure that derives from their cultural background and leads to avoiding certain things, and the local pressures from the market that sometimes require doing what the inner voice dreads.

Naturally, Russian employers and partners are experts in their own culture and accustomed to handling problems with the authorities. Language skills also have an impact on this issue. Karhunen et al, (2003) found out that Finnish businessmen were dissatisfied with their Russian partners' know-how on business management. Thus it seems natural that the Finns would be responsible for issues like, e.g., project management. Still, the perceived competencies of the partners were not the only reason for this kind of division. Some interviewees said that they regarded the corruption in relation to authorities as highly undesirable and the firm did not want to take part in any questionable arrangements. Yet, they did not absolutely deny their Russian partners or employees taking these kinds of measures, if needed in the name of survival of the business, but rather, did not want to be aware of it. The managers' solution to the dilemma between the environment's requirements and their own conscience was to let the Russian parties take care of some awkward issues.

## Discussion

The study by Pekkanen and Salmi (2006) shows that Finnish companies tend to engage in more corruption in Russia than at home in Finland, but that they are still less corrupt than companies coming from more corrupt countries. Thus, home-country factors 'follow' the foreign company into transition economies. However, the host-country context also influences behavior. Finnish companies seem to be less corrupt than their local counterparts, but they still have to cope with administrative corruption.

Whilst there is little evidence to suggest that international anti-corruption initiatives would reduce corruption, there seems to be a new openness regarding this issue. The willingness of managers to reply to the study's questionnaire was itself a positive sign and might perhaps indicate that it will be easier to investigate corruption in the future than has previously been the case.

Further, the study suggests that Russian administrators discriminate against foreign companies. Over half of the respondents were of the opinion that the Russian authorities treated Russian companies better than Finnish ones. It may well be that in all business contexts local authorities tend to treat domestic firms better than foreign firms – or that this is the common perception amongst foreign managers. The study setting by Pekkanen and Salmi (2006) tends to be biased towards the difficulties that foreign companies encounter in Russian markets. The study reveals those situations where foreign companies have had to pay extra; the most prominent examples being licensing procedures, dealing with customs issues and in securing government contracts. The key conclusion is that Finnish companies encounter corruption in Russia in various situations, and that they are adapting to this situation and usually accepting it as part of the local business culture.

The study by Ruoho and Salmi (2007) shows that the cultural background, company's (entrepreneurs') internal view on business ethics as well as the host environment all have an impact on the formation of business ethics of Finnish SMEs in Russia. The intensity of these factors varied. The internal views on business ethics were often very personal and unofficial. Finnish cultural heritage was seen as an important provider of ethical attitudes, but in practice the impact of pressures set by the host environment was strong and came especially from the authorities. Also the pressures coming from other stakeholders often concerned payments to the authorities.

Money-laundering, smuggling, large-scale corruption and other clearly 'criminal' activities were perceived as condemnable, probably due to the Finnish background. Reliance on relationships was perceived as an inseparable part of the Russian culture, yet the relationships were utilized with some cautions. Indeed, ethics cannot be separated from business, but rather the ethical norms of the company affect all its operations. Small-scale corruption, especially in relation to authorities, was perceived undesired, yet unavoidable by the majority of the respondents. The acceptable code of business behavior in Russia seems not to be established, but rather to be undergoing a constant change.

While all the interviewed companies felt pressures for unethical behavior, the personal characters of the managers and company strategies affected how the dilemmas were tackled in practice. Russians were commonly used as middlemen in handling the ethically difficult situations. Reasons for this were, among others, their 'skills of social bargaining' (Hirvensalo et. al. 2000), the company's attempt not to be directly linked to dubious activities and also, the differences in cultural backgrounds, i.e. locals know the local culture better, as in any foreign business context.

## Conclusions

The key conclusion about Finnish companies in Russian business is that the pressures coming from the stakeholders (and administration in particular) in the host country are very different from the home country, and consequently, the companies need to find special ways to deal with these, peculiar to the host country, norms. Often, locals are used as middlemen when dealing with the pressures, but still, foreigners remain easily outside the inner circles of influence.

Our key conclusion is that while the companies claim to be ethical they all note the differences in the ethical rules between the countries. Various stakeholders in the host country cause pressures for behaving differently in ethical terms than at home, and calls for extra payments come especially from the administrative sector. Both studies confirm that it is a common practice to make extra payments for several everyday services from the state.

This paper has tackled the difficult issue of corruption and ethical behavior – global phenomena that are widely discussed, but difficult to reveal in detail. In addition to discussing the literature on the subject, empirical data on Finnish companies' perceptions of corruption and relations with the administration in Russia was presented. This is quite rare, as there are only a few studies providing empirical data on corrupt practices, or perceptions of corruption. Therefore, despite the relatively small number of respondents (35 and 12) in the studies, the investigation provides new insights into the sensitive and delicate issue of corruption.

The studies show also that if provided anonymity, companies are ready to discuss quite openly even difficult issues of doing business. SME managers seem to struggle to cope with the ethically different business context in Russia. Therefore, there is a need for more analysis and discussion on these issues, by both managers and researchers. Further studies would be needed concerning e.g. more detailed analysis of the features of the managers themselves (e.g. demography, background, education) and how these influence the ethical views of the SMEs.

There are some limitations specific to the two studies. The research settings and questions replicate other Western studies on the issue, and are thus culture-bound. Corruption is different in different countries. One explanation for this is that social norms are different. What is regarded in one culture as corrupt may be considered part of a routine transaction in another. For example, it is widely recognized that in developing countries gift-exchange is an accepted social norm in business transactions (Bardhan 1997). In societies with close social relationships, the frequency of corruption is likely to be greater, its identification more difficult, and its punishment more problematic. (Tanzi 1995, 167) The present study reflects Western norms, but in future studies the formulation of the questions could be reworked to take into account different cultures. Moreover, within a country, there may be different attitudes towards bribery depending on the ethnic background of respondents. This suggests that attitudes should be compared on a cultural rather than on a national basis (Fletcher, 2001).

Furthermore, the empirical evidence is based on the perceptions of Finnish companies operating in Russia. A valuable approach for future studies would be to pose the same questions to Russian companies operating in a Western economy, like Finland's. In addition, due to the small number of respondents one needs to be cautious when generalizing the findings to other Western companies and countries and to other transition economies. However, it seems that managers too see this topic as worthy of analysis. Therefore, more analysis – both conceptual and with a larger database – is called for.

The need for analysis and discussion is further increased by the demands that transition economies make on managers. After the initial opening up and development of these emerging markets, more companies are now attracted to, and starting up business in, the transition economies. Thus, they are bound to encounter local norms. This study has focused on enterprise-state relations and SME behavior together with the pressures they encounter from different stakeholders.

It provides the following more general implications for business interaction: 1) both cooperation and competition are important for business, and even more so in transition economies. Competition is one way of avoiding relationships that are, perhaps, too intimate and binding, which in turn helps to combat corruption. 2) Although the informal aspects of business interaction are of central importance, they should not lead to secrecy in a way that enhances corruption. Openness is crucial. 3) Corruption is not limited to developing or transition countries, but is, to some extent, evident in market economies as well. When operating in such areas, Western firms will have to cope with this phenomenon. 4) Corruption mainly involves local bureaucracies and their behavior, but in dealing with the administration companies form the other half of a possibly corrupt relationship. Therefore, the corrupt behavior of both parties to this business relationship, the demand and supply of corruption needs to be analyzed. 5) Corruption involves (and means risks for) both firms and individual business people. These findings are especially relevant today when there is increasing demand for ethical behavior in global business.

## Acknowledgements

This research was partially supported by a grant from the Paulo Foundation. The data for the two reviewed studies (Pekkanen & Salmi, 2006 and Ruoho & Salmi, 2007) was collected by M.Sc. Tuomas Pekkanen and M.Sc. Elina Ruoho.

## References

Abed, G. T. & H.R. Davoodi, (2002), *Corruption, Structural Reforms, and Economic Performance in Transition Economies.* In and Gupta (Ed), *Governance, Corruption, & Economic Performance.* International Monetary Fund, Washington, D.C., USA

Abed, G. T. & S. Gupta, (2002), *The Economics of Corruption: An Overview*, In Abed and Gupta (Ed), *Governance, Corruption, & Economic Performance.* International Monetary Fund, Washington, D.C., USA

Ahmed, Mohammed M.; Ching, Kung Young.; Eichenseher, John W. (2003). Business students' perception of ethics and moral judgement:

A cross-cultural study. *Journal of Business Ethics*. (March) 43:1/2, 89-102.

Bardhan, P. (1997) "Corruption and Development: A Review of Issues", Journal of Economic Literature, Vol. XXXV (September), 1320-1346.

Beekun, R.I.; Westerman, J. and Barghouti, J. (2005). Utility of Ethical Frameworks in Determining Behavioral Intention: A Comparison of the U.S and Russia. *Journal of Business Ethics.* Dordrecht. 61:3, 235-247

Corruption and Good Governance (1997), Discussion Paper 3, Management Development and Governance Division, Bureau for Policy and Programme Support, United Nations Development Program, New York, USA

De Vel, G. & P. Csonka, (2002) *The Council of Europe Activities against Corruption,* in Fijnaut and Huberts (Ed.), *Corruption, Integrity, and Law Enforcement*, Kluwer Law International, The Hague, The Netherlands

Fletcher, R. (2001) "Attitudes Towards Bribery in a Multicultural Nation: Implications for International Marketing", *Journal Of International Marketing and Exporting*, August, pp 58-77.

Grünbaum,L.(1997). Attitudes of Future Managers towards Business Ethics: A Comparison of Finnish and American Business Students. *Journal of Business Ethics.* 16:4, 451-463

Haapaniemi, M., M. Moijanen. & K. Muradjan (2003), *Tak Ili Kak? – Venäläistä Tapakulttuuria Suomalaisille*. Suomalais-Venäläinen kauppakamariyhdistys ry. Multiprint Oy, Helsinki.

Hellman, J. S., G. Jones & D. Kaufmann (2002), *Far From Home: Do Foreign Investors Import Higher Standards of Governance in Transition Economies?* Working Paper, The World Bank.

Hellman, J.S., G. Jones & D. Kaufmann (2000), *Are Foreign Investors and Multinational Engaging in Corrupt Practices in Transition Economies?* Transition, May-June-July 2000. The World Bank/The William Davidson Institute/Stockholm Institute for Transitional Economies

Hirvensalo, I., R. Kosonen & A. Salmi (2000), "Social Bargaining and Foreign Owned Companies in Russia", *Idäntutkimus,* 2000, Special Issue for VI ICCEES world conference, 48-61.

Jaffe, E. D., Tsimerman, A. (2005) "Business Ethics in Transition Economy: Will the Next Russian Generation be any Better?" *Journal of Business Ethics*. 62:1, 87-97

Kujala, J. (2001). A Multidimensional Approach to Finnish Managers' Moral Decision-Making. Journal of Business Ethics. 34:3-4, 231-254.

—. (2004). Managers' moral perceptions: change in Finland during the 1990s. *Business Ethics: A European Review*. Oxford. (April-July)13: 2/3, 143-165

Kuula, Arja. (2006). *Tutkimusetiikka: Aineistojen käyttö, hankinta ja säilytys*. Vastapaino.

Ledeneva, A.V. (1998), *Russian Economy of Favours. Blat, Networking and Informal Exchange*. Cambridge University Press.

Lovett, S., L.C. Simmons & R. Kali (1999) "Guanxi Versus the Market: Ethics and Efficiency", *Journal of International Business Studies*, 30:2, 231-248.

Marschan-Piekkari, R.; Welch, C.. (2004) Qualitative Research Methods in International Business. The State of the Art. *in Handbook of Qualitative Business Research for International Business*. Edited by Marschan-Piekkari, R.; Welch, C. Edvar Elgar Publishing Ltd, 5-24

Pacini, C., J.A. Swingen & H. Rogers (2002), *The Role of the OECD and EU Conventions in Combating Bribery of Foreign Public Officials.* Journal of Business Ethics, 37. Kluwer Academic Publishers, The Netherlands.

Panapanaan, V.. M.; Linnanen, L., Karvonen, M-M., Phan, V. Th. (2003) "Roadmapping corporate social responsibility in Finnish companies". *Journal of Business Ethics*, 44:2/3, 133-148

Pekkanen, T. & Salmi, A (2006). Enterprise-state corruption in transition economies: An empirical analysis of Finnish companies in Russia. In: Larimo, J. and Rumpunen, S. (Eds.) *Internationalization and Management of Foreign Operations*. Proceedings of the University of Vaasa, Reports 130, 319-339. Vaasa.

Peng, M. W. & Y. Luo (2000) "Managerial ties and firm performance in a transition economy: the nature of a micro-macro ling", *Academy of Management Journal*, 43:3, 486-501.

Puffer, S.M. and McCarthy, D. J. (1995). Finding Common Ground in Russian and American Business Ethics. *California Management Review*. (Winter) 37:2, 29-46.

Puffer, S. M.(1996) *Business and Management in Russia*. Cheltenham: Elgar, 1996.

Ruoho, E. & Salmi, A. Navigating in the grey area: how do Finnish SMEs perceive ethics and tackle corruption in contemporary Russia? Paper presented to the 9th Vaasa Conference on International Business, University of Vaasa, Vaasa, Finland, August 19-21, 2007.

Salmi, A. (2000) "Corruption – do we skip unpleasant issues of business interaction?", paper presented to the 16th IMP Conference, hosted by

University of Bath and University of Birmingham, 7th-9th September 2000, Bath, UK. CD-rom Proceedings.

Shleifer, A. & R.W. Vishny (1993) "Corruption", *The Quarterly Journal of Economics*, August, 599-617.

Steves, F. & A. Rousso (2003), *Anti-corruption Programmes in Post-communist Transition Countries and Changes in the Business Environment, 1999-2002.* European Bank for Reconstruction and Development, Working Paper No. 85, London, UK.

Tanzi, V. (1995) "Corruption: arms'-length relationships and markets", in Fiorentina, Gianluca and Peltzman, Sam (eds.). The economics of organized crime, Cambridge University Press, 161-180.

—. (1998), *Corruption Around the World: Causes, Consequences, Scope, and Cures.* In Abed and Gupta (Ed.) *Governance, Corruption and Economic Performance* (2002). International Monetary Fund, Washington, D.C., USA.

Tirole, J. (1996), "A Theory of Collective reputations (with applications to the persistence of corruption and to firm quality), *The Review of Economic Studies*, January, 63:214.

Usunier, J-C. (2000), *Marketing Across Cultures*, 3rd ed., (Singapore: Prentice Hall).

World Bank (2000) *Anticorruption in Transition – A Contribution to the Policy Debate.* (2000), The World Bank, Washington, D.C., USA

—. (2004) *Anticorruption in Transition 2 – Corruption in Enterprise-State Interactions in Europe and Central Asia 1999-2002.* The European Bank for Reconstruction and Development / The World Bank, Washington, D.C., USA

Xin, K.R. & J.L. Pearce (1996) "*Guanxi*: Connections as substitutes for formal institutional support", *Academy of Management Journal*, 39:6, 1641-1658.

http://www.transparency.org/surveys/index.html

http://www.finruscc.fi

http://colostate.edu/references/research/survey/com3c1.cfm

http://info.worldbank.org/governance/beeps2002/

# RUSSIAN AND FINNISH BUSINESS OWNERS: COMPARISON OF POWER-CONTROL DIMENSIONS TO OWNERSHIP – SURVEY RESULTS

JARI JUMPPONEN, MARKKU IKÄVALKO, TUULI MIROLA AND MINNA IKÄVALKO

## Abstract

The purpose of this study is to analyze owner and owner-manager profiles among Finnish and Russian business leaders. Authors have conducted a survey among 164 business owners in Northwest Russia (SPb. area) and among 149 business owners in Southeast Finland. The survey results indicate that there are cultural differences between Finnish and Russian business managers and owners. In addition to country-wide differences the company specific variables (e.g. owners' age, firm turnover, number of personnel) affect the power-control dimension of ownership. According to the survey results the power-control dimension of ownership is more important in Russia than in Finland.

## Introduction

The small business research has shown rather clearly that one of the most distinctive characteristics of small business is the owner's identification with the business (e.g. Collins, Moore and Unwalla, 1964; Kets de Vries, 1996; Bridge, O'Neil and Cromie, 1998). The firm is a tool to fulfill economic goals, but also much more. The typologies of entrepreneurs and small business managers illustrate both the need to understand the entrepreneur and also the differences in owner/firm relationships (e.g. Stanworth and Curran, 1976). The ownership profile here means the bundle of elements through which the entrepreneur mentally links himself to his firm. The firm is both ends and means; it is partially the result of action, partially a target of actions and also an instrument to reach other targets. Owner-managers mental connection to the firm is very unique and therefore it could be stated that firms and owner-managers are not transferable. Each owner-manager has his own way to look at his firm.

In the mid-1980s there were fewer than 100,000 small companies in Russia. Small business and business managers have thus a relatively short operational history, and the role of small business is still rather modest. Currently, small business contributes some 12% of Russian GDP. The business environment in Finland could be characterized as stabilized, while in Russia the conditions for enterprises are claimed to be in constant change. The number of small firms in Russia grew quickly from 267,000 in 1991 to 865,000 in 1993. However, after this stage the number of small business units has stagnated and even declined. Kontorovich (1999) has listed likely causes for this stagnation to include 1) increased tax and regulatory burdens; 2) barriers to entry raised by the authorities; 3) the use of new businesses to plunder state-owned firms; and 4) the consequences of the banking crises in 1998.

In the end of 2003 there were 230,400 enterprises operating in Finland, which means there are 45 enterprises per 1,000 inhabitants. However, the enterprise density in Finland is lower than in several Western countries (Hyrsky and Lipponen, 2004). The respective figure for Russia was some four million enterprises, which comprises 27 companies per 1,000 inhabitants.

In the international studies of entrepreneurial activities Finland has scored rather low. In the GEM studies (Global Entrepreneurship Monitor, 1999) the activity to start up new firm was the lowest despite the facts that the attitudes towards entrepreneurship were in many cases very positive in Finland, and that the economic growth in Finland has been rather good in resent years. In Flash Euro barometer (2003) research on entrepreneurship, people were asked whether they would like to work as employees or independent entrepreneurs. Only about 35 % of Finns preferred entrepreneurship, where the average in EU was 45 % and in USA above 60%. One Finnish characteristic is that the more people are educated the less interested they are to work as entrepreneurs.

McCarthy et al. (1997) pays attention to the fact that new entrepreneurs in Russia come from diverse backgrounds. They state that some current entrepreneurs (in the mid-1990s) have been employed in State enterprises and ministries, while others have been members of the technical and cultural elite in academic and research environments. Moreover, some have been students with virtually no work experience in the centralized economy. Shama and Merrell (1997) describe the transformation of Russian management in the early 1990s by defining Russian manager's tendency to develop new managerial styles, changing from directors to managers. Besides, they state Russian managers to be active, flexible and open-minded, and have sales background with strategic and entrepreneurial risk-taking.

This paper focuses on the possible differences between Russian and Finnish business owners in regard to their power-control characteristics. It is taken as an overall pre-assumption that both different kind of economical, cultural and legal histories and the inner reality of the company would influence these ownership profiles. Therefore this research examines correlations between selected background variables (e.g. owners' age, firm turnover, number of personnel) with the power-control dimension of ownership. Power is a central element in ownership. Only when combining power with aims it is possible to achieve the results.

## Ownership, Power and Cross-Cultural Differences

### Owner and Ownership

The literature of small and medium sized enterprises is filled with notions of owner-managers mentally connecting themselves to the firm; the firm is very important for the owner-manager and a central part of his life and self-identity. In this paper psychological ownership refers to the subject–object relation comprehended by the small business owner-manager. In SME-context ownership has been rather neglected a concept.

Pierce, Kostova and Dirks (2001) proposed a frame for a theory of psychological ownership. First they defined the roots of psychological ownership, e.g. the reasons why psychological ownership exist. They summarized the previous research on the subject by stating that psychological ownership emerges because it satisfies both generic and socially generated motives of individual human beings. More specifically, these motives are: 1) efficacy, 2) self-identity, 3) having a place. This in short means that the ability to do something and "being someone somewhere" are closely connected to the concept of psychological ownership. Secondly Pierce, Kostova and Dirks (2001) defined the routes through which the individual comes to experience ownership. These separately examined but potentially interrelated routes are: 1) controlling the target, 2) coming intimately to know the target, 3) investing self into the target. Here the main elements are power, knowledge and action (targeted to the object).

Power is a central element in ownership. Theoretically, power is considered in two different ways: either with subjective or objective interpretation. Emerson (1962) treated power as a social phenomenon with persons or groups acting in a power-network. This network, in turn, is tied together with multiple power-dependence relations where dependence is a power source for individuals. In this system the "net-power" means dependence and power imbalance between actors. Thus Emerson defined power as the resistance that could be overcome, and which is a subjectively measurable phenomenon. However Rainio (1969) suggests that the definition of power by Emerson refers to power as a potential force that can be operated when needed. In that sense, the "amount" of power cannot be judged according to the outcome of an action, but by measuring the potential. Lukes (1991) also illustrated power with term capacity and social relationship, i.e. as potentiality and action. As power has several interlinked dimensions, and as power is such an important element in ownership, it leads to a conclusion that ownership is difficult to examine at one ontological level only. This creates theoretical and methodological challenges in examining psychological ownership. It is not sufficient or even possible to be studied alone without interaction with other ontological levels of ownership.

Theories of lifecycles of the firms suggest in a very straightforward way, that the development and growth of firm requires changes also in the management styles. Greiner (1972) proclaimed in his famous article that organizations do not develop in a linear manner, but via revolutionary stages, where the role and importance of managerial actions alters. Churchill and Lewis (1983) made similar conclusion when studying the development of newly established firms. In the early stages the role of the individual entrepreneur and his entrepreneurial capability is most important. In later stages the role of any individual is lesser and the firm acts more as a social entity. Without further examination of those development processes and stages it is possible to argue, that the managerial styles and other essential processes within a firm are to some extend interlinked to these development stages. Thus it could be assumed

that also ownership function, and further the ownership profile of the business owners, is affected by the development stage of the firm.
Private ownership has a long history in Finland and the basic structures of the legal regime of the company ownership have remained very much untouched during the history of Finland's independence. The share of family firms in Finland is significant and many of them are in the hands of second or third generation. The private ownership of the firms in Russia is a much newer thing. As the history obviously influences the state of being also in the case of ownership, it could be assumed that Russian and Finnish owners may have, to some extent, different opinions of themselves as business owners and decision makers. According to Cooper and Dunkelberg (1986) and Clifford, Nilakant and Hamilton (1991) the routes to business ownership and the history of the ownership are in relation to a measurable degree of entrepreneurship in later actions.

## Cultural Differences

In order to study the possible differences between Russian and Finnish business-owners, it is important to have a look at the cultural aspects of these two counties. National culture affects the everyday life in society but creates also the basis for business culture. According to Hofstede (1991) national culture is the collective programming of the mind acquired by growing up in a particular country. Business culture comprises the effective rules of the game, the boundaries between competitive and unethical behaviour, and the codes for conduct in business dealing (Terpstra and David 1985).

Even though the interest and discussion on small business issues tends to be international, the results usually originate from national level studies. The national cultures and more specifically, differences between them have been studied for decades. A great deal of the research on national cultures in broader sense has produced listings of differences. It is interesting though that the well know researches by Hofstede (1984, 1991, 1993) still remain the only serious attempts to systematically study and analyse these differences.

The value scale created by Hofstede originally included four-dimension scale (later he added the fifth dimension). Actually, Russia was not included in the original study, but Hofstede made hypotheses about the country. The first dimension of the scale is called power distance and is defined as the degree of equality between people that the population of a country considers to be a normal. Hofstede argued that Russia would be characterized by high power distance; in other words Russians would display high tolerance toward inequality in the society and business relationships. The second dimension, individualism, is the degree to which people in a country prefer to act as individuals rather than members of groups; the opposite of this is collectivism. Russia scores in this dimension in medium-range. The third dimension, masculinity/femininity, is defined as to the degree to which such 'masculine' values as assertiveness, competition, and success are emphasized as opposed to such values as quality of life, warm personal relationships, and service. Russia scores low masculinity in this dimension. The fourth dimension, uncertainty avoidance is the degree to which people in a country prefer structured to unstructured situations. Russia scores high in this dimension of uncertainty avoidance. The later added fifth dimension, short-term – long-term orientation, was not thoroughly tested in the original study. Hofstede argued that Russia would score low in long-term orientation.

Bollinger (1994) also tested these Hofstede's hypotheses in his study of Russian managers and found similar results with Hofstede's assumptions: high power distance, low tolerance for uncertainty, high appreciation for collectivism, and general equality between men and women workers.

According to Hofstede (1984, 1991, 1993) Finland could be considered quite an individualistic society, the country scored quite high on individualism scale. On the uncertainty avoidance scale, Finland has a low index (below the average), whereas Russia scores high. Furthermore, Finland and Russia differ on the power distance scale; Finland has quite a low index compared to the Russia's high score. On the Masculinity scale both Finland and Russia scores low.

## Cross-Cultural Comparisons

Ardichvili et al. (1998) illustrate in their study some characteristics of Russian entrepreneurs. Decision-making is done individually (25% of respondents of 258 total) or discussing with other executives (32% of respondents). 30% of respondents described their leadership style as democratic, whereas 11% identified themselves as autocratic leaders. Nearly 57% of respondents described themselves as situational leaders, defining this style as using both autocratic and democratic methods, depending on situation. According to Ardichivili (2001) entrepreneurs were also more likely than managers to use inspirational and charismatic leadership behaviours and to motivate by establishing a direct link between performance and rewards. Managers have higher levels of passive, laissez-faire leadership behaviours than entrepreneurs.

Puffer (1996) has also identified some differences in Western and Slavic ethical systems. According to her, one difference is in the way ethics is construed in different situations. In Slavic cultures there are often two sets of ethical standards, one for personal relationships and one for impersonal relationships in business and public life. In contrast, in the West, people are expected to employ the same set of ethical standards regardless of the situation. Another difference concerns attitudes toward conflict and compromise. Whereas Slavs often consider it a sign of weakness and cowardice to make compromises and smooth over conflicts, Western people usually consider this kind of behaviour to be positive. Puffer suggests that contemporary Russian managers tend to share power, are inclined to delegate decision-making (largely to avoid the responsibility for unforeseen consequences), prefer to concentrate on strategic decision-making, are tenacious and energetic, and have strong collectivistic attitudes.

In their study on leadership styles Fey et al. (2001) categorized most often identified Russian leadership characteristics to task-oriented, relations-oriented, authoritarian, and democratic. Besides, they extended their research to evaluate the effectiveness of those four leadership styles, which in turn revealed the task-oriented democrat and relations-oriented democrat to have been considered as most effective. As a result they concluded that Russians not only prefer directive leaders but also feel that effective leaders should prioritize task accomplishment over relationship building. Based on their results Fey et al. (2001) concluded that Russian leadership preferences are coming closer to, but not identical to, those which could be expected to be found in the United States or Western Europe. In their study Zhuplev et al. (1998), in turn, compared small-business owners' motivations and obstacles in Russia and in the United States. They found no dramatic differences in entrepreneurs' retrospective view of starting their business. Russian respondents tended to answer with an even higher rate of enthusiasm on this issue, which was explained by authors by the relative novelty of entrepreneurship for Russians.

In comparative studies between Russian and Finnish managers Suutari (1996) has revealed that Russian managers criticize actions of subordinates more and need more role clarification. Besides, they encourage participation in decision making much less than their Finnish counterparts and tend to be much more autocratic. Suutari and Bolotow (1996) continued determining differences by stating that Russians spend significantly more effort on rewarding employees.

## Survey

A 46-item survey was conducted among 313 business owners in the two countries. In Finland it was administered by mail to respondents selected from membership lists of chambers of commerce in Southeast Finland. Since in Russia there are apparent deficits for conducting such a survey by mail, the personal interviews were utilized instead. The questionnaire consisted of 46 individual statements concerning the entrepreneur/manager's opinion on himself, his company, the outside world and their relations.

A total of 164 Russian and 149 Finnish business owners and managers participated in the study. Most of the Russian companies were operating in manufacturing - out of the 164 Russian interviewees there were 106 operating in the manufacturing sector, 33 in construction, and 13 in the transport, storage and communication sector. Among Finnish companies the breakdown of the branches of economy was more even. Out of 149 Finnish respondents 31 announced to operate in manufacturing, 16 in construction, and 6 in transport, storage and communication.

**Table 1: Respondents by industrial sector**

| Code | Sector | Finland | Russia | Total |
|---|---|---|---|---|
| D | Manufacturing | 31 | 106 | 137 |
| F | Construction | 16 | 33 | 49 |
| K | Real estate, renting and business activities | 35 | 3 | 38 |
| I | Transport, storage and communications | 6 | 13 | 19 |
| G | Wholesale and retail trade; repair of motor vehicles | 5 | 3 | 8 |
| H | Hotels and restaurants | 5 | 0 | 5 |
| O | Other community, social and personal service activities | 0 | 3 | 3 |
| A | Agriculture, hunting and forestry | 2 | 0 | 2 |
| C | Mining and quarrying | 1 | 1 | 2 |
| N | Health and social work | 2 | 0 | 2 |
| J | Financial intermediation | 1 | 0 | 1 |
| | Missing | 45 | 2 | 47 |
| | **Total** | **149** | **164** | **313** |

**Table 2: Medians of selected background variables by nationality and industry**

| | | Age | | Turnover[1] | | Personnel[2] | |
|---|---|---|---|---|---|---|---|
| **Code** | **Sector** | **Russian** | **Finnish** | **Russian** | **Finnish** | **Russian** | **Finnish** |
| A | Agriculture, hunting and forestry | - | 52 | - | 800 | - | 12 |
| C | Mining and quarrying | 27 | 64 | - | 1200 | 1 | 12 |
| D | Manufacturing | 39 | 51 | 3 | 1970 | 2 | 17 |
| F | Construction | 46 | 49 | 4,5 | 900 | 3 | 11 |
| G | Wholesale and retail trade; repair of motor vehicles | 54 | 58 | 6 | 543 | 3 | 6 |
| H | Hotels and restaurants | - | 43 | - | 444 | - | 7 |
| I | Transport, storage and communications | 37 | 50 | 2 | 975 | 2 | 6,5 |
| J | Financial intermediation | - | 51 | - | 7900 | - | 53 |
| K | Real estate, renting and business activities | 45 | 52 | 3 | 550 | 1 | 10 |
| N | Health and social work | - | 45 | - | 450 | - | 10,5 |
| O | Other community, social and personal service activities | 36,5 | - | 5 | - | 3 | - |
| | **Total** | **41** | **50** | **3** | **1000** | **3** | **10** |

The median age of the Finnish respondents was 50 years, meanwhile Russian respondents were some ten years younger, except for the construction sector where managers' ages were almost the same in the both countries. Company size is represented by two variables: number of personnel and turnover. On an average, Finnish respondents had 10 employees, whereas the respective figure for Russian companies was three times more in all branches of the economy. This partly results from the fact that labour costs are remarkably lower in Russia as well as productivity and value added figures are lower. Moreover, work is more labour-intensive. However, Russian companies announce to have turnover of ten times smaller than Finnish respondents. Authors presume this firstly due to the Russian respondent's reluctance to reveal the exact figures. Secondly, the price level of goods (in nominal terms) is some four times lower in Russia. Thus, companies accumulate lower turnover figures, respectively. With these caveats in mind, it is nevertheless possible to draw some comparisons on the size effect between the two nationalities.

## Results and Analysis

In order to study the power-control attitude of the entrepreneur/manager, a sub-set of statements was selected of the original 46 statements. The set consisted of 22 individual statements concerning the entrepreneur/manager's attitude towards the power/control which he exercises in the company from three points of view: 1) in his own opinion, 2) as perceived by other people inside the company, as well as 3) in the eyes of the outside world. The opinions were measured on a 7-point Likert scale whereby respondents were asked to indicate the extent to which they agree or disagree with the statement. The anchors for the scale ranged from 1 "totally disagree" to 7 "totally agree".

In order to be able to interpret power-control dimensions a factor analysis was conducted on the data. The aim of the principle component analysis was to reduce the original set of variables i.e. statements into a smaller set of composite variables which could be interpreted as power-control factors. Varimax rotation was used to make the factors more interpretable.

The analysis produced 6 components with initial eigenvalues over 1. If 6 components were extracted, then 54 per cent of the variance would be explained. However interpreting that many components was considered not very informative, therefore the number of components was limited to 3, which explain, however, some 38 per cent of variance.

The Bartlett's test for sphericity is significant and the Kaiser-Meyer-Olkin measure of sampling adequacy is 0.816. Thus the factorability of the data is assumed. The results of the principal component analysis are presented in Table 3.

Looking at the individual variables (statements) that are strongly associated with component 1, we find that it represents the entrepreneur's own view of the power and control in the company. This component is associated with reluctance to share responsibility and need for total control of the business. The component could be thus named as "**me**"-component of power.

The second component captures strong and positive attitudes towards the social and network aspect of business. The personality type that agrees with the statements in this component is driven by social networks and very committed to the company as well as open to discussion and influence. The component represents the opinion of the "**others**" on the entrepreneur's power. This type of entrepreneur thrives when he is looked up to as a successful entrepreneur/manager.

The aspects of delegation and sharing of the power and responsibilities are emphasized in the third component. It can therefore be regarded as the "**together**" component of power and control.

The three components extracted with Varimax rotation do not totally exclude each other. Looking at the rotated component matrix we find that some of the variables (statements) have loadings of 0.3 or greater on more than one factor, i.e. they are not pure variables but complex ones. This should be taken account for when interpreting the components as they may be somewhat overlapping. However, for the purpose of this study, the interpretations are reasonably clear.

**Table 3:The principal component analysis of power-control**

| Question | Statement | 1 | 2 | 3 | Comm. |
|---|---|---|---|---|---|
| po10 | No one knows all the operational and managerial work in the company as good as I do | **,810** | -,005 | ,021 | ,657 |
| po29 | No one knows the equipment of the company as good as I do | **,729** | -,024 | -,058 | ,535 |
| po4 | No one knows the people of the company (department) as good as I do | **,699** | -,019 | ,128 | ,506 |
| po7 | My opinion is highly respected within the company | **,683** | ,190 | ,274 | ,578 |
| po2 | The company (department) has always been under my command only. There was no other manager of the company within its existence | **,662** | ,028 | -,018 | ,439 |
| po17 | The influence of the other people to company is very small | **,608** | ,049 | -,065 | ,377 |
| po24 | I do not want any new owners of the company at any circumstances | **,586** | ,160 | ,001 | ,370 |
| po1 | As a owner (or manager) of the firm I am controlling the situation | **,582** | ,287 | ,066 | ,426 |

| | | | | | |
|---|---|---|---|---|---|
| po37 | Networking with other firms will increase their power within my company | **,381** | ,139 | -,210 | ,209 |
| po41 | People know me only because I am a business owner (manager) | ,026 | **,697** | -,094 | ,495 |
| po33 | I highly value the business advice of the outsiders | -,123 | **,601** | ,025 | ,377 |
| po27 | The success of the company affects clearly my own esteem | ,367 | **,526** | ,171 | ,441 |
| po18 | The social status as an owner (manager) is very important for myself | ,343 | **,525** | -,102 | ,404 |
| po22 | My family respects me because of my working results | ,298 | **,466** | ,139 | ,325 |
| po46 | I have noticed, that people in general are very interested in the success on my firm | -,031 | **,447** | ,155 | ,224 |
| po16 | I want to know all my customers in person | ,289 | **,390** | ,127 | ,252 |
| po35 | I have often discussions with other entrepreneurs concerning my business | -,123 | **,332** | ,160 | ,151 |
| po36 | The accountant is a very valuable partner for me in decision making | ,126 | **,278** | ,020 | ,093 |
| po8 | It is very easy for me to delegate my responsibilities | ,065 | ,005 | **,740** | ,551 |

| | | | | | |
|---|---|---|---|---|---|
| po5 | I have often discussions within the company concerning the business | ,083 | ,195 | **,687** | ,517 |
| po44 | I constantly observe the product quality of the competitors | ,348 | ,147 | **,369** | ,279 |
| po42 | The account is balanced only for the tax authorities as a formal tool | ,251 | -,081 | **-,359** | ,198 |
| | Eigenvalue | 4,977 | 2,089 | 1,337 | |
| | Percent of variance | 22,621 | 9,496 | 6,076 | |
| | Cumulative | 22,621 | 32,117 | 38,194 | |
| KMO measure of sampling adequacy 0.816 (results exceeding 0.5 acceptable) | | | | | |

The independent samples t-test and Mann-Whitney test were used to find out whether there are differences between the Finnish and Russian entrepreneurs with respect to the power aspects that were identified. The Mann-Whitney test of equality of medians is used for the not-normally distributed component 1. The t-test compares the means of the factor scores by nationality and can be used to test components 2 and 3 as they are normally distributed. The Mann-Whitney test of equality of medians shows that there are statistically significant differences between Finns and Russians in the "**me**" -component of power and control. Russians are more of this type. The Levene's test for equality of variances had a probability greater than 0.05 indicating homogeneity of variance in both the factors 2 and 3. The t-value is significant in case 2 and not significant in case 3. Thus we can say that there is a significant difference between Russian and Finnish entrepreneurs in the "others" -component. The Finns are more of the "**others**" type. The test results are presented in Appendix 1.

Finns and Russian have some other dissimilarities, too. The "me" aspect of power increases the older the Russian entrepreneur is (Spearman correlation coefficient 0.237 is significant at 0.01 level). No such correlation can be found among the Finnish entrepreneurs. However, the Finnish export entrepreneurs are less of the "me" type than entrepreneurs of companies with no export business (Spearman correlation coefficient -0.225 is significant at 0.01 level). The "me" aspect of Finns decreases the larger the company is measured both by turnover and personnel. For the Russians there is no correlation between the "me" aspect and turnover. However, the larger the number of personnel, the less of the "me" type and the more of the "others" type the Russians are. These correlations are presented in Table 4. These results support the earlier discussed observations on firm lifecycles; it was stated that the development and growth of firm requires changes also in the management styles (Greiner 1972, Churchill and Lewis 1983).

**Table 4: Correlations of the power-components with background variables**

| | | Age | Export or not | Turnover[3] | N of pers. [4] |
|---|---|---|---|---|---|
| **Finns** | | | | | |
| **Me** | Correlation coeff. | ,156 | -,225** | -,256** | -,387** |
| REGR factor score 1 | Sig. (2-tailed) | ,070 | ,008 | ,003 | ,000 |
| for analysis 1 | N | 136 | 139 | 134 | 135 |
| **Others** | Correlation coeff. | ,167 | -,044 | ,070 | ,046 |
| REGR factor score 2 | Sig. (2-tailed) | ,052 | ,611 | ,421 | ,595 |
| for analysis 1 | N | 136 | 139 | 134 | 135 |
| **Together** | Correlation coeff. | ,057 | ,101 | ,023 | ,033 |
| REGR factor score 3 | Sig. (2-tailed) | ,509 | ,235 | ,796 | ,702 |
| for analysis 1 | N | 136 | 139 | 134 | 135 |
| **Russians** | | | | | |
| **Me** | Correlation coeff. | ,237** | ,074 | -,125 | -,233** |
| REGR factor score 1 | Sig. (2-tailed) | ,004 | ,375 | ,215 | ,005 |
| for analysis 1 | N | 144 | 145 | 100 | 146 |
| **Others** | Correlation coeff. | ,115 | ,096 | ,161 | ,317** |
| REGR factor score 2 | Sig. (2-tailed) | ,169 | ,252 | ,109 | ,000 |
| for analysis 1 | N | 144 | 145 | 100 | 146 |
| **Together** | Correlation coeff. | ,025 | ,053 | -,147 | -,118 |
| REGR factor score 3 | Sig. (2-tailed) | ,768 | ,528 | ,144 | ,154 |
| for analysis 1 | N | 144 | 145 | 100 | 146 |

**) Correlation is significant at the 0.01 level (2-tailed).

Ardichvili et al. (1998) stated in their study that Russian managers often make decisions individually (25% of respondents). But, even more often decisions are made after discussing with other executives (32% of respondents). Puffer (1996) noted that Russian managers not only discuss upon decisions with other executives, and moreover, they actually inclined to delegate decision-making. However, the reason for this delegation according to Puffer (1996) was that contemporary Russian managers tend to share power largely to avoid the responsibility for unforeseen consequences.

Interesting findings result from a comparison of values given by Finnish and Russian business managers to claims (Table 5). Russian respondents highly agreed that it is easy for them to delegate responsibilities (po8 average 5,6/7). Thus, our results support Puffer's (1996) in regard of responsibility delegation. In this respect it is interesting to note that Finnish respondents were slightly less willing to delegate their responsibilities (po8 average 5,2/7). In addition, like Ardichvili et al. (1998) stated, Russians also discuss with other executives before decision-making. Our respondents agreed to have discussions concerning the business within the company (po5 average 5,5/7). They discuss also with other business owners (po35 average 3,8/7), but not as often as within the company. The respective values of Finnish business owners did not differ very much from the Russians. On the other hand, both Finns and Russians highly value business advice given by outsiders (po33 average 4,6). To some extent it is controversial that even though Russians seem to be inclined to discuss with others, the influence of other people to company remains small (po17 average 4,6). Whereas Finns agreed other people to influence to their company more.

**Table 5: Comparison of Finnish and Russian business managers**

| | | Finland | | Russia | |
|---|---|---|---|---|---|
| | | **Mean** | **Median** | **Mean** | **Median** |
| | **"Me" aspect of power and control** | | | | |
| po10 | No one knows all the operational and managerial work in the company as good as I do | **3,16** | **3** | **5,13** | **5** |
| po29 | No one knows the equipment of the company as good as I do | **3,25** | **3** | **4,55** | **5** |
| po4 | No one knows the people of the company (department) as good as I do | **4,49** | **5** | **5,22** | **5** |
| po7 | My opinion is highly respected within the company | **4,84** | **5** | **5,90** | **6** |
| po2 | The company (department) has always been under my command only. There was no other manager of the company within its existence | **4,24** | **5** | **5,42** | **6** |
| po17 | The influence of the other people to company is very small | **3,34** | **3** | **4,59** | **5** |
| po24 | I do not want any new owners of the company at any circumstances | **4,05** | **4** | **5,49** | **6** |
| po1 | As a owner (or manager) of the firm I am controlling the situation | **5,09** | **5** | **5,91** | **6** |
| po37 | Networking with other firms will increase their power within my company | **2,86** | **2** | **4,02** | **4** |
| | **"Others" aspect of power and control** | | | | |
| po41 | People know me only because I am a business owner (manager) | **4,76** | **5** | **3,79** | **4** |
| po33 | I highly value the business advice of the outsiders | 4,68 | 5 | 4,63 | 5 |
| po27 | The success of the company affects clearly my own esteem | **5,39** | **6** | **5,84** | **6** |
| po18 | The social status as an owner (manager) is very important for myself | 4,87 | 5 | 5,17 | 5 |
| po22 | My family respects me because of my working results | 5,61 | 6 | 5,72 | 6 |
| po46 | I have noticed, that people in general are very interested in the success on | **5,37** | **6** | **4,52** | **5** |

| | | | | | |
|---|---|---|---|---|---|
| | my firm | | | | |
| po16 | I want to know all my customers in person | 5,43 | 6 | 5,54 | 6 |
| po35 | I have often discussions with other entrepreneurs concerning my business | 3,89 | 4 | 3,83 | 4 |
| po36 | The accountant is a very valuable partner for me in decision making | 4,89 | 5 | 4,94 | 6 |
| | **"Together" aspect of power and control** | | | | |
| **po8** | **It is very easy for me to delegate my responsibilities** | **5,16** | **6** | **5,55** | **6** |
| po5 | I have often discussions within the company concerning the business | 5,36 | 6 | 5,45 | 6 |
| **po44** | **I constantly observe the product quality of the competitors** | **4,57** | **5** | **5,33** | **5** |
| **po42** | **The account is balanced only for the tax authorities as a formal tool** | **2,11** | **2** | **3,32** | **3** |

Note: Statements in bold indicate statistically significant differences between Finnish and Russian responses (Mann-Whitney U-test)

Indeed, there are apparent similarities in the portrait of Finnish and Russian business managers. However, it is clearly seen that Russian managers tend to be more prejudiced, as responses to claim considering networking with other firms clearly shows: Finns do not consider networking to increase other companies' power in their firm (po37 average 2,9) whereas Russians are more suspicious upon this matter (average 4,0).

The effect of the background variables on the responses was tested by Spearman's correlation. Russian and Finnish data were analysed separately in order to observe the differences between the two nationalities (see Table 6).

**Table 6: Correlations between power statements and background variables**

| | | Age | | N of pers. | | Turnover | | Export or not | |
|---|---|---|---|---|---|---|---|---|---|
| | | Fin | Rus | Fin | Rus | Fin | Rus | Fin | Rus |
| | **"Me" aspect of power and control** | | | | | | | | |
| po10 | No one knows all the operational and managerial work in the company as good as I do | | ,249**<br>,002<br>158 | -,362**<br>,000<br>144 | | -,246**<br>,003<br>143 | | | |
| po29 | No one knows the equipment of the company as good as I do | | | -,361**<br>,000<br>142 | -,252**<br>,001<br>159 | -,265**<br>,001<br>141 | | -,226**<br>,006<br>146 | |
| po4 | No one knows the people of the company (department) as good as I do | | ,242**<br>,002<br>158 | -,259**<br>,002<br>144 | | | | | |
| po7 | My opinion is highly respected within the company | | ,183**<br>,022<br>156 | | -,196*<br>,013<br>158 | | | | ,179*<br>,025<br>157 |

| | | | | | | | | | |
|---|---|---|---|---|---|---|---|---|---|
| po2 | The company (department) has always been under my command. There was no other manager of the company within its existence | ,274**<br>,001<br>145 | | -,225**<br>,007<br>144 | -,288**<br>,000<br>158 | | -,199*<br>,037<br>110 | | |
| po17 | The influence of the other people to company is very small | ,203*<br>,015<br>143 | | -,307**<br>,000<br>142 | | -,279**<br>,001<br>141 | | | |
| po24 | I do not want any new owners of the company at any circumstances | | | -,299**<br>,000<br>140 | | | | -,199*<br>,017<br>144 | |
| po1 | As a owner (or manager) of the firm I am controlling the situation | | ,343**<br>,000<br>158 | | -,185*<br>,019<br>160 | | | | ,177*<br>,026<br>159 |
| po37 | Networking with other firms will increase their power within my company | | ,166*<br>,038<br>157 | | | | | | |

| | **"Others" aspect of power and control** | | | | | | | | |
|---|---|---|---|---|---|---|---|---|---|
| po41 | People know me only because I am a business owner (manager) | | | | | | | | |
| po33 | I highly value the business advice of the outsiders | ,193*<br>,020<br>144 | | | ,199*<br>,012<br>160 | | | | |
| po27 | The success of the company affects clearly my own esteem | ,167*<br>,046<br>143 | | | | | | -,220**<br>,008<br>146 | |
| po18 | The social status as an owner (manager) is very important for myself | | ,182*<br>,023<br>157 | | ,210**<br>,008<br>159 | | | | |
| po22 | My family respects me because of my working results | | ,213**<br>,007<br>157 | | | | | | |
| po46 | I have noticed, that people in general are very interested in the success on my firm | | | ,213*<br>,011<br>143 | | ,266**<br>,001<br>142 | | | |
| po16 | I want to know all my customers in person | ,258**<br>,002<br>144 | ,163*<br>,041<br>158 | | -,157*<br>,048<br>160 | | | | |

| | | | | | | | | |
|---|---|---|---|---|---|---|---|---|
| po35 | I have often discussions with other entrepreneurs concerning my business | | | | | | | |
| po36 | The accountant is a very valuable partner for me in decision making | | | | -,173*<br>,040<br>141 | | | |
| | **"Together" aspect of power and control** | | | | | | | |
| po8 | It is very easy for me to delegate my responsibilities | | | | | | | |
| po5 | I have often discussions within the company concerning the business | | | | | -,191*<br>,045<br>111 | | |
| po44 | I constantly observe the product quality of the competitors | | | | | | | |
| po42 | The account is balanced only for the tax authorities as a formal tool | | | | | | | |

Note: Numbers in cells represent correlation coefficient, significance and N.
**. Correlation is significant at the 0.01 level (2-tailed).
*. Correlation is significant at the 0.05 level (2-tailed).

In respect of the Finnish responses, respondent's age correlates with five individual power statements. The older the Finnish respondent, the more s/he agrees with the statements that depict self-esteem (po27). Interestingly, older respondents value higher the business advice of outsiders (po33) although they claim that the influence of other people to the company is small (po17). In the Russian responses, these statements did not seem to correlate with age. However, Russian respondents' age clearly correlates with more statements than in the case of Finns. Thus, age seems to be more decisive to power-control dimension in Russia than in Finland. Firstly, older respondents tend to consider networking to increase the power of others in the company. Secondly, the older the respondent the more important entrepreneurial social status is for self-esteem and the more his/her family respects him/her. Thirdly, older Russian respondents claim to know better both the personnel and work operations.

In the Finnish data, the smaller the numbers of personnel in the company, the more the respondents agree with the statements on knowledge of the people (po4), equipment (po29) and operational and managerial work (po10). In the case of Russian respondents, there was no correlation between neither the number of personnel nor turnover with statement concerning knowing both operational and managerial work. It could be assumed that in spite of increasing turnover and number of personnel the owner tends to clutch power-control.

Whether the company operates in export business or not only correlates with a few individual statements. In Finland, the owners of exporting companies tend to disagree that nobody knows the equipment of the company better than the owner. In Russia similar correlation did not exist.

## Conclusion

Our survey was conducted among 164 business owners in Northwest Russia (SPb. area) and among 149 business owners in Southeast Finland. It should be kept in mind that Russian companies on an average had more personnel and less turnover than their Finnish counterparts. It could be assumed that Russian companies have less value added production than Finnish companies. As Astrakhan and Chepurenko (2003) have noted, most of the Russian companies are not specialized in certain products or technologies, but change their fields of activities following different product markets.

On the basis of our survey results, however, it is possible to make some interesting remarks. Firstly, as stated earlier, power is a central element in ownership. Only when combining power with aims it is possible to achieve the results. Our results indicate that Russian owner-managers pursue both on knowing the personnel as well as operations better than anyone else in their company. Thus, they want to emphasize their role both in strategic as well as operational decision-making.

Secondly, even though the number of personnel and turnover of a Russian company grows, the owner still wants to persist the control. In the case of Finnish respondents the growth of company correlates negatively with statements on knowledge, people and equipment. When a company grows, a Finnish respondent tends to delegate tasks and responsibility. However, in the case of Russian respondents such phenomenon did not occur except for statement on equipment. Thus, it could be asked, whether this fact sets a limit for the growth of Russian companies.

Thirdly, respondent's age seems to be more decisive to power-control dimension in Russia than in Finland. Older Finnish respondents value higher the business advice of outsiders (po33) although they claim that the influence of other people to the company is small (po17). In the case of Russian responses these statements did not correlate with age. The older the Russian respondent, the more s/he tends to consider networking to increase the power of others in the company. Older Russian respondents claimed to know better than anyone else both the personnel and work operations.

It should be noted that the average age (41 years) of Russian respondent was almost ten years younger than his/her Finnish counterparts (50 years). On the other hand, most of the earlier studies with emphasis on Russian management have been conducted in the early 1990's, when our respondents have not yet started their working career. Thus, our respondents could be stated to represent new generation of Russian business owners. Therefore, one might ask, to which extent the new generation differs from those interviewed over 10 years ago.

Finally, our results indicate that the essence of ownership is a complex and a multifaceted phenomenon, which is intertwined with power and control. Thus, it remains to be researched, to which extent the cultural differences explain the power-control dimensions of ownership among Russian and

Finnish respondents. In any case, power-control aspect of ownership could be stated to be essential part of Russian entrepreneurship.

As the ownership is such an important factor in business and in all human actions nowadays these questions are surely worth of further studies.

## Notes

[1] Finnish data thousands of euros. Russian data in US dollars classified as follows: 0= below 10 000, 1=”10 000-49 999”, 2=”50 000-99 999”, 3=”100 000-199 999”, 4=”200 000-499 999”, 5=”500 000-999 999”, 6=”1 000 000-5 000 000”, 7= over 5 000 000.
[2] Finnish data absolute number of personnel. Russian data classified as follows: 0= below 10 persons, 1=”10-19”, 2=”20-29”, 3=”30-49”, 4=”50-74”, 5=”75-100”.
[3] Finnish data thousands of euros. Russian data in US dollars classified as follows: 0= below 10 000, 1=”10 000-49 999”, 2=”50 000-99 999”, 3=”100 000-199 999”, 4=”200 000-499 999”, 5=”500 000-999 999”, 6=”1 000 000-5 000 000”, 7= over 5 000 000.
[4] Finnish data absolute number of personnel. Russian data classified as follows:0= below 10 persons, 1=”10-19”, 2=”20-29”, 3=”30-49”, 4=”50-74”, 5=”75-100”.

## References

Ardichivili Alexander, Cardozo Richard N., and Gasparishvili Alexander (1998) Leadership styles and management practices of Russian entrepreneurs: implications for transferability of Western HRD interventions,*Human Resource Development Quarterly*, Vol. 9, No.2.

Ardichivili Alexander (2001) Leadership styles of Russian entrepreneurs and managers, *Journal of Developmental Entrepreneurship*, Vol. 6, No. 2.

Astrakhan, I. and Chepurenko (2003) A Small business in Russia: any prospects after a decade? *Futures* 35, pp. 341-359.

Bollinger Daniel (1994) The four cornerstones and three pillars in the ‘House of Russia’ management system, *The Journal of Management Development*, Vol. 13, No. 2.

Bridge Simon, O’Neil Ken, and Cromie Stan (1998) *Understanding Enterprise, Entrepreneurship and Small Business*, Macmillan Press, Wiltshire.

Camiah, N. and Hollinshead, G. (2003) Assessing the potential for effective cross-cultural working between ”new” Russian managers and western expatriates, *Journal of World Business* 38, pp. 245-261.

Churchill C. and Lewis V. L. (1983) The five stages of small business growth, *Harvard Business Review*, 61 (3), pp. 30-59.

Clifford Megan, Nilakant V. and Hamilton R. T. (1991) Management Succession and the Stages of Small Business Development, *International Small Business Journal*, 9, 4, pp. 43-55.

Collins, Orvis F., Moore, David G. and Unwalla, Darab B. (1964) *The Enterprising Man*, Bureau of Business and Economic Research, Michigan State University, East Lansing.

Cooper Arnold C., and Dunkelberg William C. (1986) Entrepreneurship and Paths to Business Ownership, *Strategic Management Journal*, Vol. 7, pp. 53-68.

Crespi Franco (1992) *Social Action & Power*, Blackwell Publishers, Cornwall.

Emerson Richard M. (1959) Power-Dependence Relations, *American Sociological Review*, Vol. 27, pp. 31-41.

Fey, Carl F., Adaeva, Margareta and Vitkovskaia, Anastasia (2001) Developing a model of leadership styles: what works best in Russia? *International Business Review* 10, pp. 615-643.

Flash Eurobarometer (2003) *Flash Eurobarometer 146 (FSD2056)*, Entrepreneurship 4, September, European commission, Press General Directorate, EOS Gallup Europe, Cologne.

French J. R. P. and Raven B. (1959) *The Basis of Social Power*, Studies in Social Power, Cartwright.

GEM (1999), *Global Entrepreneurship Monitor*, Kansakuntien yrittäjyyspotentiaali. Available at:
http://www.tuta.hut.fi/persons/etautio/reports/GEM_Finland.pdf

Greiner L. E. (1972) Evolutions and revolutions as organizations grow, *Harvard Business Review*, 50 (4), pp. 37-46.

Grunebaum James O. (1987) *Private Ownership*, Routledge & Kegan Paul, London.

Hofstede Geert (1984) *Culture's consequences – international differences in work-related values*, Sage Publications. USA.

—. (1991) *Cultures and organizations – software of the mind*, McGraw-Hill book company, London.

—. (1993) Cultural constraints in management theories. *Academy of Management Executive*, Vol. 7, No. 1.

Hyrsky, K. and Lipponen, H. (2004), *Yrittäjyyskatsaus 2004*, KTM Julkaisuja 18, Elinkeino-osasto, Edita, Helsinki.

Kets de Vries Manfred F.R. (1996), *Family Business: Human Dilemmas in the Family Firm*, International Thomson Business Press. London.

Kontorovich, V. (1999), Has new business creation in Russia come to halt? *Journal of Business Venturing* 14, pp. 451-460.

Lukes Stevens (1991) *Power: A Radical View*, Macmillan, Hong Kong.

McCarthy, D., Puffer, S. and Shekshnia, S. (1993) The resurgence of an entrepreneurial class in Russia, *Journal of Management Inquiry* 2.

McCarthy, D., Puffer, S. and Naumov, A. (1997) Partnering with Russia's New Entrepreneurs: Software Tsarina Olga Kirova, *European Management Journal*, Vol. 15, No. 6, pp. 648-657.

Pierce, Jon L., Kostova Tatiana and Dirks Kurt T (2001) Toward a Theory of Psychological Ownership in Organizations, *Academy of Management Review,* 26:2, pp. 298-310.

Puffer Sheila M. (1996) Leadership in a Russian context, In *Business and Management in Russia*, Ed. Sheila M. Puffer, Edward Elgar Publishing Company.

Radaev, V. (2001) The Development of Small Entrepreneurship in Russia, *WIDER Discussion Paper* No. 2001/135, United Nations University.

Rainio Kullervo (1969) *Valta ja vallan käyttö*, Porvoo.

Shama, Avraham and Merrell, Margaret N. (1997) Russia's True Business Performance: Inviting to International Business? *Journal of World Business* 32 (4), pp. 320-332.

Stanworth, M.J.K. and J. Curran (1976). Growth and the small firm – an alternative view, *Journal of Management Studies*, May, pp. 95–110.

Suutari, Vesa (1996) Leadership behavior in Eastern Europe: Finnish expatriates' experiences in Russia and Estonia, in Vesa Suutari (ed.) *Comparative studies on leadership beliefs and behavior of European managers,* Faculty of Business Administration, No. 50, University of Vaasa, Finland.

Suutari, Vesa and Bolotow, S. (1996) Leadership beliefs of Finnish and Russian managers: A comparative survey within two Finnish and Russian companies, in Vesa Suutari (ed.) *Comparative studies on leadership beliefs and behavior of European managers,* Faculty of Business Administration, No. 50, University of Vaasa, Finland.

Terpstra Vern, David Kenneth (1985) *The cultural environment of international business*, South-Western Publishing Co. Cincinnati.

Zhuplev, A., Konkov, A. and Kiesner, F. (1998) Russian and American Small Business: Motivations and Obstacles, *European Management Journal*, Vol. 16, No. 4, pp. 505-516.

# FOREIGNERS IN MANAGEMENT POSITIONS IN POLISH COMPANIES – POLES' ANXIETIES AND EXPECTATIONS

ARNOLD PABIAN

## Introduction

Membership of Poland in the European Union makes Polish companies more and more eager to employ employees of other nationalities, including Austrian citizens. Even though attractiveness of the Polish employment market is still arguable, particularly from the point of view of the best developed economically countries of the world, it should not be underestimated. Poland is a large European country and it quickly reduces its arrears resulting from its previous adherence to the eastern bloc. Work in many Polish companies may already bring foreigners satisfaction and profits.

A great deal of foreigners, in particular those who come from countries of the highest level of economic development, aspire to take first, middle and top level management positions in Polish companies. A foreigner employed in a management position will be in most cases subject to Poles taking higher positions and will lead groups consisting of Polish workers. This situation creates a number of complex problems. Most of these problems are caused by the fact that a foreigner is an *alien* cell in the chain of company interrelations. Although in the globalization era the word *alien* may evoke reservations, it should be remembered that foreigners are still rare in Polish companies.

Indiscriminate transfer of external management experiences to the Polish ground may result in a total failure of a foreign manager. Poland, as any other nation, has it own specificity, resulting from historical, cultural, economic and social conditions. One of the sensible principles of the international business requires that a stranger adapt to local conditions and customs (Gesteland 1999). The principle relates also to strangers taking up jobs in Poland. The purpose of this article is to at least partially approximate these conditions. The author focused on the presentation of anxieties and expectations of Polish employees, relating to their potential subordination to foreign managers. Settlements resulting from these studies are not to be found in any books on international management. This type of literature (see for example Deresky 2007; McFarlin and Sweeney 2005; Phatak and Bhagat and Koshlak 2004; Thomas 2001) is too general. It contains little specific information relating to management in individual, diversified in many respects, countries of the world.

The results of the studies presented in this article constitute only an excerpt of the author's literary output in the field of international management. The first study was intended to explain the general attitude of Poles to foreign managers to whom they may be subordinate in their native companies. The second study focused on issues relating solely to foreign directors. Through the study the author revealed some anxieties and expectations of the respondents concerning both operating of the company under the leadership of the foreigner, as well as relating to his or her decisions that may affect the professional situation of Polish employees, their work conditions and atmosphere.

## Method

The studies were conducted in different periods of time in the years 2005-2007 on two different groups of respondents. In the first study, devoted to the general attitude of Poles to foreign managers, participated 160 respondents aged 21-30, including 98 women and 62 men. 125 persons were professionally active. The remaining persons (35) were not performing any work. The working persons represented various lines and spheres of business, starting with trade, food industry, automotive industry, shoe industry, through construction, metallurgy, banking, and ending with education and public administration.

The second study, which concentrated on issues concerning foreign directors, involved 170 respondents aged 21-30, including 116 women and 54 men. 127 people were employed in different kinds of companies.

The research method called a survey interview was used in both studies. The research instruments were in a form of questionnaires consisting of open-end and close-end questions. Each questionnaire comprised two basic parts: basic questions and questions oriented towards statistical characteristics of respondents. While filling in the questionnaires the respondents did not reveal their names (they were anonymous).

## Results

In a group of 160 Poles covered by the first study the neutral attitude towards employment of foreigners in management positions in Polish companies dominated (76 people). 20 people were negatively-minded and 3 persons were very hostile-minded to such practices. Employment of foreigners in management positions was positively perceived by 61 interviewees. Among the respondents there were no people enthusiastically approaching the issue. The reserved attitude to the engagement of foreigners in management positions in Polish companies manifested itself also in answers to the question: *What is in your opinion the permissible saturation of Polish companies and institutions with managers coming from other countries (at the whole national economy level)?* 81% of the surveyed supported small saturation, up to 10, 20 or 30% (44, 42 and 44 people respectively). The number of other answers decreased with the increase of the degree of the saturation, whereas levels equal to or exceeding 70% were not supported at all.

Successive questions revealed preferences of young Poles as to the foreign manager's country of origin. The greatest support was enjoyed by the following regions of the world:

- Well developed countries of Western Europe, e.g. Germany, the United Kingdom, France
- Well developed countries of North America (the USA, Canada),
- Well developed Asian countries, e.g. Japan.

References to Australia and New Zealand, poorly developed countries of Central Europe and countries of Eastern Europe and South America were much more infrequent. African, Arabic and poorly developed Asian countries were sporadically indicated.

Young Polish people are not indifferent to a management level at which foreign managers may be employed in Polish companies. Nearly 40 % of the respondents associate them with a medium level management. Successive position is occupied by the highest management positions (30%). The smallest number of people ascribes strangers to first line management positions (20%). The remaining group (ca. 10%) believes that foreigners should not take any management positions in Poland.

What also mattered to the surveyed people was the sex of a potential foreign manager: 78% would approve of a male in a management position and only 22% would approve of a female.

One of the questionnaire questions asked about the differences the respondents would be able to approve in the appearance, behaviour and work of a foreigner. Individual issues ranked from the most to the least acceptable with the rate of positive answers are provided below:

a) Different skin colour – 78%
b) Different appearance (height, body build, face lines) – 77%
c) Different clothing style – 64%
d) Poor command of the Polish language – 37%
e) Lack of command of the Polish language – 5%
f) More easy-going attitude towards work as compared with Polish managers (e.g. unpunctuality, worse performance, lower quality of work) – 9%
g) Criticism towards Poland and Poles – 4%

All the surveyed stated that a foreign manager employed in our country should:

a) Be familiar (67%) or at least partially familiar (33%) with Polish culture and customs, including business customs,
b) Observe (60%) or at least partially observe (40%) Polish customs, including business customs.

A very important matter is the attitudes of young Poles towards the national culture represented by a foreign manager.

Expressing yourself in a manner not clear enough, not open and not always honest is the feature of partner-driven cultures. Such manner of behaviour is tolerated only by 1,8% of the respondents. The remaining group (98,2%) consider it improper (they may be treated as followers of transaction-oriented cultures).

Unpunctuality and failure to keep dates ("rubber time") underlies polychromic cultures. Only 4% of respondents approves of such attitude towards time represented by a foreign manager. The remaining group (96%) do not agree with this operation mode, declaring themselves in favour of monochromic cultures.

Non-ceremonial cultures are characterised by not attaching importance in personal contacts to professional and social status of cooperatives. 83% of the respondents favoured this approach. 17% of the surveyed, preferring ceremonial cultures, opposed to it.

Generally speaking, vivid gesticulations, expressive mimics, interrupting during conversations are characteristic for expressive cultures. 39% of the respondents have no objections towards this behaviour of foreign managers. 61% are of a different opinion; they prefer behaviours originating from reserved cultures.

The second study, in which 170 persons participated, started with a question if foreigners should actually be appointed to chief directors' positions in Polish companies. Most respondents (54%) assumed a positive attitude to this matter. The rest (46%) had a different opinion.

Will a foreigner holding a position of a director in a Polish company act better than a Pole fulfilling this function before? For such a question only 7,6 % of the surveyed answered positively. 15,9% replied in a negative way and 76,5% could not decide. The faith of Poles in abilities and knowledge of foreign directors is therefore not that great, as could be believed according to superficial observations and common opinions. Tendencies of this type revealed themselves in answers to successive questions included in the questionnaire, presented in the Table 1.

**Table 1: The attitude of the surveyed group of respondents to the results of a foreign director's activity in key areas of a company operation.**

| No. | The question and the answer structure | Yes | No | Hard to say |
|---|---|---|---|---|
| 1. | Will a foreigner holding a director's position in a Polish company lead to an increase of its income and profits? | 17,0% | 5,4% | 77,6% |
| 2. | Will a foreigner holding a director's position in a Polish company lead to its development? | 25,3% | 6,5% | 68,2% |

| | | | | |
|---|---|---|---|---|
| 3. | Will a foreigner holding a director's position in a Polish company modernise it in the technical and technological respect? | 54,8% | 2,9% | 42,3% |
| 4. | Will a foreigner holding a director's position in a Polish company improve competitiveness of manufactured products/services? | 45,3% | 5,3% | 49,4% |

Source: own study

As shown in the Table 1, a foreign director is associated by Poles first of all with higher technical and technological level of their companies and with improvement of competitiveness of manufactured products/services (questions 3 and 4). They usually rightly assume that a foreigner coming from the country that is better developed than Poland will transfer new manufacturing solutions, which will bring about manufacturing of better products and services from the market point of view. The surveyed people were less optimistic towards the skill of foreign directors as regards improvement of the financial condition of a company and its development (questions 1 and 2).

To achieve high results in all the indicated spheres right decisions should be made. Most respondents (80,0%) had no precise opinion on the issue whether a foreign director would make good or bad decisions. They stated that this depends on a candidate's knowledge, abilities and predispositions, and not on the country of origin. Only 16,4% were certain that his or her decisions would be right.

Assumed economic goals should be achieved with respect to the law and ethical principles. Therefore the respondents were asked the following two questions:

a) Will a foreigner holding a director's position in a Polish company observe legal regulations?
b) Will a foreigner holding a director's position in a Polish company behave ethically and honestly?

The first question was answered positively by 57,6% of respondents and for the second question only 28,8% answered positively. Poles are therefore more optimistic as regards observance of the law by foreigners than their abiding by ethical rules.

Poles' anxieties and expectations concerning a foreign director's decisions that may affect situations, conditions and the atmosphere at work on the positions held by them are a very important matter. Major questions relating to this issue and the respondents' answers are shown in the Table 2.

**Table 2: The attitude of the surveyed group of respondents to a foreign director's activity affecting their situation at work – selected issues**

| No. | The question and the answer structure | Yes | No | Hard to say |
|---|---|---|---|---|
| 1. | Will a foreign director have a positive attitude to Polish employees? | 39,5% | 18,2% | 42,3% |
| 2. | Will a foreign director be eager to dismiss Polish employees? | 40,6% | 12,9% | 46,5% |
| 3. | Will a foreign director be willing to raise Polish employees' salaries? | 42,3% | 15,3% | 42,4% |
| 4. | Will a foreign director promote Polish employees to higher positions? | 48,8% | 11,2% | 40,0% |
| 5. | Will a foreign director care for professional development of Polish employees? | 61,8% | 9,4% | 28,8% |
| 6. | Will a foreign director improve atmosphere at work? | 15,3% | 21,7% | 63,0% |

Source: own study

As shown in the Table 2, nearly half of the persons surveyed (apart from items 5 and 6) have no opinion on the subject discussed. The majority of the remaining respondents are optimistic; they hope that a foreign director will be eager to improve their existence and professional position. The atmosphere at work is the only exception. Only 15,3% of the surveyed believe that a foreigner holding the highest position in a company will contribute to improvement of the atmosphere.

## Conclusions

Employment of foreign managers in Polish companies having no financial connections with foreign countries is very rare today. The first part of the survey revealed that the majority of respondents have a reserved attitude towards this kind of superiors and would rather not be subordinate to them. If this type of business relation were necessary then it would be such only with respect to managers from highly-developed European, North American or Asian countries. The manager should rather be male, employed in a medium or top-level management position. A foreign manager employed in our country should be familiar at least partially with Polish culture and observe Polish customs, including business customs. The respondents would approve of the following differences in the appearance of a foreign manager: a different skin colour, different height, body build or face lines. They would not, however, accept such issues as: lack of command of the Polish language, critical attitude towards our country, or worse performance. According to the majority of the surveyed a foreigner manager should come from transaction-oriented, monochromic, non-ceremonial or reserved culture.

The second part of the survey proves that Poles cease to believe uncritically in extraordinary business abilities of a foreign management staff. The image of an infallible foreign manager who will lead a Polish company to the forefront of prosperous enterprises is becoming out-of-date. This situation results to a large extent from Poles' experiences and observations. They start to perceive more and more companies run by foreigners that poorly get along, and a growing number of dynamically prospering entities under the leadership of native directors. These tendencies are going to consolidate. The nationality of a director is soon going to become insignificant. What will matter is only their knowledge, abilities and predispositions to work on the highest levels of the organizational structure of companies. Nearly half of the surveyed people have no opinion on the effect of a foreign manager's activity on their existence and professional position. Most of the remaining respondents have high hopes as to this type of a superior, and they believe that he or she will ensure them stabilized professional position, promote them, raise salaries and care for their professional development.

## References

Deresky H., *International Management. Managing Across Borders and Cultures,* Prentice Hall 2007.

Gesteland R., *Cross-Cultural Business Behavior. Marketing, Negotiating and Managing Across Cultures,* Copenhagen Business School Press 1999.

McFarlin D., Sweeney P., *International Management: Strategic Opportunities and Cultural Challenges,* Houghton Mifflin Company 2005.

Pabian A., Kultury biznesowe w opinii młodych Polaków (Business Cultures in young Poles' opinion), *[in:]* Kierunki i metody zarządzania organizacjami w zintegrowanej Europie. Monografia (Directions and Methods of Managing Organizations in Integrated Europe. Monograph), *scientific edition L. Sobolak, Wydawnictwo Wydziału Zarządzania Politechniki Częstochowskiej (Publishing House of Management Faculty of Częstochowa Technical University), Częstochowa 2005.*

—. *Kulturowe bariery w zarządzaniu przedsiębiorstwem (Cultural Barriers in Company Management)*, „Ekonomika i Organizacja Przedsiębiorstwa" („Economics and Organization of Enterprise") 2004, no 2.

—. *Wpływ różnic kulturowych na międzynarodową działalność logistyczną (The Effect of Cultural Differences on Logistics)*, „Gospodarka Materiałowa i Logistyka" („Materials Economy and Logistics") 2004, no 4.

—. *Cudzoziemcy na rynku budowlanym (Foreigners on the Construction Market),* „Przegląd Budowlany" („Construction Review") 2006, no 6, p. 50-52.

—. *Klient Cudzoziemiec (A Foreign Client),* „Marketing w Praktyce" (Practical Marketing") 2007, no 1.

Phatak A.V., Bhagat R.S., Koshlak R., *International Management: Managing in a Diverse and Dynamic Global Environment*, McGraw-Hill 2004.

Thomas D., *Essentials of International Management*, Sage Publications, Inc. 2001.

# Ownership Structure and Firm Performance in Hungarian Manufacturing Sector

Marta Szoradi-Szabo

## Abstract

The study examines the association between corporate ownership structure and performance in Hungarian manufacturing sectors. The connection between ownership and firm performance is indirect. The influence of ownership is determined by its concentration, by the way of executing the control of the owners upon managers, by the quality of the strategic and operative management etc.

Transformation of the ownership structure of companies is a determining process in the transition to market economy. Eliminating the differences of firms' operation, the differences among companies working with different ownership structures may be the measures of the success of transition.

## Introduction

In Central-Eastern European countries, a highly important element of transition to a market economy is the transformation of the ownership structure of companies. The notion of success, as a matter of course, is linked to privately-owned companies, particularly to those founded or bought by foreign firms, while state-owned or cooperative-companies were synonymous with fragile, vulnerable or simply loss-making operations in the transition economies. The idea that different forms of ownership entail different organizational-behavioral features and operations was widespread.

This kind of segmentation of the economy has probably been lessened as the market economy gained ground since the growing market-economic compulsion affects everyone independently of the form of ownership. In this way, the development of economic factors with different ownerships in eliminating the differences of firms' operation, the differences among companies working with different ownership structures may be the measures of the success of transition. This time, our goal is to see the productivity and profitability ratios. We want to study how the different ratios have differed among the different groups of owners and what changes have taken place in the past years.

The examination of the relationship between ownership structure and firm performance is covered by extensive references. In the countries with established market institutions, the focus is rather on the importance of the concentration of ownership and only in some periods on the importance of the form of ownership for firm performance. In the transition economies both problems are important.

Regarding the Central-Eastern European countries there are analyses looking at the relations between ownership structure and firm performance. Barbone et. al. (1996) examines the relationship between productivity, size and ownership structure looking at Polish data, while Konings et.al. (1996) looks at the features of changes in staff numbers also with Polish data. Dimitrov (1996) examines ownership structures and firm performance in South-Eastern Europe. Regarding Hungary, Csermely (1997) examines the impacts of ownership structure. Fast economic changes in transition economies necessitate new and new examinations. The articles analyze the economic situation typical in the mid 90s, the period of mass privatization. Following the high wave of privatization, new examinations under different ownership conditions are very useful.

I have concentrated on the examination of three issues: introducing the characteristics of the ownership structure; examining the relationship between ownership structure and productivity-profitability features; and comparison of company groups with major domestic ownership on the one hand and with major foreign ownership on the other.

The database used for the analysis comprises: economic statistical data, aggregate data of annual financial reports and tax declarations of firms. Medium-size and big companies are examined. The statistical data at our disposal make difference between two big company groups, medium-size and big companies are the ones with double-entry book-keeping, while the small ones with single-entry book-keeping system. The analysis covers companies with double-entry book-keeping system.

## Characteristics of Ownership Structure

Ownership and property rights are one of the most intensively discussed topics in economics, especially in institutional economics. The ownership problem arises only because of the presence of scarce private goods, and only in a multi-agent world. The property rights can be called as a function of the rules to establish a relationship between scarce goods and agents. The components of property rights are conceptualised in various ways.
We distinguish the ownership rights as:

- decisions-making rights,
- control rights,
- right to derive economic benefits (narrowly called cash flow-rights).

Empirical examination of ownership structure mainly concentrates on the ownership share of different owners, the actual form of ownership rights are examined in connection with them. Characteristics of capital markets, economic development and several special features to ownership structure typical of certain economies. In the Anglo-Saxon model with extensive capital market, the examination of ownership structure focuses on privately-owned firms, among them on ownership with dispersed shareholders. Issues of control mechanism are highlighted among ownership rights, which are included in corporate governance. In the German-Japanese model, the main examination topic is also private ownership, but in accordance with the characteristics of the country, the central issue is not the control mechanism of shareholder ownership but the interpenetration of bank and firm private ownership.

In the 90s in the transition economies, the central issue was the transformation of state ownership into private ownership, the development of new circle of private owners. Now with the shrinkage of state ownership, with the dominance of private ownership, the examination of private ownership has become important. Compared to Western-European economies, research cannot be related to examination of ownership rights, decision-making or control rights, but to special problems of transition economies. The new private ownership in transition economies is dominantly foreign private or institutional ownership. Regarding size and its share, domestic private ownership takes only the second place. The question, however, is not the examination of their shares, but the difference of the economic performance of firms among domestic and foreign owners. Therefore it is important to examine whether there are still differences in the productivity-profitability of firms' operation; whether the differences have decreased; and regarding firm performance, how the gap between companies with foreign and domestic ownership can be narrowed.

Blanchard (1998) makes a difference between two important dimensions of economic transformation in transition economies, on macroeconomic level: resource allocation and on microeconomic level: resource restructuring. Resource allocation mainly refers to the transformation of former unproductive state ownership into productive private ownership related to privatization and the establishment of new private firms. Resource restructuring, on the other hand, means efficient restructuring within the firm, the enforcement of private owners' interest.

In Hungary, resource allocation has more or less taken place. The majority of former state ownership has been privatized. New privately owned firms primarily, small and medium-size ones, with the contribution of domestic private persons have been established in great numbers, mainly in the mid 90s. The ownership structure has been basically changed. Table 1 contains the most important ownership shares of the economy as a whole and of manufacturing sector.

Regarding the Hungarian economy, the rate of state ownership is 14 percent and 3 percent in the manufacturing sector. The share of state ownership in the manufacturing sector, which is considered the most dynamic sector of the economy, is negligible. 14 percent characterizing the economy as a whole is considered low. In the past years, primarily the energy sector has been privatized, in the following years, privatization of some big companies, mainly in the field of transportation and goods traffic is expected. Similarly to state ownership, cooperatives, employees and local governments also have negligible share. In 2003, their share in the economy as a whole was 6 percent and in manufacturing sector 2 percent. Ownership by cooperatives, local governments and employees both in state and other categories have to serve certain public interest, firms belonging to these categories provide services, which would not be competitive under market conditions.

**Table 1. Ownership structure in percent of subscribed capital, in companies with double entry book-keeping system**

| Owned by | Manufacture sector | | | | Economy, total |
|---|---|---|---|---|---|
| | 2000 | 2001 | 2002 | 2003 | 2003 |
| State | 3.34 | 3.29 | 3.29 | 2.77 | 14.15 |
| Foreign | 60.68 | 64.12 | 63.20 | 67.23 | 42.68 |
| Domestic firm | 22.04 | 19.72 | 20.02 | 18.07 | 24.48 |
| Domestic private person | 10.46 | 10.27 | 10.65 | 9.87 | 12.60 |
| Cooperative | 0.52 | 0.42 | 0.41 | 0.23 | 0.24 |
| Employee and management | 0.66 | 0.56 | 0.51 | 0.37 | 0.21 |
| Local government | 0.,37 | 0.27 | 0.26 | 0.16 | 4.36 |
| Other | 1.93 | 1.35 | 1.66 | 1.30 | 1.28 |
| Total | 100 | 100 | 100 | 100 | 100 |

Source: Financial Figure of Non-financial Companies. Hungarian Statistical Office, 2005

In 2003, the share of foreign ownership in the economy was 42 percent, in the manufacturing sector 67 percent. Foreign capital obtained ownership through privatization, by buying firms. This is a typical process of the early 90s, characterizing food industry, wood manufacturing, printing, press and pharmaceutical industry. Since the mid 90s foreign direct investment has accelerated. New green field investments have emerged in great numbers, primarily in the field of vehicle production and electronics industry. In the past five years foreign ownership within the manufacturing industry has decreased only in two sectors: food and wood manufacturing, in the others, mainly in the most dynamic ones, have increased (Figure 1.).

**Figure 1. A külföldi tulajdon aránya feldolgozóiparban**

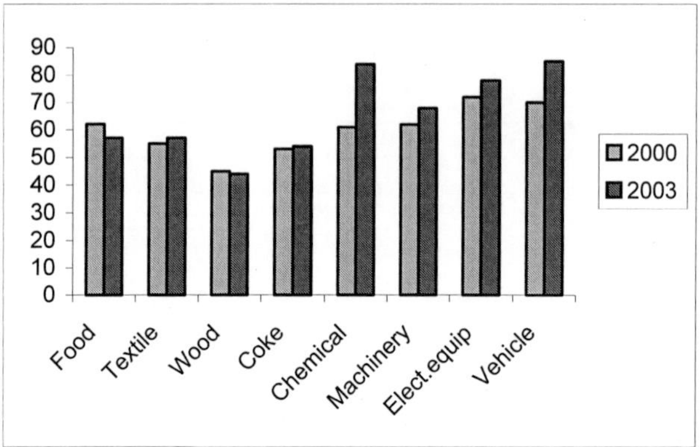


Source: Financial Figure of Non-financial Companies. Hungarian Statistical Office, 2005

Domestic owners have a 37 percent share in the economy as a whole and 28 percent in the manufacturing industry. Foreign and domestic private ownership is decisive in the Hungarian economy, by the side of the low and unchanged size of state and other ownership. Due to the dynamic growth of foreign ownership, its share has also increased in the past years. The significant share of foreign ownership also means that outside factors helped the Hungarian economy to catch up. The impact of foreign capital is summarized Figure 2.

**Figure 2. The role of foreign capital in transition process**

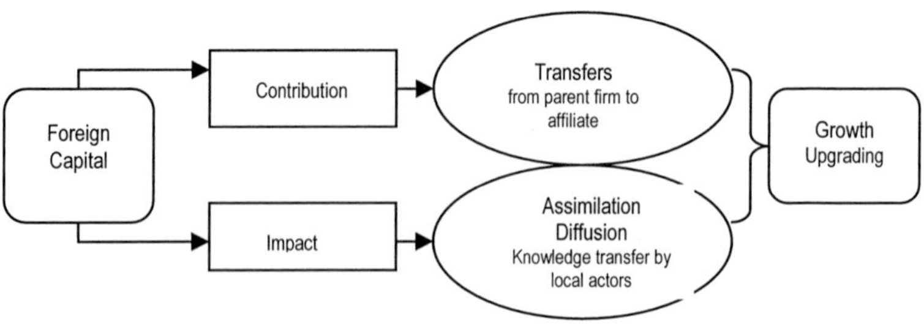


Source: Fabry (2002)

Foreign capital exerts a complex impact on the economy of the host country. On the one hand, there is a flow of real assets like machines, equipment and money capital, on the other, intangible assets like technology, expertise, know-how, methods, processes, firm functions, and organizational practices between the foreign company and its affiliate. Broadly seen, these transfers may be considered knowledge transfer. The impact of foreign capital on the host country is experienced in several fields partly by providing goods and services in accordance with western standards, partly by reorganization of firm operation and increasing productivity in the case of existing firms.

Real and intangible assets may lead to one-off, short-term effect called exogenous upgrading (Fabry, 2002). In that case foreign capital investment has localized effect only on affiliates. It increases the output and in most cases the exports of the affiliate. In addition, on the level of the affiliate it improves the quality of the product, service, and the productivity.

The secondary effect, knowledge transfer, its expansion to the sphere of the domestic firm is often more important for the host country. This effect is the endogenous-led upgrading, which transforms the economy of the host country internally. The foreign affiliates hand over higher professional knowledge for the employees and enable the reception of new methods, work culture. On the other hand, it sets new requirements for domestic suppliers, which is an incentive to adapt to western technology and methods. The affiliates providing new, quality services or goods on the Hungarian market urge other Hungarian producers to catch up.

The primary effect of foreign capital investment is intensive in the Hungarian industry; output, exports have increased significantly while the affiliates meet the western quality and cost requirements. Although it is difficult to detect and prove the secondary impact, it initiated significant catch-up also among Hungarian firms.

## Ownership Structure and Performance in Manufacturing Sector

It is difficult to put the characteristics of ownership structure, the means of control and the changes in firm performance into one model. In the next part, we are looking at the relationship between the two points: characteristics of ownership structure and firm performance. If certain groups of the owners steadily have better results, one can assume that productive firm management better serves the interests of the owners, which means the owners have more efficient control mechanisms to protect and ensure the return of their investments.

Reference articles look at the relations of owners and management regarding the relationship between ownership structure and firm performance. Corporate governance, agency theory and transaction cost theory deals with this issue. The relations between management, controlling shareholders and outside investors have a central role in modern firm theory, where insiders have relatively greater influence in managing and controlling processes than outsiders. These analyses suggest that the firm's ownership structure is a primary determinant of the extent of agency problems between controlling insiders and outside investors, which has important implications for the valuation of the firm. The impact of ownership on firms' operation is summarized Figure 3.

**Figure 3. Ownership and firm's performance**

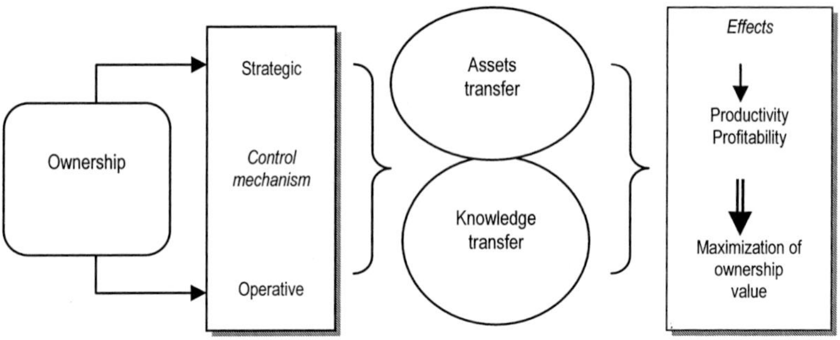


It is typical also of Hungarian medium and big companies that the owner and management functions are separate. This separation is only partial in case of several medium-size firms; the owners keep some strategic and operative management functions. The more dynamically a firm develops the less possible it is to retain direct participation of the owner in the firms' operation. Therefore the role of the owner separated from the operation of the firm is limited in the success of firm performance. However, in addition those owners expect return on the firms' capital; they transfer basic *values* to the firm management. The owners maintain their decision-making rights in strategic issues; determine the trend of product development, the expansion of the market share, and borrowing etc. issues. If western-type quality and cost requirements are set, the management will represent them in their operative decisions; it will appear in the performance of the firm (Figure 3.). Both the domestic and foreign owners typically closely control the operation of the company even if operative work is carried out by others. Few of the Hungarian manufacturing firms are listed on Stock Exchange therefore the examination of the dispersed ownership structure is only a marginal issue.

I will analyze the relationship between ownership structure and firm performance by using the database of the annual financial reports and corporate tax declarations of firms with doubly-entry book-keeping in 2002-2003. The focus of the examination is manufacturing industry and its branches. Using the database I am trying to answer the question whether there is any difference between a clearly separate circle of owners and firm performance and how the difference in performance has changed in the past few years.

Two typical circles of owners deserve special attention. One is the domestic owners, the other the foreign owners. The basic question of research is whether there is a relationship among the productivity, successfulness of manufacturing sectors and the differences of ownership forms. Table 2 summarizes the ratios employed.

To show the importance of labour productivity, a few sectors are highlighted in Table 3. The method is a so-called empirical regression. Labour productivity ratios (sales/number of employees by sectors) were computed and arranged in an ascending order. Then four groups of the sectors were distinguished. The sectoral labour productivity ratios are accompanied by the share of companies operating with foreign capital (computed as a percentage of subscribed capital). Group arithmetic averages were also calculated for the sake of simpler comparison (averages will be used in Table 4.). The computed empirical regression substitutes correlation coefficients: according to the assumed relationship, industries with higher labour productivity should feature a higher share of foreign capital.

**Table 2: Interpretation of the applied ratios**

| Ratio and calculation | Aim to examine | Expected sign |
|---|---|---|
| *Labor productivity* Gross value added product/number of employee | Labour productivity | The higher the foreign ownership, the higher the productivity |
| *Return on assets* Net income/total assets | Profitability, capital productivity | The higher the foreign ownership, the higher the profitability |
| *Profit margin* Operating income/sales | Profitability | The higher the foreign ownership, the higher the profitability |
| *Operating cost ratio* Cost of operation/sales | Cost efficiency | The higher the foreign ownership, the lower the cost level |
| *Export share* Export production/total sales | Dynamism, | The higher the foreign ownership, the higher the export share |
| *Investment growth rate* Investment and renovation/total fixed assets | Dynamism, growth opportunity | The higher the foreign ownership, the higher the investment activity |

I find it important to mention that differences among sectors can most of the time be attributed to some sectoral feature, for example in the sector of non-metallic products, building materials are most likely sold within short transportation distance, therefore the rate of exports is relatively lower. The technical-technological characteristics of the sectors often explain the sectoral differences. If in addition numerical relationship is shown for the relationship between performance and ownership, the relationship should be considered strong, which may have a certain impact beyond sectoral features

**Table 3: Productivity ratios by sectors (2003)**

| Sector | Gross value added product/number of employees (HUF million) | Foreign owned companies' share in subscribed capital, % |
|---|---|---|
| *1.1.1.1 Sector group 1* | | |
| Manufacture of textiles and textile product | 1323 | 56.9 |
| Manufacture of leather, leather product | 1468 | 68.7 |
| Manufacture of wood, wood product | 1747 | 43.6 |
| *1.1.1.2 Sector group 2* | | |
| Manufacture of machinery and equipment | 3414 | 68.2 |
| Manufacture of basic metals | 3502 | 53.3 |
| Manufacture of pulp, paper, publishing, printing | 4002 | 33.5 |
| *1.1.1.3 Sector group 3* | | |
| Manufacture of rubber and plastic product | 4443 | 62.6 |
| Manufacture of food, beverages, tobacco | 5250 | 56.8 |
| Manufacture of other non-metallic mineral product | 5275 | 60.3 |
| *1.1.1.4 Sector group 4* | | |
| Manufacture of electrical and optical equipment | 5284 | 78.7 |
| Manufacture of transport equipment | 9296 | 84.6 |
| Manufacture of chemical production | 10639 | 84.2 |

Source: Financial Figure of Non-financial Companies. Hungarian Statistical Office, 2005.

**Table 4: Average labour productivity ratios by groups of sectors (2003)**

| Group of sectors | Gross value added product/number of employee (HUF million) | Foreign owned companies' share in subscribed capital, % |
|---|---|---|
| I. | 1512.67 | 56.41 |
| II. | 3639.33 | 51.67 |
| III. | 4989.32 | 59.91 |
| IV. | 8406.33 | 82.51 |

*Empirical regression data of Hungarian manufacturing sectors show that the share of foreign capital does grow with labour productivity ratios.* The relationship shows a tendency. It differs from the regular increasing rate of foreign capital in the group 1 and 2, slightly higher in the first group than in the second one. All in all, the rate of foreign capital is substantially lower in groups 1 and 2 than in groups 3 and 4. The over fivefold difference between the first and fourth groups in labour productivity cannot be explained only by sectoral characteristics. Group four includes the most dynamic sectors (chemical industry, transport equipment, electrical and other equipment). The outstanding sectoral productivity and high rate of foreign ownership refers to exogenous-led upgrading, to the fact that the role of foreign capital is significant in increasing the productivity of Hungarian industry.

Nonetheless, one should not forget that investment by a large multinational can itself determine sectoral ownership and other characteristics on the small Hungarian market.

**Table 4: Return on assets ratios by sectors (2003)**

| Sector | ROA, % | Foreign owned companies' share in subscribed capital, % |
|---|---|---|
| *1.1.2 Sector group 1* | | |
| Manufacture of leather, leather product | -1.27 | 68.7 |
| Manufacture of food, beverages, tobacco | 3.12 | 56.8 |
| Manufacture of wood, wood product | 3.53 | 43.6 |
| *Sector group 2* | | |
| Manufacture of basic metals | 4.29 | 53.3 |
| Manufacture of machinery and equipment | 4.79 | 68.2 |
| Manufacture of textiles and textile product | 5.00 | 56.9 |
| *Sector group 3* | | |
| Manufacture of rubber and plastic product | 5.84 | 62.6 |
| Manufacture of pulp, paper, publishing, printing | 7.62 | 33.5 |
| Manufacture of chemical production | 8.23 | 84.2 |
| *Sector group 4* | | |
| Manufacture of electrical and optical equipment | 9.62 | 78.7 |
| Manufacture of other non-metallic mineral product | 10.12 | 60.3 |
| Manufacture of transport equipment | 10.22 | 84.2 |

Source: Financial Figure of Non-financial Companies. Hungarian Statistical Office, 2005.

Table 4 contains the return on assets ratios in ascending order. The groups do not include the same sectors as in the case of labour productivity. However, the order set by labour productivity and return on assets shows more similarities than differences. The first group for example includes leather and wood products, which are ranked lower regarding both productivity and efficiency of assets. Two sectors from the fourth group also were ranked into the fourth group according productivity and return on assets. A sector getting to another group indicates that other factors also influence the changes of the given ratio. The average return on assets is 1.79 percent in group 1, and 7.23 percent in group 4. Foreign ownership on average is 56 percent in group 1 and 74 percent in group 4, and the share is increasing among the different groups. Data proves that the share of foreign capital grows with return on assets ratios.

**Table 5: Average profit margin and operating cost ratios by groups of sectors (2003)**

| Group of sectors | Profit margin % | Foreign owned companies' share in subscribed capital, % | Operating cost, % | Foreign owned companies' share in subscribed capital, % |
|---|---|---|---|---|
| I. | 4.34 | 59.43 | 86.96 | 67.11 |
| II. | 5.25 | 54.37 | 92.81 | 51.96 |
| III. | 6.35 | 65.53 | 95.11 | 51.67 |
| IV. | 13.18 | 71.07 | 99.01 | 56.41 |

Profit margin and operating cost ratio in Table 5 indicate changes in profitability. The operating costs and operating income are related to each other. In case of lower cost level, the operating income is usually higher. The results, however, are not identical since different amounts are related to the sales; therefore smaller differences develop in case of ranking by groups. According to profit margin, leather, non-metallic products and chemical industry belong to group 4, the group showing the greatest profitability (the average is 13.18 percent profit margin). On the other hand, chemical industry, non-metallic products and food industry belong to group 1 showing the lowest cost ratio (average 86.3 percent cost ratio). Chemical industry and non-metallic products belong to identical groups according to both ratios. Foreign ownership is usually higher in groups with higher profitability and lower cost sectors. In case of groups 1 and 4 the connection between ownership and profit margin/operating cost is always significant.

**Table 6: Average export share and investment ratios by groups of sectors (2003)**

| Group of sectors | Export share in the Sales | Foreign owned companies' share in subscribed capital, % | Investment ratio, % | Foreign owned companies' share in subscribed capital, % |
|---|---|---|---|---|
| I. | 18.21 | 32.20 | 4.76 | 52.8 |
| II. | 42.37 | 55.03 | 6.31 | 64.86 |
| III. | 53.58 | 67.91 | 7.24 | 56.20 |
| IV. | 79.42 | 77.33 | 13.53 | 76.37 |

The share of exports in the total sales and the extent of new investments and reconstruction indicate company dynamism and possibilities of development. Table 6 includes group data. There is close relationship between the export share and foreign ownership share, which means foreign-owned companies sell at international markets, interpret operation-productivity requirements under global conditions. Investments are processes typically taking part periodically, in this way it might happen that on the basis of figures of one year no close relationship is detected with ownership share. In 2003, in sectoral groups with lower investment (groups 1, 2, 3) there was no close relationship but in group 4, where foreign ownership share was the highest, the ratio of investment was also higher.

On the whole, we can conclude that the simple method of empirical regression can indicate that ratios referring to productivity, return on assets and growth are better at companies operating with sizable foreign capital. The relationship is the strongest in case of sectoral groups showing the lowest and highest values. In case of all ratios, it is clear that the share of foreign ownership in the group with the lowest profitability/productivity value is smaller than in the sectoral group showing the highest value.

## Comparison of Performances

So far we have found a relationship primarily for foreign ownership. Indirectly, however, the comparison of foreign and domestic private ownership is behind the conclusions. Since the share of state and other ownership is low, the high/low share of foreign ownership is related to the opposite share of domestic private ownership. Related to ownership share, the tendency is opposite also in performance. Where domestic ownership compared to foreign one is higher, the performance is lower.

The most important question in current economies in transition is to what extent the economic development impact of foreign capital is isolated. In addition to the local impact on affiliates and the impact on local markets, the question is how high knowledge, technology diffuse, how the other actors of the economy are able to receive and use western-type economic management systems. The secondary impact of foreign capital, diffusion and assimilation serve economic modernization the best in the current stage. Examination of diffusion and assimilation is complex and mainly requires the examination of qualitative features. Some tendencies can be shown in this study in accordance with the characteristics of the database.

There is a close, tendency-like relationship between the sectoral data of gross value added production per capita interpreted as productivity ratio and the ownership share of domestic private persons. Tables 7 and 8 include a *productivity map*. The sectoral productivity ratios were compared with the manufacturing industry's average, in this way relative value is given for sectoral ratios. We do not use the ratio expressed in amount of currency, but the ratio compared with the average of the manufacturing industry every year. The relative values mainly facilitate to track changes in time. The ratios of sectors on the productivity map express the relationship between the performance of the sectors and the owner's capital share, and see whether the sectors are diffused or the data indicates some tendency.

Table 7 shows the productivity of manufacturing sectors by domestic ownership groups in 2003. The data indicates that in sectors with domestic ownership over 30 percent, the performance of the sectors typically reach 30-70 percent of the manufacturing industry as a whole. Out of the 12 sectors domestic ownership is over 30 percent in 8 sectors and in these sectors productivity ratios are concentrated in one field, in this field the productivity ratios do not reach the manufacturing industry average (manufacturing industry = 100 percent). A smaller group of the sectors (vehicle, electronic products, chemical industry), however, stand out of the field; their performance is over the average of the manufacturing industry (in case of chemical industry and motor-vehicle industry, almost twice as much as the average). At the same time, in the sectors, which are the most dynamic by productivity, domestic ownership is low, between 10 and 20 percent. The regression straight on the points would show close correlation, higher domestic ownership connected with lower average productivity.

The data from previous years show similar productivity map with slighter differences. One difference comes from the fact that slighter changes have taken place in ownership share in the past three years, the other one comes from the changes in productivity. In 2000, 4 sectors had over 40 percent domestic ownership share and reached 20-30 percent in the most dynamic sectors. By 2003, changes happened, the number of sectors, in which domestic ownership is 40 or 30 percent decreased and in the most dynamic sectors domestic ownership decreased below 20 percent. In 2000, the relative productivity ratios were not concentrated in one field, which means that even with higher domestic ownership they reached the average productivity of manufacturing industry or slightly exceeded it. The productivity map of 2000 shows relative lower productivity with higher domestic ownership, but its concentration is smaller. In 2003, the disadvantageously lower performance slightly increased according to the share of domestic private owners. This year the productivity map opened up both horizontally and vertically. According to productivity, horizontally the gap has slightly increased between the dynamic sectors and sectors of lower productivity. Since productivity grew in absolute numbers in all sectors, it is better to say that the productivity growth of dynamic sectors was greater than the productivity growth of the sectors in which domestic ownership is bigger.

The vertically measured increasing gap on the productivity map shows that the domestic owners are ousted from the most dynamic sectors; they could not reach the same productivity.

**Table 7: Relative labour productivity and domestic ownership by sectors, 2003**

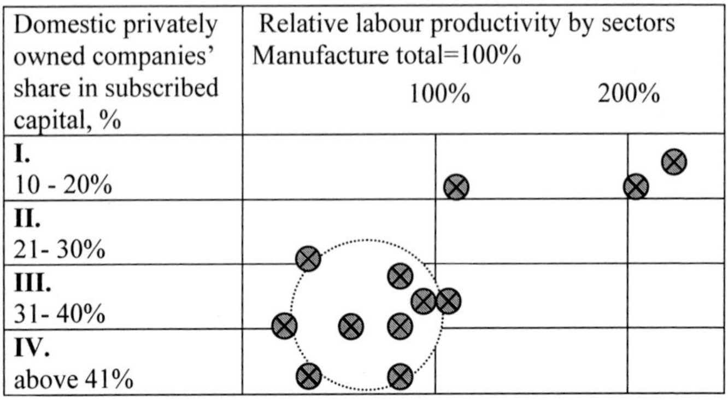


**Table 8: Relative labour productivity and domestic ownership by sectors, 2000**

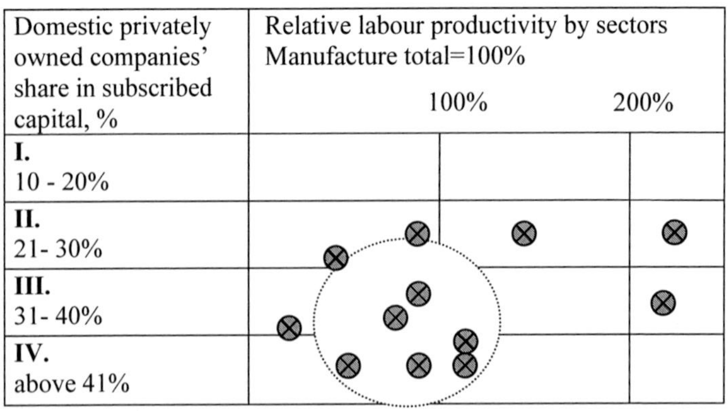


In the comparison of companies working with domestic and foreign capital, the main question is whether the difference between the two groups in productivity and profitability has increased in the past years. Comparison of the relative productivities in table 9 provides possibility for this analysis. The table highlights sectors, where domestic ownership is over 30 percent. Domestic ownership slightly increased in three sectors (food, textile and paper industries) and slightly decreased in the wood industry. The relative ratio of productivity decreased in three sectors (textile, wood, and paper) and increased in one sector, in the food industry. Relative productivity decreased in the wood and paper industry having the highest ownership share, they lagged slightly behind the manufacturing average. On the basis of three-year tendency, clear lagging of the four sectors is not evident. In 2000, they reached 65 percent of the manufacturing industry on average, which showed improvement by 2001 and 2002 (in 2001 they reached 71 percent, in 2002 68 percent of the average). At the same time, following improvement, the four sectors reached 62 percent of the average by 2003. The decline might be temporary. Only simple conclusions can be drawn from this analysis. The data does not enable the separation of the performance of companies, which work only with domestic capital or foreign capital. The temporary, relative productivity improvement in food, textile, wood and paper industries might come from foreign companies active in the sector.

**Table 9: Relative labour productivity and domestic ownership by sectors**

| Sector | Relative labour productivity, % | | | | Domestic privately owned companies' share in subscribed capital, % | | | |
|---|---|---|---|---|---|---|---|---|
| | 2000 | 2001 | 2002 | 2003 | 2000 | 2001 | 2002 | 2003 |
| Food, beverages | 87 | 125 | 119 | 101 | 32 | 36 | 37 | 40 |
| Textile production | 29 | 35 | 28 | 27 | 33 | 39 | 39 | 39 |
| Wood production | 46 | 39 | 37 | 36 | 50 | 50 | 51 | 47 |
| Paper, pulp, printing | 101 | 87 | 90 | 82 | 46 | 50 | 58 | 53 |

Source: Financial Figure of Non-financial Companies. Hungarian Statistical Office, 2005.

According to other ratios of profitability and productivity, the relative ratios developed by sectors changed only slightly. Return ratios typical of the sectors developed also in the case of return on assets. Looking at domestic owners, return on assets improved in 2001 and 2002 and declined in 2003. The most dynamitic sectors, however, improved the return on assets significantly just in 2003. Formerly return on assets showed significant fluctuation in the most dynamic sectors.

**Table 9: Relative export share and relative investment ratio by sectors**

| Sector | Relative export share, % | | | | Relative investment, % | | | |
|---|---|---|---|---|---|---|---|---|
| | 2000 | 2001 | 2002 | 2003 | 2000 | 2001 | 2002 | 2003 |
| Food, beverages | 38 | 35 | 36 | 36 | 57 | 79 | 86 | 77 |
| Textile production | 115 | 119 | 121 | 117 | 72 | 64 | 63 | 42 |
| Wood production | 135 | 128 | 141 | 134 | 151 | 150 | 151 | 81 |
| Paper, pulp, printing | 78 | 76 | 79 | 76 | 80 | 66 | 47 | 57 |

Source: Financial Figure of Non-financial Companies. Hungarian Statistical Office, 2005.

The export share ratio shows relative steadiness in food, textile, wood and paper industries. The relative values compared to the manufacturing industry as a whole also show stability, the role of export markets at sectors with domestic participation do not typically decrease. In the field of investments, greater fluctuation is experienced, but it is related to the cycles of investments. Between 2000 and 2002, the level of investments reached 90 percent of manufacturing investments, which decreased to 64 percent by 2003. All in all, by 2003 the productivity and profitability ratios worsened in the sectors, where domestic ownership is significant and improved in sectors with significant foreign ownership. On the basis of the data of one year, one cannot declare that domestic sectors are falling behind. The difference in performance is still clear, but the difference does not increase.

## Conclusion

In transition economies, modernization of production requires the improvement of product factors allocation and efficiency. Mass privatization and establishment of new companies, shrinking state and cooperative sectors enabled the reallocation of product factors and cost-efficiency has changed significantly through private ownership. Foreign capital investment is highly important for the Hungarian economy for increasing productivity. In this way, new products, new technology and new skills are adapted. Among manufacturing sectors the electronic products, motor-car industry, pharmaceutical, chemical products regarded the most dynamic ones even in developed economies and that sectors have outstandingly high foreign ownership in the Hungarian economy. The productivity and profitability ratios of these sectors are well over the average value of the manufacturing industry. Foreign capital investment resulted in significant technology and knowledge transfer in the Hungarian economy. Since the foreign direct capital investment has slightly decreased in the past 1-2 years, a basic question is how to get from the exogenous-upgrading stage to the endogenous stage. There are several indications that companies with domestic ownership began to catch up. In the late 90s, the positive impact of foreign capital failed to meet the expectations. Foreign affiliates operated as separated islands. The emergence of a dual economy was a possibility. Since the end of the 90s, the lack of relations between domestic and foreign companies has seemed to disappear slowly. In the first stage there were some approaches with the involvement of more subcontractors and improving the quality of products and services of domestic suppliers. Today the establishment of research and development bases of big multinationals in Hungary means the most important opportunity for new knowledge centres. The increasing role of technology transfer is present at other domestic companies which are not directly related to foreign companies, especially by acquisition of new machines, implement of new technology and products and adaptation of quality expectations handed over through the western products.

Foreign companies are characterized by good productivity and profitability ratios and outstanding dynamism. They have created close market competitions for domestic companies. Therefore the fact that the productivity and profitability ratios of domestic companies have not fallen behind foreign firms to a greater extent is a great achievement. The differences are great, but they do not increase significantly.

## References

Baek, J. S. – Kang, J. K. – Park, (2004): Corporate Governance and Firm Value: Evidence from the Korean Financial Crisis. Journal of Financial Economics, 71. 265-313.

Barbone,L.- Marchetti, D. –Paternostro, S. (1996): Structural Adjustment, Ownership

Transformation and Size in Polish Industry. World Bank Policy Research Working Paper.

Bayer, K. (1992): Ownership and Control: Lessons for Privatization. A Case Study of the Austrian Industries Corporation. In. Mixed Economics in Europe. Edward Elgar Publishing.

Blanchard, O. (1998): The economics of port-communist transition, Oxford, Clarendon Press.

Csernely, A. (1996): Some Characteristics of Corporate Finance in Hungary, MNB Working Paper

Dimitrov, M. (1999): Ownership Structures and Firm Performance in South Eastern Europe. In: Economies int Transition. Gorex Press, Sofia

Fabry, N. (2002): The Role of Inward-FDI in the Transition Countries of Europe.

Financial Figure of Nonfinancial Companies. Hungarian Statistical Office, 2005

La Porta, R. – Lopez, F. – Desilanes, L. – Schleifer, A. (1999): Corporate Ownership Around the Wold. The Journal of Finance, 2. 471-517.

Konings,J.-Lehmann,H. – Schaffer,M.E. (1996): Job Creation an Job Destructuring in a Transition Economy. Centre for Economic Performance, Discussion Paper, 282.

# Aspects of HRM in Foreign Subsidiaries in Russia: Training, Recruitment and Compensation

Heidi Kivelä

## Abstract

The purpose of this study is to identify HRM practices and related challenges in Finnish subsidiaries in the Leningrad Region, Russia. Based on interviews of 15 managers, the most popular training method is in-house training. The main criterion for choosing a training provider is the professionalism of the training organization. The situation in the labor market is difficult. There is less workforce available than what is needed in companies, and most candidates lack qualifications. Some companies experience problems with compensation systems, while employees are unused to bonus salaries. Lack of salary statistics in the regions also causes challenges for companies.

## Introduction

### Management Training Studies

Organizational studies concerning management in Soviet enterprises were very rare before the mid-1980s. As the societal, organizational and managerial transition started after the collapse of the Soviet Union in 1991, research on organizational behavior emerged, too. Among management studies concerning Russia the most popular research topic in the early 1990s was definitely management training. At that time the business training sector was booming in Russia because of the huge need for training the managers of the Soviet enterprises. These managers needed first and foremost information about the basics of the market economy. The focus of studies concerning management training was often on the applicability of Western management training practices in Russia and other Eastern European countries as well. The general opinion became clear soon: attempts to apply Western concepts directly, without adjusting for the specific cultural environment, would fail.

Holden & Gale (1993) stated that Russian managers saw the West as the key source of solutions to economic problems in Russia. However, at the same time Russian managers tended to misconceive the applicability of Western management concepts to the business environment in Russia. Varner & Varner (1994) suggested that anyone attempting to offer business training in Russia needs to understand the basics of Russian historical and political development, and to adapt the presentation for the Russian audience. Czinkota (1997) stated that Russians held some distinct attitudes toward business training. They were filled with national pride and angry about the seeming disrespect of outsiders for Russians' achievements. They were also suspicious toward new practices, and had a fear of the unknown.

Puffer (1996) described the business training field and its development through the years, and mentioned that management training was a booming business in early 1990s, while more than 1,000 business schools and training centers were established in Moscow alone during only a couple of years. Still, despite the huge number of training organizations, it was not clear whether there was a significant impact on Russian managers and the economy or not. Also Warner, Denezhkina and Campbell (1994) questioned whether educating managers would actually smooth the transition in Russia or not despite the high level of participation in management training. The authors did, however, admit that management training, assisted by Western institutions, had achieved a lot at the level of individual participants.

The study by May, Puffer & McCarthy (2005) about transferring management knowledge to Russia was an interesting case because, as mentioned earlier, management training studies were extremely popular in the early 1990s, but lately they seem to have been rather rare. According to the authors, what was needed in Russia was a more open culture, better communication and team building. An important aspect from the trainer's side was to show one's appreciation of the managers' past experiences and circumstances.

Usually the instructions given for managers suggest that managers need to *learn* certain skills. Kets de Vries (2000), however, stated that even if the younger group of business managers really needed to learn things, the older group was basically facing the challenge of *unlearning*. This group consisted of administrators and bureaucrats who used to supervise factories and other industrial units of the former USSR. They needed a dramatic change in their authoritarian mentality. According to Kets de Vries, most Russian executives lacked basic economic training but also knowledge of psychological concepts. Treating employees like robots and having little respect for the person would not work in a market economy.

## HRM Studies

Studies on content of human resource management in Russia became topical only in the late 1990s. Studies available before that mainly provided general guidance and information, and were rarely based on considerable survey or interview data. Some studies that have deepened the level of focus and concentrated on the insides of HRM are presented here.

Fey, Engström & Björkman (1999) underlined that in order to succeed in Russia, Western companies need to use Western "high performance" HRM practices but to adjust them to the Russian environment. The key here is to realize what kinds of adjustments are needed. Most foreign companies operating in Russia considered their HR practices as more similar to those that were used in their mother company or other foreign companies operating in Russia, compared to HRM practices in local (Russian) companies. However, the rapid growth which many companies in Russia have been experiencing increases HRM related difficulties, while there is only little time, if any, to make plans regarding the HR policy. Ardichvili, Cardozo & Gasparishvili (1998) stated that CEOs in Russian companies regularly devoted time and attention for traditional human resource management activities, such as hiring, selection and performance appraisals (59% of respondents). However, fewer managers devoted time for decision-making related to training employees: choosing training programs and implementing the plans (32% of respondents). For making comparisons, it is interesting to notice that the equivalent percentage for such an activity as strategic planning was 83,2%.

Fey, Pavlovskaya & Tang (2004) investigated HR practices in three Swedish multinationals – Ericsson, Electrolux Group and Tetra Pak – in Finland, Russia and China. The findings showed that in Russia training and development processes were much more formalized than in Finland. The central role of HR department in all the training related decision making processes was emphasized strongly especially with Tetra Pak. Sheksnia (1998) stated that just in a couple of years educational and orientating training had converted into professional, hard-competency development with in-house training centers in many cases. His survey to 73 managers of Western subsidiaries in Moscow and St. Petersburg also showed a change in employees' attitudes to training: it was no longer considered as a perk, but a career opportunity. Only a few Russian subsidiaries sent local employees abroad to training. According to Medvedev (2001), the most often used training methods during the 1990s were self-education, distance learning and coaching. In addition, many companies arranged in-house training for their managers. Also Kiriazov, Sullivan & Tu (2000) found that the most popular training method in Eastern Europe was on-the-job training. Challenges related to training included lack of financial resources in the company and shortage of professional trainers in the market. According to Fey & Björkman (2001) there was a strong connection between HR function and firm performance. In separate hypotheses both management training and development of non-managerial employees correlated with firm performance. In addition, authors suggested that by investing in employee development it was possible to produce higher organizational commitment from the employees' side. Given that, it is surprising that companies in Russia have so far invested relatively little in training and development.

According to Fey et al (2004) managers of Russian subsidiaries considered recruitment as the most important HR function on which to focus. The downside of making a bad choice in recruitment is larger in Russia than in many Western countries, such as Finland. The authors described that the importance of local managers has increased over the years, while a decade ago expatriate managers were relied heavily. Fey et al (1999) described the labor market in Russia as immature. Headhunting companies play a major role in recruitment, and actually over 50% of companies use headhunting firms. Interviews are used most often when selecting employees. Many companies interviewed indicated that they did not usually require references, although – if delivered – they were appreciated. Two important qualities that were especially valued, were working experience in a foreign company and good command of English.

Fey et al's (1999) study highlighted that even if a competitive salary was important in keeping the employees in the company, probably the most important factor was to assure the key personnel that the company was committed to Russia and there was room for them to move up in the organization in the future. However, retention was considered as a real challenge. High turnover among personnel becomes expensive for the company, and the pool of suitable candidates is limited. Also, Kiriazov et al (2000) stated that job commitment in Eastern Europe was low. The authors explained that while newly established companies often fail during their first year, employees tend not to be loyal. Kiriazov et al (2000) and Fey et al (1999) both stated that besides having money as the primary motivator, Eastern Europeans also appreciate non-wage benefits organized by their employers.

Fey et al (1999) found combining bonuses and non-monetary benefits as an optimal compensation package. Traditionally Russians have received many non-monetary benefits from their employers. Most Russians prefer the bonus to form 25% at maximum of their total salary. This is likely to be linked with the high uncertainty avoidance often perceived among Russians in cross-cultural studies. Also Kiriazov et al (2000) point out that employees are often resistant to bonuses while especially senior staff members still long for Soviet times when a monthly wage was guaranteed regardless of one's productivity. For the same reason employees are not excited about performance-based pay. According to Fey et al (2004) headquarters have the main role in determining compensation systems in foreign subsidiaries.

In order to mention a few words about the empirical data of this study, a set of interviews has been conducted within the framework of this research project. 15 representatives of Finnish companies operating in the Leningrad Region were interviewed in November 2005. Most of the interviewees have been General Directors or HR Managers of the Russian subsidiaries. The purpose of these interviews has been to hear their views on different themes related to HR. Thematic interview has been used as the research method. The data was analyzed using a qualitative method of coding topic areas, and searching for and identifying emerging themes. In addition to transcribed interview data, field notes were also used to assist in forming a broad image of the interviews.

## Examining the Empirical Data

### Training Practices

Training practices have been discussed widely during the interviews: what kind of training, how often, on which grounds and what kind of outcomes.

Various kinds of preferences, attitudes and values have been presented. Before going to further details about current training programs in the companies, some general features related to training are examined.

## Training Budget and Frequency

The question related to the training budget in the companies is answered very shortly, and no figures or exact information regarding the budget have been presented by any of the interviewees. While six interviewees have not really given any comments, nine interviewees have at least given some indication of the financial side related to training in their companies. Six out of nine admit that they have a training budget, and the remaining three interviewees say that there is no training budget in their company. It has been expected that bigger companies would have training budgets, and smaller ones would not. Thereby, it is an interesting point that a couple of interviewees state that there is a formal training budget in the company in the Russian side, even if the Russian subsidiary is relatively small.

Besides the whole existence of the training budget, also attitudes towards budgeting vary a lot. Both Interviewees A and E mention that the amount of money that is spent for training varies depending on the person and the position. However, while Interviewee A still finds it both possible and even important to create a training budget, Interviewee E considers a training budget as useless.

> "In the budget, in the cost budget I have already budgeted also expenses for the trainings. I can't remember the figures right now but I have already budgeted. So there are figures for that, for those needs. And of course they vary, depending on the position. And the need for training, it will be defined in the individual basis." (Interviewee A)

> "I don't know, if it's necessary in this situation, because we have the main factor that for people education on their own motivation. It's impossible to predict which person will want to go. —It's better not to have this training budget at all because if it comes a training budget, it comes a training policy. —It depends on the person, for example, who would like to go and study… —But if a person is willing to go and study something like English, why not. It will be for the advantage of the company anyway, and it will be for the advantage of the person oneself." (Interviewee E)

Frequency of training has been inquired from every interviewee by asking how many days one person spends for training in a year. However, only a few interviewees have been able to give such a detailed estimation. Many interviewees only say that they are training their personnel "when necessary".

> "Now we arrange the training and the development of the our employees not on the regular basis, just try to cover only current… current necessary issues. —This activity is not at the level when we can plan our training and development of the employees much beforehand." (Interviewee B)

Still, some estimations are given by a couple of interviewees. Many of them are related to the training of the accounting personnel, or chief accountant specifically, while several interviewees find that for this particular position training is really important. In some of the companies involved the chief accountant receives as much as 12 or 30 days training per year, of which the latter one can be considered as substantial.

When it comes to other managerial or middle-managerial level positions than chief accountant, the interviewees describe that the number of training days per year varies from two to five.

## Training Methods

The interviewees hold very different kinds of opinions concerning the best training methods available. While some interviewees prefer tailored trainings, some others send the employees to seminars that are open for everyone. Both short-term and long-term trainings are used, as are also interactive methods and self-learning. Basically, any kind of training is supported at least by some interviewees.

The only training method that is mentioned by the clear majority of the interviewees is in-house training. Nine out of fifteen companies involved arrange in-house training in cooperation with the mother company. These programs include training in various topics, such as human resource management, general management, product knowledge and product management.

> "Regarding (corporate) level training program, normally, the length of program something like a year and it consists from, for instance from, four, three modules. The First module is just a couple of days or induction, and then three, four days other module. And then participation for some kind of project work or some kind of home task and then they return it. And then finally that closing session. This is the main structure for many corporate programs…" (Interviewee K)

> "We have plenty of programs of our own. For example, it's ABC-management of the products. So we are doing such a, such type of project, for example. —So it's a matter of managing the product groups, and the volumes needed and of course the stock – values, volumes and so forth. So that is one part of the thing. Another part is financial control." (Interviewee A)

Several interviewees state that their in-house training programs often include a visit in the factory in Finland, or some other unit of the corporation. It is considered important that during these training periods the employees would learn the best practices from the other units – or the whole industry, as some interviewees claim.

> "Then, if needed, we can also use the knowledge we have in Finland, because there we have the main production and the main product managers, who are the best, actually, in this business." (Interviewee L)

> "Also we try to actively use our relations, internally within (our corporation). —And this is a very good opportunity for our employees to have a look at this factory, and to see big volume production, to participate in some kind of project and to get more knowledge, more expertise." (Interviewee M)

When discussing bought training as opposed to in-house programs during the interviews, both open seminars and tailored trainings are supported. One of the interviewees preferring open seminars emphasizes the affordability of them. At the same time, another interviewee, a fan of tailored training, states that even if it is more expensive to arrange training that is organized only for their company's needs, it is also more efficient.

> "I think the most cheapest way to have a training is to attend the seminars or the courses. Because there is one teacher for many, many. (The whole group.) Because we have for instance one or two persons that need the same training, extra persons need another kind of training. So it doesn't to make sense to have one teacher to one." (Interviewee D)

> "Well, I've preferred the way that it's tailored for us. Except accounting of course, it's a totally different thing. I've preferred to have the training tailored, and arranged in our premises or possibly somewhere else. But anyway, so that our issues would be handled in the training." (Interviewee H)

The length of training programs is discussed by a couple of interviewees, both of whom prefer short-term courses. According to them, the length of a training event should be two days at maximum. For long-term training programs these companies do not have either time or interest. However, at the same time, the training history of some of the interviewees themselves shows that they have received long-term training, and – at least partially – at the company's expense. Thereby, regarding the preferred length of training, the interviewees, again, have various kinds of views.

Some of the interviewees also mention the importance of developing oneself by oneself, for example by reading professional literature or magazines. Of course this is also a very cost-effective training method. Some others find it important to have interactive training instead of traditional lecturing. Interactive method is seen as a better way to make the employees actually learn and adopt something new from the training.

And finally, whatever the training method is, Interviewee A makes an important point regarding finishing the training project: some kind of feedback session needs to be arranged in the end of any training program so that the results of the training may be evaluated.

> "But if you do the training properly, there has to be get-together after some times, when it's analyzed. You got some knowledge during the training, then you worked, you implemented or not implemented. —And after some period, there has to be some kind of feedback. So the people should get together and discuss: 'Really, what did we get from this training? Or did we really get anything?' So maybe it was so theoretical that it's, it really didn't correlate of our everyday life at all. Then I would understand—that this was useful, and I can see what were the results – the real results from the training. And it would give me the perspective that I would like to have to the trainings." (Interviewee A)

This quotation is one of those rare statements that have been made in the interviews concerning training results. However, it does not really become clear, whether Interviewee A would like to arrange a reunion between all the training participants, or a meeting with one training participant and his/her colleagues. Still, most likely it would be useful either way.

## Selecting the Training Organization

When asking about the selection criteria for choosing a training provider, the opinions are fractured to a great extent. The main criterion appears to be the professionalism of the training organization, but besides that all the other factors mentioned are very diverse.

Taking into consideration that professionalism proves to be the most important piece of selection criteria, it is interesting to wonder about *how* these companies actually can assure that the training organization really is professional. Is it somehow linked with reputation or references after all, even if the interviewees tend to use the word professionalism? One of the interviewees suggests that he might make some check-up questions during the negotiations to find out the level of professionalism in the training organization at hand.

> "First of all, it has to be quite professional company. Very important to have quite good experience. It's first of all." (Interviewee N)

> "And they really had a… let's say, professional approach. They did not want to come and give the training before we had had this workshop, so that they definitely will know what we want to have." (Interviewee C)

Another factor that has been discussed quite often is the origin of the training organization and the importance of that. The comments here are very diverse, while some companies clearly prefer to cooperate with Western training providers, and the others only use the services of local training organizations. Local training is considered attractive especially when it comes to training in legislation.

> "They are basically local institutes. Because local institutes they have best knowledge of how to do it here. The legislation is the main thing why we choose local institutes, because we know that on this page law is written in that way and then we turn the page and there is completely different. So in local institutes we learn to read the law in the right way." (Interviewee F)

Some other separate factors that have been mentioned few times in the interviews are price, topic, suitable training schedule and references. The author finds it rather surprising that price has not been among the most important selection criteria. Previous market research (Fintormenta, 2003; Fintra, 2004) would have indicated a more dominant role for price.

## Recruitment Issues

This chapter focuses on recruitment issues that have been covered during the interviews. Usually these issues are related to *problems* that the interviewees have noticed in recruitment. None of the interviewees is of the opinion that recruitment has been an easy task in the company. The most common factor behind the perceived difficulties is no doubt the hard competition in the labor market, but also other problems have been recognized. In order to survive in the difficult labor market situation, the interviewees mention a couple of tools, of which establishing cooperation programs with educational organizations at different levels seems to be the most popular one.

## Recruitment Practices

In the early years of transition in Russia the most often used method of entering the Russian market was sending expatriate managers to the country. However, nowadays the situation is almost totally different, and in most cases the General Manager is the only foreigner in the subsidiary in Russia. Local managers are considered beneficial because of their understanding of the business environment. However, at the same time giving the local employees a high priority in recruitment also creates problems, while the importance of finding the right people increases. And this, as has been pointed out, has not been seen as an easy task while the pool of suitable applicants in the market is very limited.

> "So here in St. Petersburg we have altogether about 170 people. —If you take the top management, so we have approximately… It's very hard to divide sometimes but if I talk about our management group which we have once a week... Let's say, seven people for this division. And the other one… They also have some four people. —(Do you have some Finnish employees, or only Russian?) I'm the only Finnish person here in St. Petersburg." (Interviewee L)

An interesting company policy that was found in the interviews was the fact that companies are recruiting young talents, and have been doing so for some years already. It explains why the average age of employees is rather low in most of the companies involved. Apparently, the policy has been to hire young Russians in their 20s or 30s – even if they have not always fulfilled all the requirements, opposed to recruiting senior employees with mindset still oriented to Soviet times.

> "The HR strategy of our company, and the whole group, it is to employ people, not the professionals, 100%, but to give the opportunity for young, potential people to grow inside the company and with the company." (Interviewee O)

Another company policy perceived is tendency to give internal candidates the first priority when fulfilling open vacancies. Most likely this policy is linked with retention measures, while it clearly has a motivating effect for current employees.

> "...if there is a vacancy in the company, the first it's internal recruitment: we should inform everybody here inside the company, to make this advertisement of this position. And if there is somebody, who would like to get this position, so of course this person can come to HR and say that 'I would like to be that person', or 'I would like to be one of the candidates to this position'. And if, for example, his manager is not against this, so of course we can, we should give this opportunity for this person inside the company first." (Interviewee O)

## Situation in the Labor Market

Many interviewees mention that the difficult and very competitive situation in the labor market has formed an actual problem for the company. One of the interviewees even states that the competition is more fierce on the labor market, than the actual market of that particular industry.

> "At the moment the competition we have on labor market, we compete on labor resource. On this area we have competition because we have to employ a lot of people for our new plant, for our new project. —I think at the moment the competition more on the labor market than on the industry." (Interviewee M)

> "It's the biggest challenge to find qualified people, and how to then educate them. —We are in a big city where there are a lot of the same kind of business, what we are doing. And there is also a huge demand for personnel, like we have. So the biggest challenge for the coming years is to find personnel, because there is huge deficit." (Interviewee L)

These statements present two main challenges related to recruitment: first, there are less workforce available than what would be needed to fulfill the open vacancies, and second, most of the candidates are not qualified. And third, while there are only few professionals available in the labor market, these people ask for substantial salaries. High-class professionals know the value of their own expertise and competence and thereby tend to overprice themselves as employees, as Interviewee A describes.

> "(What's the usual problem when recruiting? Is there too little of professionals or...?) Too little. Other thing is that they are too expensive. So let's say so that the demand is so big compared to the amount of

> professionals available that professionals are in good position." (Interviewee A)

It also appears that recruitment is in fact very time consuming, as one of the HR Managers interviewed for this project mentions: the majority of the working time, 80%, is spent for finding new employees and organizing the recruitment processes. This share may be considered as substantial. Another interviewee describes the unstable situation by saying that the HR Department is just like a big recruitment agency.

However, not only do the interviewees see the situation in the labor market as a mere *problem* for their companies, but for some of them it has actually become a critical factor from the point of view of the company growth and survival. When the lack of qualified employees available creates a barrier for planned investments, the situation gets serious.

> "And now we are in the business on such stage that we are looking for professionals. Otherwise the growth that we are planning, we won't be able to do it." (Interviewee A)

But what is the actual background factor for the whole problem? Basically all the interviewees agree that there are not enough potential employees in the labor market. It is said that there are too little *professionals* available. Are there not enough educational organizations, then? Or do they simply organize the wrong kinds of training programs? Only one of the interviewees makes an effort to somehow explain the reasons for the current situation. Interviewee M considers the current demographic situation as the cause for the labor force deficit. In many Western countries, such as Finland, the demographic situation is very much alike – population is aging and the labor force deficit is a well-known problem that will hit the labor market with its full power within the next decade or so.

> "And just yesterday—we discussed in our business community, that demographic situation, the trend, is not really positive. We have quite big demographic gap, expected nearly ten years in Russia—which means that next years less and less young people will graduate school and college. So we have less and less people coming on the labor market, from the one side." (Interviewee M)

Even if all the interviewees are well familiar with the problem, lack of qualified personnel in St. Petersburg and the surrounding area, some of them have had more difficulties than the others. According to some HR

Managers the situation in big cities is still somewhat bearable, but outside them – in the regions – it has become impossible. It seems that the worsening situation in the countryside is facilitated by the migration trend from the regions to big cities. In spite of that, there are still not enough candidates to fulfill the vacancies in the cities, and at the same time there is less and less available workforce in the countryside.

> "I can say that it's rather difficult for us at this stage also, even in this stage to recruit people. Because there is a shortage of qualified and motivated personnel, especially in this area, in this region. And right now we have 50% of people from St. Petersburg and 50% from this region. This is not an easy issue, for every company in St. Petersburg." (Interviewee O)

> "So and the second problem is to get the recruitment problem. —There is a huge problem to get white-collar employees, or to get some, someone for managerial position. For instance, I remember just, just in spring time we had such a big trouble with getting chief engineer or chief manager. OK, we recruited him—sort of from Gatchina, from Leningrad Region, and we located him to another region. And the same problem was with our security manager, security specialty, so safety. And with accountant, so a serious problem." (Interviewee K)

The hard competition in the labor market has led in the situation where retention of the newly recruited employees is extremely hard. The interviewees tend to describe the majority of the available workforce as very opportunistic, mobile and seldom committed to the company. In fact, salary is the only matter that has any meaning at all.

Besides competing with salaries and compensation packages, a couple of interviewees have also thought of some other ways to maintain their employees and to attract new ones. These include creating an attractive, fair and employee-friendly image for the company.

> "So we are new in the labor market. And of course a year ago it was rather difficult for us to attract the potential candidates because nobody knows about the company. —Of course for us it's very important to have, to improve and to strengthen our image as a good employer. And of course we'd like that, of course not all people, in St. Petersburg and this region, want to work here. But it should be some kind of… You should be proud… And you should be proud for you're working here. That's why it's very important, and this is our main task in HR – to make that place a good working place. And we'd like to spread this information everywhere." (Interviewee O)

## Tools in Recruitment

Not too many interviewees have come up with an all-inclusive solution to the recruitment problems. However, a couple of interviewees mention having tried or even established a cooperation program with universities and institutes in order to ensure the availability of a competent workforce in future. A method that is often described as particularly Russian – using references – has only been mentioned few times. Consulting with head hunting agencies has proved to be a suitable method for some companies.

Establishing a cooperation program with universities and institutes sounds like a return to Soviet times. However, the idea is almost perfect for both companies and students: besides ensuring the availability of competent workforce in future, companies are also able to do their part in closing the gap between theoretical education and practical world in business life.

> "We have certain plans for instance. To work in the same way as actually companies and factories have worked in the Soviet times. To take direct contacts to some institutes or even universities. —We participate in the training programs of let's say, the institute that takes four years. On the third and fourth courses, we participate in the training program, and somehow train the persons for us. Actually our company has the same thing in Finland, so we are participating these vocational school programs. It's a challenge for the future and the only way perhaps to get young and educated and enthusiastic people." (Interviewee L)

Only one of the interviewees makes a statement, that using references would be the best way to recruit people in Russia. Such a small number of this kind of answers is rather surprising, while it is often said that using networks is extremely important in Russia and other post-Soviet countries when it comes to recruitment or any other business activities as well. Another interviewee points out something that might explain that matter: as the business reaches a certain point, using one's networks and references will not be enough anymore – outside assistance is absolutely needed. Thereby, consulting with head hunting agencies is seen as essential after passing a certain line.

> "But the Russian way of employing people is more or less still that you take people according to recommendation. You ask your business partners if they know anyone, if they can guarantee that this person is… —And at the moment that seems to be the best way of recruiting people. Still you make mistakes in that respect." (Interviewee F)

> "We use recruitment companies because our own... You know, when company starts a business, it's possible to start from the people you know and somebody says that OK this person might be suitable and so forth. And you can get it going. But when you come to the certain level, already… Let's call it serious business or you're taking it seriously, the volumes are already there and you have to have the business really structurized and so forth. You need to know the professionals, and know the business, that are in the business, that have the knowledge." (Interviewee A)

## Compensation Systems

In addition to challenges in recruitment, creating compensation systems has not been an easy task for the companies either. As it was already stated in the recruitment section, the lack of qualified employee candidates in the labor market is a huge problem for the companies. Finding good employees requires offering attractive salaries and paying attention to compensation packages in general. However, introducing bonus systems for the personnel – new and existing – has been found as especially tricky.

> "You know these bonus systems, they are quite popular nowadays. Bonus systems that encourage you to work a bit harder. But I'm not totally convinced, whether they have any meaning or not. But it's more... or maybe the bonus system simply isn't attractive enough. But the most important factor is that you enjoy your job and working environment at least on some level. You know, it's nice to come to work and to chat with your workmates." (Interviewee H)

> "If we continue with training and efficiency, you start to wonder, what is efficiency after all. (On what basis the bonus should be given.) Exactly, it should be easy and simple so that everyone knows, or understands it. —So, the more you invoice from the customers, the more you will get bonus euros. So this just doesn't work. I've been thinking whether our fixed salary share is set wrongly. Is the fixed salary share too high, because the bonus won't encourage you to work more and quicker and quicker. Or then it's just not understood among our employees." (Interviewee H)

Another problem is that bonus systems do not especially encourage employees to long-term thinking and planning, but leads them to pursue benefits in short-term. Of course this is a common problem in every country, not only Russia. Still, in Russia the problem may be a bit more *visible* than elsewhere, while the time scale of long-term planning in Russia is clearly shorter than in Western countries – based on the interviews it is about one year at maximum. This is most likely linked with the rapid development that is taking place in the Russian market: it seems impossible to look forward, because no one really knows what the situation will be tomorrow. Combined with the problems concerning bonus systems, the challenge is remarkable.

> "Actually, I have thought about this, because like in Russia actually, I don't think… I think always in managers and sellers, they have provision salaries, their bonus and provision. So strange of this system is, of course, they sell quite well, because they get so much salary. —But weakness of this system is they don't have to think so much of future. Because they don't see money coming from future, if they use too much time for future." (Interviewee G)

Besides not having enough qualified employees in the regions, another thing that causes a headache for HR Managers is the lack of reliable salary statistics outside big cities. Sometimes the problem is solved by asking for assistance from recruitment agencies. To solve the problem, many companies have participated into the competition with high salaries. Monitoring the salary level in the market and offering competitive compensation packages is seen as the number one solution among the interviewees. However, the best employees will probably still have other job offers with higher salaries, and thereby companies are constantly living in uncertainty.

> "…There are obviously two problems which are clear, this lack of reliable salary information or salary statistics for regions. This is quite important, because you know, sometimes it's impossible to get some reliable information on salary level in regions. OK, for Novgorod the situation more or less… OK, we can manage it, with recruitment agency for instance. -- In Carelia it's just impossible. So we should create our own way, how to calculate difference between St. Petersburg level of salary and Carelia." (Interviewee K)

> "We have to monitor very carefully the market, the salary level. We have to provide more or less competitive conditions to attract the people. In St. Petersburg there is a lot of place where people can find more or less new places and new projects, and it's going to be more and more, where people, well-educated good employees can find work. So this… The labor market in St. Petersburg quite competitive." (Interviewee M)

One of the managers interviewed finds it extremely important to "play by the book" when it comes to salary payments. Due to the history of Russia, employees intuitively look at salary payments with suspicion. This is naturally a huge burden for HR Departments, and it most likely explains at least partly the prejudices against bonus systems, as well.

> "So that our image has been risen a little bit. Because we are paying everything. We are playing by the book. So we pay the salaries to the bank, and pay the whatever fund needed." (Interviewee C)

Still, obtaining an image of an employee-friendly and fair company does not work according to Interviewee F, who demonstrates this issue with a very illustrative example. Even if the statement is clearly exaggerated, there lies a grain of truth: motivating employees with anything else but money is a real challenge.

> "And money is the main factor in every branch. Money is more important for the workers, for instance, than the circumstances where they are working. They rather sit in icy water and get 30.000 roubles, than lie on sofa and get 15.000 roubles. —They only think of their own pocket. That means that if success of company depends on that it can pay reasonable salaries, in stabile way for many years, the people rather go in company where they can in half year, during six months, they can earn twice as much per month, but, and never think of the future. That's the problem in development of the company." (Interviewee F)

What is quite surprising is the fact that none of the interviewees has presented a non-wage benefit program (health care, children's day care etc) as a part of compensation system and as a tool to decrease the high turnover figures among employees, as for example Juurikkala & Lazareva (2006) suggest. After all, non-wage benefits were very often used during the Soviet times. It is possible that this matter would have come up if the company sample had included local, Russian companies. International companies probably tend not to look for solutions from the historical practices.

## The Role of Mother Companies in Creating HR Practices in Subsidiaries

Effect of the Finnish mother companies on the HR practices in subsidiaries in Russia varies significantly. Many interviewees have not referred to their mother companies during the discussions at all. If they have, it is probably due to the fact that in many companies in-house training programs often include a visit in the factory or headquarters in Finland. It is considered important that during these training periods the employees learn the best practices from the Finnish unit – or the whole industry, as some interviewees claim. In addition to learning new things about the actual work, it is mentioned that training periods in the headquarters help the employees to *sense* the corporate culture of the mother company in general.

According to Fey et al (2004) MNCs tend to bring their standardized HR practices to foreign subsidiaries and it remains to the local HR Department's duty to implement them. Some interviewees of that study highlighted close links with their mother companies, which was also the case in this particular project. In some subsidiaries the cooperation with the mother company is on a very wide and intense basis. Policies related to training, recruitment or performance appraisal, for example, might be set totally by the mother company. Some interviewees also refer to the common values and corporate philosophy of the whole global company, and the importance of operating in line with these guidelines.

> "For this training policy we have the back-up of our mother company, so that's why they are involved in this training process. They choose the training courses, the people who can deliver these services to our company in the best way. We agree our plans for the next year and our mother company supports us, and then practically organizes training courses in St. Petersburg. -- And it's good to have the same method and technologies as our mother company has." (Interviewee B)

> "We are a very young organization and it means that plus it's the first time when we plan to have these procedures here in our Russian organization. And for us, in order to develop this procedure, of course we ask our central office, to share the information of HR practices in the company that exist. For us it is very important to be, to work in one line with our central office, of course. Because we are a global company, and for us it's important to be universal. —Because we have the same ideology as our paternal company. And we have the same values, the same mission, and all other things." (Interviewee O)

Still, it has been recognized that the policy of the mother company cannot usually be applied as entirely similar in the Russian subsidiary, but certain adaptations need to be made. For example, one of the HR Managers interviewed is of the opinion that development discussion between the superior and subordinate is not effective, if the employee will not receive a numeral grade for his/her performance. In Finland the superior evaluates the performance of the subordinate verbally, maybe making suggestions how to improve one's performance at work. In the Russian side this approach is considered as too soft and special grades have been introduced in the subsidiary.

> "It is very important to underline that of course we cannot use directly the same methods and technologies that our mother company has in Finland, because we have to adapt them to our, to our local market, to our local situation in which we have to work here in St. Petersburg. And we do it." (Interviewee B)

## Conclusion

Based on this interview data it may well be stated that HR practices in Finnish subsidiaries in the Leningrad Region, Russia, are relatively fragmented and seem to be company-specific issues to a great extent. Many of the companies in question have started their operations in Russia in the early 21st century, and it is most likely that due to the brief history of the subsidiaries the HR practices (probably among other internal practices in the company as well) are still shaping up. As usual, in large companies there is a more obvious need for formal HR practices, such as training strategies and recruitment coordination, and in small companies a specialized HR Department does not even exist and the General Director deals with HR issues among his/her other duties. At the same time, also the effect of the Finnish mother companies on the HR practices in subsidiaries in Russia varies considerably company by company. In some subsidiaries the mother company does not really affect the subsidiary's HR practices at all, while in some other subsidiaries the mother company sets the guidelines for HR practices and even makes the choice concerning the training organization to be used in the subsidiary, for example. However, the majority of the interviewees are aware of the fact that HR practices and methods cannot be directly transferred from the mother company, and certain adaptations are needed depending on the features of the business environment in question. The key issue here remains to be aware of *which* HR practices and methods need to be adapted to the realities of the business environment in Russia – or any other market in question – and *how*. For the interviewees it seems to be a question of intuition, and the conclusions are made on the basis of previous knowledge of the business environment and the characteristics of local people.

However, what remains to be similar for most companies involved is the fact that they highly value in-house training and send employees to Finland or other foreign units to learn the best practices and to get to know the whole corporation. When choosing a training organization, companies tend to emphasize the professionalism of the service provider. Recruitment is a huge challenge for almost every company involved in this study. The labor market is overheated, open vacancies exceed the amount of workforce available, and thereby most candidates lack qualifications. When making plans for compensation systems, there are some important issues to consider: the structure and applicability of bonus salary systems and availability of reliable salary information, especially in the regions. Thereby, it seems that due to HR still being such an unestablished function in many Finnish subsidiaries in Russia, there are not so many similarities regarding the actual HR practices after all. Instead, at this point the most obvious similarities concern HR related challenges, which affect every company in the market equally.

## References

Ardichvili, A., Cardozo, R. N. & Gasparishvili, A. 1998. Leadership styles and management practices of Russian entrepreneurs: Implications for transferability of Western HRD interventions. Human Resource Development Quarterly, San Francisco: Summer 1998. Vol. 9, Iss. 2, p. 145-155.

Czinkota, M. R. 1997. Russia's transition to a market economy: Learning about business. Journal of International Marketing, Chicago: 1997. Vol. 5, Iss. 4, p. 73-93.

Fey, C. & Björkman, I. 2001. The Effect of Human Resource Management Practices on MNC Subsidiary Performance in Russia. Journal of International Business Studies; 2001 1st Quarter, Vol. 32 Iss. 1, p. 59-75.

Fey, C., Engström, P. & Björkman, I. 1999. Doing Business in Russia: Effective Human Resource Management Practices for Foreign Firms in Russia. Organizational Dynamics, Autumn 1999, Vol. 28 Issue 2, p. 69-80.

Fey, C., Pavlovskaya, A. & Tang, N. 2004. Does One Shoe Fit Everyone? A Comparison of Human Resource Management in Russia, China and Finland. Organizational Dynamics. New York: Feb 2004. Vol. 33, Iss. 1, p. 79-97.

Fintormenta. 2003. ”Pääpiirteinen selvitys länsiomisteisten Venäjällä toimivien yritysten venäläisen henkilöstön keskeisimmistä koulutustarpeista” and ”Kartoitus länsimaisten organisaatioiden Venäjällä venäläisille suuntaamista avoimista koulutus- ja kehittämisohjelmista”, Fintormenta Oy in cooperation with Agency of Social Information, December 2003.

Fintra. 2004. ”Corporate preferences for training services in Saint-Petersburg”, a market research study. Agency of Social Information, September–November 2004.

Holden, N. & Gale, A. 1993. Western-sponsored training programmes: Russian managers' expectations. Leadership & Organization Development Journal, Bradford: 1993. Vol. 14, Iss. 6, p. 24-29.

Juurikkala, T. & Lazareva, O. 2006. Non-wage benefits, costs of turnover, and labor attachment: Evidence from Russian firms. Bank of Finland, BOFIT (Institute for Economies in Transition). BOFIT Discussion Papers 4/2006.

Kets de Vries, M. 2000. A Journey into the Wild East: Leadership Style and Organizational Practices in Russia. Organizational Dynamics. New York: Spring 2000. Vol. 28, Iss. 4, p. 67-81.

Kiriazov, D., Sullivan, S. E. & Tu, H. S. 2000. Business Success in Eastern Europe: Understanding and Customizing HRM. Business Horizons. Jan/Feb 2000, p. 39-43.

May, R., Puffer, S. & McCarthy, D. 2005. Transferring management knowledge to Russia: A culturally based approach. Academy of Management Executive. Vol. 19, No. 2. p. 24-35.

Medvedev, A. G. 2001. International Management: Doing Business Operations in Russia. South Carelia Polytechnic Publications, Series B: Study Materials.

Puffer, S. M. 1996. The Booming Business of Management Education. In Puffer, S.M. (ed.) Business and Management in Russia. 1996. Cheltenham: Edward Elgar Publishing Limited.

Sheksnia, S. 1998. Western Multinationals' Human Resource Practices in Russia. European Management Journal. Vol. 16, Iss. 4, p. 460-465.

Varner, I. I. & Varner, C. H. 1994. A culture-based framework for successful business training in Russia. Human Resource Development Quarterly, San Francisco: Winter 1994. Vol. 5, Iss. 4, p. 361-369.

Warner, M., Denezhkina, E. & Campbell, A. 1994. How Russian managers learn. Journal of General Management, Henley-on-Thames: Summer 1994. Vol. 19, Iss. 4, p. 69-88.

# SECTION V:

# CASE

# MACULAN GROUP

# INTERNATIONAL GROWTH THROUGH ACQUISITIONS

PETR CHADRABA, PETER HAISS
AND MARIA RAUSCHER

## Introduction

The origins of the construction company Maculan Group date back to the 1920's. It was originally known as the Hofman Construction. In 1936, fresh out of the university, Rudolf Maculan joined the company. Three years later he became a partner and the company was renamed Hofman & Maculan. The company grew steadily, but remained primarily an Austrian company. Rudolf Maculan managed the company from 1936 until his tragic death in a plane crash in 1955. Under his direction, the company pursued a very conservative strategy of growth. It focused primarily on the domestic market. The construction market in Austria was growing after World War II and Maculan Holding kept pace with that growth. Initially, the company entered international markets on a small scale. In 1952 it won a construction bid in Afghanistan, and later it completed small projects in the Middle East. The company's primary focus, however, remained the domestic market.

After the death of Rudolf Maculan, the management of the company passed on to Ernst Meissner, a long-time employee and senior manager. Meissner maintained the strategy for growth set forth by Rudolf Maculan. His main objective was to maintain the company on a path of steady and conservative growth until Rudolf Maculan's son Alexander was old enough and skilled enough to take over the operation.

Alexander Maculan assumed control of the company in 1962. Initially, the company maintained its conservative approach to bidding on construction projects. For especially large projects, the company would form a Special

Purpose Company (SPC), and bring in other Austrian construction companies as partners. Within this system, profits would be shared but financial risks involved were minimized. Under Alexander Maculan's direction the company maintained its steady growth. In 1971 the company was incorporated and renamed Maculan Holding. In 1990 the company went public and was listed on the Vienna stock exchange as the Maculan Holding, AG. One of the reasons for going public was to raise funds in preparation for a major international expansion.

Implementation of the expansion strategy begun to be implemented in the 1970s. Around that time Mr. Maculan decided to take the company "European". Through direct acquisitions, joint ventures, and bids on foreign construction projects, the company quadrupled in size and revenue from 1988 to 1993. By the end of 1993 it was the largest construction company in the former East Germany, successfully competing with German construction giants.

During the 70's and early 80's the company undertook projects beyond Austrian borders, one in Saudi Arabia and one in nearby Hungary. These were relatively small projects and easily managed from the home office. Major international expansion did not begin until the late 80's. From 1989 to 1993 the company tripled the number of employees and quadrupled its gross revenue. The primary source of this growth came from construction projects in East European countries. Mr. Maculan saw a growth potential in this region and when the former communist governments began to collapse, he quickly and aggressively moved in and established a presence.

Alexander Maculan's reputation grew with that of his company. In 1993 he was named "manager of the year" by a respected Austrian business magazine – News. The second recognition of his management skills came at the end of 1993 when the company won an award for good investor relations and corporate governance, a very prestigious award. In that year he was one of the most visible managers in Austria and approaching the status of a business legend.

## Business Environment

The Maculan Group was an established, trusted company in its domestic market. It grew slowly but steadily to become one of the top five construction companies in the Austrian market. After WWII, the Austrian government was closely involved in rebuilding the country's infrastructure. As such, the Maculan Group, being on of the major construction firms in the country, learned to work closely with government agencies. When it came to large projects, the company used a SPC arrangement to spread the financial risks. Geographically, Austria is a relatively small country with a population of approximately 8 million. The compact size of the country enabled the Maculan Group managers to personally oversee all of the projects within the country's boarders. Even when the company ventured into Hungary in the early 80's, the distance was rather small, allowing the management to oversee the project by commuting to the site. By the end of 80's, the company employed approximately 2 800 employees, all of them Austrian.

Mr. Maculan recognized the limitations of the Austrian market, and he realized that the company had to reach out to foreign markets if it were to grow. Since Austria in the 80's was not a member of the European Union, the company's ability to penetrate the European market, especially the neighboring Germany, was limited. One of the first major steps to expand outside of Austria was Mr. Maculan's decision to acquire a 51% stake in a Bavarian construction company. The acquisition was organizationally very smooth and rather quickly proved profitable. The acquisition also signaled the company's entry as a competitor in The European Union.

In 1988 the communist government in Hungary started to loosen restriction on foreign investment. The Maculan Group had a positive experience with the Hungarian market in 1982, when it bid on and completed the rebuilding of a major hotel in Budapest. This experience, and the smooth expansion into Bavaria earlier that year, encouraged the company to enter into a 50% partnership with a Polish construction company and to acquire one of the largest Hungarian construction companies. By the end of 1989 these expansion moves started to show at the company's bottom line of the balance sheet. Foreign projects added approximately 25% to the company's annual turnover for that year (Table 2).

By the end of 1989 communist governments in all of Europe began to collapse, and democratic elections were taking place. East Germany was talking about rejoining West Germany, and other Central European governments were looking for foreign investments. German reunification would mean that East Germany would be a member of the European Union. The management of the Maculan Group felt it was perfectly positioned to take advantage of the opening into these potentially lucrative market opportunities right at the country's boarders. The greatest opportunity was perceived to be in the former East Germany. Maculan Group felt its experience in Munich, and the superficial similarity of the Austrian and German cultures, made it "natural" to further expand in Germany.

## Company Growth

As stated earlier, Alexander Maculan took over the company in 1962 and immediately started to define a strategy for growth. Opportunities in Austria were limited by the size of the country. International markets provided the best venue for expansion. To raise capital required for international activities, the company was listed in 1971 on the Vienna Stock Exchange.

In 1978 Maculan Group won a bid to build schools and roads in Saudi Arabia. The project was both successful and profitable. This experience encouraged Maculan management to further pursue growth through foreign markets. Looking East of Austria, the company saw opportunities in the neighboring Hungary, at the time, a Communist country. In 1982 it won a contract to refurbish an old Hotel Elizabeth in Budapest. Since Budapest is approximately 2-hour drive from Vienna, managing this project was not a problem. The short commuting distance enabled the management to maintain close control without the need of relocating.

Encouraged by the success of these ventures, Mr. Maculan decided to pursue a more aggressive expansion strategy. The company started to look for mergers or joint ventures both inside and outside of Austria. In 1987 the company merged with Pollensky & Zollner of Austria. Since it involved another Austrian company, there were no cultural or management style issues to be overcome. To reflect the change in the corporate structure, the company is renamed Maculan Beteiligungs, AG (Maculan Group, Inc.).

In 1988, the company acquired a 51% stake in G. Hinteregger Baugesellschaft, a Munich based Construction Company. This acquisition brought Maculan Group into the European Union market; Austria would join EU in 1995. This acquisition also went smooth. The German culture, especially a Bavarian one, has great similarities with an Austria one.

Beginning in 1989 the potential for growth was enhanced by the collapse of communism. Encouraged by his company's success in 1982 in Budapest, Hungary, Mr. Maculan saw a great potential in these formerly communist countries. The company entered into a 50%/50% joint venture with a Polish company to acquire one of the largest Hungarian construction firms. This opportunity was made possible by the Hungarian government's program turning formerly state owned companies to foreign investors with capital. This would be the model followed by other governments in that region.

In 1989 the East German government collapsed and East Germany became part of West Germany. By virtue of merging with West Germany, East German territory immediately became part of the European Union. As such the existing laws and regulations were harmonized with the EU laws and regulations.

The West German government moved swiftly in taking over the former state owned companies. It formed a Treuhandanstalt Agency to take over and manage the disposal and/or privatization of approximately 4200 East German firms. The agency was given two main missions. First, privatize all companies under its management as quickly as possible. Most of the companies were undercapitalized and close to bankruptcy. Second, the agency was to assure that a collapse of these firms did not materialize. The German government feared a major economic depression leading to a massive unemployment in the region. The fear was that many of the East German workers would start to emigrate en mass to the West German region, destabilizing the economy. In return for very attractive prices, the agency typically required the foreign buyers to guarantee employment for the existing workers, and salaries that closely matched those paid in West Germany.

When Maculan Group saw the planed massive sell off, it decided on an expansion strategy into the region via Brownfield investment. Several advantages were seen in this approach over a Greenfield investment. First, the Maculan was acquiring construction equipment already owned by the companies being privatized. The management assumed it was realizing major savings since the companies were being sold off a fire sale prices. Second, Maculan was also acquiring local employees, who, it was assumed, were knowledgeable in the construction field. Third, with the purchase came contracts and bids on construction projects that were already acquired by the local firms. In other words, the acquisitions came with construction business. Relying on these assumptions, Maculan went on a major shopping spree, acquiring formerly East German construction companies at a furious pace. The economics of the region and Maculan Group's past activities in this area appeared to justify this strategy for growth.

In 1990 the company bought a 100% ownership in a Dresden based construction company – Bau Union Sud. In 1991 the Maculan Group bought outright two more companies. First it acquired a construction company – Industriebau Magedeburg and the Maculan Group also bought a 100% ownership in Risaer Hoch und Tiefbau, a structural and civil engineering company. A year later, in 1992, it acquired Kieswerk Wageleben, a gravel pit owner. Additional information on the Group's acquisitions appears in Table 3.

The growth through Brownfield investment continued in 1992 with the acquisition of SBS Specialbau, a specialty construction company and a 40% interest in Tief und Verkehrsbau Berlin, a civil and road construction company. At the time of this purchase, Maculan Group did not have enough funds to acquire the whole company. However, the company issued additional stock in 1993 and immediately raised its stake in Tief und Verkehrsbau Berlin to 90%. The remainder of the new capital was used to acquire a 49% interest in yet another Berlin based company, Ingenierhochabau Berlin. With these acquisitions completed, the Maculan Group was the largest construction company in the region. Its business activities surpassed those of West German companies which has entered the East German territory.

Mr. Maculan did not limit his corporate growth plans to the former East Germany. His company entered into joint ventures and agreements in other parts of the former Eastern Europe. In 1990 it entered into a cooperative agreement with Stavoindustria, a Slovak construction company. In 1994 the Maculan Group took a 50% stake in a Slovak cement producer – Cemmac. Table 3 shows the time line of these acquisitions.

The company also aggressively bid on construction projects in other former communist countries. It had ongoing projects in the Czech Rep., and Slovenia. In 1991, the company bid on a major project it Russia. It won a bid to build military housing for soldiers returning to Russia from Eastern European countries. The housing was to be built in two small towns, Twer and Wjasna, near St. Petersburg. The value of this bid was in the range of 1.2 Million ATS. Because of the size of this project, Maculan Group followed the approach used in the past when handling large construction projects. It formed a SPC, and took on 5 Austrian companies as partners. For the first time, the company faced serious problems managing a distant foreign construction site. Local subcontractors were unreliable, and because of privatization going on in Russia, owners changed often. The trades' people were not as efficient as expected; their work was of poor quality and work ethic very weak. The subcontractors also often lacked the proper construction equipment, and what they had was not dependable. This project required closed management oversight. It helped that Maculan was able to share management responsibilities with 5 other companies.

By 1994, the company's presence went from Munich and Dresden areas on the west all the way to St. Petersburg, Russia on the east. Table 7 shows the geographic distances of projects the company was managing out of Vienna. The various projects outside of Austria, together with the acquisitions, led to a phenomenal rise in Maculan Gross Revenue. From 1989 to 1993 the revenue growth totaled 400% (Table 5). Maculan Company, formerly an Austrian construction firm with small international activities, now became an international corporation of a significant size. In 1989 about 83% of the growth revenue came from the Austrian market. By 1993, only 28% of the Growth Revenue was generated by the domestic market. The rest came from foreign operations in Central and Eastern Europe, primarily from the former East German region. For more specific data, see Table 4. The company became international in its focus and a major player in the European construction market. Mr. Maculan has reached his goal of turning the company into a major European player.

## Organizational Structure and Culture

The Maculan Group focused its expansion plans on the former Eastern European countries, especially the former East German region. As an Austrian company, they were felt they understood the culture of these formerly communist countries. Since Austria had strong government involvement in the countries business activities, especially construction, the Maculan Group was skilled in working with governmental agencies. Overall, the company's past excursions into the region had been successful and profitable. While some of the past projects in the region had problems, such as the one in Russia, the company felt it had learned from the experience. Past experience and the general familiarity with the region was perceived as a competitive advantage over other western construction companies eying these markets.

The Maculan Group felt especially confident moving into the former East German area. They based their confidence on several factors. First, it was a German-speaking region, which made communication appear to be no problem. Second, the company had small projects in the area in the past, feeling these experiences taught them about the business environment. Third, the company's past merger with a Bavarian firm was successful with no cultural conflicts. Last, after the fall of communism, all of Eastern Europe was in need of major rebuilding of the infrastructure such as roads and bridges. The region was also short on office buildings that would meet western requirements.

The extremely fast and aggressive move into the East German market, see Table 5, forced the company to readjust its corporate structure. In a matter of 5 years, the company added over 7 000 employees. The majority of this growth came from acquisitions made in the former East Germany. This sudden growth put a strain on the Austrian middle level management. To successfully integrate this increase in labor pool, Maculan Group expected its managers to move to East Germany. Table 1 illustrates the extreme growth of Non-Austrian employees from 1989 to 1994.

Maculan Group quickly found out that its plans to move its own management into the region were not going to work out. The managers were unwilling to uproot their families a move to a different country. This relative immobility of the labor force is rather common for Europe. In many instances, Europeans have ties to the local area over several generations. Even when the language is similar, and the move is part of a promotion, the people are not always willing to relocate.

Also, since Austria was not a part of the European Union, most of the companies headquartered in Austria were concentrated on the domestic market. Mobility of management outside the country was not an important issue up to that time. However, in all fairness to the Austrians, it should be pointed out that the quality of life in the former East Germany was not that attractive. The service industry, such as restaurants and entertainment, was not on the level of Western European countries. The area had high unemployment and very weak economy. Many Austrians perceived the educational institutions and opportunities in the area as inferior to those in Austria. Last, most of the available housing was from the communist era and not up to the standards the Austrian managers and their families were accustomed to. Overall, the managers did not see this area as a good one to bring their families to.

Maculan Group realized that its own, highly trained and skilled managers were not willing to relocate. As such, the company had to develop a different strategy to solve this problem. They decided to put specially selected individuals from the acquired foreign companies on a fast track to train them into site management. Experienced construction workers and foreman were placed into the fast track site manager program. In many instances the Austrian managers would be assigned for short time to do the training. In other instances the individuals would travel to Vienna for short training periods. Since language was not a problem, it appeared that this strategy would work. Austrian managers sent to foreign sites knew that the faster they trained the local work force, the faster they would return home. Speed became the motivating factor in these instances.

An industrial construction site is a highly complex operation. It can best be described as a separate Strategic Business Unit (SBU), with millions of dollars on line. Any delays due to weather or time overruns by the individual tradesmen will have a direct impact on the overall construction costs, and as such, on the sites ultimate profitability. Since delays are inevitable, due to a variety of reasons, a site manager needs to have a multitude of skills. The site managers have to be able to properly schedule the various construction activities and tasks. They have to understand how long certain activities should take. They need to be skilled in prioritizing and coordinating all the different traits. Most of all, the managers have to be flexible and quick thinking when something does not go as planned. Any delays in the various tasks may require rescheduling of trade people, and quick improvisations. The site mangers' skills and experience are critical to managing the costs and watching for potential cost overruns. Also, one of the more important, but difficult to teach skills, is the ability to motivate the various tradesmen. On foreign sites, where the top management is geographically separated from the individual sites, fast and accurate communication between the site managers and corporate headquarters is a must.

Mr. Maculan also chose to grow the company through vertical integration within the construction industry. The company acquired several foreign operations specializing in construction material. The acquisition of

Kieswerk Wegeleben in 1991 involved a gravel pit operation. In 1994 the company acquired a 50% interest in Cemmac, a cement producer in Slovakia. The organizational chart, Table 6 shows the complexity of the company's structure and all of its subsidiaries and partnerships.

## Conclusion

The transformation of a small Austrian construction company into a major European player made Alexander Maculan a hero in his business community. When the company entered the German market in 1988, many in Austria questioned the wisdom of this move. Austrian companies were not known for competing successfully against German companies. The relationship between German and Austrian economies could be compared to that of David and Goliath. Historically, German companies were more likely to acquire Austrian companies, not vice versa. When Maculan Group became the leading construction company in the former East Germany, it overtook West German companies which also entered the region. Even before Austria entered the Union, an Austrian company is a major player in the European Union. Mr. A. Maculan became a national hero. As a result, Mr. Maculan's company received several major awards and he became a recognized and a respected business figure.

**Employees (figures rounded)**

| Year | Austria | GDR | TOTAL | Austrian employees in percent of total |
|---|---|---|---|---|
| 1989 | 2 800 | - | 2 800 | 100% |
| 1990 | 2 800 | 2 800 | 5 600 | 50% |
| 1991 | 3 300 | 3 200 | 6 500 | 51% |
| 1992 | 3 400 | 3 800 | 7 200 | 47% |
| 1993 | 2 200 | 5 500 | 7 700 | 29% |
| 1994 | 2 200 | 6 700 | 8 700 | 23% |

Data source: Maculan, Alexander (1997): Mein Fall.

**Table 1**

## Table 2

**TURNOVER and turnover growth of Maculan Holding**

**in Mio ATS= Austrian Schilling**

| Year | Austria | Germany | Other countries | TOTAL | Annual turnover growth Austria | Annual turnover growth GDR |
|---|---|---|---|---|---|---|
| 1989 | 3 300 | 350 | 430 | 4 081 | | |
| 1990 | 3 770 | 1 180 | 750 | 5 694 | ( + ) 14% | ( + ) 237% |
| 1991 | 3 970 | 3 800 | 2 000 | 9 774 | ( + ) 5% | ( + ) 222% |
| 1992 | 4 220 | 5 590 | 1 910 | 11 715 | ( + ) 6% | ( + ) 47% |
| 1993 | 5 107 | 7 621 | 1 238 | 13 966 | ( + ) 21 % | ( + ) 36% |
| 1994 | 5 096 | 8 486 | 1 986 | 15 568 | ( - ) 0,0 | ( + ) 11% |

Data source: Maculan, Alexander (1997): Mein Fall, p. 178.

## Table 3

**Maculan's Acquisitions – '90 to '94**

| Year | Acquired Company | Share of ownership | Turnover (mio ATS) |
|---|---|---|---|
| 1990 | Bau Union Sud (Dresden | 100% | 1 1591 |
| 1991 | Industriebau Magdeburg | 100% | 1 468 |
| | Risaer Hoch-und Tiefbau | 100% | 883 |
| 1992 | SB- Spezialbau Potsdam | 100% | 834 |
| | Kieswerk Wegeleben | 100% | n.a. |
| 1993 | TB Tiefbau Berlin | 40% | 1 575 |
| | Ingenieurhochabau Berlin (IHB) | 49% | 1 120 |
| 1994 | CEMMAC-Slovakia | 50% | |

**Table 4**

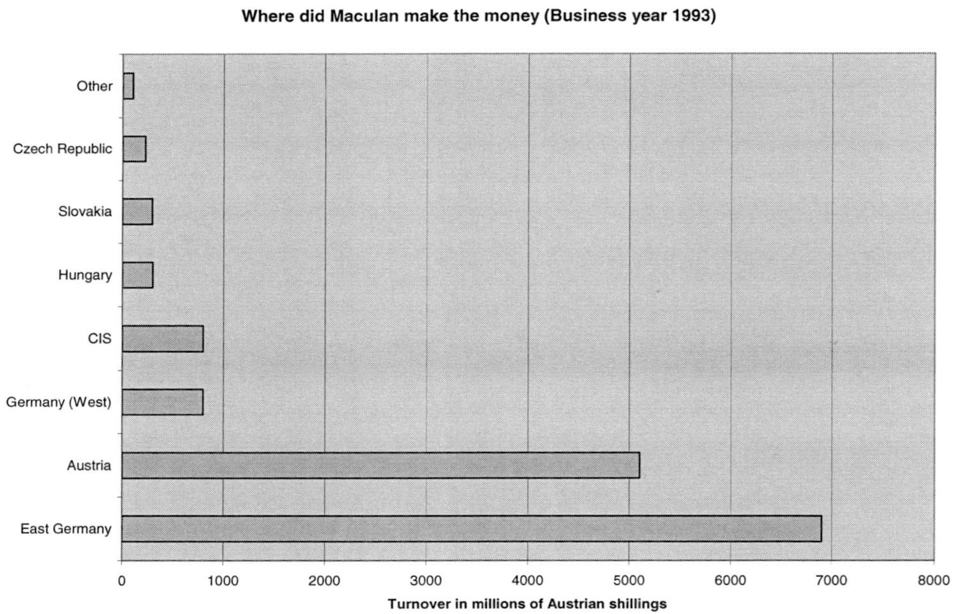
Where did Maculan make the money (Business year 1993)
Other
Czech Republic
Slovakia
Hungary
CIS
Germany (West)
Austria
East Germany
0
1000
2000
3000
4000
5000
6000
7000
8000
Turnover in millions of Austrian shillings

**Table 5**
**Maculan Sales Volume / by country**

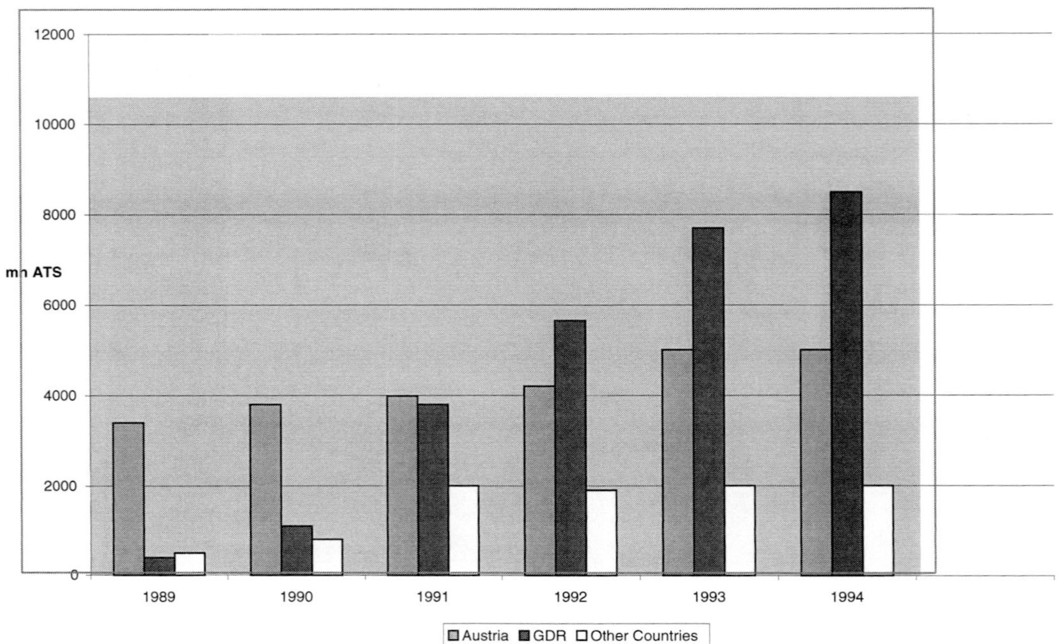

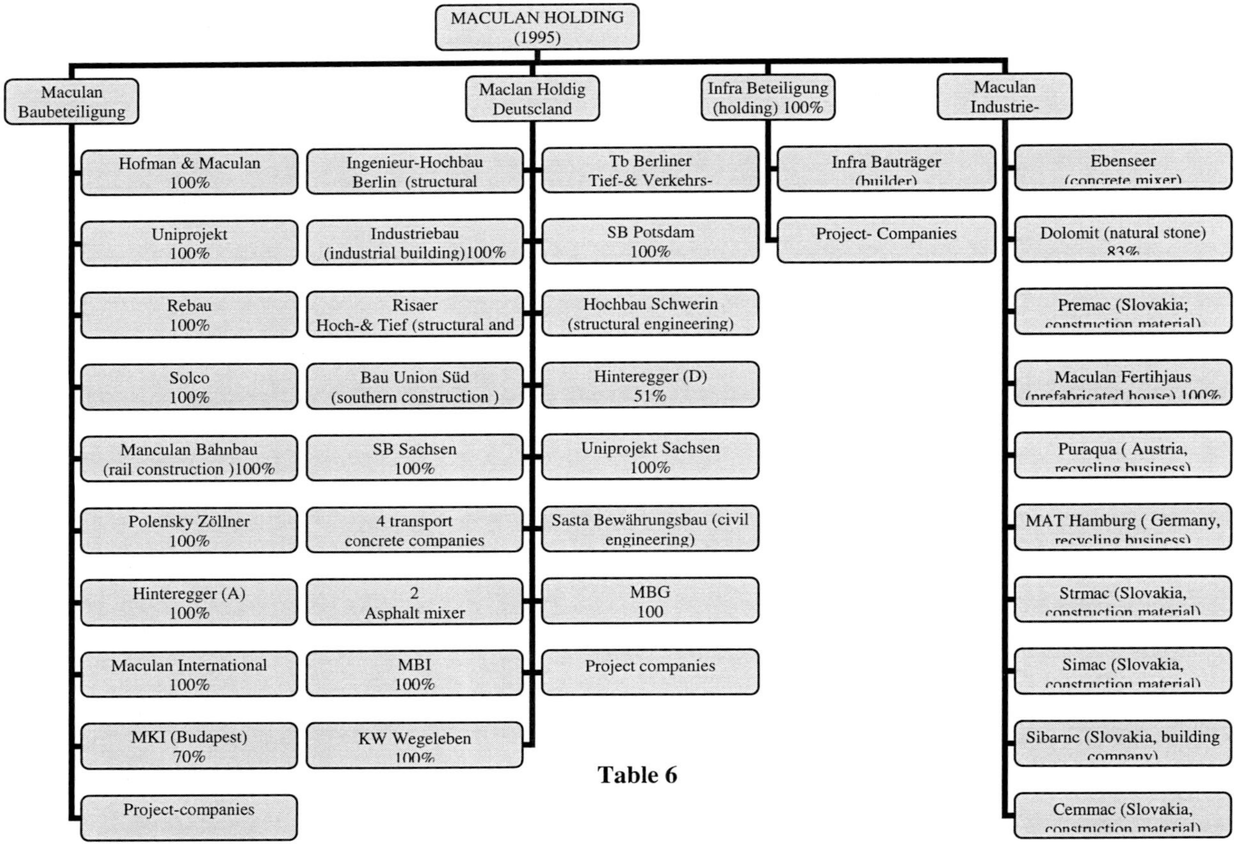
MACULAN HOLDING (1995)
Maculan Baubeteiligung
Hofman & Maculan 100%
Uniprojekt 100%
Rebau 100%
Solco 100%
Manculan Bahnbau (rail construction )100%
Polensky Zöllner 100%
Hinteregger (A) 100%
Maculan International 100%
MKI (Budapest) 70%
Project-companies
Maclan Holdig Deutscland
Ingenieur-Hochbau Berlin (structural
Industriebau (industrial building)100%
Risaer Hoch-& Tief (structural and
Bau Union Süd (southern construction )
SB Sachsen 100%
4 transport concrete companies
2 Asphalt mixer
MBI 100%
KW Wegeleben 100%
Tb Berliner Tief-& Verkehrs-
SB Potsdam 100%
Hochbau Schwerin (structural engineering)
Hinteregger (D) 51%
Uniprojekt Sachsen 100%
Sasta Bewährungsbau (civil engineering)
MBG 100
Project companies
Infra Beteiligung (holding) 100%
Infra Bauträger (builder)
Project- Companies
Maculan Industrie-
Ebenseer (concrete mixer)
Dolomit (natural stone) 83%
Premac (Slovakia; construction material)
Maculan Fertihjaus (prefabricated house) 100%
Puraqua ( Austria, recycling business)
MAT Hamburg ( Germany, recycling business)
Strmac (Slovakia, construction material)
Simac (Slovakia, construction material)
Sibarnc (Slovakia, building company)
Cemmac (Slovakia, construction material)

**Table 6**

**Table 7**

| From: | To: | Distance/Km |
|---|---|---|
| Vienna Austria | Bratislava Slovakia | 55 |
| Vienna Austria | Budapest Hungary | 215 |
| Vienna Austria | Munich Germany | 350 |
| Vienna Austria | Dresden East Germany | 385 |
| Vienna Austria | St. Petersburg Russia | 1570 |

# TEACHING NOTE[1]

# PETR CHADRABA

## Maculan Case

### Case Summary

This case addresses a variety issues dealing with a company's growth and its expansion into foreign markets. Maculan Construction Company ran into numerous problems caused by too fast expansion and also by making assumptions about foreign markets and cultures base on very superficial element – similarity in language. Initially, the company was one of the fastest growing construction companies in Austria. However, after several years of phenomenal growth, it all came crashing down and Maculan declared bankruptcy. When using this case in class, the instructor can focus on several different areas, such as culture, the need to grow mid level management before expansion, communication from and oversight of geographically distant markets and also the impact of changing conditions due legal changes. While government actions can never be predicted with a 100% certainty, a company should pay careful attention to possible changes. In this case, the instructor may want to discuss how much Maculan could expect of the governmental changes in united Germany.

## Discussion by Topic

### Culture

The management of Maculan made several assumptions about the culture in former East Germany, which showed a limited understanding of foreign cultural variables. Their assumptions were based on a common language – German spoken in the former East Germany. It was also based on their experience in Bavaria, a part of Germany. Instructor can explore these errors. They may want to discuss examples of other countries which speak a similar language yet are culturally very dissimilar. One example can be the use of English by a number of countries whose cultures have little in common. The instructor may also want to explore the use of French in many former colonies, yet in these cases no one would assume similar cultures. By using these foreign countries as an example, it may be interesting to explore the different values and attitudes that will impact the managerial strategy.

## Company Growth

After the collapse of communism, Maculan saw a great opportunity in the Central and Eastern European countries and decided to expand extremely fast to take advantage of the opportunities. Most of the former communist countries were in need of major reconstruction. Foreign companies moving into these markets needed office and factory buildings since the communist left most commercial properties in terrible condition. While construction opportunities were plentiful in Eastern Europe, was Maculan in a position to take advantage of all of them? The instructor may focus on the growth in the number of employees and on the geographic distances of some of the construction sites. How effective was the training of the new employees? Did they feel they were part of Maculan, were they managing in the way Maculan was accustomed to? How willing were the old Maculan employees to travel long distances and or to relocate families? Did the geographic expansion fit neatly into the company goals? Was the company's management comfortable delegating power to distant foreign employees and giving them significant authority? Did the new employees "skills" transfer into the Maculan way of managing construction sites?

## Government Regulations

This case illustrates the impact of a change in legal and/or regulatory environment on the competitiveness of a company. When companies enter foreign markets, they typically look at the regulatory environment to determine how it will impact their activities and competitiveness. However, as this case illustrates, one needs to do the same when entering markets undergoing economic transition. When East Germany merged with West Germany, it immediately became a member of the European Community and as such the regulatory environment had to be adjusted accordingly. This had a direct impact on Maculan and it significantly changed the market conditions. Maculan was able to purchase formerly communist owned properties on very advantageous terms. However, in return it had to make certain promises regarding employment practices. When the regulatory change took place, these legal commitments came back to haunt Maculan. Suddenly, the "cost" of the employment commitments exceeded the benefits of purchasing cheap assets.

The instructor may want to discuss the need for companies to look into the future, and price this into the cost of entering developing markets. Questions, such as, where does the country want to be in 5 to 10 years, and how will this impact the present legal environment, need to be analyzed. In the case of Maculan, many of the changes could have been anticipated since it was no secret that East Germany was going to merge with West Germany.

## Local Suppliers

Many industries rely on local suppliers when entering a foreign market. This is especially common in the construction industry. Not only will the quality of supply products impact the performance of the foreign contractor, but also the timeliness. In large construction projects the timing of the delivery of material or of the work done by subcontractors is critical. Any delays will have a snowball effect and the time lost will be very difficult to make up. This is where the construction site manager becomes critical to the timely completion of the project. The instructor may want to expand on the importance of having strong mid level management that understands the Maculan's way of doing business. When expanding its operation, a company needs to develop a mid level cadre of managers before the actual expansion takes place. The training needs to be done under close and careful supervision. This becomes even more critical as the companies geographic reach expands. In the case of Maculan, their construction operations covered a very large geographic area. At one point their activities expanded from the former East Germany all the way into the former Soviet Union.

## Communication

Fast and dependable internal communication is critical for every company. As companies expand geographically, accurate and dependable communication becomes crucial. While in Western Europe a frequent communication is common, this was not always true in the former Eastern Europe. Often times the authors of this case came across the motto "if everything is working out, why communicate?" and " if there is a problem don't tell anyone about it, try to take care of it". If we look at this motto carefully, we have to conclude there will be little communication. When companies expand they need to develop reliable channels of communication, especially if they are working in different cultures. This is when a corporate culture, overlapping different foreign cultures, becomes critical. The instructor may raise this issue with the students and pursue it further. A discussion on how to develop a corporate culture will illustrate to the students some of the inter company problems that need to be addressed before a significant corporate and geographic expansion takes place.

## Notes

[1] This teaching note was prepared by Prof. Chadraba of DePaul University. It was written for the sole purpose of aiding instructors in the classroom. Any suggestions and /or conclusions made in this note are in no way to be interpreted as a judgment or criticism of the company and/or its management. The viewpoints are presented to give students opportunity to present alternative approaches to solving management problems. The authors are not endorsing, criticizing or suggesting effective or ineffective management strategies.